MODEL CODE OF PROFESSIONAL
RESPONSIBILITY, MODEL RULES
OF PROFESSIONAL CONDUCT,
and
OTHER SELECTED STANDARDS
Including California Rules

on

PROFESSIONAL RESPONSIBILITY

By

THOMAS D. MORGAN
Oppenheim Professor of Law, George Washington University

RONALD D. ROTUNDA
Professor of Law, University of Illinois

Westbury, New York
THE FOUNDATION PRESS, INC.
1992

COPYRIGHT © 1976, 1978–1981, 1983–1991 THE FOUNDATION PRESS, INC.

COPYRIGHT © 1992
By
THE FOUNDATION PRESS, INC.
All rights reserved
ISBN 0–88277–963–X

TABLE OF CONTENTS

	Page
ABA Model Rules of Professional Conduct	1
Index to Model Rules	108
Table of Sections in the ABA Model Code Related to the ABA Model Rules	114
Table of Sections in the ABA Model Rules Related to the ABA Model Code	121
ABA Model Code of Professional Responsibility	129
Index to Model Code	198
The American Lawyer's Code of Conduct	210
California Rules of Professional Conduct	240
Selected Provisions From the California Business and Professions Code	267
Note, Some Important Statutes for Lawyers in California Government	291
New York Code of Professional Responsibility	294
Washington, D.C. Rules of Professional Conduct	319
Aspirational Goals on Lawyer Advertising	400
ABA Standards Relating to the Administration of Criminal Justice	403
The Prosecution Function	403
The Defense Function	417
Selected Federal Statutes and Rules	435
1. Bribery, Graft, and Conflicts of Interest, 18 U.S.C.A. §§ 201–18—Excerpts	435
2. 18 U.S.C.A. § 1905	452
3. 28 U.S.C.A. §§ 47, 144, 372, 454–55	453
4. 5 U.S.C.A. Appendix 6 §§ 101–112 Financial Disclosure Requirements of Federal Personnel	460
5. Sample Federal District Court Rules	486
6. Federal Rules of Appellate Procedure	488
7. U.S. Supreme Court Rules	489
ABA Model Code of Judicial Conduct (1990)	490
California Code of Judicial Conduct	518
California Rules on Confidentiality of Proceedings Before the Commission on Judicial Performance	533
ABA Canons of Professional Ethics	535
Parallel Tables Between the ABA Canons of Professional Ethics and the ABA Model Code of Professional Responsibility	548
Parallel Tables Between the ABA Model Code of Professional Responsibility and the ABA Canons of Professional Ethics	551
ABA Standing Committee on Ethics and Professional Responsibility—Composition, Jurisdiction, and Rules of Procedure	554
Lawyer's Creed of Professionalism	557

1992 SELECTED STANDARDS

on

PROFESSIONAL RESPONSIBILITY

*

AMERICAN BAR ASSOCIATION

MODEL RULES OF PROFESSIONAL CONDUCT

The Model Rules of Professional Conduct were adopted by the House of Delegates of the American Bar Association on August 2, 1983

Copyright © 1983 by the American Bar Association. All rights reserved. Permission to reprint granted by the American Bar Association. Reprinted as amended through August, 1991.

Contents

		Page
PREAMBLE: A LAWYER'S RESPONSIBILITIES		3
SCOPE		5
TERMINOLOGY		7

CLIENT–LAWYER RELATIONSHIP

Rule

1.1	Competence	8
1.2	Scope of Representation	9
1.3	Diligence	12
1.4	Communication	13
1.5	Fees	15
1.6	Confidentiality of Information	18
1.7	Conflict of Interest: General Rule	23
1.8	Conflict of Interest: Prohibited Transactions	27
1.9	Conflict of Interest: Former Client	31
1.10	Imputed Disqualification: General Rule	35
1.11	Successive Government and Private Employment	37
1.12	Former Judge or Arbitrator	39
1.13	Organization as Client	41
1.14	Client Under a Disability	45
1.15	Safekeeping Property	47
1.16	Declining or Terminating Representation	49
1.17	Sale of Law Practice	52

COUNSELOR

2.1	Advisor	56
2.2	Intermediary	57
2.3	Evaluation for Use by Third Persons	60

ADVOCATE

3.1	Meritorious Claims and Contentions	62
3.2	Expediting Litigation	63

ABA MODEL RULES

Rule		Page
3.3	Candor Toward the Tribunal	63
3.4	Fairness to Opposing Party and Counsel	68
3.5	Impartiality and Decorum of the Tribunal	70
3.6	Trial Publicity	71
3.7	Lawyer as Witness	73
3.8	Special Responsibilities of a Prosecutor	74
3.9	Advocate in Nonadjudicative Proceedings	76

TRANSACTIONS WITH PERSONS OTHER THAN CLIENTS

4.1	Truthfulness in Statements to Others	77
4.2	Communication With Person Represented by Counsel	78
4.3	Dealing With Unrepresented Person	78
4.4	Respect for Rights of Third Persons	79

LAW FIRMS AND ASSOCIATIONS

5.1	Responsibilities of a Partner or Supervisory Lawyer	79
5.2	Responsibilities of a Subordinate Lawyer	81
5.3	Responsibilities Regarding Nonlawyer Assistants	82
5.4	Professional Independence of a Lawyer	82
5.5	Unauthorized Practice of Law	83
5.6	Restrictions on Right to Practice	84
5.7	Provision of Ancillary Services	85

PUBLIC SERVICE

6.1	Pro Bono Publico Service	91
6.2	Accepting Appointments	92
6.3	Membership in Legal Services Organization	93
6.4	Law Reform Activities Affecting Client Interests	94

INFORMATION ABOUT LEGAL SERVICES

7.1	Communications Concerning a Lawyer's Services	94
7.2	Advertising	95
7.3	Direct Contact With Prospective Clients	97
7.4	Communication of Fields of Practice	100
7.5	Firm Names and Letterheads	101

MAINTAINING THE INTEGRITY OF THE PROFESSION

8.1	Bar Admission and Disciplinary Matters	102
8.2	Judicial and Legal Officials	103
8.3	Reporting Professional Misconduct	104
8.4	Misconduct	105
8.5	Jurisdiction	107
INDEX		108
TABLE A—Table of Sections in the ABA Model Code Related to the ABA Model Rules		114
TABLE B—Table of Sections in the ABA Model Rules Related to the ABA Model Code		121

Preamble: A Lawyer's Responsibilities

[1]* A lawyer is a representative of clients, an officer of the legal system and a public citizen having special responsibility for the quality of justice.

[2] As a representative of clients, a lawyer performs various functions. As advisor, a lawyer provides a client with an informed understanding of the client's legal rights and obligations and explains their practical implications. As advocate, a lawyer zealously asserts the client's position under the rules of the adversary system. As negotiator, a lawyer seeks a result advantageous to the client but consistent with requirements of honest dealing with others. As intermediary between clients, a lawyer seeks to reconcile their divergent interests as an advisor and, to a limited extent, as a spokesperson for each client. A lawyer acts as evaluator by examining a client's legal affairs and reporting about them to the client or to others.

[3] In all professional functions a lawyer should be competent, prompt and diligent. A lawyer should maintain communication with a client concerning the representation. A lawyer should keep in confidence information relating to representation of a client except so far as disclosure is required or permitted by the Rules of Professional Conduct or other law.

[4] A lawyer's conduct should conform to the requirements of the law, both in professional service to clients and in the lawyer's business and personal affairs. A lawyer should use the law's procedures only for legitimate purposes and not to harass or intimidate others. A lawyer should demonstrate respect for the legal system and for those who serve it, including judges, other lawyers and public officials. While it is a lawyer's duty, when necessary, to challenge the rectitude of official action, it is also a lawyer's duty to uphold legal process.

[5] As a public citizen, a lawyer should seek improvement of the law, the administration of justice and the quality of service rendered by the legal profession. As a member of a learned profession, a lawyer should cultivate knowledge of the law beyond its use for clients, employ that knowledge in reform of the law and work to strengthen legal education. A lawyer should be mindful of deficiencies in the administration of justice and of the fact that the poor, and sometimes persons who are not poor, cannot afford adequate legal assistance, and should therefore devote professional time and civic influence in their behalf. A lawyer should aid the legal profession in pursuing these objectives and should help the bar regulate itself in the public interest.

---

* Editors' Note: The ABA Model Rules do not number the paragraphs of the Comments. However, for ease of reference and citation, we have supplied bracketed numbers. Thus, a citation to Rule 1.6, Comment 15 refers to the fifteenth paragraph of the Comment to Model Rule 1.6; a citation to Rule 1.2, Code Comparison 5 refers to the fifth paragraph of the Code Comparison to Model Rule 1.2.

[6] Many of a lawyer's professional responsibilities are prescribed in the Rules of Professional Conduct, as well as substantive and procedural law. However, a lawyer is also guided by personal conscience and the approbation of professional peers. A lawyer should strive to attain the highest level of skill, to improve the law and the legal profession and to exemplify the legal profession's ideals of public service.

[7] A lawyer's responsibilities as a representative of clients, an officer of the legal system and a public citizen are usually harmonious. Thus, when an opposing party is well represented, a lawyer can be a zealous advocate on behalf of a client and at the same time assume that justice is being done. So also, a lawyer can be sure that preserving client confidences ordinarily serves the public interest because people are more likely to seek legal advice, and thereby heed their legal obligations, when they know their communications will be private.

[8] In the nature of law practice, however, conflicting responsibilities are encountered. Virtually all difficult ethical problems arise from conflict between a lawyer's responsibilities to clients, to the legal system and to the lawyer's own interest in remaining an upright person while earning a satisfactory living. The Rules of Professional Conduct prescribe terms for resolving such conflicts. Within the framework of these Rules many difficult issues of professional discretion can arise. Such issues must be resolved through the exercise of sensitive professional and moral judgment guided by the basic principles underlying the Rules.

[9] The legal profession is largely self-governing. Although other professions also have been granted powers of self-government, the legal profession is unique in this respect because of the close relationship between the profession and the processes of government and law enforcement. This connection is manifested in the fact that ultimate authority over the legal profession is vested largely in the courts.

[10] To the extent that lawyers meet the obligations of their professional calling, the occasion for government regulation is obviated. Self-regulation also helps maintain the legal profession's independence from government domination. An independent legal profession is an important force in preserving government under law, for abuse of legal authority is more readily challenged by a profession whose members are not dependent on government for the right to practice.

[11] The legal profession's relative autonomy carries with it special responsibilities of self-government. The profession has a responsibility to assure that its regulations are conceived in the public interest and not in furtherance of parochial or self-interested concerns of the bar. Every lawyer is responsible for observance of the Rules of Professional Conduct. A lawyer should also aid in securing their observance by other lawyers. Neglect of these responsibilities compromises the independence of the profession and the public interest which it serves.

[12] Lawyers play a vital role in the preservation of society. The fulfillment of this role requires an understanding by lawyers of their relationship to our legal system. The Rules of Professional Conduct, when properly applied, serve to define that relationship.

Scope

[1] The Rules of Professional Conduct are rules of reason. They should be interpreted with reference to the purposes of legal representation and of the law itself. Some of the Rules are imperatives, cast in the terms "shall" or "shall not." These define proper conduct for purposes of professional discipline. Others, generally cast in the term "may," are permissive and define areas under the Rules in which the lawyer has professional discretion. No disciplinary action should be taken when the lawyer chooses not to act or acts within the bounds of such discretion. Other Rules define the nature of relationships between the lawyer and others. The Rules are thus partly obligatory and disciplinary and partly constitutive and descriptive in that they define a lawyer's professional role. Many of the Comments use the term "should." Comments do not add obligations to the Rules but provide guidance for practicing in compliance with the Rules.

[2] The Rules presuppose a larger legal context shaping the lawyer's role. That context includes court rules and statutes relating to matters of licensure, laws defining specific obligations of lawyers and substantive and procedural law in general. Compliance with the Rules, as with all law in an open society, depends primarily upon understanding and voluntary compliance, secondarily upon reinforcement by peer and public opinion and finally, when necessary, upon enforcement through disciplinary proceedings. The Rules do not, however, exhaust the moral and ethical considerations that should inform a lawyer, for no worthwhile human activity can be completely defined by legal rules. The Rules simply provide a framework for the ethical practice of law.

[3] Furthermore, for purposes of determining the lawyer's authority and responsibility, principles of substantive law external to these Rules determine whether a client-lawyer relationship exists. Most of the duties flowing from the client-lawyer relationship attach only after the client has requested the lawyer to render legal services and the lawyer has agreed to do so. But there are some duties, such as that of confidentiality under Rule 1.6, that may attach when the lawyer agrees to consider whether a client-lawyer relationship shall be established. Whether a client-lawyer relationship exists for any specific purpose can depend on the circumstances and may be a question of fact.

[4] Under various legal provisions, including constitutional, statutory and common law, the responsibilities of government lawyers may include authority concerning legal matters that ordinarily reposes in the client in private client-lawyer relationships. For example, a lawyer for a government agency may have authority on behalf of the government to

decide upon settlement or whether to appeal from an adverse judgment. Such authority in various respects is generally vested in the attorney general and the state's attorney in state government, and their federal counterparts, and the same may be true of other government law officers. Also, lawyers under the supervision of these officers may be authorized to represent several government agencies in intragovernmental legal controversies in circumstances where a private lawyer could not represent multiple private clients. They also may have authority to represent the "public interest" in circumstances where a private lawyer would not be authorized to do so. These Rules do not abrogate any such authority.

[5] Failure to comply with an obligation or prohibition imposed by a Rule is a basis for invoking the disciplinary process. The Rules presuppose that disciplinary assessment of a lawyer's conduct will be made on the basis of the facts and circumstances as they existed at the time of the conduct in question and in recognition of the fact that a lawyer often has to act upon uncertain or incomplete evidence of the situation. Moreover, the Rules presuppose that whether or not discipline should be imposed for a violation, and the severity of a sanction, depend on all the circumstances, such as the willfulness and seriousness of the violation, extenuating factors and whether there have been previous violations.

[6] Violation of a Rule should not give rise to a cause of action nor should it create any presumption that a legal duty has been breached. The Rules are designed to provide guidance to lawyers and to provide a structure for regulating conduct through disciplinary agencies. They are not designed to be a basis for civil liability. Furthermore, the purpose of the Rules can be subverted when they are invoked by opposing parties as procedural weapons. The fact that a Rule is a just basis for a lawyer's self-assessment, or for sanctioning a lawyer under the administration of a disciplinary authority, does not imply that an antagonist in a collateral proceeding or transaction has standing to seek enforcement of the Rule. Accordingly, nothing in the Rules should be deemed to augment any substantive legal duty of lawyers or the extra-disciplinary consequences of violating such a duty.

[7] Moreover, these Rules are not intended to govern or affect judicial application of either the attorney-client or work product privilege. Those privileges were developed to promote compliance with law and fairness in litigation. In reliance on the attorney-client privilege, clients are entitled to expect that communications within the scope of the privilege will be protected against compelled disclosure. The attorney-client privilege is that of the client and not of the lawyer. The fact that in exceptional situations the lawyer under the Rules has a limited discretion to disclose a client confidence does not vitiate the proposition that, as a general matter, the client has a reasonable expectation that information relating to the client will not be voluntarily disclosed and that disclosure of such information may be judicially compelled only in

accordance with recognized exceptions to the attorney-client and work product privileges.

[8] The lawyer's exercise of discretion not to disclose information under Rule 1.6 should not be subject to reexamination. Permitting such reexamination would be incompatible with the general policy of promoting compliance with law through assurances that communications will be protected against disclosure.

[9] The Comment accompanying each Rule explains and illustrates the meaning and purpose of the Rule. The Preamble and this note on Scope provide general orientation. The Comments are intended as guides to interpretation, but the text of each Rule is authoritative. Research notes were prepared to compare counterparts in the ABA Model Code of Professional Responsibility (adopted 1969, as amended) and to provide selected references to other authorities. The notes have not been adopted, do not constitute part of the Model Rules, and are not intended to affect the application or interpretation of the Rules and Comments.

Terminology

[1] "Belief" or "Believes" denotes that the person involved actually supposed the fact in question to be true. A person's belief may be inferred from circumstances.

[2] "Consult" or "Consultation" denotes communication of information reasonably sufficient to permit the client to appreciate the significance of the matter in question.

[3] "Firm" or "Law firm" denotes a lawyer or lawyers in a private firm, lawyers employed in the legal department of a corporation or other organization and lawyers employed in a legal services organization. See Comment, Rule 1.10.

[4] "Fraud" or "Fraudulent" denotes conduct having a purpose to deceive and not merely negligent misrepresentation or failure to apprise another of relevant information.

[5] "Knowingly," "Known," or "Knows" denotes actual knowledge of the fact in question. A person's knowledge may be inferred from circumstances.

[6] "Partner" denotes a member of a partnership and a shareholder in a law firm organized as a professional corporation.

[7] "Reasonable" or "Reasonably" when used in relation to conduct by a lawyer denotes the conduct of a reasonably prudent and competent lawyer.

[8] "Reasonable belief" or "Reasonably believes" when used in reference to a lawyer denotes that the lawyer believes the matter in question and that the circumstances are such that the belief is reasonable.

Terminology ABA MODEL RULES

[9] "Reasonably should know" when used in reference to a lawyer denotes that a lawyer of reasonable prudence and competence would ascertain the matter in question.

[10] "Substantial" when used in reference to degree or extent denotes a material matter of clear and weighty importance.

MODEL RULES OF PROFESSIONAL CONDUCT

CLIENT–LAWYER RELATIONSHIP

RULE 1.1 Competence

A lawyer shall provide competent representation to a client. Competent representation requires the legal knowledge, skill, thoroughness and preparation reasonably necessary for the representation.

COMMENT:

Legal Knowledge and Skill

[1] In determining whether a lawyer employs the requisite knowledge and skill in a particular matter, relevant factors include the relative complexity and specialized nature of the matter, the lawyer's general experience, the lawyer's training and experience in the field in question, the preparation and study the lawyer is able to give the matter and whether it is feasible to refer the matter to, or associate or consult with, a lawyer of established competence in the field in question. In many instances, the required proficiency is that of a general practitioner. Expertise in a particular field of law may be required in some circumstances.

[2] A lawyer need not necessarily have special training or prior experience to handle legal problems of a type with which the lawyer is unfamiliar. A newly admitted lawyer can be as competent as a practitioner with long experience. Some important legal skills, such as the analysis of precedent, the evaluation of evidence and legal drafting, are required in all legal problems. Perhaps the most fundamental legal skill consists of determining what kind of legal problems a situation may involve, a skill that necessarily transcends any particular specialized knowledge. A lawyer can provide adequate representation in a wholly novel field through necessary study. Competent representation can also be provided through the association of a lawyer of established competence in the field in question.

[3] In an emergency a lawyer may give advice or assistance in a matter in which the lawyer does not have the skill ordinarily required where referral to or consultation or association with another lawyer would be impractical. Even in an emergency, however, assistance should be limited to that reasonably necessary in the circumstances, for ill considered action under emergency conditions can jeopardize the client's interest.

[4] A lawyer may accept representation where the requisite level of competence can be achieved by reasonable preparation. This applies as well to a lawyer who is appointed as counsel for an unrepresented person. See also Rule 6.2.

Thoroughness and Preparation

[5] Competent handling of a particular matter includes inquiry into and analysis of the factual and legal elements of the problem, and use of methods and procedures meeting the standards of competent practitioners. It also includes adequate preparation. The required attention and preparation are determined in part by what is at stake; major litigation and complex transactions ordinarily require more elaborate treatment than matters of lesser consequence.

Maintaining Competence

[6] To maintain the requisite knowledge and skill, a lawyer should engage in continuing study and education. If a system of peer review has been established, the lawyer should consider making use of it in appropriate circumstances.

MODEL CODE COMPARISON

DR 6–101(A)(1) provided that a lawyer shall not handle a matter "which he knows or should know that he is not competent to handle, without associating himself with a lawyer who is competent to handle it;" DR 6–101(A)(2) required "preparation adequate in the circumstances." Rule 1.1 more fully particularizes the elements of competence. Whereas DR 6–101(A)(3) prohibited the "[n]eglect of a legal matter," Rule 1.1 does not contain such a prohibition. Instead, Rule 1.1 affirmatively requires the lawyer to be competent.

RULE 1.2 Scope of Representation

(a) **A lawyer shall abide by a client's decisions concerning the objectives of representation, subject to paragraphs (c), (d) and (e), and shall consult with the client as to the means by which they are to be pursued. A lawyer shall abide by a client's decision whether to accept an offer of settlement of a matter. In a criminal case, the lawyer shall abide by the client's decision, after consultation with the lawyer, as to a plea to be entered, whether to waive jury trial and whether the client will testify.**

(b) **A lawyer's representation of a client, including representation by appointment, does not constitute an endorsement of the client's political, economic, social or moral views or activities.**

(c) **A lawyer may limit the objectives of the representation if the client consents after consultation.**

(d) **A lawyer shall not counsel a client to engage, or assist a client, in conduct that the lawyer knows is criminal or fraudulent, but a lawyer may discuss the legal consequences of any proposed course of conduct with a client and may counsel or assist a client to make a**

Rule 1.2

good faith effort to determine the validity, scope, meaning or application of the law.

(e) When a lawyer knows that a client expects assistance not permitted by the Rules of Professional Conduct or other law, the lawyer shall consult with the client regarding the relevant limitations on the lawyer's conduct.

COMMENT:

Scope of Representation

[1] Both lawyer and client have authority and responsibility in the objectives and means of representation. The client has ultimate authority to determine the purposes to be served by legal representation, within the limits imposed by law and the lawyer's professional obligations. Within those limits, a client also has a right to consult with the lawyer about the means to be used in pursuing those objectives. At the same time, a lawyer is not required to pursue objectives or employ means simply because a client may wish that the lawyer do so. A clear distinction between objectives and means sometimes cannot be drawn, and in many cases the client-lawyer relationship partakes of a joint undertaking. In questions of means, the lawyer should assume responsibility for technical and legal tactical issues, but should defer to the client regarding such questions as the expense to be incurred and concern for third persons who might be adversely affected. Law defining the lawyer's scope of authority in litigation varies among jurisdictions.

[2] In a case in which the client appears to be suffering mental disability, the lawyer's duty to abide by the client's decisions is to be guided by reference to Rule 1.14.

Independence From Client's Views or Activities

[3] Legal representation should not be denied to people who are unable to afford legal services, or whose cause is controversial or the subject of popular disapproval. By the same token, representing a client does not constitute approval of the client's views or activities.

Services Limited in Objectives or Means

[4] The objectives or scope of services provided by a lawyer may be limited by agreement with the client or by the terms under which the lawyer's services are made available to the client. For example, a retainer may be for a specifically defined purpose. Representation provided through a legal aid agency may be subject to limitations on the types of cases the agency handles. When a lawyer has been retained by an insurer to represent an insured, the representation may be limited to matters related to the insurance coverage. The terms upon which representation is undertaken may exclude specific objectives or means.

Such limitations may exclude objectives or means that the lawyer regards as repugnant or imprudent.

[5] An agreement concerning the scope of representation must accord with the Rules of Professional Conduct and other law. Thus, the client may not be asked to agree to representation so limited in scope as to violate Rule 1.1, or to surrender the right to terminate the lawyer's services or the right to settle litigation that the lawyer might wish to continue.

Criminal, Fraudulent and Prohibited Transactions

[6] A lawyer is required to give an honest opinion about the actual consequences that appear likely to result from a client's conduct. The fact that a client uses advice in a course of action that is criminal or fraudulent does not, of itself, make a lawyer a party to the course of action. However, a lawyer may not knowingly assist a client in criminal or fraudulent conduct. There is a critical distinction between presenting an analysis of legal aspects of questionable conduct and recommending the means by which a crime or fraud might be committed with impunity.

[7] When the client's course of action has already begun and is continuing, the lawyer's responsibility is especially delicate. The lawyer is not permitted to reveal the client's wrongdoing, except where permitted by Rule 1.6. However, the lawyer is required to avoid furthering the purpose, for example, by suggesting how it might be concealed. A lawyer may not continue assisting a client in conduct that the lawyer originally supposes is legally proper but then discovers is criminal or fraudulent. Withdrawal from the representation, therefore, may be required.

[8] Where the client is a fiduciary, the lawyer may be charged with special obligations in dealings with a beneficiary.

[9] Paragraph (d) applies whether or not the defrauded party is a party to the transaction. Hence, a lawyer should not participate in a sham transaction; for example, a transaction to effectuate criminal or fraudulent escape of tax liability. Paragraph (d) does not preclude undertaking a criminal defense incident to a general retainer for legal services to a lawful enterprise. The last clause of paragraph (d) recognizes that determining the validity or interpretation of a statute or regulation may require a course of action involving disobedience of the statute or regulation or of the interpretation placed upon it by governmental authorities.

MODEL CODE COMPARISON

[1] Paragraph (a) has no counterpart in the Disciplinary Rules of the Model Code. EC 7–7 stated: "In certain areas of legal representation not affecting the merits of the cause or substantially prejudicing the rights of a client, a lawyer is entitled to make decisions on his own. But otherwise the authority to make decisions is exclusively that of the client . . . ." EC 7–8 stated that "[i]n the

final analysis, however, the . . . decision whether to forego legally available objectives or methods because of nonlegal factors is ultimately for the client . . . . In the event that the client in a nonadjudicatory matter insists upon a course of conduct that is contrary to the judgment and advice of the lawyer but not prohibited by Disciplinary Rules, the lawyer may withdraw from the employment." DR 7-101(A)(1) provided that a lawyer "shall not intentionally . . . fail to seek the lawful objectives of his client through reasonably available means permitted by law . . . . A lawyer does not violate this Disciplinary Rule, however, by . . . avoiding offensive tactics . . . ."

[2] Paragraph (b) has no counterpart in the Model Code.

[3] With regard to paragraph (c), DR 7-101(B)(1) provided that a lawyer may, "where permissible, exercise his professional judgment to waive or fail to assert a right or position of his client."

[4] With regard to paragraph (d), DR 7-102(A)(7) provided that a lawyer shall not "counsel or assist his client in conduct that the lawyer knows to be illegal or fraudulent." DR 7-102(A)(6) provided that a lawyer shall not "participate in the creation or preservation of evidence when he knows or it is obvious that the evidence is false." DR 7-106 provided that a lawyer shall not "advise his client to disregard a standing rule of a tribunal or a ruling of a tribunal . . . but he may take appropriate steps in good faith to test the validity of such rule or ruling." EC 7-5 stated that a lawyer "should never encourage or aid his client to commit criminal acts or counsel his client on how to violate the law and avoid punishment therefor."

[5] With regard to paragraph (e), DR 2-110(C)(1)(c) provided that a lawyer may withdraw from representation if a client "insists" that the lawyer engage in "conduct that is illegal or that is prohibited under the Disciplinary Rules." DR 9-101(C) provided that "a lawyer shall not state or imply that he is able to influence improperly . . . any tribunal, legislative body or public official."

RULE 1.3 Diligence

A lawyer shall act with reasonable diligence and promptness in representing a client.

COMMENT:

[1] A lawyer should pursue a matter on behalf of a client despite opposition, obstruction or personal inconvenience to the lawyer, and may take whatever lawful and ethical measures are required to vindicate a client's cause or endeavor. A lawyer should act with commitment and dedication to the interests of the client and with zeal in advocacy upon the client's behalf. However, a lawyer is not bound to press for every advantage that might be realized for a client. A lawyer has professional discretion in determining the means by which a matter should be pursued. See Rule 1.2. A lawyer's workload should be controlled so that each matter can be handled adequately.

[2] Perhaps no professional shortcoming is more widely resented than procrastination. A client's interests often can be adversely affected by the passage of time or the change of conditions; in extreme instances, as when a lawyer overlooks a statute of limitations, the client's legal

position may be destroyed. Even when the client's interests are not affected in substance, however, unreasonable delay can cause a client needless anxiety and undermine confidence in the lawyer's trustworthiness.

[3] Unless the relationship is terminated as provided in Rule 1.16, a lawyer should carry through to conclusion all matters undertaken for a client. If a lawyer's employment is limited to a specific matter, the relationship terminates when the matter has been resolved. If a lawyer has served a client over a substantial period in a variety of matters, the client sometimes may assume that the lawyer will continue to serve on a continuing basis unless the lawyer gives notice of withdrawal. Doubt about whether a client-lawyer relationship still exists should be clarified by the lawyer, preferably in writing, so that the client will not mistakenly suppose the lawyer is looking after the client's affairs when the lawyer has ceased to do so. For example, if a lawyer has handled a judicial or administrative proceeding that produced a result adverse to the client but has not been specifically instructed concerning pursuit of an appeal, the lawyer should advise the client of the possibility of appeal before relinquishing responsibility for the matter.

MODEL CODE COMPARISON

DR 6–101(A)(3) required that a lawyer not "[n]eglect a matter entrusted to him." EC 6–4 stated that a lawyer should "give appropriate attention to his legal work." Canon 7 stated that "a lawyer should represent a client zealously within the bounds of law." DR 7–101(A)(1) provided that a lawyer "shall not intentionally . . . fail to seek the lawful objectives of his client through reasonably available means permitted by law and the Disciplinary Rules. . . . ." DR 7–101(A)(3) provided that a lawyer "shall not intentionally . . . [p]rejudice or damage his client during the course of the relationship . . . ."

RULE 1.4 Communication

(a) A lawyer shall keep a client reasonably informed about the status of a matter and promptly comply with reasonable requests for information.

(b) A lawyer shall explain a matter to the extent reasonably necessary to permit the client to make informed decisions regarding the representation.

COMMENT:

[1] The client should have sufficient information to participate intelligently in decisions concerning the objectives of the representation and the means by which they are to be pursued, to the extent the client is willing and able to do so. For example, a lawyer negotiating on behalf of a client should provide the client with facts relevant to the matter, inform the client of communications from another party and take other reasonable steps that permit the client to make a decision regarding a serious offer from another party. A lawyer who receives from opposing

Rule 1.4   *ABA MODEL RULES*

counsel an offer of settlement in a civil controversy or a proffered plea bargain in a criminal case should promptly inform the client of its substance unless prior discussions with the client have left it clear that the proposal will be unacceptable. See Rule 1.2(a). Even when a client delegates authority to the lawyer, the client should be kept advised of the status of the matter.

[2] Adequacy of communication depends in part on the kind of advice or assistance involved. For example, in negotiations where there is time to explain a proposal the lawyer should review all important provisions with the client before proceeding to an agreement. In litigation a lawyer should explain the general strategy and prospects of success and ordinarily should consult the client on tactics that might injure or coerce others. On the other hand, a lawyer ordinarily cannot be expected to describe trial or negotiation strategy in detail. The guiding principle is that the lawyer should fulfill reasonable client expectations for information consistent with the duty to act in the client's best interests, and the client's overall requirements as to the character of representation.

[3] Ordinarily, the information to be provided is that appropriate for a client who is a comprehending and responsible adult. However, fully informing the client according to this standard may be impracticable, for example, where the client is a child or suffers from mental disability. See Rule 1.14. When the client is an organization or group, it is often impossible or inappropriate to inform every one of its members about its legal affairs; ordinarily, the lawyer should address communications to the appropriate officials of the organization. See Rule 1.13. Where many routine matters are involved, a system of limited or occasional reporting may be arranged with the client. Practical exigency may also require a lawyer to act for a client without prior consultation.

Withholding Information

[4] In some circumstances, a lawyer may be justified in delaying transmission of information when the client would be likely to react imprudently to an immediate communication. Thus, a lawyer might withhold a psychiatric diagnosis of a client when the examining psychiatrist indicates that disclosure would harm the client. A lawyer may not withhold information to serve the lawyer's own interest or convenience. Rules or court orders governing litigation may provide that information supplied to a lawyer may not be disclosed to the client. Rule 3.4(c) directs compliance with such rules or orders.

MODEL CODE COMPARISON

Rule 1.4 has no direct counterpart in the Disciplinary Rules of the Model Code. DR 6–101(A)(3) provided that a lawyer shall not "[n]eglect a legal matter entrusted to him." DR 9–102(B)(1) provided that a lawyer shall "[p]romptly notify a client of the receipt of his funds, securities, or other properties." EC 7–8 stated that a lawyer "should exert his best efforts to insure that decisions of his client are made only after the client has been informed of relevant considerations." EC 9–2 stated that "a lawyer should fully and promptly inform his client of material developments in the matters being handled for the client."

RULE 1.5 Fees

(a) A lawyer's fee shall be reasonable. The factors to be considered in determining the reasonableness of a fee include the following:

(1) the time and labor required, the novelty and difficulty of the questions involved, and the skill requisite to perform the legal service properly;

(2) the likelihood, if apparent to the client, that the acceptance of the particular employment will preclude other employment by the lawyer;

(3) the fee customarily charged in the locality for similar legal services;

(4) the amount involved and the results obtained;

(5) the time limitations imposed by the client or by the circumstances;

(6) the nature and length of the professional relationship with the client;

(7) the experience, reputation, and ability of the lawyer or lawyers performing the services; and

(8) whether the fee is fixed or contingent.

(b) When the lawyer has not regularly represented the client, the basis or rate of the fee shall be communicated to the client, preferably in writing, before or within a reasonable time after commencing the representation.

(c) A fee may be contingent on the outcome of the matter for which the service is rendered, except in a matter in which a contingent fee is prohibited by paragraph (d) or other law. A contingent fee agreement shall be in writing and shall state the method by which the fee is to be determined, including the percentage or percentages that shall accrue to the lawyer in the event of settlement, trial or appeal, litigation and other expenses to be deducted from the recovery, and whether such expenses are to be deducted before or after the contingent fee is calculated. Upon conclusion of a contingent fee matter, the lawyer shall provide the client with a written statement stating the outcome of the matter and, if there is a recovery, showing the remittance to the client and the method of its determination.

(d) A lawyer shall not enter into an arrangement for, charge, or collect:

(1) any fee in a domestic relations matter, the payment or amount of which is contingent upon the securing of a divorce or

Rule 1.5   *ABA MODEL RULES*

upon the amount of alimony or support, or property settlement in lieu thereof; or

(2) a contingent fee for representing a defendant in a criminal case.

(e) A division of fee between lawyers who are not in the same firm may be made only if:

(1) the division is in proportion to the services performed by each lawyer or, by written agreement with the client, each lawyer assumes joint responsibility for the representation;

(2) the client is advised of and does not object to the participation of all the lawyers involved; and

(3) the total fee is reasonable.

COMMENT:

Basis or Rate of Fee

[1] When the lawyer has regularly represented a client, they ordinarily will have evolved an understanding concerning the basis or rate of the fee. In a new client-lawyer relationship, however, an understanding as to the fee should be promptly established. It is not necessary to recite all the factors that underlie the basis of the fee, but only those that are directly involved in its computation. It is sufficient, for example, to state that the basic rate is an hourly charge or a fixed amount or an estimated amount, or to identify the factors that may be taken into account in finally fixing the fee. When developments occur during the representation that render an earlier estimate substantially inaccurate, a revised estimate should be provided to the client. A written statement concerning the fee reduces the possibility of misunderstanding. Furnishing the client with a simple memorandum or a copy of the lawyer's customary fee schedule is sufficient if the basis or rate of the fee is set forth.

Terms of Payment

[2] A lawyer may require advance payment of a fee, but is obliged to return any unearned portion. See Rule 1.16(d). A lawyer may accept property in payment for services, such as an ownership interest in an enterprise, providing this does not involve acquisition of a proprietary interest in the cause of action or subject matter of the litigation contrary to Rule 1.8(j). However, a fee paid in property instead of money may be subject to special scrutiny because it involves questions concerning both the value of the services and the lawyer's special knowledge of the value of the property.

[3] An agreement may not be made whose terms might induce the lawyer improperly to curtail services for the client or perform them in a way contrary to the client's interest. For example, a lawyer should not enter into an agreement whereby services are to be provided only up to a

stated amount when it is foreseeable that more extensive services probably will be required, unless the situation is adequately explained to the client. Otherwise, the client might have to bargain for further assistance in the midst of a proceeding or transaction. However, it is proper to define the extent of services in light of the client's ability to pay. A lawyer should not exploit a fee arrangement based primarily on hourly charges by using wasteful procedures. When there is doubt whether a contingent fee is consistent with the client's best interest, the lawyer should offer the client alternative bases for the fee and explain their implications. Applicable law may impose limitations on contingent fees, such as a ceiling on the percentage.

Division of Fee

[4] A division of fee is a single billing to a client covering the fee of two or more lawyers who are not in the same firm. A division of fee facilitates association of more than one lawyer in a matter in which neither alone could serve the client as well, and most often is used when the fee is contingent and the division is between a referring lawyer and a trial specialist. Paragraph (e) permits the lawyers to divide a fee on either the basis of the proportion of services they render or by agreement between the participating lawyers if all assume responsibility for the representation as a whole and the client is advised and does not object. It does not require disclosure to the client of the share that each lawyer is to receive. Joint responsibility for the representation entails the obligations stated in Rule 5.1 for purposes of the matter involved.

Disputes Over Fees

[5] If a procedure has been established for resolution of fee disputes, such as an arbitration or mediation procedure established by the bar, the lawyer should conscientiously consider submitting to it. Law may prescribe a procedure for determining a lawyer's fee, for example, in representation of an executor or administrator, a class or a person entitled to a reasonable fee as part of the measure of damages. The lawyer entitled to such a fee and a lawyer representing another party concerned with the fee should comply with the prescribed procedure.

MODEL CODE COMPARISON

[1] DR 2-106(A) provided that a lawyer "shall not enter into an agreement for, charge, or collect an illegal or clearly excessive fee." DR 2-106(B) provided that a fee is "clearly excessive when, after a review of the facts, a lawyer of ordinary prudence would be left with a definite and firm conviction that the fee is in excess of a reasonable fee." The factors of a reasonable fee in Rule 1.5(a) are substantially identical to those listed in DR 2-106(B). EC 2-17 states that a lawyer "should not charge more than a reasonable fee . . . ."

[2] There was no counterpart to paragraph (b) in the Disciplinary Rules of the Model Code. EC 2-19 stated that it is "usually beneficial to reduce to

Rule 1.5 *ABA MODEL RULES*

writing the understanding of the parties regarding the fee, particularly when it is contingent."

[3] There was also no counterpart to paragraph (c) in the Disciplinary Rules of the Model Code. EC 2–20 provided that "[c]ontingent fee arrangements in civil cases have long been commonly accepted in the United States," but that "a lawyer generally should decline to accept employment on a contingent fee basis by one who is able to pay a reasonable fixed fee . . . ."

[4] With regard to paragraph (d), DR 2–106(C) prohibited "a contingent fee in a criminal case." EC 2–20 provided that "contingent fee arrangements in domestic relation cases are rarely justified."

[5] With regard to paragraph (e), DR 2–107(A) permitted division of fees only if: "(1) The client consents to employment of the other lawyer after a full disclosure that a division of fees will be made. (2) The division is in proportion to the services performed and responsibility assumed by each. (3) The total fee does not exceed clearly reasonable compensation . . . ." Paragraph (e) permits division without regard to the services rendered by each lawyer if they assume joint responsibility for the representation.

RULE 1.6 Confidentiality of Information *

(a) A lawyer shall not reveal information relating to representation of a client unless the client consents after consultation, except for disclosures that are impliedly authorized in order to carry out the representation, and except as stated in paragraph (b).

(b) A lawyer may reveal such information to the extent the lawyer reasonably believes necessary:

(1) to prevent the client from committing a criminal act that the lawyer believes is likely to result in imminent death or substantial bodily harm; or

---

* Editors' Note: As previously proposed by the Kutak Commission, Rule 1.6 (Revised Final Draft, June 30, 1982) read as follows:

RULE 1.6 Confidentiality of Information

(a) A lawyer shall not reveal information relating to representation of a client unless the client consents after consultation, except for disclosures that are impliedly authorized in order to carry out the representation, and except as stated in paragaraph (b).

(b) A lawyer may reveal such information to the extent the lawyer reasonably believes necessary:

(1) to prevent the client from committing a criminal or fraudulent act that the lawyer reasonably believes is likely to result in death or substantial bodily harm, or in substantial injury to the financial interests or property of another;

(2) to rectify the consequences of a client's criminal or fraudulent act in the furtherance of which the lawyer's services had been used;

(3) to establish a claim or defense on behalf of the lawyer in a controversy between the lawyer and the client, or to establish a defense to a criminal charge, civil claim or disciplinary complaint against the lawyer based upon conduct in which the client was involved; or

(4) to comply with other law.

In 1991, the ABA House of Delegates again rejected a proposal from its ethics committee to amend Rule 1.6(b) to add the rectification language found in subsection (b)(2) of the 1982 Revised Final Draft. As of the end of 1991, about a third of the states have adopted a rectification provision.

(2) to establish a claim or defense on behalf of the lawyer in a controversy between the lawyer and the client, to establish a defense to a criminal charge or civil claim against the lawyer based upon conduct in which the client was involved, or to respond to allegations in any proceeding concerning the lawyer's representation of the client.

COMMENT:

[1] The lawyer is part of a judicial system charged with upholding the law. One of the lawyer's functions is to advise clients so that they avoid any violation of the law in the proper exercise of their rights.

[2] The observance of the ethical obligation of a lawyer to hold inviolate confidential information of the client not only facilitates the full development of facts essential to proper representation of the client but also encourages people to seek early legal assistance.

[3] Almost without exception, clients come to lawyers in order to determine what their rights are and what is, in the maze of laws and regulations, deemed to be legal and correct. The common law recognizes that the client's confidences must be protected from disclosure. Based upon experience, lawyers know that almost all clients follow the advice given, and the law is upheld.

[4] A fundamental principle in the client-lawyer relationship is that the lawyer maintain confidentiality of information relating to the representation. The client is thereby encouraged to communicate fully and frankly with the lawyer even as to embarrassing or legally damaging subject matter.

[5] The principle of confidentiality is given effect in two related bodies of law, the attorney-client privilege (which includes the work product doctrine) in the law of evidence and the rule of confidentiality established in professional ethics. The attorney-client privilege applies in judicial and other proceedings in which a lawyer may be called as a witness or otherwise required to produce evidence concerning a client. The rule of client-lawyer confidentiality applies in situations other than those where evidence is sought from the lawyer through compulsion of law. The confidentiality rule applies not merely to matters communicated in confidence by the client but also to all information relating to the representation, whatever its source. A lawyer may not disclose such information except as authorized or required by the Rules of Professional Conduct or other law. See also Scope.

[6] The requirement of maintaining confidentiality of information relating to representation applies to government lawyers who may disagree with the policy goals that their representation is designed to advance.

Rule 1.6 ABA MODEL RULES

Authorized Disclosure

[7] A lawyer is impliedly authorized to make disclosures about a client when appropriate in carrying out the representation, except to the extent that the client's instructions or special circumstances limit that authority. In litigation, for example, a lawyer may disclose information by admitting a fact that cannot properly be disputed, or in negotiation by making a disclosure that facilitates a satisfactory conclusion.

[8] Lawyers in a firm may, in the course of the firm's practice, disclose to each other information relating to a client of the firm, unless the client has instructed that particular information be confined to specified lawyers.

Disclosure Adverse to Client

[9] The confidentiality rule is subject to limited exceptions. In becoming privy to information about a client, a lawyer may foresee that the client intends serious harm to another person. However, to the extent a lawyer is required or permitted to disclose a client's purposes, the client will be inhibited from revealing facts which would enable the lawyer to counsel against a wrongful course of action. The public is better protected if full and open communication by the client is encouraged than if it is inhibited.

[10] Several situations must be distinguished. First, the lawyer may not counsel or assist a client in conduct that is criminal or fraudulent. See Rule 1.2(d). Similarly, a lawyer has a duty under Rule 3.3(a)(4) not to use false evidence. This duty is essentially a special instance of the duty prescribed in Rule 1.2(d) to avoid assisting a client in criminal or fraudulent conduct.

[11] Second, the lawyer may have been innocently involved in past conduct by the client that was criminal or fraudulent. In such a situation the lawyer has not violated Rule 1.2(d), because to "counsel or assist" criminal or fraudulent conduct requires knowing that the conduct is of that character.

[12] Third, the lawyer may learn that a client intends prospective conduct that is criminal and likely to result in imminent death or substantial bodily harm. As stated in paragraph (b)(1), the lawyer has professional discretion to reveal information in order to prevent such consequences. The lawyer may make a disclosure in order to prevent homicide or serious bodily injury which the lawyer reasonably believes is intended by a client. It is very difficult for a lawyer to "know" when such a heinous purpose will actually be carried out, for the client may have a change of mind.

[13] The lawyer's exercise of discretion requires consideration of such factors as the nature of the lawyer's relationship with the client and with those who might be injured by the client, the lawyer's own involvement in the transaction and factors that may extenuate the conduct in

question. Where practical, the lawyer should seek to persuade the client to take suitable action. In any case, a disclosure adverse to the client's interest should be no greater than the lawyer reasonably believes necessary to the purpose. A lawyer's decision not to take preventive action permitted by paragraph (b)(1) does not violate this Rule.

Withdrawal

[14] If the lawyer's services will be used by the client in materially furthering a course of criminal or fraudulent conduct, the lawyer must withdraw, as stated in Rule 1.16(a)(1).

[15] After withdrawal the lawyer is required to refrain from making disclosure of the clients' confidences, except as otherwise provided in Rule 1.6. Neither this Rule nor Rule 1.8(b) nor Rule 1.16(d) prevents the lawyer from giving notice of the fact of withdrawal, and the lawyer may also withdraw or disaffirm any opinion, document, affirmation, or the like.

[16] Where the client is an organization, the lawyer may be in doubt whether contemplated conduct will actually be carried out by the organization. Where necessary to guide conduct in connection with this Rule, the lawyer may make inquiry within the organization as indicated in Rule 1.13(b).

Dispute Concerning Lawyer's Conduct

[17] Where a legal claim or disciplinary charge alleges complicity of the lawyer in a client's conduct or other misconduct of the lawyer involving representation of the client, the lawyer may respond to the extent the lawyer reasonably believes necessary to establish a defense. The same is true with respect to a claim involving the conduct or representation of a former client. The lawyer's right to respond arises when an assertion of such complicity has been made. Paragraph (b)(2) does not require the lawyer to await the commencement of an action or proceeding that charges such complicity, so that the defense may be established by responding directly to a third party who has made such an assertion. The right to defend, of course, applies where a proceeding has been commenced. Where practicable and not prejudicial to the lawyer's ability to establish the defense, the lawyer should advise the client of the third party's assertion and request that the client respond appropriately. In any event, disclosure should be no greater than the lawyer reasonably believes is necessary to vindicate innocence, the disclosure should be made in a manner which limits access to the information to the tribunal or other persons having a need to know it, and appropriate protective orders or other arrangements should be sought by the lawyer to the fullest extent practicable.

[18] If the lawyer is charged with wrongdoing in which the client's conduct is implicated, the rule of confidentiality should not prevent the lawyer from defending against the charge. Such a charge can arise in a

Rule 1.6 *ABA MODEL RULES*

civil, criminal or professional disciplinary proceeding, and can be based on a wrong allegedly committed by the lawyer against the client, or on a wrong alleged by a third person; for example, a person claiming to have been defrauded by the lawyer and client acting together. A lawyer entitled to a fee is permitted by paragraph (b)(2) to prove the services rendered in an action to collect it. This aspect of the rule expresses the principle that the beneficiary of a fiduciary relationship may not exploit it to the detriment of the fiduciary. As stated above, the lawyer must make every effort practicable to avoid unnecessary disclosure of information relating to a representation, to limit disclosure to those having the need to know it, and to obtain protective orders or make other arrangements minimizing the risk of disclosure.

Disclosures Otherwise Required or Authorized

[19] The attorney-client privilege is differently defined in various jurisdictions. If a lawyer is called as a witness to give testimony concerning a client, absent waiver by the client, Rule 1.6(a) requires the lawyer to invoke the privilege when it is applicable. The lawyer must comply with the final orders of a court or other tribunal of competent jurisdiction requiring the lawyer to give information about the client.

[20] The Rules of Professional Conduct in various circumstances permit or require a lawyer to disclose information relating to the representation. See Rules 2.2, 2.3, 3.3 and 4.1. In addition to these provisions, a lawyer may be obligated or permitted by other provisions of law to give information about a client. Whether another provision of law supersedes Rule 1.6 is a matter of interpretation beyond the scope of these Rules, but a presumption should exist against such a supersession.

Former Client

[21] The duty of confidentiality continues after the client-lawyer relationship has terminated.

MODEL CODE COMPARISON

[1] Rule 1.6 eliminates the two-pronged duty under the Model Code in favor of a single standard protecting all information about a client "relating to the representation." Under DR 4-101, the requirement applied only to information protected by the attorney-client privilege and to information "gained in" the professional relationship that "the client has requested be held inviolate or the disclosure of which would be embarrassing or would be likely to be detrimental to the client." EC 4-4 added that the duty differed from the evidentiary privilege in that it existed "without regard to the nature or source of information or the fact that others share the knowlege." Rule 1.6 imposes confidentiality on information relating to the representation even if it is acquired before or after the relationship existed. It does not require the client to indicate information that is to be confidential, or permit the lawyer to speculate whether particular information might be embarrassing or detrimental.

[2] Paragraph (a) permits a lawyer to disclose information where impliedly authorized to do so in order to carry out the representation. Under DR 4-101(B)

and (C), a lawyer was not permitted to reveal "confidences" unless the client first consented after disclosure.

[3] Paragraph (b) redefines the exceptions to the requirement of confidentiality. Regarding paragraph (b)(1), DR 4–101(C)(3) provided that a lawyer "may reveal . . . [t]he intention of his client to commit a crime and the information necessary to prevent the crime." This option existed regardless of the seriousness of the proposed crime.

[4] With regard to paragraph (b)(2), DR 4–101(C)(4) provided that a lawyer may reveal "[c]onfidences or secrets necessary to establish or collect his fee or to defend himself or his employers or associates against an accusation of wrongful conduct." Paragraph (b)(2) enlarges the exception to include disclosure of information relating to claims by the lawyer other than for the lawyer's fee; for example, recovery of property from the client.

RULE 1.7 Conflict of Interest: General Rule

(a) A lawyer shall not represent a client if the representation of that client will be directly adverse to another client, unless:

(1) the lawyer reasonably believes the representation will not adversely affect the relationship with the other client; and

(2) each client consents after consultation.

(b) A lawyer shall not represent a client if the representation of that client may be materially limited by the lawyer's responsibilities to another client or to a third person, or by the lawyer's own interests, unless:

(1) the lawyer reasonably believes the representation will not be adversely affected; and

(2) the client consents after consultation. When representation of multiple clients in a single matter is undertaken, the consultation shall include explanation of the implications of the common representation and the advantages and risks involved.

COMMENT:

Loyalty to a Client

[1] Loyalty is an essential element in the lawyer's relationship to a client. An impermissible conflict of interest may exist before representation is undertaken, in which event the representation should be declined. The lawyer should adopt reasonable procedures, appropriate for the size and type of firm and practice, to determine in both litigation and non-litigation matters the parties and issues involved and to determine whether there are actual or potential conflicts of interest.

[2] If such a conflict arises after representation has been undertaken, the lawyer should withdraw from the representation. See Rule 1.16. Where more than one client is involved and the lawyer withdraws because a conflict arises after representation, whether the lawyer may continue to represent any of the clients is determined by Rule 1.9. See also Rule 2.2(c). As to whether a client-lawyer relationship exists or,

Rule 1.7 ABA MODEL RULES

having once been established, is continuing, see Comment to Rule 1.3 and Scope.

[3] As a general proposition, loyalty to a client prohibits undertaking representation directly adverse to that client without that client's consent. Paragraph (a) expresses that general rule. Thus, a lawyer ordinarily may not act as advocate against a person the lawyer represents in some other matter, even if it is wholly unrelated. On the other hand, simultaneous representation in unrelated matters of clients whose interests are only generally adverse, such as competing economic enterprises, does not require consent of the respective clients. Paragraph (a) applies only when the representation of one client would be directly adverse to the other.

[4] Loyalty to a client is also impaired when a lawyer cannot consider, recommend or carry out an appropriate course of action for the client because of the lawyer's other responsibilities or interests. The conflict in effect forecloses alternatives that would otherwise be available to the client. Paragraph (b) addresses such situations. A possible conflict does not itself preclude the representation. The critical questions are the likelihood that a conflict will eventuate and, if it does, whether it will materially interfere with the lawyer's independent professional judgment in considering alternatives or foreclose courses of action that reasonably should be pursued on behalf of the client. Consideration should be given to whether the client wishes to accommodate the other interest involved.

Consultation and Consent

[5] A client may consent to representation notwithstanding a conflict. However, as indicated in paragraph (a)(1) with respect to representation directly adverse to a client, and paragraph (b)(1) with respect to material limitations on representation of a client, when a disinterested lawyer would conclude that the client should not agree to the representation under the circumstances, the lawyer involved cannot properly ask for such agreement or provide representation on the basis of the client's consent. When more than one client is involved, the question of conflict must be resolved as to each client. Moreover, there may be circumstances where it is impossible to make the disclosure necessary to obtain consent. For example, when the lawyer represents different clients in related matters and one of the clients refuses to consent to the disclosure necessary to permit the other client to make an informed decision, the lawyer cannot properly ask the latter to consent.

Lawyer's Interests

[6] The lawyer's own interests should not be permitted to have adverse effect on representation of a client. For example, a lawyer's need for income should not lead the lawyer to undertake matters that cannot be handled competently and at a reasonable fee. See Rules 1.1

and 1.5. If the probity of a lawyer's own conduct in a transaction is in serious question, it may be difficult or impossible for the lawyer to give a client detached advice. A lawyer may not allow related business interests to affect representation, for example, by referring clients to an enterprise in which the lawyer has an undisclosed interest.

Conflicts in Litigation

[7] Paragraph (a) prohibits representation of opposing parties in litigation. Simultaneous representation of parties whose interests in litigation may conflict, such as co-plaintiffs or co-defendants, is governed by paragraph (b). An impermissible conflict may exist by reason of substantial discrepancy in the parties' testimony, incompatibility in positions in relation to an opposing party or the fact that there are substantially different possibilities of settlement of the claims or liabilities in question. Such conflicts can arise in criminal cases as well as civil. The potential for conflict of interest in representing multiple defendants in a criminal case is so grave that ordinarily a lawyer should decline to represent more than one codefendant. On the other hand, common representation of persons having similar interests is proper if the risk of adverse effect is minimal and the requirements of paragraph (b) are met. Compare Rule 2.2 involving intermediation between clients.

[8] Ordinarily, a lawyer may not act as advocate against a client the lawyer represents in some other matter, even if the other matter is wholly unrelated. However, there are circumstances in which a lawyer may act as advocate against a client. For example, a lawyer representing an enterprise with diverse operations may accept employment as an advocate against the enterprise in an unrelated matter if doing so will not adversely affect the lawyer's relationship with the enterprise or conduct of the suit and if both clients consent upon consultation. By the same token, government lawyers in some circumstances may represent government employees in proceedings in which a government agency is the opposing party. The propriety of concurrent representation can depend on the nature of the litigation. For example, a suit charging fraud entails conflict to a degree not involved in a suit for a declaratory judgment concerning statutory interpretation.

[9] A lawyer may represent parties having antagonistic positions on a legal question that has arisen in different cases, unless representation of either client would be adversely affected. Thus, it is ordinarily not improper to assert such positions in cases pending in different trial courts, but it may be improper to do so in cases pending at the same time in an appellate court.

Interest of Person Paying for a Lawyer's Service

[10] A lawyer may be paid from a source other than the client, if the client is informed of that fact and consents and the arrangement does not compromise the lawyer's duty of loyalty to the client. See Rule

Rule 1.7 ABA MODEL RULES

1.8(f). For example, when an insurer and its insured have conflicting interests in a matter arising from a liability insurance agreement, and the insurer is required to provide special counsel for the insured, the arrangement should assure the special counsel's professional independence. So also, when a corporation and its directors or employees are involved in a controversy in which they have conflicting interests, the corporation may provide funds for separate legal representation of the directors or employees, if the clients consent after consultation and the arrangement ensures the lawyer's professional independence.

Other Conflict Situations

[11] Conflicts of interest in contexts other than litigation sometimes may be difficult to assess. Relevant factors in determining whether there is potential for adverse effect include the duration and intimacy of the lawyer's relationship with the client or clients involved, the functions being performed by the lawyer, the likelihood that actual conflict will arise and the likely prejudice to the client from the conflict if it does arise. The question is often one of proximity and degree.

[12] For example, a lawyer may not represent multiple parties to a negotiation whose interests are fundamentally antagonistic to each other, but common representation is permissible where the clients are generally aligned in interest even though there is some difference of interest among them.

[13] Conflict questions may also arise in estate planning and estate administration. A lawyer may be called upon to prepare wills for several family members, such as husband and wife, and, depending upon the circumstances, a conflict of interest may arise. In estate administration the identity of the client may be unclear under the law of a particular jurisdiction. Under one view, the client is the fiduciary; under another view the client is the estate or trust, including its beneficiaries. The lawyer should make clear the relationship to the parties involved.

[14] A lawyer for a corporation or other organization who is also a member of its board of directors should determine whether the responsibilities of the two roles may conflict. The lawyer may be called on to advise the corporation in matters involving actions of the directors. Consideration should be given to the frequency with which such situations may arise, the potential intensity of the conflict, the effect of the lawyer's resignation from the board and the possibility of the corporation's obtaining legal advice from another lawyer in such situations. If there is material risk that the dual role will compromise the lawyer's independence of professional judgment, the lawyer should not serve as a director.

Conflict Charged by an Opposing Party

[15] Resolving questions of conflict of interest is primarily the responsibility of the lawyer undertaking the representation. In litiga-

tion, a court may raise the question when there is reason to infer that the lawyer has neglected the responsibility. In a criminal case, inquiry by the court is generally required when a lawyer represents multiple defendants. Where the conflict is such as clearly to call in question the fair or efficient administration of justice, opposing counsel may properly raise the question. Such an objection should be viewed with caution, however, for it can be misused as a technique of harassment. See Scope.

MODEL CODE COMPARISON

[1] DR 5–101(A) provided that "[e]xcept with the consent of his client after full disclosure, a lawyer shall not accept employment if the exercise of his professional judgment on behalf of the client will be or reasonably may be affected by his own financial, business, property, or personal interests." DR 5–105(A) provided that a lawyer "shall decline proffered employment if the exercise of his independent professional judgment in behalf of a client will be or is likely to be adversely affected by the acceptance of the proffered employment, or if it would be likely to involve him in representing differing interests, except to the extent permitted under DR 5–105(C)." DR 5–105(C) provided that "a lawyer may represent multiple clients if it is obvious that he can adequately represent the interest of each and if each consents to the representation after full disclosure of the possible effect of such representation on the exercise of his independent professional judgment on behalf on each." DR 5–107(B) provided that a lawyer "shall not permit a person who recommends, employs, or pays him to render legal services for another to direct or regulate his professional judgment in rendering such services."

[2] Rule 1.7 clarifies DR 5–105(A) by requiring that, when the lawyer's other interests are involved, not only must the client consent after consultation but also that, independent of such consent, the representation reasonably appears not to be adversely affected by the lawyer's other interests. This requirement appears to be the intended meaning of the provision in DR 5–105(C) that "it is obvious that he can adequately represent" the client, and was implicit in EC 5–2, which stated that a lawyer "should not accept proffered employment if his personal interests or desires will, or there is a reasonable possibility that they will, affect adversely the advice to be given or services to be rendered the prospective client."

RULE 1.8 Conflict of Interest: Prohibited Transactions

(a) A lawyer shall not enter into a business transaction with a client or knowingly acquire an ownership, possessory, security or other pecuniary interest adverse to a client unless:

(1) the transaction and terms on which the lawyer acquires the interest are fair and reasonable to the client and are fully disclosed and transmitted in writing to the client in a manner which can be reasonably understood by the client;

(2) the client is given a reasonable opportunity to seek the advice of independent counsel in the transaction; and

(3) the client consents in writing thereto.

(b) A lawyer shall not use information relating to representation of a client to the disadvantage of the client unless the client consents after consultation, except as permitted or required by Rule 1.6 or Rule 3.3.

(c) A lawyer shall not prepare an instrument giving the lawyer or a person related to the lawyer as parent, child, sibling, or spouse any substantial gift from a client, including a testamentary gift, except where the client is related to the donee.

(d) Prior to the conclusion of representation of a client, a lawyer shall not make or negotiate an agreement giving the lawyer literary or media rights to a portrayal or account based in substantial part on information relating to the representation.

(e) A lawyer shall not provide financial assistance to a client in connection with pending or contemplated litigation, except that:

(1) a lawyer may advance court costs and expenses of litigation, the repayment of which may be contingent on the outcome of the matter; and

(2) a lawyer representing an indigent client may pay court costs and expenses of litigation on behalf of the client.

(f) A lawyer shall not accept compensation for representing a client from one other than the client unless:

(1) the client consents after consultation;

(2) there is no interference with the lawyer's independence of professional judgment or with the client–lawyer relationship; and

(3) information relating to representation of a client is protected as required by rule 1.6.

(g) A lawyer who represents two or more clients shall not participate in making an aggregate settlement of the claims of or against the clients, or in a criminal case an aggregated agreement as to guilty or nolo contendere pleas, unless each client consents after consultation, including disclosure of the existence and nature of all the claims or pleas involved and of the participation of each person in the settlement.

(h) A lawyer shall not make an agreement prospectively limiting the lawyer's liability to a client for malpractice unless permitted by law and the client is independently represented in making the agreement, or settle a claim for such liability with an unrepresented client or former client without first advising that person in writing that independent representation is appropriate in connection therewith.

(i) A lawyer related to another lawyer as parent, child, sibling or spouse shall not represent a client in a representation directly adverse to a person who the lawyer knows is represented by the other lawyer except upon consent by the client after consultation regarding the relationship.

(j) A lawyer shall not acquire a proprietary interest in the cause of action or subject matter of litigation the lawyer is conducting for a client, except that the lawyer may:

(1) acquire a lien granted by law to secure the lawyer's fee or expenses; and

(2) contract with a client for a reasonable contingent fee in a civil case.

COMMENT:

Transactions Between Client and Lawyer

[1] As a general principle, all transactions between client and lawyer should be fair and reasonable to the client. In such transactions a review by independent counsel on behalf of the client is often advisable. Furthermore, a lawyer may not exploit information relating to the representation to the client's disadvantage. For example, a lawyer who has learned that the client is investing in specific real estate may not, without the client's consent, seek to acquire nearby property where doing so would adversely affect the client's plan for investment. Paragraph (a) does not, however, apply to standard commercial transactions between the lawyer and the client for products or services that the client generally markets to others, for example, banking or brokerage services, medical services, products manufactured or distributed by the client, and utilities services. In such transactions, the lawyer has no advantage in dealing with the client, and the restrictions in paragraph (a) are unnecessary and impracticable.

[2] A lawyer may accept a gift from a client, if the transaction meets general standards of fairness. For example, a simple gift such as a present given at a holiday or as a token of appreciation is permitted. If effectuation of a substantial gift requires preparing a legal instrument such as a will or conveyance, however, the client should have the detached advice that another lawyer can provide. Paragraph (c) recognizes an exception where the client is a relative of the donee or the gift is not substantial.

Literary Rights

[3] An agreement by which a lawyer acquires literary or media rights concerning the conduct of the representation creates a conflict between the interests of the client and the personal interests of the lawyer. Measures suitable in the representation of the client may detract from the publication value of an account of the representation. Paragraph (d) does not prohibit a lawyer representing a client in a transaction concerning literary property from agreeing that the lawyer's fee shall consist of a share in ownership in the property, if the arrangement conforms to Rule 1.5 and paragraph (j).

Rule 1.8   *ABA MODEL RULES*

Person Paying for Lawyer's Services

[4]   Rule 1.8(f) requires disclosure of the fact that the lawyer's services are being paid for by a third party. Such an arrangement must also conform to the requirements of Rule 1.6 concerning confidentiality and Rule 1.7 concerning conflict of interest. Where the client is a class, consent may be obtained on behalf of the class by court-supervised procedure.

Family Relationships Between Lawyers

[5]   Rule 1.8(i) applies to related lawyers who are in different firms. Related lawyers in the same firm are governed by Rules 1.7, 1.9, and 1.10. The disqualification stated in Rule 1.8(i) is personal and is not imputed to members of firms with whom the lawyers are associated.

Acquisition of Interest in Litigation

[6]   Paragraph (j) states the traditional general rule that lawyers are prohibited from acquiring a proprietary interest in litigation. This general rule, which has its basis in common law champerty and maintenance, is subject to specific exceptions developed in decisional law and continued in these Rules, such as the exception for reasonable contingent fees set forth in Rule 1.5 and the exception for certain advances of the costs of litigation set forth in paragraph (e).

[7]   This Rule is not intended to apply to customary qualification and limitations in legal opinions and memoranda.

MODEL CODE COMPARISON

[1]   With regard to paragraph (a), DR 5-104(A) provided that a lawyer "shall not enter into a business transaction with a client if they have differing interests therein and if the client expects the lawyer to exercise his professional judgment therein for the protection of the client, unless the client has consented after full disclosure." EC 5-3 stated that a lawyer "should not seek to persuade his client to permit him to invest in an undertaking of his client nor make improper use of his professional relationship to influence his client to invest in an enterprise in which the lawyer is interested."

[2]   With regard to paragraph (b), DR 4-101(B)(3) provided that a lawyer should not use "a confidence or secret of his client for the advantage of himself, or of a third person, unless the client consents after full disclosure."

[3]   There was no counterpart to paragraph (c) in the Disciplinary Rules of the Model Code. EC 5-5 stated that a lawyer "should not suggest to his client that a gift be made to himself or for his benefit. If a lawyer accepts a gift from his client, he is peculiarly susceptible to the charge that he unduly influenced or overreached the client. If a client voluntarily offers to make a gift to his lawyer, the lawyer may accept the gift, but before doing so, he should urge that the client secure disinterested advice from an independent, competent person who is cognizant of all the circumstances. Other than in exceptional circumstances, a lawyer should insist that an instrument in which his client desires to name him beneficially be prepared by another lawyer selected by the client."

[4] Paragraph (d) is substantially similar to DR 5–104(B), but refers to "literary or media" rights, a more generally inclusive term than "publication" rights.

[5] Paragraph (e)(1) is similar to DR 5–103(B), but eliminates the requirement that "the client remains ultimately liable for such expenses."

[6] Paragraph (e)(2) has no counterpart in the Model Code.

[7] Paragraph (f) is substantially identical to DR 5–107(A)(1).

[8] Paragraph (g) is substantially identical to DR 5–106.

[9] The first clause of paragraph (h) is similar to DR 6–102(A). There was no counterpart in the Model Code to the second clause of paragraph (h).

[10] Paragraph (i) has no counterpart in the Model Code.

[11] Paragraph (j) is substantially identical to DR 5–103(A).

RULE 1.9 Conflict of Interest: Former Client

(a) A lawyer who has formerly represented a client in a matter shall not thereafter represent another person in the same or a substantially related matter in which that person's interests are materially adverse to the interests of the former client unless the former client consents after consultation.

(b) A lawyer shall not knowingly represent a person in the same or a substantially related matter in which a firm with which the lawyer formerly was associated had previously represented a client

(1) whose interests are materially adverse to that person; and

(2) about whom the lawyer had acquired information protected by Rules 1.6 and 1.9(c) that is material to the matter;

unless the former client consents after consultation.

(c) A lawyer who has formerly represented a client in a matter or whose present or former firm has formerly represented a client in a matter shall not thereafter:

(1) use information relating to the representation to the disadvantage of the former client except as Rule 1.6 or Rule 3.3 would permit or require with respect to a client, or when the information has become generally known; or

(2) reveal information relating to the representation except as Rule 1.6 or Rule 3.3 would permit or require with respect to a client.

COMMENT:

[1] After termination of a client-lawyer relationship, a lawyer may not represent another client except in conformity with this Rule. The principles in Rule 1.7 determine whether the interests of the present and former client are adverse. Thus, a lawyer could not properly seek to rescind on behalf of a new client a contract drafted on behalf of the former client. So also a lawyer who has prosecuted an accused person

Rule 1.9   *ABA MODEL RULES*

could not properly represent the accused in a subsequent civil action against the government concerning the same transaction.

[2] The scope of a "matter" for purposes of this Rule may depend on the facts of a particular situation or transaction. The lawyer's involvement in a matter can also be a question of degree. When a lawyer has been directly involved in a specific transaction, subsequent representation of other clients with materially adverse interests clearly is prohibited. On the other hand, a lawyer who recurrently handled a type of problem for a former client is not precluded from later representing another client in a wholly distinct problem of that type even though the subsequent representation involves a position adverse to the prior client. Similar considerations can apply to the reassignment of military lawyers between defense and prosecution functions within the same military jurisdiction. The underlying question is whether the lawyer was so involved in the matter that the subsequent representation can be justly regarded as a changing of sides in the matter in question.

Lawyers Moving Between Firms

[3] When lawyers have been associated within a firm but then end their association, the question of whether a lawyer should undertake representation is more complicated. There are several competing considerations. First, the client previously represented by the former firm must be reasonably assured that the principle of loyalty to the client is not compromised. Second, the rule should not be so broadly cast as to preclude other persons from having reasonable choice of legal counsel. Third, the rule should not unreasonably hamper lawyers from forming new associations and taking on new clients after having left a previous association. In this connection, it should be recognized that today many lawyers practice in firms, that many lawyers to some degree limit their practice to one field or another, and that many move from one association to another several times in their careers. If the concept of imputation were applied with unqualified rigor, the result would be radical curtailment of the opportunity of lawyers to move from one practice setting to another and of the opportunity of clients to change counsel.

[4] Reconciliation of these competing principles in the past has been attempted under two rubrics. One approach has been to seek per se rules of disqualification. For example, it has been held that a partner in a law firm is conclusively presumed to have access to all confidences concerning all clients of the firm. Under this analysis, if a lawyer has been a partner in one law firm and then becomes a partner in another law firm, there may be a presumption that all confidences known by the partner in the first firm are known to all partners in the second firm. This presumption might properly be applied in some circumstances, especially where the client has been extensively represented, but may be unrealistic where the client was represented only for limited purposes.

Furthermore, such a rigid rule exaggerates the difference between a partner and an associate in modern law firms.

[5] The other rubric formerly used for dealing with disqualification is the appearance of impropriety proscribed in Canon 9 of the ABA Model Code of Professional Responsibility. This rubric has a two fold problem. First, the appearance of impropriety can be taken to include any new client-lawyer relationship that might make a former client feel anxious. If that meaning were adopted, disqualification would become little more than a question of subjective judgment by the former client. Second, since "impropriety" is undefined, the term "appearance of impropriety" is question-begging. It therefore has to be recognized that the problem of disqualification cannot be properly resolved either by simple analogy to a lawyer practicing alone or by the very general concept of appearance of impropriety.

[6] A rule based on a functional analysis is more appropriate for determining the question of disqualification. Two functions are involved: preserving confidentiality and avoiding positions adverse to a client.

Confidentiality

[7] Preserving confidentiality is a question of access to information. Access to information, in turn, is essentially a question of fact in particular circumstances, aided by inferences, deductions or working presumptions that reasonably may be made about the way in which lawyers work together. A lawyer may have general access to files of all clients of a law firm and may regularly participate in discussions of their affairs; it should be inferred that such a lawyer in fact is privy to all information about all the firm's clients. In contrast, another lawyer may have access to the files of only a limited number of clients and participate in discussions of the affairs of no other clients; in the absence of information to the contrary, it should be inferred that such a lawyer in fact is privy to information about the clients actually served but not those of other clients.

[8] Application of paragraph (b) depends on a situation's particular facts. In such an inquiry, the burden of proof should rest upon the firm whose disqualification is sought.

[9] Paragraph (b) operates to disqualify the lawyer only when the lawyer involved has actual knowledge of information protected by Rules 1.6 and 1.9(b). Thus, if a lawyer while with one firm acquired no knowledge or information relating to a particular client of the firm, and that lawyer later joined another firm, neither the lawyer individually nor the second firm is disqualified from representing another client in the same or a related matter even though the interests of the two clients conflict. See Rule 1.10(b) for the restrictions on a firm once a lawyer has terminated association with the firm.

Rule 1.9 ABA MODEL RULES

[10] Independent of the question of disqualification of a firm, a lawyer changing professional association has a continuing duty to preserve confidentiality of information about a client formerly represented. See Rules 1.6 and 1.9.

Adverse Positions

[11] The second aspect of loyalty to a client is the lawyer's obligation to decline subsequent representations involving positions adverse to a former client arising in substantially related matters. This obligation requires abstention from adverse representation by the individual lawyer involved, but does not properly entail abstention of other lawyers through imputed disqualification. Hence, this aspect of the problem is governed by Rule 1.9(a). Thus, if a lawyer left one firm for another, the new affiliation would not preclude the firms involved from continuing to represent clients with adverse interests in the same or related matters, so long as the conditions of paragraphs (b) and (c) concerning confidentiality have been met.

[12] Information acquired by the lawyer in the course of representing a client may not subsequently be used or revealed by the lawyer to the disadvantage of the client. However, the fact that a lawyer has once served a client does not preclude the lawyer from using generally known information about that client when later representing another client.

[13] Disqualification from subsequent representation is for the protection of former clients and can be waived by them. A waiver is effective only if there is disclosure of the circumstances, including the lawyer's intended role in behalf of the new client.

[14] With regard to an opposing party's raising a question of conflict of interest, see Comment to Rule 1.7. With regard to disqualification of a firm with which a lawyer is or was formerly associated, see Rule 1.10.

MODEL CODE COMPARISON

[1] There was no counterpart to this Rule in the Disciplinary Rules of the Model Code. Representation adverse to a former client was sometimes dealt with under the rubric of Canon 9 of the Model Code, which provided: "A lawyer should avoid even the appearance of impropriety." Also applicable were EC 4-6 which stated that the "obligation of a lawyer to preserve the confidences and secrets of his client continues after the termination of his employment" and Canon 5 which stated that "[a] lawyer should exercise independent professional judgment on behalf of a client."

[2] The provision for waiver by the former client in paragraphs (a) and (b) is similar to DR 5-105(C).

[3] The exception in the last clause of paragraph (c)(1) permits a lawyer to use information relating to a former client that is in the "public domain," a use that was also not prohibited by the Model Code, which protected only "confidences and secrets." Since the scope of paragraphs (a) and (b) is much broader than "confidences and secrets," it is necessary to define when a lawyer may

make use of information about a client after the client-lawyer relationship has terminated.

RULE 1.10 Imputed Disqualification: General Rule

(a) While lawyers are associated in a firm, none of them shall knowingly represent a client when any one of them practicing alone would be prohibited from doing so by Rules 1.7, 1.8(c), 1.9 or 2.2.

(b) When a lawyer has terminated an association with a firm, the firm is not prohibited from thereafter representing a person with interests materially adverse to those of a client represented by the formerly associated lawyer and not currently represented by the firm, unless:

(1) the matter is the same or substantially related to that in which the formerly associated lawyer represented the client; and

(2) any lawyer remaining in the firm has information protected by Rules 1.6 and 1.9(c) that is material to the matter.

(c) A disqualification prescribed by this rule may be waived by the affected client under the conditions stated in Rule 1.7.

COMMENT:

Definition of "Firm"

[1] For purposes of the Rules of Professional Conduct, the term "firm" includes lawyers in a private firm, and lawyers in the legal department of a corporation or other organization, or in a legal services organization. Whether two or more lawyers constitute a firm within this definition can depend on the specific facts. For example, two practitioners who share office space and occasionally consult or assist each other ordinarily would not be regarded as constituting a firm. However, if they present themselves to the public in a way suggesting that they are a firm or conduct themselves as a firm, they should be regarded as a firm for the purposes of the Rules. The terms of any formal agreement between associated lawyers are relevant in determining whether they are a firm, as is the fact that they have mutual access to information concerning the clients they serve. Furthermore, it is relevant in doubtful cases to consider the underlying purpose of the Rule that is involved. A group of lawyers could be regarded as a firm for purposes of the rule that the same lawyer should not represent opposing parties in litigation, while it might not be so regarded for purposes of the rule that information acquired by one lawyer is attributed to the other.

[2] With respect to the law department of an organization, there is ordinarily no question that the members of the department constitute a firm within the meaning of the Rules of Professional Conduct. However, there can be uncertainty as to the identity of the client. For example, it may not be clear whether the law department of a corporation represents a subsidiary or an affiliated corporation, as well as the

Rule 1.10 ABA MODEL RULES

corporation by which the members of the department are directly employed. A similar question can arise concerning an unincorporated association and its local affiliates.

[3] Similar questions can also arise with respect to lawyers in legal aid. Lawyers employed in the same unit of a legal service organization constitute a firm, but not necessarily those employed in separate units. As in the case of independent practitioners, whether the lawyers should be treated as associated with each other can depend on the particular rule that is involved, and on the specific facts of the situation.

[4] Where a lawyer has joined a private firm after having represented the government, the situation is governed by Rule 1.11(a) and (b); where a lawyer represents the government after having served private clients, the situation is governed by Rule 1.11(c)(1). The individual lawyer involved is bound by the Rules generally, including Rules 1.6, 1.7 and 1.9.

[5] Different provisions are thus made for movement of a lawyer from one private firm to another and for movement of a lawyer between a private firm and the government. The government is entitled to protection of its client confidences and, therefore, to the protections provided in Rules 1.6, 1.9 and 1.11. However, if the more extensive disqualification in Rule 1.10 were applied to former government lawyers, the potential effect on the government would be unduly burdensome. The government deals with all private citizens and organizations and, thus, has a much wider circle of adverse legal interests than does any private law firm. In these circumstances, the government's recruitment of lawyers would be seriously impaired if Rule 1.10 were applied to the government. On balance, therefore, the government is better served in the long run by the protections stated in Rule 1.11.

Principles of Imputed Disqualification

[6] The rule of imputed disqualification stated in paragraph (a) gives effect to the principle of loyalty to the client as it applies to lawyers who practice in a law firm. Such situations can be considered from the premise that a firm of lawyers is essentially one lawyer for purposes of the rules governing loyalty to the client, or from the premise that each lawyer is vicariously bound by the obligation of loyalty owed by each lawyer with whom the lawyer is associated. Paragraph (a) operates only among the lawyers currently associated in a firm. When a lawyer moves from one firm to another, the situation is governed by Rules 1.9(b) and 1.10(b).

[7] Rule 1.10(b) operates to permit a law firm, under certain circumstances, to represent a person with interests directly adverse to those of a client represented by a lawyer who formerly was associated with the firm. The Rule applies regardless of when the formerly associated lawyer represented the client. However, the law firm may not represent a person with interests adverse to those of a present client of the firm,

which would violate Rule 1.7. Moreover, the firm may not represent the person where the matter is the same or substantially related to that in which the formerly associated lawyer represented the client and any other lawyer currently in the firm has material information protected by Rules 1.6 and 1.9(c).

MODEL CODE COMPARISON

DR 5–105(D) provided that "[i]f a lawyer is required to decline or to withdraw from employment under a Disciplinary Rule, no partner, or associate, or any other lawyer affiliated with him or his firm, may accept or continue such employment."

RULE 1.11 Successive Government and Private Employment

(a) Except as law may otherwise expressly permit, a lawyer shall not represent a private client in connection with a matter in which the lawyer participated personally and substantially as a public officer or employee, unless the appropriate government agency consents after consultation. No lawyer in a firm with which that lawyer is associated may knowingly undertake or continue representation in such a matter unless:

(1) the disqualified lawyer is screened from any participation in the matter and is apportioned no part of the fee therefrom; and

(2) written notice is promptly given to the appropriate government agency to enable it to ascertain compliance with the provisions of this rule.

(b) Except as law may otherwise expressly permit, a lawyer having information that the lawyer knows is confidential government information about a person acquired when the lawyer was a public officer or employee, may not represent a private client whose interests are adverse to that person in a matter in which the information could be used to the material disadvantage of that person. A firm with which that lawyer is associated may undertake or continue representation in the matter only if the disqualified lawyer is screened from any participation in the matter and is apportioned no part of the fee therefrom.

(c) Except as law may otherwise expressly permit, a lawyer serving as a public officer or employee shall not:

(1) participate in a matter in which the lawyer participated personally and substantially while in private practice or nongovernmental employment, unless under applicable law no one is, or by lawful delegation may be, authorized to act in the lawyer's stead in the matter; or

(2) negotiate for private employment with any person who is involved as a party or as attorney for a party in a matter in which the lawyer is participating personally and substantially, except that a lawyer serving as a law clerk to a judge, other adjudicative

Rule 1.11

officer or arbitrator may negotiate for private employment as permitted by Rule 1.12(b) and subject to the conditions stated in Rule 1.12(b).

(d) As used in this rule, the term "matter" includes:

(1) any judicial or other proceeding, application, request for a ruling or other determination, contract, claim, controversy, investigation, charge, accusation, arrest or other particular matter involving a specific party or parties; and

(2) any other matter covered by the conflict of interest rules of the appropriate government agency.

(e) As used in this rule, the term "confidential government information" means information which has been obtained under governmental authority and which, at the time this rule is applied, the government is prohibited by law from disclosing to the public or has a legal privilege not to disclose, and which is not otherwise available to the public.

COMMENT:

[1] This Rule prevents a lawyer from exploiting public office for the advantage of a private client. It is a counterpart of Rule 1.10(b), which applies to lawyers moving from one firm to another.

[2] A lawyer representing a government agency, whether employed or specially retained by the government, is subject to the Rules of Professional Conduct, including the prohibition against representing adverse interests stated in Rule 1.7 and the protections afforded former clients in Rule 1.9. In addition, such a lawyer is subject to Rule 1.11 and to statutes and government regulations regarding conflict of interest. Such statutes and regulations may circumscribe the extent to which the government agency may give consent under this Rule.

[3] Where the successive clients are a public agency and a private client, the risk exists that power or discretion vested in public authority might be used for the special benefit of a private client. A lawyer should not be in a position where benefit to a private client might affect performance of the lawyer's professional functions on behalf of public authority. Also, unfair advantage could accrue to the private client by reason of access to confidential government information about the client's adversary obtainable only through the lawyer's government service. However, the rules governing lawyers presently or formerly employed by a government agency should not be so restrictive as to inhibit transfer of employment to and from the government. The government has a legitimate need to attract qualified lawyers as well as to maintain high ethical standards. The provisions for screening and waiver are necessary to prevent the disqualification rule from imposing too severe a deterrent against entering public service.

[4] When the client is an agency of one government, that agency should be treated as a private client for purposes of this Rule if the lawyer thereafter represents an agency of another government, as when a lawyer represents a city and subsequently is employed by a federal agency.

[5] Paragraphs (a)(1) and (b) do not prohibit a lawyer from receiving a salary or partnership share established by prior independent agreement. They prohibit directly relating the attorney's compensation to the fee in the matter in which the lawyer is disqualified.

[6] Paragraph (a)(2) does not require that a lawyer give notice to the government agency at a time when premature disclosure would injure the client; a requirement for premature disclosure might preclude engagement of the lawyer. Such notice is, however, required to be given as soon as practicable in order that the government agency will have a reasonable opportunity to ascertain that the lawyer is complying with Rule 1.11 and to take appropriate action if it believes the lawyer is not complying.

[7] Paragraph (b) operates only when the lawyer in question has knowledge of the information, which means actual knowledge; it does not operate with respect to information that merely could be imputed to the lawyer.

[8] Paragraphs (a) and (c) do not prohibit a lawyer from jointly representing a private party and a government agency when doing so is permitted by Rule 1.7 and is not otherwise prohibited by law.

[9] Paragraph (c) does not disqualify other lawyers in the agency with which the lawyer in question has become associated.

MODEL CODE COMPARISON

[1] Paragraph (a) is similar to DR 9-101(B), except that the latter used the terms "in which he had substantial responsibility while he was a public employee."

[2] Paragraphs (b), (c), (d) and (e) have no counterparts in the Model Code.

RULE 1.12 Former Judge or Arbitrator

(a) Except as stated in paragraph (d), a lawyer shall not represent anyone in connection with a matter in which the lawyer participated personally and substantially as a judge or other adjudicative officer, arbitrator or law clerk to such a person, unless all parties to the proceeding consent after consultation.

(b) A lawyer shall not negotiate for employment with any person who is involved as a party or as attorney for a party in a matter in which the lawyer is participating personally and substantially as a judge or other adjudicative officer, or arbitrator. A lawyer serving as a law clerk to a judge, other adjudicative officer or arbitrator may negotiate for employment with a party or attorney involved in a

matter in which the clerk is participating personally and substantially, but only after the lawyer has notified the judge, other adjudicative officer or arbitrator.

(c) If a lawyer is disqualified by paragraph (a), no lawyer in a firm with which that lawyer is associated may knowingly undertake or continue representation in the matter unless:

   (1) the disqualified lawyer is screened from any participation in the matter and is apportioned no part of the fee therefrom; and

   (2) written notice is promptly given to the appropriate tribunal to enable it to ascertain compliance with the provisions of this Rule.

(d) An arbitrator selected as a partisan of a party in a multi-member arbitration panel is not prohibited from subsequently representing that party.

COMMENT:

[1] This Rule generally parallels Rule 1.11. The term "personally and substantially" signifies that a judge who was a member of a multi-member court, and thereafter left judicial office to practice law, is not prohibited from representing a client in a matter pending in the court, but in which the former judge did not participate. So also the fact that a former judge exercised administrative responsibility in a court does not prevent the former judge from acting as a lawyer in a matter where the judge had previously exercised remote or incidental administrative responsibility that did not affect the merits. Compare the Comment to Rule 1.11. The term "adjudicative officer" includes such officials as judges pro tempore, referees, special masters, hearing officers and other parajudicial officers, and also lawyers who serve as part-time judges. Compliance Canons A(2), B(2) and C of the Model Code of Judicial Conduct provide that a part-time judge, judge pro tempore or retired judge recalled to active service, may not "act as a lawyer in any proceeding in which he served as a judge or in any other proceeding related thereto." Although phrased differently from this Rule, those Rules correspond in meaning.

MODEL CODE COMPARISON

[1] Paragraph (a) is substantially similar to DR 9–101(A), which provided that a lawyer "shall not accept private employment in a matter upon the merits of which he has acted in a judicial capacity." Paragraph (a) differs, however, in that it is broader in scope and states more specifically the persons to whom it applies. There was no counterpart in the Model Code to paragraphs (b), (c) or (d).

[2] With regard to arbitrators, EC 5–20 stated that "a lawyer [who] has undertaken to act as an impartial arbitrator or mediator, . . . should not thereafter represent in the dispute any of the parties involved." DR 9–101(A) did not provide a waiver of the disqualification applied to former judges by consent of the parties. However, DR 5–105(C) was similar in effect and could be construed to permit waiver.

RULE 1.13 Organization as Client *

(a) A lawyer employed or retained by an organization represents the organization acting through its duly authorized constituents.

(b) If a lawyer for an organization knows that an officer, employee or other person associated with the organization is engaged in action, intends to act or refuses to act in a matter related to the representation that is a violation of a legal obligation to the organization, or a violation of law which reasonably might be imputed to the organization, and is likely to result in substantial injury to the organization, the lawyer shall proceed as is reasonably necessary in the best interest of the organization. In determining how to proceed,

---

* Editors' Note: As previously proposed by the Kutak Commission, Rule 1.13 (Revised Final Draft, June 30, 1982) read as follows:

RULE 1.13 Organization as the Client

(a) A lawyer employed or retained to represent an organization represents the organization as distinct from its directors, officers, employees, members, shareholders or other constituents.

(b) If a lawyer for an organization knows that an officer, employee or other person associated with the organization is engaged in action, intends to act or refuses to act in a matter related to the representation that is a violation of a legal obligation to the organization, or a violation of law which reasonably might be imputed to the organization, and is likely to result in substantial injury to the organization, the lawyer shall proceed as is reasonably necessary in the best interest of the organization. In determining how to proceed, the lawyer shall give due consideration to the seriousness of the violation and its consequences, the scope and nature of the lawyer's representation, the responsibility in the organization and the apparent motivation of the person involved, the policies of the organization concerning such matters and any other relevant considerations. Any measures taken shall be designed to minimize disruption of the organization and the risk of revealing information relating to the representation to persons outside the organization. Such measures may include among others:

(1) asking reconsideration of the matter;

(2) advising that a separate legal opinion on the matter be sought for presentation to appropriate authority in the organization; and

(3) referring the matter to higher authority in the organization, including, if warranted by the seriousness of the matter, referral to the highest authority that can act in behalf of the organization as determined by applicable law.

(c) When the organization's highest authority insists upon action, or refuses to take action, that is clearly a violation of a legal obligation to the organization, or a violation of law which reasonably might be imputed to the organization, and is likely to result in substantial injury to the organization, the lawyer may take further remedial action that the lawyer reasonably believes to be in the best interest of the organization. Such action may include revealing information otherwise protected by Rule 1.6 only if the lawyer reasonably believes that:

(1) the highest authority in the organization has acted to further the personal or financial interests of members of that authority which are in conflict with the interest of the organization; and

(2) revealing the information is necessary in the best interest of the organization.

(d) In dealing with an organization's directors, officers, employees, members, shareholders or other constituents, a lawyer shall explain the identity of the client when the lawyer believes that such explanation is necessary to avoid misunderstandings on their part.

(e) A lawyer representing an organization may also represent any of its directors, officers, employees, members, shareholders or other constituents, subject to the provisions of Rule 1.7. If the organization's consent to the dual representation is required by Rule 1.7, the consent shall be given by an appropriate official of the organization other than the individual who is to be represented or by the shareholders.

the lawyer shall give due consideration to the seriousness of the violation and its consequences, the scope and nature of the lawyer's representation, the responsibility in the organization and the apparent motivation of the person involved, the policies of the organization concerning such matters and any other relevant considerations. Any measures taken shall be designed to minimize disruption of the organization and the risk of revealing information relating to the representation to persons outside the organization. Such measures may include among others:

(1) asking reconsideration of the matter;

(2) advising that a separate legal opinion on the matter be sought for presentation to appropriate authority in the organization; and

(3) referring the matter to higher authority in the organization, including, if warranted by the seriousness of the matter, referral to the highest authority that can act in behalf of the organization as determined by applicable law.

(c) If, despite the lawyer's efforts in accordance with paragraph (b), the highest authority that can act on behalf of the organization insists upon action, or a refusal to act, that is clearly a violation of law and is likely to result in substantial injury to the organization, the lawyer may resign in accordance with rule 1.16.

(d) In dealing with an organization's directors, officers, employees, members, shareholders or other constituents, a lawyer shall explain the identity of the client when it is apparent that the organization's interests are adverse to those of the constituents with whom the lawyer is dealing.

(e) A lawyer representing an organization may also represent any of its directors, officers, employees, members, shareholders or other constituents, subject to the provisions of rule 1.7. If the organization's consent to the dual representation is required by rule 1.7, the consent shall be given by an appropriate official of the organization other than the individual who is to be represented, or by the shareholders.

COMMENT:

The Entity as the Client

[1] An organizational client is a legal entity, but it cannot act except through its officers, directors, employees, shareholders and other constituents.

[2] Officers, directors, employees and shareholders are the constituents of the corporate organizational client. The duties defined in this Comment apply equally to unincorporated associations. "Other constituents" as used in this Comment means the positions equivalent to officers, directors, employees and shareholders held by persons acting for organizational clients that are not corporations.

[3] When one of the constituents of an organizational client communicates with the organization's lawyer in that person's organizational capacity, the communication is protected by Rule 1.6. Thus, by way of example, if an organizational client requests its lawyer to investigate allegations of wrongdoing, interviews made in the course of that investigation between the lawyer and the client's employees or other constituents are covered by Rule 1.6. This does not mean, however, that constituents of an organizational client are the clients of the lawyer. The lawyer may not disclose to such constituents information relating to the representation except for disclosures explicitly or impliedly authorized by the organizational client in order to carry out the representation or as otherwise permitted by Rule 1.6.

[4] When constituents of the organization make decisions for it, the decisions ordinarily must be accepted by the lawyer even if their utility or prudence is doubtful. Decisions concerning policy and operations, including ones entailing serious risk, are not as such in the lawyer's province. However, different considerations arise when the lawyer knows that the organization may be substantially injured by action of [a] constituent that is in violation of law. In such a circumstance, it may be reasonably necessary for the lawyer to ask the constituent to reconsider the matter. If that fails, or if the matter is of sufficient seriousness and importance to the organization, it may be reasonably necessary for the lawyer to take steps to have the matter reviewed by a higher authority in the organization. Clear justification should exist for seeking review over the head of the constituent normally responsible for it. The stated policy of the organization may define circumstances and prescribe channels for such review, and a lawyer should encourage the formulation of such a policy. Even in the absence of organization policy, however, the lawyer may have an obligation to refer a matter to higher authority, depending on the seriousness of the matter and whether the constituent in question has apparent motives to act at variance with the organization's interest. Review by the chief executive officer or by the board of directors may be required when the matter is of importance commensurate with their authority. At some point it may be useful or essential to obtain an independent legal opinion.

[5] In an extreme case, it may be reasonably necessary for the lawyer to refer the matter to the organization's highest authority. Ordinarily, that is the board of directors or similar governing body. However, applicable law may prescribe that under certain conditions highest authority reposes elsewhere; for example, in the independent directors of a corporation.

Relation to Other Rules

[6] The authority and responsibility provided in paragraph (b) are concurrent with the authority and responsibility provided in other Rules. In particular, this Rule does not limit or expand the lawyer's responsibili-

Rule 1.13 ABA MODEL RULES

ty under Rules 1.6, 1.8, and 1.16, 3.3 or 4.1. If the lawyer's services are being used by an organization to further a crime or fraud by the organization, Rule 1.2(d) can be applicable.

Government Agency

[7] The duty defined in this Rule applies to governmental organizations. However, when the client is a governmental organization, a different balance may be appropriate between maintaining confidentiality and assuring that the wrongful official act is prevented or rectified, for public business is involved. In addition, duties of lawyers employed by the government or lawyers in military service may be defined by statutes and regulation. Therefore, defining precisely the identity of the client and prescribing the resulting obligations of such lawyers may be more difficult in the government context. Although in some circmstances the client may be a specific agency, it is generally the government as a whole. For example, if the action or failure to act involves the head of a bureau, either the department of which the bureau is a part or the government as a whole may be the client for purpose of this Rule. Moreover, in a matter involving the conduct of government officials, a government lawyer may have authority to question such conduct more extensively than that of a lawyer for a private organization in similar circumstances. This Rule does not limit that authority. See note on Scope.

Clarifying the Lawyer's Role

[8] There are times when the organization's interest may be or become adverse to those of one or more of its constituents. In such circumstances the lawyer should advise any constituent, whose interest the lawyer finds adverse to that of the organization of the conflict or potential conflict of interest, that the lawyer cannot represent such constituent, and that such person may wish to obtain independent representation. Care must be taken to assure that the individual understands that, when there is such adversity of interest, the lawyer for the organization cannot provide legal representation for that constituent individual, and that discussions between the lawyer for the organization and the individual may not be privileged.

[9] Whether such a warning should be given by the lawyer for the organization to any constituent individual may turn on the facts of each case.

Dual Representation

[10] Paragraph (e) recognizes that a lawyer for an organization may also represent a principal officer or major shareholder.

Derivative Actions

[11] Under generally prevailing law, the shareholders or members of a corporation may bring suit to compel the directors to perform their legal obligations in the supervision of the organization. Members of unincorporated associations have essentially the same right. Such an action may be brought nominally by the organization, but usually is, in fact, a legal controversy over management of the organization.

[12] The question can arise whether counsel for the organization may defend such an action. The proposition that the organization is the lawyer's client does not alone resolve the issue. Most derivative actions are a normal incident of an organization's affairs, to be defended by the organization's lawyer like any other suit. However, if the claim involves serious charges of wrongdoing by those in control of the organization, a conflict may arise between the lawyer's duty to the organization and the lawyer's relationship with the board. In those circumstances, Rule 1.7 governs who should represent the directors and the organization.

MODEL CODE COMPARISON

There was no counterpart to this Rule in the Disciplinary Rules of the Model Code. EC 5-18 stated that "a lawyer employed or retained by a corporation or similar entity owes his allegiance to the entity and not to a stockholder, director, officer, employee, representative, or other person connected with the entity. In advising the entity, a lawyer should keep paramount its interests and his professional judgment should not be influenced by the personal desires of any person or organization. Occasionally, a lawyer for an entity is requested by a stockholder, director, officer, employee, representative, or other person connected with the entity to represent him in an individual capacity; in such case the lawyer may serve the individual only if the lawyer is convinced that differing interests are not present." EC 5-24 stated that although a lawyer "may be employed by a business corporation with non-lawyers serving as directors or officers, and they necessarily have the right to make decisions of business policy, a lawyer must decline to accept direction of his professional judgment from any layman." DR 5-107(B) provided that a lawyer "shall not permit a person who . . . employs . . . him to render legal services for another to direct or regulate his professional judgment in rendering such legal services."

RULE 1.14 Client Under a Disability

(a) When a client's ability to make adequately considered decisions in connection with the representation is impaired, whether because of minority, mental disability or for some other reason, the lawyer shall, as far as reasonably possible, maintain a normal client–lawyer relationship with the client.

(b) A lawyer may seek the appointment of a guardian or take other protective action with respect to a client, only when the lawyer reasonably believes that the client cannot adequately act in the client's own interest.

Rule 1.14

COMMENT:

[1] The normal client-lawyer relationship is based on the assumption that the client, when properly advised and assisted, is capable of making decisions about important matters. When the client is a minor or suffers from a mental disorder or disability, however, maintaining the ordinary client-lawyer relationship may not be possible in all respects. In particular, an incapacitated person may have no power to make legally binding decisions. Nevertheless, a client lacking legal competence often has the ability to understand, deliberate upon, and reach conclusions about matters affecting the client's own well-being. Furthermore, to an increasing extent the law recognizes intermediate degrees of competence. For example, children as young as five or six years of age, and certainly those of ten or twelve, are regarded as having opinions that are entitled to weight in legal proceedings concerning their custody. So also, it is recognized that some persons of advanced age can be quite capable of handling routine financial matters while needing special legal protection concerning major transactions.

[2] The fact that a client suffers a disability does not diminish the lawyer's obligation to treat the client with attention and respect. If the person has no guardian or legal representative, the lawyer often must act as de facto guardian. Even if the person does have a legal representative, the lawyer should as far as possible accord the represented person the status of client, particularly in maintaining communication.

[3] If a legal representative has already been appointed for the client, the lawyer should ordinarily look to the representative for decisions on behalf of the client. If a legal representative has not been appointed, the lawyer should see to such an appointment where it would serve the client's best interests. Thus, if a disabled client has substantial property that should be sold for the client's benefit, effective completion of the transaction ordinarily requires appointment of a legal representative. In many circumstances, however, appointment of a legal representative may be expensive or traumatic for the client. Evaluation of these considerations is a matter of professional judgment on the lawyer's part.

[4] If the lawyer represents the guardian as distinct from the ward, and is aware that the guardian is acting adversely to the ward's interest, the lawyer may have an obligation to prevent or rectify the guardian's misconduct. See Rule 1.2(d).

Disclosure of the Client's Condition

[5] Rules of procedure in litigation generally provide that minors or persons suffering mental disability shall be represented by a guardian or next friend if they do not have a general guardian. However, disclosure of the client's disability can adversely affect the client's interests. For example, raising the question of disability could, in some circumstances, lead to proceedings for involuntary commitment. The lawyer's position

in such cases is an unavoidably difficult one. The lawyer may seek guidance from an appropriate diagnostician.

MODEL CODE COMPARISON

There was no counterpart to this Rule in the Disciplinary Rules of the Model Code. EC 7–11 stated that the "responsibilities of a lawyer may vary according to the intelligence, experience, mental condition or age of a client . . . . Examples include the representation of an illiterate or an incompetent." EC 7–12 stated that "[a]ny mental or physical condition of a client that renders him incapable of making a considered judgment on his own behalf casts additional responsibilities upon his lawyer. Where an incompetent is acting through a guardian or other legal representative, a lawyer must look to such representative for those decisions which are normally the prerogative of the client to make. If a client under disability has no legal representative, his lawyer may be compelled in court proceedings to make decisions on behalf of the client. If the client is capable of understanding the matter in question or of contributing to the advancement of his interests, regardless of whether he is legally disqualified from performing certain acts, the lawyer should obtain from him all possible aid. If the disability of a client and the lack of a legal representative compel the lawyer to make decisions for his client, the lawyer should consider all circumstances then prevailing and act with care to safeguard and advance the interests of his client. But obviously a lawyer cannot perform any act or make any decision which the law requires his client to perform or make, either acting for himself if competent, or by a duly constituted representative if legally incompetent."

RULE 1.15 Safekeeping Property

(a) **A lawyer shall hold property of clients or third persons that is in a lawyer's possession in connection with a representation separate from the lawyer's own property. Funds shall be kept in a separate account maintained in the state where the lawyer's office is situated, or elsewhere with the consent of the client or third person. Other property shall be identified as such and appropriately safeguarded. Complete records of such account funds and other property shall be kept by the lawyer and shall be preserved for a period of [five years] after termination of the representation.**

(b) **Upon receiving funds or other property in which a client or third person has an interest, a lawyer shall promptly notify the client or third person. Except as stated in this rule or otherwise permitted by law or by agreement with the client, a lawyer shall promptly deliver to the client or third person any funds or other property that the client or third person is entitled to receive and, upon request by the client or third person, shall promptly render a full accounting regarding such property.**

(c) **When in the course of representation a lawyer is in possession of property in which both the lawyer and another person claim interests, the property shall be kept separate by the lawyer until there is an accounting and severance of their interest. If a dispute arises**

Rule 1.15

concerning their respective interests, the portion in dispute shall be kept separate by the lawyer until the dispute is resolved.

COMMENT:

[1] A lawyer should hold property of others with the care required of a professional fiduciary. Securities should be kept in a safe deposit box, except when some other form of safekeeping is warranted by special circumstances. All property which is the property of clients or third persons should be kept separate from the lawyer's business and personal property and, if monies, in one or more trust accounts. Separate trust accounts may be warranted when administering estate monies or acting in similar fiduciary capacities.

[2] Lawyers often receive funds from third parties from which the lawyer's fee will be paid. If there is risk that the client may divert the funds without paying the fee, the lawyer is not required to remit the portion from which the fee is to be paid. However, a lawyer may not hold funds to coerce a client into accepting the lawyer's contention. The disputed portion of the funds should be kept in trust and the lawyer should suggest means for prompt resolution of the dispute, such as arbitration. The undisputed portion of the funds shall be promptly distributed.

[3] Third parties, such as a client's creditors, may have just claims against funds or other property in a lawyer's custody. A lawyer may have a duty under applicable law to protect such third-party claims against wrongful interference by the client, and accordingly may refuse to surrender the property to the client. However, a lawyer should not unilaterally assume to arbitrate a dispute between the client and the third party.

[4] The obligations of a lawyer under this Rule are independent of those arising from activity other than rendering legal services. For example, a lawyer who serves as an escrow agent is governed by the applicable law relating to fiduciaries even though the lawyer does not render legal services in the transaction.

[5] A "client's security fund" provides a means through the collective efforts of the bar to reimburse persons who have lost money or property as a result of dishonest conduct of a lawyer. Where such a fund has been established, a lawyer should participate.

MODEL CODE COMPARISON

[1] With regard to paragraph (a), DR 9–102(A) provided that "funds of clients" are to be kept in an identifiable bank account in the state in which the lawyer's office is situated. DR 9–102(B)(2) provided that a lawyer shall "identify and label securities and properties of a client . . . and place them in . . . safekeeping. . . ." DR 9–102(B)(3) required that a lawyer "maintain complete records of all funds, securities, and other properties of a client. . . ." Rule 1.15(a) extends these requirements to property of a third person that is in the lawyer's possession in connection with the representation.

PROFESSIONAL CONDUCT — Rule 1.16

[2] Paragraph (b) is substantially similar to DR 9–102(B)(1), (3) and (4).

[3] Paragraph (c) is similar to DR 9–102(A)(2), except that the requirement concerning disputes applies to property concerning which an interest is claimed by a third person as well as by a client.

RULE 1.16 Declining or Terminating Representation

(a) Except as stated in paragraph (c), a lawyer shall not represent a client or, where representation has commenced, shall withdraw from the representation of a client if:

(1) the representation will result in violation of the rules of professional conduct or other law;

(2) the lawyer's physical or mental condition materially impairs the lawyer's ability to represent the client; or

(3) the lawyer is discharged.

(b) Except as stated in paragraph (c), a lawyer may withdraw from representing a client if withdrawal can be accomplished without material adverse effect on the interests of the client, or if:

(1) the client persists in a course of action involving the lawyer's services that the lawyer reasonably believes is criminal or fraudulent;

(2) the client has used the lawyer's services to perpetrate a crime or fraud;

(3) a client insists upon pursuing an objective that the lawyer considers repugnant or imprudent;

(4) the client fails substantially to fulfill an obligation to the lawyer regarding the lawyer's services and has been given reasonable warning that the lawyer will withdraw unless the obligation is fulfilled;

(5) the representation will result in an unreasonable financial burden on the lawyer or has been rendered unreasonably difficult by the client; or

(6) other good cause for withdrawal exists.

(c) When ordered to do so by a tribunal, a lawyer shall continue representation notwithstanding good cause for terminating the representation.

(d) Upon termination of representation, a lawyer shall take steps to the extent reasonably practicable to protect a client's interests, such as giving reasonable notice to the client, allowing time for employment of other counsel, surrendering papers and property to which the client is entitled and refunding any advance payment of fee that has not been earned. The lawyer may retain papers relating to the client to the extent permitted by other law.

Rule 1.16 ABA MODEL RULES

COMMENT:

[1] A lawyer should not accept representation in a matter unless it can be performed competently, promptly, without improper conflict of interest and to completion.

Mandatory Withdrawal

[2] A lawyer ordinarily must decline or withdraw from representation if the client demands that the lawyer engage in conduct that is illegal or violates the Rules of Professional Conduct or other law. The lawyer is not obliged to decline or withdraw simply because the client suggests such a course of conduct; a client may make such a suggestion in the hope that a lawyer will not be constrained by a professional obligation.

[3] When a lawyer has been appointed to represent a client, withdrawal ordinarily requires approval of the appointing authority. See also Rule 6.2. Difficulty may be encountered if withdrawal is based on the client's demand that the lawyer engage in unprofessional conduct. The court may wish an explanation for the withdrawal, while the lawyer may be bound to keep confidential the facts that would constitute such an explanation. The lawyer's statement that professional considerations require termination of the representation ordinarily should be accepted as sufficient.

Discharge

[4] A client has a right to discharge a lawyer at any time, with or without cause, subject to liability for payment for the lawyer's services. Where future dispute about the withdrawal may be anticipated, it may be advisable to prepare a written statement reciting the circumstances.

[5] Whether a client can discharge appointed counsel may depend on applicable law. A client seeking to do so should be given a full explanation of the consequences. These consequences may include a decision by the appointing authority that appointment of successor counsel is unjustified, thus requiring the client to represent himself.

[6] If the client is mentally incompetent, the client may lack the legal capacity to discharge the lawyer, and in any event the discharge may be seriously adverse to the client's interests. The lawyer should make special effort to help the client consider the consequences and, in an extreme case, may initiate proceedings for a conservatorship or similar protection of the client. See Rule 1.14.

Optional Withdrawal

[7] A lawyer may withdraw from representation in some circumstances. The lawyer has the option to withdraw if it can be accomplished without material adverse effect on the client's interests. Withdrawal is also justified if the client persists in a course of action that the lawyer reasonably believes is criminal or fraudulent, for a lawyer is not required

PROFESSIONAL CONDUCT   **Rule 1.16**

to be associated with such conduct even if the lawyer does not further it. Withdrawal is also permitted if the lawyer's services were misused in the past even if that would materially prejudice the client. The lawyer also may withdraw where the client insists on a repugnant or imprudent objective.

[8] A lawyer may withdraw if the client refuses to abide by the terms of an agreement relating to the representation, such as an agreement concerning fees or court costs or an agreement limiting the objectives of the representation.

Assisting the Client Upon Withdrawal

[9] Even if the lawyer has been unfairly discharged by the client, a lawyer must take all reasonable steps to mitigate the consequences to the client. The lawyer may retain papers as security for a fee only to the extent permitted by law.

[10] Whether or not a lawyer for an organization may under certain unusual circumstances have a legal obligation to the organization after withdrawing or being discharged by the organization's highest authority is beyond the scope of these Rules.

MODEL CODE COMPARISON

[1] With regard to paragraph (a), DR 2–109(A) provided that a lawyer "shall not accept employment . . . if he knows or it is obvious that [the prospective client] wishes to . . . [b]ring a legal action . . . or otherwise have steps taken for him, merely for the purpose of harassing or maliciously injuring any person . . . ." Nor may a lawyer accept employment if the lawyer is aware that the prospective client wishes to "[p]resent a claim or defense . . . that is not warranted under existing law, unless it can be supported by good faith argument for an extension, modification, or reversal of existing law." DR 2–110(B) provided that a lawyer "shall withdraw from employment . . . if:

"(1) He knows or it is obvious that his client is bringing the legal action . . . or is otherwise having steps taken for him, merely for the purpose of harassing or maliciously injuring any person.

"(2) He knows or it is obvious that his continued employment will result in violation of a Disciplinary Rule.

"(3) His mental or physical condition renders it unreasonably difficult for him to carry out the employment effectively.

"(4) He is discharged by his client."

[2] With regard to paragraph (b), DR 2–110(C) permitted withdrawal regardless of the effect on the client if:

"(1) His client: (a) Insists upon presenting a claim or defense that is not warranted under existing law and cannot be supported by good faith argument for an extension, modification, or reversal of existing law; (b) Personally seeks to pursue an illegal course of conduct; (c) Insists that the lawyer pursue a course of conduct that is illegal or that is prohibited under the Disciplinary Rules; (d) By other conduct renders it unreasonably difficult for the lawyer to carry out his employment effectively; (e) Insists, in a matter not pending before a tribunal,

Rule 1.16 ABA MODEL RULES

that the lawyer engage in conduct that is contrary to the judgment and advice of the lawyer but not prohibited under the Disciplinary Rules; (f) Deliberately disregards an agreement or obligation to the lawyer as to expenses and fees.

"(2) His continued employment is likely to result in a violation of a Disciplinary Rule.

"(3) His inability to work with co-counsel indicates that the best interest of the client likely will be served by withdrawal.

"(4) His mental or physical condition renders it difficult for him to carry out the employment effectively.

"(5) His client knowingly and freely assents to termination of his employment.

"(6) He believes in good faith, in a proceeding pending before a tribunal, that the tribunal will find the existence of other good cause for withdrawal."

[3] With regard to paragraph (c), DR 2–110(A)(1) provided: "If permission for withdrawal from employment is required by the rules of a tribunal, the lawyer shall not withdraw . . . without its permission."

[4] The provisions of paragraph (d) are substantially identical to DR 2–110(A)(2) and (3).

RULE 1.17 Sale of Law Practice

A lawyer or a law firm may sell or purchase a law practice, including good will, if the following conditions are satisfied:

(a) The seller ceases to engage in the private practice of law [in the geographic area] [in the jurisdiction] (a jurisdiction may elect either version) in which the practice has been conducted;

(b) The practice is sold as an entirety to another lawyer or law firm;

(c) Actual written notice is given to each of the seller's clients regarding:

(1) the proposed sale;

(2) the terms of any proposed change in the fee arrangement authorized by paragraph (d);

(3) the client's right to retain other counsel or to take possession of the file; and

(4) the fact that the client's consent to the sale will be presumed if the client does not take any action or does not otherwise object within ninety (90) days of receipt of the notice.

If a client cannot be given notice, the representation of that client may be transferred to the purchaser only upon entry of an order so authorizing by a court having jurisdiction. The seller may disclose to the court in camera information relating to the representation only to the extent necessary to obtain an order authorizing the transfer of a file.

(d) The fees charged clients shall not be increased by reason of the sale. The purchaser may, however, refuse to undertake the representation unless the client consents to pay the purchaser fees at a rate not exceeding the fees charged by the purchaser for rendering substantially similar services prior to the initiation of the purchase negotiations.

COMMENT:

[1] The practice of law is a profession, not merely a business. Clients are not commodities that can be purchased and sold at will. Pursuant to this Rule, when a lawyer or an entire firm ceases to practice and another lawyer or firm takes over the representation, the selling lawyer or firm may obtain compensation for the reasonable value of the practice as may withdrawing partners of law firms. See Rules 5.4 and 5.6.

Termination of Practice by the Seller

[2] The requirement that all of the private practice be sold is satisfied if the seller in good faith makes the entire practice available for sale to the purchaser. The fact that a number of the seller's clients decide not to be represented by the purchaser but take their matters elsewhere, therefore, does not result in a violation. Neither does a return to private practice as a result of an unanticipated change in circumstances result in a violation. For example, a lawyer who has sold the practice to accept an appointment to judicial office does not violate the requirement that the sale be attendant to cessation of practice if the lawyer later resumes private practice upon being defeated in a contested or a retention election for the office.

[3] The requirement that the seller cease to engage in the private practice of law does not prohibit employment as a lawyer on the staff of a public agency or a legal services entity which provides legal services to the poor, or as in-house counsel to a business.

[4] The Rule permits a sale attendant upon retirement from the private practice of law within the jurisdiction. Its provisions, therefore, accommodate the lawyer who sells the practice upon the occasion of moving to another state. Some states are so large that a move from one locale therein to another is tantamount to leaving the jurisdiction in which the lawyer has engaged in the practice of law. To also accommodate lawyers so situated, states may permit the sale of the practice when the lawyer leaves the geographic area rather than the jurisdiction. The alternative desired should be indicated by selecting one of the two provided for in Rule 1.17(a).

Single Purchaser

[5] The Rule requires a single purchaser. The prohibition against piecemeal sale of a practice protects those clients whose matters are less

Rule 1.17 *ABA MODEL RULES*

lucrative and who might find it difficult to secure other counsel if a sale could be limited to substantial fee-generating matters. The purchaser is required to undertake all client matters in the practice, subject to client consent. If, however, the purchaser is unable to undertake all client matters because of a conflict of interest in a specific matter respecting which the purchaser is not permitted by Rule 1.7 or another rule to represent the client, the requirement that there be a single purchaser is nevertheless satisfied.

Client Confidences, Consent and Notice

[6] Negotiations between seller and prospective purchaser prior to disclosure of information relating to a specific representation of an identifiable client no more violate the confidentiality provisions of Model Rule 1.6 than do preliminary discussions concerning the possible association of another lawyer or mergers between firms, with respect to which client consent is not required. Providing the purchaser access to client-specific information relating to the representation and to the file, however, requires client consent. The Rule provides that before such information can be disclosed by the seller to the purchaser the client must be given actual written notice of the contemplated sale, including the identity of the purchaser and any proposed change in the terms of future representation, and must be told that the decision to consent or make other arrangements must be made within 90 days. If nothing is heard from the client within that time, consent to the sale is presumed.

[7] A lawyer or law firm ceasing to practice cannot be required to remain in practice because some clients cannot be given actual notice of the proposed purchase. Since these clients cannot themselves consent to the purchase or direct any other disposition of their files, the Rule requires an order from a court having jurisdiction authorizing their transfer or other disposition. The Court can be expected to determine whether reasonable efforts to locate the client have been exhausted, and whether the absent client's legitimate interests will be served by authorizing the transfer of the file so that the purchaser may continue the representation. Preservation of client confidences requires that the petition for a court order be considered in camera. (A procedure by which such an order can be obtained needs to be established in jurisdictions in which it presently does not exist.)

[8] All the elements of client autonomy, including the client's absolute right to discharge a lawyer and transfer the representation to another, survive the sale of the practice.

Fee Arrangements Between Client and Purchaser

[9] The sale may not be financed by increases in fees charged the clients of the practice. Existing agreements between the seller and the client as to fees and the scope of the work must be honored by the purchaser, unless the client consents after consultation. The purchaser

may, however, advise the client that the purchaser will not undertake the representation unless the client consents to pay the higher fees the purchaser usually charges. To prevent client financing of the sale, the higher fee the purchaser may charge must not exceed the fees charged by the purchaser for substantially similar service rendered prior to the initiation of the purchase negotiations.

[10] The purchaser may not intentionally fragment the practice which is the subject of the sale by charging significantly different fees in substantially similar matters. Doing so would make it possible for the purchaser to avoid the obligation to take over the entire practice by charging arbitrarily higher fees for less lucrative matters, thereby increasing the likelihood that those clients would not consent to the new representation.

Other Applicable Ethical Standards

[11] Lawyers participating in the sale of a law practice are subject to the ethical standards applicable to involving another lawyer in the representation of a client. These include, for example, the seller's obligation to exercise competence in identifying a purchaser qualified to assume the practice and the purchaser's obligation to undertake the representation competently (see Rule 1.1); the obligation to avoid disqualifying conflicts, and to secure client consent after consultation for those conflicts which can be agreed to (see Rule 1.7); and the obligation to protect information relating to the representation (see Rules 1.6 and 1.9).

[12] If approval of the substitution of the purchasing attorney for the selling attorney is required by the rules of any tribunal in which a matter is pending, such approval must be obtained before the matter can be included in the sale (see Rule 1.16).

Applicability of the Rule

[13] This Rule applies to the sale of a law practice by representatives of a deceased, disabled or disappeared lawyer. Thus, the seller may be represented by a non-lawyer representative not subject to these Rules. Since, however, no lawyer may participate in a sale of a law practice which does not conform to the requirements of this Rule, the representatives of the seller as well as the purchasing lawyer can be expected to see to it that they are met.

[14] Admission to or retirement from a law partnership or professional association, retirement plans and similar arrangements, and a sale of tangible assets of a law practice, do not constitute a sale or purchase governed by this Rule.

[15] This Rule does not apply to the transfers of legal representation between lawyers when such transfers are unrelated to the sale of a practice.

Rule 1.17   *ABA MODEL RULES*

MODEL CODE COMPARISON

There was no counterpart to this Rule in the Model Code.

COUNSELOR

RULE 2.1 Advisor

In representing a client, a lawyer shall exercise independent professional judgment and render candid advice. In rendering advice, a lawyer may refer not only to law but to other considerations such as moral, economic, social and political factors, that may be relevant to the client's situation.

COMMENT:

Scope of Advice

[1] A client is entitled to straightforward advice expressing the lawyer's honest assessment. Legal advice often involves unpleasant facts and alternatives that a client may be disinclined to confront. In presenting advice, a lawyer endeavors to sustain the client's morale and may put advice in as acceptable a form as honesty permits. However, a lawyer should not be deterred from giving candid advice by the prospect that the advice will be unpalatable to the client.

[2] Advice couched in narrowly legal terms may be of little value to a client, especially where practical considerations, such as cost or effects on other people, are predominant. Purely technical legal advice, therefore, can sometimes be inadequate. It is proper for a lawyer to refer to relevant moral and ethical considerations in giving advice. Although a lawyer is not a moral advisor as such, moral and ethical considerations impinge upon most legal questions and may decisively influence how the law will be applied.

[3] A client may expressly or impliedly ask the lawyer for purely technical advice. When such a request is made by a client experienced in legal matters, the lawyer may accept it at face value. When such a request is made by a client inexperienced in legal matters, however, the lawyer's responsibility as advisor may include indicating that more may be involved than strictly legal considerations.

[4] Matters that go beyond strictly legal questions may also be in the domain of another profession. Family matters can involve problems within the professional competence of psychiatry, clinical psychology or social work; business matters can involve problems within the competence of the accounting profession or of financial specialists. Where consultation with a professional in another field is itself something a competent lawyer would recommend, the lawyer should make such a recommendation. At the same time, a lawyer's advice at its best often consists of recommending a course of action in the face of conflicting recommendations of experts.

Offering Advice

[5] In general, a lawyer is not expected to give advice until asked by the client. However, when a lawyer knows that a client proposes a course of action that is likely to result in substantial adverse legal consequences to the client, duty to the client under Rule 1.4 may require that the lawyer act if the client's course of action is related to the representation. A lawyer ordinarily has no duty to initiate investigation of a client's affairs or to give advice that the client has indicated is unwanted, but a lawyer may initiate advice to a client when doing so appears to be in the client's interest.

MODEL CODE COMPARISON

There was no direct counterpart to this Rule in the Disciplinary Rules of the Model Code. DR 5-107(B) provided that a lawyer "shall not permit a person who recommends, employs, or pays him to render legal services for another to direct or regulate his professional judgment in rendering such legal services." EC 7-8 stated that "[a]dvice of a lawyer to his client need not be confined to purely legal considerations. . . . In assisting his client to reach a proper decision, it is often desirable for a lawyer to point out those factors which may lead to a decision that is morally just as well as legally permissible. . . . In the final analysis, however, . . . the decision whether to forego legally available objectives or methods because of nonlegal factors is ultimately for the client. . . ."

RULE 2.2 Intermediary

(a) A lawyer may act as intermediary between clients if:

(1) the lawyer consults with each client concerning the implications of the common representation, including the advantages and risks involved, and the effect on the attorney–client privileges, and obtains each client's consent to the common representation;

(2) the lawyer reasonably believes that the matter can be resolved on terms compatible with the clients' best interests, that each client will be able to make adequately informed decisions in the matter and that there is little risk of material prejudice to the interest of any of the clients if the contemplated resolution is unsuccessful; and

(3) the lawyer reasonably believes that the common representation can be undertaken impartially and without improper effect on other responsibilities the lawyer has to any of the clients.

(b) While acting as intermediary, the lawyer shall consult with each client concerning the decisions to be made and the considerations relevant in making them, so that each client can make adequately informed decisions.

(c) A lawyer shall withdraw as intermediary if any of the clients so request, or if any of the conditions stated in paragraph (a) is no longer satisfied. Upon withdrawal, the lawyer shall not continue to

Rule 2.2   *ABA MODEL RULES*

represent any of the clients in the matter that was the subject of the intermediation.

COMMENT:

[1] A lawyer acts as intermediary under this Rule when the lawyer represents two or more parties with potentially conflicting interests. A key factor in defining the relationship is whether the parties share responsibility for the lawyer's fee, but the common representation may be inferred from other circumstances. Because confusion can arise as to the lawyer's role where each party is not separately represented, it is important that the lawyer make clear the relationship.

[2] The Rule does not apply to a lawyer acting as arbitrator or mediator between or among parties who are not clients of the lawyer, even where the lawyer has been appointed with the concurrence of the parties. In performing such a role the lawyer may be subject to applicable codes of ethics, such as the Code of Ethics for Arbitration in Commercial Disputes prepared by a joint Committee of the American Bar Association and the American Arbitration Association.

[3] A lawyer acts as intermediary in seeking to establish or adjust a relationship between clients on an amicable and mutually advantageous basis; for example, in helping to organize a business in which two or more clients are entrepreneurs, working out the financial reorganization of an enterprise in which two or more clients have an interest, arranging a property distribution in settlement of an estate or mediating a dispute between clients. The lawyer seeks to resolve potentially conflicting interests by developing the parties' mutual interests. The alternative can be that each party may have to obtain separate representation, with the possibility in some situations of incurring additional cost, complication or even litigation. Given these and other relevant factors, all the clients may prefer that the lawyer act as intermediary.

[4] In considering whether to act as intermediary between clients, a lawyer should be mindful that if the intermediation fails the result can be additional cost, embarrassment and recrimination. In some situations the risk of failure is so great that intermediation is plainly impossible. For example, a lawyer cannot undertake common representation of clients between whom contentious litigation is imminent or who contemplate contentious negotiations. More generally, if the relationship between the parties has already assumed definite antagonism, the possibility that the clients' interests can be adjusted by intermediation ordinarily is not very good.

[5] The appropriateness of intermediation can depend on its form. Forms of intermediation range from informal arbitration, where each client's case is presented by the respective client and the lawyer decides the outcome, to mediation, to common representation where the clients' interests are substantially though not entirely compatible. One form may be appropriate in circumstances where another would not. Other

relevant factors are whether the lawyer subsequently will represent both parties on a continuing basis and whether the situation involves creating a relationship between the parties or terminating one.

Confidentiality and Privilege

[6] A particularly important factor in determining the appropriateness of intermediation is the effect on client-lawyer confidentiality and the attorney-client privilege. In a common representation, the lawyer is still required both to keep each client adequately informed and to maintain confidentiality of information relating to the representation. See Rules 1.4 and 1.6. Complying with both requirements while acting as intermediary requires a delicate balance. If the balance cannot be maintained, the common representation is improper. With regard to the attorney-client privilege, the prevailing rule is that as between commonly represented clients the privilege does not attach. Hence, it must be assumed that if litigation eventuates between the clients, the privilege will not protect any such communications, and the clients should be so advised.

[7] Since the lawyer is required to be impartial between commonly represented clients, intermediation is improper when that impartiality cannot be maintained. For example, a lawyer who has represented one of the clients for a long period and in a variety of matters might have difficulty being impartial between that client and one to whom the lawyer has only recently been introduced.

Consultation

[8] In acting as intermediary between clients, the lawyer is required to consult with the clients on the implications of doing so, and proceed only upon consent based on such a consultation. The consultation should make clear that the lawyer's role is not that of partisanship normally expected in other circumstances.

[9] Paragraph (b) is an application of the principle expressed in Rule 1.4. Where the lawyer is intermediary, the clients ordinarily must assume greater responsibility for decisions than when each client is independently represented.

Withdrawal

[10] Common representation does not diminish the rights of each client in the client-lawyer relationship. Each has the right to loyal and diligent representation, the right to discharge the lawyer as stated in Rule 1.16, and the protection of Rule 1.9 concerning obligations to a former client.

MODEL CODE COMPARISON

There was no direct counterpart to this Rule in the Disciplinary Rules of the Model Code. EC 5–20 stated that a "lawyer is often asked to serve as an

Rule 2.2

impartial arbitrator or mediator in matters which involve present or former clients. He may serve in either capacity if he first discloses such present or former relationships." DR 5–105(B) provided that a lawyer "shall not continue multiple employment if the exercise of his independent judgment in behalf of a client will be or is likely to be adversely affected by his representation of another client, or if it would be likely to involve him in representation of differing interests, except to the extent permitted under DR 5–105(C)." DR 5–105(C) provided that "a lawyer may represent multiple clients if it is obvious that he can adequately represent the interests of each and if each consents to the representation after full disclosure of the possible effect of such representation on the exercise of his independent professional judgment on behalf of each."

RULE 2.3 Evaluation for Use by Third Persons

(a) A lawyer may undertake an evaluation of a matter affecting a client for the use of someone other than the client if:

(1) the lawyer reasonably believes that making the evaluation is compatible with other aspects of the lawyer's relationship with the client; and

(2) the client consents after consultation.

(b) Except as disclosure is required in connection with a report of an evaluation, information relating to the evaluation is otherwise protected by rule 1.6.

COMMENT:

Definition

[1] An evaluation may be performed at the client's direction but for the primary purpose of establishing information for the benefit of third parties; for example, an opinion concerning the title of property rendered at the behest of a vendor for the information of a prospective purchaser, or at the behest of a borrower for the information of a prospective lender. In some situations, the evaluation may be required by a government agency; for example, an opinion concerning the legality of the securities registered for sale under the securities laws. In other instances, the evaluation may be required by a third person, such as a purchaser of a business.

[2] Lawyers for the government may be called upon to give a formal opinion on the legality of contemplated government agency action. In making such an evaluation, the government lawyer acts at the behest of the government as the client but for the purpose of establishing the limits of the agency's authorized activity. Such an opinion is to be distinguished from confidential legal advice given agency officials. The critical question is whether the opinion is to be made public.

[3] A legal evaluation should be distinguished from an investigation of a person with whom the lawyer does not have a client-lawyer relationship. For example, a lawyer retained by a purchaser to analyze a vendor's title to property does not have a client-lawyer relationship with

the vendor. So also, an investigation into a person's affairs by a government lawyer, or by special counsel employed by the government, is not an evaluation as that term is used in this Rule. The question is whether the lawyer is retained by the person whose affairs are being examined. When the lawyer is retained by that person, the general rules concerning loyalty to client and preservation of confidences apply, which is not the case if the lawyer is retained by someone else. For this reason, it is essential to identify the person by whom the lawyer is retained. This should be made clear not only to the person under examination, but also to others to whom the results are to be made available.

Duty to Third Person

[4] When the evaluation is intended for the information or use of a third person, a legal duty to that person may or may not arise. That legal question is beyond the scope of this Rule. However, since such an evaluation involves a departure from the normal client-lawyer relationship, careful analysis of the situation is required. The lawyer must be satisfied as a matter of professional judgment that making the evaluation is compatible with other functions undertaken in behalf of the client. For example, if the lawyer is acting as advocate in defending the client against charges of fraud, it would normally be incompatible with that responsibility for the lawyer to perform an evaluation for others concerning the same or a related transaction. Assuming no such impediment is apparent, however, the lawyer should advise the client of the implications of the evaluation, particularly the lawyer's responsibilities to third persons and the duty to disseminate the findings.

Access to and Disclosure of Information

[5] The quality of an evaluation depends on the freedom and extent of the investigation upon which it is based. Ordinarily a lawyer should have whatever latitude of investigation seems necessary as a matter of professional judgment. Under some circumstances, however, the terms of the evaluation may be limited. For example, certain issues or sources may be categorically excluded, or the scope of search may be limited by time constraints or the noncooperation of persons having relevant information. Any such limitations which are material to the evaluation should be described in the report. If after a lawyer has commenced an evaluation, the client refuses to comply with the terms upon which it was understood the evaluation was to have been made, the lawyer's obligations are determined by law, having reference to the terms of the client's agreement and the surrounding circumstances.

Financial Auditors' Requests for Information

[6] When a question concerning the legal situation of a client arises at the instance of the client's financial auditor and the question is referred to the lawyer, the lawyer's response may be made in accordance

with procedures recognized in the legal profession. Such a procedure is set forth in the American Bar Association Statement of Policy Regarding Lawyers' Responses to Auditors' Requests for Information, adopted in 1975.

MODEL CODE COMPARISON

There was no counterpart to this Rule in the Model Code.

ADVOCATE

RULE 3.1 Meritorious Claims and Contentions

A lawyer shall not bring or defend a proceeding, or assert or controvert an issue therein, unless there is a basis for doing so that is not frivolous, which includes a good faith argument for an extension, modification or reversal of existing law. A lawyer for the defendant in a criminal proceeding, or the respondent in a proceeding that could result in incarceration, may nevertheless so defend the proceeding as to require that every element of the case be established.

COMMENT:

[1] The advocate has a duty to use legal procedure for the fullest benefit of the client's cause, but also a duty not to abuse legal procedure. The law, both procedural and substantive, establishes the limits within which an advocate may proceed. However, the law is not always clear and never is static. Accordingly, in determining the proper scope of advocacy, account must be taken of the law's ambiguities and potential for change.

[2] The filing of an action or defense or similar action taken for a client is not frivolous merely because the facts have not first been fully substantiated or because the lawyer expects to develop vital evidence only by discovery. Such action is not frivolous even though the lawyer believes that the client's position ultimately will not prevail. The action is frivolous, however, if the client desires to have the action taken primarily for the purpose of harassing or maliciously injuring a person or if the lawyer is unable either to make a good faith argument on the merits of the action taken or to support the action taken by a good faith argument for an extension, modification or reversal of existing law.

MODEL CODE COMPARISON

DR 7–102(A)(1) provided that a lawyer may not "[f]ile a suit, assert a position, conduct a defense, delay a trial, or take other action on behalf of his client when he knows or when it is obvious that such action would serve merely to harass or maliciously injure another." Rule 3.1 is to the same general effect as DR 7–102(A)(1), with three qualifications. First, the test of improper conduct is changed from "merely to harass or maliciously injure another" to the requirement that there be a basis for the litigation measure involved that is "not frivolous." This includes the concept stated in DR 7–102(A)(2) that a lawyer may advance a claim or defense unwarranted by existing law if "it can be supported by good faith argument for an extension, modification, or reversal of existing law." Second, the test in Rule 3.1 is an objective test, whereas DR 7–102(A)(1) applied only if the lawyer "knows or when it is obvious" that the litigation is frivolous. Third, Rule 3.1 has an exception that in a criminal case, or a case in which incarceration of the client may result (for example, certain juvenile proceedings), the lawyer may put the prosecution to its proof even if there is no nonfrivolous basis for defense.

RULE 3.2 Expediting Litigation

A lawyer shall make reasonable efforts to expedite litigation consistent with the interests of the client.

COMMENT:

Dilatory practices bring the administration of justice into disrepute. Delay should not be indulged merely for the convenience of the advocates, or for the purpose of frustrating an opposing party's attempt to obtain rightful redress or repose. It is not a justification that similar conduct is often tolerated by the bench and bar. The question is whether a competent lawyer acting in good faith would regard the course of action as having some substantial purpose other than delay. Realizing financial or other benefit from otherwise improper delay in litigation is not a legitimate interest of the client.

MODEL CODE COMPARISON

DR 7–101(A)(1) stated that a lawyer does not violate the lawyer's duty to represent a client zealously "by being punctual in fulfilling all professional commitments." DR 7–102(A)(1) provided that a lawyer "shall not . . . file a suit, assert a position, conduct a defense [or] delay a trial . . . when he knows or when it is obvious that such action would serve merely to harass or maliciously injure another."

RULE 3.3 Candor Toward the Tribunal

(a) A lawyer shall not knowingly:

(1) make a false statement of material fact or law to a tribunal;

(2) fail to disclose a material fact to a tribunal when disclosure is necessary to avoid assisting a criminal or fraudulent act by the client;

(3) fail to disclose to the tribunal legal authority in the controlling jurisdiction known to the lawyer to be directly adverse to the position of the client and not disclosed by opposing counsel; or

(4) offer evidence that the lawyer knows to be false. If a lawyer has offered material evidence and comes to know of its falsity, the lawyer shall take reasonable remedial measures.

(b) The duties stated in paragraph (a) continue to the conclusion of the proceeding, and apply even if compliance requires disclosure of information otherwise protected by rule 1.6.

Rule 3.3 *ABA MODEL RULES*

(c) A lawyer may refuse to offer evidence that the lawyer reasonably believes is false.

(d) In an ex parte proceeding, a lawyer shall inform the tribunal of all material facts known to the lawyer which will enable the tribunal to make an informed decision, whether or not the facts are adverse.

COMMENT:

[1] The advocate's task is to present the client's case with persuasive force. Performance of that duty while maintaining confidences of the client is qualified by the advocate's duty of candor to the tribunal. However, an advocate does not vouch for the evidence submitted in a cause; the tribunal is responsible for assessing its probative value.

Representations by a Lawyer

[2] An advocate is responsible for pleadings and other documents prepared for litigation, but is usually not required to have personal knowledge of matters asserted therein, for litigation documents ordinarily present assertions by the client, or by someone on the client's behalf, and not assertions by the lawyer. Compare Rule 3.1. However, an assertion purporting to be on the lawyer's own knowledge, as in an affidavit by the lawyer or in a statement in open court, may properly be made only when the lawyer knows the assertion is true or believes it to be true on the basis of a reasonably diligent inquiry. There are circumstances where failure to make a disclosure is the equivalent of an affirmative misrepresentation. The obligation prescribed in Rule 1.2(d) not to counsel a client to commit or assist the client in committing a fraud applies in litigation. Regarding compliance with Rule 1.2(d), see the Comment to that Rule. See also the Comment to Rule 8.4(b).

Misleading Legal Argument

[3] Legal argument based on a knowingly false representation of law constitutes dishonesty toward the tribunal. A lawyer is not required to make a disinterested exposition of the law, but must recognize the existence of pertinent legal authorities. Furthermore, as stated in paragraph (a)(3), an advocate has a duty to disclose directly adverse authority in the controlling jurisdiction which has not been disclosed by the opposing party. The underlying concept is that legal argument is a discussion seeking to determine the legal premises properly applicable to the case.

False Evidence

[4] When evidence that a lawyer knows to be false is provided by a person who is not the client, the lawyer must refuse to offer it regardless of the client's wishes.

[5] When false evidence is offered by the client, however, a conflict may arise between the lawyer's duty to keep the client's revelations

confidential and the duty of candor to the court. Upon ascertaining that material evidence is false, the lawyer should seek to persuade the client that the evidence should not be offered or, if it has been offered, that its false character should immediately be disclosed. If the persuasion is ineffective, the lawyer must take reasonable remedial measures.

[6] Except in the defense of a criminal accused, the rule generally recognized is that, if necessary to rectify the situation, an advocate must disclose the existence of the client's deception to the court or to the other party. Such a disclosure can result in grave consequences to the client, including not only a sense of betrayal but also loss of the case and perhaps a prosecution for perjury. But the alternative is that the lawyer cooperate in deceiving the court, thereby subverting the truth-finding process which the adversary system is designed to implement. See Rule 1.2(d). Furthermore, unless it is clearly understood that the lawyer will act upon the duty to disclose the existence of false evidence, the client can simply reject the lawyer's advice to reveal the false evidence and insist that the lawyer keep silent. Thus the client could in effect coerce the lawyer into being a party to fraud on the court.

Perjury by a Criminal Defendant

[7] Whether an advocate for a criminally accused has the same duty of disclosure has been intensely debated. While it is agreed that the lawyer should seek to persuade the client to refrain from perjurious testimony, there has been dispute concerning the lawyer's duty when that persuasion fails. If the confrontation with the client occurs before trial, the lawyer ordinarily can withdraw. Withdrawal before trial may not be possible, however, either because trial is imminent, or because the confrontation with the client does not take place until the trial itself, or because no other counsel is available.

[8] The most difficult situation, therefore, arises in a criminal case where the accused insists on testifying when the lawyer knows that the testimony is perjurious. The lawyer's effort to rectify the situation can increase the likelihood of the client's being convicted as well as opening the possibility of a prosecution for perjury. On the other hand, if the lawyer does not exercise control over the proof, the lawyer participates, although in a merely passive way, in deception of the court.

[9] Three resolutions of this dilemma have been proposed. One is to permit the accused to testify by a narrative without guidance through the lawyer's questioning. This compromises both contending principles; it exempts the lawyer from the duty to disclose false evidence but subjects the client to an implicit disclosure of information imparted to counsel. Another suggested resolution, of relatively recent origin, is that the advocate be entirely excused from the duty to reveal perjury if the perjury is that of the client. This is a coherent solution but makes the advocate a knowing instrument of perjury.

[10] The other resolution of the dilemma is that the lawyer must reveal the client's perjury if necessary to rectify the situation. A criminal accused has a right to the assistance of an advocate, a right to testify and a right of confidential communication with counsel. However, an accused should not have a right to assistance of counsel in committing perjury. Furthermore, an advocate has an obligation, not only in professional ethics but under the law as well, to avoid implication in the commission of perjury or other falsification of evidence. See Rule 1.2(d).

Remedial Measures

[11] If perjured testimony or false evidence has been offered, the advocate's proper course ordinarily is to remonstrate with the client confidentially. If that fails, the advocate should seek to withdraw if that will remedy the situation. If withdrawal will not remedy the situation or is impossible, the advocate should make disclosure to the court. It is for the court then to determine what should be done—making a statement about the matter to the trier of fact, ordering a mistrial or perhaps nothing. If the false testimony was that of the client, the client may controvert the lawyer's version of their communication when the lawyer discloses the situation to the court. If there is an issue whether the client has committed perjury, the lawyer cannot represent the client in resolution of the issue and a mistrial may be unavoidable. An unscrupulous client might in this way attempt to produce a series of mistrials and thus escape prosecution. However, a second such encounter could be construed as a deliberate abuse of the right to counsel and as such a waiver of the right to further representation.

Constitutional Requirements

[12] The general rule—that an advocate must disclose the existence of perjury with respect to a material fact, even that of a client—applies to defense counsel in criminal cases, as well as in other instances. However, the definition of the lawyer's ethical duty in such a situation may be qualified by constitutional provisions for due process and the right to counsel in criminal cases. In some jurisdictions these provisions have been construed to require that counsel present an accused as a witness if the accused wishes to testify, even if counsel knows the testimony will be false. The obligation of the advocate under these Rules is subordinate to such a constitutional requirement.

Duration of Obligation

[13] A practical time limit on the obligation to rectify the presentation of false evidence has to be established. The conclusion of the proceeding is a reasonably definite point for the termination of the obligation.

Refusing to Offer Proof Believed to be False

[14] Generally speaking, a lawyer has authority to refuse to offer testimony or other proof that the lawyer believes is untrustworthy. Offering such proof may reflect adversely on the lawyer's ability to discriminate in the quality of evidence and thus impair the lawyer's effectiveness as an advocate. In criminal cases, however, a lawyer may, in some jurisdictions, be denied this authority by constitutional requirements governing the right to counsel.

Ex Parte Proceedings

[15] Ordinarily, an advocate has the limited responsibility of presenting one side of the matters that a tribunal should consider in reaching a decision; the conflicting position is expected to be presented by the opposing party. However, in an ex parte proceeding, such as an application for a temporary restraining order, there is no balance of presentation by opposing advocates. The object of an ex parte proceeding is nevertheless to yield a substantially just result. The judge has an affirmative responsibility to accord the absent party just consideration. The lawyer for the represented party has the correlative duty to make disclosures of material facts known to the lawyer and that the lawyer reasonably believes are necessary to an informed decision.

MODEL CODE COMPARISON

[1] Paragraph (a)(1) is substantially identical to DR 7–102(A)(5), which provided that a lawyer shall not "knowingly make a false statement of law or fact."

[2] Paragraph (a)(2) is implicit in DR 7–102(A)(3), which provided that "a lawyer shall not . . . knowingly fail to disclose that which he is required by law to reveal."

[3] Paragraph (a)(3) is substantially identical to DR 7–106(B)(1).

[4] With regard to paragraph (a)(4), the first sentence of this subparagraph is similar to DR 7–102(A)(4), which provided that a lawyer shall not "knowingly use" perjured testimony or false evidence. The second sentence of paragraph (a)(4) resolves an ambiguity in the Model Code concerning the action required of a lawyer who discovers that the lawyer has offered perjured testimony or false evidence. DR 7–102(A)(4), quoted above, did not expressly deal with this situation, but the prohibition against "use" of false evidence can be construed to preclude carrying through with a case based on such evidence when that fact has become known during the trial. DR 7–102(B)(1), also noted in connection with Rule 1.6, provided that a lawyer "who receives information clearly establishing that . . . his client has . . . perpetrated a fraud upon . . . a tribunal shall if the client does not rectify the situation . . . reveal the fraud to the . . . tribunal. . . ." Since use of perjured testimony or false evidence is usually regarded as "fraud" upon the court, DR 7–102(B)(1) apparently required disclosure by the lawyer in such circumstances. However, some states have amended DR 7–102(B)(1) in conformity with an ABA-recommended amendment to provide that the duty of disclosure does not apply when the "information is protected as a privileged communication." This qualification may be empty, for the rule of attorney-client privilege has been construed to exclude communications that

Rule 3.3 *ABA MODEL RULES*

further a crime, including the crime of perjury. On this interpretation of DR 7-102(B)(1), the lawyer has a duty to disclose the perjury.

[5] Paragraph (c) confers discretion on the lawyer to refuse to offer evidence that he "reasonably believes" is false. This gives the lawyer more latitude than DR 7-102(A)(4), which prohibited the lawyer from offering evidence the lawyer "knows" is false.

[6] There was no counterpart in the Model Code to paragraph (d).

RULE 3.4 Fairness to Opposing Party and Counsel

A lawyer shall not:

(a) unlawfully obstruct another party's access to evidence or unlawfully alter, destroy or conceal a document or other material having potential evidentiary value. A lawyer shall not counsel or assist another person to do any such act;

(b) falsify evidence, counsel or assist a witness to testify falsely, or offer an inducement to a witness that is prohibited by law;

(c) knowingly disobey an obligation under the rules of a tribunal except for an open refusal based on an assertion that no valid obligation exists;

(d) in pretrial procedure, make a frivolous discovery request or fail to make reasonably diligent effort to comply with a legally proper discovery request by an opposing party;

(e) in trial, allude to any matter that the lawyer does not reasonably believe is relevant or that will not be supported by admissible evidence, assert personal knowledge of facts in issue except when testifying as a witness, or state a personal opinion as to the justness of a cause, the credibility of a witness, the culpability of a civil litigant or the guilt or innocence of an accused; or

(f) request a person other than a client to refrain from voluntarily giving relevant information to another party unless:

> (1) the person is a relative or an employee or other agent of a client; and

> (2) the lawyer reasonably believes that the person's interests will not be adversely affected by refraining from giving such information.

COMMENT:

[1] The procedure of the adversary system contemplates that the evidence in a case is to be marshalled competitively by the contending parties. Fair competition in the adversary system is secured by prohibitions against destruction or concealment of evidence, improperly influencing witnesses, obstructive tactics in discovery procedure, and the like.

[2] Documents and other items of evidence are often essential to establish a claim or defense. Subject to evidentiary privileges, the right of an opposing party, including the government, to obtain evidence

PROFESSIONAL CONDUCT   Rule 3.4

through discovery or subpoena is an important procedural right. The exercise of that right can be frustrated if relevant material is altered, concealed or destroyed. Applicable law in many jurisdictions makes it an offense to destroy material for purpose of impairing its availability in a pending proceeding or one whose commencement can be foreseen. Falsifying evidence is also generally a criminal offense. Paragraph (a) applies to evidentiary material generally, including computerized information.

[3] With regard to paragrah (b), it is not improper to pay a witness's expenses or to compensate an expert witness on terms permitted by law. The common law rule in most jurisdictions is that it is improper to pay an occurrence witness any fee for testifying and that it is improper to pay an expert witness a contingent fee.

[4] Paragraph (f) permits a lawyer to advise employees of a client to refrain from giving information to another party, for the employees may identify their interests with those of the client. See also Rule 4.2.

MODEL CODE COMPARISON

[1] With regard to paragraph (a), DR 7-109(A) provided that a lawyer "shall not suppress any evidence that he or his client has a legal obligation to reveal." DR 7-109(B) provided that a lawyer "shall not advise or cause a person to secrete himself . . . for the purpose of making him unavailable as a witness. . . ." DR 7-106(C)(7) provided that a lawyer shall not "[i]ntentionally or habitually violate any established rule of procedure or of evidence."

[2] With regard to paragraph (b), DR 7-102(A)(6) provided that a lawyer shall not participate "in the creation or preservation of evidence when he knows or it is obvious that the evidence is false." DR 7-109(C) provided that a lawyer "shall not pay, offer to pay, or acquiesce in the payment of compensation to a witness contingent on the content of his testimony or the outcome of the case. But a lawyer may advance, guarantee or acquiesce in the payment of: (1) expenses reasonably incurred by a witness in attending or testifying; (2) reasonable compensation to a witness for his loss of time in attending or testifying; [or] (3) a reasonable fee for the professional services of an expert witness." EC 7-28 stated that witnesses "should always testify truthfully and should be free from any financial inducements that might tempt them to do otherwise."

[3] Paragraph (c) is substantially similar to DR 7-106(A), which provided that a lawyer "shall not disregard . . . a standing rule of a tribunal or a ruling of a tribunal made in the course of a proceeding, but he may take appropriate steps in good faith to test the validity of such rule or ruling."

[4] Paragraph (d) has no counterpart in the Model Code.

[5] Paragraph (e) substantially incorporates DR 7-106(C)(1), (2), (3) and (4). DR 7-106(C)(2) proscribed asking a question "intended to degrade a witness or other person," a matter dealt with in Rule 4.4. DR 7-106(C)(5), providing that a lawyer shall not "[f]ail to comply with known local customs of courtesy or practice," was too vague to be a rule of conduct enforceable as law.

[6] With regard to paragraph (f), DR 7-104(A)(2) provided that a lawyer shall not "[g]ive advice to a person who is not represented . . . other than the

Rule 3.4 ABA MODEL RULES

advice to secure counsel, if the interests of such person are or have a reasonable possibility of being in conflict with the interests of his client."

RULE 3.5 Impartiality and Decorum of the Tribunal

A lawyer shall not:

(a) seek to influence a judge, juror, prospective juror or other official by means prohibited by law;

(b) communicate ex parte with such a person except as permitted by law; or

(c) engage in conduct intended to disrupt a tribunal.

COMMENT:

[1] Many forms of improper influence upon a tribunal are proscribed by criminal law. Others are specified in the ABA Model Code of Judicial Conduct, with which an advocate should be familiar. A lawyer is required to avoid contributing to a violation of such provisions.

[2] The advocate's function is to present evidence and argument so that the cause may be decided according to law. Refraining from abusive or obstreperous conduct is a corollary of the advocate's right to speak on behalf of litigants. A lawyer may stand firm against abuse by a judge but should avoid reciprocation; the judge's default is no justification for similar dereliction by an advocate. An advocate can present the cause, protect the record for subsequent review and preserve professional integrity by patient firmness no less effectively than by belligerence or theatrics.

MODEL CODE COMPARISON

[1] With regard to paragraphs (a) and (b), DR 7-108(A) provided that "[b]efore the trial of a case a lawyer . . . shall not communicate with . . . anyone he knows to be a member of the venire . . . ." DR 7-108(B) provided that during the trial of a case a lawyer "shall not communicate . . . any member of the jury." DR 7-110(B) provided that a lawyer shall not "communicate . . . as to the merits of the cause with a judge or an official before whom the proceeding is pending, except . . . upon adequate notice to opposing counsel," or as "otherwise authorized by law."

[2] With regard to paragraph (c), DR 7-106(C)(6) provided that a lawyer shall not engage in "undignified or discourteous conduct which is degrading to a tribunal."

RULE 3.6 Trial Publicity

(a) A lawyer shall not make an extrajudicial statement that a reasonable person would expect to be disseminated by means of public communication if the lawyer knows or reasonably should know that it will have a substantial likelihood of materially prejudicing an adjudicative proceeding.

(b) A statement referred to in paragraph (a) ordinarily is likely to have such an effect when it refers to a civil matter triable to a jury, a criminal matter, or any other proceeding that could result in incarceration, and the statement relates to:

(1) the character, credibility, reputation or criminal record of a party, suspect in a criminal investigation or witness, or the identity of a witness, or the expected testimony of a party or witness;

(2) in a criminal case or proceeding that could result in incarceration, the possibility of a plea of guilty to the offense or the existence or contents of any confession, admission, or statement given by a defendant or suspect or that person's refusal or failure to make a statement;

(3) the performance or results of any examination or test or the refusal or failure of a person to submit to an examination or test, or the identity or nature of physical evidence expected to be presented;

(4) any opinion as to the guilt or innocence of a defendant or suspect in a criminal case or proceeding that could result in incarceration;

(5) information the lawyer knows or reasonably should know is likely to be inadmissible as evidence in a trial and would if disclosed create a substantial risk of prejudicing an impartial trial; or

(6) the fact that a defendant has been charged with a crime, unless there is included therein a statement explaining that the charge is merely an accusation and that the defendant is presumed innocent until and unless proven guilty.

(c) Notwithstanding paragraph (a) and (b)(1-5), a lawyer involved in the investigation or litigation of a matter may state without elaboration:

(1) the general nature of the claim or defense;

(2) the information contained in a public record;

(3) that an investigation of the matter is in progress, including the general scope of the investigation, the offense or claim or defense involved and, except when prohibited by law, the identity of the persons involved;

(4) the scheduling or result of any step in litigation;

(5) a request for assistance in obtaining evidence and information necessary thereto;

(6) a warning of danger concerning the behavior of a person involved, when there is reason to believe that there exists the likelihood of substantial harm to an individual or to the public interest; and

Rule 3.6 ABA MODEL RULES

(7) in a criminal case:

(i) the identity, residence, occupation and family status of the accused;

(ii) if the accused has not been apprehended, information necessary to aid in apprehension of that person;

(iii) the fact, time and place of arrest; and

(iv) the identity of investigating and arresting officers or agencies and the length of the investigation.

COMMENT:

[1] It is difficult to strike a balance between protecting the right to a fair trial and safeguarding the right of free expression. Preserving the right to a fair trial necessarily entails some curtailment of the information that may be disseminated about a party prior to trial, particularly where trial by jury is involved. If there were no such limits, the result would be the practical nullification of the protective effect of the rules of forensic decorum and the exclusionary rules of evidence. On the other hand, there are vital social interests served by the free dissemination of information about events having legal consequences and about legal proceedings themselves. The public has a right to know about threats to its safety and measures aimed at assuring its security. It also has a legitimate interest in the conduct of judicial proceedings, particularly in matters of general public concern. Furthermore, the subject matter of legal proceedings is often of direct significance in debate and deliberation over questions of public policy.

[2] No body of rules can simultaneously satisfy all interests of fair trial and all those of free expression. The formula in this Rule is based upon the ABA Model Code of Professional Responsibility and the ABA Standards Relating to Fair Trial and Free Press, as amended in 1978.

[3] Special rules of confidentiality may validly govern proceedings in juvenile, domestic relations and mental disability proceedings, and perhaps other types of litigation. Rule 3.4(c) requires compliance with such Rules.

MODEL CODE COMPARISON

Rule 3.6 is similar to DR 7–107, except as follows: First, Rule 3.6 adopts the general criteria of "substantial likelihood of materially prejudicing an adjudicative proceeding" to describe impermissible conduct. Second, Rule 3.6 transforms the particulars in DR 7–107 into an illustrative compilation that gives fair notice of conduct ordinarily posing unacceptable dangers to the fair administration of justice. Finally, Rule 3.6 omits DR 7–107(C)(7), which provided that a lawyer may reveal "[a]t the time of seizure, a description of the physical evidence seized, other than a confession, admission or statement." Such revelations may be substantially prejudicial and are frequently the subject of pretrial suppression motions, which, if successful, may be circumvented by prior disclosure to the press.

RULE 3.7 Lawyer as Witness

(a) A lawyer shall not act as advocate at a trial in which the lawyer is likely to be a necessary witness except where:

(1) the testimony relates to an uncontested issue;

(2) the testimony relates to the nature and value of legal services rendered in the case; or

(3) disqualification of the lawyer would work substantial hardship on the client.

(b) A lawyer may act as advocate in a trial in which another lawyer in the lawyer's firm is likely to be called as a witness unless precluded from doing so by rule 1.7 or rule 1.9.

COMMENT:

[1] Combining the roles of advocate and witness can prejudice the opposing party and can involve a conflict of interest between the lawyer and client.

[2] The opposing party has proper objection where the combination of roles may prejudice that party's rights in the litigation. A witness is required to testify on the basis of personal knowledge, while an advocate is expected to explain and comment on evidence given by others. It may not be clear whether a statement by an advocate-witness should be taken as proof or as an analysis of the proof.

[3] Paragraph (a)(1) recognizes that if the testimony will be uncontested, the ambiguities in the dual role are purely theoretical. Paragraph (a)(2) recognizes that where the testimony concerns the extent and value of legal services rendered in the action in which the testimony is offered, permitting the lawyers to testify avoids the need for a second trial with new counsel to resolve that issue. Moreover, in such a situation the judge has first hand knowledge of the matter in issue; hence, there is less dependence on the adversary process to test the credibility of the testimony.

[4] Apart from these two exceptions, paragraph (a)(3) recognizes that a balancing is required between the interests of the client and those of the opposing party. Whether the opposing party is likely to suffer prejudice depends on the nature of the case, the importance and probable tenor of the lawyer's testimony, and the probability that the lawyer's testimony will conflict with that of other witnesses. Even if there is risk of such prejudice, in determining whether the lawyer should be disqualified due regard must be given to the effect of disqualification on the lawyer's client. It is relevant that one or both parties could reasonably foresee that the lawyer would probably be a witness. The principle of imputed disqualification stated in Rule 1.10 has no application to this aspect of the problem.

[5] Whether the combination of roles involves an improper conflict of interest with respect to the client is determined by Rule 1.7 or 1.9.

Rule 3.7   *ABA MODEL RULES*

For example, if there is likely to be substantial conflict between the testimony of the client and that of the lawyer or a member of the lawyer's firm, the representation is improper. The problem can arise whether the lawyer is called as a witness on behalf of the client or is called by the opposing party. Determining whether or not such a conflict exists is primarily the responsibility of the lawyer involved. See Comment to Rule 1.7. If a lawyer who is a member of a firm may not act as both advocate and witness by reason of conflict of interest, Rule 1.10 disqualifies the firm also.

MODEL CODE COMPARISON

[1] DR 5–102(A) prohibited a lawyer, or the lawyer's firm, from serving as advocate if the lawyer "learns or it is obvious that he or a lawyer in his firm ought to be called as a witness on behalf of his client." DR 5–102(B) provided that a lawyer, and the lawyer's firm, may continue representation if the "lawyer learns or it is obvious that he or a lawyer in his firm may be called as a witness other than on behalf of his client . . . until it is apparent that his testimony is or may be prejudicial to his client." DR 5–101(B) permitted a lawyer to testify while representing a client: "(1) If the testimony will relate solely to an uncontested matter; (2) If the testimony will relate solely to a matter of formality and there is no reason to believe that substantial evidence will be offered in opposition to the testimony; (3) If the testimony will relate solely to the nature and value of legal services rendered in the case by the lawyer or his firm to the client; (4) As to any matter if refusal would work a substantial hardship on the client because of the distinctive value of the lawyer or his firm as counsel in the particular case."

[2] The exception stated in paragraph (a)(1) consolidates provisions of DR 5–101(B)(1) and (2). Testimony relating to a formality, referred to in DR 5–101(B)(2), in effect defined the phrase "uncontested issue," and was redundant.

RULE 3.8 Special Responsibilities of a Prosecutor

The prosecutor in a criminal case shall:

(a) refrain from prosecuting a charge that the prosecutor knows is not supported by probable cause;

(b) make reasonable efforts to assure that the accused has been advised of the right to, and the procedure for obtaining, counsel and has been given reasonable opportunity to obtain counsel;

(c) not seek to obtain from an unrepresented accused a waiver of important pretrial rights, such as the right to a preliminary hearing;

(d) make timely disclosure to the defense of all evidence or information known to the prosecutor that tends to negate the guilt of the accused or mitigates the offense, and, in connection with sentencing, disclose to the defense and to the tribunal all unprivileged mitigating information known to the prosecutor, except when the prosecutor is relieved of this responsibility by a protective order of the tribunal;

(e) exercise reasonable care to prevent investigators, law enforcement personnel, employees or other persons assisting or associated

with the prosecutor in a criminal case from making an extrajudicial statement that the prosecutor would be prohibited from making under rule 3.6; and

(f) not subpoena a lawyer in a grand jury or other criminal proceeding to present evidence about a past or present client unless:

(1) the prosecutor reasonably believes:

(i) the information sought is not protected from disclosure by any applicable privilege;

(ii) the evidence sought is essential to the successful completion of an ongoing investigation or prosecution;

(iii) there is no other feasible alternative to obtain the information; and

(2) the prosecutor obtains prior judicial approval after an opportunity for an adversarial proceeding.

COMMENT:

[1] A prosecutor has the responsibility of a minister of justice and not simply that of an advocate. This responsibility carries with it specific obligations to see that the defendant is accorded procedural justice and that guilt is decided upon the basis of sufficient evidence. Precisely how far the prosecutor is required to go in this direction is a matter of debate and varies in different jurisdictions. Many jurisdictions have adopted the ABA Standards of Criminal Justice Relating to Prosecution Function, which in turn are the product of prolonged and careful deliberation by lawyers experienced in both criminal prosecution and defense. See also Rule 3.3(d), governing ex parte proceedings, among which grand jury proceedings are included. Applicable law may require other measures by the prosecutor and knowing disregard of those obligations or a systematic abuse of prosecutorial discretion could constitute a violation of Rule 8.4.

[2] Paragraph (c) does not apply to an accused appearing pro se with the approval of the tribunal. Nor does it forbid the lawful questioning of a suspect who has knowingly waived the rights to counsel and silence.

[3] The exception in paragraph (d) recognizes that a prosecutor may seek an appropriate protective order from the tribunal if disclosure of information to the defense could result in substantial harm to an individual or to the public interest.

[4] Paragraph (f) is intended to limit the issuance of lawyer subpoenas in grand jury and other criminal proceedings to those situations in which there is a genuine need to intrude into the client-lawyer relationship. The prosecutor is required to obtain court approval for the issuance of the subpoena after an opportunity for an adversarial hearing is afforded in order to assure an independent determination that the applicable standards are met.

Rule 3.8

MODEL CODE COMPARISON

DR 7-103(A) provides that a "public prosecutor . . . shall not institute . . . criminal charges when he knows or it is obvious that the charges are not supported by probable cause." DR 7-103(B) provides that "[a] public prosecutor . . . shall make timely disclosure . . . of the existence of evidence, known to the prosecutor . . . that tends to negate the guilt of the accused, mitigate the degree of the offense, or reduce the punishment."

RULE 3.9 Advocate in Nonadjudicative Proceedings

A lawyer representing a client before a legislative or administrative tribunal in a nonadjudicative proceeding shall disclose that the appearance is in a representative capacity and shall conform to the provisions of rules 3.3(a) through (c), 3.4(a) through (c), and 3.5.

COMMENT:

[1] In representation before bodies such as legislatures, municipal councils, and executive and administrative agencies acting in a rule-making or policy-making capacity, lawyers present facts, formulate issues and advance argument in the matters under consideration. The decision-making body, like a court, should be able to rely on the integrity of the submissions made to it. A lawyer appearing before such a body should deal with the tribunal honestly and in conformity with applicable rules of procedure.

[2] Lawyers have no exclusive right to appear before nonadjudicative bodies, as they do before a court. The requirements of this Rule therefore may subject lawyers to regulations inapplicable to advocates who are not lawyers. However, legislatures and administrative agencies have a right to expect lawyers to deal with them as they deal with courts.

[3] This Rule does not apply to representation of a client in a negotiation or other bilateral transaction with a governmental agency; representation in such a transaction is governed by Rules 4.1 through 4.4.

MODEL CODE COMPARISON

EC 7-15 stated that a lawyer "appearing before an administrative agency, regardless of the nature of the proceeding it is conducting, has the continuing duty to advance the cause of his client within the bounds of the law." EC 7-16 stated that "[w]hen a lawyer appears in connection with proposed legislation, he . . . should comply with applicable laws and legislative rules." EC 8-5 stated that "[f]raudulent, deceptive, or otherwise illegal conduct by a participant in a proceeding before a . . . legislative body . . . should never be participated in . . . by lawyers." DR 7-106(B)(1) provided that "[i]n presenting a matter to a tribunal, a lawyer shall disclose . . . [u]nless privileged or irrelevant, the identity of the clients he represents and of the persons who employed him."

TRANSACTIONS WITH PERSONS OTHER THAN CLIENTS

RULE 4.1 Truthfulness in Statements to Others

In the course of representing a client a lawyer shall not knowingly:

(a) make a false statement of material fact or law to a third person; or

(b) fail to disclose a material fact to a third person when disclosure is necessary to avoid assisting a criminal or fraudulent act by a client, unless disclosure is prohibited by rule 1.6.

COMMENT:

Misrepresentation

[1] A lawyer is required to be truthful when dealing with others on a client's behalf, but generally has no affirmative duty to inform an opposing party of relevant facts. A misrepresentation can occur if the lawyer incorporates or affirms a statement of another person that the lawyer knows is false. Misrepresentations can also occur by failure to act.

Statements of Fact

[2] This Rule refers to statements of fact. Whether a particular statement should be regarded as one of fact can depend on the circumstances. Under generally accepted conventions in negotiation, certain types of statements ordinarily are not taken as statements of material fact. Estimates of price or value placed on the subject of a transaction and a party's intentions as to an acceptable settlement of a claim are in this category, and so is the existence of an undisclosed principal except where nondisclosure of the principal would constitute fraud.

Fraud by Client

[3] Paragraph (b) recognizes that substantive law may require a lawyer to disclose certain information to avoid being deemed to have assisted the client's crime or fraud. The requirement of disclosure created by this paragraph is, however, subject to the obligations created by Rule 1.6.

MODEL CODE COMPARISON

[1] Paragraph (a) is substantially similar to DR 7-102(A)(5), which stated that "[i]n his representation of a client, a lawyer shall not . . . [k]nowingly make a false statement of law or fact."

[2] With regard to paragraph (b), DR 7-102(A)(3) provided that a lawyer shall not "[c]onceal or knowingly fail to disclose that which he is required by law to reveal."

RULE 4.2 Communication With Person Represented by Counsel

In representing a client, a lawyer shall not communicate about the subject of the representation with a party the lawyer knows to be represented by another lawyer in the matter, unless the lawyer has the consent of the other lawyer or is authorized by law to do so.

COMMENT:

[1] This Rule does not prohibit communication with a party, or an employee or agent of a party, concerning matters outside the representation. For example, the existence of a controversy between a government agency and a private party, or between two organizations, does not prohibit a lawyer for either from communicating with nonlawyer representatives of the other regarding a separate matter. Also, parties to a matter may communicate directly with each other and a lawyer having independent justification for communicating with the other party is permitted to do so. Communications authorized by law include, for example, the right of a party to a controversy with a government agency to speak with government officials about the matter.

[2] In the case of an organization, this Rule prohibits communications by a lawyer for one party concerning the matter in representation with persons having a managerial responsibility on behalf of the organization, and with any other person whose act or omission in connection with that matter may be imputed to the organization for purposes of civil or criminal liability or whose statement may constitute an admission on the part of the organization. If an agent or employee of the organization is represented in the matter by his or her own counsel, the consent by that counsel to a communication will be sufficient for purposes of this Rule. Compare Rule 3.4(f). This Rule also covers any person, whether or not a party to a formal proceeding, who is represented by counsel concerning the matter in question.

MODEL CODE COMPARISON

This Rule is substantially identical to DR 7-104(A)(1).

RULE 4.3 Dealing With Unrepresented Person

In dealing on behalf of a client with a person who is not represented by counsel, a lawyer shall not state or imply that the lawyer is disinterested. When the lawyer knows or reasonably should know that the unrepresented person misunderstands the lawyer's role in the matter, the lawyer shall make reasonable efforts to correct the misunderstanding.

COMMENT:

An unrepresented person, particularly one not experienced in dealing with legal matters, might assume that a lawyer is disinterested in loyalties or is a disinterested authority on the law even when the lawyer represents a client. During the course of a lawyer's representation of a client, the lawyer should not give advice to an unrepresented person other than the advice to obtain counsel.

MODEL CODE COMPARISON

There is no direct counterpart to this Rule in the Model Code. DR 7-104(A)(2) provided that a lawyer shall not "[g]ive advice to a person who is not represented by a lawyer, other than the advice to secure counsel. . . ."

RULE 4.4 Respect for Rights of Third Persons

In representing a client, a lawyer shall not use means that have no substantial purpose other than to embarrass, delay, or burden a third person, or use methods of obtaining evidence that violate the legal rights of such a person.

COMMENT:

Responsibility to a client requires a lawyer to subordinate the interests of others to those of the client, but that responsibility does not imply that a lawyer may disregard the rights of third persons. It is impractical to catalogue all such rights, but they include legal restrictions on methods of obtaining evidence from third persons.

MODEL CODE COMPARISON

DR 7-106(C)(2) provided that a lawyer shall not "[a]sk any question that he has no reasonable basis to believe is relevant to the case and that is intended to degrade a witness or other person." DR 7-102(A)(1) provided that a lawyer shall not "take . . . action on behalf of his client when he knows or when it is obvious that such action would serve merely to harass or maliciously injure another." DR 7-108(D) provided that "[a]fter discharge of the jury . . . the lawyer shall not ask questions or make comments to a member of that jury that are calculated merely to harass or embarrass the juror. . . ." DR 7-108(E) provided that a lawyer "shall not conduct . . . a vexatious or harrassing investigation of either a venireman or a juror."

LAW FIRMS AND ASSOCIATIONS

RULE 5.1 Responsibilities of a Partner or Supervisory Lawyer

(a) A partner in a law firm shall make reasonable efforts to ensure that the firm has in effect measures giving reasonable assurance that all lawyers in the firm conform to the rules of professional conduct.

(b) A lawyer having direct supervisory authority over another lawyer shall make reasonable efforts to ensure that the other lawyer conforms to the rules of professional conduct.

(c) A lawyer shall be responsible for another lawyer's violation of the rules of professional conduct if:

(1) the lawyer orders or, with knowledge of the specific conduct, ratifies the conduct involved; or

Rule 5.1

(2) the lawyer is a partner in the law firm in which the other lawyer practices, or has direct supervisory authority over the other lawyer, and knows of the conduct at a time when its consequences can be avoided or mitigated but fails to take reasonable remedial action.

COMMENT:

[1] Paragraphs (a) and (b) refer to lawyers who have supervisory authority over the professional work of a firm or legal department of a government agency. This includes members of a partnership and the shareholders in a law firm organized as a professional corporation; lawyers having supervisory authority in the law department of an enterprise or government agency; and lawyers who have intermediate managerial responsibilities in a firm.

[2] The measures required to fulfill the responsibility prescribed in paragraphs (a) and (b) can depend on the firm's structure and the nature of its practice. In a small firm, informal supervision and occasional admonition ordinarily might be sufficient. In a large firm, or in practice situations in which intensely difficult ethical problems frequently arise, more elaborate procedures may be necessary. Some firms, for example, have a procedure whereby junior lawyers can make confidential referral of ethical problems directly to a designated senior partner or special committee. See Rule 5.2. Firms, whether large or small, may also rely on continuing legal education in professional ethics. In any event, the ethical atmosphere of a firm can influence the conduct of all its members and a lawyer having authority over the work of another may not assume that the subordinate lawyer will inevitably conform to the Rules.

[3] Paragraph (c)(1) expresses a general principle of responsibility for acts of another. See also Rule 8.4(a).

[4] Paragraph (c)(2) defines the duty of a lawyer having direct supervisory authority over performance of specific legal work by another lawyer. Whether a lawyer has such supervisory authority in particular circumstances is a question of fact. Partners of a private firm have at least indirect responsibility for all work being done by the firm, while a partner in charge of a particular matter ordinarily has direct authority over other firm lawyers engaged in the matter. Appropriate remedial action by a partner would depend on the immediacy of the partner's involvement and the seriousness of the misconduct. The supervisor is required to intervene to prevent avoidable consequences of misconduct if the supervisor knows that the misconduct occurred. Thus, if a supervising lawyer knows that a subordinate misrepresented a matter to an opposing party in negotiation, the supervisor as well as the subordinate has a duty to correct the resulting misapprehension.

[5] Professional misconduct by a lawyer under supervision could reveal a violation of paragraph (b) on the part of the supervisory lawyer

even though it does not entail a violation of paragraph (c) because there was no direction, ratification or knowledge of the violation.

[6] Apart from this Rule and Rule 8.4(a), a lawyer does not have disciplinary liability for the conduct of a partner, associate or subordinate. Whether a lawyer may be liable civilly or criminally for another lawyer's conduct is a question of law beyond the scope of these Rules.

MODEL CODE COMPARISON

There is no direct counterpart to this Rule in the Model Code. DR 1–103(A) provided that a lawyer "possessing unprivileged knowledge of a violation of DR 1–102 shall report such knowledge to . . . authority empowered to investigate or act upon such violation."

RULE 5.2 Responsibilities of a Subordinate Lawyer

(a) A lawyer is bound by the rules of professional conduct notwithstanding that the lawyer acted at the direction of another person.

(b) A subordinate lawyer does not violate the rules of professional conduct if that lawyer acts in accordance with a supervisory lawyer's reasonable resolution of an arguable question of professional duty.

COMMENT:

[1] Although a lawyer is not relieved of responsibility for a violation by the fact that the lawyer acted at the direction of a supervisor, that fact may be relevant in determining whether a lawyer had the knowledge required to render conduct a violation of the Rules. For example, if a subordinate filed a frivolous pleading at the direction of a supervisor, the subordinate would not be guilty of a professional violation unless the subordinate knew of the document's frivolous character.

[2] When lawyers in a supervisor-subordinate relationship encounter a matter involving professional judgment as to ethical duty, the supervisor may assume responsibility for making the judgment. Otherwise a consistent course of action or position could not be taken. If the question can reasonably be answered only one way, the duty of both lawyers is clear and they are equally responsible for fulfilling it. However, if the question is reasonably arguable, someone has to decide upon the course of action. That authority ordinarily reposes in the supervisor, and a subordinate may be guided accordingly. For example, if a question arises whether the interests of two clients conflict under Rule 1.7, the supervisor's reasonable resolution of the question should protect the subordinate professionally if the resolution is subsequently challenged.

MODEL CODE COMPARISON

There was no counterpart to this Rule in the Model Code.

RULE 5.3 Responsibilities Regarding Nonlawyer Assistants

With respect to a nonlawyer employed or retained by or associated with a lawyer:

(a) a partner in a law firm shall make reasonable efforts to ensure that the firm has in effect measures giving reasonable assurance that the person's conduct is compatible with the professional obligations of the lawyer;

(b) a lawyer having direct supervisory authority over the nonlawyer shall make reasonable efforts to ensure that the person's conduct is compatible with the professional obligations of the lawyer; and

(c) a lawyer shall be responsible for conduct of such a person that would be a violation of the rules of professional conduct if engaged in by a lawyer if:

(1) the lawyer orders or, with the knowledge of the specific conduct, ratifies the conduct involved; or

(2) the lawyer is a partner in the law firm in which the person is employed, or has direct supervisory authority over the person, and knows of the conduct at a time when its consequences can be avoided or mitigated but fails to take reasonable remedial action.

COMMENT:

Lawyers generally employ assistants in their practice, including secretaries, investigators, law student interns, and paraprofessionals. Such assistants, whether employees or independent contractors, act for the lawyer in rendition of the lawyer's professional services. A lawyer should give such assistants appropriate instruction and supervision concerning the ethical aspects of their employment, particularly regarding the obligation not to disclose information relating to representation of the client, and should be responsible for their work product. The measures employed in supervising nonlawyers should take account of the fact that they do not have legal training and are not subject to professional discipline.

MODEL CODE COMPARISON

There was no direct counterpart to this Rule in the Model Code. DR 4-101(D) provided that a lawyer "shall exercise reasonable care to prevent his employees, associates, and others whose services are utilized by him from disclosing or using confidences or secrets of a client. . . ." DR 7-107(J) provided that "[a] lawyer shall exercise reasonable care to prevent his employees and associates from making an extrajudicial statement that he would be prohibited from making under DR 7-107."

RULE 5.4 Professional Independence of a Lawyer

(a) A lawyer or law firm shall not share legal fees with a nonlawyer, except that:

(1) an agreement by a lawyer with the lawyer's firm, partner, or associate may provide for the payment of money, over a reasonable period of time after the lawyer's death, to the lawyer's estate or to one or more specified persons;

(2) a lawyer who purchases the practice of a deceased, disabled, or disappeared lawyer may, pursuant to the provisions of Rule 1.17, pay to the estate or other representative of that lawyer the agreed-upon purchase price; and

(3) a lawyer or law firm may include nonlawyer employees in a compensation or retirement plan, even though the plan is based in whole or in part on a profit-sharing arrangement.

(b) A lawyer shall not form a partnership with a nonlawyer if any of the activities of the partnership consist of the practice of law.

(c) A lawyer shall not permit a person who recommends, employs, or pays the lawyer to render legal services for another to direct or regulate the lawyer's professional judgment in rendering such legal services.

(d) A lawyer shall not practice with or in the form of a professional corporation or association authorized to practice law for a profit, if:

(1) a nonlawyer owns any interest therein, except that a fiduciary representative of the estate of a lawyer may hold the stock or interest of the lawyer for a reasonable time during administration;

(2) a nonlawyer is a corporate director or officer thereof; or

(3) a nonlawyer has the right to direct or control the professional judgment of a lawyer.

COMMENT:

The provisions of this Rule express traditional limitations on sharing fees. These limitations are to protect the lawyer's professional independence of judgment. Where someone other than the client pays the lawyer's fee or salary, or recommends employment of the lawyer, that arrangement does not modify the lawyer's obligation to the client. As stated in paragraph (c), such arrangements should not interfere with the lawyer's professional judgment.

MODEL CODE COMPARISON

[1] Paragraph (a) is substantially identical to DR 3–102(A).

[2] Paragraph (b) is substantially identical to DR 3–103(A).

[3] Paragraph (c) is substantially identical to DR 5–107(B).

[4] Paragraph (d) is substantially identical to DR 5–107(C).

RULE 5.5 Unauthorized Practice of Law

A lawyer shall not:

Rule 5.5

(a) practice law in a jurisdiction where doing so violates the regulation of the legal profession in that jurisdiction; or

(b) assist a person who is not a member of the bar in the performance of activity that constitutes the unauthorized practice of law.

COMMENT:

The definition of the practice of law is established by law and varies from one jurisdiction to another. Whatever the definition, limiting the practice of law to members of the bar protects the public against rendition of legal services by unqualified persons. Paragraph (b) does not prohibit a lawyer from employing the services of paraprofessionals and delegating functions to them, so long as the lawyer supervises the delegated work and retains responsibility for their work. See Rule 5.3. Likewise, it does not prohibit lawyers from providing professional advice and instruction to nonlawyers whose employment requires knowledge of law; for example, claims adjusters, employees of financial or commercial institutions, social workers, accountants and persons employed in government agencies. In addition, a lawyer may counsel nonlawyers who wish to proceed pro se.

MODEL CODE COMPARISON

[1] With regard to paragraph (a), DR 3-101(B) of the Model Code provided that "[a] lawyer shall not practice law in a jurisdiction where to do so would be in violation of regulations of the profession in that jurisdiction."

[2] With regard to paragraph (b), DR 3-101(A) of the Model Code provided that "[a] lawyer shall not aid a nonlawyer in the unauthorized practice of law."

RULE 5.6 Restrictions on Right to Practice

A lawyer shall not participate in offering or making:

(a) a partnership or employment agreement that restricts the rights of a lawyer to practice after termination of the relationship, except an agreement concerning benefits upon retirement; or

(b) an agreement in which a restriction on the lawyer's right to practice is part of the settlement of a controversy between private parties.

COMMENT:

[1] An agreement restricting the right of partners or associates to practice after leaving a firm not only limits their professional autonomy but also limits the freedom of clients to choose a lawyer. Paragraph (a) prohibits such agreements except for restrictions incident to provisions concerning retirement benefits for service with the firm.

[2] Paragraph (b) prohibits a lawyer from agreeing not to represent other persons in connection with settling a claim on behalf of a client.

[3] This Rule does not apply to prohibit restrictions that may be included in the terms of the sale of a law practice pursuant to Rule 1.17.

MODEL CODE COMPARISON

This Rule is substantially similar to DR 2–108.

RULE 5.7 Provision of Ancillary Services

(a) A lawyer shall not practice law in a law firm which owns a controlling interest in, or operates, an entity which provides non-legal services which are ancillary to the practice of law, or otherwise provides such ancillary non-legal services, except as provided in paragraph (b).

(b) A lawyer may practice law in a law firm which provides non-legal services which are ancillary to the practice of law if:

(1) The ancillary services are provided solely to clients of the law firm and are incidental to, in connection with and concurrent to, the provision of legal services by the law firm to such clients;

(2) Such ancillary services are provided solely by employees of the law firm itself and not by a subsidiary or other affiliate of the law firm;

(3) The law firm makes appropriate disclosure in writing to its clients; and

(4) The law firm does not hold itself out as engaging in any non-legal activities except in conjunction with the provision of legal services, as provided in this rule.

(c) One or more lawyers who engage in the practice of law in a law firm shall neither own a controlling interest in, nor operate, an entity which provides non-legal services which are ancillary to the practice of law, nor otherwise provide such ancillary non-legal services, except that their firms may provide such services as provided in paragraph (b).

(d) Two or more lawyers who engage in the practice of law in separate law firms shall neither own a controlling interest in, nor operate, an entity which provides non-legal services which are ancillary to the practice of law, nor otherwise provide such ancillary non-legal services.

COMMENT

General

[1] For many years, lawyers have provided to their clients non-legal services which are ancillary to the practice of law. Such services included title insurance, trust services and patent consulting. In most instances, these ancillary non-legal services were provided to law firm clients in connection with, and concurrent to, the provision of legal services by the lawyer or law firm. The provision of such services afforded benefits to clients, including making available a greater range of services from one source and maintaining technical expertise in various fields within a law firm. However, the provision of both legal

Rule 5.7   *ABA MODEL RULES*

and ancillary non-legal services raises ethical concerns, including conflicts of interest, confusion on the part of clients and possible loss (or inapplicability) of the attorney-client privilege, which may not have been addressed adequately by the other Model Rules of Professional Conduct.

[2] Eventually, law firms began to form affiliates, largely staffed by nonlawyers, to provide ancillary non-legal services to both clients and customers who were not clients for legal services. In addition to exacerbating the ethical problems of conflicts of interest, confusion and threats to confidentiality, the large-scale movement of law firms into ancillary non-legal businesses raised serious professionalism concerns, including compromising lawyers' independent judgment, the loss of the bar's right to self regulation and the provision of legal services by entities controlled by nonlawyers.

[3] Rule 5.7 addresses both the ethical and professionalism concerns implicated by the provision of ancillary non-legal services by lawyers and law firms. It preserves the ability of lawyers to provide additional services to their clients and maintain within the law firm a broad range of technical expertise. However, Rule 5.7 restricts the ability of law firms to provide ancillary non-legal services through affiliates to non-client customers and clients alike, the rendition of which raises serious ethical and professionalism concerns.

Limitations on the Provision of Non–Legal Services Which Are Ancillary to the Practice of Law

[4] Paragraph (a) attempts to forestall the ethical and professional concerns which are raised when law firms own or operate non-legal businesses which are ancillary to the practice of law or otherwise provide such services. The provision of such ancillary services by law firms has the potential of compromising a lawyer's independent professional judgment and otherwise causing harm to law firm clients (e.g., creating conflicts of interest, jeopardizing clients' expectations of confidentiality and causing confusion on the part of clients). Additionally, serious threats to lawyers' professionalism are also posed when law firms own or operate ancillary businesses which provide services to persons who are not concurrently seeking legal services from the law firm.

[5] Paragraph (a) prohibits lawyers from practicing in a law firm which owns a controlling interest in, or operates, an entity which provides non-legal services which are ancillary to the practice of law, or which provides such ancillary services from within the law firm, unless such services are incidental to the law firm's provision of legal services as set forth in Paragraph (b).

[6] The term "non-legal services which are ancillary to the practice of law" refers to those services which satisfy all or most of the following indicia: (1) are provided to clients of a law firm (or customers of a business owned or controlled by a law firm); (2) clearly do not constitute the practice of law; (3) are readily available from those not licensed to

practice law; (4) are functionally connected to the provision of legal services, i.e., services which are often sought or needed in connection with (and in addition to) legal services; (5) involve intellectual ability or learning; and (6) have the potential for creating serious ethical problems in the lawyer client relationship, such as compromising the independent professional judgment of lawyers; creating conflicts of interest; threatening the clients' (or customers') expectations of confidentiality and/or causing confusion on the part of clients or customers.

[7] Among those activities which are not included in the term "nonlegal services which are ancillary to the practice of law" because they do not pose serious ethical problems in the lawyer client relationship are:

(1) law firms or lawyers owning, for example, restaurants, shops or taxi services (since these services are not functionally connected to the practice of law);

(2) law firms providing copying services or other clerical services incidental to the practice of law;

(3) law firms owning and managing the buildings in which their offices are located or other property (since owning and managing property—even through a subsidiary or affiliate—is not functionally connected to the provision of legal services to clients);

(4) a law firm providing services or products intended for use by other lawyers, such as publications, software programs, or legal malpractice insurance (since such services or products are not functionally connected to the provision of legal services to clients);

(5) lawyers serving as fiduciaries of trusts or corporate directors or lawyers serving in quasi-judicial positions such as mediators or arbitrators.

[8] When services provided by a law firm are performed by nonlawyers, there should be an initial presumption that the services do not constitute the practice of law and may be a "non-legal service which is ancillary to the practice of law." In addition, a presumption that a service is "ancillary to the practice of law" should exist if the service is normally provided by nonlawyers in discrete professions or occupations, e.g., doctors, architects, engineers, real estate brokers, investment bankers or financial consultants.

[9] Note that Paragraph (a) does not prohibit a lawyer from practicing in a law firm which acquires a passive financial interest in an entity which provides non-legal ancillary services (i.e., purchasing shares of an investment banking firm or a consulting company), provided that the interest is not a controlling one. This rule does not define the concept of control, which is generally a fact based inquiry dependent on the particular facts and circumstances. However, the existence of an ownership interest by lawyers in other entities (especially clients) may implicate conflict of interest concerns (see Model Rules of Professional Conduct

Rule 5.7   *ABA MODEL RULES*

1.7 and 1.8) and may require disclosure by the lawyers pursuant to these rules.

Connection Between the Provision of Legal and Ancillary Non-Legal Services

[10] Paragraph (b) preserves the ability of law firms to provide non-legal services which are ancillary to the practice of law, but under conditions designed to ensure that such services are closely related to the firms' provision of legal services and not independent of, and unrelated to, such legal services.

[11] Subsection (1) of Paragraph (b) requires that ancillary non-legal services be provided solely to law firm clients (as opposed to persons who are not currently seeking legal services from a law firm) and be incidental to, in connection with, and concurrent to, the provision of legal services by the law firm. The requirement that ancillary services be "incidental to" and "in connection with" the firm's provision of legal services seeks to ensure that any non-legal services be secondary to, strictly related to, and under the supervision of those responsible for, the provision of legal services.

[12] Paragraph (b) permits law firms to employ the services of other professionals if their services are connected to the firm's provision of legal services. For example, an architect on staff at a law firm would be permitted to help clients and lawyers understand the technical issues in a construction contract negotiation, a building accident litigation or the like. However, the requirement in Paragraph (b) that such services be "incidental to" and "in connection with" the provision of legal services would proscribe a law firm from employing architects to design buildings for law firm clients or for non-client customers who do not use the law firm's legal services. Similarly, an investment banker on staff at a law firm would be permitted to assist lawyers in the negotiation of a transaction or the litigation of valuation issues or the like, as well as to consult with law firm clients when the firm is providing legal services to them, but a law firm would be prohibited from employing investment bankers to seek out acquisitions, sell securities (or otherwise secure financing) or perform other investment banking services unrelated to a pending legal representation. Likewise, a corporation pursuing an acquisition might need the assistance of non-lawyer lobbyists before a state legislature considering anti-takeover legislation. Such lobbying designed to forestall (or attain) a change in the law, if provided by nonlawyers within a law firm, could reasonably be construed to be incidental to the firm's provision of legal services.

[13] Paragraph (b) also requires that the provision of non-legal services be concurrent with the provision of legal services. In essence, law firm clients (like non-legal services customers generally) may not obtain ancillary non-legal services from the law firm (e.g., investment banking services or medical tests), and the firm may not provide them, at

a time when the client is not obtaining legal services from the law firm on a related matter.

Provision of Ancillary Non-Legal Services by Employees of Law Firms

[14] Subsection (2) of Paragraph (b), in an effort to vitiate risks of compromise to lawyers' professional judgment, conflicts of interest, client confusion and potential loss of confidentiality, provides that any ancillary services provided by a law firm must be performed within the law firm by employees of the law firm itself (who work together with, and are supervised by, the firm's lawyers), and not through a subsidiary or affiliate of the law firm. This requirement closely unites the provision of legal and non-legal services under the supervision of lawyers and thereby affords lawyers the opportunity to ensure that their non-lawyer employees are acting responsibly and in accordance with the rules of legal ethics. Such a requirement minimizes the risks of non-legal employees either providing advice with which the firm's lawyers will disagree and/or engaging in improper behavior for which the firm's lawyers would be responsible. In addition, structuring the provision of non-legal services in such a way forestalls confusion on the part of clients as to whether the non-legal services are provided subject to the limitations of the Model Rules (and will prevent lawyers from seeking to provide services outside of the protections afforded to clients by the Model Rules). Finally, if lawyers are present (or otherwise involved) in the provision of non-legal services ancillary to the practice of law, there is a greater likelihood that client confidences will be protected and a client will be able to maintain evidentiary privileges with respect to communications made by the client to the providers of non-legal ancillary services. Paragraph (b)(2) is not designed to limit the ability of lawyers to retain outside (i.e., non-affiliated) consultants such as experts, private investigators or accountants to help them provide legal services to clients.

Disclosure Requirements Relating to the Provision of Ancillary Non-Legal Services

[15] Subsection (3) of Paragraph (b) requires that before providing ancillary services to a client, a law firm must comply with appropriate disclosure requirements (as mandated in Model Rule of Professional Conduct 1.8, relevant case law and other authorities) and fully disclose in writing the firm's interest in the providers of non-legal services employed by the firm and the potential conflicts of interest inherent in the provision of such services. The law firm should also consider, in appropriate circumstances, recommending that the client seek the advice of independent counsel (or independent providers of non-legal services) before obtaining non-legal services from the firm.

Rule 5.7 ABA MODEL RULES

Representations Concerning Ancillary and Non–Legal Services

[16] Subsection (4) of Paragraph (b) ensures that when law firms deal with clients (whether prospective or actual) or the public, they do not represent themselves as providing any ancillary non-legal services independent of the firm's provision of legal services. This proscription attempts to obviate the risks of confusion on the part of clients and the public, actual or apparent overreaching by attorneys and improper solicitation. It ensures that clients and the public are aware that they are dealing with a law firm and can therefore assume that representatives of the firm are bound by the rules of legal ethics; prospective or actual clients do not feel compelled to use the firm's ancillary services; and law firms do not engage in improper solicitation by seeking business for the firm's non-legal services with an expectation that these non-legal services will serve as a "feeder" for the firm's legal services. Paragraph (b)(4) also seeks to preserve the unique and independent status of the legal profession in the public's perception by preventing law firms from representing themselves to clients and the public as multidisciplinary conglomerates or otherwise emphasizing their non-legal activities.

[17] Paragraph (b)(4) is not intended to preclude law firms from making the existence of their non-legal businesses known to clients who have retained the firm for legal services, and who, in the attorney's opinion, might have a need for the firm's ancillary services in addition to legal services (subject to appropriate disclosure requirements). In addition, Paragraph (b)(4) is not intended to prevent individual lawyers from indicating that they are qualified or licensed in other professions, e.g., accounting, where relevant jurisdictions so permit.

Provision of Ancillary Non–Legal Services by One or More Lawyers in a Law Firm

[18] Paragraph (c) prevents one or more lawyers in a single law firm from owning or operating an entity which provides non-legal services which are ancillary to the practice of law. Paragraph (c) attempts to prevent lawyers or law firms from circumventing the restrictions on law firm ownership and operation of ancillary businesses by vesting ownership not in the entire law firm, but in one or more of the attorneys in a law firm. The ethical and professional concerns inherent in the ownership of ancillary businesses are not vitiated when ownership or operation is vested in several partners in a law firm (as opposed to an entire law firm). However, a law firm itself may provide such ancillary non-legal services in accordance with Paragraph (b).

Provision of Ancillary Non–Legal Services by Lawyers from Different Law Firms

[19] Paragraph (d) addresses the concerns which may result when lawyers in separate law firms own or operate an entity which provides non-legal services which are ancillary to the practice of law. The ethical

and professional concerns inherent in the ownership and operation of such ancillary businesses by law firms (or one or more lawyers in a firm) are also present (or may be exacerbated) when lawyers in different firms own or operate such businesses.

MODEL CODE COMPARISON

There was no counterpart to this Rule in the Model Code.

PUBLIC SERVICE

RULE 6.1 Pro Bono Publico Service

A lawyer should render public interest legal service. A lawyer may discharge this responsibility by providing professional services at no fee or a reduced fee to persons of limited means or to public service or charitable groups or organizations, by service in activities for improving the law, the legal system or the legal profession, and by financial support for organizations that provide legal services to persons of limited means.

COMMENT:

[1] The ABA House of Delegates has formally acknowledged "the basic responsibility of each lawyer engaged in the practice of law to provide public interest legal services" without fee, or at a substantially reduced fee, in one or more of the following areas: poverty law, civil rights law, public rights law, charitable organization representation and the administration of justice. This Rule expresses that policy but is not intended to be enforced through disciplinary process.

[2] The rights and responsibilities of individuals and organizations in the United States are increasingly defined in legal terms. As a consequence, legal assistance in coping with the web of statutes, rules and regulations is imperative for persons of modest and limited means, as well as for the relatively well-to-do.

[3] The basic responsibility for providing legal services for those unable to pay ultimately rests upon the individual lawyer, and personal involvement in the problems of the disadvantaged can be one of the most rewarding experiences in the life of a lawyer. Every lawyer, regardless of professional prominence or professional workload, should find time to participate in or otherwise support the provision of legal services to the disadvantaged. The provision of free legal services to those unable to pay reasonable fees continues to be an obligation of each lawyer as well as the profession generally, but the efforts of individual lawyers are often not enough to meet the need. Thus, it has been necessary for the profession and government to institute additional programs to provide legal services. Accordingly, legal aid offices, lawyer referral services and other related programs have been developed, and others will be

Rule 6.1   ABA MODEL RULES

developed by the profession and government. Every lawyer should support all proper efforts to meet this need for legal services.

MODEL CODE COMPARISON

There was no counterpart of this Rule in the Disciplinary Rules of the Model Code. EC 2-25 stated that the "basic responsibility for providing legal services for those unable to pay ultimately rests upon the individual lawyer. . . . Every lawyer, regardless of professional prominence or professional workload, should find time to participate in serving the disadvantaged." EC 8-9 stated that "[t]he advancement of our legal system is of vital importance in maintaining the rule of law . . . and lawyers should encourage, and should aid in making, needed changes and improvements." EC 8-3 stated that "[t]hose persons unable to pay for legal services should be provided needed services."

RULE 6.2 Accepting Appointments

A lawyer shall not seek to avoid appointment by a tribunal to represent a person except for good cause, such as:

(a) representing the client is likely to result in violation of the Rules of Professional Conduct or other law;

(b) representing the client is likely to result in an unreasonable financial burden on the lawyer; or

(c) the client or the cause is so repugnant to the lawyer as to be likely to impair the client-lawyer relationship or the lawyer's ability to represent the client.

COMMENT:

[1] A lawyer ordinarily is not obliged to accept a client whose character or cause the lawyer regards as repugnant. The lawyer's freedom to select clients is, however, qualified. All lawyers have a responsibility to assist in providing pro bono publico service. See Rule 6.1. An individual lawyer fulfills this responsibility by accepting a fair share of unpopular matters or indigent or unpopular clients. A lawyer may also be subject to appointment by a court to serve unpopular clients or persons unable to afford legal services.

Appointed Counsel

[2] For good cause a lawyer may seek to decline an appointment to represent a person who cannot afford to retain counsel or whose cause is unpopular. Good cause exists if the lawyer could not handle the matter competently, see Rule 1.1, or if undertaking the representation would result in an improper conflict of interest, for example, when the client or the cause is so repugnant to the lawyer as to be likely to impair the client-lawyer relationship or the lawyer's ability to represent the client. A lawyer may also seek to decline an appointment if acceptance would be unreasonably burdensome, for example, when it would impose a financial sacrifice so great as to be unjust.

[3] An appointed lawyer has the same obligations to the client as retained counsel, including the obligations of loyalty and confidentiality, and is subject to the same limitations on the client-lawyer relationship, such as the obligation to refrain from assisting the client in violation of the Rules.

MODEL CODE COMPARISON

There is no counterpart to this Rule in the Disciplinary Rules of the Model Code. EC 2–29 stated that when a lawyer is "appointed by a court or requested by a bar association to undertake representation of a person unable to obtain counsel, whether for financial or other reasons, he should not seek to be excused from undertaking the representation except for compelling reason. Compelling reasons do not include such factors as the repugnance of the subject matter of the proceeding, the identity or position of a person involved in the case, the belief of the lawyer that the defendant in a criminal proceeding is guilty, or the belief of the lawyer regarding the merits of the civil case." EC 2–30 stated that "a lawyer should decline employment if the intensity of his personal feelings, as distinguished from a community attitude, may impair his effective representation of a prospective client."

RULE 6.3 Membership in Legal Services Organization

A lawyer may serve as a director, officer or member of a legal services organization, apart from the law firm in which the lawyer practices, notwithstanding that the organization serves persons having interests adverse to a client of the lawyer. The lawyer shall not knowingly participate in a decision or action of the organization:

(a) if participating in the decision or action would be incompatible with the lawyer's obligations to a client under Rule 1.7; or

(b) where the decision or action could have a material adverse effect on the representation of a client of the organization whose interests are adverse to a client of the lawyer.

COMMENT:

[1] Lawyers should be encouraged to support and participate in legal service organizations. A lawyer who is an officer or a member of such an organization does not thereby have a client-lawyer relationship with persons served by the organization. However, there is potential conflict between the interests of such persons and the interests of the lawyer's clients. If the possibility of such conflict disqualified a lawyer from serving on the board of a legal services organization, the profession's involvement in such organizations would be severely curtailed.

[2] It may be necessary in appropriate cases to reassure a client of the organization that the representation will not be affected by conflicting loyalties of a member of the board. Established, written policies in this respect can enhance the credibility of such assurances.

Rule 6.3   *ABA MODEL RULES*

MODEL CODE COMPARISON

There was no counterpart to this Rule in the Model Code.

RULE 6.4 Law Reform Activities Affecting Client Interests

A lawyer may serve as a director, officer or member of an organization involved in reform of the law or its administration notwithstanding that the reform may affect the interests of a client of the lawyer. When the lawyer knows that the interests of a client may be materially benefitted by a decision in which the lawyer participates, the lawyer shall disclose that fact but need not identify the client.

COMMENT:

Lawyers involved in organizations seeking law reform generally do not have a client-lawyer relationship with the organization. Otherwise, it might follow that a lawyer could not be involved in a bar association law reform program that might indirectly affect a client. See also Rule 1.2(b). For example, a lawyer specializing in antitrust litigation might be regarded as disqualified from participating in drafting revisions of rules governing that subject. In determining the nature and scope of participation in such activities, a lawyer should be mindful of obligations to clients under other Rules, particularly Rule 1.7. A lawyer is professionally obligated to protect the integrity of the program by making an appropriate disclosure within the organization when the lawyer knows a private client might be materially benefitted.

MODEL CODE COMPARISON

There was no countepart to this Rule in the Model Code.

INFORMATION ABOUT LEGAL SERVICES

RULE 7.1 Communications Concerning a Lawyer's Services

A lawyer shall not make a false or misleading communication about the lawyer or the lawyer's services. A communication is false or misleading if it:

(a) contains a material misrepresentation of fact or law, or omits a fact necessary to make the statement considered as a whole not materially misleading;

(b) is likely to create an unjustified expectation about results the lawyer can achieve, or states or implies that the lawyer can achieve results by means that violate the rules of professional conduct or other law; or

(c) compares the lawyer's services with other lawyers' services, unless the comparison can be factually substantiated.

COMMENT:

This Rule governs all communications about a lawyer's services, including advertising permitted by Rule 7.2. Whatever means are used to make known a lawyer's services, statements about them should be truthful. The prohibition in paragraph (b) of statements that may create "unjustified expectations" would ordinarily preclude advertisements about results obtained on behalf of a client, such as the amount of a damage award or the lawyer's record in obtaining favorable verdicts, and advertisements containing client endorsements. Such information may create the unjustified expectation that similar results can be obtained for others without reference to the specific factual and legal circumstances.

MODEL CODE COMPARISON

DR 2-101 provided that "[a] lawyer shall not . . . use . . . any form of public communication containing a false, fraudulent, misleading, deceptive, self-laudatory or unfair statement or claim." DR 2-101(B) provided that a lawyer "may publish or broadcast . . . the following information . . . in the geographic area or areas in which the lawyer resides or maintains offices or in which a significant part of the lawyer's clientele resides, provided that the information . . . complies with DR 2-101(A), and is presented in a dignified manner. . . ." DR 2-101(B) then specified 25 categories of information that may be disseminated. DR 2-101(C) provided that "[a]ny person desiring to expand the information authorized for disclosure in DR 2-101(B), or to provide for its dissemination through other forums may apply to [the agency having jurisdiction under state law]. . . . The relief granted in response to any such application shall be promulgated as an amendment to DR 2-101(B), universally applicable to all lawyers."

RULE 7.2 Advertising

(a) Subject to the requirements of Rules 7.1 and 7.3, a lawyer may advertise services through public media, such as a telephone directory, legal directory, newspaper or other periodical, outdoor advertising, radio or television, or through written or recorded communication.

(b) A copy or recording of an advertisement or communication shall be kept for two years after its last dissemination along with a record of when and where it was used.

(c) A lawyer shall not give anything of value to a person for recommending the lawyer's services except that a lawyer may

 (1) pay the reasonable costs of advertisements or communications permitted by this Rule;

 (2) pay the usual charges of a not-for-profit lawyer referral service or legal service organization; and

 (3) pay for a law practice in accordance with Rule 1.17.

(d) Any communication made pursuant to this rule shall include the name of at least one lawyer responsible for its content.

Rule 7.2

COMMENT:

[1] To assist the public in obtaining legal services, lawyers should be allowed to make known their services not only through reputation but also through organized information campaigns in the form of advertising. Advertising involves an active quest for clients, contrary to the tradition that a lawyer should not seek clientele. However, the public's need to know about legal services can be fulfilled in part through advertising. This need is particularly acute in the case of persons of moderate means who have not made extensive use of legal services. The interest in expanding public information about legal services ought to prevail over considerations of tradition. Nevertheless, advertising by lawyers entails the risk of practices that are misleading or overreaching.

[2] This Rule permits public dissemination of information concerning a lawyer's name or firm name, address and telephone number; the kinds of services the lawyer will undertake; the basis on which the lawyer's fees are determined, including prices for specific services and payment and credit arrangements; a lawyer's foreign language ability; names of references and, with their consent, names of clients regularly represented; and other information that might invite the attention of those seeking legal assistance.

[3] Questions of effectiveness and taste in advertising are matters of speculation and subjective judgment. Some jurisdictions have had extensive prohibitions against television advertising, against advertising going beyond specified facts about a lawyer, or against "undignified" advertising. Television is now one of the most powerful media for getting information to the public, particularly persons of low and moderate income; prohibiting television advertising, therefore, would impede the flow of information about legal services to many sectors of the public. Limiting the information that may be advertised has a similar effect and assumes that the bar can accurately forecast the kind of information that the public would regard as relevant.

[4] Neither this Rule nor Rule 7.3 prohibits communications authorized by law, such as notice to members of a class in class action litigation.

Record of Advertising

[5] Paragraph (b) requires that a record of the content and use of advertising be kept in order to facilitate enforcement of this Rule. It does not require that advertising be subject to review prior to dissemination. Such a requirement would be burdensome and expensive relative to its possible benefits, and may be of doubtful constitutionality.

Paying Others to Recommend a Lawyer

[6] A lawyer is allowed to pay for advertising permitted by this Rule and for the purchase of a law practice in accordance with the provisions of Rule 1.17, but otherwise is not permitted to pay another person for

channeling professional work. This restriction does not prevent an organization or person other than the lawyer from advertising or recommending the lawyer's services. Thus, a legal aid agency or prepaid legal services plan may pay to advertise legal services provided under its auspices. Likewise, a lawyer may participate in not-for-profit lawyer referral programs and pay the usual fees charged by such programs. Paragraph (c) does not prohibit paying regular compensation to an assistant, such as a secretary, to prepare communications permitted by this Rule.

MODEL CODE COMPARISON

[1] With regard to paragraph (a), DR 2–101(B) provided that a lawyer "may publish or broadcast, subject to DR 2–103, . . . in print media . . . or television or radio. . . ."

[2] With regard to paragraph (b), DR 2–101(D) provided that if the advertisement is "communicated to the public over television or radio, . . . a recording of the actual transmission shall be retained by the lawyer."

[3] With regard to paragraph (c), DR 2–103(B) provided that a lawyer "shall not compensate or give anything of value to a person or organization to recommend or secure his employment . . . except that he may pay the usual and reasonable fees or dues charged by any of the organizations listed in DR 2–103(D)." (DR 2–103(D) referred to legal aid and other legal services organizations.) DR 2–101(I) provided that a lawyer "shall not compensate or give anything of value to representatives of the press, radio, television, or other communication medium in anticipation of or in return for professional publicity in a news item."

[4] There was no counterpart to paragraph (d) in the Model Code.

RULE 7.3 Direct Contact With Prospective Clients

(a) A lawyer shall not by in-person or live telephone contact solicit professional employment from a prospective client with whom the lawyer has no family or prior professional relationship when a significant motive for the lawyer's doing so is the lawyer's pecuniary gain.

(b) A lawyer shall not solicit professional employment from a prospective client by written or recorded communication or by in-person or telephone contact even when not otherwise prohibited by paragraph (a), if:

(1) the prospective client has made known to the lawyer a desire not to be solicited by the lawyer; or

(2) the solicitation involves coercion, duress or harassment.

(c) Every written or recorded communication from a lawyer soliciting professional employment from a prospective client known to be in need of legal services in a particular matter, and with whom the lawyer has no family or prior professional relationship, shall include the words "Advertising Material" on the outside envelope and at the beginning and ending of any recorded communication.

(d) Notwithstanding the prohibitions in paragraph (a), a lawyer may participate with a prepaid or group legal service plan operated by an organization not owned or directed by the lawyer which uses in-person or telephone contact to solicit memberships or subscriptions for the plan from persons who are not known to need legal services in a particular matter covered by the plan.

COMMENT:

[1] There is a potential for abuse inherent in direct in-person or live telephone contact by a lawyer with a prospective client known to need legal services. These forms of contact between a lawyer and a prospective client subject the layperson to the private importuning of the trained advocate in a direct interpersonal encounter. The prospective client, who may already feel overwhelmed by the circumstances giving rise to the need for legal services, may find it difficult fully to evaluate all available alternatives with reasoned judgment and appropriate self-interest in the face of the lawyer's presence and insistence upon being retained immediately. The situation is fraught with the possibility of undue influence, intimidation, and over-reaching.

[2] This potential for abuse inherent in direct in-person or live telephone solicitation of prospective clients justifies its prohibition, particularly since lawyer advertising and written and recorded communication permitted under Rule 7.2 offer alternative means of conveying necessary information to those who may be in need of legal services. Advertising and written and recorded communications which may be mailed or autodialed make it possible for a prospective client to be informed about the need for legal services, and about the qualifications of available lawyers and law firms, without subjecting the prospective client to direct in-person or telephone persuasion that may overwhelm the client's judgment.

[3] The use of general advertising and written and recorded communications to transmit information from lawyer to prospective client, rather than direct in-person or live telephone contact, will help to assure that the information flows cleanly as well as freely. The contents of advertisements and communications permitted under Rule 7.2 are permanently recorded so that they cannot be disputed and may be shared with others who know the lawyer. This potential for informal review is itself likely to help guard against statements and claims that might constitute false and misleading communications, in violation of Rule 7.1. The contents of direct in-person or live telephone conversations between a lawyer to a prospective client can be disputed and are not subject to third-party scrutiny. Consequently, they are much more likely to approach (and occasionally cross) the dividing line between accurate representations and those that are false and misleading.

[4] There is far less likelihood that a lawyer would engage in abusive practices against an individual with whom the lawyer has a prior

personal or professional relationship or where the lawyer is motivated by considerations other than the lawyer's pecuniary gain. Consequently, the general prohibition in Rule 7.3(a) and the requirements of Rule 7.3(c) are not applicable in those situations.

[5] But even permitted forms of solicitation can be abused. Thus, any solicitation which contains information which is false or misleading within the meaning of Rule 7.1, which involves coercion, duress or harassment within the meaning of Rule 7.3(b)(2), or which involves contact with a prospective client who has made known to the lawyer a desire not to be solicited by the lawyer within the meaning of Rule 7.3(b)(1) is prohibited. Moreover, if after sending a letter or other communication to a client as permitted by Rule 7.2 the lawyer receives no response, any further effort to communicate with the prospective client may violate the provisions of Rule 7.3(b).

[6] This Rule is not intended to prohibit a lawyer from contacting representatives of organizations or groups that may be interested in establishing a group or prepaid legal plan for their members, insureds, beneficiaries or other third parties for the purpose of informing such entities of the availability of and details concerning the plan or arrangement which the lawyer or lawyer's firm is wiling to offer. This form of communication is not directed to a prospective client. Rather, it is usually addressed to an individual acting in a fiduciary capacity seeking a supplier of legal services for others who may, if they choose, become prospective clients of the lawyer. Under these circumstances, the activity which the lawyer undertakes in communicating with such representatives and the type of information transmitted to the individual are functionally similar to and serve the same purpose as advertising permitted under Rule 7.2.

[7] The requirement in Rule 7.3(c) that certain communications be marked "Advertising Material" does not apply to communications sent in response to requests of potential clients or their spokespersons or sponsors. General announcements by lawyers, including changes in personnel or office location, do not constitute communications soliciting professional employment from a client known to be in need of legal services within the meaning of this Rule.

[8] Paragraph (d) of this Rule would permit an attorney to participate with an organization which uses personal contact to solicit members for its group or prepaid legal service plan, provided that the personal contact is not undertaken by any lawyer who would be a provider of legal services through the plan. The organization referred to in paragraph (d) must not be owned by or directed (whether as manager or otherwise) by any lawyer or law firm that participates in the plan. For example, paragraph (d) would not permit a lawyer to create an organization controlled directly or indirectly by the lawyer and use the organization for the in-person or telephone solicitation of legal employment of the lawyer through memberships in the plan or otherwise. The communica-

tion permitted by these organizations also must not be directed to a person known to need legal services in a particular matter, but is to be designed to inform potential plan members generally of another means of affordable legal services. Lawyers who participate in a legal service plan must reasonably assure that the plan sponsors are in compliance with Rules 7.1, 7.2 and 7.3(b). See 8.4(a).

MODEL CODE COMPARISON

DR 2–104(A) provided with certain exceptions that "[a] lawyer who has given in-person unsolicited advice to a layperson that he should obtain counsel or take legal action shall not accept employment resulting from that advice. . . ." The exceptions include DR 2–104(A)(1), which provided that a lawyer "may accept employment by a close friend, relative, former client (if the advice is germane to the former employment), or one whom the lawyer reasonably believes to be a client." DR 2–104(A)(2) through DR 2–104(A)(5) provided other exceptions relating, respectively, to employment resulting from public educational programs, recommendation by a legal assistance organization, public speaking or writing and representing members of a class in class action litigation.

RULE 7.4 Communication of Fields of Practice

A lawyer may communicate the fact that the lawyer does or does not practice in particular fields of law. A lawyer shall not state or imply that the lawyer is a specialist except as follows:

(a) a lawyer admitted to engage in patent practice before the United States Patent and Trademark Office may use the designation "patent attorney" or a substantially similar designation;

(b) a lawyer engaged in admiralty practice may use the designation "admiralty," "proctor in admiralty" or a substantially similar designation; and

(c) (provisions on designation of specialization of the particular state).

COMMENT:

[1] This Rule permits a lawyer to indicate areas of practice in communications about the lawyer's services, for example, in a telephone directory or other advertising. If a lawyer practices only in certain fields, or will not accept matters except in such fields, the lawyer is permitted so to indicate. However, a lawyer is not permitted to state that the lawyer is a "specialist," practices a "specialty," or "specializes in" particular fields. These terms have acquired a secondary meaning implying formal recognition as a specialist and therefore, use of these terms is misleading. [An exception would apply in those states which provide procedures for certification or recognition of specialization and the lawyer has complied with such procedures.]

[2] Recognition of specialization in patent matters is a matter of long-established policy of the Patent and Trademark Office. Designation

of admiralty practice has a long historical tradition associated with maritime commerce and the federal courts.

MODEL CODE COMPARISON

[1] DR 2–105(A) provided that a lawyer "shall not hold himself out publicly as a specialist, as practicing in certain areas of law or as limiting his practice . . . except as follows:

"(1) A lawyer admitted to practice before the United States Patent and Trademark Office may use the designation 'Patents,' 'Patent Attorney,' 'Patent Lawyer,' or 'Registered Patent Attorney' or any combination of those terms, on his letterhead and office sign.

"(2) A lawyer who publicly discloses fields of law in which the lawyer . . . practices or states his practice is limited to one or more fields of law shall do so by using designations and definitions authorized and approved by the [agency having jurisdiction of the subject under state law].

"(3) A lawyer who is certified as a specialist in a particular field of law or law practice by [the authority having jurisdiction under state law over the subject of specialization by lawyers] may hold himself out as such, but only in accordance with the rules prescribed by that authority."

[2] EC 2–14 stated that "In the absence of state controls to insure the existence of special competence, a lawyer should not be permitted to hold himself out as a specialist, . . . other than in the fields of admiralty, trademark, and patent law where a holding out as a specialist historically has been permitted."

RULE 7.5 Firm Names and Letterheads

(a) A lawyer shall not use a firm name, letterhead or other professional designation that violates rule 7.1. A trade name may be used by a lawyer in private practice if it does not imply a connection with a government agency or with a public or charitable legal services organization and is not otherwise in violation of rule 7.1.

(b) A law firm with offices in more than one jurisdiction may use the same name in each jurisdiction, but identification of the lawyers in an office of the firm shall indicate the jurisdictional limitations on those not licensed to practice in the jurisdiction where the office is located.

(c) The name of a lawyer holding a public office shall not be used in the name of a law firm, or in communications on its behalf, during any substantial period in which the lawyer is not actively and regularly practicing with the firm.

(d) Lawyers may state or imply that they practice in a partnership or other organization only when that is the fact.

COMMENT:

[1] A firm may be designated by the names of all or some of its members, by the names of deceased members where there has been a continuing succession in the firm's identity or by a trade name such as the "ABC Legal Clinic." Although the United States Supreme Court has

Rule 7.5   *ABA MODEL RULES*

held that legislation may prohibit the use of trade names in professional practice, use of such names in law practice is acceptable so long as it is not misleading. If a private firm uses a trade name that includes a geographical name such as "Springfield Legal Clinic," an express disclaimer that it is a public legal aid agency may be required to avoid a misleading implication. It may be observed that any firm name including the name of a deceased partner is, strictly speaking, a trade name. The use of such names to designate law firms has proven a useful means of identification. However, it is misleading to use the name of a lawyer not associated with the firm or a predecessor of the firm.

[2] With regard to paragraph (d), lawyers sharing office facilities, but who are not in fact partners, may not denominate themselves as, for example, "Smith and Jones," for that title suggests partnership in the practice of law.

MODEL CODE COMPARISON

[1] With regard to paragraph (a), DR 2-102(A) provided that "[a] lawyer . . . shall not use . . . professional cards . . . letterheads, or similar professional notices, or devices, [except] . . . if they are in dignified form . . . ." DR 2-102(B) provided that "[a] lawyer in private practice shall not practice under a trade name, a name that is misleading as to the identity of the lawyer or lawyers practicing under such name, or a firm name containing names other than those of one or more of the lawyers in the firm, except that . . . a firm may use as . . . its name[,] the name or names of one or more deceased or retired members of the firm or of a predecessor firm in a continuing line of succession."

[2] With regard to paragraph (b), DR 2-102(D) provided that a partnership "shall not be formed or continued between or among lawyers licensed in different jurisdictions unless all enumerations of the members and associates of the firm on its letterhead and in other permissible listings make clear the jurisdictional limitations on those members and associates of the firm not licensed to practice in all listed jurisdictions; however, the same firm name may be used in each jurisdiction."

[3] With regard to paragraph (c), DR 2-102(B) provided that "[a] lawyer who assumes a judicial, legislative, or public executive or administrative post or office shall not permit his name to remain in the name of a law firm . . . during any significant period in which he is not actively and regularly practicing law as a member of the firm. . . ."

[4] Paragraph (d) is substantially identical to DR 2-102(C).

MAINTAINING THE INTEGRITY OF THE PROFESSION

RULE 8.1 Bar Admission and Disciplinary Matters

An applicant for admission to the bar, or a lawyer in connection with a bar admission application or in connection with a disciplinary matter, shall not:

    (a) knowingly make a false statement of material fact; or

(b) fail to disclose a fact necessary to correct a misapprehension known by the person to have arisen in the matter, or knowingly fail to respond to a lawful demand for information from an admission or disciplinary authority, except that this rule does not require disclosure of information otherwise protected by Rule 1.6.

COMMENT:

[1] The duty imposed by this Rule extends to persons seeking admission to the bar as well as to lawyers. Hence, if a person makes a material false statement in connection with an application for admission, it may be the basis for subsequent disciplinary action if the person is admitted, and in any event may be relevant in a subsequent admission application. The duty imposed by this Rule applies to a lawyer's own admission or discipline as well as that of others. Thus, it is a separate professional offense for a lawyer to knowingly make a misrepresentation or omission in connection with a disciplinary investigation of the lawyer's own conduct. This Rule also requires affirmative clarification of any misunderstanding on the part of the admissions or disciplinary authority of which the person involved becomes aware.

[2] This Rule is subject to the provisions of the Fifth Amendment of the United States Constitution and corresponding provisions of state constitutions. A person relying on such a provision in response to a question, however, should do so openly and not use the right of nondisclosure as a justification for failure to comply with this Rule.

[3] A lawyer representing an applicant for admission to the bar, or representing a lawyer who is the subject of a disciplinary inquiry or proceeding, is governed by the rules applicable to the client-lawyer relationship.

MODEL CODE COMPARISON

DR 1–101(A) provided that a lawyer "is subject to discipline if he has made a materially false statement in, or if he has deliberately failed to disclose a material fact requested in connection with, his application for admission to the bar." DR 1–101(B) provided that a lawyer "shall not further the application for admission to the bar of another person known by him to be unqualified in respect to character, education, or other relevant attribute." With respect to paragraph (b), DR 1–102(A)(5) provided that a lawyer shall not engage in "conduct that is prejudicial to the administration of justice."

RULE 8.2 Judicial and Legal Officials

(a) A lawyer shall not make a statement that the lawyer knows to be false or with reckless disregard as to its truth or falsity concerning the qualifications or integrity of a judge, adjudicatory officer or public legal officer, or of a candidate for election or appointment to judicial or legal office.

(b) A lawyer who is a candidate for judicial office shall comply with the applicable provisions of the code of judicial conduct.

Rule 8.2

COMMENT:

[1] Assessments by lawyers are relied on in evaluating the professional or personal fitness of persons being considered for election or appointment to judicial office and to public legal offices, such as attorney general, prosecuting attorney and public defender. Expressing honest and candid opinions on such matters contributes to improving the administration of justice. Conversely, false statements by a lawyer can unfairly undermine public confidence in the administration of justice.

[2] When a lawyer seeks judicial office, the lawyer should be bound by applicable limitations on political activity.

[3] To maintain the fair and independent administration of justice, lawyers are encouraged to continue traditional efforts to defend judges and courts unjustly criticized.

MODEL CODE COMPARISON

[1] With regard to paragraph (a), DR 8–102(A) provided that a lawyer "shall not knowingly make false statements of fact concerning the qualifications of a candidate for election or appointment to a judicial office." DR 8–102(B) provided that a lawyer "shall not knowingly make false accusations against a judge or other adjudicatory officer."

[2] Paragraph (b) is substantially identical to DR 8–103.

RULE 8.3 Reporting Professional Misconduct

(a) A lawyer having knowledge that another lawyer has committed a violation of the rules of professional conduct that raises a substantial question as to that lawyer's honesty, trustworthiness or fitness as a lawyer in other respects, shall inform the appropriate professional authority.

(b) A lawyer having knowledge that a judge has committed a violation of applicable rules of judicial conduct that raises a substantial question as to the judge's fitness for office shall inform the appropriate authority.

(c) This rule does not require disclosure of information otherwise protected by Rule 1.6 or information gained by a lawyer or judge while serving as a member of an approved lawyers assistance program to the extent that such information would be confidential if it were communicated subject to the attorney-client privilege.

COMMENT:

[1] Self-regulation of the legal profession requires that members of the profession initiate disciplinary investigation when they know of a violation of the Rules of Professional Conduct. Lawyers have a similar obligation with respect to judicial misconduct. An apparently isolated violation may indicate a pattern of misconduct that only a disciplinary investigation can uncover. Reporting a violation is especially important where the victim is unlikely to discover the offense.

[2] A report about misconduct is not required where it would involve violation of Rule 1.6. However, a lawyer should encourage a client to consent to disclosure where prosecution would not substantially prejudice the client's interests.

[3] If a lawyer were obliged to report every violation of the Rules, the failure to report any violation would itself be a professional offense. Such a requirement existed in many jurisdictions but proved to be unenforceable. This Rule limits the reporting obligation to those offenses that a self-regulating profession must vigorously endeavor to prevent. A measure of judgment is, therefore, required in complying with the provisions of this Rule. The term "substantial" refers to the seriousness of the possible offense and not the quantum of evidence of which the lawyer is aware. A report should be made to the bar disciplinary agency unless some other agency, such as a peer review agency, is more appropriate in the circumstances. Similar considerations apply to the reporting of judicial misconduct.

[4] The duty to report professional misconduct does not apply to a lawyer retained to represent a lawyer whose professional conduct is in question. Such a situation is governed by the rules applicable to the client-lawyer relationship.

[5] Information about a lawyer's or judge's misconduct or fitness may be received by a lawyer in the course of that lawyer's participation in an approved lawyers' or judges' assistance program. In that circumstance, providing for the confidentiality of such information encourages lawyers and judges to seek treatment through such program. Conversely, without such confidentiality, lawyers and judges may hesitate to seek assistance from these programs, which may then result in additional harm to their professional careers and additional injury to the welfare of clients and the public. The Rule therefore exempts the lawyer from the reporting requirements of paragraphs (a) and (b) with respect to information that would be privileged if the relationship between the impaired lawyer or judge and the recipient of the information were that of a client and a lawyer. On the other hand, a lawyer who receives such information would nevertheless be required to comply with the Rule 8.3 reporting provisions to report misconduct if the impaired lawyer or judge indicates an intent to engage in illegal activity, for example, the conversion of client funds to his or her use.

MODEL CODE COMPARISON

DR 1-103(A) provided that "[a] lawyer possessing unprivileged knowledge of a violation of [a Disciplinary Rule] shall report such knowledge to . . . authority empowered to investigate or act upon such violation."

RULE 8.4 Misconduct

It is professional misconduct for a lawyer to:

Rule 8.4   *ABA MODEL RULES*

(a) violate or attempt to violate the rules of professional conduct, knowingly assist or induce another to do so, or do so through the acts of another;

(b) commit a criminal act that reflects adversely on the lawyer's honesty, trustworthiness or fitness as a lawyer in other respects;

(c) engage in conduct involving dishonesty, fraud, deceit or misrepresentation;

(d) engage in conduct that is prejudicial to the administration of justice;

(e) state or imply an ability to influence improperly a government agency or official; or

(f) knowingly assist a judge or judicial officer in conduct that is a violation of applicable rules of judicial conduct or other law.

COMMENT:

[1] Many kinds of illegal conduct reflect adversely on fitness to practice law, such as offenses involving fraud and the offense of willful failure to file an income tax return. However, some kinds of offense carry no such implication. Traditionally, the distinction was drawn in terms of offenses involving "moral turpitude." That concept can be construed to include offenses concerning some matters of personal morality, such as adultery and comparable offenses, that have no specific connection to fitness for the practice of law. Although a lawyer is personally answerable to the entire criminal law, a lawyer should be professionally answerable only for offenses that indicate lack of those characteristics relevant to law practice. Offenses involving violence, dishonesty or breach of trust, or serious interference with the administration of justice are in that category. A pattern of repeated offenses, even ones of minor significance when considered separately, can indicate indifference to legal obligation.

[2] A lawyer may refuse to comply with an obligation imposed by law upon a good faith belief that no valid obligation exists. The provisions of Rule 1.2(d) concerning a good faith challenge to the validity, scope, meaning or application of the law apply to challenges of legal regulation of the practice of law.

[3] Lawyers holding public office assume legal responsibilities going beyond those of other citizens. A lawyer's abuse of public office can suggest an inability to fulfill the professional role of attorney. The same is true of abuse of positions of private trust such as trustee, executor, administrator, guardian, agent and officer, director or manager of a corporation or other organization.

MODEL CODE COMPARISON

[1] With regard to paragraphs (a) through (d), DR 1–102(A) provided that a lawyer shall not:

"(1) Violate a Disciplinary Rule.

"(2) Circumvent a Disciplinary Rule through actions of another.

"(3) Engage in illegal conduct involving moral turpitude.

"(4) Engage in conduct involving dishonesty, fraud, deceit, or misrepresentation.

"(5) Engage in conduct that is prejudicial to the administration of justice.

"(6) Engage in any other conduct that adversely reflects on his fitness to practice law."

[2] Paragraph (e) is substantially similar to DR 9-101(C).

[3] There is no direct counterpart to paragraph (f) in the Disciplinary Rules of the Model Code. EC 7-34 stated in part that "[a] lawyer . . . is never justified in making a gift or a loan to a [judicial officer] except as permitted by . . . the Code of Judicial Conduct." EC 9-1 stated that a lawyer "should promote public confidence in our [legal] system and in the legal profession."

RULE 8.5 Jurisdiction

A lawyer admitted to practice in this jurisdiction is subject to the disciplinary authority of this jurisdiction although engaged in practice elsewhere.

COMMENT:

[1] In modern practice lawyers frequently act outside the territorial limits of the jurisdiction in which they are licensed to practice, either in another state or outside the United States. In doing so, they remain subject to the governing authority of the jurisdiction in which they are licensed to practice. If their activity in another jurisdiction is substantial and continuous, it may constitute practice of law in that jurisdiction. See Rule 5.5.

[2] If the rules of professional conduct in the two jurisdictions differ, principles of conflict of laws may apply. Similar problems can arise when a lawyer is licensed to practice in more than one jurisdiction. Where the lawyer is licensed to practice law in two jurisdictions which impose conflicting obligations, applicable rules of choice of law may govern the situation. A related problem arises with respect to practice before a federal tribunal, where the general authority of the states to regulate the practice of law must be reconciled with such authority as federal tribunals may have to regulate practice before them.

MODEL CODE COMPARISON

There was no counterpart to this Rule in the Model Code.

INDEX

A

Acquiring interest in litigation, Rule 1.8(j)
    Contingent fee, Rule 1.8(j)(2)
Administration of justice,
    Lawyer's duty to seek, Preamble
Administrative agencies and tribunals,
    Appearance before, Rule 3.9 (Comment)
Admiralty practice,
    Advertising, Rule 7.4(b)
Admission to practice, Rule 8.1
Advance fee payments,
    Propriety of, Rule 1.5 (Comment)
Adversary system,
    Duty of lawyer to, Preamble
Adverse legal authority,
    Lawyer's duty to disclose, Rule 3.3(a)(3)
Advertising, *see also* Firm name, Letterheads, Solicitation, Specialization
    By mail, Rule 7.3
    Class action members, to notify, Rule 7.2 (Comment)
    Communications concerning a lawyer's services, generally Rule 7.1
    Comparisons with services of other lawyers, Rule 7.1(c)
    Endorsements by clients, Rule 7.1 (Comment)
    Fields of practice, Rule 7.4
    Material, advertising, Rule 7.3(c)
    Paying others to recommend a lawyer, Rule 7.2 (Comment)
    Permitted forms, Rule 7.2
    Prior results, Rule 7.1 (Comment)
    Record of, Rule 7.2 (Comment)
    Specialization, Rule 7.5
Advice to client,
    Candor, duty of, Rule 2.1
    Used to engage in criminal or fraudulent conduct, Rule 1.2 (Comment)
    When lawyer not competent in area, Rule 1.1
Advisor,
    Lawyer as, Preamble
Advocate,
    In nonadjudicative proceedings, Rule 3.9
    Lawyer as, Preamble
Ancillary services, law firm providing, Rule 5.7
Appeal,
    Advising client of possibility, Rule 1.3 (Comment)
Appearance of impropriety, Rule 1.10 (Comment)
Appointed counsel,
    Accepting appointments, Rule 6.2

Appointed counsel—Cont'd
    Endorsement of client's views, Rule 1.2(b)
    Requirement of competence, Rule 1.1
    Withdrawal by, Rule 1.16 (Comment)
Arbitrator,
    Former arbitrator negotiating for private employment, Rule 1.12(b)
Attorney-client privilege,
    Distinguished from confidentiality rule, Rule 1.6 (Comment)
    Intermediation, effect on, Rule 2.2(a)(1)
Attorney General,
    Authority of, Scope
Authority of lawyer,
    Decisionmaking authority, Rule 1.2(a)
    Government lawyer, Scope
Autonomy of legal profession, Preamble

B

Belief,
    Defined, Terminology
Believes,
    Defined, Terminology
Business affairs of lawyer,
    Duty to conduct in compliance with law, Preamble

C

Candor toward the tribunal,
    Requirements of, Rule 3.3
Cause of action,
    Violation of Rules as basis for, Scope
Civil disobedience,
    To test validity of statute, Rule 1.2 (Comment)
Civil liability,
    Violation of Rules as basis for, Scope
Class actions,
    Notice to members, Rule 7.2 (Comment)
Client-lawyer relationship,
    Existence of, defined by substantive law, Scope
Client's security fund,
    Participation in, Rule 1.15 (Comment)
Comments,
    Do not expand lawyer's responsibilities, Scope
Communication,
    Duty to maintain with client, Preamble, Rule 1.4 (Comment)
    With represented party, Rule 4.2
    With third persons, Rule 4.1
    With unrepresented persons, Rule 4.3

INDEX

Communication—Cont'd
　Withholding information from client, Rule 1.4 (Comment)
Competence,
　Duty of, Preamble
Competent representation,
　Requirements of, Rule 1.1
Confidences of client,
　Corporate client, Rule 1.13 (Comment)
　Disclosure of, generally, Preamble, Rule 1.6(b)
　Disclosure to disciplinary authorities, Rule 8.1
　Disclosure when charged with wrongdoing, Rule 1.6(b)(2)
　Duty to preserve, Preamble, Rule 1.6(a)
　Evaluation, information used in preparing, Rule 2.3(b)
　Imputed to members of firm, Rule 1.10 (Comment)
　Maintenance of, serves public interest, Preamble, Rule 1.6 (Comment)
　Perjury by client, Rule 3.3(b)
Conflict of interest,
　Acquiring interest in litigation, Rule 1.8(j)(2)
　Advocate, when acting as, Rule 1.7 (Comment)
　Ancillary services, Rule 5.7
　Business interests of lawyer, Rule 1.7 (Comment)
　Business transaction with client, Rule 1.8(a)
　Consent of client to, Rule 1.7 (Comment); Rule 1.7(b)(2); Rule 1.7(c)(2)
　Co-parties, representation of, Rule 1.7 (Comment)
　Declining employment because of, Rule 1.7 (Comment)
　Estate planning or administration, Rule 1.7 (Comment)
　Existing client, interest adverse to client, Rule 1.7(a)
　Fee paid by one other than client, Rule 1.7 (Comment)
　Former client, Rule 1.9
　General rule, Rule 1.7
　Interest of lawyer adverse to client, Rule 1.7(b)
　Issue conflicts, Rule 1.7 (Comment 9)
　Legal services corporation, lawyer serves as director of, Rule 6.3
　"Matter" defined, Rule 1.9 (Comment)
　Multiple representation, Rule 1.7(b)(2)
　Negotiation, Rule 1.7 (Comment)
　Opposing party raises, Rule 1.7 (Comment)
　Positional conflicts, Rule 1.7 (Comment 9)
　Third person, interest adverse to client, Rule 1.7(b)
　Unrelated matters, Rule 1.7 (Comment)
　Withdrawal because of, Rule 1.7 (Comment)

Constitutional law,
　Governing authority of government lawyer, Scope
Consult,
　Defined, Terminology
Consultation,
　Defined, Terminology
Contingent fee,
　Expert witness, Rule 3.4 (Comment)
　Prohibited representations, Rule 1.5(d)
　Requirements of, Rule 1.5(c)
Continuing legal education,
　Competence, to maintain, Rule 1.1 (Comment)
Corporate representation, *See* Organization, representation of
Corporation,
　Communicating with employees and officers of, Rule 4.2 (Comment)
Court,
　Authority over legal profession, Preamble
　Candor, duty of, Rule 3.3
　Offering false evidence to, Rule 3.3(a)(4)
Creditors of client,
　Claim funds of client, Rule 1.15 (Comment)
Criminal conduct,
　Counseling or assisting a client to engage in, Rule 1.2(d); Rule 3.3(a)(2)
　Disclosure of client's, Rule 1.2 (Comment)
Criminal representation,
　Aggregate plea bargain on behalf of multiple defendants, Rule 1.8(g)
　Co-defendants, representation of, Rule 1.7 (Comment)
　Contingent fee for, Rule 1.5(d)(2)
　Decisionmaking authority, Rule 1.2(a)
　Frivolous defense, Rule 3.1
　Perjury by client, Rule 3.3 (Comment)

D

Derivative actions, Rule 1.13 (Comment)
Dilatory practices,
　Prohibited, Rule 3.2 (Comment)
Diligence,
　Duty of, Preamble, Rule 1.3
Directors, Board of, and lawyer, Rule 1.7 (Comment 14)
Disciplinary proceedings,
　Disclosure of client confidences in connection with, Rule 1.6 (Comment)
　Failure to comply with requests for information, Rule 8.1(b)
　Jurisdiction, Rule 8.5
　Reporting professional misconduct, Rule 8.3
Discipline,
　Violation of Rules as basis for, Scope
Discovery,
　Obstructive tactics, Rule 3.4(d)
　Refusing to comply, Rule 3.4(d)

INDEX

Discretion of lawyer,
  Where Rule cast in "may", Scope
Disqualification,
  Former judge, Rule 1.12(a)
  Imputed, see Imputed disqualification
  Vicarious, see Imputed disqualification
  Waiver by client, Rule 1.9 (Comment); Rule 1.10(d)
Division of fees,
  Requirements of, Rule 1.5(e)
  With nonlawyer, Rule 5.4(a)
Domestic relations matters,
  Contingent fee in, Rule 1.5(d)(1)

E

Employees of lawyer,
  Responsibility for, Rule 5.3
Estate planning,
  Conflicts of interest in, Rule 1.7 (Comment)
Evaluation,
  Confidential information used in preparing, Rule 2.3(b)
  Third person, prepared at client's request for, Rule 2.3
Evaluator,
  Lawyer as, Preamble
Evidence,
  Destruction of, Rule 3.4(a)
  Obstructing opposing party's access to, Rule 3.4(a)
  Offering false, Rule 3.3(a)(4)
Ex parte proceedings, Rule 3.3(d)
Expediting litigation, Rule 3.2
Expenses of litigation,
  Client's right to determine, Rule 1.2 (Comment)
  Indigent client, paying on behalf of, Rule 1.8(e)(2)
  Lawyer advancing to client, Rule 1.8(e)(1)
Expert witness, See Witness
Expertise,
  As relating to competent representation, Rule 1.1

F

Fairness to opposing party and counsel, Rule 3.4
False statement,
  Made to tribunal, Rule 3.3(a)(1)
Fees,
  Acquiring ownership interest in enterprise as, Rule 1.5 (Comment)
  Advance fee payments, Rule 1.5 (Comment)
  Advertising of, Rule 7.2 (Comment)
  Arbitration of, Rule 1.5 (Comment)
  Charged upon sale of law practice, Rule 1.17(d)
  Communication of to client, Rule 1.5(b)

Fees—Cont'd
  Contingent fee,
    Prohibited representations, Rule 1.5(d)
    Requirements of, Rule 1.5(c)
  Determination of, Rule 1.5(a)
  Disclosure of confidential information to collect, Rule 1.6(b)(2)
  Division of, Rule 1.5(e)
  Paid by one other than client, Rule 1.7 (Comment); Rule 1.8(f); Rule 5.4(c)
Firm,
  Defined, Terminology
  Disqualification, Rule 1.10 (Comment)
Firm name, Rule 7.5(a)
Former client, see Conflict of interest
Former government lawyer,
  "Confidential government information" defined, Rule 1.11(e)
  "Matter" defined, Rule 1.11(d)
  Successive government and private employment, Rule 1.11
Former judge, see Judges
Fraud,
  Defined, Terminology
Fraudulent,
  Defined, Terminology
Fraudulent conduct,
  Counseling or assisting client to engage in, Rule 1.2(d)
  Disclosure of client's, Rule 1.2 (Comment)
Frivolous claims and defenses, Rule 3.1
Funds of client,
  Handling of, Rule 1.15(b)
  Lawyer claims interest in, Rule 1.15(c)

G

Gift,
  To lawyer by client, Rule 1.8(c)
Government agency,
  Representation of, Rule 1.13 (Comment)
Government lawyer,
  Authority established by constitution, statutes and common law, Scope
  Conflict of interest, Rule 1.7 (Comment)
  Duty of confidentiality, Rule 1.6 (Comment)
  Representing multiple clients, Scope
  Subject to rules, Rule 1.11 (Comment)

H

Harass,
  Law's procedures used to, Preamble

I

Impartiality and decorum of the tribunal, Rule 3.5
Imputed disqualification,
  General rule, Rule 1.10

INDEX

Imputed disqualification—Cont'd
  Government lawyers, Rule 1.11 (Comment)
  Witness, when member of firm serves as, Rule 3.7(b)
Incompetent client,
  Appointment of guardian for, Rule 1.14(b)
  Representation of, Rule 1.14(a)
Independence of the legal profession, Preamble
Independent professional judgment,
  Duty to exercise, Rule 2.1; Rule 5.4
Indigent client,
  Paying court costs and expenses on behalf of, Rule 1.8(e)(2)
Insurance representation,
  Conflict of interest, Rule 1.7 (Comment)
Intermediary,
  Between clients, Rule 2.2
  Lawyer as, Preamble
  Withdrawal as, Rule 2.2(c)
Intimidate,
  Law's procedures used to, Preamble

J

Judges,
  Duty to show respect for, Preamble
  Ex parte communication with, Rule 3.5(b)
  Former judge, disqualification, Rule 1.12
  Improper influence on, Rule 3.5(a)
  Misconduct by, Rule 8.3(b)
  Statements about, Rule 8.2
Juror,
  Improper influence on, Rule 3.5(a)
Jury trial,
  Client's right to waive, Rule 1.2(a)

L

Law clerk,
  Negotiating for private employment, Rule 1.12(b)
Law firm,
  Ancillary services, Rule 5.7
  Defined, Terminology
  Nonlawyer assistants, responsibility for, Rule 5.3
  Responsibility of partner or supervisory lawyer, Rule 5.1
  Subordinate lawyer, responsibility of, Rule 5.2
Law reform activities,
  Affecting clients' interests, Rule 6.4
Lawyer referral service,
  Advertising by way of, Rule 7.2(c)(2)
  Financial support of, Rule 6.1 (Comment)
  Legal aid and, Rule 6.1 (Comment)
Legal education,
  Duty to work to strengthen, Preamble

Legislature,
  Appearance before on behalf of client, Rule 3.8
Letterheads,
  False or misleading, Rule 7.5(a)
  Jurisdictional limitations of members, Rule 7.5(b)
  Public officials, Rule 7.5(c)
Liability to client,
  Agreements limiting, Rule 1.8(h)
Lien,
  To secure fees and expenses, Rule 1.8(j)(1)
Literary rights,
  Acquiring concerning representation, Rule 1.8(d)
Litigation,
  Expedite, duty to, Rule 3.2
Loyalty,
  Duty of to client, Rule 1.7 (Comment)

M

Malpractice,
  Limiting liability to client for, Rule 1.8(h)
Meritorious claims and contentions, Rule 3.1
Military lawyers,
  Adverse interests, representation of, Rule 1.9 (Comment)
Misconduct,
  Forms of, Rule 8.4
Misleading legal argument, Rule 3.3 (Comment)
Misrepresentation,
  In advertisements, Rule 7.1
  To court, Rule 3.3 (Comment)
Multiple representation, *see* Conflict of interest; Intermediary

N

Negotiation,
  Conflicting interest, representation of, Rule 1.7 (Comment)
  Statements made during, Rule 4.1 (Comment)
Negotiator,
  Lawyer as, Preamble
Nonlawyers,
  Division of fees with, Rule 5.4(a)
  Partnership with, Rule 5.4(b)

O

Objectives of the representation,
  Client's right to determine, Rule 1.2(a)
  Lawyer's right to limit, Rule 1.2(c)
Opposing party,
  Communications with represented party, Rule 4.2
  Duty of fairness to, Rule 3.4

INDEX

Organization, representation of,
    Board of directors, lawyer for serving on, Rule 1.7 (Comment)
    Communication with, Rule 1.4 (Comment)
    Conflict of interest, Rule 1.7 (Comment)
    Conflicting interests among officers and employees, Rule 1.7 (Comment)
    Constituents, representing, Rule 1.13(e)
    Identity of client, Rule 1.13(a); Rule 1.13(d)
    Misconduct, client engaged in, Rule 1.13(b)

P

Partner,
    Defined, Terminology
Patent practice,
    Advertising, Rule 7.4(a)
Perjury,
    Criminal defendant, Rule 3.3 (Comment)
    Disclosure of, Rule 3.3(b)
Personal affairs of lawyer,
    Duty to conduct in compliance with law, Preamble
Plea bargain,
    Client's right to accept or reject, Rule 1.2(a)
Pleadings,
    Verification of, Rule 3.3 (Comment)
Positional conflicts, Rule 1.7 (Comment 9)
Precedent,
    Failure to disclose to court, Rule 3.3(a)(3)
Prepaid legal services,
    Advertising for, Rule 7.2 (Comment)
Pro bono publico service, Rule 6.1
Procedural law,
    Lawyer's professional responsibilities proscribed by, Preamble
Professional corporation,
    Defined, Terminology
    Formation of, Rule 5.4(d)
Prompt,
    Lawyer's duty to be, Preamble
Property of client,
    Safekeeping, Rule 1.15
Prosecutor,
    Representing former defendant, Rule 1.9 (Comment)
    Special responsibilities of, Rule 3.8
    Subpoenas by, Rule 3.8(f)
Public citizen,
    Lawyer's duty as, Preamble
Public interest,
    Government lawyer's authority to represent, Rule 3.8 (Comment)
Public interest legal services, *see* Pro bono publico service
Public office, lawyer holding,
    Negotiating private employment while, Rule 1.11(c)(2)

Public officials,
    Lawyer's duty to show respect for, Preamble

R

Recordkeeping,
    Property of client, Rule 1.15(a)
Referral,
    When lawyer not competent to handle matter, Rule 1.1
Regulation of the legal profession,
    Self-governance, Preamble
Relatives of lawyer,
    Representing interests adverse to, Rule 1.8(h)
Representation of client,
    Decisionmaking authority of lawyer and client, Rule 1.2(a)
    Objectives, lawyer's right to limit, Rule 1.2(c)
    Sale of law practice, Rule 1.17
    Termination of, Rule 1.2 (Comment)
Restrictions on right to practice,
    Partnership or employment agreement imposes, Rule 5.6(a)
    Settlement imposes, Rule 5.6(b)

S

Sale of law practice, Rule 1.17
Sanction,
    Severity of, Scope
Scope of representation, Rule 1.2
Settlement,
    Aggregate settlement on behalf of clients, Rule 1.8(g)
    Client's right to refuse settlement, Rule 1.2(a)
    Informing client of settlement offers, Rule 1.4 (Comment)
Solicitation,
    By mail, Rule 7.3
    Prohibition on, Rule 7.3
Specialization, Rule 7.5
State's Attorney,
    Authority of, Scope
Statutes,
    Shape lawyer's role, Scope
Subpoenas by prosecutors, Rule 3.8(f)
Substantive law,
    Defines existence of client-lawyer relationship, Scope
    Lawyer's professional responsibilities proscribed by, Preamble
Supervising work of another lawyer,
    Responsibilities, Rule 5.1

T

Third persons,
    Respect for rights of, Rule 4.4

INDEX

Third persons—Cont'd
  Statements to, Rule 4.1
Transactions with persons other than client, *see* Third persons
Trial conduct,
  Allusion to irrelevant or inadmissable evidence, Rule 3.4(e)
  Disruptive conduct, Rule 3.5(c)
  Trial publicity, Rule 3.6
Trust accounts,
  Maintain for client funds, Rule 1.15 (Comment)

U

Unauthorized practice of law,
  Assisting in, Rule 5.5(b)
  Engaging in, Rule 5.5(a)

W

Waiver,
  Prosecutor obtaining from criminal defendant, Rule 3.8(C)
Withdrawal,
  Conflict of interest, Rule 1.7 (Comment)
  Discharge, Rule 1.16(a)(3)

Withdrawal—Cont'd
  From intermediation, Rule 2.2(c)
  Giving notice of fact of, Rule 1.6 (Comment)
  Incapacity, Rule 1.16(a)(2)
  Property of client, Rule 1.16(d)
  When client persists in criminal or fraudulent conduct, Rule 1.2 (Comment); Rule 1.6 (Comment); Rule 1.16(b)(1); Rule 1.13(c)
Witness,
  Bribing, Rule 3.4(b)
  Client's right to decide whether to testify, Rule 1.2(a)
  Expenses, payment of, Rule 3.4 (Comment)
  Expert, payment of, Rule 3.4 (Comment)
  Lawyer as, Rule 3.7
Work product privilege,
  Rules do not affect application of, Scope

Z

Zealous representation,
  Opposing party well-represented, Preamble
  Requirement of, Rule 1.3 (Comment)

TABLE A*
TABLE OF SECTIONS IN THE ABA MODEL CODE RELATED TO THE ABA MODEL RULES

ABA MODEL CODE	MODEL RULES
Canon 1: Integrity of Profession	
EC 1–1	Rules 1.1, 6.1, 8.1(a)
EC 1–2	Rules 1.1, 6.1, 8.1(a)
EC 1–3	Rules 8.1(a), 8.3
EC 1–4	Rules 6.1, 8.3
EC 1–5	Rule 8.4
EC 1–6	Rules 1.16(a)(2), 8.4(a)
DR 1–101	Rule 8.1(a)
DR 1–102(A)(1)	Rule 8.4(a)
DR 1–102(A)(2)	Rules 5.1(c), 5.3(b), 8.4(a)
DR 1–102(A)(3)	Rule 8.4(b), (f)
DR 1–102(A)(4)	Rules 3.3(a)(1), (2), & (4), 3.4(a), (b), 4.1, 8.4(c), (f)
DR 1–102(A)(5)	Rules 3.1 through 3.9, Rules 8.1, 8.4(d) & (f)
DR 1–102(A)(6)	Rules 3.4(b), 8.4(b), (f)
DR 1–103(A)	Rules 5.1, 8.3
DR 1–103(B)	Rule 8.1(b)
Canon 2: Making Counsel Available	
EC 2–1	Rules 6.1, 6.2, 7.2(a), 7.4
EC 2–2	Rules 6.1, 7.2(a)
EC 2–3	Rules 4.3, 7.3
EC 2–4	Rule 7.3
EC 2–5	Rule 7.1(b)
EC 2–6	Rule 7.2(a)
EC 2–7	Rules 7.2(a), 7.4
EC 2–8	Rules 7.1, 7.2(a), (c), 7.4
EC 2–9	Rule 7.1
EC 2–10	Rule 7.1(a), (c)
EC 2–11	Rule 7.5
EC 2–12	Rule 7.5(c)
EC 2–13	Rule 7.5(a) & (d)
EC 2–14	Rule 7.4
EC 2–15	Rule 7.2(a), (c)

* This Table and Table B provide cross-references to related provisions, but only in the sense that the provisions consider substantially similar subject matter or reflect similar concerns. A cross-reference does not indicate that a provision of the ABA Model Code of Professional Responsibility has been incorporated by the provision of a Model Rule. The Canons of the Code are not cross-referenced.

TABLE OF SECTIONS

ABA MODEL CODE	MODEL RULES
EC 2-16	Rules 1.5(a), 6.1, 6.2(b)
EC 2-17	Rule 1.5(a)
EC 2-18	Rule 1.5(a)
EC 2-19	Rule 1.5(b)
EC 2-20	Rule 1.5(c), (d)
EC 2-21	Rules 1.7(b), 1.8(f)
EC 2-22	Rule 1.5(e)
EC 2-23	Rule 1.5 Comment ¶ 5
EC 2-24	Rules 6.1, 6.2
EC 2-25	Rules 6.1, 6.2
EC 2-26	Rules 1.16(a), 6.2
EC 2-27	Rule 6.2(a), (c)
EC 2-28	Rule 6.2(a)
EC 2-29	Rules 1.16(a), 6.2
EC 2-30	Rules 1.16(a), (b)(3), 4.2, 6.2
EC 2-31	Rules 1.3, 1.16, 6.2
EC 2-32	Rule 1.16
EC 2-33	Rules 5.4, 6.3, 6.4
DR 2-101(A)	Rule 7.1
DR 2-101(B)	Rules 7.1, 7.2(a)
DR 2-101(C)	Rules 7.1, 7.2
DR 2-101(D)	Rule 7.2(b)
DR 2-101(E)	Rule 7.1(a)
DR 2-101(F)	Rule 7.1
DR 2-101(G)	Rule 7.1
DR 2-101(H)	Rules 7.1, 7.2
DR 2-101(I)	Rule 7.2(c)
DR 2-102(A)	Rules 7.2(a), 7.4, 7.5
DR 2-102(B)	Rules 7.2(a), 7.5(a), (c)
DR 2-102(C)	Rule 7.5(d)
DR 2-102(D)	Rule 7.5(a), (b)
DR 2-102(E)	Rules 7.1(a), 7.4, 7.5(a)
DR 2-103(A)	Rules 7.2(a), 7.3
DR 2-103(B)	Rules 5.4(c), 7.2(a), (c)
DR 2-103(C)	Rules 5.4(a), 7.2(c), 7.3
DR 2-103(D)	Rules 5.4, 7.2(c), 7.3
DR 2-103(E)	Rules 1.16(a), 8.4(a)
DR 2-104	Rules 1.16(a), 7.3
DR 2-105	Rule 7.4
DR 2-106(A)	Rule 1.5(a)
DR 2-106(B)	Rule 1.5(a)
DR 2-106(C)	Rule 1.5(d)(2)
DR 2-107(A)	Rule 1.5(e)
DR 2-107(B)	Rule 5.4(a)(1)
DR 2-108(A)	Rule 5.6(a)
DR 2-108(B)	Rule 5.6(b)

ABA MODEL CODE—ABA MODEL RULES

ABA MODEL CODE	MODEL RULES
DR 2–109(A)	Rules 1.16(a), 3.1, 3.2
DR 2–110(A)	Rule 1.16(c), (d)
DR 2–110(B)	Rules 1.16(a), 3.1, 4.4
DR 2–110(C)	Rules 1.2(e), 1.16(a), (b)

Canon 3: Unauthorized Practice

EC 3–1	Rules 5.4, 5.5
EC 3–2	Rules 5.4, 5.5
EC 3–3	Rules 5.4, 5.5
EC 3–4	Rules 5.4, 5.5
EC 3–5	Rules 5.4, 5.5
EC 3–6	Rule 5.3
EC 3–7	Rule 5.5
EC 3–8	Rules 5.4(a), (b), (d), 5.5(b)
EC 3–9	Rules 5.5(a), 8.5
DR 3–101(A)	Rule 5.5(b)
DR 3–101(B)	Rule 5.5(a)
DR 3–102	Rule 5.4(a)
DR 3–103	Rule 5.4(b)

Canon 4: Confidences and Secrets

EC 4–1	Rule 1.6
EC 4–2	Rules 1.6(a), (b)(1), 2.2(a)(1), 5.3(a)
EC 4–3	Rule 1.6(a)
EC 4–4	Rule 1.6(a)
EC 4–5	Rules 1.8(b), 1.9(b), 1.10(a) & (b), 5.1(a), (b) & (c), 5.3(a)
EC 4–6	Rule 1.9(b), (c)
DR 4–101(A)	Rule 1.6(a)
DR 4–101(B)	Rules 1.6(a), (b), 1.8(b), 1.9(b)
DR 4–101(C)	Rules 1.6, 1.9(b)
DR 4–101(D)	Rules 5.1(a), (b), 5.3(a), (b)

Canon 5: Independent Judgment

EC 5–1	Rules 1.7, 1.8(c), (d), (e), (f), (g), (j)
EC 5–2	Rules 1.7, 1.8(a), (c), (d), (e), (f), (j)
EC 5–3	Rules 1.7, 1.8(a), (d), (e)
EC 5–4	Rule 1.8(d)
EC 5–5	Rule 1.8(a), (c)
EC 5–6	Rule 1.8(c)
EC 5–7	Rules 1.5(c), 1.8(e), (j), 1.15
EC 5–8	Rule 1.8(e)
EC 5–9	Rules 1.7(b), 3.7
EC 5–10	Rule 3.7
EC 5–11	Rules 1.7, 2.1
EC 5–12	Rule 1.2(a)
EC 5–13	Rule 1.7(b)
EC 5–14	Rules 1.7, 2.2(a)

TABLE OF SECTIONS

ABA MODEL CODE	MODEL RULES
EC 5–15	Rules 1.7, 2.2(a), (c)
EC 5–16	Rules 1.2(e), 1.7(b), 1.13(d), (e), 2.2(a), (b)
EC 5–17	Rule 1.7
EC 5–18	Rule 1.13
EC 5–19	Rules 1.7(b), 2.2(c)
EC 5–20	Rules 1.12, 2.2
EC 5–21	Rules 1.7, 1.16(a)(1)
EC 5–22	Rules 1.7, 1.8(f)
EC 5–23	Rules 1.7(b), 1.8(f), 5.4(c)
EC 5–24	Rules 1.13, 5.4(a), (d)
DR 5–101(A)	Rules 1.7, 1.8(j), 6.3, 6.4
DR 5–101(B)	Rules 1.7, 3.7
DR 5–102(A)	Rules 1.7, 3.7
DR 5–102(B)	Rules 1.7, 3.7
DR 5–103(A)	Rules 1.5(c), 1.8(e), (j), 1.15
DR 5–103(B)	Rule 1.8(e)
DR 5–104(A)	Rules 1.7(b), 1.8(a)
DR 5–104(B)	Rule 1.8(d)
DR 5–105(A)	Rules 1.7, 2.2
DR 5–105(B)	Rules 1.7, 1.13(e), 2.2
DR 5–105(C)	Rules 1.7, 1.9, 1.10(c), 1.13(e), 2.2
DR 5–105(D)	Rules 1.10(a), 1.12(c)
DR 5–106	Rule 1.8(g)
DR 5–107(A)	Rules 1.7, 1.8(f)
DR 5–107(B)	Rules 1.7, 1.8(f), 1.13(b), (c), 2.1, 5.4(c)
DR 5–107(C)	Rule 5.4(d)
Canon 6: Competence	
EC 6–1	Rule 1.1
EC 6–2	Rules 1.1, 5.1(a), (b), 6.1
EC 6–3	Rules 1.1, 1.3
EC 6–4	Rules 1.1, 1.3
EC 6–5	Rule 1.1
EC 6–6	Rule 1.8(h)
DR 6–101	Rules 1.1, 1.3, 1.4, 1.5(e)
DR 6–102	Rule 1.8(h)
Canon 7: Zeal within the Law	
EC 7–1	Rules 1.2(d), 1.3, 3.1
EC 7–2	Rule 1.2(d)
EC 7–3	Rules 1.4(b), 2.1
EC 7–4	Rule 3.1
EC 7–5	Rules 1.2(d), 1.4(a), 3.1
EC 7–6	Rule 3.4(a), (b)
EC 7–7	Rule 1.2(a)

ABA MODEL CODE—ABA MODEL RULES

ABA MODEL CODE	MODEL RULES
EC 7–8	Rules 1.2(a), (c), 1.4, 2.1
EC 7–9	Rule 1.2(c)
EC 7–10	Rule 4.4
EC 7–11	Rules 1.14(a), 3.8, 3.9
EC 7–12	Rule 1.14
EC 7–13	Rule 3.8
EC 7–14	Rules 3.1, 3.8, 4.4
EC 7–15	Rule 3.9
EC 7–16	Rule 3.9
EC 7–17	Rule 1.2(b)
EC 7–18	Rules 3.8(c), 4.2, 4.3
EC 7–19	Rules 3.1 through 3.5
EC 7–20	Rules 3.1 through 3.6
EC 7–21	Rule 4.4
EC 7–22	Rules 1.2(d), 3.4(c)
EC 7–23	Rule 3.3(a)(3)
EC 7–24	Rule 3.4(e)
EC 7–25	Rules 3.1, 3.4(c), (e), 3.5, 3.6, 4.4
EC 7–26	Rule 3.3(a)(4), (c)
EC 7–27	Rules 3.3(a)(d), 3.4(a), (f)
EC 7–28	Rules 3.4(b), 5.3(a), (b)
EC 7–29	Rules 3.5(a), 4.4
EC 7–30	Rule 4.4
EC 7–31	Rules 3.5(a), (b), 4.4
EC 7–32	Rule 8.3
EC 7–33	Rule 3.6
EC 7–34	Rules 3.5(a), 8.4(f)
EC 7–35	Rule 3.5(b)
EC 7–36	Rule 3.5(c)
EC 7–37	Rules 3.5(c), 4.4
EC 7–38	Rules 1.3, 3.4(c)
EC 7–39	Rules 3.1 through 3.8
DR 7–101(A)	Rules 1.2(a), (d), 1.3, 3.2, 3.5(c), 4.4
DR 7–101(B)	Rules 1.2(a), (c), (d), 1.16(b)
DR 7–102(A)(1)	Rules 3.1, 3.2, 4.4
DR 7–102(A)(2)	Rule 3.1
DR 7–102(A)(3)	Rules 3.3(a)(2), (3), 4.1
DR 7–102(A)(4)	Rule 3.3(a)(4), (c)
DR 7–102(A)(5)	Rules 3.3(a)(1), 4.1
DR 7–102(A)(6)	Rules 1.2(b), 3.4(b)
DR 7–102(A)(7)	Rules 1.2(d), 3.3(a), 4.1
DR 7–102(A)(8)	Rules 1.2(d), 8.4(a), (b)
DR 7–102(B)	Rules 1.6(b), 3.3(a)(4), (b), 4.1(b)
DR 7–103(A)	Rule 3.8(a)
DR 7–103(B)	Rule 3.8(d)

TABLE OF SECTIONS

ABA MODEL CODE	MODEL RULES
DR 7–104	Rules 3.4(f), 4.2, 4.3
DR 7–105	None
DR 7–106(A)	Rules 1.2(d), 3.4(c), (d)
DR 7–106(B)	Rules 3.3(a)(3), 3.9
DR 7–106(C)	Rules 3.4(a), (c), (d), (e), 3.5, 4.4
DR 7–107(A)–(I)	Rule 3.6
DR 7–107(J)	Rules 5.1(a), (b), 5.3(a), (b)
DR 7–108(A)	Rule 3.5(a), (b)
DR 7–108(B)	Rules 3.5(a), (b), 5.1(c), 5.3(a), (b), 8.4(a)
DR 7–108(C)	Rule 3.5(a), (b)
DR 7–108(D)	Rules 3.5(b), 4.4
DR 7–108(E)	Rules 3.5(b), 4.4, 5.1(c), 5.3(a), (b), 8.4(a)
DR 7–108(F)	Rule 4.4
DR 7–108(G)	None
DR 7–109(A)	Rules 3.3(a)(2), 3.4(a)
DR 7–109(B)	Rule 3.4(a), (f)
DR 7–109(C)	Rule 3.4(b)
DR 7–110(A)	Rules 3.5(a), 8.4(f)
DR 7–110(B)	Rule 3.5(a), (b)
Canon 8: Improving Legal System	
DR 8–1	Rules 1.2(b), 6.1
DR 8–2	Rule 6.1
DR 8–3	Rules 6.1, 6.2
DR 8–4	Rule 3.9
DR 8–5	Rules 3.3(a)(1), (2), (4), (b), 3.9
DR 8–6	Rule 8.2(a)
DR 8–7	Rules 5.5, 8.1
DR 8–8	Rule 1.11(c)
DR 8–9	Rule 6.1
DR 8–101	Rules 1.11(c), 3.5(a), 8.4(e), (f)
DR 8–102	Rule 8.2(a)
DR 8–103	Rule 8.2(b)
Canon 9: Appearance of Impropriety	
EC 9–1	Rules 3.1 through 3.8, 4.1, 8.4
EC 9–2	Rules 1.4, 3.1 through 3.8, 4.1
EC 9–3	Rules 1.11(a), 1.12(a)
EC 9–4	Rules 7.1(b), 8.4(c), (e)
EC 9–5	Rule 1.15
EC 9–6	Preamble, Rule 8.4(e)
EC 9–7	Rule 1.15
DR 9–101(A)	Rule 1.12
DR 9–101(B)	Rules 1.11(a), 1.12(a), (b)

TABLE OF SECTIONS

ABA MODEL CODE	MODEL RULES
DR 9–101(C)	Rules 1.2(e), 7.1(b), 8.4(e)
DR 9–102	Rules 1.4, 1.15

TABLE B *
TABLE OF SECTIONS
IN THE ABA MODEL RULES RELATED TO THE
ABA MODEL CODE

ABA MODEL RULES OF PROFESSIONAL CONDUCT	ABA MODEL CODE OF PROFESSIONAL RESPONSIBILITY
Competence	
Rule 1.1	EC 1-1, EC 1-2, EC 6-1, EC 6-2, EC 6-3, EC 6-4, EC 6-5, DR 6-101(A)
Scope of Representation	
Rule 1.2(a)	EC 5-12, EC 7-7, EC 7-8, DR 7-101(A)(1)
Rule 1.2(b)	EC 7-17
Rule 1.2(c)	EC 7-8, EC 7-9, DR 7-101(B)(1)
Rule 1.2(d)	EC 7-1, EC 7-2, EC 7-5, EC 7-22, DR 7-102(A)(6), (7)&(8), DR 7-106
Rule 1.2(e)	DR 2-110(C)(1)(c), DR 9-101(C)
Diligence	
Rule 1.3	EC 2-31, EC 6-4, EC 7-1, EC 7-38, DR 6-101(A)(3), DR 7-101(A)(1)&(3)
Communication	
Rule 1.4(a)	EC 7-8, EC 9-2, DR 6-101(A)(3), DR 9-102(B)(1)
Rule 1.4(b)	EC 7-8
Fees	
Rule 1.5(a)	EC 2-16, EC 2-17, EC 2-18, DR 2-106(A)&(B)
Rule 1.5(b)	EC 2-19
Rule 1.5(c)	EC 2-20, EC 5-7
Rule 1.5(d)	EC 2-20, DR 2-106(C)
Rule 1.5(e)	EC 2-22, DR 2-107(A), DR 6-101(A)(1)
Confidentiality of Information	
Rule 1.6(a)	EC 4-1, EC 4-2, EC 4-3, EC 4-4, DR 4-101(A), (B)&(C)

* This Table and Table A provide cross-references to related provisions, but only in the sense that the provisions consider substantially similar subject matter or reflect similar concerns. A cross-reference does not indicate that a provision of the ABA Model Code of Professional Responsibility has been incorporated by the provision of a Model Rule. The Canons of the Code are not cross-referenced.

ABA MODEL CODE—ABA MODEL RULES

ABA MODEL RULES OF PROFESSIONAL CONDUCT	ABA MODEL CODE OF PROFESSIONAL RESPONSIBILITY
Rule 1.6(b)(1)	EC 4-2, DR 4-101(C)(3), DR 7-102(B)
Rule 1.6(b)(2)	DR 4-101(C)(4)
Conflict of Interest	
Rule 1.7(a)	EC 5-1, EC 5-14, EC 5-15, EC 5-17, EC 5-21, EC 5-22, DR 5-101(A), DR 5-105(A)&(B), DR 5-107(B)
Rule 1.7(b)&(b)(1)	EC 2-21, EC 5-1, EC 5-2, EC 5-3, EC 5-9, EC 5-11, EC 5-13, EC 5-14, EC 5-15, EC 5-16, EC 5-17, EC 5-19, EC 5-21, EC 5-22, EC 5-23, DR 5-101(A)&(B), DR 5-102, DR 5-104(A), DR 5-105(A), (B)&(C), DR 5-107(A)
Rule 1.7(b)(2)	EC 5-16, EC 5-17, DR 7-106(B)(2)
Prohibited Transactions	
Rule 1.8(a)	EC 5-3, EC 5-5, DR 5-104(A)
Rule 1.8(b)	EC 4-5, DR 4-101(B)
Rule 1.8(c)	EC 5-1, EC 5-2, EC 5-5, EC 5-6
Rule 1.8(d)	EC 5-1, EC 5-3, EC 5-4, DR 5-104(B)
Rule 1.8(e)	EC 5-1, EC 5-3, EC 5-7, EC 5-8, DR 5-103(B)
Rule 1.8(f)	EC 2-21, EC 5-1, DR 5-107(A)&(B)
Rule 1.8(g)	EC 5-1, DR 5-106(A)
Rule 1.8(h)	EC 6-6, DR 6-102(A)
Rule 1.8(i)	None
Rule 1.8(j)	EC 5-1, EC 5-7, DR 5-101(A), DR 5-103(A)
Former Client	
Rule 1.9(a)	DR 5-105(C)
Rule 1.9(b)	EC 4-5, EC 4-6
Rule 1.9(c)	EC 4-6, DR 4-101
Imputed Disqualification	
Rule 1.10(a)	EC 4-5, DR 5-105(D)
Rule 1.10(b)	EC 4-5, DR 5-105(D)
Rule 1.10(c)	DR 5-105(C)
Successive Government and Private Employment	
Rule 1.11(a)	EC 9-3, DR 9-101(B)
Rule 1.11(b)	None
Rule 1.11(c)	EC 8-8

TABLE OF SECTIONS

ABA MODEL RULES OF PROFESSIONAL CONDUCT	ABA MODEL CODE OF PROFESSIONAL RESPONSIBILITY
Rule 1.11(d)	None
Rule 1.11(e)	None
Former Judge or Arbitrator	
Rule 1.12(a)&(b)	EC 5–20, EC 9–3, DR 9–101(A)&(B)
Rule 1.12(c)	DR 5–105(D)
Rule 1.12(d)	None
Organization as Client	
Rule 1.13(a)	EC 5–18, EC 5–24
Rule 1.13(b)	EC 5–18, EC 5–24, DR 5–107(B)
Rule 1.13(c)	EC 5–18, EC 5–24, DR 5–105(D), DR 5–107(B)
Rule 1.13(d)	EC 5–16
Rule 1.13(e)	EC 4–4, EC 5–16, DR 5–105(B)&(C)
Disabled Client	
Rule 1.14(a)	EC 7–11, EC 7–12
Rule 1.14(b)	EC 7–12
Safekeeping Property	
Rule 1.15	EC 5–7, EC 9–5, EC 9–7, DR 5–103(A)(1), DR 9–102
Declining or Terminating Representation	
Rule 1.16(a)(1)	EC 2–30, EC 2–31, EC 2–32, DR 2–103(E), DR 2–104(A), DR 2–109(A), DR 2–110(B)(1)&(2)
Rule 1.16(a)(2)	EC 1–6, EC 2–30, EC 2–31, EC 2–32, DR 2–110(B)(3), DR 2–110(C)(4)
Rule 1.16(a)(3)	EC 2–31, EC 2–32, DR 2–110(B)(4)
Rule 1.16(b)(1)	EC 2–31, EC 2–32, DR 2–110(C)(1)(b)&(c), DR 2–110(C)(2)
Rule 1.16(b)(2)	EC 2–31, EC 2–32, DR 2–110(C)(2)
Rule 1.16(b)(3)	EC 2–30, EC 2–31, EC 2–32, DR 2–110(C)(1)(d)
Rule 1.16(b)(4)	EC 2–31, EC 2–32, DR 2–110(C)(1)(f)(i)(j)
Rule 1.16(b)(5)	EC 2–32, DR 2–110(C)(1)(d)&(e)
Rule 1.16(b)	EC 2–32, DR 2–110(C)(6)
Rule 1.16(c)	EC 2–32, DR 2–110(A)(1)
Rule 1.16(d)	EC 2–32, DR 2–110(A)(2)&(3)
Sale of Law Practice	
Rule 1.17	None

ABA MODEL CODE—ABA MODEL RULES

ABA MODEL RULES OF PROFESSIONAL CONDUCT	ABA MODEL CODE OF PROFESSIONAL RESPONSIBILITY
Advisor	
Rule 2.1	EC 5–11, EC 7–3, EC 7–8, DR 5–107(B)
Intermediary	
Rule 2.2(a)(1)	EC 4–2, EC 5–14, EC 5–15, EC 5–16, EC 5–20, DR 5–105(A)&(C)
Rule 2.2(a)(2)&(3)	EC 5–14, EC 5–15, DR 5–105(A)&(C)
Rule 2.2(b)	EC 5–16
Rule 2.2(c)	EC 5–15, EC 5–19, DR 5–105(B)&(C)
Evaluation for Use by Third Persons	
Rule 2.3	None
Meritorious Claims and Contentions	
Rule 3.1	EC 7–1, EC 7–4, EC 7–5, EC 7–14, EC 7–25, DR 1–102(A)(5), DR 2–109(A)(B)(1), DR 7–102(A)(1)&(2)
Expediting Litigation	
Rule 3.2	EC 7–20, DR 1–102(A)(5), DR 7–101(A)(1)&(2)
Candor Toward the Tribunal	
Rule 3.3(a)(1)	EC 7–4, EC 7–32, EC 8
Fairness to Opposing Party and Counsel	
Rule 3.4(a)	EC 7–6, EC 7–27, DR 1–102(A)(4)&(5), DR 7–106(C)(7), DR 7–109(A)&(B)
Rule 3.4(b)	EC 7–6, EC 7–28, DR 1–102(A)(4), (5)&(6), DR 7–102(A)(6), DR 7–109(C)
Rule 3.4(c)	EC 7–22, EC 7–25, EC 7–38, DR 1–102(a)(5), DR 7–106(A), DR 7–106(C)(5)&(7)
Rule 3.4(d)	DR 1–102(A)(5), DR 7–106(A), DR 7–106(C)(7)
Rule 3.4(e)	EC 7–24, EC 7–25, DR 1–102(A)(5), DR 7–106(C)(1), (2), (3)&(4)
Rule 3.4(f)	EC 7–27, DR 1–102(A)(5), DR 7–104(A)(2), DR 7–109(B)

TABLE OF SECTIONS

ABA MODEL RULES OF PROFESSIONAL CONDUCT	ABA MODEL CODE OF PROFESSIONAL RESPONSIBILITY
Impartiality and Decorum	
Rule 3.5(a)	EC 7–20, EC 7–29, EC 7–31, EC 7–32, EC 7–34, DR 7–106, DR 7–108, DR 7–109, DR 7–110, DR 8–101(A)
Rule 3.5(b)	EC 7–35, DR 7–108, DR 7–110(A)&(B)
Rule 3.5(c)	EC 7–20, EC 7–25, EC 7–36, EC 7–37, DR 7–101(A)(1), DR 7–106(C)(6)
Trial Publicity	
Rule 3.6	EC 7–25, EC 7–33, DR 7–107
Lawyer as Witness	
Rule 3.7(a)	EC 5–9, EC 5–10, DR 5–101(B)(1)&(2), DR 5–102
Rule 3.7(b)	EC 5–9, DR 5–101(B), DR 5–102
Special Responsibilities of a Prosecutor	
Rule 3.8(a)	EC 7–11, EC 7–13, EC 7–14, DR 7–103(A)
Rule 3.8(b)	EC 7–11, EC 7–13
Rule 3.8(c)	EC 7–11, EC 7–13, EC 7–18
Rule 3.8(d)	EC 7–11, EC 7–13, DR 7–103(B)
Rule 3.8(e)	None
Rule 3.8(f)	None
Advocate in Nonadjudicative Proceedings	
Rule 3.9	EC 7–11, EC 7–15, EC 7–16, EC 8–4, EC 8–5, DR 7–106(B)(2), DR 9–101(C)
Truthfulness to Others	
Rule 4.1	EC 7–5, DR 7–102(A)(3), (4), (5)&(7), DR 7–102(B)
Communication with Represented Persons	
Rule 4.2	EC 2–30, EC 7–18, DR 7–104(A)(1)
Dealing with Unrepresented Persons	
Rule 4.3	EC 2–3, EC 7–8, DR 7–104(A)(2)

ABA MODEL RULES OF PROFESSIONAL CONDUCT

ABA MODEL CODE OF PROFESSIONAL RESPONSIBILITY

Respect for Rights of Third Persons

Rule 4.4	EC 7–10, EC 7–14, EC 7–21, EC 7–25, EC 7–29, EC 7–30, EC 7–37, DR 2–110(B)(1), DR 7–101(A)(1), DR 7–102(A)(1), DR 7–106(C)(2), DR 7–107(D), (E)&(F), DR 7–108(D), (E)&(F)

Responsibilities of a Partner or Supervisory Lawyer

Rule 5.1(a)&(b)	EC 4–4, DR 4–101(d), DR 7–107(J)
Rule 5.1(c)	DR 1–102(A)(2), DR 1–103(A), DR 7–108(E)

Responsibilities of a Subordinate Lawyer

Rule 5.2	None

Responsibilities Regarding Nonlawyer Assistants

Rule 5.3(a)	EC 3–6, EC 4–2, EC 4–5, EC 7–28, DR 4–101(D), DR 7–107(J)
Rule 5.3(b)	DR 1–102(A)(2), DR 7–107(J), DR 7–108(B), DR 7–108(E)

Professional Independence of Lawyer

Rule 5.4(a)	EC 2–33, EC 3–8, EC 5–24, DR 2–103(D)(4)(d), (e)&(f), DR 3–102(A), DR 5–107(C)(3)
Rule 5.4(b)	EC 2–33, EC 3–8, DR 3–103(A)
Rule 5.4(c)	EC 2–33, EC 5–23, DR 2–103(C), DR 5–107(B)
Rule 5.4(d)	EC 2–33, EC 3–8, DR 5–107(C)

Unauthorized Practice of Law

Rule 5.5	DR 3–101(A)&(B)

Restrictions on Right to Practice

Rule 5.6	DR 2–108

Provision of Ancillary Services

Rule 5.7	None

Pro Bono Publico Service

Rule 6.1	EC 1–2, EC 1–4, EC 2–1, EC 2–2, EC 2–16, EC 2–24, EC 2–25, EC 6–2, EC 8–1, EC 8–2, EC 8–3, EC 8–7, EC 8–9

TABLE OF SECTIONS

ABA MODEL RULES OF PROFESSIONAL CONDUCT	ABA MODEL CODE OF PROFESSIONAL RESPONSIBILITY
Accepting Appointments	
Rule 6.2(a)	EC 2-1, EC 2-25, EC 2-27, EC 2-28, EC 2-29, EC 8-3
Rule 6.2(b)	EC 2-16, EC 2-25, EC 2-29, EC 2-30
Rule 6.2(c)	EC 2-25, EC 2-27, EC 2-29, EC 2-30
Membership in Legal Services Organization	
Rule 6.3	EC 2-33, DR 5-101(A)
Law Reform Activities Affecting Client Interests	
Rule 6.4	EC 2-33, DR 5-101(A), DR 8-101
Communication Concerning Lawyer's Services	
Rule 7.1(a)	EC 2-8, EC 2-9, EC 2-10, DR 2-101(A), (B), (C), (E), (F)&(G), DR 2-102(E)
Rule 7.1(b)	EC 2-5, EC 2-8, EC 2-9, EC 9-4, DR 2-101(A), (B), (C), (E), (F)&(G), DR 9-101(C)
Rule 7.1(c)	EC 2-8, EC 2-9, EC 2-10, DR 2-101(A), (B), (C), (E), (F)&(G)
Advertising	
Rule 7.2(a)	EC 2-1, EC 2-2, EC 2-6, EC 2-7, EC 2-8, EC 2-15, DR 2-101(B)&(H), DR 2-102(A)&(B), DR 2-103(B), DR 2-104(A)(4)&(5)
Rule 7.2(b)	DR 2-101(D)
Rule 7.2(c)	EC 2-8, EC 2-15, DR 2-101(I), DR 2-103(B), (C)&(D)
Rule 7.2(d)	None
Direct Contact with Prospective Clients	
Rule 7.3	EC 2-3, EC 2-4, EC 5-6, DR 2-103(A), DR 2-103(C)(1), DR 2-103(D)(4)(b)&(c), DR 2-104(A)(1), (2), (3)&(5)

ABA MODEL CODE—ABA MODEL RULES

ABA MODEL RULES OF PROFESSIONAL CONDUCT	ABA MODEL CODE OF PROFESSIONAL RESPONSIBILITY
Communication of Fields of Practice	
Rule 7.4	EC 2–1, EC 2–7, EC 2–8, EC 2–14, DR 2–101(B)(2), DR 2–102(A)(3), DR 2–102(E), DR 2–105(A)
Rule 7.4(a)	DR 2–105(A)(1)
Rule 7.4(b)	EC 2–14
Rule 7.4(c)	DR 2–105(A)(2)&(3)
Firm Names and Letterheads	
Rule 7.5(a)	EC 2–11, EC 2–13, DR 2–102(A)(4), DR 2–102(B), (D)&(E), DR 2–105
Rule 7.5(b)	EC 2–11, DR 2–102(D)
Rule 7.5(c)	EC 2–11, EC 2–12, DR 2–102(B)
Rule 7.5(d)	EC 2–11, EC 2–13, DR 2–102(C)
Bar Admission and Disciplinary Matters	
Rule 8.1(a)	EC 1–1, EC 1–2, EC 1–3, DR 1–101(A)&(B)
Rule 8.1(b)	DR 1–102(A)(5), DR 1–103(B)
Judges and Legal Officials	
Rule 8.2(a)	EC 8–6, DR 8–102
Rule 8.2(b)	DR 8–103
Reporting Professional Misconduct	
Rule 8.3	EC 1–3, DR 1–103(A)
Misconduct	
Rule 8.4(a)	EC 1–5, EC 1–6, EC 9–6, DR 1–102(A)(1)&(2), DR 2–103(E), DR 7–102(A)&(B)
Rule 8.4(b)	EC 1–5, DR 1–102(A)(3)&(6), DR 7–102(A)(8), DR 8–101(A)(3)
Rule 8.4(c)	EC 1–5, EC 9–4, DR 1–102(A)(4), DR 8–101(A)(3)
Rule 8.4(d)	EC 3–9, EC 8–3, DR 1–102(A)(5), DR 3–101(B)
Rule 8.4(e)	EC 1–5, EC 9–2, EC 9–4, EC 9–6, DR 9–101(C)
Rule 8.4(f)	EC 1–5, EC 7–34, EC 9–1, DR 1–102(A)(3), (4), (5)&(6), DR 7–110(A), DR 8–101(A)(2)
Jurisdiction	
Rule 8.5	None

AMERICAN BAR ASSOCIATION

MODEL CODE OF PROFESSIONAL RESPONSIBILITY

As Amended

Copyright © American Bar Association 1981. All rights reserved. Reprinted with permission.

PREAMBLE AND PRELIMINARY STATEMENT

Preamble [1]

The continued existence of a free and democratic society depends upon recognition of the concept that justice is based upon the rule of law grounded in respect for the dignity of the individual and his capacity through reason for enlightened self-government.[2] Law so grounded makes justice possible, for only through such law does the dignity of the individual attain respect and protection. Without it, individual rights become subject to unrestrained power, respect for law is destroyed, and rational self-government is impossible.

Lawyers, as guardians of the law, play a vital role in the preservation of society. The fulfillment of this role requires an understanding by lawyers of their relationship with and function in our legal system.[3] A consequent obligation of lawyers is to maintain the highest standards of ethical conduct.

In fulfilling his professional responsibilities, a lawyer necessarily assumes various roles that require the performance of many difficult tasks. Not every situation which he may encounter can be foreseen,[4] but fundamental ethical principles are always present to guide him. Within the framework of these principles, a lawyer must with courage and foresight be able and ready to shape the body of the law to the ever-changing relationships of society.[5]

The Code of Professional Responsibility points the way to the aspiring and provides standards by which to judge the transgressor. Each lawyer must find within his own conscience the touchstone against which to test the extent to which his actions should rise above minimum standards. But in the

---

1. The footnotes are intended merely to enable the reader to relate the provisions of this Code to the ABA Canons of Professional Ethics adopted in 1908, as amended, the Opinions of the ABA Committee on Professional Ethics, and a limited number of other sources; they are not intended to be an annotation of the views taken by the ABA Special Committee on Evaluation of Ethical Standards. Footnotes citing ABA Canons refer to the ABA Canons of Professional Ethics, adopted in 1908, as amended.

2. Cf. ABA Canons, Preamble.

3. "[T]he lawyer stands today in special need of a clear undertstanding of his obligations and of the vital connection between these obligations and the role his profession plays in society." *Professional Responsibility: Report of the Joint Conference*, 44 A.B.A.J. 1159, 1160 (1958).

4. "No general statement of the responsibilities of the legal profession can encompass all the situations in which the lawyer may be placed. Each position held by him makes its own peculiar demands. These demands the lawyer must clarify for himself in the light of the particular role in which he serves." *Professional Responsibility: Report of the Joint Conference*, 44 A.B.A.J. 1159, 1218 (1958).

5. "The law and its institutions change as social conditions change. They must change if they are to preserve, much less advance, the political and social values from which they derive their purposes and their life. This is true of the most important of legal institutions, the profession of law. The profession, too, must change when conditions change in order to preserve and advance the social values that are its reasons for being." Cheatham, *Availability of Legal Services: The Responsibility of the Individual Lawyer and the Organized Bar*, 12 U.C.L.A.L.Rev. 438, 440 (1965).

Preamble *ABA*

last analysis it is the desire for the respect and confidence of the members of his profession and of the society which he serves that should provide to a lawyer the incentive for the highest possible degree of ethical conduct. The possible loss of that respect and confidence is the ultimate sanction. So long as its practitioners are guided by these principles, the law will continue to be a noble profession. This is its greatness and its strength, which permit of no compromise.

Preliminary Statement

In furtherance of the principles stated in the Preamble, the American Bar Association has promulgated this Code of Professional Responsibility, consisting of three separate but interrelated parts: Canons, Ethical Considerations, and Disciplinary Rules.[6] The Code is designed to be adopted by appropriate agencies both as an inspirational guide to the members of the profession and as a basis for disciplinary action when the conduct of a lawyer falls below the required minimum standards stated in the Disciplinary Rules.

Obviously the Canons, Ethical Considerations, and Disciplinary Rules cannot apply to non-lawyers; however, they do define the type of ethical conduct that the public has a right to expect not only of lawyers but also of their non-professional employees and associates in all matters pertaining to professional employment. A lawyer should ultimately be responsible for the conduct of his employees and associates in the course of the professional representation of the client.

The Canons are statements of axiomatic norms, expressing in general terms the standards of professional conduct expected of lawyers in their relationships with the public, with the legal system, and with the legal profession. They embody the general concepts from which the Ethical Considerations and the Disciplinary Rules are derived.

The Ethical Considerations are aspirational in character and represent the objectives toward which every member of the profession should strive. They constitute a body of principles upon which the lawyer can rely for guidance in many specific situations.[7]

The Disciplinary Rules, unlike the Ethical Considerations, are mandatory in character. The Disciplinary Rules state the minimum level of conduct below which no lawyer can fall without being subject to disciplinary action. Within the framework of fair trial,[8] the Disciplinary Rules should be uniformly

---

6. The Supreme Court of Wisconsin adopted a Code of Judicial Ethics in 1967. "The code is divided into standards and rules, the standards being statements of what the general desirable level of conduct should be, the rules being particular canons, the violation of which shall subject an individual judge to sanctions." In re Promulgation of a Code of Judicial Ethics, 36 Wis.2d 252, 255, 153 N.W.2d 873, 874 (1967).

The portion of the Wisconsin Code of Judicial Ethics entitled "Standards" states that "[t]he following standards set forth the significant qualities of the ideal judge . . . ." Id., 36 Wis.2d at 256, 153 N.W.2d at 875. The portion entitled "Rules" states that "[t]he court promulgates the following rules because the requirements of judicial conduct embodied therein are of sufficient gravity to warrant sanctions if they are not obeyed . . . ." Id., 36 Wis.2d at 259, 153 N.W.2d at 876.

7. "Under the conditions of modern practice it is peculiarly necessary that the lawyer should understand, not merely the established standards of professional conduct, but the reasons underlying these standards. Today the lawyer plays a changing and increasingly varied role. In many developing fields the precise contribution of the legal profession is as yet undefined." *Professional Responsibility: Report of the Joint Conference*, 44 A.B.A.J. 1159 (1958).

"A true sense of professional responsibility must derive from an understanding of the reasons that lie back of specific restraints, such as those embodied in the Canons. The grounds for the lawyer's peculiar obligations are to be found in the nature of his calling. The lawyer who seeks a clear understanding of his duties will be led to reflect on the special services his profession renders to society and the services it might render if its full capacities were realized. When the lawyer fully understands the nature of his office, he will then discern what restraints are necessary to keep that office wholesome and effective." *Id.*

8. "Disbarment, designed to protect the public, is a punishment or penalty imposed on the lawyer. * * * He is accordingly entitled to procedural due process, which includes fair notice of the charge." In re Ruffalo, 390 U.S. 544, 550, 20 L.Ed.2d 117, 122, 88 S.Ct. 1222, 1226 (1968), rehearing denied, 391 U.S. 961, 20 L.Ed.2d 874, 88 S.Ct. 1833 (1968).

"A State cannot exclude a person from the practice of law or from any other occupation in a manner or for reasons that contravene the Due Process or Equal Protection Clause of the Fourteenth Amendment. . . . A State can require high standards of qualification . . . but any qualification must have a rational connection with the applicant's fitness or capacity to practice law."

applied to all lawyers,[9] regardless of the nature of their professional activities.[10] The Code makes no attempt to prescribe either disciplinary procedures or penalties [11] for violation of a Disciplinary Rule,[12] nor does it undertake to define standards for civil liability of lawyers for professional conduct. The severity of judgment against one found guilty of violating a Disciplinary Rule should be determined by the character of the offense and the attendant circumstances.[13] An enforcing agency, in applying the Disciplinary Rules, may find interpretive guidance in the basic principles embodied in the Canons and in the objectives reflected in the Ethical Considerations.

CANON 1

A Lawyer Should Assist in Maintaining the Integrity and Competence of the Legal Profession

ETHICAL CONSIDERATIONS

EC 1-1 A basic tenet of the professional responsibility of lawyers is that every person in our society should have ready access to the independent professional services of a lawyer of integrity and competence. Maintaining the integrity and improving the competence of the bar to meet the highest standards is the ethical responsibility of every lawyer.

EC 1-2 The public should be protected from those who are not qualified to be lawyers by reason of a deficiency in education [1]

Schware v. Bd. of Bar Examiners, 353 U.S. 232, 239, 1 L.Ed.2d 796, 801–02, 77 S.Ct. 752, 756 (1957).

"[A]n accused lawyer may expect that he will not be condemned out of a capricious self-righteousness or denied the essentials of a fair hearing." Kingsland v. Dorsey, 338 U.S. 318, 320, 94 L.Ed. 123, 126, 70 S.Ct. 123, 124–25 (1949).

"The attorney and counsellor being, by the solemn judicial act of the court, clothed with his office, does not hold it as a matter of grace and favor. The right which it confers upon him to appear for suitors, and to argue causes is something more than a mere indulgence, revocable at the pleasure of the court, or at the command of the legislature. It is a right of which he can only be deprived by the judgment of the court, for moral or professional delinquency." Ex parte Garland, 71 U.S. (4 Wall.) 333, 378–79, 18 L.Ed. 366, 370 (1866).

See generally Comment, *Procedural Due Process and Character Hearings for Bar Applicants*, 15 Stan.L.Rev. 500 (1963).

9. "The canons of professional ethics must be enforced by the Courts and must be respected by members of the Bar if we are to maintain public confidence in the integrity and impartiality of the administration of justice." In re Meeker, 76 N.M. 354, 357, 414 P.2d 862, 864 (1966), appeal dismissed, 385 U.S. 449 (1967).

10. See ABA Canon 45.

"The Canons of this Association govern all its members, irrespective of the nature of their practice, and the application of the Canons is not affected by statutes or regulations governing certain activities of lawyers which may prescribe less stringent standards." ABA Comm. on Professional Ethics, Opinions, No. 203 (1940) [hereinafter each Opinion is cited as "ABA Opinion"].

Cf. *ABA Opinion* 152 (1936).

11. "There is generally no prescribed discipline for any particular type of improper conduct. The disciplinary measures taken are discretionary with the courts, which may disbar, suspend, or merely censure the attorney as the nature of the offense and past indicia of character may warrant." Note, 43 Cornell L.Q. 489, 495 (1958).

12. The Code seeks only to specify conduct for which a lawyer should be disciplined. Recommendations as to the procedures to be used in disciplinary actions and the gravity of disciplinary measures appropriate for violations of the Code are within the jurisdiction of the American Bar Association Special Committee on Evaluation of Disciplinary Enforcement.

13. "The severity of the judgment of this court should be in proportion to the gravity of the offenses, the moral turpitude involved, and the extent that the defendant's acts and conduct affect his professional qualifications to practice law." Louisiana State Bar Ass'n v. Steiner, 204 La. 1073, 1092–93, 16 So.2d 843, 850 (1944) (Higgins, J., concurring in decree).

"Certainly an erring lawyer who has been disciplined and who having paid the penalty has given satisfactory evidence of repentance and has been rehabilitated and restored to his place at the bar by the court which knows him best ought not to have what amounts to an order of permanent disbarment entered against him by a federal court solely on the basis of an earlier criminal record and without regard to his subsequent rehabilitation and present good character . . . . We think, therefore, that the district court should reconsider the appellant's application for admission and grant it unless the court finds it to be a fact that the appellant is not presently of good moral or professional character." In re Dreier, 258 F.2d 68, 69–70 (3d Cir.1958).

1. "[W]e cannot conclude that all educational restrictions [on bar admission are unlawful. We assume that few would deny that a grammar school education requirement, before taking the bar examination, was reasonable. Or that an applicant had to be able to read or write. Once we conclude that *some* restriction is proper, then it becomes a matter of degree—the problem of drawing the line.

or moral standards[2] or of other relevant factors[3] but who nevertheless seek to practice law. To assure the maintenance of high moral and educational standards of the legal profession, lawyers should affirmatively assist courts and other appropriate bodies in promulgating, enforcing, and improving requirements for admission to the bar.[4] In like manner, the bar has a positive obligation to aid in the continued improvement of all phases of pre-admission and post-admission legal education.

EC 1–3 Before recommending an applicant for admission, a lawyer should satisfy himself that the applicant is of good moral character. Although a lawyer should not become a self-appointed investigator or judge of applicants for admission, he should report to proper officials all unfavorable information he possesses relating to the character or other qualifications of an applicant.[5]

EC 1–4 The integrity of the profession can be maintained only if conduct of lawyers in violation of the Disciplinary Rules is brought to the attention of the proper officials. A lawyer should reveal voluntarily to those officials all unprivileged knowledge of conduct of lawyers which he believes clearly to be in violation of the Disciplinary Rules.[6] A lawyer should, upon request, serve on and assist committees and boards having responsibility for the administration of the Disciplinary Rules.[7]

EC 1–5 A lawyer should maintain high standards of professional conduct and should encourage fellow lawyers to do likewise. He should be temperate and dignified, and he should refrain from all illegal and morally reprehensible conduct.[8] Because of his posi-

---

. . .

"We conclude the fundamental question here is whether Rule IV, Section 6 of the Rules Pertaining to Admission of Applicants to the State Bar of Arizona is 'arbitrary, capricious and unreasonable.' We conclude an educational requirement of graduation from an accredited law school is not." Hackin v. Lockwood, 361 F.2d 499, 503–04 (9th Cir.1966), cert. denied, 385 U.S. 960, 17 L.Ed. 2d 305, 87 S.Ct. 396 (1966).

2. "Every state in the United States, as a prerequisite for admission to the practice of law, requires that applicants possess 'good moral character.' Although the requirement is of judicial origin, it is now embodied in legislation in most states." Comment, *Procedural Due Process and Character Hearings for Bar Applicants*, 15 Stan.L.Rev. 500 (1963).

"Good character in the members of the bar is essential to the preservation of the integrity of the courts. The duty and power of the court to guard its portals against intrusion by men and women who are mentally and morally dishonest, unfit because of bad character, evidenced by their course of conduct, to participate in the administrative law, would seem to be unquestioned in the matter of preservation of judicial dignity and integrity." In re Monaghan, 126 Vt. 53, 222 A.2d 665, 670 (1966).

"Fundamentally, the question involved in both situations [i.e. admission and disciplinary proceedings] is the same—is the applicant for admission or the attorney sought to be disciplined a fit and proper person to be permitted to practice law, and that usually turns upon whether he has committed or is likely to continue to commit acts of moral turpitude. At the time of oral argument the attorney for respondent frankly conceded that the test for admission and for discipline is and should be the same. We agree with this concession." Hallinan v. Comm. of Bar Examiners, 65 Cal.2d 447, 453, 421 P.2d 76, 81, 55 Cal.Rptr. 228, 233 (1966).

3. "Proceedings to gain admission to the bar are for the purpose of protecting the public and the courts from the ministrations of persons unfit to practice the profession. Attorneys are officers of the court appointed to assist the court in the administration of justice. Into their hands are committed the property, the liberty and sometimes the lives of their clients. This commitment demands a high degree of intelligence, knowledge of the law, respect for its function in society, sound and faithful judgment and, above all else, integrity of character in private and professional conduct." In re Monaghan, 126 Vt. 53, 222 A.2d 665, 676 (1966) (Holden, C.J., dissenting).

4. "A bar composed of lawyers of good moral character is a worthy objective but it is unnecessary to sacrifice vital freedoms in order to obtain that goal. It is also important both to society and the bar itself that lawyers be unintimidated—free to think, speak, and act as members of an Independent Bar." Konigsberg v. State Bar, 353 U.S. 252, 273, 1 L.Ed.2d 810, 825, 77 S.Ct. 722, 733 (1957).

5. See ABA Canon 29.

6. ABA Canon 28 designates certain conduct as unprofessional and then states that: "A duty to the public and to the profession devolves upon every member of the Bar having knowledge of such practices upon the part of any practitioner immediately to inform thereof, to the end that the offender may be disbarred." ABA Canon 29 states a broader admonition: "Lawyers should expose without fear or favor before the proper tribunals corrupt or dishonest conduct in the profession."

7. "It is the obligation of the organized Bar and the individual lawyer to give unstinted cooperation and assistance to the highest court of the state in discharging its function and duty with respect to discipline and in purging the profession of the unworthy." *Report of the Special Committee on Disciplinary Procedures*, 80 A.B.A.Rep. 463, 470 (1955).

8. Cf. ABA Canon 32.

tion in society, even minor violations of law by a lawyer may tend to lessen public confidence in the legal profession. Obedience to law exemplifies respect for law. To lawyers especially, respect for the law should be more than a platitude.

EC 1-6 An applicant for admission to the bar or a lawyer may be unqualified, temporarily or permanently, for other than moral and educational reasons, such as mental or emotional instability. Lawyers should be diligent in taking steps to see that during a period of disqualification such person is not granted a license or, if licensed, is not permitted to practice.[9] In like manner, when the disqualification has terminated, members of the bar should assist such person in being licensed, or, if licensed, in being restored to his full right to practice.

DISCIPLINARY RULES

DR 1-101 Maintaining Integrity and Competence of the Legal Profession.

(A) A lawyer is subject to discipline if he has made a materially false statement in, or if he has deliberately failed to disclose a material fact requested in connection with, his application for admission to the bar.[10]

(B) A lawyer shall not further the application for admission to the bar of another person known by him to be unqualified in respect to character, education, or other relevant attribute.[11]

DR 1-102 Misconduct.

(A) A lawyer shall not:

(1) Violate a Disciplinary Rule.

(2) Circumvent a Disciplinary Rule through actions of another.[12]

(3) Engage in illegal conduct involving moral turpitude.[13]

---

9. "We decline, on the present record, to disbar Mr. Sherman or to reprimand him—not because we condone his actions, but because, as heretofore indicated, we are concerned with whether he is mentally responsible for what he has done.

"The logic of the situation would seem to dictate the conclusion that, if he was mentally responsible for the conduct we have outlined, he should be disbarred; and, if he was not mentally responsible, he should not be permitted to practice law.

"However, the flaw in the logic is that he may have been mentally irresponsible [at the time of his offensive conduct] . . ., and, yet, have sufficiently improved in the almost two and one-half years intervening to be able to capably and competently represent his clients. . . .
. . .

"We would make clear that we are satisfied that a case has been made against Mr. Sherman, warranting a refusal to permit him to further practice law in this state unless he can establish his mental irresponsibility at the time of the offenses charged. The burden of proof is upon him.

"If he establishes such mental irresponsibility, the burden is then upon him to establish his present capability to practice law." In re Sherman, 58 Wash.2d 1, 6–7, 354 P.2d 888, 890 (1960), cert. denied, 371 U.S. 951, 9 L.Ed.2d 499, 83 S.Ct. 506 (1963).

10. "This Court has the inherent power to revoke a license to practice law in this State, where such license was issued by this Court, and its issuance was procured by the fraudulent concealment, or by the false and fraudulent representation by the applicant of a fact which was manifestly material to the issuance of the license." North Carolina ex rel. Attorney General v. Gorson, 209 N.C. 320, 326, 183 S.E. 392, 395 (1936), cert. denied, 298 U.S. 662, 80 L.Ed. 1387, 56 S.Ct. 752 (1936).

See also Application of Patterson, 318 P.2d 907, 913 (Or.1957), cert. denied, 356 U.S. 947, 2 L.Ed.2d 822, 78 S.Ct. 795 (1958).

11. See ABA Canon 29.

12. In *ABA Opinion* 95 (1933), which held that a municipal attorney could not permit police officers to interview persons with claims against the municipality when the attorney knew the claimants to be represented by counsel, the Committee on Professional Ethics said:

"The law officer is, of course, responsible for the acts of those in his department who are under his supervision and control." *Opinion 85.* In re Robinson, 136 N.Y.S. 548 (affirmed 209 N.Y. 354–1912) held that it was a matter of disbarment for an attorney to adopt a general course of approving the unethical conduct of employees of his client, even though he did not actively participate therein.

" '. . . The attorney should not advise or sanction acts by his client which he himself should not do.' *Opinion 75.*"

13. "The most obvious non-professional ground for disbarment is conviction for a felony. Most states make conviction for a felony grounds for automatic disbarment.

Canon 1   ABA

(4) **Engage in conduct involving dishonesty, fraud, deceit, or misrepresentation.**

(5) **Engage in conduct that is prejudicial to the administration of justice.**

(6) **Engage in any other conduct that adversely reflects on his fitness to practice law.**[14]

DR 1–103 Disclosure of Information to Authorities.

(A) **A lawyer possessing unprivileged knowledge of a violation of DR 1–102 shall report such knowledge to a tribunal or other authority empowered to investigate or act upon such violation.**[15]

(B) **A lawyer possessing unprivileged knowledge or evidence concerning another lawyer or a judge shall reveal fully such knowledge or evidence upon proper request of a tribunal or other authority empowered to investigate or act upon the conduct of lawyers or judges.**[16]

CANON 2

A Lawyer Should Assist the Legal Profession in Fulfilling Its Duty to Make Legal Counsel Available

ETHICAL CONSIDERATIONS

EC 2–1 The need of members of the public for legal services [1] is met only if they recognize their legal problems, appreciate the im-

---

Some of these states, including New York, make disbarment mandatory upon conviction for *any* felony, while others require disbarment only for those felonies which involve moral turpitude. There are strong arguments that some felonies, such as involuntary manslaughter, reflect neither on an attorney's fitness, trustworthiness, nor competence and, therefore, should not be grounds for disbarment, but most states tend to disregard these arguments and, following the common law rule, make disbarment mandatory on conviction for any felony." Note, 43 Cornell L.Q. 489, 490 (1958).

"Some states treat conviction for misdemeanors as grounds for automatic disbarment . . . . However, the vast majority, accepting the common law rule, require that the misdemeanor involve moral turpitude. While the definition of moral turpitude may prove difficult, it seems only proper that those minor offenses which do not affect the attorney's fitness to continue in the profession should not be grounds for disbarment. A good example is an assault and battery conviction which would not involve moral turpitude unless done with malice and deliberation." Id. at 491.

"The term 'moral turpitude' has been used in the law for centuries. It has been the subject of many decisions by the courts but has never been clearly defined because of the nature of the term. Perhaps the best general definition of the term 'moral turpitude' is that it imports an act of baseness, vileness or depravity in the duties which one person owes to another or to society in general, which is contrary to the usual, accepted and customary rule of right and duty which a person should follow. 58 C.J.S. at page 1201. Although offenses against revenue laws have been held to be crimes of moral turpitude, it has also been held that the attempt to evade the payment of taxes due to the government or any subdivision thereof, while wrong and unlawful, does not involve moral turpitude. 58 C.J.S. at page 1205." Comm. on Legal Ethics v. Scheer, 149 W.Va. 721, 726–27, 143 S.E.2d 141, 145 (1965).

"The right and power to discipline an attorney, as one of its officers, is inherent in the court. . . . This power is not limited to those instances of misconduct wherein he has been employed, or has acted, in a professional capacity; but, on the contrary, this power may be exercised where his misconduct outside the scope of his professional relations shows him to be an unfit person to practice law." In re Wilson, 391 S.W.2d 914, 917–18 (Mo.1965).

14. "It is a fair characterization of the lawyer's responsibility in our society that he stands 'as a shield,' to quote Devlin, J., in defense of right and to ward off wrong. From a profession charged with these responsibilities there must be exacted those qualities of truthspeaking, of a high sense of honor, of granite discretion, of the strictest observance of fiduciary responsibility, that have, throughout the centuries, been compendiously described as 'moral character.' " Schware v. Bd. of Bar Examiners, 353 U.S. 232, 247 L.Ed.2d 796, 806, 77 S.Ct. 752, 761 (1957) (Frankfurter, J., concurring).

"Particularly applicable here is Rule 4.47 providing that 'A lawyer should always maintain his integrity; and shall not willfully commit any act against the interest of the public; nor shall he violate his duty to the courts or his clients; *nor shall he, by any misconduct, commit any offense against the laws of Missouri or the United States of America, which amounts to a crime involving acts done by him contrary to justice, honesty, modesty or good morals;* nor shall he be guilty of any other misconduct whereby, for the protection of the public and those charged with the administration of justice, he should no longer be entrusted with the duties and responsibilities belonging to the office of an attorney.' " In re Wilson, 391 S.W.2d 914, 917 (Mo.1965).

15. See ABA Canon 29; cf. ABA Canon 28.

16. Cf. ABA Canons 28 and 29.

1. "Men have need for more than a system of law; they have need for a system of law which functions, and that means they have need for lawyers." Cheatham, *The Lawyer's Role and Surroundings*, 25 Rocky Mt.L.Rev. 405 (1953).

portance of seeking assistance,[2] and are able to obtain the services of acceptable legal counsel.[3] Hence, important functions of the legal profession are to educate laymen to recognize their problems, to facilitate the process of intelligent selection of lawyers, and to assist in making legal services fully available.[4]

Recognition of Legal Problems

EC 2-2 The legal profession should assist lay-persons to recognize legal problems because such problems may not be self-revealing and often are not timely noticed. Therefore, lawyers should encourage and participate in educational and public relations programs concerning our legal system with particular reference to legal problems that frequently arise. Preparation of advertisements and professional articles for lay publications [5] and participation in seminars, lectures, and civic programs should be motivated by a desire to educate the public to an awareness of legal needs and to provide information relevant to the selection of the most appropriate counsel rather than to obtain publicity for particular lawyers. The problems of advertising on television require special consideration, due to the style, cost, and transitory nature of such media. If the interests of laypersons in receiving relevant lawyer advertising are not adequately served by print media and radio advertising, and if adequate safeguards to protect the public can reasonably be formulated, television advertising may serve a public interest.

EC 2-3 Whether a lawyer acts properly in volunteering in-person advice to a layperson to seek legal services depends upon the circumstances.[6] The giving of advice that one should take legal action could well be in fulfillment of the duty of the legal profession to assist laypersons in recognizing legal problems.[7] The advice is proper only if moti-

---

2. "Law is not self-applying; men must apply and utilize it in concrete cases. But the ordinary man is incapable. He cannot know the principles of law or the rules guiding the machinery of law administration; he does not know how to formulate his desires with precision and to put them into writing; he is ineffective in the presentation of his claims." Cheatham, *The Lawyer's Role and Surroundings*, 25 Rocky Mt.L.Rev. 405 (1953).

3. "This need [to provide legal services] was recognized by . . . Mr. [Lewis F.] Powell [Jr., President, American Bar Association, 1963–64], who said: 'Looking at contemporary America realistically, we must admit that despite all our efforts to date (and these have not been insignificant), far too many persons are not able to obtain equal justice under law. This usually results because their poverty or their ignorance has prevented them from obtaining legal counsel.'" Address by E. Clinton Bamberger, Association of American Law Schools 1965 Annual Meeting, Dec. 28, 1965, in Proceedings, Part II, 1965, 61, 63–64 (1965).

"A wide gap separates the need for legal services and its satisfaction, as numerous studies reveal. Looked at from the side of the layman, one reason for the gap is poverty and the consequent inability to pay legal fees. Another set of reasons is ignorance of the need for and the value of legal services, and ignorance of where to find a dependable lawyer. There is fear of the mysterious processes and delays of the law, and there is fear of overreaching and overcharging by lawyers, a fear stimulated by the occasional exposure of shysters." Cheatham, *Availability of Legal Services: The Responsibility of the Individual Lawyer and of the Organized Bar*, 12 U.C.L.A.L.Rev. 438 (1965).

4. "It is not only the right but the duty of the profession as a whole to utilize such methods as may be developed to bring the services of its members to those who need them, so long as this can be done ethically and with dignity." ABA Opinion 320 (1968).

"[T]here is a responsibility on the bar to make legal services available to those who need them. The maxim, 'privilege brings responsibilities,' can be expanded to read, exclusive privilege to render public service brings responsibility to assure that the service is available to those in need of it." Cheatham, *Availability of Legal Services: The Responsibility of the Individual Lawyer and of the Organized Bar*, 12 U.C.L.A.L.Rev. 438, 443 (1965).

"The obligation to provide legal services for those actually caught up in litigation carries with it the obligation to make preventive legal advice accessible to all. It is among those unaccustomed to business affairs and fearful of the ways of the law that such advice is often most needed. If it is not received in time, the most valiant and skillful representation in court may come too late." *Professional Responsibility: Report of the Joint Conference*, 44 A.B.A.J. 1159, 1216 (1958).

5. "A lawyer may with propriety write articles for publications in which he gives information upon the law. . . ." A.B.A. Canon 40.

6. See ABA Canon 28.

7. This question can assume constitutional dimensions: "We meet at the outset the contention that 'solicitation' is wholly outside the area of freedoms protected by the First Amendment. To this contention there are two answers. The first is that a State cannot foreclose the exercise of constitutional rights by mere labels. The second is that abstract discussion is not the only species of communication which the Constitution protects; the First Amendment also protects vigorous advocacy, certainly of lawful ends, against governmental intrusion. . . .

vated by a desire to protect one who does not recognize that he may have legal problems or who is ignorant of his legal rights or obligations. It is improper if motivated by a desire to obtain personal benefit, secure personal publicity, or cause legal action to be taken merely to harass or injure another. A lawyer should not initiate an in-person contact with a non-client, personally or through a representative, for the purpose of being retained to represent him for compensation.

EC 2–4 Since motivation is subjective and often difficult to judge, the motives of a lawyer who volunteers in-person advice likely to produce legal controversy may well be suspect if he receives professional employment or other benefits as a result.[8] A lawyer who volunteers in-person advice that one should obtain the services of a lawyer generally should not himself accept employment, compensation, or other benefit in connection with that matter. However, it is not improper for a lawyer to volunteer such advice and render resulting legal services to close friends, relatives, former clients (in regard to matters germane to former employment), and regular clients.[9]

EC 2–5 A lawyer who writes or speaks for the purpose of educating members of the public to recognize their legal problems should carefully refrain from giving or appearing to give a general solution applicable to all apparently similar individual problems,[10] since slight changes in fact situations may require a material variance in the applicable advice; otherwise, the public may be mislead and misadvised. Talks and writings by lawyers for laypersons should caution them not to attempt to solve individual problems upon the basis of the information contained therein.[11]

Selection of a Lawyer

EC 2–6 Formerly a potential client usually knew the reputations of local lawyers for competency and integrity and therefore could select a practitioner in whom he had confidence. This traditional selection process worked well because it was initiated by the client and the choice was an informed one.

EC 2–7 Changed conditions, however, have seriously restricted the effectiveness of the traditional selection process. Often the reputations of lawyers are not sufficiently known to enable laypersons to make intelli-

---

"However valid may be Virginia's interest in regulating the traditionally illegal practice of barratry, maintenance and champerty, that interest does not justify the prohibition of the NAACP activities disclosed by this record. Malicious intent was of the essence of the common-law offenses of fomenting or stirring up litigation. And whatever may be or may have been true of suits against governments in other countries, the exercise in our own, as in this case of First Amendment rights to enforce Constitutional rights through litigation, as a matter of law, cannot be deemed malicious." NAACP v. Button, 371 U.S. 415, 429, 439–40, 9 L.Ed.2d 405, 415–16, 422, 83 S.Ct. 328, 336, 341 (1963).

8. It is disreputable for an attorney to breed litigation by seeking out those who have claims for personal injuries or other grounds of action in order to secure them as clients, or to employ agents or runners, or to reward those who bring or influence the bringing of business to his office. . . . Moreover, it tends quite easily to the institution of baseless litigation and the manufacture of perjured testimony. From early times, this danger has been recognized in the law by the condemnation of the crime of common barratry, or the stirring up of suits or quarrels between individuals at law or otherwise." In re Ades, 6 F.Supp. 467, 474–75 (D.Mary.1934).

9. "Rule 2.

"§ a. . . .

"[A] member of the State Bar shall not solicit professional employment by

"(1) Volunteering counsel or advice except where ties of blood relationship or trust make it appropriate." Cal. Business and Professions Code § 6076 (West 1962).

10. "Rule 18 . . . A member of the State Bar shall not advise inquirers or render opinions to them through or in connection with a newspaper, radio or other publicity medium of any kind in respect to their specific legal problems, whether or not such attorney shall be compensated for his services." Cal.Business and Professions Code § 6076 (West 1962).

11. "In any case where a member might well apply the advice given in the opinion to his individual affairs, the lawyer rendering the opinion [concerning problems common to members of an association and distributed to the members through a periodic bulletin] should specifically state that this opinion should not be relied on by any member as a basis for handling his individual affairs, but that in every case he should consult his counsel. In the publication of the opinion the association should make a similar statement." *ABA Opinion* 273 (1946).

gent choices.[12] The law has become increasingly complex and specialized. Few lawyers are willing and competent to deal with every kind of legal matter, and many laypersons have difficulty in determining the competence of lawyers to render different types of legal services. The selection of legal counsel is particularly difficult for transients, persons moving into new areas, persons of limited education or means, and others who have little or no contact with lawyers.[13] Lack of information about the availability of lawyers, the qualifications of particular lawyers, and the expense of legal representation leads laypersons to avoid seeking legal advice.

EC 2-8 Selection of a lawyer by a layperson should be made on an informed basis. Advice and recommendation of third parties—relatives, friends, acquaintances, business associates, or other lawyers—and disclosure of relevant information about the lawyer and his practice may be helpful. A layperson is best served if the recommendation is disinterested and informed. In order that the recommendation be disinterested, a lawyer should not seek to influence another to recommend his employment. A lawyer should not compensate another person for recommending him, for influencing a prospective client to employ him, or to encourage future recommendations.[14] Advertisements and public communications, whether in law lists, telephone directories, newspapers, other forms of print media, television or radio, should be formulated to convey only information that is necessary to make an appropriate selection. Such information includes: (1) office information, such as, name, including name of law firm and names of professional associates; addresses; telephone numbers; credit card acceptability; fluency in foreign languages; and office hours; (2) relevant biographical information; (3) description of the practice, but only by using designations and definitions authorized by [the agency having jurisdiction of the subject under state law], for example, one or more fields of law in which the lawyer or law firm practices; a statement that practice is limited to one or more fields of law; and/or a statement that the lawyer or law firm specializes in a particular field of law practice, but only by using designations, definitions and standards authorized by [the agency having jurisdiction of the subject under state law]; and (4) permitted fee information. Self-laudation should be avoided.

Selection of a Lawyer: Lawyer Advertising

EC 2-9 The lack of sophistication on the part of many members of the public concerning legal services, the importance of the interests affected by the choice of a lawyer and prior experience with unrestricted lawyer advertising, require that special care be taken by lawyers to avoid misleading the public and to assure that the information set forth in any advertising is relevant to the selection of a lawyer. The lawyer must be mindful that the benefits of lawyer advertising depend upon its reliability and accuracy. Examples of information in lawyer advertising that would be deceptive include misstatements of fact, suggestions that the ingenuity or prior record of a lawyer rather than the justice of the claim are the principal factors likely to determine the result, inclusion of information irrelevant to selecting a lawyer, and representations concerning the quality of service, which cannot be measured or verified. Since lawyer advertising is calculated and not spontaneous, reasonable regulation of lawyer advertising designed to foster compliance with appropriate standards serves the public interest without impeding the flow of useful, meaningful, and relevant information to the public.

---

12. "A group of recent interrelated changes bears directly on the availability of legal services. . . . [One] change is the constantly accelerating urbanization of the country and the decline of personal and neighborhood knowledge of whom to retain as a professional man." Cheatham, *Availability of Legal Services: The Responsibility of the Individual Lawyer and of the Organized Bar*, 12 U.C.L.A.L.Rev. 438, 440 (1965).

13. Cf. Cheatham, *A Lawyer When Needed: Legal Services for the Middle Classes*, 63 Colum.L.Rev. 973, 974 (1963).

14. See ABA Canon 28.

EC 2-10 A lawyer should ensure that the information contained in any advertising which the lawyer publishes, broadcasts or causes to be published or broadcast is relevant, is disseminated in an objective and understandable fashion, and would facilitate the prospective client's ability to compare the qualifications of the lawyers available to represent him. A lawyer should strive to communicate such information without undue emphasis upon style and advertising strategems which serve to hinder rather than to facilitate intelligent selection of counsel. Because technological change is a recurrent feature of communications forms, and because perceptions of what is relevant in lawyer selection may change, lawyer advertising regulations should not be cast in rigid, unchangeable terms. Machinery is therefore available to advertisers and consumers for prompt consideration of proposals to change the rules governing lawyer advertising. The determination of any request for such change should depend upon whether the proposal is necessary in light of existing Code provisions, whether the proposal accords with standards of accuracy, reliability and truthfulness, and whether the proposal would facilitate informed selection of lawyers by potential consumers of legal services. Representatives of lawyers and consumers should be heard in addition to the applicant concerning any proposed change. Any change which is approved should be promulgated in the form of an amendment to the Code so that all lawyers practicing in the jurisdiction may avail themselves of its provisions.

EC 2-11 The name under which a lawyer conducts his practice may be a factor in the selection process.[15] The use of a trade name or an assumed name could mislead laypersons concerning the identity, responsibility, and status of those practicing thereunder.[16] Accordingly, a lawyer in private practice should practice only under a designation containing his own name, the name of a lawyer employing him, the name of one or more of the lawyers practicing in a partnership, or, if permitted by law, the name of a professional legal corporation, which should be clearly designated as such. For many years some law firms have used a firm name retaining one or more names of deceased or retired partners and such practice is not improper if the firm is a bona fide successor of a firm in which the deceased or retired person was a member, if the use of the name is authorized by law or by contract, and if the public is not misled thereby.[17] However, the name of a partner who withdraws from a firm but continues to practice law should be omitted from the firm name in order to avoid misleading the public.

EC 2-12 A lawyer occupying a judicial, legislative, or public executive or administrative position who has the right to practice law concurrently may allow his name to remain in the name of the firm if he actively continues to practice law as a member thereof. Otherwise, his name should be removed from the firm name,[18] and he should not be

---

15. *Cf. ABA Opinion* 303 (1961).
16. *See* ABA Canon 33.
17. Id.

"The continued use of a firm name by one or more surviving partners after the death of a member of the firm whose name is in the firm title is expressly permitted by the Canons of Ethics. The reason for this is that all of the partners have by their joint and several efforts over a period of years contributed to the good will attached to the firm name. In the case of a firm having widespread connections, this good will is disturbed by a change in firm name every time a name partner dies, and that reflects a loss in some degree of the good will to the building up of which the surviving partners have contributed their time, skill and labor through a period of years. To avoid this loss the firm name is continued, and to meet the requirements of the Canon the individuals constituting the firm from time to time are listed." *ABA Opinion* 267 (1945).

"Accepted local custom in New York recognizes that the name of a law firm does not necessarily identify the individual members of the firm, and hence the continued use of a firm name after the death of one or more partners is not a deception and is permissible. . . . The continued use of a deceased partner's name in the firm title is not affected by the fact that another partner withdraws from the firm and his name is dropped, or the name of the new partner is added to the firm name." Opinion No. 45, Committee on Professional Ethics, New York State Bar Ass'n, 39 N.Y.St.B.J. 455 (1967).

Cf. *ABA Opinion* 258 (1943).

18. Cf. ABA Canon 33 and *ABA Opinion* 315 (1965).

identified as a past or present member of the firm; and he should not hold himself out as being a practicing lawyer.

EC 2-13 In order to avoid the possibility of misleading persons with whom he deals, a lawyer should be scrupulous in the representation of his professional status.[19] He should not hold himself out as being a partner or associate of a law firm if he is not one in fact,[20] and thus should not hold himself out as partner or associate if he only shares offices with another lawyer.[21]

EC 2-14 In some instances a lawyer confines his practice to a particular field of law.[22] In the absence of state controls to insure the existence of special competence, a lawyer should not be permitted to hold himself out as a specialist or as having official recognition as a specialist, other than in the fields of admiralty, trademark, and patent law where a holding out as a specialist historically has been permitted. A lawyer may, however, indicate in permitted advertising, if it is factual, a limitation of his practice or one or more particular areas or fields of law in which he practices using designations and definitions authorized for that purpose by [the state agency having jurisdiction]. A lawyer practicing in a jurisdiction which certifies specialists must also be careful not to confuse laypersons as to his status. If a lawyer discloses areas of law in which he practices or to which he limits his practice, but is not certified in [the jurisdiction], he, and the designation authorized in [the jurisdiction], should avoid any implication that he is in fact certified.

EC 2-15 The legal profession has developed lawyer referral systems designed to aid individuals who are able to pay fees but need assistance in locating lawyers competent to handle their particular problems. Use of a lawyer referral system enables a layman to avoid an uninformed selection of a lawyer because such a system makes possible the employment of competent lawyers who have indicated an interest in the subject matter involved. Lawyers should support the principle of lawyer referral systems and should encourage the evolution of other ethical plans which aid in the selection of qualified counsel.

Financial Ability to Employ Counsel: Generally

EC 2-16 The legal profession cannot remain a viable force in fulfilling its role in our society unless its members receive adequate compensation for services rendered, and reasonable fees [23] should be charged in appropriate cases to clients able to pay them. Nevertheless, persons unable to pay all or a portion of a reasonable fee should be able to obtain necessary legal services,[24] and lawyers should support and participate in ethical activities designed to achieve that objective.[25]

---

19. Cf. *ABA Opinions* 283 (1950) and 81 (1932).

20. See *ABA Opinion* 316 (1967).

21. "The word 'associates' has a variety of meanings. Principally through custom the word when used on the letterheads of law firms has come to be regarded as describing those who are employees of the firm. Because the word has acquired this special significance in connection with the practice of the law the use of the word to describe lawyer relationships other than employer-employee is likely to be misleading." In re Sussman and Tanner, 241 Ore. 246, 248, 405 P.2d 355, 356 (1965).

According to *ABA Opinion* 310 (1963), use of the term "associates" would be misleading in two situations: (1) where two lawyers are partners and they share both responsibility and liability for the partnership; and (2) where two lawyers practice separately, sharing no responsibility or liability, and only share a suite of offices and some costs.

22. "For a long time, many lawyers have, of necessity, limited their practice to certain branches of law. The increasing complexity of the law and the demand of the public for more expertness on the part of the lawyer has, in the past few years—particularly in the last ten years—brought about specialization on an increasing scale." *Report of the Special Committee on Specialization and Specialized Legal Services*, 79 A.B.A.Rep. 582, 584 (1954).

23. See ABA Canon 12.

24. Cf. ABA Canon 12.

25. "If there is any fundamental proposition of government on which all would agree, it is that one of the highest goals of society must be to achieve and maintain equality before the law. Yet this ideal remains an empty form of words unless the legal profession is ready to provide adequate representation for those unable to pay the usual fees." *Professional Representation: Report of the Joint Conference*, 44 A.B.A.J. 1159, 1216 (1958).

Financial Ability to Employ Counsel: Persons Able to Pay Reasonable Fees

EC 2-17 The determination of a proper fee requires consideration of the interests of both client and lawyer.[26] A lawyer should not charge more than a reasonable fee,[27] for excessive cost of legal service would deter laymen from utilizing the legal system in protection of their rights. Furthermore, an excessive charge abuses the professional relationship between lawyer and client. On the other hand, adequate compensation is necessary in order to enable the lawyer to serve his client effectively and to preserve the integrity and independence of the profession.[28]

EC 2-18 The determination of the reasonableness of a fee requires consideration of all relevant circumstances,[29] including those stated in the Disciplinary Rules. The fees of a lawyer will vary according to many factors, including the time required, his experience, ability, and reputation, the nature of the employment, the responsibility involved, and the results obtained. It is a commendable and long-standing tradition of the bar that special consideration is given in the fixing of any fee for services rendered a brother lawyer or a member of his immediate family.

EC 2-19 As soon as feasible after a lawyer has been employed, it is desirable that he reach a clear agreement with his client as to the basis of the fee charges to be made. Such a course will not only prevent later misunderstanding but will also work for good relations between the lawyer and the client. It is usually beneficial to reduce to writing the understanding of the parties regarding the fee, particularly when it is contingent. A lawyer should be mindful that many persons who desire to employ him may have had little or no experience with fee charges of lawyers, and for this reason he should explain fully to such persons the reasons for the particular fee arrangement he proposes.

EC 2-20 Contingent fee arrangements [30] in civil cases have long been commonly accepted in the United States in proceedings to enforce claims. The historical bases of their acceptance are that (1) they often, and in a variety of circumstances, provide the only practical means by which one having a claim against another can economically afford, finance, and obtain the services of a competent lawyer to prosecute his claim, and (2) a successful prosecution of the claim produces a *res* out of which the fee can be paid.[31] Although a lawyer generally should decline to accept employment on a contingent fee basis by one who is able to pay a reasonable fixed fee, it is not necessarily improper for a lawyer, where justified by the particular circumstances of a case, to enter into a contingent fee contract in a civil case with any client who, after being fully informed of all relevant factors, desires that arrangement. Because of the human relationships involved and the unique character of the proceedings, contingent fee arrangements in domestic relation cases are rarely justified. In administrative agency proceedings contingent fee contracts should be governed by the same consideration as in other civil cases. Public policy properly condemns contingent fee ar-

---

26. See ABA Canon 12.
27. Cf. ABA Canon 12.
28. "When members of the Bar are induced to render legal services for inadequate compensation as a consequence the quality of the service rendered may be lowered, the welfare of the profession injured and the administration of justice made less efficient." *ABA Opinion* 302 (1961).

Cf. *ABA Opinion* 307 (1962).

29. See ABA Canon 12.
30. See ABA Canon 13; see also MacKinnon, Contingent Fees for Legal Services (1964) (A report of the American Bar Foundation).

"A contract for a reasonable contingent fee where sanctioned by law is permitted by *Canon 13*, but the client must remain responsible to the lawyer for expenses advanced by the latter. 'There is to be no barter of the privilege of prosecuting a cause for gain in exchange for the promise of the attorney to prosecute at his own expense.' (Cardozo, C.J. In Matter of Gilman, 251 N.Y. 265, 270-271.)" *ABA Opinion* 246 (1942).

31. See Comment, *Providing Legal Services for the Middle Class in Civil Matters: The Problem, the Duty and a Solution,* 26 U.Pitt.L.Rev. 811, 829 (1965).

rangements in criminal cases, largely on the ground that legal services in criminal cases do not produce a *res* with which to pay the fee.

EC 2-21 A lawyer should not accept compensation or any thing of value incident to his employment or services from one other than his client without the knowledge and consent of his client after full disclosure.[32]

EC 2-22 Without the consent of his client, a lawyer should not associate in a particular matter another lawyer outside his firm. A fee may properly be divided between lawyers [33] properly associated if the division is in proportion to the services performed and the responsibility assumed by each lawyer [34] and if the total fee is reasonable.

EC 2-23 A lawyer should be zealous in his efforts to avoid controversies over fees with clients [35] and should attempt to resolve amicably any differences on the subject.[36] He should not sue a client for a fee unless necessary to prevent fraud or gross imposition by the client.[37]

Financial Ability to Employ Counsel: Persons Unable to Pay Reasonable Fees

EC 2-24 A layman whose financial ability is not sufficient to permit payment of any fee cannot obtain legal services, other than in cases where a contingent fee is appropriate, unless the services are provided for him. Even a person of moderate means may be unable to pay a reasonable fee which is large because of the complexity, novelty, or difficulty of the problem or similar factors.[38]

EC 2-25 Historically, the need for legal services of those unable to pay reasonable fees has been met in part by lawyers who donated their services or accepted court appointments on behalf of such individuals.

---

32. See ABA Canon 38.

"Of course, as . . . [Informal Opinion 679] points out, there must be full disclosure of the arrangement [that an entity other than the client pays the attorney's fee] by the attorney to the client. . . ." *ABA Opinion* 320 (1968).

33. "Only lawyers may share in . . . a division of fees, but . . . it is not necessary that both lawyers be admitted to practice in the same state, so long as the division was based on the division of services or responsibility." *ABA Opinion* 316 (1967).

34. See ABA Canon 34.

"We adhere to our previous rulings that where a lawyer merely brings about the employment of another lawyer *but renders no service and assumes no responsibility in the matter*, a division of the latter's fee is improper. (Opinions 18 and 153).

"It is assumed that the bar, generally, understands what acts or conduct of a lawyer may constitute 'services' to a client within the intendment of *Canon 12*. Such acts or conduct invariably, if not always, involve 'responsibility' on the part of the lawyer, whether the word 'responsibility' be construed to denote the possible resultant legal or moral liability on the part of the lawyer to the client or to others, or the onus of deciding what should or should not be done in behalf of the client. The word 'services' in *Canon 12* must be construed in this broad sense and may apply to the selection and retainer of associate counsel as well as to others acts or conduct in the client's behalf." *ABA Opinion* 204 (1940).

35. See ABA Canon 14.

36. Cf. *ABA Opinion* 320 (1968).

37. See ABA Canon 14.

"Ours is a learned profession, not a mere money-getting trade. . . . Suits to collect fees should be avoided. Only where the circumstances imperatively require, should resort be had to a suit to compel payment. And where a lawyer does resort to a suit to enforce payment of fees which involves a disclosure, he should carefully avoid any disclosure not clearly necessary to obtaining or defending his rights." *ABA Opinion* 250 (1943).

But cf. *ABA Opinion* 320 (1968).

38. "As a society increases in size, sophistication and technology, the body of laws which is required to control that society also increases in size, scope and complexity. With this growth, the law directly affects more and more facets of individual behavior, creating an expanding need for legal services on the part of the individual members of the society. . . . As legal guidance in social and commercial behavior increasingly becomes necessary, there will come a concurrent demand from the layman that such guidance be made available to him. This demand will not come from those who are able to employ the best legal talent, nor from those who can obtain legal assistance at little or no cost. It will come from the large 'forgotten middle income class,' who can neither afford to pay proportionately large fees nor qualify for ultra-low-cost services. The legal profession must recognize this inevitable demand and consider methods whereby it can be satisfied. If the profession fails to provide such methods, the laity will." Comment, *Providing Legal Services for the Middle Class in Civil Matters: The Problem, the Duty and a Solution,* 26 U.Pitt.L.Rev. 811, 811-12 (1965).

"The issue is not whether we shall do something or do nothing. The demand for ordinary everyday legal justice is so great and the moral nature of the demand is so strong that the issue has become whether we devise, maintain, and support suitable agencies able to satisfy the demand or, by our own default, force the government to take over the job, supplant us, and ultimately dominate us." Smith, *Legal Service Offices for Persons of Moderate Means,* 1949 Wis.L.Rev. 416, 418 (1949).

The basic responsibility for providing legal services for those unable to pay ultimately rests upon the individual lawyer, and personal involvement in the problems of the disadvantaged can be one of the most rewarding experiences in the life of a lawyer. Every lawyer, regardless of professional prominence or professional workload, should find time to participate in serving the disadvantaged. The rendition of free legal services to those unable to pay reasonable fees continues to be an obligation of each awyer, but the efforts of individual lawyers are often not enough to meet the need.[39] Thus it has been necessary for the profession to institute additional programs to provide legal services.[40] Accordingly, legal aid offices,[41] lawyer referral services, and other related programs have been developed, and others will be developed, by the profession.[42] Every lawyer should support all proper efforts to meet this need for legal services.[43]

Acceptance and Retention of Employment

EC 2–26 A lawyer is under no obligation to act as advisor or advocate for every person who may wish to become his client; but in furtherance of the objective of the bar to make legal services fully available, a lawyer should not lightly decline proffered employment. The fulfillment of this objective requires acceptance by a lawyer of his share of tendered employment which may be unattractive both to him and the bar generally.[44]

EC 2–27 History is replete with instances of distinguished and sacrificial services by lawyers who have represented unpopular clients and causes. Regardless of his personal feelings, a lawyer should not decline representation because a client or a cause is unpopular or community reaction is adverse.[45]

---

39. "Lawyers have peculiar responsibilities for the just administration of the law, and these responsibilities include providing advice and representation for needy persons. To a degree not always appreciated by the public at large, the bar has performed these obligations with zeal and devotion. The Committee is persuaded, however, that a system of justice that attempts, in mid-twentieth century America, to meet the needs of the financially incapacitated accused through primary or exclusive reliance on the uncompensated services of counsel will prove unsuccessful and inadequate. . . . A system of adequate representation, therefore, should be structured and financed in a manner reflecting its public importance. . . . We believe that fees for private appointed counsel should be set by the court within maximum limits established by the statute." Report of the Att'y Gen's Comm. on Poverty and the Administration of Criminal Justice 41–43 (1963).

40. "At present this representation [of those unable to pay usual fees] is being supplied in some measure through the spontaneous generosity of individual lawyers, through legal aid societies, and—increasingly—through the organized efforts of the Bar. If those who stand in need of this service know of its availability and their need is in fact adequately met, the precise mechanism by which this service is provided becomes of secondary importance. It is of great importance, however, that both the impulse to render this service, and the plan for making that impulse effective, should arise within the legal profession itself." *Professional Responsibility: Report of the Joint Conference*, 44 A.B.A.J. 1159, 1216 (1958).

41. "Free legal clinics carried on by the organized bar are not ethically objectionable. On the contrary, they serve a very worthwhile purpose and should be encouraged." *ABA Opinion* 191 (1939).

42. "Whereas the American Bar Association believes that it is a fundamental duty of the bar to see to it that all persons requiring legal advice be able to attain it, irrespective of their economic status . . . .

"Resolved, that the Association approves and sponsors the setting up by state and local bar associations of lawyer referral plans and low-cost legal service methods for the purpose of dealing with cases of persons who might not otherwise have the benefit of legal advice . . . ." *Proceedings of the House of Delegates of the American Bar Association*, Oct. 30, 1946, 71 A.B.A.Rep. 103, 109–10 (1946).

43. "The defense of indigent citizens, without compensation, is carried on throughout the country by lawyers representing legal aid societies, not only with the approval, but with the commendation of those acquainted with the work. Not infrequently services are rendered out of sympathy or for other philanthropic reasons, by individual lawyers who do not represent legal aid societies. There is nothing whatever in the Canons to prevent a lawyer from performing such an act, nor should there be." *ABA Opinion* 148 (1935).

44. But cf. ABA Canon 31.

45. "One of the highest services the lawyer can render to society is to appear in court on behalf of clients whose causes are in disfavor with the general public." *Professional Responsibility: Report of the Joint Conference*, 44 A.B.A.J. 1159, 1216 (1958).

One author proposes the following proposition to be included in "A Proper Oath for Advocates": "I recognize that it is sometimes difficult for clients with unpopular causes to obtain proper legal representation. I will do all that I can to assure that the client with the unpopular cause is properly represented, and that the lawyer representing such a client receives credit from and support of the bar for handling such a matter." Thode, *The Ethical Standard for the Advocate*, 39 Texas L.Rev. 575, 592 (1961).

"§ 6068. . . . It is the duty of an attorney:

MODEL CODE OF PROFESSIONAL RESPONSIBILITY — Canon 2

EC 2-28 The personal preference of a lawyer to avoid adversary alignment against judges, other lawyers,[46] public officials, or influential members of the community does not justify his rejection of tendered employment.

EC 2-29 When a lawyer is appointed by a court or requested by a bar association to undertake representation of a person unable to obtain counsel, whether for financial or other reasons, he should not seek to be excused from undertaking the representation except for compelling reasons.[47] Compelling reasons do not include such factors as the repugnance of the subject matter of the proceeding, the identity[48] or position of a person involved in the case, the belief of the lawyer that the defendant in a criminal proceeding is guilty,[49] or the belief of the lawyer regarding the merits of the civil case.[50]

EC 2-30 Employment should not be accepted by a lawyer when he is unable to render competent service[51] or when he knows or it is obvious that the person seeking to employ him desires to institute or maintain an action merely for the purpose of harassing or maliciously injuring another.[52] Likewise, a lawyer should decline employment if the intensity of his personal feeling, as distinguished from a community attitude, may impair his effective representation of a prospective client. If a lawyer knows a client has previously obtained counsel, he should not accept employment in the matter unless the other counsel approves[53] or withdraws, or the client terminates the prior employment.[54]

EC 2-31 Full availability of legal counsel requires both that persons be able to obtain counsel and that lawyers who undertake representation complete the work involved. Trial counsel for a convicted defendant should continue to represent his client by advising whether to take an appeal and, if the appeal is prosecuted, by representing him through the appeal unless new counsel is substituted or withdrawal is permitted by the appropriate court.

EC 2-32 A decision by a lawyer to withdraw should be made only on the basis of

---

. . .

"(h) Never to reject, for any consideration personal to himself, the cause of the defenseless or the oppressed." Cal.Business and Professions Code § 6068 (West 1962). Virtually the same language is found in the Oregon statutes at Ore.Rev.Stats. Ch. 9, § 9.460(8).

See Rostow, *The Lawyer and His Client*, 48 A.B.A.J. 25 and 146 (1962).

46. See ABA Canons 7 and 29.

"We are of the opinion that it is not professionally improper for a lawyer to accept employment to compel another lawyer to honor the just claim of a layman. On the contrary, it is highly proper that he do so. Unfortunately, there appears to be a widespread feeling among laymen that it is difficult, if not impossible, to obtain justice when they have claims against members of the Bar because other lawyers will not accept employment to proceed against them. The honor of the profession, whose members proudly style themselves officers of the court, must surely be sullied if its members bind themselves by custom to refrain from enforcing just claims of laymen against lawyers." *ABA Opinion* 144 (1935).

47. ABA Canon 4 uses a slightly different test, saying, "A lawyer assigned as counsel for an indigent prisoner ought not to ask to be excused for any trivial reason. . . ."

48. Cf. ABA Canon 7.

49. See ABA Canon 5.

50. Dr. Johnson's reply to Boswell upon being asked what he thought of "supporting a cause which you know to be bad" was: "Sir, you do not know it to be good or bad till the Judge determines it. I have said that you are to state facts fairly; so that your thinking, or what you call knowing, a cause to be bad, must be from reasoning, must be from supposing your arguments to be weak and inconclusive. But, Sir, that is not enough. An argument which does not convince yourself, may convince the Judge to whom you urge it; and if it does convince him, why, then, Sir, you are wrong, and he is right." 2 Boswell, The Life of Johnson 47–48 (Hill ed. 1887).

51. "The lawyer deciding whether to undertake a case must be able to judge objectively whether he is capable of handling it and whether he can assume its burdens without prejudice to previous commitments.. . . ." *Professional Responsibility: Report of the Joint Conference*, 44 A.B.A.J. 1158, 1218 (1958).

52. "The lawyer must decline to conduct a civil cause or to make a defense when convinced that it is intended merely to harass or to injure the opposite party or to work oppression or wrong." ABA Canon 30.

53. See ABA Canon 7.

54. Id.

"From the facts stated we assume that the client has discharged the first attorney and given notice of the discharge. Such being the case, the second attorney may properly accept employment. *Canon 7; Opinions 10, 130, 149.*" *ABA Opinion* 209 (1941).

compelling circumstances,[55] and in a matter pending before a tribunal he must comply with the rules of the tribunal regarding withdrawal. A lawyer should not withdraw without considering carefully and endeavoring to minimize the possible adverse effect on the rights of his client and the possibility of prejudice to his client[56] as a result of his withdrawal. Even when he justifiably withdraws, a lawyer should protect the welfare of his client by giving due notice of his withdrawal,[57] suggesting employment of other counsel, delivering to the client all papers and property to which the client is entitled, cooperating with counsel subsequently employed, and otherwise endeavoring to minimize the possibility of harm. Further, he should refund to the client any compensation not earned during the employment.[58]

EC 2–33 As a part of the legal profession's commitment to the principle that high quality legal services should be available to all, attorneys are encouraged to cooperate with qualified legal assistance organizations providing prepaid legal services. Such participation should at all times be in accordance with the basic tenets of the profession: independence, integrity, competence and devotion to the interests of individual clients. An attorney so participating should make certain that his relationship with a qualified legal assistance organization in no way interferes with his independent, professional representation of the interests of the individual client. An attorney should avoid situations in which officials of the organization who are not lawyers attempt to direct attorneys concerning the manner in which legal services are performed for individual members, and should also avoid situations in which considerations of economy are given undue weight in determining the attorneys employed by an organization or the legal services to be performed for the member or beneficiary rather than competence and quality of service. An attorney interested in maintaining the historic traditions of the profession and preserving the function of a lawyer as a trusted and independent advisor to individual members of society should carefully assess such factors when accepting employment by, or otherwise participating in, a particular qualified legal assistance organization, and while so participating should adhere to the highest professional standards of effort and competence.

DISCIPLINARY RULES

DR 2–101 Publicity.

(A) **A lawyer shall not, on behalf of himself, his partner, associate or any other lawyer affiliated with him or his firm, use or participate in the use of any form of public communication containing a false, fraudulent, misleading, deceptive, self-laudatory or unfair statement or claim.**

(B) **In order to facilitate the process of informed selection of a lawyer by potential consumers of legal services, a lawyer may publish or broadcast, subject to DR 2–103, the following information in print media distributed or over television or radio broadcast in the geographic area or areas in which the lawyer resides or maintains offices or in which a significant part of the lawyer's clientele resides, provided that the information disclosed by the lawyer in such publication or broadcast complies with DR 2–101(A),**

---

55. See ABA Canon 44.

"I will carefully consider, before taking a case, whether it appears that I can fully represent the client within the framework of law. If the decision is in the affirmative, then it will take extreme circumstances to cause me to decide later that I cannot so represent him." Thode, *The Ethical Standard for the Advocate*, 39 Texas L.Rev. 575, 592 (1961) (from "A Proper Oath for Advocates").

56. *ABA Opinion* 314 (1965) held that a lawyer should not disassociate himself from a cause when "it is obvious that the very act of disassociation would have the effect of violating *Canon 37*."

57. ABA Canon 44 enumerates instances in which ". . . the lawyer may be warranted in withdrawing on due notice to the client, allowing him time to employ another lawyer."

58. *See* ABA Canon 44.

MODEL CODE OF PROFESSIONAL RESPONSIBILITY   Canon 2

and is presented in a dignified manner:

(1) Name, including name of law firm and names of professional associates; addresses and telephone numbers;

(2) One or more fields of law in which the lawyer or law firm practices, a statement that practice is limited to one or more fields of law, or a statement that the lawyer or law firm specializes in a particular field of law practice, to the extent authorized under DR 2-105;

(3) Date and place of birth;

(4) Date and place of admission to the bar of state and federal courts;

(5) Schools attended, with dates of graduation, degrees and other scholastic distinctions;

(6) Public or quasi-public offices;

(7) Military service;

(8) Legal authorships;

(9) Legal teaching positions;

(10) Memberships, offices, and committee assignments, in bar associations;

(11) Membership and offices in legal fraternities and legal societies;

(12) Technical and professional licenses;

(13) Memberships in scientific, technical and professional associations and societies;

(14) Foreign language ability;

(15) Names and addresses of bank references;

(16) With their written consent, names of clients regularly represented;

(17) Prepaid or group legal services programs in which the lawyer participates;

(18) Whether credit cards or other credit arrangements are accepted;

(19) Office and telephone answering service hours;

(20) Fee for an initial consultation;

(21) Availability upon request of a written schedule of fees and/or an estimate of the fee to be charged for specific services;

(22) Contingent fee rates subject to DR 2-106(C), provided that the statement discloses whether percentages are computed before or after deduction of costs;

(23) Range of fees for services, provided that the statement discloses that the specific fee within the range which will be charged will vary depending upon the particular matter to be handled for each client and the client is entitled without obligation to an estimate of the fee within the range likely to be charged, in print size equivalent to the largest print used in setting forth the fee information;

(24) Hourly rate, provided that the statement discloses that the total fee charged will depend upon the number of hours which must be devoted to the particular matter to be handled for each client and the client is entitled to without obligation an estimate of the fee likely to be charged, in print size at least equivalent to the largest print used in setting forth the fee information;

(25) Fixed fees for specific legal services,* the description of which

---

* The agency having jurisdiction under state law may desire to issue appropriate guidelines defining "specific legal services."

would not be misunderstood or be deceptive, provided that the statement discloses that the quoted fee will be available only to clients whose matters fall into the services described and that the client is entitled without obligation to a specific estimate of the fee likely to be charged in print size at least equivalent to the largest print used in setting forth the fee information.

(C) Any person desiring to expand the information authorized for disclosure in DR 2–101(B), or to provide for its dissemination through other forums may apply to [the agency having jurisdiction under state law]. Any such application shall be served upon [the agencies having jurisdiction under state law over the regulation of the legal profession and consumer matters] who shall be heard, together with the applicant, on the issue of whether the proposal is necessary in light of the existing provisions of the Code, accords with standards of accuracy, reliability and truthfulness, and would facilitate the process of informed selection of lawyers by potential consumers of legal services. The relief granted in response to any such application shall be promulgated as an amendment to DR 2–101(B), universally applicable to all lawyers.**

(D) If the advertisement is communicated to the public over television or radio, it shall be prerecorded, approved for broadcast by the lawyer, and a recording of the actual transmission shall be retained by the lawyer.

(E) If a lawyer advertises a fee for a service, the lawyer must render that service for no more than the fee advertised.

(F) Unless otherwise specified in the advertisement if a lawyer publishes any fee information authorized under DR 2–101(B) in a publication that is published more frequently than one time per month, the lawyer shall be bound by any representation made therein for a period of not less than 30 days after such publication. If a lawyer publishes any fee information authorized under DR 2–101(B) in a publication that is published once a month or less frequently, he shall be bound by any representation made therein until the publication of the succeeding issue. If a lawyer publishes any fee information authorized under DR 2–101(B) in a publication which has no fixed date for publication of a succeeding issue, the lawyer shall be bound by any representation made therein for a reasonable period of time after publication but in no event less than one year.

(G) Unless otherwise specified, if a lawyer broadcasts any fee information authorized under DR 2–101(B), the lawyer shall be bound by any representation made therein for a period of not less than 30 days after such broadcast.

(H) This rule does not prohibit limited and dignified identification of a lawyer as a lawyer as well as by name:

(1) In political advertisements when his professional status is germane to the political campaign or to a political issue.

(2) In public notices when the name and profession of a lawyer are required or authorized by law or are reasonably pertinent for a purpose other than the attraction of potential clients.

(3) In routine reports and announcements of a bona fide

** The agency having jurisdiction under state law should establish orderly and expeditious procedures for ruling on such applications.

MODEL CODE OF PROFESSIONAL RESPONSIBILITY Canon 2

business, civic, professional, or political organization in which he serves as a director or officer.

(4) In and on legal documents prepared by him.

(5) In and on legal textbooks, treatises, and other legal publications, and in dignified advertisements thereof.

(I) A lawyer shall not compensate or give any thing of value to representatives of the press, radio, television, or other communication medium in anticipation of or in return for professional publicity in a news item.

DR 2-102 Professional Notices, Letterheads and Offices.

(A) A lawyer or law firm shall not use or participate in the use of professional cards, professional announcement cards, office signs, letterheads, or similar professional notices or devices, except that the following may be used if they are in dignified form:

(1) A professional card of a lawyer identifying him by name and as a lawyer, and giving his addresses, telephone numbers, the name of his law firm, and any information permitted under DR 2-105. A professional card of a law firm may also give the names of members and associates. Such cards may be used for identification.

(2) A brief professional announcement card stating new or changed associations or addresses, change of firm name, or similar matters pertaining to the professional offices of a lawyer or law firm, which may be mailed to lawyers, clients, former clients, personal friends, and relatives.[59] It shall not state biographical data except to the extent reasonably necessary to identify the lawyer or to explain the change in his association, but it may state the immediate past position of the lawyer.[60] It may give the names and dates of predecessor firms in a continuing line of succession. It shall not state the nature of the practice except as permitted under DR 2-105.[61]

(3) A sign on or near the door of the office and in the building directory identifying the law office. The sign shall not state the nature of the practice, except as permitted under DR 2-105.

(4) A letter head of a lawyer identifying him by name and as a lawyer, and giving his addresses, telephone numbers, the name of his law firm, associates and any information permitted under DR 2-105. A letterhead of a law firm may also give the names of members and associates,[62] and names and dates relating to deceased and retired members.[63] A lawyer may be designated "Of Counsel" on a letterhead if he has a continuing relationship with a lawyer or law firm, other than as a partner or associate. A lawyer or law firm may be

---

59. See *ABA Opinion* 301 (1961).

60. "[I]t has become commonplace for many lawyers to participate in government service; to deny them the right, upon their return to private practice, to refer to their prior employment in a brief and dignified manner, would place an undue limitation upon a large element of our profession. It is entirely proper for a member of the profession to explain his absence from private practice, where such is the primary purpose of the announcement, by a brief and dignified reference to the prior employment.

". . . [A]ny such announcement should be limited to the immediate past connection of the lawyer with the government, made upon his leaving that position to enter private practice." *ABA Opinion* 301 (1961).

61. See *ABA Opinion* 251 (1943).

62. "Those lawyers who are working for an individual lawyer or a law firm may be designated on the letterhead and in other appropriate places as 'associates'." *ABA Opinion* 310 (1963).

63. See ABA Canon 33.

designated as "General Counsel" or by similar professional reference on stationary of a client if he or the firm devotes a substantial amount of professional time in the representation of that client.[64] The letterhead of a law firm may give the names and dates of predecessor firms in a continuing line of succession.

(B) A lawyer in private practice shall not practice under a trade name, a name that is misleading as to the identity of the lawyer or lawyers practicing under such name, or a firm name containing names other than those of one or more of the lawyers in the firm, except that the name of a professional corporation or professional association may contain "P.C." or "P.A." or similar symbols indicating the nature of the organization, and if otherwise lawful a firm may use as, or continue to include in, its name the name or names of one or more deceased or retired members of the firm or of a predecessor firm in a continuing line of succession.[65] A lawyer who assumes a judicial, legislative, or public executive or administrative post or office shall not permit his name to remain in the name of a law firm or to be used in professional notices of the firm during any significant period in which he is not actively and regularly practicing law as a member of the firm,[66] and during such period other members of the firm shall not use his name in the firm name or in professional notices of the firm.[67]

(C) A lawyer shall not hold himself out as having a partnership with one or more other lawyers or professional corporations unless they are in fact partners.[68]

(D) A partnership shall not be formed or continued between or among lawyers licensed in different jurisdictions unless all enumerations of the members and associates of the firm on its letterhead and in other permissible listings make clear the jurisdictional limitations on those members and associates of the firm not licensed to practice in all listed jurisdictions;[69] however, the same firm name may be used in each jurisdiction.

(E) Nothing contained herein shall prohibit a lawyer from using or permitting the use of, in connection with his name, an earned degree or title derived therefrom indicating his training in the law.

DR 2–103 Recommendation of Professional Employment.[70]

(A) A lawyer shall not, except as authorized in DR 2–101(B), recommend employment as a private practitioner,[71] of himself, his partner, or associate to a layperson who has not sought his

---

64. But see *ABA Opinion* 285 (1951).

65. See ABA Canon 33; cf. *ABA Opinions* 318 (1967), 267 (1945), 219 (1941), 208 (1940), 192 (1939), 97 (1933), and 6 (1925).

66. *ABA Opinion* 318 (1967) held, "anything to the contrary in Formal Opinion 315 or in the other opinions cited notwithstanding that: "Where a partner whose name appears in the name of a law firm is elected or appointed to high local, state or federal office, which office he intends to occupy only temporarily, at the end of which time he intends to return to his position with the firm, and provided that he is not precluded by holding such office from engaging in the practice of law and does not in fact sever his relationship with the firm but only takes a leave of absence, and provided that there is no local law, statute or custom to the contrary, his name may be retained in the firm name during his term or terms of office, but only if proper precautions are taken not to mislead the public as to his degree of participation in the firm's affairs."

Cf. *ABA Opinion* 143 (1935). New York County Opinion 67, and New York City Opinions 36 and 798; but cf. *ABA Opinion* 192 (1939) and Michigan Opinion 164.

67. Cf. ABA Canon 33.

68. See *ABA Opinion* 277 (1948); cf. ABA Canon 33 and *ABA Opinions* 318 (1967), 126 (1935), 115 (1934), and 106 (1934).

69. See *ABA Opinions* 318 (1967) and 316 (1967); cf. ABA Canon 33.

70. Cf. ABA Canon 28.

71. "We think it clear that a lawyer's seeking employment in an ordinary law office, or appointment to a civil service position, is not prohibited by . . . [Canon 27]." *ABA Opinion* 197 (1939).

advice regarding employment of a lawyer.[72]

(B) A lawyer shall not compensate or give anything of value to a person or organization to recommend or secure his employment[73] by a client, or as a reward for having made a recommendation resulting in his employment[74] by a client, except that he may pay the usual and reasonable fees or dues charged by any of the organizations listed in DR 2-103(D).

(C) A lawyer shall not request a person or organization to recommend or promote the use of his services or those of his partner or associate, or any other lawyer affiliated with him or his firm, as a private practitioner,[75] except as authorized in DR 2-101, and except that

(1) He may request referrals from a lawyer referral service operated, sponsored, or approved by a bar association and may pay its fees incident thereto.[76]

(2) He may cooperate with the legal service activities of any of the offices or organizations enumerated in DR 2-103(D)(1) through (4) and may perform legal services for those to whom he was recommended by it to do such work if:

(a) The person to whom the recommendation is made is a member or beneficiary of such office or organization; and

(b) The lawyer remains free to exercise his independent professional judgment on behalf of his client.

(D) A lawyer or his partner or associate or any other lawyer affiliated with him or his firm may be recommended, employed or paid by, or may cooperate with, one of the following offices or organizations that promote the use of his services or those of his partner or associate or any other lawyer affiliated with him or his firm if there is no interference with the exercise of independent professional judgment in behalf of his client:

(1) A legal aid office or public defender office:

(a) Operated or sponsored by a duly accredited law school.

(b) Operated or sponsored by a bona fide nonprofit community organization.

(c) Operated or sponsored by a governmental agency.

(d) Operated, sponsored, or approved by a bar association.[77]

(2) A military legal assistance office.

(3) A lawyer referral service operated, sponsored, or approved by a bar association.

---

72. "[A] lawyer may not seek from persons not his clients the opportunity to perform . . . a [legal] checkup." *ABA Opinion* 307 (1962).

73. Cf. *ABA Opinion* 78 (1932).

74. " 'No financial connection of any kind between the Brotherhood and any lawyer is permissible. No lawyer can properly pay any amount whatsoever to the Brotherhood or any of its departments, officers or members as compensation, reimbursement of expenses or gratuity in connection with the procurement of a case.' " In re Brotherhood of R.R. Trainmen, 13 Ill.2d 391, 398, 150 N.E.2d 163, 167 (1958), quoted in In re Ratner, 194 Kan. 362, 372, 399 P.2d 865, 873 (1956).

See *ABA Opinion* 147 (1935).

75. "This Court has condemned the practice of ambulance chasing through the media of runners and touters. In similar fashion we have with equal emphasis condemned the practice of direct solicitation by a lawyer. We have classified both offenses as serious breaches of the Canons of Ethics demanding severe treatment of the offending lawyer." State v. Dawson, 111 So.2d 427, 431 (Fla.1959).

76. "Registrants [of a lawyer referral plan] may be required to contribute to the expense of operating it by a reasonable registration charge or by a reasonable percentage of fees collected by them." *ABA Opinion* 291 (1956).

Cf. *ABA Opinion* 227 (1941).

77. Cf. *ABA Opinion* 148 (1935).

(4) Any bona fide organization that recommends, furnishes or pays for legal services to its members or beneficiaries [78] provided the following conditions are satisfied:

    (a) Such organization, including any affiliate, is so organized and operated that no profit is derived by it from the rendition of legal services by lawyers, and that, if the organization is organized for profit, the legal services are not rendered by lawyers employed, directed, supervised or selected by it except in connection with matters where such organization bears ultimate liability of its member or beneficiary.

    (b) Neither the lawyer, nor his partner, nor associate, nor any other lawyer affiliated with him or his firm, nor any non-lawyer, shall have initiated or promoted such organization for the primary purpose of providing financial or other benefit to such lawyer, partner, associate or affiliated lawyer.

    (c) Such organization is not operated for the purpose of procuring legal work or financial benefit for any lawyer as a private practitioner outside of the legal services program of the organization.

    (d) The member or beneficiary to whom the legal services are furnished, and not such organization, is recognized as the client of the lawyer in the matter.

    (e) Any member or beneficiary who is entitled to have legal services furnished or paid for by the organization may, if such member or beneficiary so desires, select counsel other than that furnished, selected or approved by the organization for the particular matter involved; and the legal service plan of such organization provides appropriate relief for any member or beneficiary who asserts a claim that representation by counsel furnished, selected or approved would be unethical, improper or inadequate under the circumstances of the matter involved and the plan provides an appropriate procedure for seeking such relief.

    (f) The lawyer does not know or have cause to know that such organization is in violation of applicable laws, rules of court and other legal requirements that govern its legal service operations.

    (g) Such organization has filed with the appropriate disciplinary authority at least annually a report with respect to its legal service plan, if any, showing its terms, its schedule of benefits, its subscription charges, agreements with counsel, and financial results of its legal service ac-

---

78. United Mine Workers v. Ill. State Bar Ass'n., 389 U.S. 217, 19 L.Ed.2d 426, 88 S.Ct. 353 (1967); Brotherhood of R.R. Trainmen v. Virginia, 371 U.S. 1, 12 L.Ed.2d 89, 84 S.Ct. 1113 (1964); NAACP v. Button, 371 U.S. 415, 9 L.Ed.2d 405, 83 S.Ct. 328 (1963).

tivities or, if it has failed to do so, the lawyer does not know or have cause to know of such failure.

(E) A lawyer shall not accept employment when he knows or it is obvious that the person who seeks his services does so as a result of conduct prohibited under this Disciplinary Rule.

DR 2-104 Suggestion of Need of Legal Services.[79, 80]

(A) A lawyer who has given in-person unsolicited advice to a layperson that he should obtain counsel or take legal action shall not accept employment resulting from that advice,[81] except that:

 (1) A lawyer may accept employment by a close friend, relative, former client (if the advice is germane to the former employment), or one whom the lawyer reasonably believes to be a client.[82]

 (2) A lawyer may accept employment that results from his participation in activities designed to educate laypersons to recognize legal problems, to make intelligent selection of counsel, or to utilize available legal services if such activities are conducted or sponsored by a qualified legal assistance organization.

 (3) A lawyer who is recommended, furnished or paid by a qualified legal assistance organization enumerated in DR 2-103(D)(1) through (4) may represent a member or beneficiary thereof, to the extent and under the conditions prescribed therein.

 (4) Without affecting his right to accept employment, a lawyer may speak publicly or write for publication on legal topics[83] so long as he does not emphasize his own professional experience or reputation and does not undertake to give individual advice.

 (5) If success in asserting rights or defenses of his client in litigation in the nature of a class action is dependent upon the joinder of others, a lawyer may accept, but shall not seek, employment from those contacted for the purpose of obtaining their joinder.[84]

DR 2-105 Limitation of Practice.[85]

(A) A lawyer shall not hold himself out publicly as a specialist, as practicing in certain areas of law or as limiting

---

79. "If a bar association has embarked on a program of institutional advertising for an annual legal check-up and provides brochures and reprints, it is not improper to have these available in the lawyer's office for persons to read and take." *ABA Opinion* 307 (1962).

Cf. *ABA Opinion* 121 (1934).

80. ABA Canon 28.

81. Cf. *ABA Opinions* 229 (1941) and 173 (1937).

82. "It certainly is not improper for a lawyer to advise his regular clients of new statutes, court decisions, and administrative rulings, which may affect the client's interests, provided the communication is strictly limited to such information. . . ."

"When such communications go to concerns or individuals other than regular clients of the lawyer, they are thinly disguised advertisements for professional employment, and are obviously improper." *ABA Opinion* 213 (1941).

"It is our opinion that where the lawyer has no reason to believe that he has been supplanted by another lawyer, it is not only his right, but it might even be his duty to advise his client of any change of fact or law which might defeat the client's testamentary purpose as expressed in the will.

"Periodic notices might be sent to the client for whom a lawyer has drawn a will, suggesting that it might be wise for the client to reexamine his will to determine whether or not there has been any change in his situation requiring a modification of his will." *ABA Opinion* 210 (1941).

Cf. ABA Canon 28.

83. Cf. *ABA Opinion* 168 (1937).

84. But cf. *ABA Opinion* 111 (1934).

85. See ABA Canon 45; cf. ABA Canons 43, and 46.

Canon 2

his practice permitted under DR 2–101(B), except as follows:

(1) A lawyer admitted to practice before the United States Patent and Trademark Office may use the designation "Patents," "Patent Attorney," "Patent Lawyer," or "Registered Patent Attorney" or any combination of those terms, on his letterhead and office sign.

(2) A lawyer who publicly discloses fields of law in which the lawyer or the law firm practices or states that his practice is limited to one or more fields of law shall do so by using designations and definitions authorized and approved by [the agency having jurisdiction of the subject under state law].

(3) A lawyer who is certified as a specialist in a particular field of law or law practice by [the authority having jurisdiction under state law over the subject of specialization by lawyers] may hold himself out as such, but only in accordance with the rules prescribed by that authority.[86]

DR 2–106 Fees for Legal Services.[87]

(A) A lawyer shall not enter into an agreement for, charge, or collect an illegal or clearly excessive fee.[88]

(B) A fee is clearly excessive when, after a review of the facts, a lawyer of ordinary prudence would be left with a definite and firm conviction that the fee is in excess of a reasonable fee. Factors to be considered as guides in determining the reasonableness of a fee include the following:

(1) The time and labor required, the novelty and difficulty of the questions involved, and the skill requisite to perform the legal service properly.

(2) The likelihood, if apparent to the client, that the acceptance of the particular employment will preclude other employment by the lawyer.

(3) The fee customarily charged in the locality for similar legal services.

(4) The amount involved and the results obtained.

(5) The time limitations imposed by the client or by the circumstances.

(6) The nature and length of the professional relationship with the client.

(7) The experience, reputation, and ability of the lawyer or lawyers performing the services.

(8) Whether the fee is fixed or contingent.[89]

(C) A lawyer shall not enter into an arrangement for, charge, or collect a contingent fee for representing a defendant in a criminal case.[90]

---

86. This provision is included to conform to action taken by the ABA House of Delegates at the Mid-Winter Meeting, January, 1969.

87. See ABA Canon 12.

88. The charging of a "clearly excessive fee" is a ground for discipline. State ex rel. Nebraska State Bar Ass'n. v. Richards, 165 Neb. 80, 90, 84 N.W.2d 136, 143 (1957).

"An attorney has the right to contract for any fee he chooses so long as it is not excessive (see Opinion 190), and this Committee is not concerned with the amount of such fees unless so excessive as to constitute a misappropriation of the client's funds (see Opinion 27)." *ABA Opinion* 320 (1968).

Cf. *ABA Opinions* 209 (1940), 190 (1939), and 27 (1930) and State ex rel. Lee v. Buchanan, 191 So.2d 33 (Fla. 1966).

89. Cf. ABA Canon 13; see generally MacKinnon, Contingent Fees for Legal Services (1964) (A Report of the American Bar Foundation).

90. "Contingent fees, whether in civil or criminal cases, are a special concern of the law.. . . . .

"In criminal cases, the rule is stricter because of the danger of corrupting justice. The second part of Section 542 of the Restatement [of Contracts] reads: 'A bargain

DR 2-107 Division of Fees Among Lawyers

(A) A lawyer shall not divide a fee for legal services with another lawyer who is not a partner in or associate of his law firm or law office, unless:

  (1) The client consents to employment of the other lawyer after a full disclosure that a division of fees will be made.

  (2) The division is made in proportion to the services performed and responsibility assumed by each.[91]

  (3) The total fee of the lawyers does not clearly exceed reasonable compensation for all legal services they rendered the client.[92]

(B) This Disciplinary Rule does not prohibit payment to a former partner or associate pursuant to a separation or retirement agreement.

DR 2-108 Agreements Restricting the Practice of a Lawyer.

(A) A lawyer shall not be a party to or participate in a partnership or employment agreement with another lawyer that restricts the right of a lawyer to practice law after the termination of a relationship created by the agreement, except as a condition to payment of retirement benefits.[93]

(B) In connection with the settlement of a controversy or suit, a lawyer shall not enter into an agreement that restricts his right to practice law.

DR 2-109 Acceptance of Employment.

(A) A lawyer shall not accept employment on behalf of a person if he knows or it is obvious that such person wishes to:

  (1) Bring a legal action, conduct a defense, or assert a position in litigation, or otherwise have steps taken for him, merely for the purpose of harassing or maliciously injuring any person.[94]

  (2) Present a claim or defense in litigation that is not warranted under existing law, unless it can be supported by good faith argument for an extension, modification, or reversal of existing law.

DR 2-110 Withdrawal from Employment.[95]

(A) In general.

  (1) If permission for withdrawal from employment is required by

---

to conduct a criminal case . . . in consideration of a promise of a fee contingent on success is illegal. . . .'" Peyton v. Margiotti, 398 Pa. 86, 156 A.2d 865, 967 (1959).

"The third area of practice in which the use of the contingent fee is generally considered to be prohibited is the prosecution and defense of criminal cases. However, there are so few cases, and these are predominantly old, that it is doubtful that there can be said to be any current law on the subject. . . . In the absence of cases on the validity of contingent fees for defense attorneys, it is necessary to rely on the consensus among commentators that such a fee is void as against public policy. The nature of criminal practice itself makes unlikely the use of contingent fee contracts." MacKinnon, Contingent Fees for Legal Services 52 (1964) (A Report of the American Bar Foundation).

91. See ABA Canon 34 and *ABA Opinions* 316 (1967) and 294 (1958); see generally *ABA Opinions* 265 (1945), 204 (1940), 190 (1939), 171 (1937), 153 (1936), 97 (1933), 63 (1932), 28 (1930), 27 (1930), and 18 (1930).

92. "*Canon 12* contemplates that a lawyer's fee should not exceed *the value of the services* rendered. . . .

"*Canon 12* applies, whether joint or separate fees are charged [by associate attorneys] . . . ." *ABA Opinion* 204 (1940).

93. "[A] general covenant restricting an employed lawyer, after leaving the employment, from practicing in the community for a stated period, appears to this Committee to be an unwarranted restriction on the right of a lawyer to choose where he will practice and inconsistent with our professional status. Accordingly, the Committee is of the opinion it would be improper for the employing lawyer to require the covenant and likewise for the employed lawyer to agree to it." *ABA Opinion* 300 (1961).

94. See ABA Canon 30.

"*Rule 13*. . . . A member of the State Bar shall not accept employment to prosecute or defend a case solely out of spite, or solely for the purpose of harassing or delaying another. . . ." Cal.Business and Professions Code § 6067 (West 1962).

95. Cf. ABA Canon 44.

the rules of a tribunal, a lawyer shall not withdraw from employment in a proceeding before that tribunal without its permission.

(2) In any event, a lawyer shall not withdraw from employment until he has taken reasonable steps to avoid foreseeable prejudice to the rights of his client, including giving due notice to his client, allowing time for employment of other counsel, delivering to the client all papers and property to which the client is entitled, and complying with applicable laws and rules.

(3) A lawyer who withdraws from employment shall refund promptly any part of a fee paid in advance that has not been earned.

(B) Mandatory Withdrawal.

A lawyer representing a client before a tribunal, with its permission if required by its rules, shall withdraw from employment, and a lawyer representing a client in other matters shall withdraw from employment, if:

(1) He knows or it is obvious that his client is bringing the legal action, conducting the defense, or asserting a position in the litigation, or is otherwise having steps taken for him, merely for the purpose of harassing or maliciously injuring any person.

(2) He knows or it is obvious that his continued employment will result in violation of a Disciplinary Rule.[96]

(3) His mental or physical condition renders it unreasonably difficult for him to carry out the employment effectively.

(4) He is discharged by his client.

(C) Permissive withdrawal.[97]

If DR 2–110(B) is not applicable, a lawyer may not request permission to withdraw in matters pending before a tribunal, and may not withdraw in other matters, unless such request or such withdrawal is because:

(1) His client:

(a) Insists upon presenting a claim or defense that is not warranted under existing law and cannot be supported by good faith argument for an extension, modification, or reversal of existing law.[98]

(b) Personally seeks to pursue an illegal course of conduct.

(c) Insists that the lawyer pursue a course of conduct that is illegal or that is prohibited under the Disciplinary Rules.

(d) By other conduct renders it unreasonably difficult for the lawyer to carry out his employment effectively.

(e) Insists, in a matter not pending before a tribunal, that the lawyer engage in conduct that is contrary to the judgment and advice of the lawyer but not prohibited under the Disciplinary Rules.

(f) Deliberately disregards an agreement or obligation to the lawyer as to expenses or fees.

---

96. See also Code of Professional Responsibility, DR 5–102 and DR 5–105.
97. Cf. ABA Canon 4.
98. Cf. Anders v. California, 386 U.S. 738, 18 L.Ed.2d 493, 87 S.Ct. 1396 (1967), rehearing denied, 388 U.S. 924, 18 L.Ed.2d 1377, 87 S.Ct. 2094 (1967).

(2) His continued employment is likely to result in a violation of a Disciplinary Rule.

(3) His inability to work with co-counsel indicates that the best interests of the client likely will be served by withdrawal.

(4) His mental or physical condition renders it difficult for him to carry out the employment effectively.

(5) His client knowingly and freely assents to termination of his employment.

(6) He believes in good faith, in a proceeding pending before a tribunal, that the tribunal will find the existence of other good cause for withdrawal.

CANON 3

A Lawyer Should Assist in Preventing the Unauthorized Practice of Law

Ethical Considerations

EC 3-1 The prohibition against the practice of law by a layman is grounded in the need of the public for integrity and competence of those who undertake to render legal services. Because of the fiduciary and personal character of the lawyer-client relationship and the inherently complex nature of our legal system, the public can better be assured of the requisite responsibility and competence if the practice of law is confined to those who are subject to the requirements and regulations imposed upon members of the legal profession.

EC 3-2 The sensitive variations in the considerations that bear on legal determinations often make it difficult even for a lawyer to exercise appropriate professional judgment, and it is therefore essential that the personal nature of the relationship of client and lawyer be preserved. Competent professional judgment is the product of a trained familiarity with law and legal processes, a disciplined, analytical approach to legal problems, and a firm ethical commitment.

EC 3-3 A non-lawyer who undertakes to handle legal matters is not governed as to integrity or legal competence by the same rules that govern the conduct of a lawyer. A lawyer is not only subject to that regulation but also is committed to high standards of ethical conduct. The public interest is best served in legal matters by a regulated profession committed to such standards.[1] The Disciplinary Rules protect the public in that they prohibit a lawyer from seeking employment by improper overtures, from acting in cases of divided loyalties, and from submitting to the control of others in the exercise of his judgment. Moreover, a person who entrusts legal matters to a lawyer is protected by the attorney-client privilege and by the duty of the lawyer to hold inviolate the confidences and secrets of his client.

EC 3-4 A layman who seeks legal services often is not in a position to judge whether he will receive proper professional attention. The entrustment of a legal matter may well involve the confidences, the reputation, the property, the freedom, or even the life of the client. Proper protection of members of the public demands that no person be permitted to act in the confidential and demanding capacity of a lawyer unless he is subject to the regulations of the legal profession.

EC 3-5 It is neither necessary nor desirable to attempt the formulation of a single, specific definition of what constitutes the practice of law.[2] Functionally, the practice of law relates to the rendition of services for others that call for the professional judg-

---

1. "The condemnation of the unauthorized practice of law is designed to protect the public from legal services by persons unskilled in the law. The prohibition of lay intermediaries is intended to insure the loyalty of the lawyer to the client unimpaired by intervening and possibly conflicting interests." Cheatham, *Availability of Legal Services: The Responsibility of the Individual Lawyer and of the Organized Bar*, 12 U.C.L.A.L.Rev. 438, 439 (1965).

2. "What constitutes unauthorized practice of the law in a particular jurisdiction is a matter for determination by the courts of that jurisdiction." *ABA Opinion* 198 (1939).

ment of a lawyer. The essence of the professional judgment of the lawyer is his educated ability to relate the general body and philosophy of law to a specific legal problem of a client; and thus, the public interest will be better served if only lawyers are permitted to act in matters involving professional judgment. Where this professional judgment is not involved, non-lawyers, such as court clerks, police officers, abstracters, and many governmental employees, may engage in occupations that require a special knowledge of law in certain areas. But the services of a lawyer are essential in the public interest whenever the exercise of professional legal judgment is required.

EC 3–6 A lawyer often delegates tasks to clerks, secretaries, and other lay persons. Such delegation is proper if the lawyer maintains a direct relationship with his client, supervises the delegated work, and has complete professional responsibility for the work product.[3] This delegation enables a lawyer to render legal service more economically and efficiently.

EC 3–7 The prohibition against a non-lawyer practicing law does not prevent a layman from representing himself, for then he is ordinarily exposing only himself to possible injury. The purpose of the legal profession is to make educated legal representation available to the public; but anyone who does not wish to avail himself of such representation is not required to do so. Even so, the legal profession should help members of the public to recognize legal problems and to understand why it may be unwise for them to act for themselves in matters having legal consequences.

EC 3–8 Since a lawyer should not aid or encourage a layman to practice law, he should not practice law in association with a layman or otherwise share legal fees with a layman.[4] This does not mean, however, that the pecuniary value of the interest of a deceased lawyer in his firm or practice may not be paid to his estate or specified persons such as his widow or heirs.[5] In like manner, profit-sharing retirement plans of a lawyer or law firm which include non-lawyer office

---

"In the light of the historical development of the lawyer's functions, it is impossible to lay down an exhaustive definition of 'the practice of law' by attempting to enumerate every conceivable act performed by lawyers in the normal course of their work." State Bar of Arizona v. Arizona Land Title & Trust Co., 90 Ariz. 76, 87, 366 P.2d 1, 8–9 (1961), modified, 91 Ariz. 293, 371 P.2d 1020 (1962).

3. "A lawyer can employ lay secretaries, lay investigators, lay detectives, lay researchers, accountants, lay scriveners, nonlawyer draftsmen or nonlawyer researchers. In fact, he may employ nonlawyers to do any task for him except counsel clients about law matters, engage directly in the practice of law, appear in court or appear in formal proceedings a part of the judicial process, so long as it is he who takes the work and vouches for it to the client and becomes responsible to the client." ABA Opinion 316 (1967).

ABA Opinion 316 (1967) also stated that if a lawyer practices law as part of a law firm which includes lawyers from several states, he may delegate tasks to firm members in other states so long as he "is the person who, on behalf of the firm, vouched for the work of all of the others and, with the client and in the courts, did the legal acts defined by that state as the practice of law."

"A lawyer cannot delegate his professional responsibility to a law student employed in his office. He may avail himself of the assistance of the student in many of the fields of the lawyer's work, such as examination of case law, finding and interviewing witnesses, making collections of claims, examining court records, delivering papers, conveying important messages, and other similar matters. But the student is not permitted, until he is admitted to the Bar, to perform the professional functions of a lawyer, such as conducting court trials, giving professional advice to clients or drawing legal documents for them. The student in all his work must act as agent for the lawyer employing him, who must supervise his work and be responsible for his good conduct." ABA Opinion 85 (1932).

4. "No division of fees for legal services is proper, except with another lawyer . . . ." ABA Canon 34. Otherwise, according to ABA Opinion 316 (1967), "[t]he Canons of Ethics do not examine into the method by which such persons are remunerated by the lawyer. . . . They may be paid a salary, a per diem charge, a flat fee, a contract price, etc."

See ABA Canons 33 and 47.

5. "Many partnership agreements provide that the active partners, on the death of any one of them, are to make payments to the estate or to the nominee of a deceased partner on a pre-determined formula. It is only where the effect of such an arrangement is to make the estate or nominee a member of the partnership along with the surviving partners that it is prohibited by Canon 34. Where the payments are made in accordance with a pre-existing agreement entered into by the deceased partner during his lifetime and providing for a fixed method for determining their amount based upon the value of services rendered during the partner's lifetime and providing for a fixed period over which the payments are to be made, this is not the case. Under these circumstances, whether the payments are considered to be delayed payment of compensation earned but withheld during the partner's lifetime, or whether they are considered to be

employees are not improper.[6] These limited exceptions to the rule against sharing legal fees with laymen are permissible since they do not aid or encourage laymen to practice law.

EC 3-9 Regulation of the practice of law is accomplished principally by the respective states.[7] Authority to engage in the practice of law conferred in any jurisdiction is not per se a grant of the right to practice elsewhere, and it is improper for a lawyer to engage in practice where he is not permitted by law or by court order to do so. However, the demands of business and the mobility of our society pose distinct problems in the regulation of the practice of law by the states.[8] In furtherance of the public interest, the legal profession should discourage regulation that unreasonably imposes territorial limitations upon the right of a lawyer to handle the legal affairs of his client or upon the opportunity of a client to obtain the services of a lawyer of his choice in all matters including the presentation of a contested matter in a tribunal before which the lawyer is not permanently admitted to practice.[9]

DISCIPLINARY RULES

DR 3-101 Aiding Unauthorized Practice of Law.[10]

(A) A lawyer shall not aid a non-lawyer in the unauthorized practice of law.[11]

(B) A lawyer shall not practice law in a jurisdiction where to do so would be in violation of regulations of the profession in that jurisdiction.[12]

DR 3-102 Dividing Legal Fees with a Non-Lawyer.

(A) A lawyer or law firm shall not share legal fees with a non-lawyer,[13] except that:

(1) An agreement by a lawyer with his firm, partner, or associate may provide for the payment of money, over a reasonable period of time after his death, to his estate or to one or more specified persons.[14]

(2) A lawyer who undertakes to complete unfinished legal business of a deceased lawyer may pay to the estate of the deceased

---

an approximation of his interest in matters pending at the time of his death, is immaterial. In either event, as Henry S. Drinker says in his book, Legal Ethics, at page 189: 'It would seem, however, that a reasonable agreement to pay the estate a proportion of the receipts for a reasonable period is a proper practical settlement for the lawyer's services to his retirement or death.'" *ABA Opinion* 308 (1963).

6. Cf. ABA Opinion 311 (1964).

7. "That the States have broad power to regulate the practice of law is, of course, beyond question." United Mine Workers v. Ill. State Bar Ass'n, 389 U.S. 217, 222 (1967).

"It is a matter of law, not of ethics, as to where an individual may practice law. Each state has its own rules." *ABA Opinion* 316 (1967).

8. "Much of clients' business crosses state lines. People are mobile, moving from state to state. Many metropolitan areas cross state lines. It is common today to have a single economic and social community involving more than one state. The business of a single client may involve legal problems in several states." *ABA Opinion* 316 (1967).

9. "[W]e reaffirmed the general principle that legal services to New Jersey residents with respect to New Jersey matters may ordinarily be furnished only by New Jersey counsel; but we pointed out that there may be multistate transactions where strict adherence to this thesis would not be in the public interest and that, under the circumstances, it would have been not only more costly to the client but also 'grossly impractical and inefficient' to have had the settlement negotiations conducted by separate lawyers from different states." In re Estate of Waring, 47 N.J. 367, 376, 221 A.2d 193, 197 (1966).

Cf. ABA Opinion 316 (1967).

10. Conduct permitted by the Disciplinary Rules of Canons 2 and 5 does not violate DR 3-101.

11. See ABA Canon 47.

12. It should be noted, however, that a lawyer may engage in conduct, otherwise prohibited by this Disciplinary Rule, where such conduct is authorized by preemptive federal legislation. See Sperry v. Florida, 373 U.S. 379, 10 L.Ed.2d 428, 83 S.Ct. 1322 (1963).

13. See ABA Canon 34 and *ABA Opinions* 316 (1967), 180 (1938), and 48 (1931).

"The receiving attorney shall not under any guise or form share his fee for legal services with a lay agency, personal or corporate, without prejudice, however, to the right of the lay forwarder to charge and collect from the creditor proper compensation for non-legal services rendered by the law [sic] forwarder which are separate and apart from the services performed by the receiving attorney." *ABA Opinion* 294 (1958).

14. See *ABA Opinion* 266 (1945).

lawyer that proportion of the total compensation which fairly represents the services rendered by the deceased lawyer.

(3) A lawyer or law firm may include non-lawyer employees in a compensation or retirement plan, even though the plan is based in whole or in part on a profit-sharing arrangement [15] providing such plan does not circumvent another disciplinary rule.[16]

DR 3–103 Forming a Partnership with a Non-Lawyer.

(A) A lawyer shall not form a partnership with a non-lawyer if any of the activities of the partnership consist of the practice of law.[17]

CANON 4

A Lawyer Should Preserve the Confidences and Secrets of a Client

ETHICAL CONSIDERATIONS

EC 4–1 Both the fiduciary relationship existing between lawyer and client and the proper functioning of the legal system require the preservation by the lawyer of confidences and secrets of one who has employed or sought to employ him.[1] A client must feel free to discuss whatever he wishes with his lawyer and a lawyer must be equally free to obtain information beyond that volunteered by his client.[2] A lawyer should be fully informed of all the facts of the matter he is handling in order for his client to obtain the full advantage of our legal system. It is for the lawyer in the exercise of his independent professional judgment to separate the relevant and important from the irrelevant and unimportant. The observance of the ethical obligation of a lawyer to hold inviolate the confidences and secrets of his client not only facilitates the full development of facts essential to proper representa-

---

15. Cf. *ABA Opinion* 311 (1964).

16. See ABA Informal Opinion 1440 (1979).

17. See ABA Canon 33; cf. *ABA Opinions* 239 (1942) and 201 (1940).

ABA Opinion 316 (1967) states that lawyers licensed in different jurisdictions may, under certain conditions, enter "into an arrangement for the practice of law" and that a lawyer licensed in State A is not, for such purpose a layman in State B.

1. See ABA Canons 6 and 37 and *ABA Opinion* 287 (1953). "The reason underlying the rule with respect to confidential communications between attorney and client is well stated in Mechem on Agency, 2d Ed., Vol. 2, § 2297, as follows: 'The purposes and necessities of the relation between a client and his attorney require, in many cases, on the part of the client, the fullest and freest disclosures to the attorney of the client's objectives, motives and acts. This disclosure is made in the strictest confidence, relying upon the attorney's honor and fidelity. To permit the attorney to reveal to others what is so disclosed, would be not only a gross violation of a sacred trust upon his part, but it would utterly destroy and prevent the usefulness and benefits to be derived from professional assistance. Based upon considerations of public policy, therefore, the law wisely declares that all confidential communications and disclosures, made by a client to his legal adviser for the purpose of obtaining his professional aid or advice, shall be strictly privileged:—that the attorney shall not be permitted, without the consent of his client,—and much less will he be compelled—to reveal or disclose communications made to him under such circumstances.'" *ABA Opinion* 250 (1943).

"While it is true that complete revelation of relevant facts should be encouraged for trial purposes, nevertheless an attorney's dealings with his client, if both are sincere, and if the dealings involve more than mere technical matters, should be immune to discovery proceedings. There must be freedom from fear of revealment of matters disclosed to an attorney because of the peculiarly intimate relationship existing." Ellis-Foster Co. v. Union Carbide & Carbon Corp., 159 F.Supp. 917, 919 (D.N.J.1958).

Cf. *ABA Opinions* 314 (1965), 274 (1946) and 268 (1945).

2. "While it is the great purpose of law to ascertain the truth, there is the countervailing necessity of insuring the right of every person to freely and fully confer and confide in one having knowledge of the law, and skilled in its practice, in order that the former may have adequate advice and a proper defense. This assistance can be made safely and readily available only when the client is free from the consequences of apprehension of disclosure by reason of the subsequent statements of the skilled lawyer." Baird v. Koerner, 279 F.2d 623, 629–30 (9th Cir. 1960).

Cf. *ABA Opinion* 150 (1936).

tion of the client but also encourages laymen to seek early legal assistance.

EC 4-2 The obligation to protect confidences and secrets obviously does not preclude a lawyer from revealing information when his client consents after full disclosure,[3] when necessary to perform his professional employment, when permitted by a Disciplinary Rule, or when required by law. Unless the client otherwise directs, a lawyer may disclose the affairs of his client to partners or associates of his firm. It is a matter of common knowledge that the normal operation of a law office exposes confidential professional information to non-lawyer employees of the office, particularly secretaries and those having access to the files; and this obligates a lawyer to exercise care in selecting and training his employees so that the sanctity of all confidences and secrets of his clients may be preserved. If the obligation extends to two or more clients as to the same information, a lawyer should obtain the permission of all before revealing the information. A lawyer must always be sensitive to the rights and wishes of his client and act scrupulously in the making of decisions which may involve the disclosure of information obtained in his professional relationship.[4] Thus, in the absence of consent of his client after full disclosure, a lawyer should not associate another lawyer in the handling of a matter; nor should he, in the absence of consent, seek counsel from another lawyer if there is a reasonable possibility that the identity of the client or his confidences or secrets would be revealed to such lawyer. Both social amenities and professional duty should cause a lawyer to shun indiscreet conversations concerning his clients.

EC 4-3 Unless the client otherwise directs, it is not improper for a lawyer to give limited information from his files to an outside agency necessary for statistical, bookkeeping, accounting, data processing, banking, printing, or other legitimate purposes, provided he exercises due care in the selection of the agency and warns the agency that the information must be kept confidential.

EC 4-4 The attorney-client privilege is more limited than the ethical obligation of a lawyer to guard the confidences and secrets of his client. This ethical precept, unlike the evidentiary privilege, exists without regard to the nature or source of information or the fact that others share the knowledge. A lawyer should endeavor to act in a manner which preserves the evidentiary privilege; for example, he should avoid professional discussions in the presence of persons to whom the privilege does not extend. A lawyer owes an obligation to advise the client of the attorney-client privilege and timely to assert the privilege unless it is waived by the client.

EC 4-5 A lawyer should not use information acquired in the course of the representation of a client to the disadvantage of the client and a lawyer should not use, except with the consent of his client after full disclosure, such information for his own purposes.[5] Likewise, a lawyer should be diligent in his efforts to prevent the misuse of such information by his employees and associates.[6] Care should be exercised by a lawyer to prevent the disclosure of the confidences and secrets of one client to another,[7]

---

3. "Where . . . [a client] knowingly and after full disclosure participates in a [legal fee] financing plan which requires the furnishing of certain information to the bank, clearly by his conduct he has waived any privilege as to that information." *ABA Opinion* 320 (1968).

4. "The lawyer must decide when he takes a case whether it is a suitable one for him to undertake and after this decision is made, he is not justified in turning against his client by exposing injurious evidence entrusted to him. . . . [D]oing something intrinsically regrettable, because the only alternative involves worse consequences, is a necessity in every profession." Williston, Life and Law 271 (1940).

Cf. *ABA Opinions* 177 (1938) and 83 (1932).

5. See ABA Canon 11.

6. See ABA Canon 37.

7. See ABA Canons 6 and 37.

"[A]n attorney must not accept professional employment against a client or a former client which will, or even *may* require him to use confidential information obtained by the attorney in the course of his professional and no employment should be accepted that might require such disclosure.

EC 4–6 The obligation of a lawyer to preserve the confidences and secrets of his client continues after the termination of his employment.[8] Thus a lawyer should not attempt to sell a law practice as a going business because, among other reasons, to do so would involve the disclosure of confidences and secrets.[9] A lawyer should also provide for the protection of the confidences and secrets of his client following the termination of the practice of the lawyer, whether termination is due to death, disability, or retirement. For example, a lawyer might provide for the personal papers of the client to be returned to him and for the papers of the lawyer to be delivered to another lawyer or to be destroyed. In determining the method of disposition, the instructions and wishes of the client should be a dominant consideration.

DISCIPLINARY RULES

DR 4–101 Preservation of Confidences and Secrets of a Client.[10]

(A) "Confidence" refers to information protected by the attorney-client privilege under applicable law, and "secret" refers to other information gained in the professional relationship that the client has requested be held inviolate or the disclosure of which would be embarrassing or would be likely to be detrimental to the client.

(B) Except when permitted under DR 4–101(C), a lawyer shall not knowingly:

(1) Reveal a confidence or secret of his client.[11]

(2) Use a confidence or secret of his client to the disadvantage of the client.

(3) Use a confidence or secret of his client for the advantage of himself [12] or of a third person,[13] unless the client consents after full disclosure.

(C) A lawyer may reveal:

(1) Confidences or secrets with the consent of the client or clients affected, but only after a full disclosure to them.[14]

(2) Confidences or secrets when permitted under Disciplinary

---

relations with such client regarding the subject matter of the employment . . . ." *ABA Opinion* 165 (1936).

8. See ABA Canon 37.

"Confidential communications between an attorney and his client, made because of the relationship and concerning the subject-matter of the attorney's employment, are generally privileged from disclosure without the consent of the client, and this privilege outlasts the attorney's employment. Canon 37." *ABA Opinion* 154 (1936).

9. Cf. *ABA Opinion* 266 (1945).

10. See ABA Canon 37; cf. ABA Canon 6.

11. "§ 6068 . . . It is the duty of an attorney: . . . .

"(e) To maintain inviolate the confidence, and at every peril to himself to preserve the secrets, of his client." Cal. Business and Professions Code § 6068 (West 1962). Virtually the same provision is found in the Oregon statutes. Ore.Rev.Stat. ch. 9, § 9.460(5).

"Communications between lawyer and client are privileged (Wigmore on Evidence, 3d Ed., Vol. 8, §§ 2290–2329). The modern theory underlying the privilege is subjective and is to give the client freedom of apprehension in consulting his legal advisor (ibid., § 2290, p. 548). The privilege applies to communications made in seeking legal advice for any purpose (ibid., § 2294, p. 563). The mere circumstance that the advice is given without charge therefore does not nullify the privilege (ibid., § 2303)." *ABA Opinion* 216 (1941).

"It is the duty of an attorney to maintain the confidence and preserve inviolate the secrets of his client . . . ." *ABA Opinion* 155 (1936).

12. See ABA Canon 11.

"The provision respecting employment is in accord with the general rule announced in the adjudicated cases that a lawyer may not make use of knowledge or information acquired by him through his professional relations with his client, or in the conduct of his client's business, to his own advantage or profit (7 C.J.S., § 125, p. 958; Healy v. Gray, 184 Iowa 111, 168 N.W. 222; Baumgardner v. Hudson, D.C.App., 277 F. 552; Goodrum v. Clement, D.C. App., 277 F. 586)." *ABA Opinion* 250 (1943).

13. See *ABA Opinion* 177 (1938).

14. "[A lawyer] may not divulge confidential communications, information, and secrets imparted to him by the client or acquired during their professional relations, unless he is authorized to do so by the client (People v. Gerold, 265 Ill. 448, 107 N.E. 165, 178; Murphy v. Riggs, 238 Mich. 151, 213 N.W. 110, 112; Opinion of this Committee, No. 91)." *ABA Opinion* 202 (1940).

Cf. *ABA Opinion* 91 (1933).

Rules or required by law or court order.[15]

(3) The intention of his client to commit a crime [16] and the information necessary to prevent the crime.[17]

(4) Confidences or secrets necessary to establish or collect his fee [18] or to defend himself or his employees or associates against an accusation of wrongful conduct.[19]

(D) A lawyer shall exercise reasonable care to prevent his employees, associates, and others whose services are utilized by him from disclosing or using confidences or secrets of a client, except that a lawyer may reveal the information allowed by DR 4-101(C) through an employee.

CANON 5

A Lawyer Should Exercise Independent Professional Judgment on Behalf of a Client

ETHICAL CONSIDERATIONS

EC 5-1 The professional judgment of a lawyer should be exercised, within the

---

15. "A defendant in a criminal case when admitted to bail is not only regarded as in the custody of his bail, but he is also in the custody of the law, and admission to bail does not deprive the court of its inherent power to deal with the person of the prisoner. Being in lawful custody, the defendant is guilty of an escape when he gains his liberty before he is delivered in due process of law, and is guilty of a separate offense for which he may be punished. In failing to disclose his client's whereabouts as a fugitive under these circumstances the attorney would not only be aiding his client to escape trial on the charge for which he was indicted, but would likewise be aiding him in evading prosecution for the additional offense of escape.

"It is the opinion of the committee that under such circumstances the attorney's knowledge of his client's whereabouts is not privileged, and that he may be disciplined for failing to disclose that information to the proper authorities. . . ." *ABA Opinion* 155 (1936).

"We held in *Opinion* 155 that a communication by a client to his attorney in respect to the future commission of an unlawful act or to a continuing wrong is not privileged from disclosure. Public policy forbids that the relation of attorney and client should be used to conceal wrongdoing on the part of the client.

. . .

"When an attorney representing a defendant in a criminal case applies on his behalf for probation or suspension of sentence, he represents to the court, by implication at least, that his client will abide by the terms and conditions of the court's order. When that attorney is later advised of a violation of that order, it is his duty to advise his client of the consequences of his act, and endeavor to prevent a continuance of the wrongdoing. If his client thereafter persists in violating the terms and conditions of his probation, it is the duty of the attorney as an officer of the court to advise the proper authorities concerning his client's conduct. Such information, even though coming to the attorney from the client in the course of his professional relations with respect to other matters in which he represents the defendant, is not privileged from disclosure. . . ." *ABA Opinion* 156 (1936).

See *ABA Opinion* 155 (1936).

16. *ABA Opinion* 314 (1965) indicates that a lawyer must disclose even the confidences of his clients if "the facts in the attorney's possession indicate beyond reasonable doubt that a crime will be committed."
See *ABA Opinion* 155 (1936).

17. See ABA Canon 37 and *ABA Opinion* 202 (1940).

18. Cf. *ABA Opinion* 250 (1943).

19. See ABA Canon 37 and *ABA Opinions* 202 (1940) and 19 (1930).

"[T]he adjudicated cases recognize an exception to the rule [that a lawyer shall not reveal the confidences of his client], where disclosure is necessary to protect the attorney's interests arising out of the relation of attorney and client in which disclosure was made.

"The exception is stated in Mechem on Agency, 2d Ed., Vol. 2, § 2313, as follows: 'But the attorney may disclose information received from the client when it becomes necessary for his own protection, as if the client should bring an action against the attorney for negligence or misconduct, and it became necessary for the attorney to show what his instructions were, or what was the nature of the duty which the client expected him to perform. So if it became necessary for the attorney to bring an action against the client, the client's privilege could not prevent the attorney from disclosing what was essential as a means of obtaining or defending his own rights.'

"Mr. Jones, in his Commentaries on Evidence, 2d Ed., Vol. 5, § 2165, states the exception thus: 'It has frequently been held that the rule as to privileged communications does not apply when litigation arises between attorney and client to the extent that their communications are relevant to the issue. In such cases, if the disclosure of privileged communications becomes necessary to protect the attorney's rights, he is released from those obligations of secrecy which the law places upon him. He should not, however, disclose more than is necessary for his own protection. It would be a manifest injustice to allow the client to take advantage of the rule of exclusion as to professional confidence to the prejudice of his attorney, or that it should be carried to the extent of depriving the attorney of the means of obtaining or defending his own rights. In such cases the attorney is exempted from the obligations of secrecy.'" *ABA Opinion* 250 (1943).

bounds of the law, solely for the benefit of his client and free of compromising influences and loyalties.[1] Neither his personal interests, the interests of other clients, nor the desires of third persons should be permitted to dilute his loyalty to his client.

Interests of a Lawyer That May Affect His Judgment

EC 5–2 A lawyer should not accept proffered employment if his personal interests or desires will, or there is a reasonable probability that they will, affect adversely the advice to be given or services to be rendered the prospective client.[2] After accepting employment, a lawyer carefully should refrain from acquiring a property right or assuming a position that would tend to make his judgment less protective of the interests of his client.

EC 5–3 The self-interest of a lawyer resulting from his ownership of property in which his client also has an interest or which may affect property of his client may interfere with the exercise of free judgment on behalf of his client. If such interference would occur with respect to a prospective client, a lawyer should decline employment proffered by him. After accepting employment, a lawyer should not acquire property rights that would adversely affect his professional judgment in the representation of his client. Even if the property interests of a lawyer do not presently interfere with the exercise of his independent judgment, but the likelihood of interference can reasonably be foreseen by him, a lawyer should explain the situation to his client and should decline employment or withdraw unless the client consents to the continuance of the relationship after full disclosure. A lawyer should not seek to persuade his client to permit him to invest in an undertaking of his client nor make improper use of his professional relationship to influence his client to invest in an enterprise in which the lawyer is interested.

EC 5–4 If, in the course of his representation of a client, a lawyer is permitted to receive from his client a beneficial ownership in publication rights relating to the subject matter of the employment, he may be tempted to subordinate the interests of his client to his own anticipated pecuniary gain. For

---

1. Cf. ABA Canon 35.

"[A lawyer's] fiduciary duty is of the highest order and he must not represent interests adverse to those of the client. It is true that because of his professional responsibility and the confidence and trust which his client may legitimately repose in him, he must adhere to a high standard of honesty, integrity and good faith in dealing with his client. He is not permitted to take advantage of his position or superior knowledge to impose upon the client; nor to conceal facts or law, nor in any way deceive him without being held responsible therefor." Smoot v. Lund, 13 Utah 2d 168, 172, 369 P.2d 933, 936 (1962).

"When a client engages the services of a lawyer in a given piece of business he is entitled to feel that, until that business is finally disposed of in some manner, he has the undivided loyalty of the one upon whom he looks as his advocate and champion. If, as in this case, he is sued and his home attached by his own attorney, who is representing him in another matter, all feeling of loyalty is necessarily destroyed, and the profession is exposed to the charge that it is interested only in money." Grievance Comm. v. Rattner, 152 Conn. 59, 65, 203 A.2d 82, 84 (1964).

"One of the cardinal principles confronting every attorney in the representation of a client is the requirement of complete loyalty and service in good faith to the best of his ability. In a criminal case the client is entitled to a fair trial, but not a perfect one. These are fundamental requirements of due process under the Fourteenth Amendment. . . . The same principles are applicable in Sixth Amendment cases (not pertinent herein) and suggest that an attorney should have no conflict of interest and that he must devote his full and faithful efforts toward the defense of his client." Johns v. Smyth, 176 F.Supp. 949, 952 (E.D.Va.1959), modified, United States ex rel. Wilkins v. Banmiller, 205 F.Supp. 123, 128 n. 5 (E.D.Pa.1962), aff'd 325 F.2d 514 (3d Cir. 1963), cert. denied, 379 U.S. 847, 13 L.Ed.2d 51, 85 S.Ct. 87 (1964).

2. "Attorneys must not allow their private interests to conflict with those of their clients. . . . They owe their entire devotion to the interests of their clients." United States v. Anonymous, 215 F.Supp. 111, 113 (E.D.Tenn. 1963).

"[T]he court [below] concluded that a firm may not accept any action against a person whom they are presently representing even though there is no relationship between the two cases. In arriving at this conclusion, the court cites an opinion of the Committee on Professional Ethics of the New York County Lawyers' Association which stated in part: 'While under the circumstances . . . there may be no actual conflict of interest . . . "maintenance of public confidence in the Bar requires an attorney who has accepted representation of a client to decline, while representing such client, any employment from an adverse party in any matter even though wholly unrelated to the original retainer." See Question and Answer No. 350, N.Y. County L. Ass'n, Question and Answer No. 450 (June 21, 1956).'" Grievance Comm. v. Rattner, 152 Conn. 59, 65, 203 A.2d 82, 84 (1964).

example, a lawyer in a criminal case who obtains from his client television, radio, motion picture, newspaper, magazine, book, or other publication rights with respect to the case may be influenced, consciously or unconsciously, to a course of conduct that will enhance the value of his publication rights to the prejudice of his client. To prevent these potentially differing interests, such arrangements should be scrupulously avoided prior to the termination of all aspects of the matter giving rise to the employment, even though his employment has previously ended.

EC 5–5 A lawyer should not suggest to his client that a gift be made to himself or for his benefit. If a lawyer accepts a gift from his client, he is peculiarly susceptible to the charge that he unduly influenced or overreached the client. If a client voluntarily offers to make a gift to his lawyer, the lawyer may accept the gift, but before doing so, he should urge that his client secure disinterested advice from an independent, competent person who is cognizant of all the circumstances.[3] Other than in exceptional circumstances, a lawyer should insist that an instrument in which his client desires to name him beneficially be prepared by another lawyer selected by the client.[4]

EC 5–6 A lawyer should not consciously influence a client to name him as executor, trustee, or lawyer in an instrument. In those cases where a client wishes to name his lawyer as such, care should be taken by the lawyer to avoid even the appearance of impropriety.[5]

EC 5–7 The possibility of an adverse effect upon the exercise of free judgment by a lawyer on behalf of his client during litigation generally makes it undesirable for the lawyer to acquire a proprietary interest in the cause of his client or otherwise to become financially interested in the outcome of the litigation.[6] However, it is not improper for a lawyer to protect his right to collect a fee for his services by the assertion of legally permissible liens, even though by doing so he may acquire an interest in the outcome of litigation. Although a contingent fee arrangement[7] gives a lawyer a financial interest in the outcome of litigation, a reasonable contingent fee is permissible in civil cases because it may be the only means by which a layman can obtain the services of a lawyer of his choice. But a lawyer, because he is in a better position to evaluate a cause of action, should enter into a continent fee arrangement only in those instances where the arrangement will be beneficial to the client.

EC 5–8 A financial interest in the outcome of litigation also results if monetary advances are made by the lawyer to his client.[8] Although this assistance generally is not encouraged, there are instances when it is not improper to make loans to a client. For example, the advancing or guaranteeing of payment of the costs and expenses of litigation by a lawyer may be the only way a client can enforce his cause of action,[9] but

---

3. "Courts of equity will scrutinize with jealous vigilance transactions between parties occupying fiduciary relations toward each other. . . . A deed will not be held invalid, however, if made by the grantor with full knowledge of its nature and effect, and because of the deliberate, voluntary and intelligent desire of the grantor. . . . Where a fiduciary relation exists, the burden of proof is on the grantee or beneficiary of an instrument executed during the existence of such relationship to show the fairness of the transaction, that it was equitable and just and that it did not proceed from undue influence. . . . The same rule has application where an attorney engages in a transaction with a client during the existence of the relation and is benefited thereby. . . . Conversely, an attorney is not prohibited from dealing with his client or buying his property, and such contracts, if open, fair and honest, when deliberately made, are as valid as contracts between other parties. . . . [I]mportant factors in determining whether a transaction is fair include a showing by the fiduciary (1) that he made a full and frank disclosure of all the relevant information that he had; (2) that the consideration was adequate; and (3) that the principal had independent advice before completing the transaction." McFail v. Braden, 19 Ill.2d 108, 117–18, 166 N.E.2d 46, 52 (1960).

4. See State ex rel. Nebraska State Bar Ass'n v. Richards, 165 Neb. 80, 94–95, 84 N.W.2d 136, 146 (1957).

5. See ABA Canon 9.

6. See ABA Canon 10.

7. See Code of Professional Responsibility, EC 2–20.

8. See ABA Canon 42.

9. "*Rule 3a.* . . . A member of the State Bar shall not directly or indirectly pay or agree to pay, or represent or sanction the representation that he will pay, medical, hospital or nursing bills or other personal expenses in-

the ultimate liability for such costs and expenses must be that of the client.

EC 5–9 Occasionally a lawyer is called upon to decide in a particular case whether he will be a witness or an advocate. If a lawyer is both counsel and witness, he becomes more easily impeachable for interest and thus may be a less effective witness. Conversely, the opposing counsel may be handicapped in challenging the credibility of the lawyer when the lawyer also appears as an advocate in the case. An advocate who becomes a witness is in the unseemly and ineffective position of arguing his own credibility. The roles of an advocate and of a witness are inconsistent; the function of an advocate is to advance or argue the cause of another, while that of a witness is to state facts objectively.

EC 5–10 Problems incident to the lawyer-witness relationship arise at different stages; they relate either to whether a lawyer should accept employment or should withdraw from employment.[10] Regardless of when the problem arises, his decision is to be governed by the same basic considerations. It is not objectionable for a lawyer who is a potential witness to be an advocate if it is unlikely that he will be called as a witness because his testimony would be merely cumulative or if his testimony will relate only to an uncontested issue.[11] In the exceptional situation where it will be manifestly unfair to the client for the lawyer to refuse employment or to withdraw when he will likely be a witness on a contested issue, he may serve as advocate even though he may be a witness.[12] In making such decision, he should determine the personal or financial sacrifice of the client that may result from his refusal of employment or withdrawal therefrom, the materiality of his testimony, and the effectiveness of his representation in view of his personal involvement. In weighing these factors, it should be clear that refusal or withdrawal will impose an unreasonable hardship upon the client before the lawyer accepts or continues the employment.[13] Where the question arises, doubts should be resolved in favor of the lawyer testifying and against his becoming or continuing as an advocate.[14]

---

curred by or for a client, prospective or existing; provided this rule shall not prohibit a member:

"(1) with the consent of the client, from paying or agreeing to pay to third persons such expenses from funds collected or to be collected for the client; or

"(2) after he has been employed, from lending money to his client upon the client's promise in writing to repay such loan; or

"(3) from advancing the costs of prosecuting or defending a claim or action. Such costs within the meaning of this subparagraph (3) include all taxable costs or disbursements, costs of investigation and costs of obtaining and presenting evidence." Cal. Business and Professions Code § 6076 (West Supp.1967).

10. "When a lawyer knows, prior to trial, that he will be a necessary witness, except as to merely formal matters such as identification or custody of a document or the like, neither he nor his firm nor associates should conduct the trial. If, during the trial, he discovers that the ends of justice require his testimony, he should, from that point on, if feasible and not prejudicial to his client's case, leave further conduct of the trial to other counsel. If circumstances do not permit withdrawal from the conduct of the trial, the lawyer should not argue the credibility of his own testimony." *A Code of Trial Conduct: Promulgated by the American College of Trial Lawyers*, 43 A.B.A.J. 223, 224–25 (1957).

11. Cf. Canon 19: "When a lawyer is a witness for his client, except as to merely formal matters, such as the attestation or custody of an instrument and the like, he should leave the trial of the case to other counsel."

12. "It is the general rule that a lawyer may not testify in litigation in which he is an advocate unless circumstances arise which could not be anticipated and it is necessary to prevent a miscarriage of justice. In those rare cases where the testimony of an attorney is needed to protect his client's interests, it is not only proper but mandatory that it be forthcoming." Schwartz v. Wenger, 267 Minn. 40, 43–44, 124 N.W.2d 489, 492 (1963).

13. "The great weight of authority in this country holds that the attorney who acts as counsel and witness, in behalf of his client, in the same cause on a material matter, not of a merely formal character, and not in an emergency, but having knowledge that he would be required to be a witness in ample time to have secured other counsel and given up his service in the case, violates a highly important provision of the Code of Ethics and a rule of professional conduct, but does not commit a legal error in so testifying, as a result of which a new trial will be granted." Erwin M. Jennings Co. v. DiGenova, 107 Conn. 491, 499, 141 A. 866, 869 (1928).

14. "[C]ases may arise, and in practice often do arise, in which there would be a failure of justice should the attorney withhold his testimony. In such a case it would be a vicious professional sentiment which would deprive the client of the benefit of his attorney's testimony." Connolly v. Straw, 53 Wis. 645, 649, 11 N.W. 17, 19 (1881).

EC 5-11 A lawyer should not permit his personal interests to influence his advice relative to a suggestion by his client that additional counsel be employed.[15] In like manner, his personal interests should not deter him from suggesting that additional counsel be employed; on the contrary, he should be alert to the desirability of recommending additional counsel when, in his judgment, the proper representation of his client requires it. However, a lawyer should advise his client not to employ additional counsel suggested by the client if the lawyer believes that such employment would be a disservice to the client, and he should disclose the reasons for his belief.

EC 5-12 Inability of co-counsel to agree on a matter vital to the representation of their client requires that their disagreement be submitted by them jointly to their client for his resolution, and the decision of the client shall control the action to be taken.[16]

EC 5-13 A lawyer should not maintain membership in or be influenced by any organization of employees that undertakes to prescribe, direct, or suggest when or how he should fulfill his professional obligations to a person or organization that employs him as a lawyer. Although it is not necessarily improper for a lawyer employed by a corporation or similar entity to be a member of an organization of employees, he should be vigilant to safeguard his fidelity as a lawyer to his employer, free from outside influences.

Interests of Multiple Clients

EC 5-14 Maintaining the independence of professional judgment required of a lawyer precludes his acceptance or continuation of employment that will adversely affect his judgment on behalf of or dilute his loyalty to a client.[17] This problem arises whenever a lawyer is asked to represent two or more clients who may have differing interests, whether such interests be conflicting, inconsistent, diverse, or otherwise discordant.[18]

EC 5-15 If a lawyer is requested to undertake or to continue representation of multiple clients having potentially differing interests, he must weigh carefully the possibility that his judgment may be impaired or his loyalty divided if he accepts or continues the employment. He should resolve all doubts against the propriety of the representation. A lawyer should never represent in litigation multiple clients with differing interests;[19] and there are few situations in which he would be justified in representing in litigation multiple clients with potentially differing interests. If a lawyer accepted such employment and the interests did become actually differing, he would have to withdraw from employment with likelihood of resulting hardship on the clients; and for this reason it is preferable that he refuse the employment initially. On the other hand,

---

But see canon 19: "Except when essential to the ends of justice, a lawyer should avoid testifying in court in behalf of his client."

15. Cf. ABA Canon 7.

16. See ABA Canon 7.

17. See ABA Canon 6; cf. *ABA Opinions* 261 (1944), 242 (1942), 142 (1935), and 30 (1931).

18. The ABA Canons speak of "conflicting interests" rather than "differing interests" but make no attempt to define such other than the statement in Canon 6: "Within the meaning of this canon, a lawyer represents conflicting interests when, in behalf of one client, it is his duty to contend for that which duty to another client requires him to oppose."

19. "Canon 6 of the Canons of Professional Ethics, adopted by the American Bar Association on September 30, 1937, and by the Pennsylvania Bar Association on January 7, 1938, provides in part that 'It is unprofessional to represent conflicting interests, except by express consent of all concerned given after a full disclosure of the facts. Within the meaning of this Canon, a lawyer represents conflicting interests when, in behalf of one client, it is his duty to contend for that which duty to another client requires him to oppose.' The full disclosure required by this canon contemplates that the possibly adverse effect of the conflict be fully explained by the attorney to the client to be affected and by him thoroughly understood. . . .

"The foregoing canon applies to cases where the circumstances are such that possibly conflicting interests may permissibly be represented by the same attorney. But manifestly, there are instances where the conflicts of interest are so critically adverse as not to admit of one attorney's representing both sides. Such is the situation which this record presents. No one could conscionably contend that the same attorney may represent both the plaintiff and defendant in an adversary action. Yet, that is what is being done in this case." Jedwabny v. Philadelphia Transportation Co., 390 Pa. 231, 235, 135 A.2d 252, 254 (1957), cert. denied, 355 U.S. 966, 2 L.Ed.2d 541, 78 S.Ct. 557 (1958).

there are many instances in which a lawyer may properly serve multiple clients having potentially differing interests in matters not involving litigation. If the interests vary only slightly, it is generally likely that the lawyer will not be subjected to an adverse influence and that he can retain his independent judgment on behalf of each client; and if the interests become differing, withdrawal is less likely to have a disruptive effect upon the causes of his clients.

EC 5–16 In those instances in which a lawyer is justified in representing two or more clients having differing interests, it is nevertheless essential that each client be given the opportunity to evaluate his need for representation free of any potential conflict and to obtain other counsel if he so desires.[20] Thus before a lawyer may represent multiple clients, he should explain fully to each client the implications of the common representation and should accept or continue employment only if the clients consent.[21] If there are present other circumstances that might cause any of the multiple clients to question the undivided loyalty of the lawyer, he should also advise all of the clients of those circumstances.[22]

EC 5–17 Typically recurring situations involving potentially differing interests are those in which a lawyer is asked to represent co-defendants in a criminal case, co-plaintiffs in a personal injury case, an insured and his insurer,[23] and beneficiaries of the estate of a decedent. Whether a lawyer can fairly and adequately protect the interests of multiple clients in these and similar situations depends upon an analysis of each case. In certain circumstances, there may exist little chance of the judgment of the lawyer being adversely affected by the slight possibility that the interests will become actually differing; in other circumstances, the chance of adverse effect upon his judgment is not unlikely.

EC 5–18 A lawyer employed or retained by a corporation or similar entity owes his allegiance to the entity and not to a stockholder, director, officer, employee, representative, or other person connected with the entity. In advising the entity, a lawyer should keep paramount its interests and his professional judgment should not be influenced by the personal desires of any person or organization. Occasionally a lawyer for an entity is requested by a stockholder, director, officer, employee, representative, or other person connected with the entity to represent him in an individual capacity; in such case the lawyer may serve the individual only if the

---

20. "Glasser wished the benefit of the undivided assistance of counsel of his own choice. We think that such a desire on the part of an accused should be respected. Irrespective of any conflict of interest, the additional burden of representing another party may conceivably impair counsel's effectiveness.

"To determine the precise degree of prejudice sustained by Glasser as a result of the court's appointment of Stewart as counsel for Kretske is at once difficult and unnecessary. The right to have the assistance of counsel is too fundamental and absolute to allow courts to indulge in nice calculations as to the amount of prejudice arising from its denial." Glasser v. United States, 315 U.S. 60, 75–76, 86 L.Ed. 680, 62 S.Ct. 457, 467 (1942).

21. See ABA Canon 6.

22. Id.

23. Cf. *ABA Opinion* 282 (1950).

"When counsel, although paid by the casualty company, undertakes to represent the policyholder and files his notice of appearance, he owes to his client, the assured, an undeviating and single allegiance. His fealty embraces the requirement to produce in court all witnesses, fact and expert, who are available and necessary for the proper protection of the rights of his client. . . .

". . . The Canons of Professional Ethics make it pellucid that there are not two standards, one applying to counsel privately retained by a client, and the other to counsel paid by an insurance carrier." American Employers Ins. Co. v. Goble Aircraft Specialties, 205 Misc. 1066, 1075, 131 N.Y.S.2d 393, 401 (1954), motion to withdraw appeal granted, 1 App.Div.2d 1008, 154 N.Y.S.2d 835 (1956).

"[C]ounsel, selected by State Farm to defend Dorothy Walker's suit for $50,000 damages, was apprised by Walker that his earlier version of the accident was untrue and that actually the accident occurred because he lost control of his car in passing a Cadillac just ahead. At that point, Walker's counsel should have refused to participate further in view of the conflict of interest between Walker and State Farm. . . . Instead he participated in the ensuing deposition of the Walkers, even took an *ex parte* sworn statement from Mr. Walker in order to advise State Farm what action it should take, and later used the statement against Walker in the District Court. This action appears to contravene an Indiana attorney's duty 'at every peril to himself, to preserve the secrets of his client' . . . ." State Farm Mut. Auto Ins. Co. v. Walker, 382 F.2d 548, 552 (1967), cert. denied, 389 U.S. 1045, 19 L.Ed.2d 837, 88 S.Ct. 789 (1968).

lawyer is convinced that differing interests are not present.

EC 5-19 A lawyer may represent several clients whose interests are not actually or potentially differing. Nevertheless, he should explain any circumstances that might cause a client to question his undivided loyalty.[24] Regardless of the belief of a lawyer that he may properly represent multiple clients, he must defer to a client who holds the contrary belief and withdraw from representation of that client.

EC 5-20 A lawyer is often asked to serve as an impartial arbitrator or mediator in matters which involve present or former clients. He may serve in either capacity if he first discloses such present or former relationships. After a lawyer has undertaken to act as an impartial arbitrator or mediator, he should not thereafter represent in the dispute any of the parties involved.

Desires of Third Persons

EC 5-21 The obligation of a lawyer to exercise professional judgment solely on behalf of his client requires that he disregard the desires of others that might impair his free judgment.[25] The desires of a third person will seldom adversely affect a lawyer unless that person is in a position to exert strong economic, political, or social pressures upon the lawyer. These influences are often subtle, and a lawyer must be alert to their existence. A lawyer subjected to outside pressures should make full disclosure of them to his client;[26] and if he or his client believes that the effectiveness of his representation has been or will be impaired thereby, the lawyer should take proper steps to withdraw from representation of his client.

EC 5-22 Economic, political, or social pressures by third persons are less likely to impinge upon the independent judgment of a lawyer in a matter in which he is compensated directly by his client and his professional work is exclusively with his client. On the other hand, if a lawyer is compensated from a source other than his client, he may feel a sense of responsibility to someone other than his client.

EC 5-23 A person or organization that pays or furnishes lawyers to represent others possesses a potential power to exert strong pressures against the independent judgment of those lawyers. Some employers may be interested in furthering their own economic, political, or social goals without regard to the professional responsibility of the lawyer to his individual client. Others may be far more concerned with establishment or extension of legal principles than in the immediate protection of the rights of the lawyer's individual client. On some occasions, decisions on priority of work may be made by the employer rather than the lawyer with the result that prosecution of work already undertaken for clients is postponed to their detriment. Similarly, an employer may seek, consciously or unconsciously, to further its own economic interests through the action of the lawyers employed by it. Since a lawyer must always be free to exercise his professional judgment without regard to the interests or motives of a third person, the lawyer who is employed by one to represent another must constantly guard against erosion of his professional freedom.[27]

EC 5-24 To assist a lawyer in preserving his professional independence, a number of

---

24. See ABA Canon 6.
25. See ABA Canon 35.

"Objection to the intervention of a lay intermediary, who may control litigation or otherwise interfere with the rendering of legal services in a confidential relationship, . . . derives from the element of pecuniary gain. Fearful of dangers thought to arise from that element, the courts of several States have sustained regulations aimed at these activities. We intimate no view one way or the other as to the merits of those decisions with respect to the particular arrangements against which they are directed. It is enough that the superficial resemblance in form between those arrangements and that at bar cannot obscure the vital fact that here the entire arrangement employs constitutionally privileged means of expression to secure constitutionally guaranteed civil rights." NAACP v. Button, 371 U.S. 415, 441-42, 9 L.Ed.2d 405, 423-24, 83 S.Ct. 328, 342-43 (1963).

26. Cf. ABA Canon 38.

27. "Certainly it is true that 'the professional relationship between an attorney and his client is highly personal, involving an intimate appreciation of each individual client's particular problem.' And this Committee does not condone practices which interfere with that relationship.

Canon 5 ABA

courses are available to him. For example, a lawyer should not practice with or in the form of a professional legal corporation, even though the corporate form is permitted by law,[28] if any director, officer, or stockholder of it is a non-lawyer. Although a lawyer may be employed by a business corporation with non-lawyers serving as directors or officers, and they necessarily have the right to make decisions of business policy, a lawyer must decline to accept direction of his professional judgment from any layman. Various types of legal aid offices are administered by boards of directors composed of lawyers and laymen. A lawyer should not accept employment from such an organization unless the board sets only broad policies and there is no interference in the relationship of the lawyer and the individual client he serves. Where a lawyer is employed by an organization, a written agreement that defines the relationship between him and the organization and provides for his independence is desirable since it may serve to prevent misunderstanding as to their respective roles. Although other innovations in the means of supplying legal counsel may develop, the responsibility of the lawyer to maintain his professional independence remains constant, and the legal profession must insure that changing circumstances do not result in loss of the professional independence of the lawyer.

DISCIPLINARY RULES

DR 5–101 Refusing Employment When the Interests of the Lawyer May Impair His Independent Professional Judgment.

(A) **Except with the consent of his client after full disclosure, a lawyer shall not accept employment if the exercise of his professional judgment on behalf of his client will be or reasonably may be affected by his own financial, business, property, or personal interests.**[29]

(B) **A lawyer shall not accept employment in contemplated or pending litigation if he knows or it is obvious that he or a lawyer in his firm ought to be called as a witness, except that he may undertake the employment and he or a lawyer in his firm may testify:**

   (1) **If the testimony will relate solely to an uncontested matter.**

   (2) **If the testimony will relate solely to a matter of formality and there is no reason to believe that substantial evidence will be offered in opposition to the testimony.**

   (3) **If the testimony will relate solely to the nature and value of legal services rendered in the**

However, the mere fact the lawyer is actually paid by some entity other than the client does not affect that relationship, so long as the lawyer is selected by and is directly responsible to the client. See Informal Opinions 469 and 679. Of course, as the latter decision points out, there must be full disclosure of the arrangement by the attorney to the client. . . ." *ABA Opinion* 320 (1968).

"[A] third party may pay the cost of legal services as long as control remains in the client and the responsibility of the lawyer is solely to the client. Informal Opinions 469 ad [sic] 679. See also *Opinion* 237." Id.

28. *ABA Opinion* 303 (1961) recognized that "[s]tatutory provisions now exist in several states which are designed to make [the practice of law in a form that will be classified as a corporation for federal income tax purposes] legally possible, either as a result of lawyers incorporating or forming associations with various corporate characteristics."

29. Cf. ABA Canon 6 and *ABA Opinions* 181 (1938), 104 (1934), 103 (1933), 72 (1932), 50 (1931), 49 (1931), and 33 (1931).

"New York County [Opinion] 203. . . . [A lawyer] should not advise a client to employ an investment company in which he is interested, without informing him of this." Drinker, *Legal Ethics* 956 (1953).

"In *Opinions* 72 and 49 this Committee held: The relations of partners in a law firm are such that neither the firm nor any member or associate thereof, may accept any professional employment which any member of the firm cannot properly accept.

"In *Opinion* 16 this Committee held that a member of a law firm could not represent a defendant in a criminal case which was being prosecuted by another member of the firm who was public prosecuting attorney. The Opinion stated that it was clearly unethical for one member of the firm to oppose the interest of the state while another member represented those interests . . . . Since the prosecutor himself could not represent both the public and the defendant, no member of his law firm could either." *ABA Opinion* 296 (1959).

MODEL CODE OF PROFESSIONAL RESPONSIBILITY   Canon 5

case by the lawyer or his firm to the client.

(4) As to any matter, if refusal would work a substantial hardship on the client because of the distinctive value of the lawyer or his firm as counsel in the particular case.

DR 5–102 Withdrawal as Counsel When the Lawyer Becomes a Witness.[30]

(A) If, after undertaking employment in contemplated or pending litigation, a lawyer learns or it is obvious that he or a lawyer in his firm ought to be called as a witness on behalf of his client, he shall withdraw from the conduct of the trial and his firm, if any, shall not continue representation in the trial, except that he may continue the representation and he or a lawyer in his firm may testify in the circumstances enumerated in DR 5–101(B)(1) through (4).

(B) If, after undertaking employment in contemplated or pending litigation, a lawyer learns or it is obvious that he or a lawyer in his firm may be called as a witness other than on behalf of his client, he may continue the representation until it is apparent that his testimony is or may be prejudicial to his client.[31]

DR 5–103 Avoiding Acquisition of Interest in Litigation.

(A) A lawyer shall not acquire a proprietary interest in the cause of action or subject matter of litigation he is conducting for a client,[32] except that he may:

(1) Acquire a lien granted by law to secure his fee or expenses.

(2) Contract with a client for a reasonable contingent fee in a civil case.[33]

(B) While representing a client in connection with contemplated or pending litigation, a lawyer shall not advance or guarantee financial assistance to his client,[34] except that a lawyer may advance or guarantee the expenses of litigation, including court costs, expenses of investigation, expenses of medical examination, and costs of obtaining and presenting evidence, provided the client remains ultimately liable for such expenses.

DR 5–104 Limiting Business Relations with a Client.

(A) A lawyer shall not enter into a business transaction with a client if they have differing interests therein and if the client expects the lawyer to exercise his professional judgment therein for the protection of the client, unless the client has consented after full disclosure.

(B) Prior to conclusion of all aspects of the matter giving rise to his employment, a lawyer shall not enter into any arrangement or understanding with a client or a prospective client by which he acquires an interest in publication rights with respect to the subject matter of his employment or proposed employment.

---

30. Cf. ABA Canon 19 and *ABA Opinions* 220 (1941), 185 (1938), 50 (1931), and 33 (1931); but cf. Erwin M. Jennings Co. v. DiGenova, 107 Conn. 491, 498–99, 141 A. 866, 868 (1928).

31. "This *Canon* [19] *of Ethics* needs no elaboration to be applied to the facts here. Apparently, the object of this precept is to avoid putting a lawyer in the obviously embarrassing predicament of testifying and then having to argue the credibility and effect of his own testimony. It was not designed to permit a lawyer to call opposing counsel as a witness and thereby disqualify him as counsel." Galarowicz v. Ward, 119 Utah 611, 620, 230 P.2d 576, 580 (1951).

32. ABA Canon 10 and *ABA Opinions* 279 (1949), 246 (1942) and 176 (1938).

33. See Code of Professional Responsibility, DR 2–106(C).

34. See ABA Canon 42; cf. *ABA Opinion* 288 (1954).

Canon 5

DR 5–105 Refusing to Accept or Continue Employment if the Interests of Another Client May Impair the Independent Professional Judgment of the Lawyer.

(A) A lawyer shall decline proffered employment if the exercise of his independent professional judgment in behalf of a client will be or is likely to be adversely affected by the acceptance of the proffered employment,[35] or if it would be likely to involve him in representing differing interests, except to the extent permitted under DR 5–105(C).[36]

(B) A lawyer shall not continue multiple employment if the exercise of his independent professional judgment in behalf of a client will be or is likely to be adversely affected by his representation of another client, or if it would be likely to involve him in representing differing interests, except to the extent permitted under DR 5–105(C).[37]

(C) In the situations covered by DR 5–105(A) and (B), a lawyer may represent multiple clients if it is obvious that he can adequately represent the interest of each and if each consents to the representation after full disclosure of the possible effect of such representation on the exercise of his independent professional judgment on behalf of each.

(D) If a lawyer is required to decline employment or to withdraw from employment under a Disciplinary Rule, no partner or associate, or any other lawyer affiliated with him or his firm may accept or continue such employment.

As amended in 1974.

DR 5–106 Settling Similar Claims of Clients.[38]

(A) A lawyer who represents two or more clients shall not make or participate in the making of an aggregate settlement of the claims of or against his clients, unless each client has consented to the settlement after being advised of the existence and nature of all the claims involved in the proposed settlement, of the total amount of the settlement, and of the participation of each person in the settlement.

DR 5–107 Avoiding Influence by Others Than the Client.

(A) Except with the consent of his client after full disclosure, a lawyer shall not:

(1) Accept compensation for his legal services from one other than his client.

(2) Accept from one other than his client any thing of value related to his representation of or his employment by his client.[39]

(B) A lawyer shall not permit a person who recommends, employs, or pays him to render legal services for another to direct or regulate his profes-

---

35. See ABA Canon 6; cf. *ABA Opinions* 167 (1937), 60 (1931), and 40 (1931).

36. *ABA Opinion* 247 (1942) held that an attorney could not investigate a night club shooting on behalf of one of the owner's liability insurers, obtaining the cooperation of the owner, and later represent the injured patron in an action against the owner and a different insurance company unless the attorney obtain the "express consent of all concerned given after a full disclosure of the facts," since to do so would be to represent conflicting interests.

See *ABA Opinions* 247 (1942), 224 (1941), 222 (1941), 218 (1941), 112 (1934), 83 (1932), and 86 (1932).

37. Cf. *ABA Opinions* 231 (1941) and 160 (1936).

38. Cf. *ABA Opinions* 243 (1942) and 235 (1941).

39. See ABA Canon 38.

"A lawyer who receives a commission (whether delayed or not) from a title insurance company or guaranty fund for recommending or selling the insurance to his client, or for work done for the client or the company, without either fully disclosing to the client his financial interest in the transaction, or crediting the client's bill with the amount thus received, is guilty of unethical conduct." *ABA Opinion* 304 (1962).

sional judgment in rendering such legal services.[40]

(C) A lawyer shall not practice with or in the form of a professional corporation or association authorized to practice law for a profit, if:

(1) A non-lawyer owns any interest therein,[41] except that a fiduciary representative of the estate of a lawyer may hold the stock or interest of the lawyer for a reasonable time during administration;

(2) A non-lawyer is a corporate director or officer thereof;[42] or

(3) A non-lawyer has the right to direct or control the professional judgment of a lawyer.[43]

CANON 6

A Lawyer Should Represent a Client Competently

ETHICAL CONSIDERATIONS

EC 6–1 Because of his vital role in the legal process, a lawyer should act with competence and proper care in representing clients. He should strive to become and remain proficient in his practice [1] and should accept employment only in matters which he is or intends to become competent to handle.

EC 6–2 A lawyer is aided in attaining and maintaining his competence by keeping abreast of current legal literature and developments, participating in continuing legal education programs,[2] concentrating in particular areas of the law, and by utilizing other available means. He has the additional ethical obligation to assist in improving the legal

---

40. See ABA Canon 35; cf. *ABA Opinion* 237 (1941).

"When the lay forwarder, as agent for the creditor, forwards a claim to an attorney, the direct relationship of attorney and client shall then exist between the attorney and the creditor, and the forwarder shall not interpose itself as an intermediary to control the activities of the attorney." *ABA Opinion* 294 (1958).

41. "Permanent beneficial and voting rights in the organization set up to practice law, whatever its form, must be restricted to lawyers while the organization is engaged in the practice of law." *ABA Opinion* 303 (1961).

42. "*Canon 33* . . . promulgates underlying principles that must be observed no matter in what form of organization lawyers practice law. Its requirement that no person shall be admitted or held out as a practitioner or member who is not a member of the legal profession duly authorized to practice, and amendable to professional discipline, makes it clear that any centralized management must be in lawyers to avoid a violation of this Canon." *ABA Opinion* 303 (1961).

43. "There is no intervention of any lay agency between lawyer and client when centralized management provided only by lawyers may give guidance or direction to the services being rendered by a lawyer-member of the organization to a client. The language in *Canon 35* that a lawyer should avoid all relations which direct the performance of his duties by or in the interest of an intermediary refers to lay intermediaries and not lawyer intermediaries with whom he is associated in the practice of law." *ABA Opinion* 303 (1961).

1. "[W]hen a citizen is faced with the need for a lawyer, he wants, and is entitled to, the best informed counsel he can obtain. Changing times produce changes in our laws and legal procedures. The natural complexities of law require continuing intensive study by a lawyer if he is to render his clients a maximum of efficient service. And, in so doing, he maintains the high standards of the legal profession; and he also increases respect and confidence by the general public." Rochelle & Payne, *The Struggle for Public Understanding*, 25 Texas B.J. 109, 160 (1962).

"We have undergone enormous changes in the last fifty years within the lives of most of the adults living today who may be seeking advice. Most of these changes have been accompanied by changes and developments in the law. . . . Every practicing lawyer encounters these problems and is often perplexed with his own inability to keep up, not only with changes in the law, but also with changes in the lives of his clients and their legal problems.

"To be sure, no client has a right to expect that his lawyer will have all of the answers at the end of his tongue or even in the back of his head at all times. But the client does have the right to expect that the lawyer will have devoted his time and energies to maintaining and improving his competence to know where to look for the answers, to know how to deal with the problems, and to know how to advise to the best of his legal talents and abilities." Levy & Sprague, *Accounting and Law: Is Dual Practice in the Public Interest?*, 52 A.B.A.J. 1110, 1112 (1966).

2. "The whole purpose of continuing legal education, so enthusiastically supported by the ABA, is to make it possible for lawyers to make themselves better lawyers. But there are no nostrums for proficiency in the law; it must come through the hard work of the lawyer himself. To the extent that that work, whether it be in attending institutes or lecture courses, in studying after hours or in the actual day in and day out practice of his profession, can be concentrated within a limited field, the greater the proficiency and expertness that can be developed." *Report of the Special Committee on Specialization and Specialized Legal Education*, 79 A.B.A.Rep. 582, 588 (1954).

profession, and he may do so by participating in bar activities intended to advance the quality and standards of members of the profession. Of particular importance is the careful training of his younger associates and the giving of sound guidance to all lawyers who consult him. In short, a lawyer should strive at all levels to aid the legal profession in advancing the highest possible standards of integrity and competence and to meet those standards himself.

EC 6–3 While the licensing of a lawyer is evidence that he has met the standards then prevailing for admission to the bar, a lawyer generally should not accept employment in any area of the law in which he is not qualified.[3] However, he may accept such employment if in good faith he expects to become qualified through study and investigation, as long as such preparation would not result in unreasonable delay or expense to his client. Proper preparation and representation may require the association by the lawyer of professionals in other disciplines. A lawyer offered employment in a matter in which he is not and does not expect to become so qualified should either decline the employment or, with the consent of his client, accept the employment and associate a lawyer who is competent in the matter.

EC 6–4 Having undertaken representation, a lawyer should use proper care to safeguard the interests of his client. If a lawyer has accepted employment in a matter beyond his competence but in which he expected to become competent, he should diligently undertake the work and study necessary to qualify himself. In addition to being qualified to handle a particular matter, his obligation to his client requires him to prepare adequately for and give appropriate attention to his legal work.

EC 6–5 A lawyer should have pride in his professional endeavors. His obligation to act competently calls for higher motivation than that arising from fear of civil liability or disciplinary penalty.

EC 6–6 A lawyer should not seek, by contract or other means, to limit his individual liability to his client for his malpractice. A lawyer who handles the affairs of his client properly has no need to attempt to limit his liability for his professional activities and one who does not handle the affairs of his client properly should not be permitted to do so. A lawyer who is a stockholder in or is associated with a professional legal corporation may, however, limit his liability for malpractice of his associates in the corporation, but only to the extent permitted by law.[4]

DISCIPLINARY RULES

DR 6–101 Failing to Act Competently.

(A) A lawyer shall not:

(1) Handle a legal matter which he knows or should know that he is not competent to handle, without associating with him a lawyer who is competent to handle it.

(2) Handle a legal matter without preparation adequate in the circumstances.

(3) Neglect a legal matter entrusted to him.[5]

DR 6–102 Limiting Liability to Client.

(A) A lawyer shall not attempt to exonerate himself from or limit his liability to his client for his personal malpractice.

---

3. "If the attorney is not competent to skillfully and properly perform the work, he should not undertake the service." Degen v. Steinbrink, 202 App.Div. 477, 481, 195 N.Y.S. 810, 814 (1922), aff'd mem., 236 N.Y. 669, 142 N.E. 328 (1923).

4. See *ABA Opinion* 303 (1961); cf. Code of Professional Responsibility EC 2–11.

5. The annual report for 1967–1968 of the Committee on Grievances of the Association of the Bar of the City of New York showed a receipt of 2,232 complaints; of the 828 offenses against clients, 76 involved conversion, 49 involved "overreaching," and 452, or more than half of all such offenses, involved neglect. *Annual Report of the Committee on Grievances of the Association of the Bar of the City of New York*, N.Y.L.J., Sept. 12, 1968, at 4, col. 5.

CANON 7

A Lawyer Should Represent a Client Zealously Within the Bounds of the Law

ETHICAL CONSIDERATIONS

EC 7-1 The duty of a lawyer, both to his client [1] and to the legal system, is to represent his client zealously [2] within the bounds of the law,[3] which includes Disciplinary Rules and enforceable professional regulations.[4] The professional responsibility of a lawyer derives from his membership in a profession which has the duty of assisting members of the public to secure and protect available legal rights and benefits. In our government of laws and not of men, each member of our society is entitled to have his

---

1. "The right to be heard would be, in many cases, of little avail if it did not comprehend the right to be heard by counsel. Even the intelligent and educated layman has small and sometimes no skill in the science of law." Powell v. Alabama, 287 U.S. 45, 68–69, 77 L.Ed. 158, 170, 53 S.Ct. 55, 64 (1932).

2. Cf. ABA Canon 4.

"At times . . . [the tax lawyer] will be wise to discard some arguments and he should exercise discretion to emphasize the arguments which in his judgment are most likely to be persuasive. But this process involves legal judgment rather than moral attitudes. The tax lawyer should put aside private disagreements with Congressional and Treasury policies. His own notions of policy, and his personal view of what the law should be, are irrelevant. The job entrusted to him by his client is to use all his learning and ability to protect his client's rights, not to help in the process of promoting a better tax system. The tax lawyer need not accept his client's economic and social opinions, but the client is paying for technical attention and undivided concentration upon his affairs. He is equally entitled to performance unfettered by his attorney's economic and social predilections." Paul, *The Lawyer as a Tax Advisor*, 25 Rocky Mt.L.Rev. 412, 418 (1953).

3. See ABA Canons 15 and 32.

ABA Canon 5, although only speaking of one accused of crime, imposes a similar obligation on the lawyer: "[T]he lawyer is bound, by all fair and honorable means, to present every defense that the law of the land permits, to the end that no person may be deprived of life or liberty, but by due process of law."

"Any persuasion or pressure on the advocate which deters him from planning and carrying out the litigation on the basis of 'what, within the framework of the law, is best for my client's interest?' interferes with the obligation to represent the client fully within the law.

"This obligation, in its fullest sense, is the heart of the adversary process. Each attorney, as an advocate, acts for and seeks that which in his judgment is best for his client, within the bounds authoritatively established. The advocate does not *decide* what is just in this case—he would be usurping the function of the judge and jury—he acts for and seeks for his client that which he is entitled to under the law. He can do no less and properly represent the client." Thode, *The Ethical Standard for the Advocate*, 39 Texas L.Rev. 575, 584 (1961).

"The [Texas public opinion] survey indicates that distrust of the lawyer can be traced directly to certain factors. Foremost of these is a basic misunderstanding of the function of the lawyer as an advocate in an adversary system.

"Lawyers are accused of taking advantage of 'loopholes' and 'technicalities' to win. Persons who make this charge are unaware, or do not understand, that the lawyer is hired to win, and if he does not exercise every legitimate effort in his client's behalf, then he is betraying a sacred trust." Rochelle & Payne, *The Struggle for Public Understanding*, 25 Texas B.J. 109, 159 (1962).

"The importance of the attorney's undivided allegiance and faithful service to one accused of crime, irrespective of the attorney's personal opinion as to the guilt of his client, lies in Canon 5 of the American Bar Association Canon of Ethics.

"The difficulty lies, of course, in ascertaining whether the attorney has been guilty of an error of judgment, such as an election with respect to trial tactics, or has otherwise been actuated by his conscience or belief that his client should be convicted in any event. All too frequently courts are called upon to review actions of defense counsel which are, at the most, errors of judgment, not properly reviewable on habeas corpus unless the trial is a farce and a mockery of justice which requires the court to intervene. . . . But when defense counsel, in a truly adverse proceeding, admits that his conscience would not permit him to adopt certain customary trial procedures, this extends beyond the realm of judgment and strongly suggests an invasion of constitutional rights." Johns v. Smyth, 176 F.Supp. 949, 952 (E.D.Va.1959), modified, United States ex rel. Wilkins v. Banmiller, 205 F.Supp. 123, 128, n. 5 (E.D. Pa.1962), aff'd 325 F.2d 514 (3d Cir.1963), cert. denied, 379 U.S. 847, 13 L.Ed.2d 51, 85 S.Ct. 87 (1964).

"The adversary system in law administration bears a striking resemblance to the competitive economic system. In each we assume that the individual through partisanship or through self-interest will strive mightily for his side, and that kind of striving we must have. But neither system would be tolerable without restraints and modifications, and at times without outright departures from the system itself. Since the legal profession is entrusted with the system of law administration, a part of its task is to develop in its members appropriate restraints without impairing the values of partisan striving. An accompanying task is to aid in the modification of the adversary system or departure from it in areas to which the system is unsuited." Cheatham, *The Lawyer's Role and Surroundings*, 25 Rocky Mt.L.Rev. 405, 410 (1953).

4. "Rule 4.15 prohibits, in the pursuit of a client's cause, 'any manner of fraud or chicane'; Rule 4.22 requires 'candor and fairness' in the conduct of the lawyer, and forbids the making of knowing misquotations; Rule 4.47 provides that a lawyer 'should always maintain his integrity,' and generally forbids all misconduct injurious to the interests of the public, the courts, or his clients, and acts contrary to 'justice, honesty, modesty or good

conduct judged and regulated in accordance with the law;[5] to seek any lawful objective[6] through legally permissible means;[7] and to present for adjudication any lawful claim, issue, or defense.

EC 7–2 The bounds of the law in a given case are often difficult to ascertain.[8] The language of legislative enactments and judicial opinions may be uncertain as applied to varying factual situations. The limits and specific meaning of apparently relevant law may be made doubtful by changing or developing constitutional interpretations, inadequately expressed statutes or judicial opinions, and changing public and judicial attitudes. Certainty of law ranges from well-settled rules through areas of conflicting authority to areas without precedent.

EC 7–3 Where the bounds of law are uncertain, the action of a lawyer may depend on whether he is serving as advocate or adviser. A lawyer may serve simultaneously as both advocate and adviser, but the two roles are essentially different.[9] In asserting a position on behalf of his client, an advocate for the most part deals with past conduct and must take the facts as he finds them. By contrast, a lawyer serving as adviser primarily assists his client in determining the course of future conduct and relationships. While serving as advocate, a lawyer should resolve in favor of his client doubts as to the bounds of the law.[10] In serving a client as

---

morals.' Our Commissioner has accurately paraphrased these rules as follows: 'An attorney does not have the duty to do all and whatever he can that may enable him to win his client's cause or to further his client's interest. His duty and efforts in these respects, although they should be prompted by his "entire devotion" to the interest of his client, must be within and not without the bounds of the law.'" In re Wines, 370 S.W.2d 328, 333 (Mo.1963).

See Note, 38 Texas L.Rev. 107, 110 (1959).

5. "Under our system of government the process of adjudication is surrounded by safeguards evolved from centuries of experience. These safeguards are not designed merely to lend formality and decorum to the trial of causes. They are predicated on the assumption that to secure for any controversy a truly informed and dispassionate decision is a difficult thing, requiring for its achievement a special summoning and organization of human effort and the adoption of measures to exclude the biases and prejudgments that have free play outside the courtroom. All of this goes for naught if the man with an unpopular cause is unable to find a competent lawyer courageous enough to represent him. His chance to have his day in court loses much of its meaning if his case is handicapped from the outset by the very kind of prejudgment our rules of evidence and procedure are intended to prevent." *Professional Responsibility: Report of the Joint Conference*, 44 A.B.A.J. 1159, 1216 (1958).

6. "[I]t is . . . [the tax lawyer's] positive duty to show the client how to avail himself to the full of what the law permits. He is not the keeper of the Congressional conscience." Paul, *The Lawyer as a Tax Adviser*, 25 Rocky Mt.L.Rev. 412, 418 (1953).

7. See ABA Canons 15 and 30.

8. "The fact that it desired to evade the law, as it is called, is immaterial, because the very meaning of a line in the law is that you intentionally may go as close to it as you can if you do not pass it . . . . It is a matter of proximity and degree as to which minds will differ . . . ." Justice Holmes, in Superior Oil Co. v. Mississippi, 280 U.S. 390, 395–96, 74 L.Ed. 504, 508, 50 S.Ct. 169, 170 (1930).

9. "Today's lawyers perform two distinct types of functions, and our ethical standards should, but in the main do not, recognize these two functions. Judge Philbrick McCoy recently reported to the American Bar Association the need for a reappraisal of the Canons in light of the new and distinct function of counselor, as distinguished from advocate, which today predominates in the legal profession. . . .

". . . In the first place, any revision of the canons must take into account and speak to this new and now predominant function of the lawyer. . . . It is beyond the scope of this paper to discuss the ethical standards to be applied to the counselor except to state that in my opinion such standards should require a greater recognition and protection for the interest of the public generally than is presently expressed in the canons. Also, the counselor's obligation should extend to requiring him to inform and to impress upon the client a just solution of the problem, considering all interests involved." Thode, *The Ethical Standard for the Advocate*, 39 Texas L.Rev. 575, 578–79 (1961).

"The man who has been called into court to answer for his own actions is entitled to fair hearing. Partisan advocacy plays its essential part in such a hearing, and the lawyer pleading his client's case may properly present it in the most favorable light. A similar resolution of doubts in one direction becomes inappropriate when the lawyer acts as counselor. The reasons that justify and even require partisan advocacy in the trial of a cause do not grant any license to the lawyer to participate as legal advisor in a line of conduct that is immoral, unfair, or of doubtful legality. In saving himself from this unworthy involvement, the lawyer cannot be guided solely by an unreflective inner sense of good faith; he must be at pains to preserve a sufficient detachment from his client's interests so that he remains capable of a sound and objective appraisal of the propriety of what his client proposes to do." *Professional Responsibility: Report of the Joint Conference*, 44 A.B.J. 1159, 1161 (1958).

10. "[A] lawyer who is asked to advise his client . . . may freely urge the statement of positions most favorable to the client just as long as there is reasonable basis for those positions." *ABA Opinion* 314 (1965).

adviser, a lawyer in appropriate circumstances should give his professional opinion as to what the ultimate decisions of the courts would likely be as to the applicable law.

Duty of the Lawyer to a Client

EC 7-4 The advocate may urge any permissible construction of the law favorable to his client, without regard to his professional opinion as to the likelihood that the construction will ultimately prevail.[11] His conduct is within the bounds of the law, and therefore permissible, if the position taken is supported by the law or is supportable by a good faith argument for an extension, modification, or reversal of the law. However, a lawyer is not justified in asserting a position in litigation that is frivolous.[12]

EC 7-5 A lawyer as adviser furthers the interest of his client by giving his professional opinion as to what he believes would likely be the ultimate decision of the courts on the matter at hand and by informing his client of the practical effect of such decision.[13] He may continue in the representation of his client even though his client has elected to pursue a course of conduct contrary to the advice of the lawyer so long as he does not thereby knowingly assist the client to engage in illegal conduct or to take a frivolous legal position. A lawyer should never encourage or aid his client to commit criminal acts or counsel his client on how to violate the law and avoid punishment therefor.[14]

EC 7-6 Whether the proposed action of a lawyer is within the bounds of the law may be a perplexing question when his client is contemplating a course of conduct having

---

11. "The lawyer . . . is not an umpire, but an advocate. He is under no duty to refrain from making every proper argument in support of any legal point because he is not convinced of its inherent soundness. . . . His personal belief in the soundness of his cause or of the authorities supporting it, is irrelevant." *ABA Opinion* 280 (1949).

"Counsel apparently misconceived his role. It was his duty to honorably present his client's contentions in the light most favorable to his client. Instead he presumed to advise the court as to the validity and sufficiency of prisoner's motion, by letter. We therefore conclude that the prisoner had no effective assistance of counsel and remand this case to the District Court with instructions to set aside the Judgment, appoint new counsel to represent the prisoner if he makes no objection thereto, and proceed anew." McCartney v. United States, 343 F.2d 471, 472 (9th Cir.1965).

12. "Here the court-appointed counsel had the transcript but refused to proceed with the appeal because he found no merit in it. . . . We cannot say that there was a finding of frivolity by either of the California courts or that counsel acted in any greater capacity than merely as *amicus curiae* which was condemned in *Ellis*, supra. Hence California's procedure did not furnish petitioner with counsel acting in the role of an advocate nor did it provide that full consideration and resolution of the matter as is obtained when counsel is acting in that capacity. . . .

"The constitutional requirement of substantial equality and fair process can only be attained where counsel acts in the role of an active advocate in behalf of his client, as opposed to that of *amicus curiae*. The no-merit letter and the procedure it triggers do not reach that dignity. Counsel should, and can with honor and without conflict, be of more assistance to his client and to the court. His role as advocate requires that he support his client's appeal to the best of his ability. Of course, if counsel finds his case to be wholly frivolous, after a conscientious examination of it, he should so advise the court and request permission to withdraw. That request must, however, be accompanied by a brief referring to anything in the record that might arguably support the appeal. A copy of counsel's brief should be furnished the indigent and time allowed him to raise any points that he chooses; the court—not counsel—then proceeds, after a full examination of all the proceedings, to decide whether the case is wholly frivolous. If it so finds it may grant counsel's request to withdraw and dismiss the appeal insofar as federal requirements are concerned, or proceed to a decision on the merits, if state law so requires. On the other hand, if it finds any of the legal points arguable on their merits (and therefore not frivolous) it must, prior to decision, afford the indigent the assistance of counsel to argue the appeal." Anders v. California, 386 U.S. 738, 744, 18 L.Ed.2d 493, 498, 87 S.Ct. 1396, 1399–1400 (1967), rehearing denied, 388 U.S. 924, 18 L.Ed.2d 1377, 87 S.Ct. 2094 (1967).

See Paul, *The Lawyer As a Tax Adviser*, 25 Rocky Mt. L.Rev. 412, 432 (1953).

13. See ABA Canon 32.

14. "For a lawyer to represent a syndicate notoriously engaged in the violation of the law for the purpose of advising the members how to break the law and at the same time escape it, is manifestly improper. While a lawyer may see to it that anyone accused of crime, no matter how serious and flagrant, has a fair trial, and present all available defenses, he may not co-operate in planning violations of the law. There is a sharp distinction, of course, between advising what can lawfully be done and advising how unlawful acts can be done in a way to avoid conviction. Where a lawyer accepts a retainer from an organization, known to be unlawful, and agrees in advance to defend its members when from time to time they are accused of crime arising out of its unlawful activities, this is equally improper."

"See also *Opinion* 155." *ABA Opinion* 281 (1952).

legal consequences that vary according to the client's intent, motive, or desires at the time of the action. Often a lawyer is asked to assist his client in developing evidence relevant to the state of mind of the client at a particular time. He may properly assist his client in the development and preservation of evidence of existing motive, intent, or desire; obviously, he may not do anything furthering the creation or preservation of false evidence. In many cases a lawyer may not be certain as to the state of mind of his client, and in those situations he should resolve reasonable doubts in favor of his client.

EC 7-7 In certain areas of legal representation not affecting the merits of the cause or substantially prejudicing the rights of a client, a lawyer is entitled to make decisions on his own. But otherwise the authority to make decisions is exclusively that of the client and, if made within the framework of the law, such decisions are binding on his lawyer. As typical examples in civil cases, it is for the client to decide whether he will accept a settlement offer or whether he will waive his right to plead an affirmative defense. A defense lawyer in a criminal case has the duty to advise his client fully on whether a particular plea to a charge appears to be desirable and as to the prospects of success on appeal, but it is for the client to decide what plea should be entered and whether an appeal should be taken.[15]

EC 7-8 A lawyer should exert his best efforts to insure that decisions of his client are made only after the client has been informed of relevant considerations. A lawyer ought to initiate this decision-making process if the client does not do so. Advice of a lawyer to his client need not be confined to purely legal considerations.[16] A lawyer should advise his client of the possible effect of each legal alternative.[17] A lawyer should bring to bear upon this decision-making process the fullness of his experience as well as his objective viewpoint.[18] In assisting his client to reach a proper decision, it is often desirable for a lawyer to point out those factors which may lead to a decision that is morally just as well as legally permissible.[19] He may emphasize the possibility of harsh consequences that might result from assertion of legally permissible positions. In the final analysis, however, the lawyer should always remember that the decision whether to forego legally available objectives or methods because of non-legal factors is ultimately for the client and not for himself. In the event that the client in a non-adjudicatory matter insists upon a course of conduct that is contrary to the judgment and advice of the lawyer but not prohibited by Disciplinary

---

15. See ABA Special Committee on Minimum Standards for the Administration of Criminal Justice, *Standards Relating to Pleas of Guilty*, pp. 69-70 (1968).

16. "First of all, a truly great lawyer is a wise counselor to all manner of men in the varied crises of their lives when they most need disinterested advice. Effective counseling necessarily involves a thoroughgoing knowledge of the principles of the law not merely as they appear in the books but as they actually operate in action." Vanderbilt, *The Five Functions of the Lawyer: Service to Clients and the Public*, 40 A.B.A.J. 31 (1954).

17. "A lawyer should endeavor to obtain full knowledge of his client's cause before advising thereon. . . ." ABA Canon 8.

18. "[I]n devising charters of collaborative effort the lawyer often acts where all of the affected parties are present as participants. But the lawyer also performs a similar function in situations where this is not so, as, for example, in planning estates and drafting wills. Here the instrument defining the terms of collaboration may affect persons not present and often not born. Yet here, too, the good lawyer does not serve merely as a legal conduit for his client's desires, but as a wise counselor, experienced in the art of devising arrangements that will put in workable order the entangled affairs and interests of human beings." *Professional Responsibility: Report of the Joint Conference*, 44 A.B.A.J. 1159, 1162 (1958).

19. See ABA Canon 8.

"Vital as is the lawyer's role in adjudication, it should not be thought that it is only as an advocate pleading in open court that he contributes to the administration of the law. The most effective realization of the law's aims often takes place in the attorney's office, where litigation is forestalled by anticipating its outcome, where the lawyer's quiet counsel takes the place of public force. Contrary to popular belief, the compliance with the law thus brought about is not generally lip-serving and narrow, for by reminding him of its long-run costs the lawyer often deters his client from a course of conduct technically permissible under existing law, though inconsistent with its underlying spirit and purpose." *Professional Responsibility: Report of the Joint Conference*, 44 A.B.A.J. 1159, 1161 (1958).

Rules, the lawyer may withdraw from the employment.[20]

EC 7-9 In the exercise of his professional judgment on those decisions which are for his determination in the handling of a legal matter,[21] a lawyer should always act in a manner consistent with the best interests of his client.[22] However, when an action in the best interest of his client seems to him to be unjust, he may ask his client for permission to forego such action.[23]

EC 7-10 The duty of a lawyer to represent his client with zeal does not militate against his concurrent obligation to treat with consideration all persons involved in the legal process and to avoid the infliction of needless harm.

EC 7-11 The responsibilities of a lawyer may vary according to the intelligence, experience, mental condition or age of a client, the obligation of a public officer, or the nature of a particular proceeding. Examples include the representation of an illiterate or an incompetent, service as a public prosecutor or other government lawyer, and appearances before administrative and legislative bodies.

EC 7-12 Any mental or physical condition of a client that renders him incapable of making a considered judgment on his own behalf casts additional responsibilities upon his lawyer. Where an incompetent is acting through a guardian or other legal representative, a lawyer must look to such representative for those decisions which are normally the prerogative of the client to make. If a client under disability has no legal representative, his lawyer may be compelled in court proceedings to make decisions on behalf of the client. If the client is capable of understanding the matter in question or of contributing to the advancement of his interests, regardless of whether he is legally disqualified from performing certain acts, the lawyer should obtain from him all possible aid. If the disability of a client and the lack of a legal representative compel the lawyer to make decisions for his client, the lawyer should consider all circumstances then prevailing and act with care to safeguard and advance the interests of his client. But obviously a lawyer cannot perform any act or make any decision which the law requires his client to perform or make, either acting for himself if competent, or by a duly constituted representative if legally incompetent.

EC 7-13 The responsibility of a public prosecutor differs from that of the usual advocate; his duty is to seek justice, not merely to convict.[24] This special duty exists because: (1) the prosecutor represents the sovereign and therefore should use restraint in the discretionary exercise of governmental powers, such as in the selection of cases to prosecute; (2) during trial the prosecutor is not only an advocate but he also may make decisions normally made by an individ-

---

20. "My summation of Judge Sharswood's view of the advocate's duty to the client is that he owes to the client the duty to use all legal means in support of the client's case. However, at the same time Judge Sharswood recognized that many advocates would find this obligation unbearable if applicable without exception. Therefore, the individual lawyer is given the choice of representing his client fully within the bounds set by the law *or of telling his client that he cannot do so*, so that the client may obtain another attorney if he wishes." Thode, *The Ethical Standard for the Advocate*, 39 Texas L.Rev. 575, 582 (1961).

Cf. Code of Professional Responsibility, DR 2–110(C).

21. See ABA Canon 24.

22. Thode, *The Ethical Standard for the Advocate*, 39 Texas L.Rev. 575, 592 (1961).

23. Cf. *ABA Opinions* 253 (1946) and 178 (1938).

24. See ABA Canon 5 and Berger v. United States, 295 U.S. 78, 79 L.Ed. 1314, 55 S.Ct. 629 (1935).

"The public prosecutor cannot take as a guide for the conduct of his office the standards of an attorney appearing on behalf of an individual client. The freedom elsewhere wisely granted to a partisan advocate must be severely curtailed if the prosecutor's duties are to be properly discharged. The public prosecutor must recall that he occupies a dual role, being obligated, on the one hand, to furnish that adversary element essential to the informed decision of any controversy, but being possessed, on the other, of important governmental powers that are pledged to the accomplishment of one objective only, that of impartial justice. Where the prosecutor is recreant to the trust implicit in his office, he undermines confidence, not only in his profession, but in government and the very ideal of justice itself." *Professional Responsibility: Report of the Joint Conference*, 44 A.B. A.J. 1159, 1218 (1958).

"The prosecuting attorney is the attorney for the state, and it is his primary duty not to convict but to see that justice is done." *ABA Opinion* 150 (1936).

ual client, and those affecting the public interest should be fair to all; and (3) in our system of criminal justice the accused is to be given the benefit of all reasonable doubts. With respect to evidence and witnesses, the prosecutor has responsibilities different from those of a lawyer in private practice; the prosecutor should make timely disclosure to the defense of available evidence, known to him, that tends to negate the guilt of the accused, mitigate the degree of the offense, or reduce the punishment. Further, a prosecutor should not intentionally avoid pursuit of evidence merely because he believes it will damage the prosecutor's case or aid the accused.

EC 7–14 A government lawyer who has discretionary power relative to litigation should refrain from instituting or continuing litigation that is obviously unfair. A government lawyer not having such discretionary power who believes there is lack of merit in a controversy submitted to him should so advise his superiors and recommend the avoidance of unfair litigation. A government lawyer in a civil action or administrative proceeding has the responsibility to seek justice and to develop a full and fair record, and he should not use his position or the economic power of the government to harass parties or to bring about unjust settlements or results.

EC 7–15 The nature and purpose of proceedings before administrative agencies vary widely. The proceedings may be legislative or quasi-judicial, or a combination of both. They may be *ex parte* in character, in which event they may originate either at the instance of the agency or upon motion of an interested party. The scope of an inquiry may be purely investigative or it may be truly adversary looking toward the adjudication of specific rights of a party or of classes of parties. The foregoing are but examples of some of the types of proceedings conducted by administrative agencies. A lawyer appearing before an administrative agency,[25] regardless of the nature of the proceeding it is conducting, has the continuing duty to advance the cause of his client within the bounds of the law.[26] Where the applicable rules of the agency impose specific obligations upon a lawyer, it is his duty to comply therewith, unless the lawyer has a legitimate basis for challenging the validity thereof. In all appearances before administrative agencies, a lawyer should identify himself, his client if identity of his client is not privileged,[27] and the representative nature of his appearance. It is not improper, however, for a lawyer to seek from an agency information available to the public without identifying his client.

EC 7–16 The primary business of a legislative body is to enact laws rather than to adjudicate controversies, although on occasion the activities of a legislative body may take on the characteristics of an adversary proceeding, particularly in investigative and impeachment matters. The role of a lawyer supporting or opposing proposed legislation normally is quite different from his role in representing a person under investigation or on trial by a legislative body. When a lawyer appears in connection with proposed legislation, he seeks to affect the lawmaking process, but when he appears on behalf of a client in investigatory or impeachment proceedings, he is concerned with the protection of the rights of his client. In either event, he should identify himself and his client, if identity of his client is not privileged, and should comply with applicable laws and legislative rules.[28]

EC 7–17 The obligation of loyalty to his client applies only to a lawyer in the dis-

---

25. As to appearances before a department of government, Canon 26 provides: "A lawyer openly . . . may render professional services . . . in advocacy of claims before departments of government, upon the same principles of ethics which justify his appearance before the Courts . . . ."

26. "But as an advocate before a service which itself represents the adversary point of view, where his client's case is fairly arguable, a lawyer is under no duty to disclose its weaknesses, any more than he would be to make such a disclosure to a brother lawyer. The limitations within which he must operate are best expressed in Canon 22 . . . ." *ABA Opinion* 314 (1965).

27. See Baird v. Koerner, 279 F.2d 623 (9th Cir.1960).

28. See ABA Canon 26.

charge of his professional duties and implies no obligation to adopt a personal viewpoint favorable to the interests or desires of his client.[29] While a lawyer must act always with circumspection in order that his conduct will not adversely affect the rights of a client in a matter he is then handling, he may take positions on public issues and espouse legal reforms he favors without regard to the individual views of any client.

EC 7-18 The legal system in its broadest sense functions best when persons in need of legal advice or assistance are represented by their own counsel. For this reason a lawyer should not communicate on the subject matter of the representation of his client with a person he knows to be represented in the matter by a lawyer, unless pursuant to law or rule of court or unless he has the consent of the lawyer for that person.[30] If one is not represented by counsel, a lawyer representing another may have to deal directly with the unrepresented person; in such an instance, a lawyer should not undertake to give advice to the person who is attempting to represent himself,[31] except that he may advise him to obtain a lawyer.

Duty of the Lawyer to the Adversary System of Justice

EC 7-19 Our legal system provides for the adjudication of disputes governed by the rules of substantive, evidentiary, and procedural law. An adversary presentation counters the natural human tendency to judge too swiftly in terms of the familiar that which is not yet fully known;[32] the advocate, by his zealous preparation and presentation of facts and law, enables the tribunal to come to the hearing with an open and neutral mind and to render impartial judgments.[33] The duty of a lawyer to his client and his duty to the legal system are the same: to represent his client zealously within the bounds of the law.[34]

EC 7-20 In order to function properly, our adjudicative process requires an informed, impartial tribunal capable of administering justice promptly and efficiently[35] according to procedures that command public confidence and respect.[36] Not only must there be competent, adverse presentation of evidence and issues, but a tribunal must be aided by rules appropriate to an effective and dignified process. The procedures under which tribunals operate in our adversary system have been prescribed largely by legislative enactments, court rules and decisions, and

---

29. "Law should be so practiced that the lawyer remains free to make up his own mind how he will vote, what causes he will support, what economic and political philosophy he will espouse. It is one of the glories of the profession that it admits of this freedom. Distinguished examples can be cited of lawyers whose views were at variance from those of their clients, lawyers whose skill and wisdom make them valued advisers to those who had little sympathy with their views as citizens." *Professional Responsibility: Report of the Joint Conference*, 44 A.B.A.J. 1159, 1217 (1958).

"No doubt some tax lawyers feel constrained to abstain from activities on behalf of a better tax system because they think that their clients may object. Clients have no right to object if the tax adviser handles their affairs competently and faithfully and independently of his private views as to tax policy. They buy his expert services, not his private opinions or his silence on issues that gravely affect the public interest." Paul, *The Lawyer as a Tax Adviser*, 25 Rocky Mt.L.Rev. 412, 434 (1953).

30. See ABA Canon 9.

31. Id.

32. See *Professional Responsibility: Report of the Joint Conference*, 44 A.B.A.J. 1159, 1160 (1958).

33. "Without the participation of someone who can act responsibly for each of the parties, this essential narrowing of the issues [by exchange of written pleadings or stipulations of counsel] becomes impossible. But here again the true significance of partisan advocacy lies deeper, touching once more the integrity of the adjudicative process itself. It is only through the advocate's participation that the hearing may remain in fact what it purports to be in theory: a public trial of the facts and issues. Each advocate comes to the hearing prepared to present his proofs and arguments, knowing at the same time that his arguments may fail to persuade and that his proof may be rejected as inadequate. . . . The deciding tribunal, on the other hand, comes to the hearing uncommitted. It has not represented to the public that any fact can be proved, that any argument is sound, or that any particular way of stating a litigant's case is the most effective expression of its merits." *Professional Responsibility: Report of the Joint Conference*, 44 A.B.A.J. 1159, 1160–61 (1958).

34. Cf. ABA Canons 15 and 32.

35. Cf. ABA Canon 21.

36. See *Professional Responsibility: Report of the Joint Conference*, 44 A.B.A.J. 1159, 1216 (1958).

administrative rules. Through the years certain concepts of proper professional conduct have become rules of law applicable to the adversary adjudicative process. Many of these concepts are the bases for standards of professional conduct set forth in the Disciplinary Rules.

EC 7-21 The civil adjudicative process is primarily designed for the settlement of disputes between parties, while the criminal process is designed for the protection of society as a whole. Threatening to use, or using, the criminal process to coerce adjustment of private civil claims or controversies is a subversion of that process;[37] further, the person against whom the criminal process is so misused may be deterred from asserting his legal rights and thus the usefulness of the civil process in settling private disputes is impaired. As in all cases of abuse of judicial process, the improper use of criminal process tends to diminish public confidence in our legal system.

EC 7-22 Respect for judicial rulings is essential to the proper administration of justice; however, a litigant or his lawyer may, in good faith and within the framework of the law, take steps to test the correctness of a ruling of a tribunal.[38]

EC 7-23 The complexity of law often makes it difficult for a tribunal to be fully informed unless the pertinent law is presented by the lawyers in the cause. A tribunal that is fully informed on the applicable law is better able to make a fair and accurate determination of the matter before it. The adversary system contemplates that each lawyer will present and argue the existing law in the light most favorable to his client.[39] Where a lawyer knows of legal authority in the controlling jurisdiction directly adverse to the position of his client, he should inform the tribunal of its existence unless his adversary has done so; but, having made such disclosure, he may challenge its soundness in whole or in part.[40]

EC 7-24 In order to bring about just and informed decisions, evidentiary and procedural rules have been established by tribunals to permit the inclusion of relevant evidence and argument and the exclusion of all other considerations. The expression by a lawyer of his personal opinion as to the justness of a cause, as to the credibility of a witness, as to the culpability of a civil litigant, or as to the guilt or innocence of an accused is not a proper subject for argument to the trier of fact.[41] It is improper as to factual matters because admissible evidence possessed by a lawyer should be presented only as sworn testimony. It is improper as to all other matters because, were the rule otherwise, the silence of a lawyer on a given occasion could be construed unfavorably to his client. However, a lawyer may argue, on his analy-

---

37. "We are of the opinion that the letter in question was improper, and that in writing and sending it respondent was guilty of unprofessional conduct. This court has heretofore expressed its disapproval of using threats of criminal prosecution as a means of forcing settlement of civil claims. . . .

"Respondent has been guilty of a violation of a principle which condemns any confusion of threats of criminal prosecution with the enforcement of civil claims. For this misconduct he should be severely censured." Matter of Gelman, 230 App.Div. 524, 527, 245 N.Y.S. 416, 419 (1930).

38. "An attorney has the duty to protect the interests of his client. He has a right to press legitimate argument and to protest an erroneous ruling." Gallagher v. Municipal Court, 31 Cal.2d 784, 796, 192 P.2d 905, 913 (1948).

"There must be protection, however, in the far more frequent case of the attorney who stands on his rights and combats the order in good faith and without disrespect believing with good cause that it is void, for it is here that the independence of the bar becomes valuable." Note, 39 Colum.L.Rev. 433, 438 (1939).

39. "Too many do not understand that accomplishment of the layman's abstract ideas of justice is the function of the judge and jury, and that it is the lawyer's sworn duty to portray his client's case in its most favorable light." Rochelle and Payne, *The Struggle for Public Understanding*, 25 Texas B.J. 109, 159 (1962).

40. "We are of the opinion that this Canon requires the lawyer to disclose such decisions [that are adverse to his client's contentions] to the court. He may, of course, after doing so, challenge the soundness of the decisions or present reasons which he believes would warrant the court in not following them in the pending case." *ABA Opinion* 146 (1935).

Cf. *ABA Opinion* 280 (1949) and Thode, *The Ethical Standard for the Advocate*, 39 Texas L.Rev. 575, 585–86 (1961).

41. See ABA Canon 15.

"The traditional duty of an advocate is that he honorably uphold the contentions of his client. He should not voluntarily undermine them." Harders v. State of California, 373 F.2d 839, 842 (9th Cir.1967).

sis of the evidence, for any position or conclusion with respect to any of the foregoing matters.

EC 7-25 Rules of evidence and procedure are designed to lead to just decisions and are part of the framework of the law. Thus while a lawyer may take steps in good faith and within the framework of the law to test the validity of rules, he is not justified in consciously violating such rules and he should be diligent in his efforts to guard against his unintentional violation of them.[42] As examples, a lawyer should subscribe to or verify only those pleadings that he believes are in compliance with applicable law and rules; a lawyer should not make any prefatory statement before a tribunal in regard to the purported facts of the case on trial unless he believes that his statement will be supported by admissible evidence; a lawyer should not ask a witness a question solely for the purpose of harassing or embarrassing him; and a lawyer should not by subterfuge put before a jury matters which it cannot properly consider.

EC 7-26 The law and Disciplinary Rules prohibit the use of fraudulent, false, or perjured testimony or evidence.[43] A lawyer who knowingly[44] participates in introduction of such testimony or evidence is subject to discipline. A lawyer should, however, present any admissible evidence his client desires to have presented unless he knows, or from facts within his knowledge should know, that such testimony or evidence is false, fraudulent, or perjured.[45]

EC 7-27 Because it interferes with the proper administration of justice, a lawyer should not suppress evidence that he or his client has a legal obligation to reveal or produce. In like manner, a lawyer should not advise or cause a person to secrete himself or to leave the jurisdiction of a tribunal for the purpose of making him unavailable as a witness therein.[46]

EC 7-28 Witnesses should always testify truthfully[47] and should be free from any financial inducements that might tempt them to do otherwise.[48] A lawyer should not pay or agree to pay a non-expert witness an amount in excess of reimbursement for expenses and financial loss incident to his being a witness; however, a lawyer may pay or agree to pay an expert witness a reasonable fee for his services as an expert. But in no event should a lawyer pay or agree to pay a contingent fee to any witness. A lawyer should exercise reasonable diligence to see that his client and lay associates conform to these standards.[49]

EC 7-29 To safeguard the impartiality that is essential to the judicial process, veniremen and jurors should be protected against extra-

---

42. See ABA Canon 22.
43. Id. Cf. ABA Canon 41.
44. See generally *ABA Opinion* 287 (1953) as to a lawyer's duty when he unknowingly participates in introducing perjured testimony.
45. "Under any standard of proper ethical conduct an attorney should not sit by silently and permit his client to commit what may have been perjury, and which certainly would mislead the court and the opposing party on a matter vital to the issue under consideration. . . .

"Respondent next urges that it was his duty to observe the utmost good faith toward his client, and therefore he could not divulge any confidential information. This duty to the client of course does not extend to the point of authorizing collaboration with him in the commission of fraud." In re Carroll, 244 S.W.2d 474, 474-75 (Ky.1951).
46. See ABA Canon 5; cf. *ABA Opinion* 131 (1935).
47. Cf. ABA Canon 39.
48. "The prevalence of perjury is a serious menace to the administration of justice, to prevent which no means have as yet been satisfactorily devised. But there certainly can be no greater incentive to perjury than to allow a party to make payments to its opponents witnesses under any guise or on any excuse, and at least attorneys who are officers of the court to aid it in the administration of justice, must keep themselves clear of any connection which in the slightest degree tends to induce witnesses to testify in favor of their clients." In re Robinson, 151 App.Div. 589, 600, 136 N.Y.S. 548, 556-57 (1912), aff'd, 209 N.Y. 354, 103 N.E. 160 (1913).

49. "It will not do for an attorney who seeks to justify himself against charges of this kind to show that he has escaped criminal responsibility under the Penal Law, nor can he blindly shut his eyes to a system which tends to suborn witnesses, to produce perjured testimony, and to suppress the truth. He has an active affirmative duty to protect the administration of justice from perjury and fraud, and that duty is not performed by allowing his subordinates and assistants to attempt to subvert justice and procure results for his clients based upon false testimony and perjured witnesses." Id., 151 App.Div. at 592, 136 N.Y.S. at 551.

neous influences.[50] When impartiality is present, public confidence in the judicial system is enhanced. There should be no extrajudicial communication with veniremen prior to trial or with jurors during trial by or on behalf of a lawyer connected with the case. Furthermore, a lawyer who is not connected with the case should not communicate with or cause another to communicate with a venireman or a juror about the case. After the trial, communication by a lawyer with jurors is permitted so long as he refrains from asking questions or making comments that tend to harass or embarrass the juror[51] or to influence actions of the juror in future cases. Were a lawyer to be prohibited from communicating after a trial with a juror, he could not ascertain if the verdict might be subject to legal challenge, in which event the invalidity of a verdict might go undetected.[52] When an extrajudicial communication by a lawyer with a juror is permitted by law, it should be made considerately and with deference to the personal feelings of the juror.

EC 7–30 Vexatious or harassing investigations of veniremen or jurors seriously impair the effectiveness of our jury system. For this reason, a lawyer or anyone on his behalf who conducts an investigation of veniremen or jurors should act with circumspection and restraint.

EC 7–31 Communications with or investigations of members of families of veniremen or jurors by a lawyer or by anyone on his behalf are subject to the restrictions imposed upon the lawyer with respect to his communications with or investigations of veniremen and jurors.

EC 7–32 Because of his duty to aid in preserving the integrity of the jury system, a lawyer who learns of improper conduct by or towards a venireman, a juror, or a member of the family of either should make a prompt report to the court regarding such conduct.

EC 7–33 A goal of our legal system is that each party shall have his case, criminal or civil, adjudicated by an impartial tribunal. The attainment of this goal may be defeated by dissemination of news or comments which tend to influence judge or jury.[53] Such news or comments may prevent prospective jurors

---

50. See ABA Canon 23.

51. "[I]t is unfair to jurors to permit a disappointed litigant to pick over their private associations in search of something to discredit them and their verdict. And it would be unfair to the public too if jurors should understand that they cannot convict a man of means without risking an inquiry of that kind by paid investigators, with, to boot, the distortions an inquiry of that kind can produce." State v. LaFera, 42 N.J. 97, 107, 199 A.2d 630, 636 (1964).

52. *ABA Opinion* 319 (1968) points out that "[m]any courts today, and the trend is in this direction, allow the testimony of jurors as to all irregularities in and out of the courtroom except those irregularities whose existence can be determined only by exploring the consciousness of a single particular juror, New Jersey v. Kociolek, 20 N.J. 92, 118 A.2d 812 (1955). Model Code of Evidence Rule 301. Certainly as to states in which the testimony and affidavits of jurors may be received in support of or against a motion for new trial, a lawyer, in his obligation to protect his client, must have the tools for ascertaining whether or not grounds for a new trial exist and it is not unethical for him to talk to and question jurors."

53. Generally see ABA Advisory Committee on Fair Trial and Free Press, Standards Relating to Fair Trial and Free Press (1966).

"[T]he trial court might well have proscribed extrajudicial statements by any lawyer, party, witness, or court official which divulged prejudicial matters . . . . See State v. Van Dwyne, 43 N.J. 369, 389, 204 A.2d 841, 852 (1964), in which the court interpreted Canon 20 of the American Bar Association's Canons of Professional Ethics to prohibit such statements. Being advised of the great public interest in the case, the mass coverage of the press, and the potential prejudicial impact of publicity, the court could also have requested the appropriate city and county officials to promulgate a regulation with respect to dissemination of information about the case by their employees. In addition, reporters who wrote or broadcast prejudicial stories, could have been warned as to the impropriety of publishing material not introduced in the proceedings. . . . In this manner, Sheppard's right to a trial free from outside interference would have been given added protection without corresponding curtailment of the news media. Had the judge, the other officers of the court, and the police placed the interest of justice first, the news media would have soon learned to be content with the task of reporting the case as it unfolded in the courtroom—not pieced together from extrajudicial statements." Sheppard v. Maxwell, 384 U.S. 333, 361–62, 16 L.Ed.2d 600, 619–20, 86 S.Ct. 1507, 1521–22 (1966).

"Court proceedings are held for the solemn purpose of endeavoring to ascertain the truth which is the *sine qua non* of a fair trial. Over the centuries Anglo-American courts have devised careful safeguards by rule and otherwise to protect and facilitate the performance of this high function. As a result, at this time those safeguards do not permit the televising and photographing of a criminal trial, save in two States and there only under restrictions. The federal courts prohibit it by specific rule. This is weighty evidence that our concepts of a fair trial do not tolerate such an indulgence. We have always held that the atmosphere essential to the preservation of a fair

from being impartial at the outset of the trial [54] and may also interfere with the obligation of jurors to base their verdict solely upon the evidence admitted in the trial.[55] The release by a lawyer of out-of-court statements regarding an anticipated or pending trial may improperly affect the impartiality of the tribunal.[56] For these reasons, standards for permissible and prohibited conduct of a lawyer with respect to trial publicity have been established.

EC 7-34 The impartiality of a public servant in our legal system may be impaired by the receipt of gifts or loans. A lawyer,[57] therefore, is never justified in making a gift or a loan to a judge, a hearing officer, or an official or employee of a tribunal, except as permitted by Section C(4) of Canon 5 of the Code of Judicial Conduct, but a lawyer may make a contribution to the campaign fund of a candidate for judicial office in conformity with Section B(2) under Canon 7 of the Code of Judicial Conduct.[58]

EC 7-35 All litigants and lawyers should have access to tribunals on an equal basis. Generally, in adversary proceedings a lawyer should not communicate with a judge relative to a matter pending before, or which is to be brought before, a tribunal over which he presides in circumstances which might have the effect or give the appearance

---

trial—the most fundamental of all freedoms—must be maintained at all costs." Estes v. State of Texas, 381 U.S. 532, 540, 14 L.Ed.2d 543, 549, 85 S.Ct. 1628, 1631–32 (1965), rehearing denied, 382 U.S. 875, 15 L.Ed.2d 118, 86 S.Ct. 18 (1965).

54. "Pretrial can create a major problem for the defendant in a criminal case. Indeed, it may be more harmful than publicity during the trial for it may well set the community opinion as to guilt or innocence. . . . The trial witnesses present at the hearing, as well as the original jury panel, were undoubtedly made aware of the peculiar public importance of the case by the press and television coverage being provided, and by the fact that they themselves were televised live and their pictures rebroadcast on the evening show." Id., 381 U.S. at 536–37, 14 L.Ed.2d at 546–47, 85 S.Ct. at 1629–30.

55. "The undeviating rule of this Court was expressed by Mr. Justice Holmes over half a century ago in Patterson v. Colorado, 205 U.S. 454, 462 (1907):

"The theory of our system is that the conclusions to be reached in a case will be induced only by evidence and argument in open court, and not by any outside influence, whether of private talk or public print."

Sheppard v. Maxwell, 384 U.S. 333, 351, 16 L.Ed.2d 600, 614, 86 S.Ct. 1507, 1516 (1966).

"The trial judge has a large discretion in ruling on the issue of prejudice resulting from the reading by jurors of news articles concerning the trial. . . . Generalizations beyond that statement are not profitable, because each case must turn on its special facts. We have here the exposure of jurors to information of a character which the trial judge ruled was so prejudicial it could not be directly offered as evidence. The prejudice to the defendant is almost certain to be as great when that evidence reaches the jury through news accounts as when it is a part of the prosecution's evidence. . . . It may indeed be greater for it is then not tempered by protective procedures." Marshall v. United States, 360 U.S. 310, 312–13, 3 L.Ed.2d 1250, 1252, 79 S.Ct. 1171, 1173 (1959).

"The experienced trial lawyer knows that an adverse public opinion is a tremendous disadvantage to the defense of his client. Although grand jurors conduct their deliberations in secret, they are selected from the body of the public. They are likely to know what the general public knows and to reflect the public attitude. Trials are open to the public, and aroused public opinion respecting the merits of a legal controversy creates a court room atmosphere which, without any vocal expression in the presence of the petit jury, makes itself felt and has its effect upon the action of the petit jury. Our fundamental concepts of justice and our American sense of fair play requires that the petit jury shall be composed of persons with fair and impartial minds and without preconceived views as to the merits of the controversy, and that it shall determine the issues presented to it solely upon the evidence adduced at the trial and according to the law given in the instructions of the trial judge.

"While we may doubt that the effect of public opinion would sway or bias the judgment of the trial judge in an equity proceeding, the defendant should not be called upon to run that risk and the trial court should not have his work made more difficult by any dissemination of statements to the public that would be calculated to create a public demand for a particular judgment in a prospective or pending case." ABA Opinion 199 (1940).

Cf. Estes v. State of Texas, 381 U.S. 532, 544–45, 14 L.Ed.2d 543, 551, 85 S.Ct. 1628, 1634 (1965), rehearing denied, 381 U.S. 875, 15 L.Ed.2d 118, 86 S.Ct. 18 (1965).

56. See ABA Canon 20.

57. Canon 3 observes that a lawyer "deserves rebuke and denunciation for any device or attempt to gain from a Judge special personal consideration or favor."

See ABA Canon 32.

58. "*Judicial Canon 32* provides:

"'A judge should not accept any presents or favors from litigants, or from lawyers practicing before him or from others whose interests are likely to be submitted to him for judgment.'

"The language of this Canon is perhaps broad enough to prohibit campaign contributions by lawyers, practicing before the court upon which the candidate hopes to sit. However, we do not think it was intended to prohibit such contributions when the candidate is obligated, by force of circumstances over which he has no control, to conduct a campaign, the expense of which exceeds that which he should reasonably be expected to personally bear!" *ABA Opinion* 226 (1941).

Canon 7   ABA

of granting undue advantage to one party.[59] For example, a lawyer should not communicate with a tribunal by a writing unless a copy thereof is promptly delivered to opposing counsel or to the adverse party if he is not represented by a lawyer. Ordinarily an oral communication by a lawyer with a judge or hearing officer should be made only upon adequate notice to opposing counsel, or, if there is none, to the opposing party. A lawyer should not condone or lend himself to private importunities by another with a judge or hearing officer on behalf of himself or his client.

EC 7–36 Judicial hearings ought to be conducted through dignified and orderly procedures designed to protect the rights of all parties. Although a lawyer has the duty to represent his client zealously, he should not engage in any conduct that offends the dignity and decorum of proceedings.[60] While maintaining his independence, a lawyer should be respectful, courteous, and aboveboard in his relations with a judge or hearing officer before whom he appears.[61] He should avoid undue solicitude for the comfort or convenience of judge or jury and should avoid any other conduct calculated to gain special consideration.

EC 7–37 In adversary proceedings, clients are litigants and though ill feeling may exist between clients, such ill feeling should not influence a lawyer in his conduct, attitude, and demeanor towards opposing lawyers.[62] A lawyer should not make unfair or derogatory personal reference to opposing counsel. Haranguing and offensive tactics by lawyers interfere with the orderly administration of justice and have no proper place in our legal system.

EC 7–38 A lawyer should be courteous to opposing counsel and should accede to reasonable requests regarding court proceedings, settings, continuances, waiver of procedural formalities, and similar matters which do not prejudice the rights of his client.[63] He should follow local customs of courtesy or practice, unless he gives timely notice to opposing counsel of his intention not to do so.[64] A lawyer should be punctual in fulfilling all professional commitments.[65]

EC 7–39 In the final analysis, proper functioning of the adversary system depends upon cooperation between lawyers and tribunals in utilizing procedures which will preserve the impartiality of tribunals and make their decisional processes prompt and just, without impinging upon the obligation of lawyers to represent their clients zealously within the framework of the law.

DISCIPLINARY RULES

DR 7–101 Representing a Client Zealously.

(A) A lawyer shall not intentionally:[66]

(1) Fail to seek the lawful objectives of his client through reasonably available means[67] permitted by law and the Disciplinary Rules, except as provided by DR 7–101(B). A lawyer does not violate this Disciplinary Rule, however, by acceding to reasonable requests of opposing counsel which do not prejudice the rights of his client, by being punctual in fulfilling all professional commitments, by avoiding offensive tactics, or by treating with courtesy and consideration all persons involved in the legal process.

(2) Fail to carry out a contract of employment entered into with a client for professional services, but he may withdraw as permit-

---

59. See ABA Canons 3 and 32.
60. Cf. ABA Canon 18.
61. See ABA Canons 1 and 3.
62. See ABA Canon 17.
63. See ABA Canon 24.
64. See ABA Canon 25.
65. See ABA Canon 21.
66. See ABA Canon 15.
67. See ABA Canons 5 and 15; cf. ABA Canons 4 and 32.

ted under DR 2–110, DR 5–102, and DR 5–105.

(3) Prejudice or damage his client during the course of the professional relationship [68] except as required under DR 7–102(B).

(B) In his representation of a client, a lawyer may:

(1) Where permissible, exercise his professional judgment to waive or fail to assert a right or position of his client.

(2) Refuse to aid or participate in conduct that he believes to be unlawful, even though there is some support for an argument that the conduct is legal.

DR 7–102 Representing a Client Within the Bounds of the Law.

(A) In his representation of a client, a lawyer shall not:

(1) File a suit, assert a position, conduct a defense, delay a trial, or take other action on behalf of his client when he knows or when it is obvious that such action would serve merely to harass or maliciously injure another.[69]

(2) Knowingly advance a claim or defense that is unwarranted under existing law, except that he may advance such claim or defense it if can be supported by good faith argument for an extension, modification, or reversal of existing law.

(3) Conceal or knowingly fail to disclose that which he is required by law to reveal.

(4) Knowingly use perjured testimony or false evidence.[70]

(5) Knowingly make a false statement of law or fact.

(6) Participate in the creation or preservation of evidence when he knows or it is obvious that the evidence is false.

(7) Counsel or assist his client in conduct that the lawyer knows to be illegal or fraudulent.

(8) Knowingly engage in other illegal conduct or conduct contrary to a Disciplinary Rule.

(B) A lawyer who receives information clearly establishing that:

(1) His client has, in the course of the representation, perpetrated a fraud upon a person or tribunal shall promptly call upon his client to rectify the same, and if his client refuses or is unable to do so, he shall reveal the fraud to the affected person or tribunal, except when the information is protected as a privileged communication.[71]

(2) A person other than his client has perpetrated a fraud upon a tribunal shall promptly reveal the fraud to the tribunal.[72]

As amended in 1974.

DR 7–103 Performing the Duty of Public Prosecutor or Other Government Lawyer.[73]

(A) A public prosecutor or other government lawyer shall not institute or cause to be instituted criminal charges when he knows or it is obvious that the charges are not supported by probable cause.

(B) A public prosecutor or other government lawyer in criminal litigation shall make timely disclosure to coun-

---

68. Cf. ABA Canon 24.
69. See ABA Canon 30.
70. Cf. ABA Canons 22 and 29.
71. See ABA Canon 41; cf. Hinds v. State Bar, 19 Cal. 2d 87, 92–93, 119 P.2d 134, 137 (1941); but see ABA Opinion 287 (1953) and Texas Canon 38. Also see Code of Professional Responsibility. DR 4–101(C)(2).

72. See Precision Inst. Mfg. Co. v. Automotive M.M. Co., 324 U.S. 806, 89 L.Ed. 1381, 65 S.Ct. 993 (1945).

73. Cf. ABA Canon 5.

sel for the defendant, or to the defendant if he has no counsel, of the existence of evidence, known to the prosecutor or other government lawyer, that tends to negate the guilt of the accused, mitigate the degree of the offense, or reduce the punishment.

DR 7-104 Communicating With One of Adverse Interest.[74]

(A) During the course of his representation of a client a lawyer shall not:

(1) Communicate or cause another to communicate on the subject of the representation with a party he knows to be represented by a lawyer in that matter unless he has the prior consent of the lawyer representing such other party [75] or is authorized by law to do so.

(2) Give advice to a person who is not represented by a lawyer, other than the advice to secure counsel,[76] if the interests of such person are or have a reasonable possibility of being in conflict with the interests of his client.[77]

DR 7-105 Threatening Criminal Prosecution.

(A) A lawyer shall not present, participate in presenting, or threaten to present criminal charges solely to obtain an advantage in a civil matter.

DR 7-106 Trial Conduct.

(A) A lawyer shall not disregard or advise his client to disregard a standing rule of a tribunal or a ruling of a tribunal made in the course of a proceeding, but he may take appropriate steps in good faith to test the validity of such rule or ruling.

(B) In presenting a matter to a tribunal, a lawyer shall disclose:[78]

(1) Legal authority in the controlling jurisdiction known to him to be directly adverse to the position of his client and which is not disclosed by opposing counsel.[79]

(2) Unless privileged or irrelevant, the identities of the clients he represents and of the persons who employed him.[80]

---

74. "Rule 12. . . . A member of the State Bar shall not communicate with a party represented by counsel upon a subject of controversy, in the absence and without the consent of such counsel. This rule shall not apply to communications with a public officer, board, committee or body." Cal. Business and Professions Code § 6076 (West 1962).

75. See ABA Canon 9; cf. *ABA Opinions* 124 (1934), 108 (1934), 95 (1933), and 75 (1932); also see In re Schwabe, 242 Or. 169, 174–75, 408 P.2d 922, 924 (1965).

"It is clear from the earlier opinions of this committee that *Canon 9* is to be construed literally and does not allow a communication with an opposing party, without the consent of his counsel, though the purpose merely be to investigate the facts. *Opinions 117, 55, 66,*" ABA Opinion 187 (1938).

76. Cf. *ABA Opinion* 102 (1933).

77. Cf. ABA Canon 9 and *ABA Opinion* 58 (1931).

78. Cf. Note, 38 Texas L.Rev. 107, 108–09 (1959).

79. "In the brief summary in the 1947 edition of the Committee's decisions (p. 17), *Opinion 146* was thus summarized: *Opinion 146*—A lawyer should disclose to the court a decision directly adverse to his client's case that is unknown to his adversary.

. . .

"We would not confine the Opinion to 'controlling authorities'—i.e., those decisive of the pending case—but, in accordance with the tests hereafter suggested, would apply it to a decision directly adverse to any proposition of law on which the lawyer expressly relies, which would reasonably be considered important by the judge sitting on the case.

. . .

". . . The test in every case should be: Is the decision which opposing counsel has overlooked one which the court should clearly consider in deciding the case? Would a reasonable judge properly feel that a lawyer who advanced, as the law, a proposition adverse to the undisclosed decision, was lacking in candor and fairness to him? Might the judge consider himself misled by an implied representation that the lawyer knew of no adverse authority?" *ABA Opinion* 280 (1949).

80. "The authorities are substantially uniform against any privilege as applied to the fact of retainer or identity of the client. The privilege is limited to confidential communications, and a retainer is not a confidential communication, although it cannot come into existence without some communication between the attorney and the— at that stage prospective—client." United States v. Pape, 144 F.2d 778, 782 (2d Cir. 1944), cert. denied, 323 U.S. 752, 89 L.Ed.2d 602, 65 S.Ct. 86 (1944).

MODEL CODE OF PROFESSIONAL RESPONSIBILITY — Canon 7

(C) In appearing in his professional capacity before a tribunal, a lawyer shall not:

(1) State or allude to any matter that he has no reasonable basis to believe is relevant to the case or that will not be supported by admissible evidence.[81]

(2) Ask any question that he has no reasonable basis to believe is relevant to the case and that is intended to degrade a witness or other person.[82]

(3) Assert his personal knowledge of the facts in issue, except when testifying as a witness.

(4) Assert his personal opinion as to the justness of a cause, as to the credibility of a witness, as to the culpability of a civil litigant, or as to the guilt or innocence of an accused;[83] but he may argue, on his analysis of the evidence, for any position or conclusion with respect to the matters stated herein.

(5) Fail to comply with known local customs of courtesy or practice of the bar or a particular tribunal without giving to opposing counsel timely notice of his intent not to comply.[84]

(6) Engage in undignified or discourteous conduct which is degrading to a tribunal.

(7) Intentionally or habitually violate any established rule of procedure or of evidence.

DR 7–107 Trial Publicity.[85]

(A) A lawyer participating in or associated with the investigation of a crimi-

---

"To be sure, there may be circumstances under which the identification of a client may amount to the prejudicial disclosure of a confidential communication, as where the substance of a disclosure has already been revealed but not its source." Colton v. United States, 306 F.2d 633, 637 (2d Cir. 1962).

81. See ABA Canon 22; cf. ABA Canon 17.

"The rule allowing counsel when addressing the jury the widest latitude in discussing the evidence and presenting the client's theories falls far short of authorizing the statement by counsel of matter not in evidence, or indulging in argument founded on no proof, or demanding verdicts for purposes other than the just settlement of the matters at issue between the litigants, or appealing to prejudice or passion. The rule confining counsel to legitimate argument is not based on etiquette, but on justice. Its violation is not merely an overstepping of the bounds of propriety, but a violation of a party's rights. The jurors must determine the issues upon the evidence. Counsel's address should help them do this, not tend to lead them astray." Cherry Creek Nat. Bank v. Fidelity & Cas. Co., 207 App.Div. 787, 790–91, 202 N.Y.S. 611, 614 (1924).

82. Cf. ABA Canon 18.

§ 6068. . . . It is the duty of an attorney:

. . .

"(f) To abstain from all offensive personality, and to advance no fact prejudicial to the honor or reputation of a party or witness, unless required by the justice of the cause with which he is charged." Cal.Business and Professions Code § 6068 (West 1962).

83. "The record in the case at bar was silent concerning the qualities and character of the deceased. It is especially improper, in addressing the jury in a murder case, for the prosecuting attorney to make reference to his knowledge of the good qualities of the deceased where there is no evidence in the record bearing upon his character. . . . A prosecutor should never inject into his argument evidence not introduced at the trial." People v. Dukes, 12 Ill.2d 334, 341, 146 N.E.2d 14, 17–18 (1957).

84. "A lawyer should not ignore known customs or practice of the Bar or of a particular Court, even when the law permits, without giving timely notice to the opposing counsel." ABA Canon 25.

85. The provisions of Sections (A), (B), (C), and (D) of this Disciplinary Rule incorporate the fair trial-free press standards which apply to lawyers as adopted by the ABA House of Delegates, Feb. 19, 1968, upon the recommendation of the Fair Trial and Free Press Advisory Committee of the ABA Special Committee on Minimum Standards for the Administration of Criminal Justice.

Cf. ABA Canon 20; see generally ABA Advisory Committee on Fair Trial and Free Press, Standards Relating to Fair Trial and Free Press (1966).

"From the cases coming here we note that unfair and prejudicial news comment on pending trials has become increasingly prevalent. Due process requires that the accused receive a trial by an impartial jury free from outside influences. Given the pervasiveness of modern communications and the difficulty of effacing prejudicial publicity from the minds of the jurors, the trial courts must take strong measures to ensure that the balance is never weighed against the accused. And appellate tribunals have the duty to make an independent evaluation of the circumstances. Of course, there is nothing that prescribes the press from reporting events that transpire in the courtroom. But where there is a reasonable likelihood that prejudicial news prior to trial will prevent a fair trial, the judge should continue the case until the threat abates, or transfer it to another county not so permeated

nal matter shall not make or participate in making an extrajudicial statement that a reasonable person would expect to be disseminated by means of public communication and that does more than state without elaboration:

(1) Information contained in a public record.

(2) That the investigation is in progress.

(3) The general scope of the investigation including a description of the offense and, if permitted by law, the identity of the victim.

(4) A request for assistance in apprehending a suspect or assistance in other matters and the information necessary thereto.

(5) A warning to the public of any dangers.

(B) A lawyer or law firm associated with the prosecution or defense of a criminal matter shall not, from the time of the filing of a complaint, information, or indictment, the issuance of an arrest warrant, or arrest until the commencement of the trial or disposition without trial, make or participate in making an extrajudicial statement that a reasonable person would expect to be disseminated by means of public communication and that relates to:

(1) The character, reputation, or prior criminal record (including arrests, indictments, or other charges of crime) of the accused.

(2) The possibility of a plea of guilty to the offense charged or to a lesser offense.

(3) The existence or contents of any confession, admission, or statement given by the accused or his refusal or failure to make a statement.

(4) The performance or results of any examinations or tests or the refusal or failure of the accused to submit to examinations or tests.

(5) The identity, testimony, or credibility of a prospective witness.

(6) Any opinion as to the guilt or innocence of the accused, the evidence, or the merits of the case.

(C) DR 7–107(B) does not preclude a lawyer during such period from announcing:

(1) The name, age, residence, occupation, and family status of the accused.

(2) If the accused has not been apprehended, any information necessary to aid in his apprehension or to warn the public of any dangers he may present.

(3) A request for assistance in obtaining evidence.

(4) The identity of the victim of the crime.

(5) The fact, time, and place of arrest, resistance, pursuit, and use of weapons.

(6) The identity of investigating and arresting officers or agencies and the length of the investigation.

(7) At the time of seizure, a description of the physical evidence seized, other than a confession, admission, or statement.

(8) The nature, substance, or text of the charge.

---

with publicity. . . . The courts must take such steps by rule and regulation that will protect their processes from prejudicial outside interferences. Neither prosecutors, counsel for defense, the accused, witnesses, court staff nor enforcement officers coming under the jurisdiction of the court should be permitted to frustrate its function. Collaboration between counsel and the press as to information affecting the fairness of a criminal trial is not only subject to regulation, but is highly censurable and worthy of disciplinary measures." Sheppard v. Maxwell, 384 U.S. 333, 362–63, 16 L.Ed.2d 600, 620, 86 S.Ct. 1507, 1522 (1966).

- (9) Quotations from or references to public records of the court in the case.
- (10) The scheduling or result of any step in the judicial proceedings.
- (11) That the accused denies the charges made against him.

(D) During the selection of a jury or the trial of a criminal matter, a lawyer or law firm associated with the prosecution or defense of a criminal matter shall not make or participate in making an extra-judicial statement that a reasonable person would expect to be disseminated by means of public communication and that relates to the trial, parties, or issues in the trial or other matters that are reasonably likely to interfere with a fair trial, except that he may quote from or refer without comment to public records of the court in the case.

(E) After the completion of a trial or disposition without trial of a criminal matter and prior to the imposition of sentence, a lawyer or law firm associated with the prosecution or defense shall not make or participate in making an extra-judicial statement that a reasonable person would expect to be disseminated by public communication and that is reasonably likely to affect the imposition of sentence.

(F) The foregoing provisions of DR 7-107 also apply to professional disciplinary proceedings and juvenile disciplinary proceedings when pertinent and consistent with other law applicable to such proceedings.

(G) A lawyer or law firm associated with a civil action shall not during its investigation or litigation make or participate in making an extra-judicial statement, other than a quotation from or reference to public records, that a reasonable person would expect to be disseminated by means of public communication and that relates to:

- (1) Evidence regarding the occurrence or transaction involved.
- (2) The character, credibility, or criminal record of a party, witness, or prospective witness.
- (3) The performance or results of any examinations or tests or the refusal or failure of a party to submit to such.
- (4) His opinion as to the merits of the claims or defenses of a party, except as required by law or administrative rule.
- (5) Any other matter reasonably likely to interfere with a fair trial of the action.

(H) During the pendency of an administrative proceeding, a lawyer or law firm associated therewith shall not make or participate in making a statement, other than a quotation from or reference to public records, that a reasonable person would expect to be disseminated by means of public communication if it is made outside the official course of the proceeding and relates to:

- (1) Evidence regarding the occurrence or transaction involved.
- (2) The character, credibility, or criminal record of a party, witness, or prospective witness.
- (3) Physical evidence or the performance or results of any examinations or tests or the refusal or failure of a party to submit to such.
- (4) His opinion as to the merits of the claims, defenses, or positions of an interested person.
- (5) Any other matter reasonably likely to interfere with a fair hearing.

(I) The foregoing provisions of DR 7-107 do not preclude a lawyer from replying to charges of misconduct publicly made against him or from participating in the proceedings of legislative,

Canon 7 ABA

administrative, or other investigative bodies.

(J) A lawyer shall exercise reasonable care to prevent his employees and associates from making an extra-judicial statement that he would be prohibited from making under DR 7-107.

DR 7-108 Communication with or Investigation of Jurors.

(A) Before the trial of a case a lawyer connected therewith shall not communicate with or cause another to communicate with anyone he knows to be a member of the venire from which the jury will be selected for the trial of the case.

(B) During the trial of a case:

(1) A lawyer connected therewith shall not communicate with or cause another to communicate with any member of the jury.[86]

(2) A lawyer who is not connected therewith shall not communicate with or cause another to communicate with a juror concerning the case.

(C) DR 7-108(A) and (B) do not prohibit a lawyer from communicating with veniremen or jurors in the course of official proceedings.

(D) After discharge of the jury from further consideration of a case with which the lawyer was connected, the lawyer shall not ask questions of or make comments to a member of that jury that are calculated merely to harass or embarrass the juror or to influence his actions in future jury service.[87]

(E) A lawyer shall not conduct or cause, by financial support or otherwise, another to conduct a vexatious or harassing investigation of either a venireman or a juror.

(F) All restrictions imposed by DR 7-108 upon a lawyer also apply to communications with or investigations of members of a family of a venireman or a juror.

(G) A lawyer shall reveal promptly to the court improper conduct by a venireman or a juror, or by another toward a venireman or a juror or a member of his family, of which the lawyer has knowledge.

DR 7-109 Contact with Witnesses.

(A) A lawyer shall not suppress any evidence that he or his client has a legal obligation to reveal or produce.[88]

(B) A lawyer shall not advise or cause a person to secrete himself or to leave the jurisdiction of a tribunal for the purpose of making him unavailable as a witness therein.[89]

(C) A lawyer shall not pay, offer to pay, or acquiesce in the payment of compensation to a witness contingent upon the content of his testimony or the outcome of the case.[90] But a lawyer may advance, guarantee, or acquiesce in the payment of:

(1) Expenses reasonably incurred by a witness in attending or testifying.

(2) Reasonable compensation to a witness for his loss of time in attending or testifying.

(3) A reasonable fee for the professional services of an expert witness.

---

86. See ABA Canon 23.

87. "[I]t would be unethical for a lawyer to harass, entice, induce or exert influence on a juror to obtain his testimony." *ABA Opinion* 319 (1968).

88. See ABA Canon 5.

89. Cf. ABA Canon 5.

"*Rule 15.* . . . A member of the State Bar shall not advise a person, whose testimony could establish or tend to establish a material fact, to avoid service of process, or secrete himself, or otherwise to make his testimony unavailable." Cal.Business and Professions Code § 6076 (West 1962).

90. See In re O'Keefe, 49 Mont. 369, 142 P. 638 (1914).

MODEL CODE OF PROFESSIONAL RESPONSIBILITY   Canon 8

DR 7-110 Contact with Officials.[91]

(A) A lawyer shall not give or lend any thing of value to a judge, official, or employee of a tribunal, except as permitted by Section C(4) of Canon 5 of the Code of Judicial Conduct, but a lawyer may make a contribution to the campaign fund of a candidate for judicial office in conformity with Section B(2) under Canon 7 of the Code of Judicial Conduct.

(B) In an adversary proceeding, a lawyer shall not communicate, or cause another to communicate, as to the merits of the cause with a judge or an official before whom the proceeding is pending, except:

   (1) In the course of official proceedings in the cause.

   (2) In writing if he promptly delivers a copy of the writing to opposing counsel or to the adverse party if he is not represented by a lawyer.

   (3) Orally upon adequate notice to opposing counsel or to the adverse party if he is not represented by a lawyer.

   (4) As otherwise authorized by law, or by Section A(4) under Canon 3 of the Code of Judicial Conduct.[92]

As amended in 1974.

CANON 8

A Lawyer Should Assist in Improving the Legal System

ETHICAL CONSIDERATIONS

EC 8-1 Changes in human affairs and imperfections in human institutions make necessary constant efforts to maintain and improve our legal system.[1] This system should function in a manner that commands public respect and fosters the use of legal remedies to achieve redress of grievances. By reason of education and experience, lawyers are especially qualified to recognize deficiencies in the legal system and to initiate corrective measures therein. Thus they should participate in proposing and supporting legislation and programs to improve the system,[2] without regard to the general interests or desires of clients or former clients.[3]

EC 8-2 Rules of law are deficient if they are not just, understandable, and responsive to the needs of society. If a lawyer believes

---

91. Cf. ABA Canon 3.

92. *"Rule 16. . . .* A member of the State Bar shall not, in the absence of opposing counsel, communicate with or argue to a judge or judicial officer except in open court upon the merits of a contested matter pending before such judge or judicial officer; nor shall he, without furnishing opposing counsel with a copy thereof, address a written communication to a judge or judicial officer concerning the merits of a contested matter pending before such judge or judicial officer. This rule shall not apply to ex parte matters." Cal.Business and Professions Code § 6076 (West 1962).

1. ". . . [Another] task of the great lawyer is to do his part individually and as a member of the organized bar to improve his profession, the courts, and the law. As President Theodore Roosevelt aptly put it, 'Every man owes some of his time to the upbuilding of the profession to which he belongs.' Indeed, this obligation is one of the great things which distinguishes a profession from a business. The soundness and the necessity of President Roosevelt's admonition insofar as it relates to the legal profession cannot be doubted. The advances in natural science and technology are so startling and the velocity of change in business and in social life is so great that the law along with the other social sciences, and even human life itself, is in grave danger of being extinguished by new gods of its own invention if it does not awake from its lethargy. Vanderbilt, *The Five Functions of the Lawyer: Service to Clients and the Public*, 40 A.B.A.J. 31, 31–32 (1954).

2. See ABA Cannon 29; Cf. Cheatham, *The Lawyer's Role and Surroundings*, 25 Rocky Mt.L.Rev. 405, 406–07 (1953).

"The lawyer tempted by repose should recall the heavy costs paid by his profession when needed legal reform has to be accomplished through the initiative of public-spirited laymen. Where change must be thrust from without upon an unwilling Bar, the public's least flattering picture of the lawyer seems confirmed. The lawyer concerned for the standing of his profession will, therefore, interest himself actively in the improvement of the law. In doing so he will not only help to maintain confidence in the Bar, but will have the satisfaction of meeting a responsibility inhering in the nature of his calling." *Professional Responsibility: Report of the Joint Conference*, 44 A.B.A.J. 1159, 1217 (1958).

3. See Stayton, *Cum Honore Officium*, 19 Tex.B.J. 765, 766 (1956); *Professional Responsibility: Report of the Joint Conference*, 44 A.B.A.J. 1159, 1162 (1958); and Paul, *The Lawyer as a Tax Adviser*, 25 Rocky Mt.L.Rev. 412, 433–34 (1953).

that the existence or absence of a rule of law, substantive or procedural, causes or contributes to an unjust result, he should endeavor by lawful means to obtain appropriate changes in the law. He should encourage the simplification of laws and the repeal or amendment of laws that are outmoded.[4] Likewise, legal procedures should be improved whenever experience indicates a change is needed.

EC 8–3 The fair administration of justice requires the availability of competent lawyers. Members of the public should be educated to recognize the existence of legal problems and the resultant need for legal services, and should be provided methods for intelligent selection of counsel. Those persons unable to pay for legal services should be provided needed services. Clients and lawyers should not be penalized by undue geographical restraints upon representation in legal matters, and the bar should address itself to improvements in licensing, reciprocity, and admission procedures consistent with the needs of modern commerce.

EC 8–4 Whenever a lawyer seeks legislative or administrative changes, he should identify the capacity in which he appears, whether on behalf of himself, a client, or the public.[5] A lawyer may advocate such changes on behalf of a client even though he does not agree with them. But when a lawyer purports to act on behalf of the public, he should espouse only those changes which he conscientiously believes to be in the public interest.

EC 8–5 Fraudulent, deceptive, or otherwise illegal conduct by a participant in a proceeding before a tribunal or legislative body is inconsistent with fair administration of justice, and it should never be participated in or condoned by lawyers. Unless constrained by his obligation to preserve the confidences and secrets of his client, a lawyer should reveal to appropriate authorities any knowledge he may have of such improper conduct.

EC 8–6 Judges and administrative officials having adjudicatory powers ought to be persons of integrity, competence, and suitable temperament. Generally, lawyers are qualified, by personal observation or investigation, to evaluate the qualifications of persons seeking or being considered for such public offices, and for this reason they have a special responsibility to aid in the selection of only those who are qualified.[6] It is the duty of lawyers to endeavor to prevent political considerations from outweighing judicial fitness in the selection of judges. Lawyers should protest earnestly against the appointment or election of those who are unsuited for the bench and should strive to have elected [7] or appointed thereto only those who are willing to forego pursuits, whether of a business, political, or other nature, that may interfere with the free and fair consideration

---

4. "There are few great figures in the history of the Bar who have not concerned themselves with the reform and improvement of the law. The special obligation of the profession with respect to legal reform rests on considerations too obvious to require enumeration. Certainly it is the lawyer who has both the best chance to know when the law is working badly and the special competence to put it in order." *Professional Responsibility: Report of the Joint Conference*, 44 A.B.A.J. 1159, 1217 (1958).

5. "*Rule 14.* . . . A member of the State Bar shall not communicate with, or appear before, a public officer, board, committee or body, in his professional capacity, without first disclosing that he is an attorney representing interests that may be affected by action of such officer, board, committee or body." Cal.Business and Professions Code § 6076 (West 1962).

6. See ABA Canon 2.

"Lawyers are better able than laymen to appraise accurately the qualifications of candidates for judicial office. It is proper that they should make that appraisal known to the voters in a proper and dignified manner. A lawyer may with propriety endorse a candidate for judicial office and seek like endorsement from other lawyers. But the lawyer who endorses a judicial candidate or seeks that endorsement from other lawyers should be actuated by a sincere belief in the superior qualifications of the candidate for judicial service and not by personal or selfish motives; and a lawyer should not use or attempt to use the power or prestige of the judicial office to secure such endorsement. On the other hand, the lawyer whose endorsement is sought, if he believes the candidate lacks the essential qualifications for the office or believes the opposing candidate is better qualified, should have the courage and moral stamina to refuse the request for endorsement." *ABA Opinion* 189 (1938).

7. "[W]e are of the opinion that, whenever a candidate for judicial office merits the endorsement and support of lawyers, the lawyers may make financial contributions toward the campaign if its cost, when reasonably conducted, exceeds that which the candidate would be expected to bear personally." *ABA Opinion* 226 (1941).

of questions presented for adjudication. Adjudicatory officials, not being wholly free to defend themselves, are entitled to receive the support of the bar against unjust criticism.[8] While a lawyer as a citizen has a right to criticize such officials publicly,[9] he should be certain of the merit of his complaint, use appropriate language, and avoid petty criticisms, for unrestrained and intemperate statements tend to lessen public confidence in our legal system.[10] Criticisms motivated by reasons other than a desire to improve the legal system are not justified.

EC 8-7 Since lawyers are a vital part of the legal system, they should be persons of integrity, of professional skill, and of dedication to the improvement of the system. Thus a lawyer should aid in establishing, as well as enforcing, standards of conduct adequate to protect the public by insuring that those who practice law are qualified to do so.

EC 8-8 Lawyers often serve as legislators or as holders of other public offices. This is highly desirable, as lawyers are uniquely qualified to make significant contributions to the improvement of the legal system. A lawyer who is a public officer, whether full or part-time, should not engage in activities in which his personal or professional interests are or foreseeably may be in conflict with his official duties.[11]

EC 8-9 The advancement of our legal system is of vital importance in maintaining the rule of law and in facilitating orderly changes; therefore, lawyers should encourage, and should aid in making, needed changes and improvements.

DISCIPLINARY RULES

DR 8-101 Action as a Public Official.

(A) **A lawyer who holds public office shall not:**

(1) **Use his public position to obtain, or attempt to obtain, a special advantage in legislative matters for himself or for a client under circumstances where he knows or it is obvious that such action is not in the public interest.**

---

8. See ABA Canon 1.

9. "Citizens have a right under our constitutional system to criticize governmental officials and agencies. Courts are not, and should not be, immune to such criticism." Konigsberg v. State Bar of California, 353 U.S. 252, 269 (1957).

10. "[E]very lawyer, worthy of respect, realizes that public confidence in our courts is the cornerstone of our governmental structure, and will refrain from unjustified attack on the character of the judges, while recognizing the duty to denounce and expose a corrupt or dishonest judge." Kentucky State Bar Ass'n v. Lewis, 282 S.W.2d 321, 326 (Ky.1955).

"We should be the last to deny that Mr. Meeker has the right to uphold the honor of the profession and to expose without fear or favor corrupt or dishonest conduct in the profession, whether the conduct be that of a judge or not. . . . However, this Canon [29] does not permit one to make charges which are false and untrue and unfounded in fact. When one's fancy leads him to make false charges, attacking the character and integrity of others, he does so at his peril. He should not do so without adequate proof of his charges and he is certainly not authorized to make careless, untruthful and vile charges against his professional brethren." In re Meeker, 76 N.M. 354, 364-65, 414 P.2d 862, 869 (1966), appeal dismissed, 385 U.S. 449, 17 L.Ed.2d 510, 87 S.Ct. 613 (1967).

11. "*Opinions 16, 30, 34, 77, 118* and *134* relate to Canon 6, and pass on questions concerning the propriety of the conduct of an attorney who is a public officer, in representing private interests adverse to those of the public body which he represents. The principle applied in those opinions is that an attorney holding public office should avoid all conduct which might lead the layman to conclude that the attorney is utilizing his public position to further his professional success or personal interests." *ABA Opinion* 192 (1939).

"The next question is whether a lawyer-member of a legislative body may appear as counsel or co-counsel at hearings before a zoning board of appeals, or similar tribunal, created by the legislative group of which he is a member. We are of the opinion that he may practice before fact-finding officers, hearing bodies and commissioners, since under our views he may appear as counsel in the courts where his municipality is a party. Decisions made at such hearings are usually subject to administrative review by the courts upon the record there made. It would be inconsistent to say that a lawyer-member of a legislative body could not participate in a hearing at which the record is made, but could appear thereafter when the cause is heard by the courts on administrative review. This is subject to an important exception. He should not appear as counsel where the matter is subject to review by the legislative body of which he is a member. . . . We are of the opinion that where a lawyer does so appear there would be conflict of interests between his duty as an advocate for his client on the one hand and the obligation to his governmental unit on the other." In re Becker, 16 Ill.2d 488, 494-95, 158 N.E.2d 753, 756-57 (1959).

Cf. *ABA Opinions* 186 (1938), 136 (1935), 118 (1934), and 77 (1932).

Canon 8   ABA

    (2) Use his public position to influence, or attempt to influence, a tribunal to act in favor of himself or of a client.

    (3) Accept any thing of value from any person when the lawyer knows or it is obvious that the offer is for the purpose of influencing his action as a public official.

DR 8-102 Statements Concerning Judges and Other Adjudicatory Officers.[12]

(A) A lawyer shall not knowingly make false statements of fact concerning the qualifications of a candidate for election or appointment to a judicial office.

(B) A lawyer shall not knowingly make false accusations against a judge or other adjudicatory officer.

DR 8-103 Lawyer Candidate for Judicial Office.

(A) A lawyer who is a candidate for judicial office shall comply with the applicable provisions of Canon 7 of the Code of Judicial Conduct.

Added in 1974.

CANON 9

A Lawyer Should Avoid Even the Appearance of Professional Impropriety

ETHICAL CONSIDERATIONS

EC 9-1 Continuation of the American concept that we are to be governed by rules of law requires that the people have faith that justice can be obtained through our legal system.[1] A lawyer should promote public confidence in our system and in the legal profession.[2]

EC 9-2 Public confidence in law and lawyers may be eroded by irresponsible or improper conduct of a lawyer. On occasion, ethical conduct of a lawyer may appear to laymen to be unethical. In order to avoid misunderstandings and hence to maintain confidence, a lawyer should fully and promptly inform his client of material developments in the matters being handled for the client. While a lawyer should guard against otherwise proper conduct that has a tendency to diminish public confidence in the legal system or in the legal profession, his duty to clients or to the public should never be subordinate merely because the full discharge of his obligation may be misunderstood or may tend to subject him or the legal profession to criticism. When explicit ethical guidance does not exist, a lawyer should determine his conduct by acting in a manner that promotes public confidence in the integrity and efficiency of the legal system and the legal profession.[3]

EC 9-3 After a lawyer leaves judicial office or other public employment, he should not accept employment in connection with any matter in which he had substantial responsibility prior to his leaving, since to accept employment would give the appearance of impropriety even if none exists.[4]

EC 9-4 Because the very essence of the legal system is to provide procedures by which matters can be presented in an impartial manner so that they may be decided solely upon the merits, any statement or suggestion by a lawyer that he can or would attempt to circumvent those procedures is detrimental to the legal system and tends to undermine public confidence in it.

---

12. Cf. ABA Canons 1 and 2.

1. "Integrity is the very breath of justice. Confidence in our law, our courts, and in the administration of justice is our supreme interest. No practice must be permitted to prevail which invites towards the administration of justice a doubt or distrust of its integrity." Erwin M. Jennings Co. v. DiGenova, 107 Conn. 491, 499, 141 A. 866, 868 (1928).

2. "A lawyer should never be reluctant or too proud to answer unjustified criticism of his profession, of himself, or of his brother lawyer. He should guard the reputation of his profession and of his brothers as zealously as he guards his own." Rochelle and Payne, *The Struggle for Public Understanding*, 25 Texas B.J. 109, 162 (1962).

3. See ABA Canon 29.

4. See ABA Canon 36.

EC 9-5 Separation of the funds of a client from those of his lawyer not only serves to protect the client but also avoids even the appearance of impropriety, and therefore commingling of such funds should be avoided.

EC 9-6 Every lawyer owes a solemn duty to uphold the integrity and honor of his profession; to encourage respect for the law and for the courts and the judges thereof; to observe the Code of Professional Responsibility; to act as a member of a learned profession, one dedicated to public service; to cooperate with his brother lawyers in supporting the organized bar through the devoting of his time, efforts, and financial support as his professional standing and ability reasonably permit; to conduct himself so as to reflect credit on the legal profession and to inspire the confidence, respect, and trust of his clients and of the public; and to strive to avoid not only professional impropriety but also the appearance of impropriety.[5]

EC 9-7 A lawyer has an obligation to the public to participate in collective efforts of the bar to reimburse persons who have lost money or property as a result of the misappropriation or defalcation of another lawyer, and contribution to a clients' security fund is an acceptable method of meeting this obligation.

DISCIPLINARY RULES

DR 9-101 Avoiding Even the Appearance of Impropriety.[6]

(A) **A lawyer shall not accept private employment in a matter upon the merits of which he has acted in a judicial capacity.**[7]

(B) **A lawyer shall not accept private employment in a matter in which he had**

---

5. "As said in Opinion 49 of the Committee on Professional Ethics and Grievances of the American Bar Association, page 134: 'An attorney should not only avoid impropriety but should avoid the appearance of impropriety.'" State ex rel. Nebraska State Bar Ass'n v. Richards, 165 Neb. 80, 93, 84 N.W.2d 136, 145 (1957).

"It would also be preferable that such contribution [to the campaign of a candidate for judicial office] be made to a campaign committee rather than to the candidate personally. In so doing, possible appearances of impropriety would be reduced to a minimum." *ABA Opinion* 226 (1941).

"The lawyer assumes high duties, and has imposed upon him grave responsibilities. He may be the means of much good or much mischief. Interests of vast magnitude are entrusted to him; confidence is reposed in him; life, liberty, character and property should be protected by him. He should guard, with jealous watchfulness, his own reputation, as well as that of his profession." People ex rel. Cutler v. Ford, 54 Ill. 520, 522 (1870), and also quoted in State Board of Law Examiners v. Sheldon, 43 Wyo. 522, 526, 7 P.2d 226, 227 (1932).

See *ABA Opinion* 150 (1936).

6. Cf. Code of Professional Responsibility, EC 5-6.

7. See *ABA* Canon 36.

"It is the duty of the judge to rule on questions of law and evidence in misdemeanor cases and examinations in felony cases. That duty calls for impartial and uninfluenced judgment, regardless of the effect on those immediately involved or others who may, directly or indirectly, be affected. Discharge of that duty might be greatly interfered with if the judge, in another capacity, were permitted to hold himself out to employment by those who are to be, or who may be, brought to trial in felony cases, even though he did not conduct the examination. His private interests as a lawyer in building up his clientele, his duty as such zealously to espouse the cause of his private clients and to defend against charges of crime brought by law-enforcement agencies of which he is a part, might prevent, or even destroy, that unbiased judicial judgment which is so essential in the administration of justice.

"In our opinion, acceptance of a judgeship with the duties of conducting misdemeanor trials, and examinations in felony cases to determine whether those accused should be bound over for trial in a higher court, ethically bars the judge from acting as attorney for the defendants upon such trial, whether they were examined by him or by some other judge. Such a practice would not only diminish public confidence in the administration of justice in both courts, but would produce serious conflict between the private interests of the judge as a lawyer, and of his clients, and his duties as a judge in adjudicating important phases of criminal processes in other cases. The public and private duties would be incompatible. The prestige of the judicial office would be diverted to private benefit, and the judicial office would be demeaned thereby." *ABA Opinion* 242 (1942).

"A lawyer, who has previously occupied a judicial position or acted in a judicial capacity, should refrain from accepting employment in any matter involving the same facts as were involved in any specific question which he acted upon in a judicial capacity and, for the same reasons, should also refrain from accepting any employment which might reasonably appear to involve the same facts." *ABA Opinion* 49 (1931).

See *ABA Opinion* 110 (1934).

Canon 9   ABA

substantial responsibility while he was a public employee.[8]

(C) A lawyer shall not state or imply that he is able to influence improperly or upon irrelevant grounds any tribunal, legislative body,[9] or public official.

DR 9–102 Preserving Identity of Funds and Property of a Client.[10]

(A) All funds of clients paid to a lawyer or law firm, other than advances for costs and expenses, shall be deposited in one or more identifiable bank accounts maintained in the state in which the law office is situated and no funds belonging to the lawyer or law firm shall be deposited therein except as follows:

    (1) Funds reasonably sufficient to pay bank charges may be deposited therein.

    (2) Funds belonging in part to a client and in part presently or potentially to the lawyer or law firm must be deposited therein, but the portion belonging to the lawyer or law firm may be withdrawn when due unless the right of the lawyer or law firm to receive it is disputed by the client, in which event the disputed portion shall not be withdrawn until the dispute is finally resolved.

(B) A lawyer shall:

    (1) Promptly notify a client of the receipt of his funds, securities, or other properties.

    (2) Identify and label securities and properties of a client promptly upon receipt and place them in a safe deposit box or other place of safekeeping as soon as practicable.

    (3) Maintain complete records of all funds, securities, and other properties of a client coming into the possession of the lawyer and render appropriate accounts to his client regarding them.

    (4) Promptly pay or deliver to the client as requested by a client the funds, securities, or other properties in the possession of the lawyer which the client is entitled to receive.

DEFINITIONS *

As used in the Disciplinary Rules of the Code of Professional Responsibility:

    (1) "Differing interests" include every interest that will adversely affect either the judgment or the

---

8. See *ABA Opinions* 135 (1935) and 134 (1935); cf. ABA Canon 36 and *ABA Opinions* 39 (1931) and 26 (1930). But see *ABA Opinion* 37 (1931).

9. "[A statement by a governmental department or agency with regard to a lawyer resigning from its staff that includes a laudation of his legal ability] carries implications, probably not founded in fact, that the lawyer's acquaintance and previous relations with the personnel of the administrative agencies of the government place him in an advantageous position in practicing before such agencies. So to imply would not only represent what probably is untrue, but would be highly reprehensible." *ABA Opinion* 184 (1938).

10. See ABA Canon 11.

"Rule 9. . . . A member of the State Bar shall not commingle the money or other property of a client with his own; and he shall promptly report to the client the receipt by him of all money and other property belonging to such client. Unless the client otherwise directs in writing, he shall promptly deposit his client's funds in a bank or trust company . . . in a bank account separate from his own account and clearly designated as 'Clients' Funds Account' or 'Trust Funds Account' or words of similar import. Unless the client otherwise directs in writing, securities of a client in bearer form shall be kept by the attorney in a safe deposit box at a bank or trust company, . . . which safe deposit box shall be clearly designated as 'Clients' Account' or 'Trust Account' or words of similar import, and be separate from the attorney's own safe deposit box." Cal.Business and Professions Code § 6076 (West 1962).

"[C]ommingling is committed when a client's money is intermingled with that of his attorney and its separate identity lost so that it may be used for the attorney's personal expenses or subjected to claims of his creditors. . . . The rule against commingling was adopted to provide against the probability in some cases, the possibility in many cases, and the danger in all cases that such commingling will result in the loss of clients' money." Black v. State Bar, 57 Cal.2d 219, 225–26, 368 P.2d 118, 122, 18 Cal.Rptr. 518, 522 (1962).

* "Confidence" and "secret" are defined in DR 4–101(A).

loyalty of a lawyer to a client, whether it be a conflicting, inconsistent, diverse, or other interest.

(2) "Law firm" includes a professional legal corporation.

(3) "Person" includes a corporation, an association, a trust, a partnership, and any other organization or legal entity.

(4) "Professional legal corporation" means a corporation, or an association treated as a corporation, authorized by law to practice law for profit.

(5) "State" includes the District of Columbia, Puerto Rico, and other federal territories and possessions.

(6) "Tribunal" includes all courts and all other adjudicatory bodies.

(7) "A Bar association" includes a bar association of specialists as referred to in DR 2-105(A)(1) or (3).

(8) "Qualified legal assistance organization" means an office or organization of one of the four types listed in DR 2-103(D)(1)-(4), inclusive that meets all the requirements thereof.

As amended in 1974.

INDEX TO MODEL CODE

A

Acceptance of Employment. *See* Employment, acceptance of
Acquiring interest in litigation. *See* Adverse effect on professional judgment, interests of lawyer
Address change, notification of, 2–102(A)(2)
Administrative agencies and tribunals,
  Former employee, rejection of employment by, EC 9–3, DR 9–101(B)
  Improper influences on, EC 5–13, 5–21, 5–24, 8–5, 8–6, 9–4, DR 5–107(A), (B), 7–110, 8–101(A)(2), 9–101(C)
  Representation of client, generally, EC 7–11, 7–15, 7–16, 8–4, 8–5, 8–8, DR 8–101(A)
Admiralty practitioner, EC 2–14
Admission to practice,
  Duty of lawyers as to applicants, EC 1–3, 1–6, DR 1–101(B)
  Requirements for, EC 1–2, 1–3, 1–6, DR 1–101(A)
Advancing funds to clients, EC 5–8, DR 5–103(B)
  Court costs, EC 5–8, DR 5–103(B)
  Investigation expenses, EC 5–8, DR 5–103(B)
  Litigation expenses, EC 5–7, 5–8, DR 5–103(B)
  Medical examination, EC 5–8, DR 5–103(B)
  Personal expenses, EC 5–8, DR 5–103(B)
Adversary system, duty of lawyer to, EC 7–19 to 7–30, DR 7–101, 7–102
Adverse effect on professional judgment,
  Canon 5, definitions, (1)
  Desires of third persons, EC 5–1, 5–21 to 5–24, DR 5–107
  Interests of lawyer, EC 5–1, 5–2 to 5–13, DR 5–101 to 5–104
  Interests of other clients, EC 5–1, 5–14 to 5–20, DR 5–105, 5–106
Adverse legal authority, duty to reveal, EC 7–23, DR 7–106(B)(1)
Advertising, EC 2–2, 2–6 to 2–15, DR 2–101, 2–102(A)
  See also Name, use of
  Admission to bar, date and place of, EC 2–8
  Announcement of change of association, DR 2–102(A)(2)
  Announcement of change of firm name. DR 2–102(A)(2)
  Announcement of change of office address, DR 2–102(A)(2)

Advertising—Cont'd
  Announcement of establishment of law office, DR 2–102(A)(2)
  Announcement of office opening, DR 2–102(A)(2)
  Announcement of organization of which lawyer is officer or director, inclusion of name and profession of lawyer in, DR 2–101(H)(3)
  Authorships, DR 2–101(B)(8)
  Birthdate and place of birth, EC 2–8
  Books written by lawyer, DR 2–101(H)(5)
  Building directory, DR 2–102(A)(3)
  Cards,
    Announcement, DR 2–102(A)(2)
    Professional, DR 2–102(A)(1)
  Clients, regular, DR 2–101(B)(16)
  Commercial publicity, EC 2–8 to 2–10, DR 2–101, 2–102(A)
  Compensation for, EC 2–8, DR 2–101(B), (I), 2–103(B)
  Credit arrangements, EC 2–8, DR 2–101(B)(18)
  Deceptive, EC 2–9, DR 2–101(A)
  Display, DR 2–101(B)
  Fees, EC 2–8, DR 2–101(B)(18), (20), (25), (E), (F), (G)
    Consultation, DR 2–101(B)(20)
    Contingent, rates, DR 2–101(B)(22)
    Credit arrangements, DR 2–101(B)(18)
    Estimate, DR 2–101(B)(21), (23), (24), (25)
    Fixed, for specific services, DR 2–101(B)(25)
    Hourly rate, DR 2–101(B)(24)
    Schedule, DR 2–101(B)(23)
  Foreign language, fluency in, EC 2–8, DR 2–101(B)(14)
  Jurisdictional limitations of members of firm, required notice of, DR 2–102(D)
  Justification for, EC 2–2, 2–7, 2–8
  Law lists, EC 2–8
  Law office establishment, DR 2–102(A)(2)
  Law office, identification of, DR 2–102(A)(3)
  Legal directories, EC 2–8
  Legal documents, DR 2–101(H)(4)
  Legal notices, DR 2–101(B)(2)
  Legal publications, DR 2–101(B)(8), (H)(5)
  Letterheads,
    Of clients, DR 2–102(A)(4)
    Of law firm, DR 2–102(A)(4)
    Of lawyer, DR 2–102(A)(4), 2–102(B)
  Limited practice, EC 2–7, 2–8, 2–14, DR 2–101(B)(2), 2–105(A)(2)

ABA CODE

Advertising—Cont'd
Magazine, EC 2-8, DR 2-101
Memberships,
  Bar association, DR 2-101(B)(10)
  Legal fraternities and societies, DR 2-101(B)(11)
  Scientific, professional and technical associations, DR 2-101(B)(11)
Military service, DR 2-101(B)(7)
Name. See Name, use of
Newspaper, EC 2-8, DR 2-101
Office,
  Establishment, DR 2-102(A)(2)
  Identification of, DR 2-101(B)(1), 2-102(A)(3)
Office address change, DR 2-102(A)(2)
Office building directory, DR 2-102(A)(3)
Office hours, EC 2-8, DR 2-101(B)(19)
Office sign, DR 2-102(A)(3)
Political, DR 2-101(H)(1)
Prepaid or group service programs, participation in, DR 2-101(17)
Public notices, DR 2-101(H)(2)
Public office, DR 2-101(B)(6)
Quality of service, representation concerning, EC 2-9
Radio, EC 2-8, DR 2-101(B), (D), (I)
References, bank, DR 2-101(B)(15)
Regulation, reasons for, EC 2-2, 2-6 to 2-13
Rules, change in, EC 2-10, DR 2-101(C)
Schools and degrees, DR 2-101(B)(5)
Self-laudation, EC 2-8, 2-101(A)
Sign, DR 2-102(A)(3)
Specialization, EC 2-8, 2-14, DR 2-101(B)(2), 2-105
Teaching positions, DR 2-101(B)(9)
Technical and professional licenses, DR 2-101(B)(12)
Telephone directory, EC 2-8
Television, EC 2-8, DR 2-101(B), (D), (I)
Textbook, DR 2-101(H)(5)
Trade names, EC 2-11, DR 2-102(A)(4)
Treatises, DR 2-101(H)(5)
Advice by lawyer to secure legal services, EC 2-3 to 2-5, 7-18, DR 2-104, 7-104(A)(2)
  Client, former or regular, EC 2-4, DR 2-104(A)(1)
  Close friend, EC 2-4, DR 2-104(A)(1)
  Employment resulting from, EC 2-4, 2-104
  Motivation, effect of, EC 2-4
  One with adverse interest, EC 7-18, DR 7-104(A)(2)
  Other laymen parties to class action, DR 2-104(A)(5)
  Relative, EC 2-4, DR 2-104(A)(1)
  Volunteered, EC 2-3, 2-4, DR 2-104
  Within permissible legal service programs, DR 2-103(D), 2-104(A)(3)
Advocacy, professional, Canon 7

Aiding unauthorized practice of law, EC 3-8, DR 3-101
Ambulance chasing. See Recommendation of professional employment
Announcement card. See Advertising, cards
Appeal, duty to handle, EC 2-31
Appearance of impropriety, avoiding, EC 5-6, 9-2, 9-3, 9-5, 9-6, DR 9-101.
Appearance of lawyer. See Administrative agencies and tribunals, representation of client before; Courts, representation of client before; Legislature, representation of client before; Witness, lawyer acting as
Application for bar admission. See Admission to practice
Arbitrator, lawyer as, EC 5-20
Argument,
  Before administrative agency, EC 7-15
  Before jury, EC 7-24, 7-25, 7-37, DR 7-102(A), 7-106(C)
  Before legislature, EC 7-16, 7-17
  Before tribunal, EC 7-19 to 7-25, DR 7-102(A), 7-106,
Associates of lawyer, duty to control, EC 1-4, 3-8, 3-9, 4-2, 4-5, 6-2, DR 2-103, 4-101(D), 7-107(J)
Association of counsel,
  See also Co-counsel; Division of legal fees
  Client's consent, requirement of, EC 2-22
  Client's suggestion of, EC 5-10, 5-11
  Lawyer's suggestion of, EC 5-10, 5-11, 6-3, DR 6-101(A)(1)
Assumed name. See Name, use of, assumed name
Attempts to exert personal influence on tribunal, EC 7-24, 7-29, 7-34 to 7-36, DR 7-110, 8-101(A)(2)
Attorney-client privilege. DR 1-103, EC 3-3, Canon 4, DR 7-101(B)(1), 7-102(B)(1). See also Confidences of client; Secrets of client
Attorney's lien. See Fee for legal services, collection of
Availability of counsel, EC 2-1, 2-7, 2-24 to 2-33

B

Bank accounts for clients' funds, EC 9-5, DR 9-102(A)
Bank charges on clients' accounts, EC 9-5, DR 9-102(A)(1)
Bar applicant,
  See also Admission to practice
  Bar examiners, assisting, EC 1-2, 1-3, DR 1-101(B)
Bar associations,
  Advertising, DR 2-101(B)(10)
  Definitions, (7)

Bar associations—Cont'd
Disciplinary authorities, assisting, EC 1-4, DR 1-103
Educational activities, EC 6-2
Lawyer referral service, DR 2-103(C)(1), (D)(3)
Legal service programs, DR 2-103(D)(1)(d)
Requesting lawyer's representation of individual, EC 2-29
Barratry. *See* Advice by lawyer to secure legal services; Recommendation of professional employment
Bequest by client to lawyer, EC 5-5
Best efforts. *See* Zeal
Bounds of law,
Difficulty of ascertaining, EC 7-2 to 7-6
Duty to observe, EC 7-1, DR 7-102
Bribes. *See* Gifts to tribunal officer or employee by lawyer
Building directory. *See* Advertising, building directory
Business card. *See* Advertising, cards, professional
Business relations with clients, EC 5-3 to 5-7, DR 5-104

C

Calling card. *See* Advertising, cards, professional
Candidate. *See* Political activity
Canons, purpose of, preliminary statement
Card. *See* Advertising, cards
Change of association. *See* Advertising, announcement of change of association
Change of firm name. *See* Advertising, announcement of change of firm name
Change of office address. *See* Advertising, announcement of change of office
Character requirements, Canon 1, EC 1-3
Circumvention of disciplinary rule, DR 1-102(A)(2)
Class action. *See* Advice by lawyer to secure legal services
Clients,
See also Employment; Adverse effect on professional judgment; Fee for legal services; Indigents, representation of; Mental competence of client; Unpopular party, representation of
Appearance as witness for, EC 5-9, 5-10, DR 5-101(B), 5-102
Attorney-client privilege, EC 3-3, Canon 4
Commingling of funds of, EC 9-5, DR 9-102
Confidences of, Canon 4
Counseling, EC 7-3, 7-5 to 7-9, 7-12, DR 7-102(A)(7), (B)(1), 7-106(A), 7-109(B)
Decisions of, EC 5-12, 7-7, 7-8, 7-12

Clients—Cont'd
Property, protection of, DR 9-102
Secrets of, EC 3-3, Canon 4
Co-counsel,
See also Association of counsel
Disagreements with, EC 5-12
Division of fee with, DR 2-107(A)
Inability to work with, DR 2-110(C)(3)
Commercial publicity. *See* Advertising, commercial publicity
Commingling of funds, EC 9-5, DR 9-102
Communications with,
Judicial officers, EC 7-34, 7-35, 7-36, DR 7-110(B)
Jurors, EC 7-29 to 7-32, DR 7-108
One of adverse interests, EC 7-18, DR 7-104
Opposing party, EC 7-21, DR 7-104
Veniremen, EC 7-29 to 7-32, DR 7-108
Witnesses, EC 7-27, 7-28, DR 7-109
Compensation for recommendation of employment, prohibition against, EC 2-8, DR 2-103(B)
Competence, mental. *See* Mental competence of bar applicant; Mental competence of client, effect on representation; Mental competence of lawyer
Competence, professional, EC 2-30, Canon 6
Confidences of client, EC 3-3, 3-4, Canon 4
Conflicting interests. *See* Adverse effect on professional judgment
Consent of client, requirement of,
Acceptance of employment though interests conflict, EC 5-3, 5-14 to 5-20, DR 5-101(A), 5-104(A), 5-105(C)
Acceptance of value from third person, EC 2-21, 5-22, 5-23, DR 5-107(A), (B)
Advice requested from another lawyer, EC 4-2
Aggregate settlement of claims, DR 5-106
Association of lawyer, EC 2-22, DR 2-107(A)(1)
Division of legal fees, DR 2-107(A)(1)
Foregoing legal action, EC 7-7, 7-8, 7-9
Multiple representation, EC 5-16, DR 5-105(C)
Revelation of client's confidences and secrets, EC 4-2, 4-4, 4-5, DR 4-101(B)(3), (C)
Use of client's confidences and secrets, EC 4-2, 4-5, DR 4-101(B)(3), (C)
Withdrawal from employment, EC 2-32, DR 2-110(A)(2), (C)(5)
Consent of tribunal to lawyer's withdrawal, requirement of, EC 2-32, DR 2-110(A)(1), (C)
Contingent fee, propriety of,
In administrative actions, EC 2-20
In civil actions, EC 2-20, 5-7, DR 5-103(A)(2)
In criminal actions, EC 2-20, DR 2-106(C)

Contingent fee, propriety of—Cont'd
　In domestic relation actions, EC 2-20
Continuing legal education programs, EC 1-2, 6-2
Contract of employment,
　Fee provisions, desirability of writing, EC 2-19
　Restrictive covenant in, DR 2-108
Controversy over fee, avoiding, EC 2-19, 2-23
Corporation,
　Lawyer employed by, EC 5-18, 5-24, DR 5-107(C)
　Professional legal, EC 2-11, 5-24, DR 5-107(C), definitions (4)
Counsel, designation as,
　"General Counsel" designation, DR 2-102(A)(4)
　"Of Counsel" designation, DR 2-102(A)(4)
Counseling, client, EC 7-3, 7-5 to 7-8, DR 7-102(A)(7), (B)(1), 7-106(A)
Courts,
　See also Consent of tribunal to lawyer's withdrawal, requirement of; Evidence, conduct regarding; Trial tactics
　Appointment of lawyer as counsel, EC 2-29
　Courtesy, known customs of, EC 7-36, 7-38, DR 7-106(C)(5), (6)
　Personal influence, prohibitions against exerting, EC 7-34 to 7-36, DR 7-110
　Representation of client before, Canon 7
Criminal conduct,
　As basis for discipline of lawyer, EC 1-5, DR 1-102(A)(3), 7-102(A)
Criticism of judges and administrative officials, EC 8-6, DR 8-102
Cross-examination of witness. See Witnesses, questioning of
Duty to reveal information as to, EC 1-4, DR 1-103
Providing counsel for those accused of, EC 2-26 to 2-31

D

De facto specialization, EC 2-8, 2-14, DR 2-101(B)(2), 2-105(A)(2)
Deceased lawyer,
　Payment to estate of, EC 3-8, DR 3-102(A)(1), (2)
　Use of name by law firm, EC 2-11, DR 2-102(A)(4), (B)
Defender, public, working with. See Public defender office, working with
Defense against accusation by client, privilege to disclose confidences and secrets, DR 4-101(C)(4)
Defense of those accused of crime, EC 2-26 to 2-31

Definitions, following, Canon 9
　A bar association, definitions (7)
　Differing interests, definitions (1), EC 5-14
　Law firm, definitions (2)
　Person, definitions (3)
　Professional legal corporation, definitions (4)
　Qualified legal assistance organization, definitions (8)
　State, definitions (5)
　Tribunal, definitions (6)
Delegation of tasks to lay employees, EC 3-6
Desires of third parties, duty to avoid influence of, EC 5-21 to 5-24, DR 5-107
Differing interests, definitions (1), EC 5-14. See also Adverse effect on professional judgment
Disciplinary procedures, preliminary statement
Disciplinary rules, preliminary statement,
　Application of, preliminary statement
　Fair trial, requirement of, preliminary statement
　Penalties imposed, preliminary statement
　Purpose and function of, preliminary statement
Disciplinary sanction, preliminary statement
Discipline of lawyer, grounds for,
　Advertising, improper, DR 1-102, 2-101(A), 2-102
　Associates, failure to exercise reasonable care toward, DR 4-101(D)
　Bribery of legal officials, DR 7-110(A)
　Circumvention of disciplinary rule, DR 1-102(A)(2)
　Clients' funds, mismanagement of, DR 9-102
　Communication with adverse party, improper, DR 7-104
　Communication with jurors, improper, DR 7-108
　Communication with tribunal, improper, DR 7-110(B)
　Compensation, accepting from third party, DR 5-107
　Confidences, improper use of, DR 4-101(B), (D)
　Confidential information, disclosure of, DR 4-101(B), (D)
　Conflict of interest with clients, disregard of duty to avoid, DR 5-101 to 5-107
　Conflicting interests, representation of, DR 5-105, 5-106, 5-107
　Crime of moral turpitude, DR 1-102(A)(3)
　Criminal conduct, DR 1-102, 7-102, 7-109(A)
　Criminal prosecution threatening, DR 7-105
　Differing interests, improper representation of, DR 5-105, 5-106
　Disregard of tribunal ruling, DR 7-106(A)

201

PROFESSIONAL RESPONSIBILITY

Discipline of lawyer, grounds for—Cont'd
Division of fee, improper, DR 2–107(A), 3–102
Employees, failure to exercise reasonable care toward, DR 3–102, 4–101(D)
Evidence,
  False or misleading, use of, DR 7–102(A)(4), (6)
  Suppression of, DR 7–103(B), 7–109(A)
Extra-judicial statement, improper, DR 7–107
Failure to act competently, DR 6–101
Failure to act zealously, DR 7–101(A)
Failure to disclose information concerning another lawyer or judge, DR 1–103
Failure to disclose information to tribunal, DR 1–103, 7–102, 7–106(B)
False accusations, DR 8–102(B)
False statements concerning adjudicating officers, DR 8–102
False statements in bar application, DR 1–101(A)
Fees,
  Charging contingent fee in criminal case, DR 2–106(C)
  Charging illegal or clearly excessive, DR 2–106(A)
  Failure to return unearned, DR 2–110(A)(3)
Fraud, dishonesty, deceit, misrepresentation, DR 1–102(A)(4)
Further application of unqualified bar applicant, DR 1–101(B)
Gift or loan to public official, DR 7–110(A)
Guaranty of financial assistance, DR 5–103(B)
Holding out as having limited practice, DR 2–105
Holding out as a specialist, DR 2–105
Illegal conduct, DR 1–102(A)(3), 7–102
Improper argument before tribunal, DR 7–102(A), 7–106(C)(1), (3), (4)
Institution of criminal charges, DR 7–103(A)
Investigation of jurors, DR 7–108
Limiting liability, DR 6–102
Malpractice, DR 6–101, 6–102
Moral turpitude, crime of, DR 1–102(A)(3)
Negligence, DR 6–101
Nonmeritorious claim, DR 2–109
Nonmeritorious prosecution, DR 2–109
Professional affiliation with nonlawyers, DR 3–103, 5–107(C)
Public office, improper use of, DR 8–101
Publicity, improper, DR 2–101, 2–102
Recommendation of professional employment, prohibited, DR 2–103
Restrictive covenant, entering prohibited, DR 2–108
Secrets,
  Disclosure of, DR 4–101(B), (D)
  Improper use of, DR 4–101(B), (D)

Discipline of lawyer, grounds for—Cont'd
Solicitation of business, DR 2–103, 2–104
Specialization, notice of, DR 2–105
Suggestion of need of legal services, prohibited, DR 2–104
Unauthorized practice of law, 3–101(B)
  Aiding laymen in, DR 3–101(A)
Violation of disciplinary rule, DR 1–102(A)(1)
Withdrawal,
  Failure to, DR 2–110(B)
  Improper, DR 2–110
Disclosure of improper conduct,
  Of another lawyer, EC 1–4, DR 1–103
  Of bar applicant, EC 1–2, 1–3, DR 1–101(B)
  Of judge, DR 1–103(B)
  Toward juror or venireman, EC 7–32, DR 7–108(G)
Discretion of government lawyer, exercise of, EC 7–13, 7–14
Discussion of pending litigation with news media, EC 7–33, DR 7–107
Disregarding court ruling, DR 7–106(A)
Diverse interests. *See* Adverse effect on professional judgment
Division of legal fees,
  Consent of client, when required for, EC 2–22, DR 2–107(A)(1)
  Reasonableness of total fee, requirement of, EC 2–22, DR 2–107(A)(3)
  With associated lawyer, EC 2–22, DR 2–107
  With estate of deceased lawyer, EC 3–8, DR 3–102(A)(1), (2), (3)
  With laymen, EC 3–8, DR 3–102

E

Education,
  Continuing legal education programs, EC 6–2
  Of laymen to recognize legal problems, EC 2–1 to 2–5, 8–1, 8–3, DR 2–104
  Of laymen to select lawyers, EC 2–6 to 2–15, 18–1, DR 2–104(A)(2)
  Requirement of education for bar applicant, EC 1–2
Elections, DR 2–101(H)(1), 8–102(A)
Emotional instability. *See* Mental competence of lawyer
Employees of lawyer,
  Delegation of tasks, EC 3–6
  Duty of lawyer to control, EC 3–6, 4–2, 4–3, DR 4–101(D), 7–107(J)
Employment,
  See also Advice by lawyer to secure legal services; Recommendation of professional employment
  Acceptance of,
    Generally, EC 2–26 to 2–33

Employment—Cont'd
  Indigent client, on behalf of, EC 2-25, 2-29
  Instances when improper, EC 2-3, 2-4, 2-30, 4-6, 5-2, 5-3, 5-10, 5-14 to 5-16, 5-20, 5-24, 6-1, 6-3, 9-3, DR 2-103(E), 2-104, 2-109, 5-101, 5-105, 6-101(A)(1), 9-101(A), (B)
  Multiple clients, on behalf of, EC 5-14 to 5-19, DR 5-105(A), (C)
  Unpopular cause, on behalf of, EC 2-26 to 2-30
  Unpopular client, on behalf of, EC 2-26 to 2-30
  When able to render competent service, EC 2-30, 6-1, 6-3, DR 6-101
Arbitrator, in capacity as, EC 5-20
Contract,
  Desirability of, EC 2-19
  Restrictive covenant in, DR 2-108
Mediator, in capacity as, EC 5-20
Public, retirement from, EC 9-3, DR 9-101(A), (B)
Rejection of, EC 2-26 to 2-33, 4-5, 6-1, 6-3, 9-3, DR 2-103, 2-104, 2-109, 2-110, 6-101, 9-101(A), (B)
Withdrawal from,
  Generally, EC 2-32, 5-3, 5-10, 5-14 to 5-16, 5-19, 7-8, DR 2-110, 5-102, 5-105, 7-101(A)(2)
  Harm to client, avoidance of, EC 2-32, 4-6, 5-10, 5-15, DR 2-110(A)(2), 5-102(B), 5-105(B)
  Mandatory withdrawal, DR 2-110(B), 5-102, 5-105(B), (D)
  Permissive withdrawal, EC 7-8, DR 2-110(C)
  Refund of unearned fee paid in advance, requirement of, EC 2-32, DR 2-110(A)(3)
  Tribunal, consent to, EC 2-32, DR 2-110(A)(1)
  When arbitrator or mediator, EC 5-20
Estate of deceased lawyer,
Ethical considerations, purpose and function of, preliminary statement
Evidence, conduct regarding, EC 7-13, 7-24 to 7-28, DR 7-102(A), 7-103(B), 7-106(C), 7-109(A)
Excessive fee, EC 2-17, DR 2-106(A), (B)
Executor, client naming lawyer as, EC 5-6
Expenses of client, advancing or guaranteeing payment of, EC 5-8, DR 5-103(B)
Expert witness, payment to, EC 7-28, DR 7-109(C)(3)

F

False or perjured evidence, use of, EC 7-6, 7-26, DR 7-102(A)(4), EC 8-4
Fee for legal services,
  See also Advertising, fees

Fee for legal services—Cont'd
  Adequate fee, need for, EC 2-17
  Agreement as to, EC 2-19, DR 2-106
  Amount of,
    Determination of, EC 2-18, DR 2-106(B)
    Excessive, clearly, EC 2-17, DR 2-106(A), (B)
    Rationale for, EC 2-17
    Reasonable, desirability of, EC 2-17, 2-18
  Collection of,
    Avoiding litigation with client, EC 2-23
    Client's secrets, use of in collecting or establishing, DR 4-101(C)(4)
    Liens, use of, EC 5-7, DR 5-103(A)(1)
  Contingent fee, EC 2-18, 2-20, 2-24, 5-7, 5-8, DR 2-106(B)(8), (C), 5-103(A)(2)
  Contract as to, desirability of written, EC 2-19
  Controversy over, avoiding, EC 2-19, 2-23
  Determination of, factors to consider, EC 2-18, DR 2-106(B)
    Ability of lawyer, EC 2-18, DR 2-106(B)(7)
    Amount involved, DR 2-106(B)(4)
    Customary, DR 2-106(B)(3)
    Effort required, DR 2-106(B)(1)
    Employment, likelihood of preclusion of other, DR 2-106(B)(2)
    Experience of lawyer, EC 2-18, DR 2-106(B)(7)
    Interests of client and lawyer, EC 2-16 to 2-18
    Labor required, DR 2-106(B)(1)
    Nature of employment, EC 2-18
    Question involved, difficulty and novelty of, DR 2-106(B)(1)
    Relationship with client, professional, EC 2-17, DR 2-106(B)(6)
    Reputation of lawyer, EC 2-18, DR 2-106(B)(7)
    Responsibility assumed by lawyer, EC 2-18
    Results obtained, EC 2-18, DR 2-106(B)(4)
    Skill requisite to services, EC 2-18, DR 2-106(B)(1)
    Time required, EC 2-18, DR 2-106(B)(1)
    Type of fee, fixed or contingent, EC 2-18, 5-7, 5-8, DR 2-106(B)(8), 5-103
  Division of,
    Among lawyers, EC 2-22, DR 2-107
    With laypersons, EC 3-8, DR 3-102
  Establishment of fee, use of client's confidences and secrets, DR 4-101(C)(4)
  Excessive fee, EC 2-17, DR 2-106(A), (B)
  Explanation of, EC 2-17, 2-18, 2-19
  Illegal fee, prohibition against, DR 2-106(A)
  Persons able to pay reasonable fee, EC 2-17 to 2-23

Fee for legal services—Cont'd
  Persons only able to pay a partial fee, EC 2–16
  Persons without means to pay a fee, EC 2–24, 2–25
  Reasonable fee, EC 2–17, 2–18, DR 2–106(B)
  Rebate, propriety of accepting, EC 2–21, 22, DR 2–107, 5–107(A)
  Refund of unearned portion to client, EC 2–32, DR 2–110(A)(3)
Fee of lawyer referral service, propriety of paying, DR 2–103(C)(1)
Felony. See Criminal conduct; Discipline of lawyer, grounds for, illegal conduct
Firm name. See Name, use of, firm name
Framework of law. See Bounds of law
Fraud, duty to reveal, EC 8–5, DR 7–102(B)
Frivolous position avoiding, EC 7–4, DR 7–102(A)(1), (2), 7–106(C)(1)
Funds of client, protection of, EC 9–5, DR 9–102
Future conduct of client, counseling as to. See Clients, counseling

G

"General counsel" designation, DR 2–102(A)(4)
Gift to lawyer by client, EC 5–5
Gifts to tribunal officer or employee by lawyer, EC 7–34, 7–110(A)
Government, employment in,
  Civil cases, EC 7–14
  Criminal cases, EC 7–11, 7–13, 7–14, DR 7–103
    Name in partnership name, EC 2–12, DR 2–102(B)
    Retirement from government service, EC 9–3, DR 9–101(B)
Government legal assistance agencies, working with, DR 2–103(C)(2), (D)(1)(c)
Grievance committee. See Bar applicant, disciplinary authority, assisting
Guaranteeing payment of client's costs and expenses, EC 5–8, DR 5–103(B)

H

Harassment, duty to avoid litigation involving, EC 2–30, DR 2–109(A)(1), 2–110(B)(1), 7–102(A)(1)
Holding out,
  As being engaged in both law and another field, DR 2–102(E)
  As limiting practice, EC 2–8, 2–14, DR 2–101(B)(2), 2–105
  As partnership, EC 2–13, DR 2–102(C)
  As specialist, EC 2–8, 2–14, DR 2–101(B)(2), 2–105

I

Identity of client, duty to reveal, EC 7–15, 7–16, 8–4, 8–5, DR 7–106(B)(2)
Illegal conduct, as cause for discipline, EC 1–5, 7–26, DR 1–102(A)(3), 7–102(A)
Impartiality of tribunal, aiding in the, EC 7–34, 7–35, DR 7–110
Improper influences,
  Gift or loan to judicial officer, EC 7–34, DR 7–110(A)
  On judgment of lawyer. See Adverse effect on professional judgment
Improvement of legal system, Canon 8
Incompetence,
  Mental. See Mental competence of bar applicant; Mental competence of client; Mental competence of lawyer
  Professional. See Competence, professional
Independent professional judgment, duty to preserve, Canon 5
Indigents,
  Provision of legal services to, EC 2–16, 2–24, 2–25, 8–3, DR 2–103(D)(1)
  Representation of, EC 2–24, 2–25, 2–29
Integrity of legal profession, maintaining, Canon 1, EC 1–1, 1–4, 8–7, 9–1, 9–2, 9–6, DR 1–101
Intent of client, as factor in giving advice, EC 7–5, 7–6, DR 7–102(A)(7)
Interests of lawyer. See Adverse effect on professional judgment, interests of lawyer
Interests of other client. See Adverse effect on professional judgment, interests of other clients
Interests of third person. See Adverse effect on professional judgment, desires of third persons
Intermediary, prohibition against use of, EC 5–21 to 5–24, DR 5–107
Interview,
  With opposing party, EC 7–18, DR 7–104
  With news media, EC 7–33, DR 7–107
  With witness, EC 7–27, 7–28, DR 7–109
Investigation expenses, advancing or guaranteeing payment, EC 5–8, DR 5–103(B)

J

Judges,
  False statements concerning, DR 8–102
  Improper influences on,
    Gifts or loans to, EC 7–34, 7–110(A)
    Private communication with, EC 7–35, 7–39, DR 7–110(B)
  Misconduct toward,
    Criticisms of, EC 8–6, DR 8–102
    Disobedience of orders, EC 7–36, DR 7–106(A)
    False statement regarding, DR 8–102

ABA CODE

Judges—Cont'd
  Name in partnership name, EC 2-12, DR 2-102(B)
  Retirement from bench, EC 9-3, DR 9-101
  Selection of, EC 8-6, DR 8-102, 8-103
Judgment of lawyer, EC 3-2.
  See also Adverse effect on professional judgment
Judicial rulings, EC 7-22, DR 7-106(A)
Jury,
  Arguments before, EC 7-24, 7-25, 7-37, DR 7-102(A), 7-106(C)
  Communications with,
    After dismissal, EC 7-29, DR 7-108(D)
    Before trial, EC 7-29, 7-31, 7-33, DR 7-108(A), 7-108(C)
    During trial, EC 7-29, 7-31, 7-33, DR 7-108(B), 7-108(C)
  Improper influences on,
    Extra judicial statements, EC 7-29, 7-31, 7-33, DR 7-108
    Undue solicitude for, EC 7-36
  Investigation of members, EC 7-30, 7-31, DR 7-108(E), (F)
  Misconduct of, duty to reveal, EC 7-32, DR 7-108(G)
  Misconduct toward, EC 7-30, 7-31, DR 7-108(E), (G)
  Questioning members of after their dismissal, EC 7-29, DR 7-108(D)

K

Knowledge of intended crime, revealing, DR 4-101(C)(3)

L

Law firm, definitions (2)
Law lists. See Advertising law lists
Law office. See Partnership
Law school, working with legal aid office or public defender office sponsored by, DR 2-103(D)(1)(a)
Lawyer-client privilege. See Attorney-client privilege
Lawyer referral services, EC 2-15
  Fee for listing, propriety of paying, DR 2-103(C)(1)
  Listing of type referrals accepted, propriety of, DR 2-105(A)(2)
  Request for referrals, propriety of, DR 2-103(C)(1), (D)
  Working with, DR 2-103(C), (D)
Laypersons,
  See also Unauthorized practice of law,
  Need to legal services, EC 2-1 to 2-3, 2-6 to 2-8, 3-3, DR 2-104
  Recognition of legal problems, need to improve, EC 2-1 to 2-3, 8-3

Laypersons—Cont'd
  Selection of lawyer, need to facilitate, EC 2-7 to 2-10, 8-3
Legal aid offices, working with, EC 2-25, DR 2-103(D)(1)
Legal corporation. See Professional legal corporation
Legal directory. See Advertising, law lists
Legal documents of clients, duty to safeguard, EC 4-2, 4-3
Legal education programs. See Continuing legal education programs
Legal problems, recognition of by laymen, EC 2-1 to 2-3, 8-3, DR 2-104
Legal system, duty to improve, Canon 8
Legislature,
  Improper influence upon, EC 9-2, 9-3, 9-4, DR 8-101(A)(1), 9-101(B), (C)
  Representation of client before, EC 7-16, 7-17, 8-4, 8-5
  Serving as member of, EC 8-8, DR 8-101
Letterhead. See Advertising, letterheads
Liability to client, limiting, EC 6-6, DR 6-102
Licensing of lawyers,
  As evidence of competence, EC 6-3
  Control of, EC 3-1, 3-3 to 3-6, 3-9, DR 3-101
  Modernization of, EC 3-5, 3-9, 8-3
Liens, attorneys', EC 5-7, DR 5-103(A)(1)
Limited practice, holding out as having, EC 2-8, 2-14, DR 2-101(B)(2), 2-105(A)(2)
Litigation,
  Acquiring an interest in, EC 5-7, 5-8, DR 5-103
  Expenses of, advancing or guaranteeing payment of, EC 5-7, 5-8, DR 5-103(B)
  Pending, media discussion of, EC 7-33, DR 7-107(A) to (D), (F), (G), (I), (J)
  Responsibility of lawyer for conduct of, EC 7-4, 7-5, 7-7, 7-10, 7-13, 7-14, 7-20, 7-22 to 7-25, DR 7-102, 7-103, 7-106
  To harass or maliciously harm another, duty to avoid, EC 2-30, 7-10, 7-14, DR 2-109, 2-110(B)(1), 7-102(A)(1), 7-103(A)(1)
Living expenses of client, advances to client of, EC 5-8, DR 5-103(B)
Loan to judicial officer, EC 7-34, DR 7-110(A)
Loyalty to client. See Zeal
Lump-sum settlements, DR 5-106

M

Malpractice, Canon 6
Mandatory withdrawal. See Employment, withdrawal from, mandatory
Mediator, lawyer as, EC 5-20
Medical expenses, EC 5-8, DR 5-103(B)

Mental competence of bar applicant, EC 1–6
Mental competence of client, effect on representation, EC 7–11, 7–12
Mental competence of lawyer,
  Generally, EC 1–6, DR 2–110(B)(3), (C) (4)
  Recognition of rehabilitation, EC 1–6
Military legal service office, working with, DR 2–103(D)(2)
Misappropriation,
  Confidences or secrets of client, EC 4–1, 4–5, 4–6, DR 4–101(B)(3), (D)
  Property of client, EC 9–5, 9–6, DR 9–102
Misconduct,
  See also Discipline of lawyer,
  Of client, EC 2–23, 2–30, 7–5 to 7–10, 7–26, DR 2–109, 2–110(B)(1), (C), 4–101(C)(3), 7–101(B)(2), 7–102
  Of juror, EC 7–32, DR 7–108(D), (F), (G)
  Of lawyer, duty to reveal to proper officials, EC 1–4, DR 1–103
Misleading advertisement or professional notice, prohibition of, EC 2–9, 2–11, 2–13, 2–14, DR 2–101, 2–102(B), (C)
Moral character, requirement of, Canon 1, EC 1–2, 1–3, 1–5, DR 1–102
Moral factors, considered in counseling, EC 7–3, 7–5, 7–8, 7–9
Moral turpitude, crime of as ground for discipline, DR 1–102(A)(3)
Multiple clients, representation of, EC 5–14 to 5–20, DR 5–105, 5–106

N

Name, use of,
  Assumed name, EC 2–11, DR 2–102(B)
  Deceased partner's, EC 2–11, DR 2–102(A)(4), (B)
  Firm name, EC 2–11 to 2–13, DR 2–102(B)
  Misleading name, EC 2–11, 2–13, DR 2–102(B), (C)
  Partners who hold public office, EC 2–12, DR 2–102(B)
  Predecessor firms, EC 2–11, DR 2–102(A)(4), (B)
  Proper for law firm, EC 2–11, DR 2–102(B)
  Proper for lawyer in law practice, EC 2–11, DR 2–102(B)
  Retired partner, EC 2–11, DR 2–102(A)(4), (B)
  Trade name, EC 2–11, DR 2–102(B)
  Withdrawn partner's, EC 2–11, 2–12, DR 2–102(B)
Need for legal services, suggestion of. *See* Advice by lawyer to secure legal services
Negligence of lawyer, Canon 6
Negotiations with opposite party, EC 7–18, 7–20, DR 7–104, 7–105
Neighborhood law offices, working with, EC 2–6, 2–7, 2–25, DR 2–103(D)(1)(b)

Newspapers,
  Advertising in, EC 2–8 to 2–10, DR 2–101(A) to (C), (E), (F), (I)
  News releases in, during or pending trial, EC 7–33, DR 7–107
  News stories in, DR 2–101(I)
Non-meritorious position, duty to avoid, EC 7–4, 7–5, 7–14, DR 2–109, 2–110(B)(1), 7–102(A)(1), (2), 7–103(A), 7–106(C)(1)
Non-profit organization, legal aid services of, EC 2–24, 2–25, DR 2–103(D)(1), (4) (a), 2–104(A)(2), (3)
Notices. *See* Advertising

O

Objectives of client, duty to seek, EC 7–1, 7–10, DR 7–101(A)(1), 7–102
"Of Counsel" designation, DR 2–102(A)(4)
Offensive tactics by lawyer, EC 7–4, 7–5, 7–10, DR 7–101, 7–102, 7–104, 7–105
Office building directory. *See* Advertising, building directory
Office sign, DR 2–102(A)(3)
Opposing counsel, EC 5–9, 7–20, 7–23, 7–35, 7–37, 7–38, DR 7–101(A)(1), 7–104(A)(1), 7–106(C)(5), 7–110(B)(2), (3)
Opposing party, communications with, EC 7–18, DR 7–104

P

Partnership,
  Advertising. *See* Advertising
  Conflicts of interest, DR 5–105(D)
  Deceased member,
    Payments to estate of, EC 3–8, DR 3–102(A)(1), (2)
    Use of name, EC 2–11, DR 2–102(A)(4), (B)
  Dissolved, use of name of, EC 2–11 to 2–13, DR 2–102(A)(4), (B), (C)
  Holding out as, falsely, EC 2–13, DR 2–102(B), (C)
  Imputed disability of partner and associates, DR 5–105(D)
  Layperson, partnership with, EC 3–8, DR 3–103
  Members licensed in different jurisdictions, DR 2–102(D)
  Name, EC 2–11, 2–12, 2–13, DR 2–102(B)
  Nonexistent, holding out falsely, EC 2–13, DR 2–102(B), (C)
Patent practitioner, EC 2–14, DR 2–105(A)(1)
Payment to obtain recommendation of employment, prohibition against, EC 2–8, DR 2–103(B), (D)
Pending litigation, discussion of in media, EC 7–33, DR 7–107
Perjury, EC 7–5, 7–6, 7–26, 7–28, DR 7–102(A)(4), (6), (7), 7–102(B)

Person, definitions (3)

Personal interests of lawyer. *See* Adverse effect on professional judgment, interests of lawyer

Personal opinion of client's cause, EC 2–27 to 2–30, 7–24, DR 7–106(C)(4)

Phone directory, listing in. *See* Advertising, telephone directory

Political activity, EC 8–6, 8–8, DR 2–101(H)(1), 8–101, 8–102, 8–103

Political considerations in selection of judges, EC 8–6, DR 8–103

Potentially differing interest. *See* Adverse effect on professional judgment

Prejudice to right of client, duty to avoid, EC 2–32, DR 2–110(A)(2), (C)(3), (C)(4), 7–101(A)(3)

Prepaid legal services, EC 2–33, 5–23, DR 2–101(B)(17), 2–103(D)(4)

Preservation of confidences and secrets of client, EC 3–3, Canon 4

Pressure on lawyer by third person. *See* Adverse effect on professional judgment of lawyer

Privilege, attorney-client. *See* Attorney-client privilege

Procedures, duty to help improve, EC 8–1, 8–2, 8–9

Professional card of lawyer. *See* Advertising cards, professional

Professional impropriety, avoiding appearance of, EC 5–1, 5–6, Canon 9

Professional judgment, duty to protect independence of, EC 2–33, Canon 5

Professional legal corporations, EC 2–11, 5–24, DR 2–102(B)(C), 5–107(C), definitions (4)

Partnership with, DR 2–102(C)

Professional notices. *See* Advertising

Professional status, responsibility not to mislead concerning, EC 2–11 to 2–14, DR 2–102(B) to (D)

Profit-sharing with lay employees, authorization of, EC 3–8, DR 3–102(A)(3)

Property of client, handling, EC 9–5, DR 9–102

Prosecuting attorney, duty of, EC 7–13, 7–14, DR 7–103

Public defender office, working with, DR 2–103(C)(2), (D)(1)

Public employment, retirement from, EC 9–3, DR 9–101(A), (B)

Public office, duty of holder, EC 8–8, DR 8–101

Public opinion, irrelevant to acceptance of employment, EC 2–26 to 2–29

Public prosecutor. *See* Prosecuting attorney, duty of

Publication of articles for lay press, EC 2–2, 2–5, DR 2–104(A)(4)

Publication rights of lawyer, relating to subject matter of employment, EC 5–4, DR 5–104(B)

Publication of articles for lay press—Cont'd

Publicity,
Commercial. *See* Advertising, commercial publicity
Trial. *See* Trial publicity

Q

Qualified legal assistance organization, EC 2–33, DR 2–103(C)(2), (D), 2–104(A)(2), (3), definitions (8)

Quasi-judicial proceedings, EC 7–15, 7–16, 8–4, DR 7–107(H)

R

Radio, broadcasting. *See* Advertising, radio

Reasonable fee. *See* Fee for legal services, amount of

Rebate, propriety of accepting, EC 2–21, 2–22, 5–22, DR 2–107, 5–107

Recognition of legal problems, aiding laymen in, EC 2–1 to 2–5, 8–3, DR 2–104

Recommendation of bar applicant, duty of lawyer to satisfy himself that applicant is qualified, EC 1–3, DR 1–101(B)

Recommendation of professional employment, EC 2–8, 2–15, DR 2–103

Records of funds, securities, and properties of clients, EC 9–5, DR 9–102(B)(3)

Referral service. *See* Lawyer referral services

Refund of unearned fee when withdrawing, duty to give to client, EC 2–32, DR 2–110(A)(3)

Regulation of legal profession, EC 3–1, 3–3, 3–9, 8–3, 8–7, DR 3–101(B)

Rehabilitation of bar applicant or lawyer, recognition of, EC 1–6

Representation of multiple clients. *See* Adverse effect on professional judgment, interests of other clients

Reputation of lawyer, EC 2–6, 2–7

Requests for recommendation for employment, EC 2–8, DR 2–103(C)

Requirements for bar admission, EC 1–2, 1–6, DR 1–101(B)

Respect for law, EC 1–5, 9–6

Restrictive covenant, DR 2–108

Retention of employment. *See* Employment

Retirement,
See also Name, use of, retired partner
From judicial office, EC 9–3, DR 9–101(A)
From public employment, EC 9–3, DR 9–101(B)
Plan for laymen employees', EC 3–8, DR 3–102(A)(3)

Revealing of confidences, Canon 4

Revealing of secrets, Canon 4

Revealing to tribunal,
  Jury misconduct, EC 7–32, DR 7–108(G)
Representative capacity in which appearing, EC 7–15, 7–16, DR 7–106(B)(2)
Runner, prohibition against use of. *See* Recommendation of professional employment

S

Sanction for violating disciplinary rules, preliminary statement
Secrets of client, Canon 4
Selection of lawyer. EC 2–6 to 2–15, DR 2–101 to 2–105
Selection of judges, duty of lawyers, EC 8–6, DR 8–102
Self-interest of lawyer. *See* Adverse effect on professional judgment, interests of lawyer
Self-representation, privilege of, EC 3–7
Settlement agreement. EC 7–7, DR 5–106
Solicitation of business. *See* Advertising; Advice by lawyer to secure legal services; Recommendation of professional employment
Specialist, holding out as, EC 2–8, 2–14, DR 2–101(B)(2), 2–105
Specialization, EC 2–8, 2–14, DR 2–101(B)(2), 2–105
  Admiralty, EC 2–14
  Holding out as having, EC 2–8, 2–14, DR 2–101(B)(2), 2–105
  Patents, EC 2–14, DR 2–105(A)(1)
  Trademark, EC 2–14, DR 2–105(A)(1)
Speeches to lay groups, EC 2–2, 2–5, DR 2–104(A)(4)
State, definitions (5)
State of mind of client, effect of in advising him, EC 7–6, 7–11, 7–12
State's attorney. *See* Prosecuting attorney
"Stirring up litigation." *See* Advertising; Advice by lawyer to secure legal services; Recommendation of; professional employment
Stockholders of corporation, corporate counsel's allegiance to, EC 5–18
Suggestion of need for legal services. *See* Advice by lawyer to secure legal services
Suit to harass or maliciously harm another, duty to avoid, EC 2–30, 7–10, 7–14, DR 2–109, 2–110(B)(1), 7–102(A)(1)
Suppression of evidence, EC 7–27, DR 7–102(A)(3), 7–103(B), 7–106(C)(7), 7–109(A)

T

Technical and professional licenses. *See* Advertising, technical and professional licenses

Telephone directory. *See* Advertising, telephone directory
Television. *See* Advertising, television
Termination of employment. *See* Confidences of client; Employment, withdrawal from
Third persons, desires of. *See* Adverse effect on professional judgment, desires of third persons
Threatening criminal process, EC 7–21, DR 7–105
Trade name, EC 2–11, DR 2–102(B)
Trademark practitioner, EC 2–14, DR 2–105(A)(1)
Trial publicity, EC 7–33, DR 7–107
Trial tactics, EC 7–19 to 7–39, DR 7–101(A)(1), 7–102, 7–103(B), 7–105 to 7–110
Tribunal,
  Definitions (6)
  Representation of client before, Canon 7
Trustee, client naming lawyer as, EC 5–6

U

Unauthorized practice of law, Canon 3
  See also Division of legal fees, with laymen; Partnership, laypersons with
  Aiding a layman in the prohibited, EC 3–8, DR 3–101
  Distinguished from delegation of tasks to subprofessionals, EC 3–5, 3–6, DR 3–102(A)(3)
  Functional meaning of, EC 3–5, 3–9
  Self-representation by layman not included in, EC 3–7
Undignified conduct, duty to avoid, EC 7–36 to 7–38, DR 7–106(C)(6)
Unions, lawyers as members of, EC 5–13
Unlawful conduct, aiding client in, EC 7–5, 7–6, DR 7–102(A)(6), (7), (B)(1)
Unpopular party, representation of, EC 2–27, 2–29 to 2–31
Unreasonable fees. *See* Fee for legal services, amount of, excessive
Unsolicited advice. *See* Advice by lawyer to secure legal services

V

Varying interests of clients. *See* Adverse effect on professional judgment, interests of other clients
Veniremen. *See* Communications with, venireman; Jury
Violation of disciplinary rule as cause for discipline, DR 1–102(A)(1), (2)
Violation of law as cause for discipline, EC 1–5, 7–6, DR 1–102(A)(3), (A)(4), 7–102(A)(3) to (A)(8)
Voluntary gifts by client to lawyer, EC 5–5

Volunteered advice to secure legal services. *See* Advice by lawyer to secure legal services

W

Waiver of position of client, DR 7-101(B)(1)
Will of client, gift to lawyer in, EC 5-5
Withdrawal. *See* Employment, withdrawal from
Witness,
   Communications with. *See* Communications with, witnesses
   Expert, EC 7-28, DR 7-109(C)(3)
   False testimony by, EC 7-26, 7-28, DR 7-102(A)(4), (B)(2)
   Lawyer acting as, EC 5-9, 5-10, DR 5-101(B), 5-102

Witness—Cont'd
   Member of lawyer's firm acting as, DR 5-101(B), 5-102
   Payment to, EC 7-28, DR 7-109(C)
   Questioning of, EC 7-25, DR 7-106(C)(2)
   Secreting of, EC 7-27, DR 7-109(B)
   Writing for lay publication, avoiding appearance of giving general solution, EC 2-2, 2-5, DR 2-104(4)

Z

Zeal,
   General duty of, EC 7-1, 7-8 to 7-10, DR 7-101(A)
   Limitations upon, Canon 7

THE AMERICAN LAWYER'S CODE OF CONDUCT *

Revised Draft—May 1982
Commission on Professional Responsibility
The Roscoe Pound—American Trial Lawyers Foundation

Preface
By Theodore I. Koskoff **

On the following pages, we provide you with the text of an important new document: the May 1982 Revised Draft of The American Lawyer's Code of Conduct. This Code was prepared under the auspices of the Roscoe Pound—American Trial Lawyers Foundation, by a Commission on Professional Responsibility of which I am co-chairman. A Public Discussion Draft was issued in June 1980, and published in TRIAL magazine in August of that year.

This Code is quite frankly presented as an alternative to the old Code of Professional Responsibility previously promulgated by the American Bar Association (ABA), and to the new Rules of Professional Conduct that the ABA is apparently about to hawk as the latest thing in legal ethics. It was dissatisfaction with both of these ABA products that both got us going on this Code, and kept us going.

That dissatisfaction was not reduced when the ABA's Kutak Commission published a new draft in mid-1981. It grew. It grew still more when the ABA House of Delegates voted in January 1982 to drop its "old" Code of 1969, and to frame its new Rules only in a new, untried format. Many of us deeply resent the take-it-or-leave-it attitude of the ABA, which seems to be switching codes on us for no better reason than that it has spent so much money on the Kutak Rules that rejecting them would cause it to lose face.

This is not just a squabble over form. It is a serious disagreement over substance. The ABA Commission evidently is trying to win the debate over the substance of legal ethics by side-stepping it. It is trying to make us all not only debate whether and how to amend the present Code, but also debate that question in this very peculiar form: whether and how to amend a code that the Commission has already amended, in ways that even the Commission does not fully understand.

The National Organization of Bar Counsel (NOBC) has demonstrated that the ideas of the Kutak Commission can be integrated into the present Code, so that its proposals can be compared to others, and judged on their merits. NOBC has done this twice, once with each of the Kutak Commission's drafts. The Commission has ignored NOBC's efforts, probably because NOBC rejected some of its proposals. Chairman Kutak and his friends have ramrodded through the ABA a resolution committing the ABA to dropping the present Code.

By publishing this Code in two formats, we are giving notice that we are not going to let the ABA dictate the terms for the debate on lawyer's ethics. We regard the proposed

---

* *The American Lawyer's Code of Conduct* was drafted under the auspices of the Roscoe Pound-American Trial Lawyers Foundation, is copyrighted by the Foundation, and is reproduced here by permission.

** *Theodore I. Koskoff was President of ATLA from 1979 to 1980. His practice is in Bridgeport, Connecticut.*

Kutak Rules as fundamentally flawed, and we intend to force Kutak & Co. to debate the issues before the state courts and bar bodies that will really decide what the law of lawyers' ethics is to be.

When you write a new code, you have to be careful not just about what you are putting in, but also about what you are leaving out. For example, the Kutak Commission would drop DR 7-105 of the Code, which forbids threatening criminal prosecution solely to gain an advantage in a civil matter. No provision of the Kutak Rules covers such situations. Does this mean that adopting the Kutak Rules would legitimize blackmail? The Commission gives no explanation.

If you are not careful, you may leave out something whose absence completely changes the context, and thus the meaning, of something you are putting in. One of the purposes of codifying a body of law is to make it clear, and to make clear to everyone just what you are doing when you change it. Amending a code should not be like writing a zero-based budget. You want to keep those portions of existing law that work well, and to change only what needs to be changed. Continuity is not a negligible virtue.

That is why our Commission has taken issue with the ABA's conclusion that the Code of Professional Responsibility is old hat. "With all its serious flaws," my co-chairman Irwin Birnbaum said in the Preface to our June 1980 Draft, "the Code of Professional Responsibility is preferable to the Model Rules" of the Kutak Commission.

We have tried to make it clear just what we think should be changed in today's Code of Professional Responsibility * * *. Just what we have changed in our own Code, between the June 1980 Draft and this one, is not quite so clear, and should be spelled out.

The introductory materials, including the preamble, have been substantially pruned, without changing our meaning. Similar trimming may be found in the Comment portions, and in the lengthy "Introductory Comment on Knowing" of the 1980 Draft, replaced by two brief paragraphs of "Terminology." None of these omissions will be missed.

The truly substantive changes are in the Rules, and they are not numerous.

First, and most important, is the Commission's resolution of its ambivalence about the alternative versions of Chapter I, on confidentiality, published in the 1980 Draft. Alternative A was a fairly traditional approach. Alternative B was probably the most thoroughgoing embodiment of the lawyer's "first duty . . . is to keep the secrets of . . . clients," ever included in a draft code of ethics. It would have allowed lawyers to reveal clients' confidences, without client consent, in only two circumstances:

1) where a client impliedly waived confidentiality, or "opened the door," by accusing the lawyer of misconduct; and

2) when the lawyer's lips were pried open by compulsion of law.

We have tried to keep the spirit of that recommendation, although we have tempered it somewhat. Our first principle remains that a client must be able to confide absolutely in a lawyer, or there may be little point in anyone's having a lawyer. We have rejected one concept that the Kutak Commission apparently espouses, that lawyers have a general duty to do good for society that often overrides their specific duty to serve their clients. Serving clients is the lawyer's basic reason for being a lawyer, and the exceptions to the fundamental rule of absolute loyalty to clients must be minimal, and must be strictly construed.

As revised, Chapter I is closer to the traditional approach of our old Alternative A than it is to the radical position of Alternative B. It is still, however, the strictest set of rules on preserving client confidences in any proposed code of lawyers' conduct. In my view, the Sixth Amendment guarantee of the effective assistance of counsel requires no less.

In Chapter IV, a new Rule 4.2 places a special burden of competence on the lawyer who is held out to a client as having special expertise. This follows the law that has developed in malpractice cases, holding people who call themselves specialists to the standard of care required of such specialists.

A number of other rules have been tightened, but not substantially changed. For example, Rule 2.3 now explicitly requires the client's consent before a lawyer may accept compensation from someone other than the client.

In short, the Commission has refined its product without changing its approach.

We continue to disagree with the Kutak Commission in our basic approach to legal ethics. We believe that a code of lawyers' conduct is important legislation for the entire community, because it affects every person's ability to exercise basic rights. We believe that the basic purpose of such a code should be to enable lawyers to help people—to leave the individual lawyer free to help the individual client.

The Kutak Commission sees lawyers as ombudsmen, who serve the system as much as they serve clients. This is a collectivist, bureaucratic concept. It is the sort of thinking you get from a commission made up of lawyers who work for institutional clients, in institutional firms, and who have lost sight of the lawyer's basic function. Lawyers are not licensed to write prospectuses for giant corporations, or to haggle with federal agencies over regulations and operating rights. We are licensed to represent people in court, which often means people in trouble with the law, and with the government. We are the citizens' champions against official tyranny.

We cannot continue to have a democratic system, as we know it, without a legal profession whose members are free to perform that function. The Kutak Rules contain some useful changes in regulating peripheral aspects of law practice, but they embody a core conviction about the lawyer's role that is fundamentally at odds with the American constitutional system.

That is why we have continued to work on our Code, and why we have issued this Revised Draft. We are not willing to take dictation from the ABA on the standards governing our life's work. We are not willing to allow the Kutak Rules to become the law of legal ethics by default. We intend to fight in the state bar associations, and in the state courts, to preserve the constitutional concept of what a lawyer is, and what a lawyer's duties are.

I invite you to join with us in the fight.

THE COMMISSION ON PROFESSIONAL RESPONSIBILITY

Irwin Birnbaum, Esquire, Chair
Syracuse, New York

Theodore I. Koskoff, Esquire, Chair
Bridgeport, Connecticut

John A. Burgess, Esquire, Associate Chair
Berkeley, California

MEMBERS

Professor Robert H. Aronson
University of Washington School of Law

Professor Hugo A. Bedau
Department of Philosophy
Tufts University

Professor Gary Bellow
Legal Services Institute
Harvard University

Charles N. Carter, Legal Counsel
National Association for the Advancement of Colored People

Barney Dreyfus, Esquire
San Francisco, California

Daniel Fogel, Esquire
Los Angeles, California

Ira Glasser, Executive Director
American Civil Liberties Union

LAWYER'S CODE OF CONDUCT

Neil N. Glazer, Esquire
Boston, Massachusetts

The Honorable Thomas L. Hayes
Superior Court of Vermont

C. Richard Henrickson, Esquire
Salt Lake City, Utah

LeRoy Hersh, Esquire
San Francisco, California

Sherri Jeans, Esquire
Kansas City, Missouri

J.D. Lee, Esquire
Madisonville, Tennessee

Terry W. Mackey, Esquire
Cheyenne, Wyoming

Richard T. Marshall, Esquire
El Paso, Texas

Professor Gary T. Marx
Department of Urban Studies and Planning
Massachusetts Institute of Technology

Arlo A. McKinnon, Esquire
Milwaukee, Wisconsin

Kathleen O'Reilly, Executive Director
Consumer Federation of America
(Resigned January 1980)

Margie T. Searcy, Esquire
Tuscaloosa, Alabama

Karl P. Seuthe, Esquire
Los Angeles, California

David S. Shrager, Esquire
Philadelphia, Pennsylvania

Edward T. Sullivan, Business Manager
Local 254, Service Employees
International Union, AFL–CIO

The Honorable William S. Thompson
District of Columbia Superior Court

Stephen L. Tober, Esquire
Portsmouth, New Hampshire

Bill Wagner, Esquire
Tallahassee, Florida

REPORTERS

Professor Monroe H. Freedman
Hofstra Law School
(Public Discussion Draft, June 1980)

Thomas Lumbard, Esquire
Washington, DC
(Revised Draft and Appendix, May 1982)

CONTENTS

Chairmen's Introduction by Theodore I. Koskoff and Irwin Birnbaum
Preamble
Terminology

I. The Client's Trust and Confidences
   Rules
   Comment
   Illustrative Cases

II. Fidelity to the Client's Interests
   Rules
   Comment
   Illustrative Cases

III. Zealousness on the Client's Behalf
   Rules
   Comment
   Illustrative Cases

IV. Competence
   Rules
   Comment

V. Retainer Agreements and Financial Arrangements With Clients
   Rules
   Comment
   Illustrative Cases

VI. Withdrawal From Representation

    Rules

    Comment

    Illustrative Cases

VII. Informing the Public About Legal Services

    Rules

    Comment

    Illustrative Cases

VIII. Maintaining Professional Integrity and Competence

    Rules

    Comment

    Illustrative Cases

IX. Responsibilities of Government Lawyers

    Rules

    Supplementary Provisions

    Comment

    Illustrative Cases

Appendix: A Proposed Revision of the Code of Professional Responsibility

---

Copyright © 1982, The Roscoe Pound—American Trial Lawyers Foundation

This revised draft reflects extensive comments by the Commission on Professional Responsibility, but has not been finally approved by it. The Commission will continue to review the draft in the light of comments received from members of the bar and the public. Comments should be sent to: Thomas Lumbard, Reporter, The Commission on Professional Responsibility, Roscoe Pound—American Trial Lawyers Foundation, 1050 31st Street, N.W., Washington, DC 20007.

CHAIRMEN'S INTRODUCTION

By Irwin Birnbaum and Theodore I. Koskoff

This Revised Draft of The American Lawyer's Code of Conduct is the second published product of the Commission on Professional Responsibility. It consists of two parts. The primary text is the June, 1980, Public Discussion Draft of the Code, amended to reflect both the comments on that Draft, and the Commission's second thoughts on some matters. The appendix is a reworking of our Code in the form of proposed amended Disciplinary Rules of the Code of Professional Responsibility, now the law of lawyers' conduct in almost every state. The purpose of this second part is to show how the provisions of our Code can be adopted, in whole or in part, as amendments to existing law.

We are presenting the Commission's work in these two formats, because we view the substance of the lawyers' code of conduct as more important than its form. The purpose of our work has been to produce a code that embodies the principles we believe are essential to the effective functioning of the legal profession in a democratic society, and to get such a code adopted, as the law of lawyers' conduct, by the courts. We have no special pride of authorship that compels us to insist that the courts adopt all of our ideas, or none of them, or that our ideas be adopted only in a particular form. The issues involved are too important to play such games with them.

Only the first of these drafts, the American Lawyers' Code of Conduct proper, has been voted upon and approved by the Commission, or bears the stamp of the Commission's original Reporter, Professor Monroe H. Freedman. The reworking of the Code of

Professional Responsibility is the work of Professor Freedman's successor as Reporter to the Commission, Mr. Thomas Lumbard of Washington, formerly our Associate Reporter, and a consultant to the Commission since its inception.

This Commission was called the Commission on Professional Responsibility for Trial Practice, when founded in 1979. We quickly found that we could not write a code of conduct solely for trial lawyers. We also found that another Commission, that of the American Bar Association "on Evaluation of Professional Standards," was rewriting the profession's basic code in a way that demanded from us a viable alternative code, applicable to all lawyers.

We obviously believe that our Code is better than the so-called "Model" Rules of Professional Conduct produced by the A.B.A. Commission.[1] Even as amended in 1981, significantly and substantially, and in part reflecting (if not acknowledging) doctrine that we had published, the proposed Model Rules are inferior to the existing Code of Professional Responsibility. With all its flaws, the Code is preferable to the proposed Rules.

Accordingly, we here present our views both in the form we prefer, the *ALCC*, and in the generally accepted form of the *CPR*. This avoids the "take it or leave it" attitude expressed by the A.B.A.'s recent endorsement of the proposed Rules drafted by its Commission. It also acknowledges that we, and all other members of today's generation of revisers of the law of lawyers' conduct, are only able to reach higher than our predecessors because we stand upon their shoulders. While flattering ourselves that we are correcting their mistakes, we are neither so blithe as to suggest that we are not introducing errors of our own, nor so foolhardy as not to try to reduce such errors to a minimum.

Our work and our attitude thus stand in stark contrast to those of the A.B.A. Commission. That Commission has refused to build on the wisdom of the past. It has rejected the good faith efforts of others, such as the National Organization of Bar Counsel, to accommodate its ideas to the form of the *CPR*. It has even gone so far as to publish a huge "Alternative Draft" that the New York State Bar Association correctly concluded was not a good faith effort to amend the *CPR*. It was merely an elaborate charade, designed to make the Commission's "Proposed Final Draft" look good by invidious comparison.

The reader will find no such deception in the present document. Unlike the A.B.A. Commission's "Alternative Draft," our Code's Appendix is a good faith effort to improve upon the *CPR* by preserving and amending it. It was drafted by a Reporter who believes in the wisdom of that approach.[2] It is relatively short, and considerably easier to read than either the elephantine "Alternative Draft" or the "Proposed Final Draft" of the proposed A.B.A. Rules.

We have not called this a "Final Draft," because experience has shown that no draft of such a code is ever "final." The A.B.A. has published amendments to the "Final Draft" of its Code almost annually since 1969. We continue to seek suggestions to improve this Code.

PREAMBLE

This Code of Conduct embodies a traditional and constitutional concept of the role of the American lawyer in our limited form of government, which seeks to maximize individual liberty within a rule of law. The

---

1. The A.B.A. first added the adjective "Model" to the title of its Code to avoid federal charges that its promulgation of The Code was restraint of trade. The A.B.A. Commission now seems to make a virtue of necessity; it always refers to its work-product as the *Model* Rules, although it courts federal displeasure by always calling the CPR "the Code," never the "Model Code."

Refusing to take any A.B.A. product for a model, we consistently refer to existing law as "the Code of Professional Responsibility" and to what the A.B.A. Commission has recommended as "the proposed Rules of Professional Conduct."

2. See Lumbard, Setting Standards: The Courts, the Bar, and the Lawyers' Code of Conduct, 30 Cath.Univ.Law Rev. 249 (1981).

fundamental structure of the role of the American lawyer is fixed by the Bill of Rights of the Constitution; rules of conduct should be designed and interpreted to enhance those rights, not to inhibit them.

The individual rights most relevant to lawyers' duties relate to what we call one's "day in court"—the rights to due process of law, counsel, and trial by jury. Also relevant are rights relating to self-incrimination, confrontation, bail, search and seizure, and cruel and unusual punishment. The right to litigate is also an essential aspect of freedom of speech and of the right to petition for redress of grievances.

As a result of the enormous volume and complexity of our law, ordinary citizens need the assistance of lawyers simply to comprehend and cope with the rules governing their actions. The lawyer therefore serves the most basic individual right, that of personal autonomy: the right to make those decisions that most affect one's own life and values. Without professional assistance, the individual citizen is often unaware of the range of choices available, and of the means to pursue particular choices.

The assistance of counsel is thus essential to justice under law, and to equal protection of the laws. Leaving each person to his or her own resources, without the aid of counsel in comprehending and coping with the complexities of the legal system, would produce gross disparities in justice under law.

All these basic rights, individually and together, express the high value placed by our constitutional democracy on the dignity of the individual. Before any person is significantly affected by society in his or her person, relationships, or property, our system requires that certain processes be duly followed—processes to which competent, independent, and zealous lawyers are essential. And if it be observed that the stated ideal is too frequently denied in fact, our response must be that standards for lawyers be so drafted and enforced as to strive to make that ideal a reality.

The legal system that gives context and meaning to basic American rights is the adversary system. It is the adversary system which assures each of us a "champion against a hostile world," and which thereby helps to preserve and enhance our dignity as individuals.

Recognizing that the American attorney functions in an adversary system, and that such a system expresses fundamental American values, helps us to appreciate the emptiness of some cliches of lawyers' ethics. It is said, for example, that the lawyer is an "officer of the court," or an "officer of the legal system." Out of context, such phrases are at best meaningless, and at worst misleading. In the context of the adversary system, it is clear that the lawyer for a private party is and should be an officer of a court only in the sense of serving a court as a zealous, partisan advocate of one side of the case before it, and in the sense of having been licensed by a court to play that very role.

Further, the lawyer who litigates is not the only one who serves in an adversarial role. Lawyers function in an adversary system even when their clients are not actually involved in litigation. Parties to negotiations are usually adversaries, and are always potential adversaries. The lawyer drafting a contract or a will must anticipate and guard against interests adverse to the client's that may exist or that may develop in the course of time. The lawyer who prepares tax returns or other documents for filing with the government can adequately protect a client's interests only by recognizing the possibility of an adverse reaction. Any lawyer who counsels a client about rights, liabilities, and legal choices must be conscious of numerous possible reactions of an adversarial nature.

Unquestionably, there are differences among cases involving litigation, negotiating, drafting, and counseling. Thus, the opportunities to withdraw without prejudicing a client's interests are likely to be greater in counseling than in litigation, and greater in civil litigation than in criminal cases. But the basic principle will remain the same:

avoid withdrawal unless significant prejudice to the client can be avoided. We have therefore rejected the idea of writing this Code in separate sections for lawyers in litigation, negotiation, and so forth; at the same time, we have tried throughout to be aware of the variety of services lawyers perform and to make distinctions when they appear appropriate.

In sum, the following American Lawyer's Code of Conduct has been drafted with a recognition that all American lawyers function in an adversary system, and with a commitment to strengthening that system as the embodiment of the constitutional values inherent in the administration of justice in the United States.

The format of this Code embodies an effort to make it as readable and as clear as possible. The Rules are intended to be used for disciplinary purposes; they are written in declarative sentences stating what the lawyer "shall" or "shall not" do. The Rules are followed by Comments, which are not intended to be the basis of disciplinary action, but to enhance understanding of the disciplinary rules. In addition, when useful to avoid ambiguity or to resolve possible conflict between rules, Illustrative Cases are provided.

TERMINOLOGY

Attorney is used as a synonym for "lawyer," but only to distinguish between the lawyer to whom the rule applies and another attorney.

A **client's confidence**, protected by this Code, includes any information obtained by the client's lawyer in the course of and by reason of the lawyer-client relationship.

A lawyer **knows** certain facts, or acts **knowingly** or with **knowledge** of facts, when a person with that lawyer's professional training and experience would be reasonably certain of those facts in view of all the circumstances of which the lawyer is aware. A duty to investigate or inquire is not implied by the use of these words, but may be explicitly required under particular rules. Even in the absence of a duty to investigate, however, a studied rejection of reasonable inferences is inadequate to avoid ethical responsibility.

Reasonable belief, reasonably believes or **reasonable understanding** is the standard used to denote a lawyer's mental state when the lawyer may be required or permitted to act on the basis of incomplete knowledge of relevant facts, as when the lawyer is predicting future events, or is compelled to act on the basis of assumptions or inferences because all the relevant facts cannot be ascertained. The lawyer must understand or suppose the fact or circumstance to be so, and the circumstances must make that understanding or supposition a reasonable one.

CHAPTER I. THE CLIENT'S TRUST AND CONFIDENCES

Rules

1.1. Beginning with the initial interview with a prospective client, a lawyer shall strive to establish and maintain a relationship of trust and confidence with the client. The lawyer shall impress upon the client that the lawyer cannot adequately serve the client without knowing everything that might be relevant to the client's problem, and that the client should not withhold information that the client might think is embarrassing or harmful to the client's interests. The lawyer shall explain to the client the lawyer's obligation of confidentiality.

1.2. Without the client's knowing and voluntary consent, a lawyer shall not directly or indirectly reveal a confidence of a client or former client, or use it in any way detrimental to the interests of the client, except as provided in Rules 1.3 to 1.6, and Rule 6.5. (Rules 1.3 to 1.6 permit divulgence under compulsion of law; to avoid proceeding before a corrupted judge or juror; to defend the lawyer or the lawyer's associates from charges of misconduct; and to prevent imminent danger to human life. Rule 6.5 permits withdrawal in non-criminal cases when the client has induced the lawyer to act through material misrepresentation, even though withdrawal might indirectly divulge a confidence.)

1.3. A lawyer may reveal a client's confidence to the extent required to do so by law, rule of court, or court order, but only after good faith efforts to test the validity of the law, rule, or order have been exhausted.

1.4. A lawyer may reveal a client's confidence when the lawyer knows that a judge or juror in a pending proceeding in which the lawyer is involved has been bribed or subjected to extortion. In such a case, the lawyer shall use all reasonable means to protect the client, consistent with preventing the case from going forward with a corrupted judge or juror.

1.5. A lawyer may reveal a client's confidence to the extent necessary to defend the lawyer or the lawyer's associate or employee against charges of criminal, civil, or professional misconduct asserted by the client, or against formally instituted charges of such conduct in which the client is implicated.

[1.6. A lawyer may reveal a client's confidence when and to the extent that the lawyer reasonably believes that divulgence is necessary to prevent imminent danger to human life. The lawyer shall use all reasonable means to protect the client's interests that are consistent with preventing loss of life.]

Note: Rule 1.6 was not approved by the Commission, but was supported by so many members that it is included in this Revised Draft as a Supplemental Rule.

Comment

One of the most difficult and delicate responsibilities of the lawyer is to establish and maintain a relationship of trust and confidence with the client. Clients frequently mistrust their lawyers, are embarrassed about the truth, or assume that their lawyers would prefer not to be burdened with knowledge about illegal or immoral conduct. For lawyers to provide effective assistance, however, it is essential that they know everything about the clients' affairs that might be relevant.

If the client were able to distinguish the legally relevant from the legally irrelevant, the useful from the useless, and the incriminatory from the exculpatory, the client would have little need for the lawyer's professional training and skills. And when the lawyer does not have all of the relevant facts, the lawyer's professional abilities are of limited value. Accordingly, the effective functioning of the lawyer-client relationship requires complete candor by the client to the lawyer.

Such candor is in the public interest because only through the counsel and advocacy of a lawyer can each individual fully exercise his or her autonomy and realize other important rights under our Constitution and laws. Further, as every experienced lawyer knows, a substantial part of the lawyer's time is devoted to advising clients that a particular course of conduct should not be followed on grounds of legality or morality. Unless clients are candid with lawyers, those critical functions cannot be served. The client's sense of trust in the lawyer is therefore vital, and the lawyer's obligation of confidentiality is essential to establishing and maintaining that trust.

The most obvious concern of confidentiality is, of course, with protecting the client's direct communications to the lawyer. But the lawyer must also obtain relevant information from sources other than the client, often through leads provided by the client, and unauthorized divulgence of such information to the client's detriment would seriously impair lawyer-client relationships and could induce clients to limit the scope of their lawyers' investigatory efforts. Accordingly, "confidence," as protected by these rules, is any information obtained by the lawyer in the course of the lawyer-client relationship.

Since candor may be no less important in preliminary interviews, the lawyer-client relationship includes discussions between the lawyer and client to determine whether the lawyer will be retained by the client. Also, the obligation to maintain confidentiality extends beyond the lawyer-client relationship.

It is sometimes suggested that confidentiality is inimical to the truth-seeking function of our system of justice. That is true, however, only in a superficial and short-sighted sense. Certainly, under the adversary system, lawyers frequently have knowledge that the court or other parties would want to have. Most often, however, lawyers have such knowledge precisely because of the established rule of confidentiality. If we were to remove that safeguard, by permitting lawyers to divulge their clients' confidences, lawyers would come to have few truths to divulge.

Nevertheless, in some narrowly circumscribed exceptions, this Code permits lawyers to reveal some confidences. Such exceptions should reflect values of such overriding concern that some minimal systemic risk would be justified. Also, such exceptions should be limited to situations that arise infrequently, to further minimize the risk of impairing lawyer-client trust.

The Rules to this Chapter are more protective of confidentiality than the Code of Professional Responsibility or the A.B.A. Commission's Rules. The exceptions permit divulgence, but do not require it, under compulsion of law; to avoid proceeding before a corrupted judge or juror; to defend the lawyer or the lawyer's associates against formally instituted charges of misconduct, or charges made by the client; and to prevent imminent danger to human life. (Rules 1.3 to 1.6.) Also, withdrawal is permitted in non-criminal cases, even when a confidence might thereby be divulged indirectly, when the client has induced the lawyer to act through material misrepresentation (Rule 6.5; see also Rule 6.6).

The corruption cases are an appropriate exception because the corruption of the impartial judge or jury vitiates the adversary system itself. Since cases of corruption are infrequent, the exception should not have significant impact on the lawyer-client relationship. By contrast, cases of false testimony are more frequent, and the adversary system anticipates and is specifically designed to cope with false testimony through cross-examination, rebuttal, and observation of demeanor during testimony.

These Rules reject the previously recognized exception permitting lawyers to violate confidentiality to collect an unpaid fee. The reason for that exception—the lawyer's financial interest—is not sufficiently weighty to justify impairing confidentiality. On the other hand, a limited exception is permitted, when a lawyer or the lawyer's associate is formally charged with criminal or unprofessional conduct.

Rule 1.2 refers to using a confidence in a way detrimental to "the interests of the client." Here, as elsewhere in this Code, the interests of the client are determined by the client after having been counseled by the lawyer. (See Rules 2.1, 3.1 and 3.2, and the Comment to Chapter II.) If there is inadequate opportunity for consultation, the lawyer should act in accordance with the lawyer's reasonable understanding of what the client would perceive to be in the client's interest.

This Code rejects permitting violation of confidentiality in all cases of "future (or continuing) crimes." First, the category of "crimes" is too broad; it lumps offenses that are openly done and relatively harmless, with those that are clandestine and involve life and death. At the same time, the requirement of a crime may be too narrow; if saving a life, for example, is sufficiently important to justify an exception to confidentiality, then the exception should not turn on technicalities. The exception for "future or continuing" offenses has also proved unsatisfactory; it is all too easily interpreted to include a failure to relinquish the proceeds of a past crime, or a fugitive's refusal to surrender, thereby permitting or even requiring lawyers to violate confidentiality in situations where their clients are desperately in need of counsel.

Illustrative Cases

1(a). A lawyer representing the wife in a divorce and custody case learns from his client that she had sexual relations with a man other than her husband during the time of separation. The client insists upon not disclosing that fact. The lawyer knows that the judge would want to know it, and would weigh it against the wife in deciding custody. The lawyer would commit a disciplinary violation by informing the judge.

1(b). The same facts as 1(a), and the wife testifies falsely on deposition that she has not had sexual relations with anyone other than her husband during the marriage. The lawyer would commit a disciplinary violation by revealing the perjury.

1(c). A lawyer representing the husband in a divorce case learns that his client's tax returns have understated his income. At deposition, the client produces his tax returns, and testifies that they are complete and accurate. The lawyer would commit a disciplinary violation by revealing knowledge of the false returns to the wife, her lawyer, the judge, or the Internal Revenue Service.

1(d). A lawyer represents a client negotiating the purchase of real estate. During negotiations, the parties and their lawyers discuss the adverse effect of existing zoning restrictions, which prevent commercial development of the property. Just prior to formalizing an agreement of sale, however, the buyer learns that his lawyer has persuaded the zoning board to change the zoning to permit commercial use. The buyer decides not to tell the seller about the imminent zoning change. The buyer's lawyer would commit a disciplinary violation by informing the seller.

1(e). A lawyer representing a client accused of murdering a man learns from his client that the client has killed a young woman and hidden the body in a woods. The lawyer goes to the woods and finds the dead body. Because the client could be implicated through his relationship with the lawyer, or even through circumstantial evidence alone, the lawyer tells no one about the body. The lawyer has not committed a disciplinary violation.

1(f). The same facts as 1(e), but the lawyer, without authorization of the client, tells the young woman's parents. The lawyer has committed a disciplinary violation.

1(g). The same facts as 1(e), but the woman is not dead. However, she is seriously injured and unable to help herself or to get help. The lawyer calls an ambulance for her, but takes care not to be personally identified. The lawyer has committed a disciplinary violation, if supplementary Rule 1.6 is not adopted as part of the Code.

1(h). A lawyer learns from a client that the latter is hiding out, in violation of bail or probation. The lawyer would commit a disciplinary violation by revealing the client's location to the authorities.

1(i). A lawyer learns from a client during the trial of a civil or criminal case that the client intends to give testimony that the lawyer knows to be false. The lawyer does not present the client's testimony as she otherwise would, but instead simply requests a narrative from the client and returns to her seat at the counsel table. On summation to the jury, the lawyer makes no reference to her client's false testimony, contrary to what she would have done had she not known it to be false. The lawyer has committed disciplinary violations, both in the manner of presenting the client's testimony and in the manner of summation.

1(j). A lawyer learns from a client during the trial of a civil or criminal case that the client intends to give testimony that the lawyer knows to be false. The lawyer reasonably believes that a request for leave to withdraw would be denied and/or would be understood by the judge and by opposing counsel as an indication that the testimony is false. The lawyer does not seek leave to withdraw, presents the client's testimony in the ordinary manner, and refers to it in summation as evidence in the case. The lawyer has not committed a disciplinary violation.

1(k). A lawyer represents a client charged with possessing narcotics. The client is acquitted. In the course of the representation, however, the lawyer has learned from the client that the client is regularly engaged in selling heroin. If the lawyer does not disclose the information about the client to the police, therefore, the client will continue to sell drugs, thereby causing death or serious bodily harm to others. The lawyer would commit a disciplinary violation by revealing the client's confidence.

1(*l*). A lawyer is retained by an insurance company to represent its insured, who is being sued in a personal injury action. Without the insured client's consent, the lawyer informs the insurance company of possible defenses of the company against the insured client under the policy. The lawyer has committed a disciplinary violation.

CHAPTER II. FIDELITY TO THE CLIENT'S INTERESTS

Rules

2.1. In a matter entrusted to a lawyer by a client, the lawyer shall give undivided fidelity to the client's interests as perceived by the client, unaffected by any interest of the lawyer or of any other person, or by the lawyer's perception of the public interest.

2.2. A lawyer may limit the scope of the matter entrusted to the lawyer, subject to Rules 5.1 and 5.2, which relate to the obligation to treat a client fairly and in good faith, and to make clear the scope of the representation.

2.3. With the consent of a client, a lawyer may accept a fee or salary from a person or organization other than the client, subject to Rules 2.1, 2.2, and 2.4.

2.4. A lawyer may serve one or more clients, despite a divided loyalty, if each client who is or may be adversely affected by the divided loyalty is fully informed of the actual or potential adverse effects, and voluntarily consents.

2.5. A lawyer representing a corporation shall, as early as possible in the lawyer-client relationship, inform the board of directors of potential conflicts that might develop among the interests of the board, corporate officers, and shareholders. The lawyer shall receive from the board instructions in advance as to how to resolve such conflicts, and shall take reasonable steps to ensure that officers with whom the lawyer deals, and the shareholders, are made aware of how the lawyer has been instructed to resolve conflicts of interest.

Comment

Because our society places the highest value on the dignity and autonomy of the individual, its lawyers serve the public interest by undivided fidelity to each client's interests as the client perceives them.

That is not to say that lawyers should ignore possible harm to other persons or to public interests, or assume that clients' choices will be made in narrowly selfish terms. On the contrary, in counseling clients, lawyers should advise them fully of all significant potential consequences of particular courses of conduct, and that advice should include moral and public interest concerns along with strictly legal ones. The lawyer's ultimate fidelity, however, is to the client. By maintaining that fidelity, the lawyer acts in the highest public interest.

Just as it would be improper for a lawyer to impose other values upon a client, the lawyer should not impose upon the client an adversarial attitude toward others. For example, if two people seeking a divorce prefer to proceed in an amicable way with a single lawyer, it may be entirely proper for the lawyer to represent both at once. (Whether it would be prudent for the lawyer to do so, and risk subsequent criticism by one party or the other, is a matter of judgment for the lawyer.) Similarly, a lawyer might properly represent two or more partners, or co-defendants in a criminal or civil case, or the driver and the passenger in an automobile negligence action against a third party. In each such case, the clients might well decide that it is in their financial interest and/or in the best interest of their personal relationship to conduct their affairs in a cooperative rather than an adversarial way.

The essential responsibility of the lawyer in such a case is to make sure that each party is fully aware of the actual and potential conflicts of interest, and that each voluntarily consents. One problem that should be addressed particularly is the effect of joint representation on the lawyer-client privilege under applicable law. The clients should also be informed of the likelihood that the lawyer would subsequently be disqualified from representing either party in any dispute that might arise between them.

One of the conundrums of professional ethics has been the responsibility of a corporate lawyer who learns from a corporate official that the official has engaged in illegal conduct, either against or on behalf of the company. In informing the lawyer, the official assumes a confidential relationship. Nevertheless, the lawyer may feel compelled to inform the board of directors, which is generally regarded as the embodiment of the corporate entity. If the board fails to take appropriate action, however, the lawyer may then feel an obligation to inform the shareholders (although the general public will then learn about the problem, to the likely disadvantage of the company). As the question is frequently posed, who is the lawyer's client in such circumstances?

Although it has not been generally recognized, the problem is basically a familiar and relatively simple one of conflict of interest. The lawyer's difficulty is insoluble only because the lawyer has failed to inform the board of readily foreseeable conflicts of interest and to receive guidance in advance. On the basis of the board's instructions, the lawyer can then make sure that each interested party is informed in advance and is thereby in a position to seek adequate protection.

For example, one board might prefer to maximize candor between its officers and the lawyer, and therefore instruct the lawyer to honor the officers' confidences, even in reporting to the board. The shareholders would then be in a position to approve or disapprove that policy, or to relinquish their shares. Another board might prefer to know everything the lawyer knows. In that event the officers would be on notice that they might want to consult with personal counsel before disclosing certain information to corporate counsel. Rule 2.5 requires the lawyer to take the reasonable steps necessary to avoid the situation in which the lawyer has awkward information, and cannot either disclose it or keep it confidential without betraying someone's reasonable expectations of trust.

The requirement is that the lawyer have the issue resolved as early as possible in the lawyer-client relationship. If a conflict arises before the issue is resolved, the lawyer should act in accordance with the lawyer's reasonable belief as to what the board of directors would consider to be in the best interests of the corporation.

Illustrative Cases

2(a). A lawyer represents a defendant charged with tax fraud. It is apparent to the lawyer that the fraud was actually committed by the client's wife, who has not been charged. The client insists that the lawyer conduct the defense without in any way implicating the client's wife. The lawyer would commit a disciplinary violation by violating those instructions.

2(b). A lawyer represents the accused in a criminal case. The lawyer interviews a potential witness whose story strongly supports the defense. Shortly thereafter, however, the lawyer learns that the prosecution has interviewed the same witness and has received a story highly damaging to the defense. At trial, the prosecution does not present the witness. The defendant insists upon calling the witness for the defense. The defense lawyer does not do so, because of concern with the conflicting story the witness has given the prosecution, and the lawyer's judgment that the witness will hurt the defense. The lawyer has committed a disciplinary violation.

2(c). A lawyer represents the driver and passenger of an automobile, who were both injured through the alleged negligence of the driver of another car in an intersection accident. The lawyer has not advised them of potential conflicts in their interests. The lawyer has committed a disciplinary violation.

2(d). A lawyer represents the plaintiff in a civil action. The case is one in which the defendant can be held responsible for the plaintiff's attorney's fees. The lawyer negotiates a settlement for the client, and also negotiates with the defense regarding the lawyer's own fee. The lawyer does not inform the client of the conflict thereby created between the client's interests and the lawyer's. (For example, the client might feel, if fully informed of the circumstances, that the liability settlement should be larger in view of what is available for the lawyer's fee.) Because the client was not in a position to evaluate the settlement with full awareness of the lawyer's conflict, or to consider having additional counsel represent the client's interests in the negotiations, the lawyer has committed a disciplinary violation, even though the ultimate liability settlement and fee were in fact fair.

CHAPTER III. ZEALOUSNESS ON THE CLIENT'S BEHALF

Rules

3.1. A lawyer shall use all legal means that are consistent with the retainer agreement, and reasonably available, to advance a client's interests as the client perceives them.

3.2. A lawyer shall fully inform a client of the client's rights, liabilities, and possible lawful alternatives regarding issues of substantial importance related to the matter for which the lawyer has been retained, except (a) to the extent that the client has instructed the lawyer to exercise the lawyer's judgment without further consultation with the client, or (b) as provided in Rule 3.3.

3.3. A lawyer shall not advise a client about the law when the lawyer knows that the client is requesting the advice for an unlawful purpose likely to cause death or serious physical injury to another person.

3.4. A lawyer shall not knowingly encourage a client to engage in illegal conduct, except in a good faith effort to test the validity or scope of the law.

3.5. A lawyer shall not knowingly participate in unlawfully concealing or destroying evidence, or discourage a witness or potential witness from talking to counsel for another party.

3.6. A lawyer shall not knowingly participate in creating false evidence, or a misrepresentation upon which another person is likely to rely and suffer material detriment.

3.7. A lawyer shall not knowingly file a materially false pleading, present materially false evidence, or make a materially false representation to a court or other tribunal, except as required to do so by Rule 1.2, which proscribes direct or indirect divulgence of a client's confidence.

3.8. A lawyer shall not give legal advice to a person who the lawyer knows is not represented by an attorney, other than the advice to secure counsel, when the lawyer knows that the interests of that person are in conflict or likely to be in conflict with the interests of the lawyer's client.

3.9. A lawyer shall not communicate regarding a legal matter with an adverse party who the lawyer knows is represented in that matter by an attorney, unless the lawyer has been authorized to do so by that party's attorney. However, a lawyer may send a written offer of settlement directly to an adverse party, seven days or more after that party's attorney has received the same offer of settlement in writing.

3.10. A lawyer shall not give a witness money or anything of substantial value, or threaten a witness with harm, in order to induce the witness to testify or dissuade the witness from testifying. However, a lawyer may pay a fee to an expert witness; a lawyer may reimburse a witness' actual, reasonable financial losses and expenses of appearing; a lawyer may give a witness protection against physical harm; and a prosecutor may immunize a witness from prosecution in order to avoid an assertion of the constitutional privilege against self-incrimination.

3.11. Except as permitted by law, a lawyer representing an interested party shall not initiate communication with a judge or hearing officer about the facts or issues in a case that the lawyer knows is pending or likely to be pending before the judge or hearing officer, unless the lawyer has first made a good faith effort to apprise opposing counsel. If a lawyer has an *ex parte* discussion with a judge or hearing officer regarding the issues in a case, the lawyer shall fully inform opposing counsel of the *ex parte* communication at the earliest opportunity, except to the extent prohibited by Rule 1.2, which proscribes unauthorized divulgence of a client's confidences.

Comment

Except when ordered by a court to represent a client, a lawyer has complete discretion whether to accept a particular client. Once a lawyer is committed to represent a client, however, the lawyer has no discretion, short of grounds for withdrawal, to fail to provide the client with every legal recourse that is consistent with the retainer agreement, reasonably available, and in the client's interests as the client perceives them. When there is inadequate opportunity for consultation regarding the client's interests, the lawyer shall act in accordance with the lawyer's reasonable belief as to what the client would perceive to be in the client's interest.

This Code both emphasizes the client's autonomy as a basic value and assumes that the client is competent to make the decisions at issue. Accordingly, the lawyer who represents a person who is incompetent is not bound by the literal terms of those rules. Nor does it appear to be possible to draft disciplinary rules that will adequately deal with the many variations that might arise regarding clients who are altogether or in part incompetent to make decisions in their own interest. Two guidelines can be stated, however. First, the lawyer's controlling concern should be the client's interest as the client would be most likely to perceive it if competent to make the decision. Second, depending upon the circumstances, the lawyer might be well advised to seek guidance from other professionals, such as psychiatrists or social workers, and from members of the client's family.

The phrase "materially false" in Rule 3.7 means false and likely to affect the resolution of one or more issues before the tribunal.

Illustrative Cases

3(a). A lawyer represents the defendant in a bank robbery. The lawyer suggests that the client give the lawyer the gun used in the robbery and the stolen money, so that the lawyer can put them in a place less likely to be searched. The lawyer has committed a disciplinary violation.

3(b). A lawyer represents a client in a murder case. The client leaves the murder weapon with the lawyer. The lawyer fails to advise the client that the weapon might be more accessible to the prosecution in the lawyer's possession than in the client's, and that, if the lawyer retains the weapon, he will produce it if ordered to do so by a valid subpoena. The lawyer has committed a disciplinary violation by failing to fully advise the client.

3(c). The same facts as 3(b). The lawyer would not commit a disciplinary violation by returning the weapon to the client, unless the lawyer also encouraged the client to make it unavailable as evidence.

3(d). The same facts as 3(b). The lawyer would not commit a disciplinary violation by producing the gun in response to a subpoena, unless the lawyer failed first to make a good faith effort to test the validity of the subpoena.

3(e). A lawyer is conducting the defense of a criminal prosecution. The judge calls the lawyer to the bench and asks her whether the defendant is guilty. The lawyer knows that the defendant is guilty, and reasonably believes that an equivocal answer will be taken by the judge as an admission of guilt. The lawyer assures the judge that the defendant is innocent. The lawyer has not committed a disciplinary violation.

3(f). The same facts as in 3(e), but the lawyer replies to the judge, "I'm sorry, Your Honor, but it would be improper for me to answer that question." The lawyer has committed a disciplinary violation.

3(g). The same facts as in 3(e), but the lawyer is an assistant public defender, and the public defender has publicly announced that the office's policy is to refuse to answer such questions and to report every judge who asks such questions to the state Judicial Discipline Commission. For that reason, a refusal to answer would not be taken as an admission of guilt. The lawyer reminds the judge of her office's policy, and asks the judge to withdraw the question. The lawyer has not committed a disciplinary violation.

CHAPTER IV. COMPETENCE

Rules

4.1. At a minimum, a lawyer shall serve a client with skill and care commensurate with that generally afforded to clients by other lawyers in similar matters.

4.2. A lawyer who has held himself or herself out to a client as having special skill and competence relative to a matter in which the client has retained the laywer shall serve the client with that skill and care generally afforded to clients by lawyers of such skill and competence.

4.3. A lawyer shall take such legal action as is necessary and reasonably available to protect and advance a client's interests in the matter entrusted to the lawyer by the client.

4.4. A lawyer shall seek out all facts and legal authorities that are reasonably available and relevant to a client's interests in the matter entrusted to the lawyer by the client. In so doing, the lawyer shall give due regard not only to established rules of law, but also to developing legal concepts that might affect the client's interests.

4.5. A lawyer shall keep a client currently apprised of all significant developments in the matter entrusted to the lawyer by the client, unless the client has instructed the lawyer to do otherwise.

4.6. A lawyer shall seek out reasonably available resources that are necessary to protect and advance a client's interests, such as experts in specialized areas of the law or experts in non-legal disciplines.

4.7. If a lawyer forms a partnership with a non-lawyer for the purpose of more effectively serving clients' interests, the terms of the partnership shall be consistent with the lawyer's obligations under this Code, with particular reference to Rule 2.1, requiring undivided fidelity to the client.

Comment

It is generally agreed that a lack of competence is unprofessional and that a code of professional conduct should prescribe competence. Drafting rules to that end, however, has proved difficult.

Canon 6 of the Code of Professional Responsibility proscribes the failure to act competently, but defines competence in circular terms as conduct that the lawyer "knows or should know . . . is not competent." The CPR also requires preparation that is "adequate in the circumstances," but adequacy is neither defined nor given a reference point.

This Code requires, at a minimum, a level of skill and care commensurate with that generally provided by other lawyers in similar matters. Recognizing, however, that what is provided by other lawyers may not always amount to an adequate standard of competence, the Rules prescribe specific duties that are defined in terms of what is relevant or necessary to protect and advance the client's interests, and is reasonably available. The client's interests are determined by the client, and delineated by "the matter entrusted to the lawyer." (See Rules 2.2, 5.1, and 5.2, permitting the lawyer to limit the scope of the matter, subject to the requirements of fairness and good faith.)

CHAPTER V. RETAINER AGREEMENTS AND FINANCIAL ARRANGEMENTS WITH CLIENTS

Rules

5.1. A lawyer shall treat a client fairly and in good faith, giving due regard to the client's position of dependence upon the lawyer, the lawyer's special training and experience, and the high degree of trust which a client is entitled to place in a lawyer.

5.2. As soon as practicable after being retained, a lawyer shall make clear to a client, in writing, the material terms of the retainer agreement, including the scope of what the lawyer is undertaking to do for the client, the limits of that undertaking, and the fee and any other obligations the client is assuming.

5.3. A lawyer shall not contract with a client to limit the lawyer's liability to the client for malpractice.

5.4. Lawyers who are not openly associated in the same firm shall not share a fee unless: (a) the division reflects the proportion of work performed by each attorney and the normal billing rate of each; or (b) the client has been informed pursuant to Rule 5.2 of the fact of fee-sharing and the effect on the total fee, and the client consents.

5.5. A lawyer shall not impose a lien upon any part of a client's files, except upon the lawyer's own work product, and then only to the extent that the work product has not been paid for. This work-product exception shall be inapplicable when the client is in fact unable to pay, or when withholding the lawyer's work product would present a significant risk to the client of imprisonment, deportation, destruction of essential evidence, loss of custody of a child, or similar irreparable harm.

5.6. A lawyer shall not give money or anything of substantial value to any person in order to induce that person to become or to remain a client, or to induce that person to retain or to continue the lawyer as counsel on behalf of someone else. However, a lawyer may (a) advance money to a client on any terms that are fair; (b) give money to a client as an act of charity; (c) give money to a client to enable the client to withstand delays in litigation that would otherwise induce the client to settle a case because of financial hardship, rather than on the merits of the client's claim; or (d) charge a fee that is contingent in whole or in part on the outcome of the case.

Comment

Rule 5.4, governing the division of fees by lawyers not openly associated in the same firm, is less restrictive than any other provision or proposal known to the Commission. First, it allows a fee to be divided, without express client consent, if the division reflects the proportion of each lawyer's contribution to the work of the client, and each lawyer's normal billing rate. (Note that each lawyer would have been retained either by the client, pursuant to Rule 5.2, or by another lawyer pursuant to Rule 4.6, which requires the lawyer to seek out experts in specialized areas of the law to the extent available and necessary, with such notice to the client as is required by Rule 4.5.) Compare DR 2–107 of the Code of Professional Responsibility, and Rule 1.5(d) of the proposed Rules of Professional Conduct.

Second, Rule 5.4 allows any division to which the client consents after being informed of the fact that the lawyers intend to divide the fee, and of the effect of the division on the total fee. In addition, Rule 5.2 requires that this information be provided in writing, including the scope of what each lawyer is to do for the client. That requirement should be sufficient to prevent unfairness to clients.

It must be emphasized that the purpose of allowing fee splitting is to encourage lawyers to refer clients to competent specialists. The proposed Rules of Professional Conduct would continue the existing practice of penalizing such referrals outside one's own firm; even the Massachusetts and California rules prohibit a division that increases the amount of the fee (but only when the two lawyers are not members of the same firm). Such rules exalt the form of association over the substance of client consent and providing better service for the client, particularly in the context of recent increases in the number and size of multi-office firms. It prohibits some lawyers from doing something that other lawyers may do with impunity, and that many lawyers in fact do. It is more realistic to regulate a common practice than to prohibit it on a discriminatory basis, especially when the practice may actually improve the quality of service made available to clients.

Rule 5.6(c) permits a lawyer to give money to a client to enable the client to have access to the legal system or to withstand delay as a form of coercion to settle on unfavorable terms not related to the merits of the case. A not uncommon practice is revealed, for example, in *Abramson v. Kenwood Laboratories, Inc.*, 223 N.Y.S.2d 1005 (1961). There the attorney "frankly stated in the course of the . . . pretrial hearings that he is 'running a business.' He indicated the generally known policy of his insurance carrier to offer payment in settlements of personal injury suits of sums less than what may reasonably be anticipated as the probable recovery upon trial."

Such a practice conflicts most clearly with the fair administration of justice when a plaintiff is in need of immediate funds for food, housing, medical attention, etc., and is therefore under unconscionable pressure to settle for less than a claim is worth. In such a case, the lawyer contributes to the fair administration of justice by giving or lending the funds that are necessary to enable the client to obtain a fair recovery on the merits of the case, uninfluenced by financial pressures resulting from delay.

Rule 5.6(d) permits fees to be contingent in whole or in part on the outcome of any case. Such fees have long been recognized as proper when the client is a plaintiff in civil litigation. The principal reason is that, as a practical matter, most people would not be in a position to seek vindication of their legal rights, however meritorious, if litigating those rights could result in substantial financial loss as well as loss in time and the other burdens of litigation. Since there is little if any incentive to lawyers to take frivolous cases on contingent fees, such cases are screened out through a contingent fee system more effectively than they might be in a system based exclusively upon retainers. Moreover, any concern that contingent fees will induce unethical conduct on the part of lawyers seems fanciful. A lawyer unscrupulous enough to fabricate a case to earn a contingent fee will undoubtedly not hesitate to do so to earn a retainer or to establish a reputation for winning cases.

Similarly, there appears to be no justification, on ethical grounds, to forbid contingent fees to defendants in civil cases. Indeed, the only apparent reason for such a prohibition is that anyone who is worth suing is likely to be able to pay a retainer, and is effectively coerced into doing so because of the pending claim. Thus, a rule against charging contingent fees to defendants has every appearance of being less a matter of ethics than a restraint of trade. If a lawyer considers a complaint to be so lacking in merit as to justify basing the fee in whole or in part on the lawyer's success in defending against it, the lawyer and client should be free to contract on that basis.

There is even more reason for allowing contingent fees for the accused in criminal cases, because the accused who goes to prison, thereby losing any opportunity to earn a living, is far less able to pay a fee than is the accused who is acquitted. Also, lawyers would accept such arrangements only when the defense appeared sufficiently strong to warrant it, and the unscrupulous lawyer would be no more likely to fabricate a defense to earn a contingent fee than to earn a retainer.

When a contingent fee is proposed by an attorney, it is desirable, although it is not required, that a reasonable retainer arrangement be offered to the client in the alternative.

These rules do not preclude any particular mode or terms of payment, such as credit cards or interest on unpaid fees. The lawyer may also accept in payment shares of stock, literary rights, or other property. The only limitation is that the mode and terms of payment be consistent with fairness, good faith, full disclosure, and undivided fidelity to the client's interests, and otherwise be consistent with the provisions of this Code.

Illustrative Cases

5(a). A lawyer represents the widow of a railroad employee killed in a switching accident; the railroad is the defendant. After many months, the case is near trial, but the plaintiff tells the lawyer that she urgently needs money for food and rent, and must therefore settle immediately for whatever she can get. The lawyer reasonably believes that she will receive substantially more in settlement on the eve of the trial or as a result of jury verdict. He therefore gives her money, with the understanding that she will pay it back only if there is a recovery in the case. The lawyer has not committed a disciplinary violation.

5(b). A lawyer advances litigation expenses on behalf of a client on the clear understanding, in writing, that the client will reimburse the lawyer on a monthly basis, and that the client will pay interest at a specified, reasonable rate for any amounts in default. The lawyer has not committed a disciplinary violation.

5(c). A law firm is counsel to a corporation. An officer of the corporation asks a member of the firm to represent him in a divorce. The lawyer does so, without charging the firm's customary fee. The lawyer has committed a disciplinary violation.

CHAPTER VI. WITHDRAWAL FROM REPRESENTATION

Rules

6.1. A lawyer shall withdraw from representing a client when the lawyer is discharged by the client.

6.2. A lawyer may withdraw from representing a client at any time and for any reason if (a) withdrawal will cause no significant harm to the client's interests, (b) the client is fully informed of the consequences of withdrawal and voluntarily assents to it, or (c) withdrawal is pursuant to the terms of the retainer agreement required by Rules 5.1 and 5.2 of this Code.

6.3. A lawyer may withdraw from representing a client if the lawyer reasonably believes that continued employment in the case would be likely to have a seriously adverse effect upon the lawyer's health.

6.4. Unless the lawyer knows that withdrawal would result in significant and irreparable harm to the client, a lawyer may withdraw from representing a client if (a) the client commits a clear and substantial violation of a written agreement regarding fees or expenses, or (b) the lawyer encounters continuing, unavoidable and substantial difficulties in working with co-counsel or with the client.

6.5. In any matter other than criminal litigation, a lawyer may withdraw from representing a client if the lawyer comes to know that the client has knowingly induced the lawyer to take the case or to take action on behalf of the client on the basis of material misrepresentations about the facts of the case, and if withdrawal can be accomplished without a direct violation of confidentiality.

6.6. A lawyer shall decline or withdraw from representing a client when the lawyer knows that such action is necessary to avoid commission by the lawyer of a disciplinary violation, unless such action would result in a violation of Rule 1.2, proscribing direct or indirect divulgence of a client's confidences.

6.7. Whatever the reason for withdrawing from representation, a lawyer shall take reasonable care to avoid foreseeable harm to a client, including giving due notice to the client, allowing reasonable time for substitution of new counsel, cooperating with new counsel, promptly turning over all papers and property to which the client is entitled, and promptly returning any unearned advances.

Comment

Withdrawal from representing a client is the termination of the lawyer's authority to act for the client. What that entails will vary in different situations. Some of the duties that attach at the time of withdrawal are stated by Rule 6.7; others appear in Rule 1.2, relating to continuing confidentiality, and Rule 5.5, limiting the assertion of attorney's liens.

Most of the Rules in this Part state the circumstances under which lawyers are permitted to initiate withdrawal, and the conditions that may circumscribe such withdrawals.

Rule 6.1 is absolute. The lawyer discharged by the client must terminate the representation.

It sometimes appears that this Rule is overridden by a court's refusal to accept the withdrawal of counsel. In such cases, however, the client has the right either to persist in discharging the lawyer, and to go forward without counsel, or to revoke the discharge. Continuing with an unwanted lawyer is a true Hobson's choice, but it is still the client's choice of that course that continues, or revives, the representation.

Rule 6.6 is not absolute, because the duty it embodies, that of avoiding violating the Code, is sometimes subordinate to the paramount duty not to reveal clients' confidences. It should also be noted that Rule 6.5 allows indirect divulgence of confidences by withdrawal from a class of cases also covered by Rule 6.6, those non-criminal matters where the client has knowingly induced the lawyer either to take the case or to take action on the client's behalf, on the basis of material factual misrepresentations.

A lawyer is forbidden by Rule 3.7 to knowingly present false evidence. Therefore, withdrawal from representation would be required by Rule 6.6 when the lawyer knows through a confidence that the client intends to present false evidence, and when withdrawal would not result in violating a confidence. When the lawyer reasonably believes that refusal to present false evidence could result in violating a confidence, however, Rules 1.2, 3.7, and 6.6 require the lawyer to continue in the case.

Rule 6.5 permits withdrawal in a matter, other than criminal litigation, when the lawyer has been induced to take action by misrepresentations by the client, even though withdrawal might result indirectly in divulging a confidence. When the facts of a case fall within Rule 6.5, therefore, Rules 1.2, 3.7, and 6.6 are in part subordinated to it.

Illustrative Cases

6(a). A lawyer representing the accused in a criminal case learns from the client that he intends to present a false alibi. The lawyer knows that he will be required to give an explanation to the judge if he makes motion for leave to withdraw as counsel; he also knows that the judge will take an equivocal explanation as an indication that the client intends to commit perjury. The lawyer nevertheless asks leave to withdraw, telling the judge only, "I have an ethical problem," or, "My client and I do not see eye to eye." The lawyer has committed a disciplinary violation.

6(b). A lawyer represents a client required to file documents with a government agency. The lawyer comes to know that there are material misrepresentations in documents filed by the lawyer on the client's behalf, and subsequent uncorrected filings would further the misrepresentation. The client insists upon making the subsequent filings. The lawyer's withdrawal would cause no significant harm to the client's interest. The lawyer would commit a disciplinary violation by failing to withdraw.

6(c). The same facts as in 6(b), but the agency has a rule requiring a lawyer to give the agency the reason for any withdrawal. The lawyer would commit a disciplinary violation by withdrawing and thereby directly violating the client's confidences in making the required explanation.

6(d). The same facts as in 6(b). In addition, the lawyer was induced to particiate in the earlier filing by knowing misrepresentations by the client to the lawyer; the lawyer's withdrawal would adversely affect the client's ability to meet important deadlines; and the lawyer would not be required to explain his withdrawal to the agency, but the agency would be likely to scrutinize the client's filings more closely. The lawyer would not commit a disciplinary violation either by withdrawing or by going forward with the client.

CHAPTER VII. INFORMING THE PUBLIC ABOUT LEGAL SERVICES

Rules

7.1. A lawyer shall not knowingly make any representation that is materially false or misleading, and that might reasonably be expected to induce reliance by a member of the public in the selection of counsel.

7.2. A lawyer shall not advertise for or solicit clients in a way that violates a valid law imposing reasonable restrictions regarding time or place.

7.3. A lawyer shall not advertise for or solicit clients through another person when the lawyer knows, or could reasonably ascertain, that such conduct violates a contractual or other legal obligation of that other person.

7.4. A lawyer shall not solicit a member of the public when the lawyer has been told by that person or someone acting on that person's behalf that he or she does not want to receive communications from the lawyer.

7.5. A lawyer who advertises for or solicits clients through another person shall be as responsible for that person's representations to and dealings with potential clients as if the lawyer acted personally.

Comment

Access to the legal system is essential to the exercise of fundamental rights, particularly those rights relating to personal autonomy, freedom of expression, counsel, due process, and equal protection of the laws. Yet members of the public are frequently unaware of their need for legal assistance and of its availability. It is thus important for lawyers to provide members of the public with information regarding the availability of lawyers to serve them, the ways in which legal services can be useful, and the costs of legal services. Lawyers are therefore encouraged to advertise and to solicit clients, subject only to restrictions relating to false and misleading representations, harassment, violation of reasonable time and place regulations, and inducing violations by others of contractual or other legal obligations.

Solicitation refers to spoken communication, in person or by telephone, intended to induce the other person to become a client.

Illustrative Cases

7(a). A lawyer advertises truthfully that she has been certified as a specialist in international law by the Trans-World Bar Association, which is a bona fide association of lawyers imposing substantial requirements for such certification. The lawyer has not committed a disciplinary violation.

7(b). A lawyer advertises truthfully that he has been certified as a specialist in Family Law by the State Lawyers Association. The membership of the State Lawyers Association consists only of the lawyer himself, his two partners, and his neighbor. The advertisement is materially misleading, and the lawyer has committed a disciplinary violation.

7(c). A lawyer telephones the fifteen-year-old victim of a recent automobile accident, and is told by her parents that they are arranging for legal representation for their daughter, that she is in the hospital, and that they do not want him to contact her. The lawyer nevertheless calls upon the girl in the hospital and attempts to induce her to retain him. The lawyer has committed a disciplinary violation.

7(d). A lawyer visits the fifteen-year-old victim of an automobile accident in the hospital, and she retains him on reasonable terms for work he is competent to perform. He has not been instructed not to visit the girl, and the hospital has no regulations against solicitation of patients by lawyers. The lawyer has not committed a disciplinary violation.

Note: A client can discharge a lawyer with or without cause. The liability of the client to the lawyer in that event is a matter of state contract law.

7(e). A lawyers pays a hospital orderly a fee to distribute his professional cards to patients. The hospital has a rule against such conduct by its personnel. The lawyer has committed a disciplinary violation.

CHAPTER VIII. MAINTAINING PROFESSIONAL INTEGRITY AND COMPETENCE

Rules

8.1. A lawyer shall not engage in criminal or otherwise unlawful conduct that creates a substantial doubt that the lawyer will comply with this Code of Conduct.

8.2. Subject to Rule 1.2, proscribing unauthorized divulgence of a client's confidences, a lawyer who knows that an attorney or judge has committed a disciplinary violation, or who has material, adverse information about a candidate for the bar, shall convey that knowledge to the appropriate disciplinary or admission authorities.

8.3. When a lawyer has represented a client, or when, because of the lawyer's association with a law firm, a client of that firm could reasonably believe that the lawyer has had access to the client's confidences, the lawyer shall not thereafter accept employment by any other party whose interests are in any way adverse to the client's and could be materially affected by the lawyer's presumed knowledge of the client's confidences.

8.4. When a lawyer knows that the lawyer's testimony is likely to be offered on a material, disputed issue in a case, the lawyer shall decline or withdraw from representation in the case, unless doing so would cause serious and irreparable injury to the client.

8.5. When a lawyer is disqualified from representing a client under Rule 8.3 no partner or associate of that lawyer, and no one with an of counsel relation to the lawyer, shall represent the client.

8.6. When a lawyer is disqualified by Rule 8.3, 8.4, or 8.5 from representing a client, the disqualification may be waived by the voluntary and informed consent of each person whose interests are protected by the applicable rule.

8.7. A lawyer shall not enter into a commercial transaction or other business relationship with a person who is or was recently a client, unless that person is represented by independent counsel. This Rule does not affect the specific transactions covered by Chapter V of this Code, relating to retainer agreements and financial arrangements with clients.

8.8. A lawyer shall not commence having sexual relations with a client during the lawyer-client relationship.

8.9. A lawyer shall not act as officer or director of a publicly held corporation that is a client of the lawyer, of the lawyer's partner or associate, or of any firm or attorney with whom the lawyer has an of counsel relationship.

8.10. A lawyer serving on the board of a charitable or public organization shall not participate in discussing or voting upon any matter before the board that the lawyer knows might materially affect the interests of a client of the lawyer or of the lawyer's firm.

8.11. A lawyer shall not participate in arranging for a gift from a client to the lawyer, to a member of the lawyer's family, or to one who is a partner, associate, or of counsel to the lawyer.

8.12. When a lawyer holds money or property in whole or in part for the benefit of someone else, the lawyer shall hold it in trust, separate from the lawyer's own money and property, and appropriately identified, recorded, and safeguarded. When another person becomes entitled to receive any part of the money or property, the lawyer shall promptly deliver it to that person. If a dispute develops regarding entitlement to any part of the money or property, the lawyer may take action in accordance with applicable law, such as by depositing with a court the money or property that is in dispute, pending determination of the dispute.

8.13. A lawyer shall not enter into an agreement that unreasonably restricts a lawyer's right to practice law or to communicate with members of the public, and which thereby interferes with the freedom of clients to obtain counsel of their choice. However, lawyers in a partnership or similar professional relationship may make reasonable agreements regarding the allocation of fees among themselves with respect to clients who elect to continue with one or another lawyer upon termination of the professional relationship between the lawyers.

8.14. A lawyer shall not knowingly assist or seek to induce a disciplinary violation by another lawyer.

8.15. A lawyer shall take reasonable care to assure that none of the lawyer's partners, associates, or employees commits an act that would be a disciplinary violation if committed by the lawyer.

Comment

Satisfying each person's sense of justice is a high value in a society that respects the dignity of the individual, and public confidence in the administration of justice is necessary to maintain respect for law. For those reasons, it is a truism that justice must not only be done but that it must be seen to be done.

The role of lawyers is an essential element of the administration of justice, and rules of lawyers' conduct define that role. Thus, lawyers not only must comply with rules of professional conduct; they also must be seen as complying with them. For the profession to promulgate ethical rules, yet appear to wink at violations, can only result in disrespect for the profession and thereby in disrespect for the administration of justice. Thus, the concept that a lawyer should avoid the appearance of impropriety is an extremely important one. Embodying that concept in specific rules is, however, exceedingly difficult.

An early draft of this Code included the following provision:

> A lawyer shall avoid acting in such a way that a fair-minded person, knowing all of the relevant facts that are readily available, would conclude that, in the generality of such cases, disciplinary violations are likely to occur in a significant number of instances.

This views the appearance of impropriety from the perspective of a fair-minded person, not that of either a naif or a cynic. The appearance depends upon the facts readily available. The question is not whether the lawyer has in fact acted improperly, since the issue of appearances ordinarily arises in situations in which the impropriety would be extremely difficult to detect or to prove. The focus is on the generality of cases, and on whether improprieties are likely to occur in a significant number of instances.

Phrased otherwise: lawyers should avoid situations in which temptation and opportunity for wrongdoing are high, and detection or proof of wrongdoing would be difficult—situations, that is, in which common sense and experience inform us that a significant number of people will not be able to resist temptation. An obvious example is the lawyer who puts the client's funds into the lawyer's checking account.

The Commission accepted the proposed Rule as an aspirational guide, but found it too vague to be an acceptable basis for disciplinary action. Instead, this Chapter consists solely of rules proscribing particular conduct that gives rise to reasonable inferences of impropriety.

For example, Rule 8.8 forbids a lawyer to commence having sexual relations with a client during the lawyer-client relationship. This rule, like Rule 5.1, recognizes the dependency of a client upon a lawyer, the high degree of trust that a client is entitled to place in a lawyer, and the potential for unfair advantage in such a relationship. Other professionals, such as psychiatrists, have begun to face up to analogous problems.

Rule 8.1 provides for discipline of a lawyer who, either as a lawyer or as a private citizen, engages in unlawful conduct not specifically covered by other provisions of this Code if that conduct is relevant to one's performance as a lawyer.

Here again, an effort has been made to avoid unfairly vague terms. The elusive concept of moral turpitude is not used, nor is the undefined standard of "fitness to practice law." To warrant professional sanctions, the conduct must be unlawful—a felony, misdemeanor, or violation of rule of court—and must create a substantial doubt that the lawyer will comply with the rules of conduct required of lawyers.

This Code has no rule requiring each lawyer to do a particular amount of uncompensated public interest or *pro bono publico* work, on pain of professional discipline. That does not mean that the attorney members of the Commission are unwilling to perform such services or that the non-lawyer members do not want to share in the benefits of *pro bono* work. Rather, it is apparent to the Commission that such a rule would be inherently so vague as to be unenforceable and unenforced, and therefore hypocritical.

All lawyers should do work in the public interest. But some lawyers should not be telling other lawyers how much *pro bono* work they should be doing, and for whom, and disciplining them if they do not. Nor should codes of conduct purport to impose disciplinary requirements that the codifiers know will not be enforced.

Illustrative Cases

8(a). A lawyer represents the D Company, which is the defendant in an anti-trust action brought by the government. Subsequently, the lawyer represents the P Company, which is suing the D Company in a private anti-trust action involving the same alleged violation. Unless the D Company has knowingly and voluntarily assented to the lawyer's representation of the P Company, the lawyer has committed a disciplinary violation.

8(b). The same facts as in 8(a), but another attorney in the lawyer's firm represents the P Company, and the firm undertakes to "insulate" the lawyer from any involvement in the case. Unless the D Company has knowingly and voluntarily assented to the insulating or screening arrangement, and to the other attorney's representation of the P Company, the other attorney has committed a disciplinary violation.

8(c). A lawyer expects to cross examine a witness who previously was acquitted in a criminal case. The lawyer offers to pay the witness' previous attorney to provide information, learned by representing the witness in the criminal case, that could be used to discredit the witness on cross examination. The lawyer has committed a disciplinary violation.

CHAPTER IX.
RESPONSIBILITIES OF GOVERNMENT LAWYERS

Rules

9.1. A lawyer serving as public prosecutor shall not seek evidence to support a prosecution against a particular individual unless that individual is identified as a suspect in the course of a good faith investigation into suspected criminal conduct.

9.2. In exercising discretion to investigate or to prosecute, a lawyer serving as public prosecutor shall not show favoritism for, or invidiously discriminate against, one person among others similarly situated.

9.3. A lawyer serving as public prosecutor shall not seek or sign formal charges, or proceed to trial, unless a fair-minded juror could conclude beyond a reasonable doubt that the accused is guilty, on the basis of all of the facts that are known to the prosecutor and likely to be admissible into evidence.

9.4. A lawyer serving as public prosecutor before a grand jury shall not interfere with the independence of the grand jury, preempt a function of the grand jury, or use the processes of the grand jury for purposes not approved by the grand jury.

9.5. A lawyer serving as public prosecutor shall not use unconscionable pressures in plea bargaining, such as charging an accused in several counts for what is essentially a single offense, or charging an accused with a more serious offense than is warranted under Rule 9.3.

9.6. A lawyer serving as public prosecutor shall not condition a dismissal, nolle prosequi, or similar action on an accused's relinquishment of constitutional rights, or of rights against the government, a public official, or any other person, other than relinquishment of those rights inherent in pleading not guilty and proceeding to trial.

9.7. A lawyer serving as public prosecutor shall promptly make available to defense counsel, without request for it, any information that the prosecutor knows is likely to be useful to the defense.

9.8. A lawyer serving as public prosecutor shall not strike jurors on grounds of race, religion, national or ethnic background, or sex, except to counteract the use of such tactics initiated by the defense.

9.9. A lawyer serving as public prosecutor, who knows that a defendant is not receiving or has not received effective assistance of counsel, shall promptly advise the court, on the record when possible.

9.10. A lawyer representing the government before a court or other tribunal shall inform the tribunal of any facts or legal authorities that might materially affect the decision in the case, and that have not been brought to the attention of the tribunal by other counsel.

9.11. A lawyer in public service shall not engage in publicity regarding a criminal investigation or proceeding, or an administrative investigation or proceeding involving charges of wrongdoing, until after the announcement of a disposition of the case. However, the lawyer may publicize information that is (a) necessary to protect the public from an accused who is at large and reasonably believed to be dangerous; (b) necessary to help in apprehending a suspect; or (c) necessary to rebut publicized allegations of improper conduct on the part of the lawyer or the lawyer's staff.

9.12. A lawyer in public service shall not knowingly violate the rights of any person, or knowingly tolerate the violation of any person's rights by any other public employee.

9.13. A lawyer in public service shall not use the powers of public office for personal advantage, favoritism, or retaliation.

9.14. A lawyer shall not accept private employment relating to any matter in which the lawyer participated personally and substantially while in public service.

9.15. When a lawyer is disqualified from representing a client under Rule 9.14, no partner or associate of the lawyer, and no one with an of counsel relationship to the lawyer, shall represent the client.

9.16. A lawyer in public service shall not participate in any matter in which the lawyer participated personally and substantially in private practice.

9.17. While a lawyer in public service is participating personally and substantially in a matter in which a private attorney's client has a material interest, neither lawyer shall comment to the other about the government lawyer's private employment possibilities.

Supplementary Provisions*

9.18. For one year after leaving public service, a lawyer shall not counsel or otherwise represent a client who was previously involved in any matter in which the lawyer participated personally and substantially within one year prior to leaving public service.

9.19. For one year after leaving public service, a lawyer shall not become a partner or associate of, or have an of counsel relationship with, any law firm that represented an interested party in any matter in which the lawyer participated personally and substantially within one year prior to leaving public service.

9.20. For one year after entering public service, a lawyer shall not participate in any matter in which an interested party was the lawyer's client within one year before the lawyer entered public service, or in which an interested party is represented by a lawyer who was the partner or associate of, or had

---

* These provisions have not been approved by the Commission, principally because of concern about their effect in smaller communities served by very few lawyers.

an of counsel relationship to, the lawyer within one year before the lawyer entered public service, unless (a) the lawyer was appointed to office by the chief executive officer of the jurisdiction, with approval of a legislative body, or (b) the lawyer's participation is approved by a superior who was appointed by the chief executive officer with approval of a legislative body, or (c) the lawyer was elected to office.

9.21. When a lawyer is disqualified from representing a client under Rules 9.18 or 9.19, no partner or associate of the lawyer, and no one of counsel to the lawyer, shall represent the client.

Comment

Government lawyers are, of course, covered by rules that relate to lawyers generally. But government lawyers have significantly different roles and functions from lawyers representing private parties, and their ethical difficulties and the solutions to them must vary accordingly. Those differences stem principally from important distinctions between the government and the individual citizen. One such distinction is the paramount value given the sanctity of the individual in our society. Another is the awesome power of the government, a power that the founders of our nation had good reason to circumscribe in the Bill of Rights and elsewhere in the Constitution. A third difference is the majesty and dignity of our government. Conduct that may be tolerable in individuals may be reprehensible when done under color of law on behalf of the nation or a state.

In addition, the prosecutor has extraordinary powers of a quasi-judicial nature. The discretion to select a person to investigate has been described by Justice Robert Jackson (a former Attorney General) as "the most dangerous power" of the prosecutor. The prosecutor also decides the crime to be charged, affects the punishment, and even decides whether to prosecute at all. In the course of exercising that awesome discretion, the prosecutor is frequently called upon to make decisions which, in private litigation, would be made by a client rather than by the lawyer. Thus, to say that the prosecutor has special responsibilities in wielding the vast discretionary powers of government, is simply to recognize that the prosecutor is the person who has that discretionary power.

Defense counsel has special professional responsibilities deriving from the importance of confidentiality between attorney and client, the presumption of innocence, the constitutional right to counsel, and the constitutional privilege against self-incrimination. The prosecutor, who does not represent a private client, is not affected by those considerations in the same way.

Thus a defense attorney may be professionally bound to withhold evidence. There is nothing unethical in keeping a guilty defendant off the stand and putting the government to its proof; the Constitution guarantees the defendant nothing less. Obviously, however, the prosecutor is not similarly privileged to withhold material evidence; the constitutional command is precisely the contrary.

In recognition of the different roles of defense counsel and prosecutor, the American Bar Association and the Association of American Law Schools, in their Joint Conference Report on Professional Responsibility, concluded: "The public prosecutor cannot take as a guide for the conduct of his ofice the standards of an attorney appearing on the behalf of an individual client. The freedom elsewhere wisely granted to partisan advocacy must be severely curtailed if the prosecutor's duties are to be properly discharged."

As the Code of Professional Responsibility states, the responsibility of a public prosecutor "differs from that of the usual advocate; his duty is to seek justice, not merely to convict." The ABA Standards Relating to the Prosecution and the Defense Function also emphasize the unique role of the prosecutor: "Although the prosecutor operates within the adversary system, it is fundamental that his obligation is to protect the innocent as well as to convict the guilty; to guard the rights of the accused as well as to enforce the rights of the public." Unfortunately, however, neither the Code nor the Standards provides adequate rules governing prosecutorial misconduct, and the proposed Rules of Professional Conduct are similarly deficient.

Rule 9.3 forbids a prosecutor to seek an indictment or proceed to trial unless a fair-minded juror could conclude that the accused is guilty beyond a reasonable doubt, on the basis of the facts known to the prosecutor and likely to be admissible at trial. A further ethical obligation is assumed by many conscientious prosecutors; they will not seek an indictment or proceed to trial unless they are satisfied that the accused is guilty beyond a reasonable doubt, on the basis of all the facts known to them, regardless of admissibility. That rule should be followed in all cases, but is not here made the basis of a disciplinary violation, because the subjective nature of the standard makes it impossible to enforce.

Along with other unique powers of office, a prosecutor is privileged, in an indictment, to publish severely defamatory information against a private person. Despite their inherent harmfulness, indictments must be publicly available to prevent the abuses of secret proceedings. There is no similar justification, however, for a prosecutor to engage in press conferences, press releases, and other publicity efforts that have the effect of impairing or destroying the reputation of an accused without the due process of a trial or hearing. Yet, on the other hand, an accused may never be more in need of the First Amendment rights to freedom of speech than when officially labeled a wrongdoer before family, friends, neighbors, and business associates. Many defendants are inarticulate; almost all need the special skills of a lawyer as spokesperson. That is why this Code places restrictions on preconviction publicity by public officials, who act under color of law, but recognizes that the First Amendment precludes such restrictions on the speech of private persons and their attorneys.

The prosecutor working with a grand jury has peculiar responsibilities. The grand jury resembles an adjudicative tribunal, but its procedures are usually not adversary. Suspects who appear before it usually cannot be accompanied by counsel. The entire process is usually conducted *ex parte*; one side, the defense, cannot appear. The prosecutor presents evidence before the grand jury, as an advocate does before other tribunals, but also advises the grand jury, which is the representative of the people, regarding the course of action it should take.

This function is sometimes described as quasi-judicial: the prosecutor has much the same relation to a grand jury as a judge instructing a petit jury on the law. It is also, however, akin to the relationship of a lawyer in private practice to a client, particularly to the board of directors of a corporate client. The prosecutor has much the same obligations to a grand jury as the private lawyer to the private client, particularly the duty to serve the client's interests not as the lawyer perceives them, but as the client perceives them, and therefore to act as the servant, not the master, of the grand jury. Indeed, the grand jury prosecutor is almost the only lawyer for the public who has a real opportunity to consult directly with a duly constituted body, representative of the public, whose members have no conflicting interest (such as the desire to stay in office).

Ironically, however, the American grand jury has been criticized as a "rubber stamp for the prosecutor," because some prosecutors have used it improperly as an investigative tool and as a device for obtaining unwarranted indictments. Prosecutors have had grand juries dissolved because they would not indict, or because they wished to indict, quite properly, persons the prosecutor did not want indicted. Prosecutors have routinely isssued "grand jury subpoenas" for documents they wished to examine, without obtaining the consent of "their" grand juries, or even consulting the grand jury.

Rule 9.4 proscribes such abuses by prosecutors of the extraordinary powers of grand juries, when it is read in conjunction with other applicable rules in this Chapter. Particularly applicable are Rule 9.1, which proscribes seeking evidence to prosecute persons not identified as bona fide suspects; Rule 9.2, proscribing discriminating among potential defendants; and Rule 9.3, prohibiting seeking or signing indictments not likely to result in proper convictions. Most significant is Rule 9.10, which requires the prosecutor to inform the grand jury of all facts and legal authorities that might materially affect its decisions, because it is a tribunal before which no other counsel has the right to present facts or argument. Taken together with Rule 9.4, these rules should substantially contribute to returning the grand jury to its constitutional role as a bulwark between the citizen and the power of the state, and reducing its use as a cat's paw for the overzealous prosecutor.

Rule 9.13 forbids a lawyer in public service to use the powers of public office for personal advantage, favoritism, or retaliation. The use of an Enemies List in a prosecutor's office would be a clear violation of that rule. See also Rule 9.1. A lawyer in public service should also take pains to avoid participating in any matter in which members of the public might reasonably, though erroneously, believe that the lawyer is motivated by personal concern, such as a grudge. One way for a prosecutor to attempt to avoid such appearances is to move for the appointment of special prosecutors in cases in which the prosecutor's own motives might reasonably be questioned.

There is a common error of ethical discourse that should be avoided in interpreting the rules in this Code: When an appellate court affirms a conviction, that does not necessarily mean that the prosecutor's conduct has comported with professional ethics. A court might well decide that particular conduct by a prosecutor does not warrant reversal of a conviction on constitutional grounds, yet that same conduct might be a serious disciplinary violation.

Whenever this Chapter imposes special obligations upon lawyers serving as public prosecutors, that category includes enforcement lawyers for regulatory agencies, regardless of whether criminal or civil sanctions are being invoked. Also included are lawyers serving as bar counsel or in a similar disciplinary role.

One of the most controversial areas of appearance of impropriety has been, paradoxically, that in which the public nature of the profession is most obvious—conflicts of interest of the lawyer in (or formerly in) public service. In order to resolve that problem, it is important to note how narrow the area of dispute actually is.

First, there is virtual unanimity that when a lawyer has had substantial, personal participation in a matter while in public service, that lawyer should be disqualified from subsequently participating in the same matter on behalf of a private client.* Also, a lawyer in public service should not negotiate for private employment with a party or law firm whose interests the lawyer is able to affect.

There are several reasons for such rules. The present or former government attorney might be in a position to give one private party an unfair advantage over others through the favored use of confidential government information. There is also the possibility of favoritism to the former colleague on the part of lawyers still involved in the matter. The Association of the Bar of the City of New York has found "inevitable pressure" on government lawyers to show favoritism to private firms with whom they might later seek employment. Cases have also arisen in which there was an appearance of abuse of official power to create subsequent private employment for an attorney, or to give an attorney an advantage against a private party in subsequent private litigation.

---

* The reference to lawyers "in public service" includes judges and their law clerks; "matter" includes any judicial administrative, or other proceeding, application, request for a ruling or other determination, contract negotiation, claim, controversy, charge, accusation, arrest, or other particular matter.

A second principle on which there is general agreement is that of imputed disqualification. That is, when a lawyer is disqualified from representing a private client because of previous public service in the same matter, then that lawyer's partners and associates—those with whom the lawyer shares daily conversation and annual profits—should also be disqualified.

The narrow focus of disagreement has been whether the imputed disqualification of partners and associates should be subject to a waiver. A waiver would be based on a determination by the government agency involved that the disqualified attorney has been "screened" or "insulated" from any participation in the case. There are three major objections to the screening-waiver device, however, and none of them has been successfully answered.

The first unanswered objection is that no adequate standards for screening and granting waivers have been articulated: once we recognize that disqualification is appropriate, it is hardly sufficient to base a waiver on the mere assurance of the disqualified lawyers that they will not do anything improper.

The second unanswered objection is the virtual impossibility of policing violations once a waiver has been given.

Finally, the screening-waiver device compounds the initial conflict of interest by adding another. Agency lawyers who are called upon to grant or deny a waiver on behalf of a former colleague's law firm will have a substantial personal incentive to be generous in granting the waiver, because they will expect to make similar requests when they leave government service.

The principal argument in favor of permitting a screening-waiver device is that the government would find it impossible to hire competent lawyers if the screening-waiver exception is rejected, because lawyers would fear becoming unemployable. But if concern over the denial of waivers would indeed result in the unemployability of former government lawyers, that problem would prevail as long as there were any significant risk that waivers would be denied in particular cases. That is, unless the waiver device were a sham, and waivers were to be granted as a matter of course whenever requested, the asserted risks of hiring former government employees would still discourage law firms from employing them, and would thus discourage lawyers from entering government service.

In fact, however, no instance has ever been given of a government employee who would be rendered unemployable by the rejection of a waiver-screening exception. Unquestionably, a particular lawyer might have to forgo employment with a paricular law firm, or even with three or four firms, but that is hardly the sweeping effect that has been projected by opponents of the ethical rule.

It should be emphasized, however, that these rules are not motivated by disapproval of the so-called revolving door between government service and private practice, but by the serious likelihood of professional impropriety inherent in the lawyer's switching from one side to the other.

In addition to dealing with the problem of the lawyer who switches sides in the same matter, these rules seek also to discourage the situation in which a lawyer is representing the government's interests and, at the same time, may be contemplating leaving government service and going to work for a party or a law firm whose interests the government lawyer is able to affect. Because it is easy for understandings of future employment to be reached without any realistic opportunity to discover or to prove that to have been the case, the Supplementary Provisions establish time bars to employment of former government lawyers by some parties and firms in some circumstances.

Illustrative Cases

9(a). A police officer tells a prosecutor that he is sure a cache of contraband can be found in a particular dwelling. The prosecutor learns, in questioning the officer, that the officer cannot substantiate his hunch with evidence sufficient to obtain a search warrant. The prosecutor does not tell the officer to invent a pretext for entering the premises and to seize the contraband, but says nothing when the officer says he is going to do so. The prosecutor has committed a disciplinary violation.

9(b). A lawyer with the Public Contracts Award Board is advising the Board regarding the award of a contract for widgets. The attorney for Multinational Widgets, Inc., discusses his client's proposal with the Board lawyer. During the discussion, the attorney comments to the Board lawyer that his firm is looking for young lawyers with the Board lawyer's background, and that the Board lawyer should be sure to see him if he decides to leave government service. The attorney for Multinational has committed a disciplinary violation.

9(c). The same facts as 9(b). The Board lawyer fails to report the Multinational lawyer's comment to the disciplinary board. The Board lawyer has committed a disciplinary violation.

CALIFORNIA RULES OF PROFESSIONAL CONDUCT

(Approved by the California Supreme Court on November 28, 1988, operative on May 27, 1989)

Table of Rules

CHAPTER 1. PROFESSIONAL INTEGRITY IN GENERAL

Rule		Page
1-100.	Rules of Professional Conduct, in General	241
1-110.	Disciplinary Authority of State Bar	243
1-120.	Assisting, Soliciting, or Inducing Violations	243
1-200.	False Statement Regarding Admission to the State Bar	243
1-300.	Unauthorized Practice of Law	243
1-310.	Forming a Partnership With a Non-lawyer	244
1-320.	Financial Arrangements With Non-lawyers	244
1-400.	Advertising and Solicitation	245
1-500.	Agreements Restricting a Member's Practice	248
1-600.	Legal Service Programs	248

CHAPTER 2. RELATIONSHIP AMONG MEMBERS

2-100.	Communication With a Represented Party	249
2-200.	Financial Agreements Among Lawyers	250
2-300.	Sale or Purchase of a Law Practice of a Member, Living or Deceased	251

CHAPTER 3. PROFESSIONAL RELATIONSHIP WITH CLIENTS

3-110.	Failing to Act Competently	252
3-200.	Prohibited Objectives of Employment	253
3-210.	Advising the Violation of Law	253
3-300.	Avoiding Adverse Interests	254
3-310.	Avoiding the Representation of Adverse Interests	254
3-320.	Relationship With Other Party's Lawyer	256
3-400.	Limiting Liability to Client	256
3-500.	Communication	256
3-510.	Communication of Settlement Offer	256
3-600.	Organization as Client	257
3-700.	Termination of Employment	258

CHAPTER 4. FINANCIAL RELATIONSHIP WITH CLIENTS

4-100.	Preserving Identity of Funds and Property of a Client	260
4-200.	Fees for Legal Services	261
4-210.	Payment of Personal or Business Expenses Incurred by or for a Client	262

Rule		Page
4–300.	Purchasing Property at a Foreclosure or a Sale Subject to Judicial Review	262
4–400.	Gifts From Client	263

CHAPTER 5. ADVOCACY AND REPRESENTATION

5–100.	Threatening Criminal, Administrative, or Disciplinary Charges	263
5–110.	Performing the Duty of Member in Government Service	263
5–200.	Trial Conduct	264
5–210.	Member as Witness	264
5–220.	Suppression of Evidence	265
5–300.	Contact With Officials	265
5–310.	Prohibited Contact With Witnesses	265
5–320.	Contact With Jurors	266

CHAPTER 1. PROFESSIONAL INTEGRITY IN GENERAL

RULE 1–100. Rules of Professional Conduct, in General

(A) **Purpose and Function**. The following rules are intended to regulate professional conduct of members of the State Bar through discipline. They have been adopted by the Board of Governors of the State Bar of California and approved by the Supreme Court of California pursuant to Business and Professions Code sections 6076 and 6077 to protect the public and to promote respect and confidence in the legal profession. These rules together with any standards adopted by the Board of Governors pursuant to these rules shall be binding upon all members of the State Bar.

For a willful breach of any of these rules, the Board of Governors has the power to discipline members as provided by law.

The prohibition of certain conduct in these rules is not exclusive. Members are also bound by applicable law including the State Bar Act (Bus. & Prof.Code, § 6000 et seq.) and opinions of California courts. Although not binding, opinions of ethics committees in California should be consulted by members for guidance on proper professional conduct. Ethics opinions and rules and standards promulgated by other jurisdictions and bar associations may also be considered.

These rules are not intended to create new civil causes of action. Nothing in these rules shall be deemed to create, augment, diminish, or eliminate any substantive legal duty of lawyers or the non-disciplinary consequences of violating such a duty.

(B) **Definitions**.

(1) "Law Firm" means:

(a) two or more lawyers whose activities constitute the practice of law, and who share its profits, expenses, and liabilities; or

Rule 1-100   CALIFORNIA RULES

(b) a law corporation which employes more than one member; or

(c) a division, department, office, or group within a business entity, which includes more than one lawyer who performs legal services for the business entity; or

(d) a publicly funded entity which employs more than one lawyer to perform legal services.

(2) "Member" means a member of the State Bar of California.

(3) "Lawyer" means a member of the State Bar of California or a person who is admitted in good standing of and eligible to practice before the bar of any United States court or the highest court of the District of Columbia or any state, territory, or insular possession of the United States.

(4) "Associate" means an employee or fellow employee who is employed as a lawyer.

(5) "Shareholder" means a shareholder in a professional corporation pursuant to Business and Professions Code section 6160 et seq.

(C) Purpose of Discussions. Because it is a practical impossibility to convey in black letter form all of the nuances of these disciplinary rules, the comments contained in the Discussions of the rules, while they do not add independent basis for imposing discipline, are intended to provide guidance for interpreting the rules and practicing in compliance with them.

(D) Geographic Scope of Rules.

(1) *As to members:* These rules shall govern the activities of members in and outside this state, except as members lawfully practicing outside this state may be specifically required by a jurisdiction in which they are practicing to follow rules of professional conduct different from these rules.

(2) *As to lawyers from other jurisdictions:* These rules shall also govern the activities of lawyers while engaged in the performance of lawyer functions in this state; but nothing contained in these rules shall be deemed to authorize the performance of such functions by such persons in this state except as otherwise permitted by law.

(E) These rules may be cited and referred to as "Rules of Professional Conduct of the State Bar of California."

Comment

The Rules of Professional Conduct are intended to establish the standards for members for purposes of discipline. (See *Ames v. State Bar* (1973) 8 Cal.3d 910 [106 Cal.Rptr. 489].) The fact that a member has engaged in conduct that may be contrary to these rules does not automatically give rise to a civil cause of action. (See *Noble v. Sears, Roebuck & Co.* (1973) 33 Cal.App.3d 654 [109 Cal.Rptr. 269]; *Wilhelm v. Pray, Price, Williams &*

Russell (1986) 186 Cal.App.3d 1324 [231 Cal.Rptr. 355].) These rules are not intended to supercede existing law relating to members in non-disciplinary contexts. (See, e.g., *Klemm v. Superior Court* (1977) 75 Cal.App.3d 893 [142 Cal.Rptr. 509] (motion for disqualification of counsel due to a conflict of interest); *Academy of California Optometrists, Inc. v. Superior Court* (1975) 51 Cal.App.3d 999 [124 Cal.Rptr. 668] (duty to return client files); *Chronometrics, Inc. v. Sysgen, Inc.* (1980) 110 Cal.App.3d 597 [168 Cal.Rptr. 196] (disqualification of member appropriate remedy for improper communication with adverse party).

Law firm, as defined by subparagraph (B)(1), is not intended to include an association of members who do not share profits, expenses, and liabilities. The subparagraph is not intended to imply that a law firm may include a person who is not a member in violation of the law governing the unauthorized practice of law.

RULE 1-110. Disciplinary Authority of the State Bar

A member shall comply with conditions attached to public or private reprovals or other discipline administered by the State Bar pursuant to Business and Professions Code sections 6077 and 6078 and rule 956, California Rules of Court.

RULE 1-120. Assisting, Soliciting, or Inducing Violations

A member shall not knowingly assist in, solicit, or induce any violation of these rules or the State Bar Act.

RULE 1-200. False Statement Regarding Admission to the State Bar

(A) A member shall not knowingly make a false statement regarding a material fact or knowingly fail to disclose a material fact in connection with an application for admission to the State Bar.

(B) A member shall not further an application for admission to the State Bar of a person whom the member knows to be unqualified in respect to character, education, or other relevant attributes.

(C) This rule shall not prevent a member from serving as counsel of record for an applicant for admission to practice in proceedings related to such admission.

Comment

For purposes of rule 1-200 "admission" includes readmission.

RULE 1-300. Unauthorized Practice of Law

(A) A member shall not aid any person or entity in the unauthorized practice of law.

(B) A member shall not practice law in a jurisdiction where to do so would be in violation of regulations of the profession in that jurisdiction.

RULE 1-310. Forming a Partnership With a Non-lawyer

A member shall not form a partnership with a person not licensed to practice law if any of the activities of that partnership consist of the practice of law.

Comment

Rule 1-310 is not intended to govern members' activities which cannot be considered to constitute the practice of law. It is intended solely to preclude a member from being involved in the practice of law with a person not licensed to practice law.

RULE 1-320. Financial Arrangements With Non-lawyers

(A) Neither a member nor a law firm shall directly or indirectly share legal fees with a person or entity not licensed to practice law, except that:

(1) An agreement between a member and a law firm, partner, or associate may provide for the payment of money after the member's death to the member's estate or to one or more specified persons over a reasonable period of time; or

(2) A member or law firm undertaking to complete unfinished legal business of a deceased member may pay to the estate of the deceased member or other person legally entitled thereto that proportion of the total compensation which fairly represents the services rendered by the deceased member;

(3) A member or law firm may include non-member employees in a compensation, profit-sharing, or retirement plan even though the plan is based in whole or in part on a profit-sharing arrangement, if such plan does not circumvent these rules or Business and Professions Code section 6000 et seq.; or

(4) A member may pay a prescribed registration, referral, or participation fee to a lawyer referral service established, sponsored, and operated in accordance with the State Bar of California's Minimum Standards for a Lawyer Referral Service in California.

(B) A member shall not compensate, give, or promise anything of value to any person or entity for the purpose of recommending or securing employment of the member or the member's law firm by a client, or as a reward for having made a recommendation resulting in employment of the member or the member's law firm by a client. A member's offering of or giving a gift or gratuity to any person or entity having made a recommendation resulting in the employment of the member or the member's law firm shall not of itself violate this rule, provided that the gift or gratuity was not offered or given in consideration of any promise, agreement, or understanding that such a gift or gratuity would be forthcoming or that referrals would be made or encouraged in the future.

(C) A member shall not compensate, give, or promise anything of value to any representative of the press, radio, television, or other communication medium in anticipation of or in return for publicity of the member, the law firm, or any other member as such in a news item, but the incidental provision of food or beverage shall not of itself violate this rule.

Comment

Rule 1–320(C) is not intended to preclude compensation to the communications media in exchange for advertising the member's or law firm's availability for professional employment.

RULE 1–400. Advertising and Solicitation

(A) For purposes of this rule, "communication" means any message or offer made by or on behalf of a member concerning the availability for professional employment of a member or a law firm directed to any former, present, or prospective client, including but not limited to the following:

(1) Any use of firm name, trade name, fictitious name, or other professional designation of such member or law firm; or

(2) Any stationery, letterhead, business card, sign, brochure, or other comparable written material describing such member, law firm, or lawyers; or

(3) Any advertisement (regardless of medium) of such member or law firm directed to the general public or any substantial portion thereof; or

(4) Any unsolicited correspondence from a member or law firm directed to any person or entity.

(B) For purposes of this rule, a "solicitation" means any communication:

(1) Concerning the availability for professional employment of a member or a law firm in which a significant motive is pecuniary gain; and

(2) Which is;

(a) delivered in person or by telephone, or

(b) directed by any means to a person known to the sender to be represented by counsel in a matter which is a subject of the communication.

(C) A solicitation shall not be made by or on behalf of a member or law firm to a prospective client with whom the member or law firm has no family or prior professional relationship, unless the solicitation is protected from abridgment by the Constitution of the United States or by the Constitution of the State of California. A solicitation to a former

Rule 1-400 CALIFORNIA RULES

or present client in the discharge of a member's or law firm's professional duties is not prohibited.

(D) A communication or a solicitation (as defined herein) shall not:

(1) Contain any untrue statement; or

(2) Contain any matter, or present or arrange any matter in a manner or format which is false, deceptive, or which tends to confuse, deceive, or mislead the public; or

(3) Omit to state any fact necessary to make the statements made, in the light of circumstances under which they are made, not misleading to the public; or

(4) Fail to indicate clearly, expressly, or by context, that it is a communication or solicitation, as the case may be; or

(5) Be transmitted in any manner which involves intrusion, coercion, duress, compulsion, intimidation, threats, or vexatious or harassing conduct; or

(6) State that a member is a "certified specialist" unless the member holds a current certificate as a specialist issued by the California Board of Legal Specialization pursuant to a plan for specialization approved by the Supreme Court.

(E) The Board of Governors of the State Bar shall formulate and adopt standards as to communications which will be presumed to violate this rule 1-400. The standards shall only be used as presumptions affecting the burden of proof in disciplinary proceedings involving alleged violations of these rules. "Presumption affecting the burden of proof" means that presumption defined in Evidence Code sections 605 and 606. Such standards formulated and adopted by the Board, as from time to time amended, shall be effective and binding on all members.

(F) A member shall retain for two years a true and correct copy or recording of any communication made by written or electronic media. Upon written request, the member shall make any such copy or recording available to the State Bar, and, if requested, shall provide to the State Bar evidence to support any factual or objective claim contained in the communication.

Standards:

Pursuant to rule 1-400(E) the Board of Governors of the State Bar has adopted the following standards, effective May 27, 1989 as forms of "communication" defined in rule 1-400(A) which are presumed to be in violation of rule 1-400.

(1) A "communication" which contains guarantees, warranties, or predictions regarding the result of the representation.

(2) A "communication" which contains testimonials about or endorsements of a member unless such communication also contains an express disclaimer such as "this testimonial or endorsement does not

constitute a guarantee, warranty, or prediction regarding the outcome of your legal matter."

(3) A "communication" which is delivered to a potential client whom the member knows or should reasonably have known is in such a physical, emotional, or mental state that he or she would not be expected to exercise reasonable judgment as to the retention of counsel.

(4) A "communication" which is transmitted at the scene of an accident or at or en route to a hospital, emergency care center, or other health care facility.

(5) A "communication" except professional announcements, seeking professional employment primarily for pecuniary gain which is transmitted by mail or equivalent means which does not clearly identify itself as an advertisement. If transmitted in an envelope, the envelope shall be identified as an advertisement on the outside thereof.

(6) A "communication" in the form of a firm name, trade name, fictitious name, or other professional designation which states or implies a relationship between any member in private practice and a government agency or instrumentality or a public or non-profit legal services organization.

(7) A "communication" in the form of a firm name, trade name, fictitious name, or other professional designation which states or implies that a member has a relationship to any other member or a law firm as a partner or associate, or officer or shareholder pursuant to Business and Professions Code sections 6160–6172 unless such relationship in fact exists.

(8) A "communication" which states or implies that a member or law firm is "of counsel" to another member or a law firm unless the former has a relationship with the latter (other than as a partner or associate, or officer or shareholder pursuant to Business and Professions Code sections 6160–6172) which is close, personal, continuous, and regular.

(9) A "communication" in the form of a firm name, trade name, fictitious name, or other professional designation used by a member or law firm in private practice which differs materially from any other such designation used by such member or law firm at the same time in the same community.

(10) A "communication" which implies that the member or member's firm is participating in a lawyer referral service which has been certified by the State Bar of California or as having satisfied the Minimum Standards for Lawyer Referral Services in California, when that is not the case.

RULE 1–500. Agreements Restricting a Member's Practice

(A) A member shall not be a party to or participate in offering or making an agreement, whether in connection with the settlement of a lawsuit or otherwise, if the agreement restricts the right of a member to practice law.

(B) Nothing in paragraph (A) of this rule shall be construed as prohibiting such a restrictive agreement which:

(1) Is a part of an employment, shareholders', or partnership agreement among members provided the restrictive agreement does not survive the termination of the employment, shareholder, or partnership relationship; or

(2) Requires payments to a member upon the member's retirement from the practice of law.

(C) A member shall not be a party to or participate in offering or making an agreement which precludes the reporting of a violation of these rules.

Comment

Paragraph (A) makes it clear that the practice, in connection with settlement agreements, of proposing that a member refrain from representing other clients in similar litigation, is prohibited. Neither counsel may demand or suggest such provisions nor may opposing counsel accede or agree to such provisions.

Paragraph (B) permits a restrictive covenant in a law corporation, partnership, or employment agreement. The law corporation shareholder, partner, or associate may agree not to have a separate practice during the existence of the relationship; however, upon termination of the relationship (whether voluntary or involuntary), the member is free to practice law without any contractual restriction except in the case of retirement from the active practice of law.

RULE 1–600. Legal Service Programs

(A) A member shall not participate in a nongovernmental program, activity, or organization furnishing, recommending, or paying for legal services, which allows any third person or organization to interfere with the member's independence of professional judgment, or with the client-lawyer relationship, or allows unlicensed persons to practice law, or allows any third person or organization to receive directly or indirectly any part of the consideration paid to the member except as permitted by these rules, or otherwise violates the State Bar Act or these rules.

(B) The Board of Governors of the State Bar shall formulate and adopt Minimum Standards for Lawyer Referral Services, which, as from time to time amended, shall be binding on members.

Comment

The participation of a member in a lawyer referral service established, sponsored, supervised, and operated in conformity with the Minimum Standards for a Lawyer Referral Service in California is encouraged and is not, of itself, a violation of these rules.

Rule 1-600 is not intended to override any contractual agreement or relationship between insurers and insureds regarding the provision of legal services.

Rule 1-600 is not intended to apply to the activities of a public agency responsible for providing legal services to a government or to the public.

For purposes of paragraph (A), "a nongovernmental program, activity, or organization" includes, but is not limited to group, prepaid, and voluntary legal service programs, activities, or organizations.

CHAPTER 2. RELATIONSHIP AMONG MEMBERS

RULE 2-100. Communication With a Represented Party

(A) While representing a client, a member shall not communicate directly or indirectly about the subject of the representation with a party the member knows to be represented by another lawyer in the matter, unless the member has the consent of the other lawyer.

(B) For purposes of this rule, a "party" includes:

(1) An officer, director, or managing agent of a corporation or association, and a partner or managing agent of a partnership; or

(2) An association member or an employee of an association, corporation, or partnership, if the subject of the communication is any act or omission of such person in connection with the matter which may be binding upon or imputed to the organization for purposes of civil or criminal liability or whose statement may constitute an admission on the part of the organization.

(C) This rule shall not prohibit:

(1) Communications with a public officer, board, committee, or body;

(2) Communications initiated by a party seeking advice or representation from an independent lawyer of the party's choice; or

(3) Communications otherwise authorized by law.

Comment

Rule 2-100 is intended to control communications between a member and persons the member knows to be represented by counsel unless a statutory scheme or case law will override the rule. There are a number of express statutory schemes which authorize communications between a member and person who would otherwise be subject to this rule. These statutes protect a variety of other rights such as the right of employees to organize and to engage in collective bargaining, employee health and safety, or equal employment opportunity. Other applicable law also includes the authority of government prosecutors and investigators to conduct criminal investigations, as limited by the relevant decisional law.

Rule 2–100 is not intended to prevent the parties themselves from communicating with respect to the subject matter of the representation, and nothing in the rule prevents a member from advising the client that such communication can be made. Moreover, the rule does not prohibit a member who is also a party to a legal matter from directly or indirectly communicating on his or her own behalf with a represented party. Such a member has independent rights as a party which should not be abrogated because of his or her professional status. To prevent any possible abuse in such situations, the counsel for the opposing party may advise that party (1) about the risks and benefits of communications with a lawyer-party, and (2) not to accept or engage in communications with the lawyer-party.

Rule 2–100 also addresses the situation in which member A is contacted by an opposing party who is represented and, because of dissatisfaction with that party's counsel, seeks A's independent advice. Since A is employed by the opposition, the member cannot give independent advice.

As used in paragraph (A), "the subject of the representation," "matter," and "party" are not limited to a litigation context.

Paragraph (B) is intended to apply only to persons employed at the time of the communication.

Subparagraph (C)(2) is intended to permit a member to communicate with an individual seeking to hire new counsel or to obtain a second opinion. A member contacted by such an individual continues to be bound by other Rules of Professional Conduct. (See, e.g., rules 1–400 and 3–310.)

RULE 2–200. Financial Arrangements Among Lawyers

(A) A member shall not divide a fee for legal services with a lawyer who is not a partner of, associate of, or shareholder with the member unless:

> (1) The client has consented in writing thereto after a full disclosure has been made in writing that a division of fees will be made and the terms of such division; and
>
> (2) The total fee charged by all lawyers is not increased solely by reason of the provision for division of fees and is not unconscionable as that term is defined in rule 4–200.

(B) Except as permitted in paragraph (A) of this rule or rule 2–300, a member shall not compensate, give, or promise anything of value to any lawyer for the purpose of recommending or securing employment of the member or the member's law firm by a client, or as a reward for having made a recommendation resulting in employment of the member or the member's law firm by a client. A member's offering of or giving a gift or gratuity to any lawyer who has made a recommendation resulting in the employment of the member or the member's law firm shall not of itself violate this rule, provided that the gift or gratuity was not offered

PROFESSIONAL CONDUCT — Rule 2-300

in consideration of any promise, agreement, or understanding that such a gift or gratuity would be forthcoming or that referrals would be made or encouraged in the future.

RULE 2-300. Sale or Purchase of a Law Practice of a Member, Living or Deceased

All or substantially all of the law practice of a member, living or deceased, including goodwill, may be sold to another member or law firm subject to all the following conditions:

(A) Fees charged to clients shall not be increased solely by reason of such sale.

(B) If the sale contemplates the transfer of responsibility for work not yet completed or responsibility for client files or information protected by Business and Professions Code section 6068, subdivision (e), then;

　(1) if the seller is deceased, has a conservator or other person acting in a representative capacity, prior to the transfer;

　　(a) the purchaser shall cause a written notice to be given to the client stating that the interest in the law practice is being transferred to the purchaser; that the client has the right to retain other counsel; that the client may take possession of any client papers and property, as required by rule 3-700(D); and that if no response is received to the notification within 90 days of the sending of such notice, or in the event the client's rights would be prejudiced by a failure to act during that time, the purchaser may act on behalf of the client until otherwise notified by the client. Such notice shall comply with the requirements as set forth in rule 1-400(D) and any provisions relating to attorney-client fee arrangements, and

　　(b) the purchaser shall obtain the written consent of the client provided that such consent shall be presumed until otherwise notified by the client if no response is received to the notification specified in subparagraph (a) within 90 days of the date of the sending of such notification to the client's last address as shown on the records of the seller, or the client's rights would be prejudiced by a failure to act during such 90-day period.

　(2) in all other circumstances, not less than 90 days prior to the transfer;

　　(a) the seller shall cause a written notice to be given to the client stating that the interest in the law practice is being transferred to the purchaser; that the client has the right to retain other counsel; that the client may take possession of any client papers and property, as required by rule 3-700(D); and that if no response is received to the notification within 90 days of the sending of such notice, the purchaser may act on behalf of the client until otherwise notified by the client. Such notice shall

Rule 2–300 CALIFORNIA RULES

comply with the requirements as set forth in rule 1–400(D) and any provisions relating to attorney-client fee arrangements, and

(b) the seller shall obtain the written consent of the client prior to the transfer provided that such consent shall be presumed until otherwise notified by the client if no response is received to the notification specified in subparagraph (a) within 90 days of the date of the sending of such notification to the client's last address as shown on the records of the seller.

(C) If substitution is required by the rules of a tribunal in which a matter is pending, all steps necessary to substitute a member shall be taken.

(D) All activity of a purchaser or potential purchaser under this rule shall be subject to compliance with rules 3–300 and 3–310 where applicable.

(E) Confidential information shall not be disclosed to a non-member in connection with a sale under this rule.

(F) Admission to or retirement from a law partnership or law corporation, retirement plans and similar arrangements, or sale of tangible assets of a law practice shall not be deemed a sale or purchase under this rule.

Comment

Paragraph (A) is intended to prohibit the purchaser from charging the former clients of the seller a higher fee than the purchaser is charging his or her existing clients.

"All or substantially all of the law practice of a member" means, for purposes of rule 2–300 that, for example, a member may retain one or two clients who have such a longstanding personal and professional relationship with the member that transfer of those clients' files is not feasible. Conversely, rule 2–300 is not intended to authorize the sale of a law practice in a piecemeal fashion except as may be required by subparagraph (B)(1)(a) or paragraph (D).

Transfer of individual client matters, where permitted, is governed by rule 2–200. Payment of a fee to a non-lawyer broker for arranging the sale or purchase of a law practice is governed by rule 1–320.

CHAPTER 3. PROFESSIONAL RELATIONSHIP WITH CLIENTS

RULE 3–110. Failing to Act Competently

(A) A member shall not intentionally, or with reckless disregard, or repeatedly fail to perform legal services competently.

(B) To perform legal services competently means diligently to apply the learning and skill necessary to perform the member's duties arising from employment or representation. If the member does not have sufficient learning and skills when the employment or representation is undertaken, or during the course of the employment or representation, the member may nonetheless perform such duties competently by associating or, where appropriate, professionally consulting another member reasonably believed to be competent, or by acquiring sufficient learning and skill before performance is required, if the member has sufficient time, resources, and ability to do so.

(C) As used in this rule, the term "ability" means a quality or state of having sufficient learning and skill and being mentally, emotionally, and physically able to perform legal services.

Comment

The duties set forth in rule 3–110 include the duty to supervise the work of subordinate attorney and non-attorney employees or agents. (See, e.g., *Waysman v. State Bar* (1986) 41 Cal.3d 452; *Trousil v. State Bar* (1985) 38 Cal.3d 337, 342 [211 Cal.Rptr. 525]; *Palomo v. State Bar* (1984) 36 Cal.3d 785 [205 Cal.Rptr. 834]; *Crane v. State Bar* (1981) 30 Cal.3d 117, 122; *Black v. State Bar* (1972) 7 Cal.3d 676, 692 [103 Cal.Rptr. 288; 499 P.2d 968]; *Vaughn v. State Bar* (1972) 6 Cal.3d 847, 857–858 [100 Cal.Rptr. 713; 494 P.2d 1257]; *Moore v. State Bar* (1964) 62 Cal.2d 74, 81 [41 Cal.Rptr. 161; 396 P.2d 577].)

RULE 3–200. Prohibited Objectives of Employment

A member shall not seek, accept, or continue employment if the member knows or should know that the objective of such employment is:

(A) To bring an action, conduct a defense, assert a position in litigation, or take an appeal, without probable cause and for the purpose of harassing or maliciously injuring any person; or

(B) To present a claim or defense in litigation that is not warranted under existing law, unless it can be supported by a good faith argument for an extension, modification, or reversal of such existing law.

RULE 3–210. Advising the Violation of Law

A member shall not advise the violation of any law, rule, or ruling of a tribunal unless the member believes in good faith that such law, rule, or ruling is invalid. A member may take appropriate steps in good faith to test the validity of any law, rule, or ruling of a tribunal.

Comment

Rule 3–210 is intended to apply not only to the prospective conduct of a client but also to the interaction between the member and client and to the specific legal service sought by the client from the member. An example of the former is the handling of physical evidence of a crime in the possession of the client and offered to the member. (See *People v. Meredith* (1981) 29 Cal.3d 682 [175 Cal.Rptr. 612].) An example of the latter is a request that the member negotiate the return of stolen property in exchange for the owner's agreement not to report the theft to the police or prosecutorial authorities. (See *People v. Pic'l* (1982) 31 Cal.3d 731 [183 Cal.Rptr. 685].)

RULE 3–300. Avoiding Adverse Interests

A member shall not enter into a business transaction with a client; or knowingly acquire an ownership, possessory, security, or other pecuniary interest adverse to a client, unless each of the following requirements has been satisfied:

(A) The transaction or acquisition and its terms are fair and reasonable to the client and are fully disclosed and transmitted in writing to the client in a manner which should reasonably have been understood by the client; and

(B) The client is advised in writing that the client may seek the advice of an independent lawyer of the client's choice and is given a reasonable opportunity to seek that advice; and

(C) The client thereafter consents in writing to the terms of the transaction or the terms of the acquisition.

Comment

Rule 3–300 is not intended to apply to the agreement by which the member is retained by the client, unless the agreement confers on the member an ownership, possessory, security, or other pecuniary interest adverse to the client. Such an agreement is governed, in part, by rule 4–200.

Rule 3–300 is not intended to apply where the member and client each make an investment on terms offered to the general public or a significant portion thereof. For example, rule 3–300 is not intended to apply where A, a member, invests in a limited partnership syndicated by a third party. B, A's client, makes the same investment. Although A and B are each investing in the same business, A did not enter into the transaction "with" B for the purposes of the rule.

Rule 3–300 is intended to apply where the member wishes to obtain an interest in client's property in order to secure the amount of the member's past due or future fees.

RULE 3–310. Avoiding the Representation of Adverse Interests

(A) If a member has or had a relationship with another party interested in the representation, or has an interest in its subject matter, the member shall not accept or continue such representation without all affected clients' informed written consent.

(B) A member shall not concurrently represent clients whose interests conflict, except with their informed written consent.

(C) A member who represents two or more clients shall not enter into an aggregate settlement of the claims of or against the clients, except with their informed written consent.

(D) A member shall not accept employment adverse to a client or former client where, by reason of the representation of the client or former client, the member has obtained confidential information material to the employment except with the informed written consent of the client or former client.

(E) A member shall not accept compensation for representing a client from one other than the client unless:

(1) There is no interference with the member's independence of professional judgment or with the client-lawyer relationship; and

(2) Information relating to representation of a client is protected as required by Business and Professions Code section 6068, subdivision (e); and

(3) The client consents after disclosure, provided that no disclosure is required if;

(a) such nondisclosure is otherwise authorized by law, or

(b) the member is rendering legal services on behalf of any public agency which provides legal services to other public agencies or members of the public.

(F) As used in this rule "informed" means full disclosure to the client of the circumstances and advice to the client of any actual or reasonably foreseeable adverse effects of those circumstances upon the representation.

Comment

Rule 3-310 is not intended to prohibit a member from representing parties having antagonistic positions on the same legal question that has arisen in different cases, unless representation of either client would be adversely affected.

Paragraph (A) is intended to apply to all types of legal employment, including the representation of multiple parties in litigation or in a single transaction or other common enterprise or legal relationship. Examples of the latter include the formation of a partnership for several partners or a corporation for several shareholders, the preparation of an ante-nuptial agreement, or joint or reciprocal wills for a husband and wife, or the resolution of an "uncontested" marital dissolution. In such situations, for the sake of convenience or economy, the parties may well prefer to employ a single counsel, but a member must disclose the potential adverse aspects of such multiple representation (e.g., Evid.Code, § 962) and must obtain the consent of the clients thereto. Moreover, if the potential adversity should become actual, the member must obtain the further consent of the clients pursuant to paragraph (B).

Paragraph (E) is not intended to abrogate existing relationships between insurers and insureds whereby the insurer has the contractual right to unilaterally select counsel for the insured, where there is no conflict of interest. (See *San Diego Navy Federal Credit Union v. Cumis Insurance Society* (1984) 162 Cal.App.3d 358 [208 Cal.Rptr. 494].)

RULE 3-320. Relationship With Other Party's Lawyer

A member shall not represent a client in a matter in which another party's lawyer is a spouse, parent, child, or sibling of the member, lives with the member, is a client of the member, or has an intimate personal relationship with the member, unless the member informs the client in writing of the relationship.

Comment

Rule 3-320 is not intended to apply to circumstances in which a member fails to advise the client of a relationship with another member who is merely a partner or associate in the same law firm as the adverse party's counsel, and who has no direct involvement in the matter.

RULE 3-400. Limiting Liability to Client

A member shall not:

(A) Contract with a client prospectively limiting the member's liability to the client for the member's professional malpractice; or

(B) Settle a claim or potential claim for such liability unless the client is informed in writing that the client may seek the advice of an independent lawyer of the client's choice regarding the settlement and is given a reasonable opportunity to seek that advice.

Comment

Rule 3-400 is not intended to apply to customary qualifications and limitations in legal opinions and memoranda, nor is it intended to prevent a member from reasonably limiting the scope of the member's employment or representation.

RULE 3-500. Communication

A member shall keep a client reasonably informed about significant developments relating to the employment or representation and promptly comply with reasonable requests for information.

Comment

Rule 3-500 is not intended to change a member's duties to his or her clients. It is intended to make clear that, while a client must be informed of significant developments in the matter, a member will not be disciplined for failing to communicate insignificant or irrelevant information. (See Bus. & Prof.Code, § 6068, subd. (m).)

RULE 3-510. Communication of Settlement Offer

(A) A member shall promptly communicate to the member's client:

(1) All terms and conditions of any offer made to the client in a criminal matter; and

(2) All amounts, terms, and conditions of any written offer of settlement made to the client in all other matters.

(B) As used in this rule, "client" includes a person who possesses the authority to accept an offer of settlement or plea, or, in a class action, all the named representatives of the class.

Comment

Rule 3-510 is intended to require that counsel in a criminal matter convey all offers, whether written or oral, to the client, as give and take negotiations are less common in criminal matters, and, even were they to occur, such negotiations should require the participation of the accused.

Any oral offers of settlement made to the client in a civil matter should also be communicated if they are "significant" for the purposes of rule 3-500.

RULE 3-600. Organization as Client

(A) In representing an organization, a member shall conform his or her representation to the concept that the client is the organization itself, acting through its highest authorized officer, employee, body, or constituent overseeing the particular engagement.

(B) If a member acting on behalf of an organization knows that an actual or apparent agent of the organization acts or intends or refuses to act in a manner that is or may be a violation of law reasonably imputable to the organization, or in a manner which is likely to result in substantial injury to the organization, the member shall not violate his or her duty of protecting all confidential information as provided in Business and Professions Code section 6068, subdivision (e). Subject to Business and Professions Code section 6068, subdivision (e), the member may take such actions as appear to the member to be in the best lawful interest of the organization. Such actions may include among others:

(1) Urging reconsideration of the matter while explaining its likely consequences to the organization; or

(2) Referring the matter to the next higher authority in the organization, including, if warranted by the seriousness of the matter, referral to the highest internal authority that can act on behalf of the organization.

(C) If, despite the member's actions in accordance with paragraph (B), the highest authority that can act on behalf of the organization insists upon action or a refusal to act that is a violation of law and is likely to result in substantial injury to the organization, the member's response is limited to the member's right, and, where appropriate, duty to resign in accordance with rule 3-700.

(D) In dealing with an organization's directors, officers, employees, members, shareholders, or other constituents, a member shall explain the identity of the client for whom the member acts, whenever it is or becomes apparent that the organization's interests are or may become adverse to those of the constituent(s) with whom the member is dealing. The member shall not mislead such a constituent into believing that the constituent may communicate confidential information to the member in a way that will not be used in the organization's interest if that is or becomes adverse to the constituent.

(E) A member representing an organization may also represent any of its directors, officers, employees, members, shareholders, or other constituents, subject to the provisions of rule 3-310. If the organization's consent to the dual representation is required by rule 3-310, the consent shall be given by an appropriate constituent of the organization other than the individual or constituent who is to be represented, or by the shareholder(s) or organization members.

Comment

Rule 3-600 is not intended to enmesh members in the intricacies of the entity and aggregate theories of partnership.

Rule 3-600 is not intended to prohibit members from representing both an organization and other parties connected with it, as for instance (as simply one example) in establishing employee benefit packages for closely held corporations or professional partnerships.

Rule 3-600 is not intended to create or to validate artificial distinctions between entities and their officers, employees, or members, nor is it the purpose of the rule to deny the existence or importance of such formal distinctions. In dealing with a close corporation or small association, members commonly perform professional engagements for both the organization and its major constituents. When a change in control occurs or is threatened, members are faced with complex decisions involving personal and institutional relationships and loyalties and have frequently had difficulty in perceiving their correct duty. (See *People ex rel. Deukmejian v. Brown* (1981) 29 Cal.3d 150 [172 Cal.Rptr. 478]; *Goldstein v. Lees* (1975) 46 Cal.App.3d 614 [120 Cal. Rptr. 253]; *Woods v. Superior Court* (1983) 149 Cal.App.3d 931 [197 Cal. Rptr. 185]; *In re Banks* (1978) 283 Ore. 459 [584 P.2d 284]; 1 A.L.R. 4th 1105.) In resolving such multiple relationships, members must rely on case law.

RULE 3-700. Termination of Employment

(A) In General.

(1) If permission for termination of employment is required by the rules of a tribunal, a member shall not withdraw from employment in a proceeding before that tribunal without its permission.

(2) A member shall not withdraw from employment until the member has taken reasonable steps to avoid reasonably foreseeable prejudice to the rights of the client, including giving due notice to the client, allowing time for employment of other counsel, complying with rule 3-700(D), and complying with applicable laws and rules.

(B) Mandatory Withdrawal. A member representing a client before a tribunal shall withdraw from employment with the permission of the tribunal, if required by its rules, and a member representing a client in other matters shall withdraw from employment, if:

(1) The member knows or should know that the client is bringing an action, conducting a defense, asserting a position in litigation, or taking an appeal, without probable cause and for the purpose of harassing or maliciously injuring any person; or

(2) The member knows or should know that continued employment will result in violation of these rules or of the State Bar Act; or

(3) The member's mental or physical condition renders it unreasonably difficult to carry out the employment effectively.

(C) Permissive Withdrawal. If rule 3–700(B) is not applicable, a member may not request permission to withdraw in matters pending before a tribunal, and may not withdraw in other matters, unless such request or such withdrawal is because:

(1) The client

(a) insists upon presenting a claim or defense that is not warranted under existing law and cannot be supported by good faith argument for an extension, modification, or reversal of existing law, or

(b) seeks to pursue an illegal course of conduct, or

(c) insists that the member pursue a course of conduct that is illegal or that is prohibited under these rules or the State Bar Act, or

(d) by other conduct renders it unreasonably difficult for the member to carry out the employment effectively, or

(e) insists, in a matter not pending before a tribunal, that the member engage in conduct that is contrary to the judgment and advice of the member but not prohibited under these rules or the State Bar Act, or

(f) breaches an agreement or obligation to the member as to expenses or fees.

(2) The continued employment is likely to result in a violation of these rules or of the State Bar Act; or

(3) The inability to work with co-counsel indicates that the best interests of the client likely will be served by withdrawal; or

(4) The member's mental or physical condition renders it difficult for the member to carry out the employment effectively; or

(5) The client knowingly and freely assents to termination of the employment; or

(6) The member believes in good faith, in a proceeding pending before a tribunal, that the tribunal will find the existence of other good cause for withdrawal.

(D) Papers, Property, and Fees. A member whose employment has terminated shall:

Rule 3-700   CALIFORNIA RULES

(1) Subject to any protective order or non-disclosure agreement, promptly release to the client, at the request of the client, all the client papers and property. "Client papers and property" includes correspondence, pleadings, deposition transcripts, exhibits, physical evidence, expert's reports, and other items reasonably necessary to the client's representation, whether the client has paid for them or not; and

(2) Promptly refund any part of a fee paid in advance that has not been earned. This provision is not applicable to a true retainer fee which is paid solely for the purpose of ensuring the availability of the member for the matter.

Comment

Subparagraph (A)(2) provides that "a member shall not withdraw from employment until the member has taken reasonable steps to avoid reasonably foreseeable prejudice to the rights of the clients." What such steps would include, of course, will vary according to the circumstances. Absent special circumstances, "reasonable steps" do not include providing additional services to the client once the successor counsel has been employed and rule 3-700(D) has been satisfied.

Paragraph (D) makes clear the member's duties in the recurring situation in which new counsel seeks to obtain client files from a member discharged by the client. It codifies existing case law. (See *Academy of California Optometrists v. Superior Court* (1975) 51 Cal.App.3d 999 [124 Cal.Rptr. 668]; *Weiss v. Marcus* (1975) 51 Cal.App.3d 590 [124 Cal.Rptr. 297].) Paragraph (D) also requires that the member "promptly" return unearned fees paid in advance. If a client disputes the amount to be returned, the member shall comply with rule 4-100(A)(2).

Paragraph (D) is not intended to prohibit a member from making, at the member's own expense, and retaining copies of papers released to the client, nor to prohibit a claim for the recovery of the member's expense in any subsequent legal proceeding.

CHAPTER 4. FINANCIAL RELATIONSHIP WITH CLIENTS

RULE 4-100. Preserving Identity of Funds and Property of a Client

(A) All funds received or held for the benefit of clients by a member or law firm, including advances for costs and expenses, shall be deposited in one or more identifiable bank accounts labelled "Trust Account," "Client's Funds Account" or words of similar import, maintained in the State of California, or, with written consent of the client, in any other jurisdiction where there is a substantial relationship betwen the client or the client's business and the other jurisdiction. No funds belonging to the member or the law firm shall be deposited therein or otherwise commingled therewith except as follows:

(1) Funds reasonably sufficient to pay bank charges.

(2) In the case of funds belonging in part to a client and in part presently or potentially to the member or the law firm, the portion belonging to the member or law firm must be withdrawn at the earliest reasonable time after the member's interest in that portion becomes fixed. However, when the right of the member or law firm to receive a portion of trust funds is disputed by the client, the disputed portion shall not be withdrawn until the dispute is finally resolved.

(B) A member shall:

(1) Promptly notify a client of the receipt of the client's funds, securities, or other properties.

(2) Identify and label securities and properties of a client promptly upon receipt and place them in a safe deposit box or other place of safekeeping as soon as practicable.

(3) Maintain complete records of all funds, securities, and other properties of a client coming into the possession of the member or law firm and render appropriate accounts to the client regarding them; preserve such records for a period of no less than five years after final appropriate distribution of such funds or properties; and comply with any order for an audit of such records issued pursuant to the Rules of Procedure of the State Bar.

(4) Promptly pay or deliver, as requested by the client, any funds, securities, or other properties in the possession of the member which the client is entitled to receive.

(C) The Board of Governors of the State Bar shall have the authority to formulate and adopt standards as to what "records" shall be maintained by members and law firms in accordance with subparagraph (B)(3). The standards formulated and adopted by the Board, as from time to time amended, shall be effective and binding on all members.

RULE 4–200. Fees for Legal Services

(A) A member shall not enter into an agreement for, charge, or collect an illegal or unconscionable fee.

(B) Unconscionability of a fee agreement shall be determined on the basis of all the facts and circumstances existing at the time the agreement is entered into except where the parties contemplate that the fee will be affected by later events. Among the factors to be considered, where appropriate, in determining the conscionability of a fee are the following:

(1) The amount of the fee in proportion to the value of the services performed.

(2) The relative sophistication of the member and the client.

(3) The novelty and difficulty of the questions involved and the skill requisite to perform the legal service properly.

Rule 4-200

(4) The likelihood, if apparent to the client, that the acceptance of the particular employment will preclude other employment by the member.

(5) The amount involved and the results obtained.

(6) The time limitations imposed by the client or by the circumstances.

(7) The nature and length of the professional relationship with the client.

(8) The experience, reputation, and ability of the member or members performing the services.

(9) Whether the fee is fixed or contingent.

(10) The time and labor required.

(11) The informed consent of the client to the fee agreement.

RULE 4-210. Payment of Personal or Business Expenses Incurred by or for a Client

(A) A member shall not directly or indirectly pay or agree to pay, guarantee, represent, or sanction a representation that the member or member's law firm will pay the personal or business expenses of a prospective or existing client, except that this rule shall not prohibit a member:

(1) With the consent of the client, from paying or agreeing to pay such expenses to third persons from funds collected or to be collected for the client as a result of the representation; or

(2) After employment, from lending money to the client upon the client's promise in writing to repay such loan; or

(3) From advancing the costs of prosecuting or defending a claim or action or otherwise protecting or promoting the client's interests, the repayment of which may be contingent on the outcome of the matter. Such costs within the meaning of this subparagraph (3) shall be limited to all reasonable expenses of litigation or reasonable expenses in preparation for litigation or in providing any legal services to the client.

(B) Nothing in rule 4-210 shall be deemed to limit rules 3-300, 3-310, and 4-300.

RULE 4-300. Purchasing Property at a Foreclosure or a Sale Subject to Judicial Review

A member shall not directly or indirectly purchase property at a probate, foreclosure, receiver's, trustee's, or judicial sale in an action or proceeding in which such member or any member affiliated by reason of personal, business, or professional relationship with that member or with that member's law firm is an attorney for a party or is acting as executor, receiver, trustee, administrator, guardian, or conservator.

RULE 4–400. Gifts From Client

A member shall not induce a client to make a substantial gift, including a testamentary gift, to the member or to the member's parent, child, sibling, or spouse, except where the client is related to the member.

Comment

A member may accept a gift from a member's client, subject to general standards of fairness and absence of undue influence. The member who participates in the preparation of an instrument memorializing a gift which is otherwise permissible ought not to be subject to professional discipline. On the other hand, where impermissible influence occurred, discipline is appropriate. (See *Magee v. State Bar* (1962) 58 Cal.2d 423 [24 Cal.Rptr. 839].)

CHAPTER 5. ADVOCACY AND REPRESENTATION

RULE 5–100. Threatening Criminal, Administrative, or Disciplinary Charges

(A) A member shall not threaten to present criminal, administrative, or disciplinary charges to obtain an advantage in a civil dispute.

(B) As used in paragraph (A) of this rule, the term "administrative charges" means the filing or lodging of a complaint with a federal, state, or local governmental entity which may order or recommend the loss or suspension of a license, or may impose or recommend the imposition of a fine, pecuniary sanction, or other sanction of a quasi-criminal nature but does not include filing charges with an administrative entity required by law as a condition precedent to maintaining a civil action.

(C) As used in paragraph (A) of this rule, the term "civil dispute" means a controversy or potential controversy over the rights and duties of two or more parties under civil law, whether or not an action has been commenced, and includes an administrative proceeding of a quasi-civil nature pending before a federal, state, or local governmental entity.

Comment

Rule 5–100 is not intended to apply to a member's threatening to initiate contempt proceedings against a party for a failure to comply with a court order.

Paragraph (B) is intended to exempt the threat of filing an administrative charge which is a prerequisite to filing a civil complaint on the same transaction or occurrence.

For purposes of paragraph (C), the definition of "civil dispute" makes clear that the rule is applicable prior to the formal filing of a civil action.

RULE 5–110. Performing the Duty of Member in Government Service

A member in government service shall not institute or cause to be instituted criminal charges when the member knows or should know that

Rule 5–110

the charges were not supported by probable cause. If, after the institution of criminal charges, the member in government service having responsibility for prosecuting the charges becomes aware that those charges are not supported by probable cause, the member shall promptly so advise the court in which the criminal matter is pending.

RULE 5–200. Trial Conduct

In presenting a matter to a tribunal, a member:

(A) Shall employ, for the purpose of maintaining the causes confided to the member such means only as are consistent with truth;

(B) Shall not seek to mislead the judge, judicial officer, or jury by an artifice or false statement of fact or law;

(C) Shall not intentionally misquote to a tribunal the language of a book, statute, or decision;

(D) Shall not, knowing its invalidity, cite as authority a decision that has been overruled or a statute that has been repealed or declared unconstitutional; and

(E) Shall not assert personal knowledge of the facts at issue, except when testifying as a witness.

RULE 5–210. Member as Witness

A member shall not act as an advocate before a jury which will hear testimony from the member unless:

(A) The testimony relates to an uncontested matter; or

(B) The testimony relates to the nature and value of legal services rendered in the case; or

(C) The member has the informed, written consent of the client. If the member represents the People or a governmental entity, the consent shall be obtained from the head of the office or a designee of the head of the office by which the member is employed and shall be consistent with principles of recusal.

Comment

Rule 5–210 is intended to apply to situations in which the member knows or should know that he or she ought to be called as a witness in litigation in which there is a jury. This rule is not intended to encompass situations in which the member is representing the client in an adversarial proceeding and is testifying before a judge. In non-adversarial proceedings, as where the lawyer testifies on behalf of the client in a hearing before a legislative body, rule 5–210 is not applicable.

Rule 5–210 is not intended to apply to circumstances in which a partner or associate in an advocate's firm will be a witness.

RULE 5–220. Suppression of Evidence

A member shall not suppress any evidence that the member or the member's client has a legal obligation to reveal or to produce.

RULE 5–300. Contact With Officials

(A) A member shall not directly or indirectly give or lend anything of value to a judge, official, or employee of a tribunal unless the personal or family relationship between the member and the judge, official, or employee is such that gifts are customarily given and exchanged. Nothing contained in this rule shall prohibit a member from contributing to the campaign fund of a judge running for election or confirmation pursuant to applicable law pertaining to such contributions.

(B) A member shall not directly or indirectly communicate with or argue to a judge or judicial officer upon the merits of a contested matter pending before such judge or judicial officer, except:

(1) In open court; or

(2) With the consent of all other counsel in such matter; or

(3) In the presence of all other counsel in such matter; or

(4) In writing with a copy thereof furnished to such other counsel; or

(5) In ex parte matters.

(C) As used in this rule, the phrase "judge or judicial officer" shall include law clerks, research attorneys, or other court personnel who participate in the decision-making process.

RULE 5–310. Prohibited Contact With Witnesses

A member shall not:

(A) Advise or directly or indirectly cause a person to secrete himself or herself or to leave the jurisdiction of a tribunal for the purpose of making that person unavailable as a witness therein.

(B) Directly or indirectly pay, offer to pay, or acquiesce in the payment of compensation to a witness contingent upon the content of the witness's testimony or the outcome of the case. Except where prohibited by law, a member may advance, guarantee, or acquiesce in the payment of:

(1) Expenses reasonably incurred by a witness in attending or testifying.

(2) Reasonable compensation to a witness for loss of time in attending or testifying.

(3) A reasonable fee for the professional services of an expert witness.

RULE 5–320. Contact With Jurors

(A) A member connected with a case shall not communicate directly or indirectly with anyone the member knows to be a member of the venire from which the jury will be selected for trial of that case.

(B) During trial a member connected with the case shall not communicate directly or indirectly with any member of the jury.

(C) During trial a member who is not connected with the case shall not communicate directly or indirectly concerning the case with anyone a member knows is a juror in the case.

(D) After discharge of the jury from further consideration of a case a member shall not ask questions of or make comments to a member of that jury that are intended to harass or embarrass the juror or to influence the juror's actions in future jury service.

(E) A member shall not conduct directly or indirectly an out of court investigation of either a venireman or a juror of a type likely to influence the state of mind of such venireman or juror in present or future jury service.

(F) All restrictions imposed by rule 5–320 upon a member also apply to communications with or investigations of members of the family of a venireman or a juror.

(G) A member shall reveal promptly to the court improper conduct by a venireman or a juror, or by another toward a venireman or a juror or a member of his or her family, of which the member has knowledge.

(H) Rule 5–320 does not prohibit a member from communicating with veniremen or jurors as a part of the official proceedings.

SELECTED PROVISIONS FROM THE CALIFORNIA BUSINESS AND PROFESSIONS CODE

Table of Sections

ARTICLE 4. ADMISSION TO THE PRACTICE OF LAW

Sec.		Page
6067.	Oath	269
6068.	Duties of Attorney	269

ARTICLE 6. DISCIPLINARY AUTHORITY OF THE COURTS

6100.	Disbarment or Suspension	271
6101.	Conviction of Crime; Notice of Pendency of Action; Record of Conviction; Proceedings	271
6102.	Immediate Suspension and Subsequent Disbarment Upon Conviction of Crime; Crimes Involving Moral Turpitude or Felonies; Procedure	272
6103.	Disobedience of Court Order; Violation of Oath or Attorney's Duties	273
6103.5	Written Offers of Settlement; Required Communication to Client; Discovery	273
6104.	Unauthorized Appearance	274
6105.	Permitting Misuse of Name	275
6106.	Moral Turpitude, Dishonesty or Corruption Irrespective of Criminal Conviction	275
6106.1	Advocacy of Overthrow of Government	275
6106.5	Insurance Claims; Fraud	275
6106.7	Professional Sport Service Contracts; Violation of Requirements	275
6106.8	Sexual Involvement Between Lawyers and Clients; Rule of Professional Conduct	275

ARTICLE 7. UNLAWFUL PRACTICE OF LAW

6128.	Deceit, Collusion, Delay of Suit and Improper Receipt of Money as Misdemeanor	275
6129.	Buying Claim as Misdemeanor	275
6130.	Disbarred or Suspended Attorney Suing as Assignee	276
6131.	Aiding Defense Where Partner or Self Has Acted as Public Prosecutor; Misdemeanor and Disbarment	276

SELECTED PROVISIONS

ARTICLE 8.5 CONTINGENCY FEE AGREEMENTS

Sec.		Page
6146.	Limitations; Periodic Payments	276
6147.	Contingency Fee Contract: Contents; Effect of Noncompliance; Application to Contracts for Recovery of Workers' Compensation Benefits	277
6148.	Written Fee Contract: Contents; Effect of Noncompliance	278
6149.	Written Fee Contract: Confidential Communication	279

ARTICLE 9. UNLAWFUL SOLICITATION

6151.	Definitions	279
6152.	Prohibition of Solicitation	279
6153.	Violation as Misdemeanor; Forfeiture of Public Office or Employment	280
6154.	Invalidity of Contract for Services	280

ARTICLE 13. ARBITRATION OF ATTORNEY'S FEES

6200.	Establishment of System and Procedure; Applicability of Article; Voluntary or Mandatory Nature; Rules; Immunity of Arbitrator; Powers of Arbitrator	280

ARTICLE 14. FUNDS FOR THE PROVISION OF LEGAL SERVICES TO INDIGENT PERSONS

6210.	Legislative Findings; Purpose	282
6211.	Establishment by Attorney of Demand Trust Account; Interest Earned to Be Paid to State Bar; Other Accounts Not Prohibited; Rules of Professional Conduct, Authority of Supreme Court or State Bar Not Affected	282
6212.	Establishment by Attorney of Demand Trust Account; Amount of Interest; Remittance to State Bar; Statements and Reports	283
6213.	Definitions	283
6214.	Qualified Legal Service Projects	285
6214.5	Qualified Legal Services Projects; Eligibility for Distributions of Funds	286
6215.	Qualified Support Centers	286
6216.	Distribution of Funds	286
6217.	Maintenance of Quality Services, Professional Standards, Attorney-Client Privilege; Funds to Be Expended in Accordance With Article; Interference With Attorney Prohibited	288
6218.	Eligibility for Services; Establishment of Guidelines; Funds to Be Expended in Accordance With Article	288
6219.	Provision of Work Opportunities and Scholarships for Disadvantaged Law Students	288
6220.	Private Attorneys Providing Legal Services Without Charge; Support Center Services	289
6221.	Services for Indigent Members of Disadvantaged and Underserved Groups	289
6222.	Financial Statements; Submission to State Bar; State Bar Report	
6223.	Expenditure of Funds; Prohibitions	289

Sec.		Page
6224.	State Bar; Powers; Determination of Qualifications to Receive Funds; Denial of Funds; Termination; Procedures	289
6225.	Implementation of Article; Adoption of Rules and Regulations; Procedures	290
6226.	Implementation of Article; Resolution	290
6227.	Credit of State Not Pledged	290
6228.	Severability	291

ARTICLE 4. ADMISSION TO THE PRACTICE OF LAW

§ 6067. Oath

Every person on his admission shall take an oath to support the Constitution of the United States and the Constitution of the State of California, and faithfully to discharge the duties of any attorney at law to the best of his knowledge and ability. A certificate of the oath shall be indorsed upon his license.

§ 6068. Duties of Attorney

It is the duty of an attorney to do all of the following:

(a) To support the Constitution and laws of the United States and of this state.

(b) To maintain the respect due to the courts of justice and judicial officers.

(c) To counsel or maintain such actions, proceedings, or defenses only as appear to him or her legal or just, except the defense of a person charged with a public offense.

(d) To employ, for the purpose of maintaining the causes confided to him or her, such means only as are consistent with truth, and never to seek to mislead the judge or any judicial officer by an artifice or false statement of fact or law.

(e) To maintain inviolate the confidence, and at every peril to himself or herself to preserve the secrets, of his or her client.

(f) To abstain from all offensive personality, and to advance no fact prejudicial to the honor or reputation of a party or witness, unless required by the justice of the cause with which he or she is charged.

(g) Not to encourage either the commencement or the continuance of an action or proceeding from any corrupt motive of passion or interest.

(h) Never to reject, for any consideration personal to himself or herself, the cause of the defenseless or the oppressed.

(i) To cooperate and participate in any disciplinary investigation or other regulatory or disciplinary proceeding pending against the attorney. However, this subdivision shall not be construed to deprive an attorney of any privilege guaranteed by the Fifth Amendment to the Constitution of the United States or any other constitutional or statutory privileges.

(j) To comply with the requirements of Section 6002.1.

(k) To comply with all conditions attached to any disciplinary probation, including a probation imposed with the concurrence of the attorney.

(*l*) To keep all agreements made in lieu of disciplinary prosecution with the agency charged with attorney discipline.

(m) To respond promptly to reasonable status inquiries of clients and to keep clients reasonably informed of significant developments in matters with regard to which the attorney has agreed to provide legal services.

(n) To provide copies to the client of certain documents under time limits and as is prescribed in a rule of professional conduct which the board shall adopt.

(o) To report to the agency charged with attorney discipline, in writing, within 30 days of the time the attorney has knowledge of any of the following:

(1) The filing of three or more lawsuits in a 12-month period against the attorney for malpractice or other wrongful conduct committed in a professional capacity.

(2) The entry of judgment against the attorney in any civil action for fraud, misrepresentation, breach of fiduciary duty, or gross negligence committed in a professional capacity.

(3) The imposition of any judicial sanctions against the attorney, except for sanctions for failure to make discovery or monetary sanctions of less than one thousand dollars ($1,000).

(4) The bringing of an indictment or information charging a felony against the attorney.

(5) The conviction of the attorney, including any verdict of guilty, or plea of guilty or no contest, of any felony, or any misdemeanor committed in the course of the practice of law, or in any manner such that a client of the attorney was the victim, or a necessary element of which, as determined by the statutory or common law definition of the misdemeanor, involves improper conduct of an attorney, including dishonesty or other moral turpitude, or an attempt or a conspiracy or solicitation of another to commit a felony or any such misdemeanor.

(6) The imposition of discipline against the attorney by any professional or occupational disciplinary agency or licensing board, whether in California or elsewhere.

(7) Reversal of judgment in a proceeding based in whole or in part upon misconduct, grossly incompetent representation, or wilful misrepresentation by an attorney.

(8) As used in this subdivision, "against the attorney" includes claims and proceedings against any firm of attorneys for the practice of law in which the attorney was a partner at the time of the conduct complained of and any law corporation in which the attorney was a shareholder at the time of the conduct complained of unless the matter has to the attorney's knowledge already been reported by the law firm or corporation.

(9) The State Bar may develop a prescribed form for the making of reports required by this section, usage of which it may require by rule or regulation.

(10) This subdivision is only intended to provide that the failure to report as required herein may serve as a basis of discipline.

ARTICLE 6. DISCIPLINARY AUTHORITY OF THE COURTS

§ 6100. Disbarment or Suspension

For any of the causes provided in this article, arising after an attorney's admission to practice, he or she may be disbarred or suspended by the Supreme Court. Nothing in this article limits the inherent power of the Supreme Court to discipline, including to summarily disbar, any attorney.

§ 6101. Conviction of Crime; Notice of Pendency of Action; Record of Conviction; Proceedings

(a) Conviction of a felony or misdemeanor, involving moral turpitude, constitutes a cause for disbarment or suspension.

In any proceeding, whether under this article or otherwise, to disbar or suspend an attorney on account of that conviction, the record of conviction shall be conclusive evidence of guilt of the crime of which he or she has been convicted.

(b) The district attorney, city attorney, or other prosecuting agency shall notify the Office of the State Bar of the State Bar of California of the pendency of an action against an attorney charging a felony or misdemeanor immediately upon obtaining information that the defendant is an attorney. The notice shall identify the attorney and describe the crimes charged and the alleged facts. The prosecuting agency shall also notify the clerk of the court in which the action is pending that the defendant is an attorney, and the clerk shall record prominently in the file that the defendant is an attorney.

(c) The clerk of the court in which an attorney is convicted of a crime shall, within 48 hours after the conviction, transmit a certified copy of the record of conviction to the Office of the State Bar. Within five days of receipt, the Office of the State Bar shall transmit the record of any conviction which involves or may involve moral turpitude to the Supreme Court with such other records and information as may be appropriate to establish the Supreme Court's jurisdiction. The State Bar of California may procure and transmit the record of conviction to the Supreme Court when the clerk has not done so or when the conviction was had in a court other than a court of this state.

(d) The proceedings to disbar or suspend an attorney on account of such a conviction shall be undertaken by the Supreme Court pursuant to the procedure provided in this section and Section 6102, upon the receipt of the certified copy of the record of conviction.

(e) A plea or verdict of guilty or a conviction after a plea of nolo contendere is deemed to be a conviction within the meaning of those sections.

§ 6102. Immediate Suspension and Subsequent Disbarment Upon Conviction of Crime; Crimes Involving Moral Turpitude or Felonies; Procedure

(a) Upon the receipt of the certified copy of the record of conviction, if it appears therefrom that the crime of which the attorney was convicted involved or that there is probable cause to believe that it involved moral turpitude or is a felony under the laws of California or of the United States, the Supreme Court shall suspend the attorney until the time for appeal has elapsed, if no appeal has been taken, or until the judgment of conviction has been affirmed on appeal, or has otherwise become final, and until the further order of the court. Upon its own motion or upon good cause shown the court may decline to impose, or may set aside, the suspension when it appears to be in the interest of justice to do so, with due regard being given to maintaining the integrity of and confidence in the profession.

(b) For the purposes of this section, a crime is a felony under the law of California if it is declared to be so specifically or by subdivision (a) of Section 17 of the Penal Code, unless it is charged as a misdemeanor pursuant to paragraph (4) or (5) of subdivision (b) of Section 17 of the Penal Code, irrespective of whether in a particular case the crime may be considered a misdemeanor as a result of postconviction proceedings, including proceedings resulting in punishment or probation set forth in paragraph (1) or (3) of subdivision (b) of Section 17 of the Penal Code.

(c) After the judgment of conviction of an offense specified in subdivision (a) has become final or, irrespective of any subsequent order under Section 1203.4 of the Penal Code, an order granting probation has been made suspending the imposition of sentence, the Supreme Court shall summarily disbar the attorney if the conviction is a felony under the laws of California or of the United States which meets both of the following criteria:

(1) An element of the offense is the specific intent to deceive, defraud, steal, or make or suborn a false statement.

(2) The offense was committed in the course of the practice of law or in any manner such that a client of the attorney was a victim.

(d) Except as provided in subdivision (c), if after adequate notice and opportunity to be heard (which hearing shall not be had until the judgment of conviction has become final or, irrespective of any subsequent order under Section 1203.4 of the Penal Code, an order granting probation has been made suspending the imposition of sentence), the court finds that the crime of which the attorney was convicted, or the circumstances of its commission, involved moral turpitude, it shall enter an order disbarring the attorney or suspending him or her from practice for a limited time, according to the gravity of the crime and the circumstances of the case; otherwise it shall dismiss the proceedings. In determining the extent of the discipline to be imposed in a proceeding pursuant to this article any prior discipline imposed upon the attorney may be considered.

(e) The court may refer the proceedings or any part thereof or issue therein, including the nature or extent of discipline, to the State Bar for hearing, report, and recommendation.

(f) The record of the proceedings resulting in the conviction, including a transcript of the testimony therein, may be received in evidence.

(g) The Supreme Court shall prescribe rules for the practice and procedure in proceedings had pursuant to this section and Section 6101.

(h) The other provisions of this article providing a procedure for the disbarment or suspension of an attorney do not apply to proceedings pursuant to this section and Section 6101, unless expressly made applicable.

§ 6103. Disobedience of Court Order; Violation of Oath or Attorney's Duties

A wilful disobedience or violation of an order of the court requiring him to do or forbear an act connected with or in the course of his profession, which he ought in good faith to do or forbear, and any violation of the oath taken by him, or of his duties as such attorney, constitute causes for disbarment or suspension.

§ 6103.5 Written Offers of Settlement; Required Communication to Client; Discovery

(a) A member of the State Bar shall promptly communicate to the member's client all amounts, terms, and conditions of any written offer of settlement made by or on behalf of an opposing party. As used in this section, "client" includes any person employing the member of the State Bar who possesses the authority to accept an offer of settlement, or in a class action, who is a representative of the class.

(b) Any written offer of settlement or any required communication of a settlement offer, as described in subdivision (a), shall be discoverable by either party in any action in which the existence or communication of the offer of settlement is an issue before the trier of fact.

§ 6104. Unauthorized Appearance

Corruptly or wilfully and without authority appearing as attorney for a party to an action or proceeding constitutes a cause for disbarment or suspension.

§ 6105. Permitting Misuse of Name

Lending his name to be used as attorney by another person who is not an attorney constitutes a cause for disbarment or suspension.

§ 6106. Moral Turpitude, Dishonesty or Corruption Irrespective of Criminal Conviction

The commission of any act involving moral turpitude, dishonesty or corruption, whether the act is committed in the course of his relations as an attorney or otherwise, and whether the act is a felony or misdemeanor or not, constitutes a cause for disbarment or suspension.

If the act constitutes a felony or misdemeanor, conviction thereof in a criminal proceeding is not a condition precedent to disbarment or suspension from practice therefor.

§ 6106.1 Advocacy of Overthrow of Government

Advocating the overthrow of the Government of the United States or of this State by force, violence, or other unconstitutional means, constitutes a cause for disbarment or suspension.

§ 6106.5 Insurance Claims; Fraud

It shall constitute cause for disbarment or suspension for an attorney to engage in any conduct prohibited under Section 556 of the Insurance Code.

§ 6106.7 Professional Sport Service Contracts; Violation of Requirements

(a) It shall constitute cause for the imposition of discipline of an attorney within the meaning of this chapter for an attorney to negotiate a professional sport service contract, as defined by subdivision (d) of Section 1500 of the Labor Code, and in willful violation of subdivision (b) of Section 1531 of the Labor Code, to collect a fee that in any calendar year exceeds 10 percent of the compensation the athlete is receiving in that calendar year under the contract.

(b) Willful violation of Section 1530.5, subdivision (b) or (c) of Section 1531, or Section 1535.5, 1535.7, or 1539 of the Labor Code constitutes cause for the imposition of discipline of an attorney within the meaning of this chapter.

§ 6106.8 Sexual Involvement Between Lawyers and Clients; Rule of Professional Conduct

(a) The Legislature hereby finds and declares that there is no rule that governs propriety of sexual relationships between lawyers and clients. The Legislature further finds and declares that it is difficult to separate sound judgment from emotion or bias which may result from sexual involvement between a lawyer and his or her client during the period that an attorney-client relationship exists, and that emotional detachment is essential to the lawyer's ability to render competent legal services. Therefore, in order to ensure that a lawyer acts in the best interest of his or her client, a rule of professional conduct governing sexual relations between attorneys and their clients shall be adopted.

(b) With the approval of the Supreme Court, the State Bar shall adopt a rule of professional conduct governing sexual relations between attorneys and their clients in cases involving, but not limited to, probate matters and domestic relations, including dissolution proceedings, child custody cases, and settlement proceedings.

(c) The State Bar shall submit the proposed rule to the Supreme Court for approval no later than January 1, 1991.

(d) Intentional violation of this rule shall constitute a cause for suspension or disbarment.

ARTICLE 7. UNLAWFUL PRACTICE OF LAW

§ 6128. Deceit, Collusion, Delay of Suit and Improper Receipt of Money as Misdemeanor

Every attorney is guilty of a misdemeanor who either:

(a) Is guilty of any deceit or collusion, or consents to any deceit or collusion, with intent to deceive the court or any party.

(b) Willfully delays his client's suit with a view to his own gain.

(c) Willfully receives any money or allowance for or on account of any money which he has not laid out or become answerable for.

Any violation of the provisions of this section is punishable by imprisonment in the county jail not exceeding six months, or by a fine not exceeding two thousand five hundred dollars ($2,500), or by both.

§ 6129. Buying Claim as Misdemeanor

Every attorney who, either directly or indirectly, buys or is interested in buying any evidence of debt or thing in action, with intent to bring suit thereon, is guilty of a misdemeanor.

Any violation of the provisions of this section is punishable by imprisonment in the county jail not exceeding six months, or by a fine not exceeding two thousand five hundred dollars ($2,500), or by both.

§ 6130. Disbarred or Suspended Attorney Suing as Assignee

No person, who has been an attorney, shall while a judgment of disbarment or suspension is in force appear on his own behalf as plaintiff in the prosecution of any action where the subject of the action has been assigned to him subsequent to the entry of the judgment of disbarment or suspension and solely for purpose of collection.

§ 6131. Aiding Defense Where Partner or Self Has Acted as Public Prosecutor; Misdemeanor and Disbarment

Every attorney is guilty of a misdemeanor and, in addition to the punishment prescribed therefor, shall be disbarred:

(a) Who directly or indirectly advises in relation to, or aids, or promotes the defense of any action or proceeding in any court the prosecution of which is carried on, aided or promoted by any person as district attorney or other public prosecutor with whom such person is directly or indirectly connected as a partner.

(b) Who, having himself prosecuted or in any manner aided or promoted any action or proceeding in any court as district attorney or other public prosecutor, afterwards, directly or indirectly, advises in relation to or takes any part in the defense thereof, as attorney or otherwise, or who takes or receives any valuable consideration from or on behalf of any defendant in any such action upon any understanding or agreement whatever having relation to the defense thereof.

This section does not prohibit an attorney from defending himself in person, as attorney or counsel, when prosecuted, either civilly or criminally.

ARTICLE 8.5 CONTINGENCY FEE AGREEMENTS

§ 6146. Limitations; Periodic Payments

(a) An attorney shall not contract for or collect a contingency fee for representing any person seeking damages in connection with an action for injury or damage against a health care provider based upon such person's alleged professional negligence in excess of the following limits:

(1) Forty percent of the first fifty thousand dollars ($50,000) recovered.

(2) Thirty-three and one-third percent of the next fifty thousand dollars ($50,000) recovered.

(3) Twenty-five percent of the next five hundred thousand dollars ($500,000) recovered.

(4) Fifteen percent of any amount on which the recovery exceeds six hundred thousand dollars ($600,000).

The limitations shall apply regardless of whether the recovery is by settlement, arbitration, or judgment, or whether the person for whom the recovery is made is a responsible adult, an infant, or a person of unsound mind.

(b) If periodic payments are awarded to the plaintiff pursuant to Section 667.7 of the Code of Civil Procedure, the court shall place a total value on these payments based upon the projected life expectancy of the plaintiff and include this amount in computing the total award from which attorney's fees are calculated under this section.

(c) For purposes of this section:

(1) "Recovered" means the net sum recovered after deducting any disbursements or costs incurred in connection with prosecution or settlement of the claim. Costs of medical care incurred by the plaintiff and the attorney's office-overhead costs or charges are not deductible disbursements or costs for such purpose.

(2) "Health care provider" means any person licensed or certified pursuant to Division 2 (commencing with Section 500), or licensed pursuant to the Osteopathic Initiative Act, or the Chiropractic Initiative Act, or licensed pursuant to Chapter 2.5 (commencing with Section 1440) of Division 2 of the Health and Safety Code; and any clinic, health dispensary, or health facility, licensed pursuant to Division 2 (commencing with Section 1200) of the Health and Safety Code. "Health care provider" includes the legal representatives of a health care provider.

(3) "Professional negligence" is a negligent act or omission to act by a health care provider in the rendering of professional services, which act or omission is the proximate cause of a personal injury or wrongful death, provided that the services are within the scope of services for which the provider is licensed and which are not within any restriction imposed by the licensing agency or licensed hospital.

§ 6147. Contingency Fee Contract: Contents; Effect of Noncompliance; Application to Contracts for Recovery of Workers' Compensation Benefits

(a) An attorney who contracts to represent a plaintiff on a contingency fee basis shall, at the time the contract is entered into, provide a duplicate copy of the contract, signed by both the attorney and the plaintiff, or his guardian or representative, to the plaintiff, or to the plaintiff's guardian or representative. The contract shall be in writing and shall include, but is not limited to, all of the following:

(1) A statement of the contingency fee rate which the client and attorney have agreed upon.

(2) A statement as to how disbursements and costs incurred in connection with the prosecution or settlement of the claim will affect the contingency fee and the client's recovery.

(3) A statement as to what extent, if any, the plaintiff could be required to pay any compensation to the attorney for related matters that arise out of their relationship not covered by their contingency fee

§ 6147

contract. This may include any amounts collected for the plaintiff by the attorney.

(4) Unless the claim is subject to the provisions of Section 6146, a statement that the fee is not set by law but is negotiable between attorney and client.

(5) If the claim is subject to the provisions of Section 6146, a statement that the rates set forth in that section are the maximum limits for the contingency fee agreement, and that the attorney and client may negotiate a lower rate.

(b) Failure to comply with any provision of this section renders the agreement voidable at the option of the plaintiff, and the attorney shall thereupon be entitled to collect a reasonable fee.

(c) This section shall not apply to contingency fee contracts for the recovery of workers' compensation benefits.

§ 6148. Written Fee Contract: Contents; Effect of Noncompliance

(a) In any case not coming within Section 6147 in which it is reasonably foreseeable that total expense to a client, including attorney fees will exceed one thousand dollars ($1,000), the contract for services in the case shall be in writing and shall contain all of the following:

(1) The hourly rate and other standard rates, fees, and charges applicable to the case.

(2) The general nature of the legal services to be provided to the client.

(3) The respective responsibilities of the attorney and the client as to the performance of the contract.

(b) All bills rendered by an attorney to a client shall clearly state the basis thereof. Bills for the fee portion of the bill shall include the amount, rate, basis for calculation, or other method of determination of the attorney's fees and costs. Bills for the cost and expense portion of the bill shall clearly identify the costs and expenses incurred and the amount of the costs and expenses. Upon request by the client, the attorney shall provide a bill to the client no later than 10 days following the request unless the attorney has provided a bill to the client within 31 days prior to the request, in which case the attorney may provide a bill to the client no later than 31 days following the date the most recent bill was provided. The client is entitled to make similar requests at intervals of no less than 30 days following the initial request. In providing responses to client requests for billing information, the attorney may use billing data that is currently effective on the date of the request, or, if the fee or costs to that date cannot be accurately determined, they shall be described and estimated.

(c) Failure to comply with any provision of this section renders the agreement voidable at the option of the client, and the attorney shall, upon the agreement being voided, be entitled to collect a reasonable fee.

(d) This section shall not apply to any of the following:

(1) Services rendered in an emergency to avoid foreseeable prejudice to the rights or interests of the client or where a writing is otherwise impractical.

(2) An arrangement as to the fee implied by the fact that the attorney's services are of the same general kind as previously rendered to and paid for by the client.

(3) If the client knowingly states in writing, after full disclosure of this section, that a writing concerning fees is not required.

(4) If the client is a corporation.

(e) This section applies prospectively only to fee agreements following its operative date.

§ 6149. Written Fee Contract: Confidential Communication

A written fee contract shall be deemed to be a confidential communication within the meaning of subdivision (e) of Section 6068 and of Section 952 of the Evidence Code.

ARTICLE 9. UNLAWFUL SOLICITATION

§ 6151. Definitions

As used in this article:

(a) A runner or capper is any person, firm, association or corporation acting in any manner or in any capacity as an agent for an attorney at law, whether the attorney is admitted in California or any other jurisdiction, in the solicitation or procurement of business for such attorney at law as provided in this article.

(b) An agent is one who represents another in dealings with one or more third persons.

§ 6152. Prohibition of Solicitation

(a) It is unlawful for:

(1) Any person, in his individual capacity or in his capacity as a public or private employee, or for any firm, corporation, partnership or association to act as a runner or capper for any such attorneys or to solicit any business for any such attorneys in and about the state prisons, county jails, city jails, city prisons, or other places of detention of persons, city receiving hospitals, city and county receiving hospitals, county hospitals, justice courts, municipal courts, superior courts, or in any public institution or in any public place or upon any public street or highway or in and about private hospitals, sanitariums or in and about any private institution or upon private property of any character whatsoever.

(2) Any person to solicit another person to commit or join in the commission of a violation of subdivision (a).

(b) A general release from a liability claim obtained from any person during the period of the first physical confinement, whether as an inpatient or outpatient, in a clinic or health facility as defined in Sections 1203 and 1250 of the Health and Safety Code, as a result of the injury alleged to have given rise to such claim and primarily for treatment of such injury, is presumed fraudulent if such release is executed within 15 days after the commencement of such confinement or prior to release from such confinement, whichever occurs first.

(c) Nothing in this section shall be construed to prevent the recommendation of professional employment where such recommendation is not prohibited by the Rules of Professional Conduct of the State Bar of California.

(d) Nothing in this section shall be construed to mean that a public defender or assigned counsel may not make known his or her services as a criminal defense attorney to persons unable to afford legal counsel whether such persons are in custody or otherwise.

§ 6153. Violation as Misdemeanor; Forfeiture of Public Office or Employment

Any person, firm, partnership, association, or corporation violating subdivision (a) of Section 6152 is guilty of a misdemeanor, and is punishable by imprisonment in the county jail not exceeding six months, or by a fine not exceeding two thousand five hundred dollars ($2,500), or by both.

Any person employed either as an officer, director, trustee, clerk, servant or agent of this state or of any county or other municipal corporation or subdivision thereof, who is found guilty of violating any of the provisions of this article, shall forfeit the right to his office and employment in addition to any other penalty provided in this article.

§ 6154. Invalidity of Contract for Services

Any contract for professional services secured by any attorney at law in this State through the services of a runner or capper is void.

ARTICLE 13. ARBITRATION OF ATTORNEYS' FEES

§ 6200. Establishment of System and Procedure; Applicability of Article; Voluntary or Mandatory Nature; Rules; Immunity of Arbitrator; Powers of Arbitrator

(a) The board of governors shall, by rule, establish, maintain, and administer a system and procedure for the arbitration of disputes concerning fees charged for professional services by members of the State Bar or by members of the bar of other jurisdictions. The rules may include provision for a filing fee in such amount as the board may, from time to time determine.

(b) This article shall not apply to any of the following:

(1) Disputes where a member of the State Bar of California is also admitted to practice in another jurisdiction or where an attorney is only admitted to practice in another jurisdiction, and he or she maintains no office in the State of California, and no material portion of the services were rendered in the State of California.

(2) Claims for affirmative relief against the attorney for damages or otherwise based upon alleged malpractice or professional misconduct, except as provided in subdivision (a) of Section 6203.

(3) Disputes where the fee to be paid by the client or on his or her behalf has been determined pursuant to statute or court order.

(c) Arbitration under this article shall be voluntary for a client and shall be mandatory for an attorney if commenced by a client.

(d) The board of governors shall adopt rules to allow arbitration of attorney fee disputes under this article to proceed under arbitration systems sponsored by local bar associations in this state. Rules of procedure promulgated by local bar associations are subject to review by the board to insure that they provide for a fair, impartial, and speedy hearing and award. In adopting or reviewing these rules, the board may provide for one lay member of any arbitration panel of three arbitrators.

(e) In adopting or reviewing rules of arbitration under this section the board shall provide that the panel shall include one attorney member whose area of practice is either, at the option of the client, civil or criminal law, as follows:

(1) If the panel is composed of three members the panel shall include one attorney member whose area of practice is either, at the option of the client, civil or criminal law, and shall include one lay member.

(2) If the panel is composed of one member, that member shall be an attorney whose area of practice is either, at the option of the client, civil or criminal law.

(f) In any arbitration conducted pursuant to this article by the State Bar or by a local bar association, pursuant to rules of procedure approved by the board of governors, the arbitrator or arbitrators, as well as the arbitrating association and its directors, officers, and employees, shall have the same immunity which attaches in judicial proceedings.

(g) In the conduct of arbitrations under this article the arbitrator or arbitrators may do all of the following:

(1) Take and hear evidence pertaining to the proceeding.

(2) Administer oaths and affirmations.

(3) Compel, by subpoena, the attendance of witnesses and the production of books, papers, and documents pertaining to the proceeding.

ARTICLE 14. FUNDS FOR THE PROVISION OF LEGAL SERVICES TO INDIGENT PERSONS

§ 6210. Legislative Findings; Purpose

The Legislature finds that, due to insufficient funding, existing programs providing free legal services in civil matters to indigent persons, especially underserved client groups, such as the elderly, the disabled, juveniles, and non-English-speaking persons, do not adequately meet the needs of these persons. It is the purpose of this article to expand the availability and improve the quality of existing free legal services in civil matters to indigent persons, and to initiate new programs that will provide services to them. The Legislature finds that the use of funds collected by the State Bar pursuant to this article for these purposes is in the public interest, is a proper use of the funds, and is consistent with essential public and governmental purposes in the judicial branch of government. The Legislature further finds that the expansion, improvement, and initiation of legal services to indigent persons will aid in the advancement of the science of jurisprudence and the improvement of the administration of justice.

§ 6211. Establishment by Attorney of Demand Trust Account; Interest Earned to Be Paid to State Bar; Other Accounts Not Prohibited; Rules of Professional Conduct, Authority of Supreme Court or State Bar Not Affected

(a) An attorney or law firm, which in the course of the practice of law receives or disburses trust funds, shall establish and maintain an interest bearing demand trust account and shall deposit therein all client deposits that are nominal in amount or are on deposit for a short period of time. All such client funds may be deposited in a single unsegregated account. The interest earned on all such accounts shall be paid to the State Bar of California to be used for the purposes set forth in this article.

(b) Nothing in this article shall be construed to prohibit an attorney or law firm from establishing one or more interest bearing bank accounts or other trust investments as may be permitted by the Supreme Court, with the interest or dividends earned on the accounts payable to clients for trust funds not deposited in accordance with subdivision (a).

(c) With the approval of the Supreme Court, the State Bar may formulate and enforce rules of professional conduct pertaining to the use by attorneys or law firms of interest bearing trust accounts for unsegregated client funds pursuant to this article.

(d) Nothing in this article shall be construed as affecting or impairing the disciplinary powers and authority of the Supreme Court or of the State Bar or as modifying the statutes and rules governing the conduct of members of the State Bar.

§ 6212. Establishment by Attorney of Demand Trust Account; Amount of Interest; Remittance to State Bar; Statements and Reports

An attorney who, or a law firm which, establishes an interest bearing demand trust account pursuant to subdivision (a) of Section 6211 shall comply with all of the following provisions:

(a) The interest bearing trust account shall be established with a bank or such other financial institutions as are authorized by the Supreme Court.

(b) The rate of interest payable on any interest bearing demand trust account shall not be less than the rate paid by the depository institution to regular, nonattorney depositors. Higher rates offered by the institution to customers whose deposits exceed certain time or quantity qualifications, such as those offered in the form of certificates of deposit, may be obtained by an attorney or law firm so long as there is no impairment of the right to withdraw or transfer principal immediately (except as accounts generally may be subject to statutory notification requirements), even though interest may be sacrificed thereby.

(c) The depository institution shall be directed to do all of the following:

(1) To remit interest on the average daily balance in the account, less reasonable service charges, to the State Bar, at least quarterly.

(2) To transmit to the State Bar with each remittance a statement showing the name of the attorney or law firm for whom the remittance is sent, the rate of interest applied, and the amount of service charges deducted, if any.

(3) To transmit to the depositing attorney or law firm at the same time a report showing the amount paid to the State Bar for that period, the rate of interest applied, the amount of service charges deducted, if any, and the average daily account balance for each month of the period for which the report is made.

§ 6213. Definitions

As used in this article:

(a) "Qualified legal services project" means either of the following:

(1) A nonprofit project incorporated and operated exclusively in California which provides as its primary purpose and function legal services without charge to indigent persons and which has quality control procedures approved by the State Bar of California.

(2) A program operated exclusively in California by a nonprofit law school accredited by the State Bar of California which meets the requirements of subparagraphs (A) and (B).

(A) The program shall have operated for at least two years at a cost of at least twenty thousand dollars ($20,000) per year as an identifiable law school unit with a primary purpose and function of providing legal services without charge to indigent persons.

(B) The program shall have quality control procedures approved by the State Bar of California.

(b) "Qualified support center" means an incorporated nonprofit legal services center, which has as its primary purpose and function the provision of legal training, legal technical assistance, or advocacy support without charge and which actually provides through an office in California a significant level of legal training, legal technical assistance, or advocacy support without charge to qualified legal services projects on a statewide basis in California.

(c) "Recipient" means a qualified legal services project or support center receiving financial assistance under this article.

(d) "Indigent person" means a person whose income is (1) 125 percent or less of the current poverty threshold established by the United States Office of Management and Budget, or (2) who is eligible for Supplemental Security Income or free services under the Older Americans Act or Developmentally Disabled Assistance Act. With regard to a project which provides free services of attorneys in private practice without compensation, "indigent person" also means a person whose income is 75 percent or less of the maximum levels of income for lower income households as defined in Section 50079.5 of the Health and Safety Code. For the purpose of this subdivision, the income of a person who is disabled shall be determined after deducting the costs of medical and other disability-related special expenses.

(e) "Fee generating case" means any case or matter which, if undertaken on behalf of an indigent person by an attorney in private practice, reasonably may be expected to result in payment of a fee for legal services from an award to a client, from public funds, or from the opposing party. A case shall not be considered fee generating if adequate representation is unavailable and any of the following circumstances exist:

(1) The recipient has determined that free referral is not possible because of any of the following reasons:

(A) The case has been rejected by the local lawyer referral service, or if there is no such service, by two attorneys in private practice who have experience in the subject matter of the case.

(B) Neither the referral service nor any attorney will consider the case without payment of a consultation fee.

(C) The case is of the type that attorneys in private practice in the area ordinarily do not accept, or do not accept without prepayment of a fee.

(D) Emergency circumstances compel immediate action before referral can be made, but the client is advised that, if appropriate and consistent with professional responsibility, referral will be attempted at a later time.

(2) Recovery of damages is not the principal object of the case and a request for damages is merely ancillary to an action for equitable or other nonpecuniary relief, or inclusion of a counterclaim requesting damages is necessary for effective defense or because of applicable rules governing joinder of counterclaims.

(3) A court has appointed a recipient or an employee of a recipient pursuant to a statute or a court rule or practice of equal applicability to all attorneys in the jurisdiction.

(4) The case involves the rights of a claimant under a publicly supported benefit program for which entitlement to benefit is based on need.

(f) "Legal Services Corporation" means the Legal Services Corporation established under the Legal Services Corporation Act of 1974 (Public Law 93-355; 42 U.S.C. Sec. 2996 et seq.).

(g) "Older Americans Act" means the Older Americans Act of 1965, as amended (Public Law 89-73; 42 U.S.C. Sec. 3001 et seq.).

(h) "Developmentally Disabled Assistance Act" means the Developmentally Disabled Assistance and Bill of Rights Act of 1975, as amended (Public Law 94-103; 42 U.S.C. Sec. 6001 et seq.).

(i) "Supplemental security income recipient" means an individual receiving or eligible to receive payments under Title XVI of the federal Social Security Act, or payments under Chapter 3 (commencing with Section 12000) of Part 3 of Division 9 of the Welfare and Institutions Code.

§ 6214. Qualified Legal Service Projects

(a) Projects meeting the requirements of subdivision (a) of Section 6213 which are funded either in whole or part by the Legal Services Corporation or with Older American Act funds shall be presumed qualified legal services projects for the purpose of this article.

(b) Projects meeting the requirements of subdivision (a) of Section 6213 but not qualifying under the presumption specified in subdivision (a) shall qualify for funds under this article if they meet all of the following additional criteria:

(1) They receive cash funds from other sources in the amount of at least twenty thousand dollars ($20,000) per year to support free legal representation to indigent persons.

(2) They have demonstrated community support for the operation of a viable ongoing program.

(3) They provide one or both of the following special services:

(A) The coordination of the recruitment of substantial numbers of attorneys in private practice to provide free legal representation to indigent persons or to qualified legal services projects in California.

(B) The provision of legal representation, training, or technical assistance on matters concerning special client groups, including the elderly, the disabled, juveniles, and non-English-speaking groups, or on matters of specialized substantive law important to the special client groups.

§ 6214.5 Qualified Legal Services Projects; Eligibility for Distributions of Funds

A law school program that meets the definition of a "qualified legal services project" as defined in paragraph (2) of subdivision (a) of Section 6213, and that applied to the State Bar for funding under this article not later than February 17, 1984, shall be deemed eligible for all distributions of funds made under Section 6216.

§ 6215. Qualified Support Centers

(a) Support centers satisfying the qualifications specified in subdivision (b) of Section 6213 which were operating an office and providing services in California on December 31, 1980, shall be presumed to be qualified support centers for the purposes of this article.

(b) Support centers not qualifying under the presumption specified in subdivision (a) may qualify as a support center by meeting both of the following additional criteria:

(1) Meeting quality control standards established by the State Bar.

(2) Being deemed to be of special need by a majority of the qualified legal services projects.

§ 6216. Distribution of Funds

The State Bar shall distribute all moneys received under the program established by this article for the provision of civil legal services to indigent persons. The funds first shall be distributed 18 months from the effective date of this article, or upon such a date, as shall be determined by the State Bar, that adequate funds are available to initiate the program. Thereafter, the funds shall be distributed on an annual basis. All distributions of funds shall be made in the following order and in the following manner:

(a) To pay the actual administrative costs of the program, including any costs incurred after the adoption of this article and a reasonable reserve therefor.

(b) Eighty-five percent of the funds remaining after payment of administrative costs allocated pursuant to this article shall be distributed to qualified legal services projects. Distribution shall be by a pro rata county-by-county formula based upon the number of persons whose income is 125 percent or less of the current poverty threshold per county. For the purposes of this section, the source of data identifying the number of persons per county shall be the latest available figures from the United States Department of Commerce, Bureau of the Census. Projects from more than one county may pool their funds to operate a joint, multicounty legal services project serving each of their respective counties.

(1)(A) In any county which is served by more than one qualified legal services project, the State Bar shall distribute funds for the county to those projects which apply on a pro rata basis, based upon the amount of their total budget expended in the prior year for legal services in that county as compared to the total expended in the prior year for legal services by all qualified legal services projects applying therefor in the county. In determining the amount of funds to be allocated to a qualified legal services project specified in paragraph (2) of subdivision (a) of Section 6213, the State Bar shall recognize only expenditures attributable to the representation of indigent persons as constituting the budget of the program.

(B) The State Bar shall reserve 10 percent of the funds allocated to the county for distribution to programs meeting the standards of subparagraph (A) of paragraph (3) and paragraphs (1) and (2) of subdivision (b) of Section 6214 and which perform the services described in subparagraph (A) of paragraph (3) of Section 6214 as their principal means of delivering legal services. The State Bar shall distribute the funds for that county to those programs which apply on a pro rata basis, based upon the amount of their total budget expended for free legal services in that county as compared to the total expended for free legal services by all programs meeting the standards of subparagraph (A) of paragraph (3) and paragraphs (1) and (2) of subdivision (b) of Section 6214 in that county. The State Bar shall distribute any funds for which no program has qualified pursuant hereto, in accordance with the provisions of subparagraph (A) of paragraph (1) of this subdivision.

(2) In any county in which there is no qualified legal services project providing services, the State Bar shall reserve for the remainder of the fiscal year for distribution the pro rata share of funds as provided for by this article. Upon application of a qualified legal services project proposing to provide legal services to the indigent of the county, the State Bar shall distribute the funds to the project. Any funds not so distributed shall be added to the funds to be distributed the following year.

(c) Fifteen percent of the funds remaining after payment of administrative costs allocated for the purposes of this article shall be distributed equally by the State Bar to qualified support centers which apply for the funds. The funds provided to support centers shall be used only for the provision of legal services within California. Qualified support centers that receive funds to provide services to qualified legal services projects from sources other than this article, shall submit and shall have ap-

§ 6216　　　　SELECTED PROVISIONS

proved by the State Bar a plan assuring that the services funded under this article are in addition to those already funded for qualified legal services projects by other sources.

§ 6217. Maintenance of Quality Services, Professional Standards, Attorney-Client Privilege; Funds to Be Expended in Accordance With Article; Interference With Attorney Prohibited

With respect to the provision of legal assistance under this article, each recipient shall ensure all of the following:

(a) The maintenance of quality service and professional standards.

(b) The expenditure of funds received in accordance with the provisions of this article.

(c) The preservation of the attorney-client privilege in any case, and the protection of the integrity of the adversary process from any impairment in furnishing legal assistance to indigent persons.

(d) That no one shall interfere with any attorney funded in whole or in part by this article in carrying out his or her professional responsibility to his or her client as established by the rules of professional responsibility and this chapter.

§ 6218. Eligibility for Services; Establishment of Guidelines; Funds to Be Expended in Accordance With Article

All legal services projects and support centers receiving funds pursuant to this article shall adopt financial eligibility guidelines for indigent persons.

(a) Qualified legal services programs shall ensure that funds appropriated pursuant to this article shall be used solely to defray the costs of providing legal services to indigent persons or for such other purposes as set forth in this article.

(b) Funds received pursuant to this article by support centers shall only be used to provide services to qualified legal services projects as defined in subdivision (a) of Section 6213 which are used pursuant to a plan as required by subdivision (c) of Section 6216, or as permitted by Section 6219.

§ 6219. Provision of Work Opportunities and Scholarships for Disadvantaged Law Students

Qualified legal services projects and support centers may use funds provided under this article to provide work opportunities with pay, and where feasible, scholarships for disadvantaged law students to help defray their law school expenses.

§ 6220. Private Attorneys Providing Legal Services Without Charge; Support Center Services

Attorneys in private practice who are providing legal services without charge to indigent persons shall not be disqualified from receiving the services of the qualified support centers.

§ 6221. Services for Indigent Members of Disadvantaged and Underserved Groups

Qualified legal services projects shall make significant efforts to utilize 20 percent of the funds allocated under this article for increasing the availability of services to the elderly, the disabled, juveniles, or other indigent persons who are members of disadvantaged and underserved groups within their service area.

§ 6222. Financial Statements; Submission to State Bar; State Bar Report

A recipient of funds allocated pursuant to this article annually shall submit a financial statement to the State Bar, including an audit of the funds by a certified public accountant or a fiscal review approved by the State Bar, a report demonstrating the programs on which they were expended, a report on the recipient's compliance with the requirements of Section 6217, and progress in meeting the service expansion requirements of Section 6221.

The Board of Governors of the State Bar shall include a report of receipts of funds under this article, expenditures for administrative costs, and disbursements of the funds, on a county-by-county basis, in the annual report of State Bar receipts and expenditures required pursuant to Section 6145.

§ 6223. Expenditure of Funds; Prohibitions

No funds allocated by the State Bar pursuant to this article shall be used for any of the following purposes:

(a) The provision of legal assistance with respect to any fee generating case, except in accordance with guidelines which shall be promulgated by the State Bar.

(b) The provision of legal assistance with respect to any criminal proceeding.

(c) The provision of legal assistance, except to indigent persons or except to provide support services to qualified legal services projects as defined by this article.

§ 6224. State Bar; Powers; Determination of Qualifications to Receive Funds; Denial of Funds; Termination; Procedures

The State Bar shall have the power to determine that an applicant for funding is not qualified to receive funding, to deny future funding, or to terminate existing funding because the recipient is not operating in compliance with the requirements or restrictions of this article.

A denial of an application for funding or for future funding or an action by the State Bar to terminate an existing grant of funds under this article shall not become final until the applicant or recipient has been afforded reasonable notice and an opportunity for a timely and fair hearing. Pending final determination of any hearing held with reference to termination of funding, financial assistance shall be continued at its existing level on a month-to-month basis. Hearings for denial shall be conducted by an impartial hearing officer whose decision shall be final. The hearing officer shall render a decision no later than 30 days after the conclusion of the hearing. Specific procedures governing the conduct of the hearings of this section shall be determined by the State Bar pursuant to Section 6225.

§ 6225. Implementation of Article; Adoption of Rules and Regulations; Procedures

The Board of Governors of the State Bar shall adopt the regulations and procedures necessary to implement this article and to ensure that the funds allocated herein are utilized to provide civil legal services to indigent persons, especially underserved client groups such as but not limited to the elderly, the disabled, juveniles, and non-English-speaking persons.

In adopting the regulations the Board of Governors shall comply with the following procedures:

(a) The board shall publish a preliminary draft of the regulations and procedures, which shall be distributed, together with notice of the hearings required by subdivision (b), to commercial banking institutions, to members of the State Bar, and to potential recipients of funds.

(b) The board shall hold at least two public hearings, one in southern California and one in northern California where affected and interested parties shall be afforded an opportunity to present oral and written testimony regarding the proposed regulations and procedures.

§ 6226. Implementation of Article; Resolution

The program authorized by this article shall become operative only upon the adoption of a resolution by the Board of Governors of the State Bar stating that regulations have been adopted pursuant to Section 6225 which conform the program to all applicable tax and banking statutes, regulations, and rulings.

§ 6227. Credit of State Not Pledged

Nothing in this article shall create an obligation or pledge of the credit of the State of California or of the State Bar of California. Claims arising by reason of acts done pursuant to this article shall be limited to the moneys generated hereunder.

§ 6228. Severability

If any provision of this article or the application thereof to any group or circumstances is held invalid, such invalidity shall not affect the other provisions or applications of this article which can be given effect without the invalid provision or application, and to this end the provisions of this article are severable.

NOTE, SOME IMPORTANT STATUTES FOR LAWYERS IN CALIFORNIA GOVERNMENT

The State has a large number of statutes dealing with professional responsibilities of governmental officials, particularly if they are lawyers. West's California Government Code, provides in part:

§ 8920. Prohibited Acts

(a) No Member of the Legislature, state elective or appointive officer, or judge or justice shall, while serving as such, have any interest, financial or otherwise, direct or indirect, or engage in any business or transaction or professional activity, or incur any obligation of any nature, which is in substantial conflict with the proper discharge of his duties in the public interest and of his responsibilities as prescribed in the laws of this state.

(b) No Member of the Legislature shall do any of the following:

(1) Accept other employment which he has reason to believe will either impair his independence of judgment as to his official duties or require him, or induce him, to disclose confidential information acquired by him in the course of and by reason of his official duties.

(2) Willfully and knowingly disclose, for pecuniary gain, to any other person, confidential information acquired by him in the course of and by reason of his official duties or use any such information for the purpose of pecuniary gain.

(3) Accept or agree to accept, or be in partnership with any person who accepts or agrees to accept, any employment, fee, or other thing of monetary value, or portion thereof, in consideration of his appearing, agreeing to appear, or taking any other action on behalf of another person before any state board or agency.

This subdivision shall not be construed to prohibit a member who is an attorney at law from practicing in that capacity before any court or before the Workers' Compensation Appeals Board and receiving compensation therefor. This subdivision shall not act to prohibit a member from acting as an advocate without compensation or making inquiry for information on behalf of a constituent before a state board or agency, or from engaging in activities on behalf of another which require purely ministerial acts by the board or agency and which in no way require the board or agency to exercise any discretion, or from engaging in activities involving a board or agency which are strictly on his or her own behalf. The prohibition contained in this subdivision shall not apply to a partnership or firm of which the Member of the Legislature is a member if the Member of the Legislature does not share directly or indirectly in the fee, less any expenses attributable to that fee, resulting from the transaction. The prohibition contained in this subdivision as it read immediately prior to January 1, 1983, shall not apply in connection with any matter pending before any state board or agency on or before January 2, 1967, if the affected member of the Legislature was an attorney of record or representative in the matter prior to January 2, 1967. The prohibition contained in this subdivision, as amended and operative on January 1, 1983, shall not apply to any activity of any Member in connection with a matter pending before any state board or agency on January 1, 1983, which was not prohibited by this section prior to that date, if the affected Member of the Legislature was an attorney of record or representative in the matter prior to January 1, 1983.

(4) Receive or agree to receive, directly or indirectly, any compensation, reward, or gift from any source except the State of California for any service, advice, assistance or other matter related to the legislative process, except fees for speeches or published works on legislative subjects and except, in connection therewith, reimbursement of expenses for actual expenditures for travel and reasonable subsistence for which no payment or reimbursement is made by the State of California;

(5) Participate, by voting or any other action, on the floor of either house, or in committee or elsewhere, in the passage or defeat of legislation in which he has a personal interest, except as follows:

(i) If, on the vote for final passage by the house of which he is a member, of the legislation in which he has a personal interest, he first files a statement (which shall be entered verbatim on the journal) stating in substance that he has a personal interest in the legislation to be voted on and notwithstanding that interest, he is able to cast a fair and objective vote on that legislation, he may cast his vote without violating any provision of this article;

(ii) If the member believes that, because of his personal interest, he should abstain from participating in the vote on the legislation, he shall so advise the presiding officer prior to the commencement of the vote and shall be excused from voting on the legislation without any entry on the journal of the fact of his personal interest. In the event a rule of the house, requiring that each member who is present vote aye or nay is invoked, the presiding officer shall order the member excused from compliance and shall order entered on the journal a simple statement that the member was excused from voting on the legislation pursuant to law.

The provisions of this section do not apply to persons who are members of the state civil service as defined in Article VII of the California Constitution.

§ 8921. Interest in Substantial Conflict With Proper Discharge of Duties

A person subject to this article has an interest which is in substantial conflict with the proper discharge of his duties in the public interest and of his responsibilities as prescribed in the laws of this state or a personal interest, arising from any situation, within the scope of this article, if he has reason to believe or expect that he will derive a direct monetary gain or suffer a direct monetary loss, as the case may be, by reason of his official activity. He does not have an interest which is in substantial conflict with the proper discharge of his duties in the public interest and of his responsibilities as prescribed in the laws of this state or a personal interest, arising from any situation, within the scope of this article, if any benefit or detriment accrues to him as a member of a business, profession, occupation, or group to no greater extent than any other member of such business, profession, occupation, or group.

See also: West California Government Code, Section 24004—restrictions on practice of law by sheriff, clerk, constable, or any of their deputies.

Id. Section 31000.6—employment of legal counsel by board of supervisors to assist county assessor where county counsel or district attorney have a conflict of interest; in the event of a dispute as to whether a conflict exists, the presiding judge of superior court decides.

Id. Section 41805—representation of defendants in criminal matters by city attorney (or his partner or associate) if the defendant is not accused of violation of such city's ordinances, the city expressly relieves the city attorney of all prosecutorial functions on his behalf, and the defendant is "informed of and expressly waives any rights created as a result of any potential conflict * * *."

NEW YORK CODE OF PROFESSIONAL RESPONSIBILITY
DISCIPLINARY RULES OF THE CODE OF PROFESSIONAL RESPONSIBILITY

Promulgated as joint rules of the Appellate Divisions of the Supreme Court effective Sept. 1, 1990.*

Definitions		295
DR 1-101.	Maintaining Integrity and Competence of the Legal Profession	296
DR 1-102.	Misconduct	296
DR 1-103.	Disclosure of Information to Authorities	296
DR 1-104.	Responsibilities of a Supervisory Lawyer	297
DR 2-101.	Publicity and Advertising	297
DR 2-102.	Professional Notices, Letterheads, and Signs	299
DR 2-103.	Solicitation and Recommendation of Professional Employment	300
DR 2-104.	Suggestion of Need of Legal Services	302
DR 2-105.	Identification of Practice and Specialty	302
DR 2-106.	Fee for Legal Services	302
DR 2-107.	Division of Fees Among Lawyers	303
DR 2-108.	Agreements Restricting the Practice of a Lawyer	303
DR 2-109.	Acceptance of Employment	303
DR 2-110.	Withdrawal From Employment	304
DR 3-101.	Aiding Unauthorized Practice of Law	305
DR 3-102.	Dividing Legal Fees With a Non-lawyer	305
DR 3-103.	Forming a Partnership With a Non-lawyer	305
DR 4-101.	Preservation of Confidences and Secrets of a Client	305
DR 5-101.	Refusing Employment When the Interests of the Lawyer May Impair Independent Professional Judgment	306
DR 5-102.	Withdrawal as Counsel When the Lawyer Becomes a Witness	307
DR 5-103.	Avoiding Acquisition of Interest in Litigation	307
DR 5-104.	Limiting Business Relations With a Client	307
DR 5-105.	Refusing to Accept or Continue Employment if the Interests of Another Client May Impair the Independent Professional Judgment of the Lawyer	308
DR 5-106.	Settling Similar Claims of Clients	308
DR 5-107.	Avoiding Influence by Others Than the Client	308
DR 5-108.	Conflict of Interest—Former Client	309
DR 5-109.	____ Organization as Client	309
DR 5-110.	Membership in Legal Services Organization	309
DR 6-101.	Failing to Act Competently	309
DR 6-102.	Limiting Liability to Client	309
DR 7-101.	Representing a Client Zealously	310
DR 7-102.	Representing a Client Within the Bounds of the Law	310
DR 7-103.	Performing the Duty of Public Prosecutor or Other Government Lawyer	311
DR 7-104.	Communicating With One of Adverse Interest	311

* Editors' Note: New York did not adopt any Ethical Considerations.

N.Y. CODE OF PROFESSIONAL RESPONSIBILITY

DR 7-105.	Threatening Criminal Prosecution	311
DR 7-106.	Trial Conduct	311
DR 7-107.	Trial Publicity	312
DR 7-108.	Communication With or Investigation of Jurors	313
DR 7-109.	Contact With Witnesses	314
DR 7-110.	Contact With Officials	314
DR 8-101.	Action as a Public Official	314
DR 8-102.	Statements Concerning Judges and Other Adjudicatory Officers	315
DR 8-103.	Lawyers Candidate for Judicial Office	315
DR 9-101.	Avoiding Even the Appearance of Impropriety	315
DR 9-102.	Preserving Identity of Funds and Property of Others; Fiduciary Responsibility; Maintenance of Bank Accounts; Recordkeeping; Examination of Records	316

DEFINITIONS *

As used in the Disciplinary Rules of the Code of Professional Responsibility:

1. "Differing interests" include every interest that will adversely affect either the judgment or the loyalty of a lawyer to a client, whether it be a conflicting, inconsistent, diverse, or other interest.

2. "Law firm" includes, but is not limited to, a professional legal corporation, the legal department of a corporation or other organization and a legal services organization.

3. "Person" includes a corporation, an association, a trust, a partnership, and any other organization or legal entity.

4. "Professional legal corporation" means a corporation, or an association treated as a corporation, authorized by law to practice law for profit.

5. "State" includes the District of Columbia, Puerto Rico, and other federal territories and possessions.

6. "Tribunal" includes all courts and all other adjudicatory bodies. A tribunal shall be deemed "available" when it would have jurisdiction to hear a complaint, if timely brought.

7. "Bar association" includes a bar association of specialists as referred to in DR 2-105(B).

8. "Qualified legal assistance organization" means an office or organization of one of the four types listed in DR 2-103(D)(1) through (4), inclusive, that meets all the requirements thereof.

9. "Fraud" does not include conduct, although characterized as fraudulent by statute or administrative rule, which lacks an element of scienter, deceit, intent to mislead, or knowing failure to correct misrepresentations which can be reasonably expected to induce detrimental reliance by another.

* "Confidence" and "Secret" are defined in DR 4-101(A).

DISCIPLINARY RULES

DR 1-101. Maintaining Integrity and Competence of the Legal Profession

A. A lawyer is subject to discipline if the lawyer has made a materially false statement in, or has deliberately failed to disclose a material fact requested in connection with, the lawyer's application for admission to the bar.

B. A lawyer shall not further the application for admission to the bar of another person that the lawyer knows to be unqualified in respect to character, education, or other relevant attribute.

DR 1-102. Misconduct

A.[1] A lawyer shall not:

1. Violate a Disciplinary Rule.

2. Circumvent a Disciplinary Rule through actions of another.

3. Engage in illegal conduct involving moral turpitude.

4. Engage in conduct involving dishonesty, fraud, deceit, or misrepresentation.

5. Engage in conduct that is prejudicial to the administration of justice.

6. Unlawfully discriminate in the practice of law, including in hiring, promoting or otherwise determining conditions of employment, on the basis of age, race, creed, color, national origin, sex, disability, or marital status.

Where there is available a tribunal of competent jurisdiction, other than a Departmental Disciplinary Committee, a complaint of professional misconduct based on unlawful discrimination shall be brought before such tribunal in the first instance. A certified copy of a determination by such a tribunal, which has become final and enforceable, and as to which the right to judicial or appellate review has been exhausted, finding that the lawyer has engaged in an unlawful discriminatory practice shall constitute *prima facie* evidence of professional misconduct in a disciplinary proceeding.

7. Engage in any other conduct that adversely reflects on the lawyer's fitness to practice law.

DR 1-103. Disclosure of Information to Authorities

A. A lawyer possessing knowledge, not protected as a confidence or secret, of a violation of DR 1-102 that raises a substantial question as to another lawyer's honesty, trustworthiness or fitness in other respects as a lawyer shall report such knowledge to a tribunal or other authority empowered to investigate or act upon such violation.

B. A lawyer possessing knowledge or evidence, not protected as a confidence or secret, concerning another lawyer or a judge shall reveal fully such knowledge or evidence upon proper request of a tribunal or other authority empowered to investigate or act upon the conduct of lawyers or judges.

1. So in original. No par. B has been enacted.

DR 1-104. Responsibilities of a Supervisory Lawyer

A.[1] A lawyer shall be responsible for a violation of the Disciplinary Rules by another lawyer or for conduct of a non-lawyer employed or retained by or associated with the lawyer that would be a violation of the Disciplinary Rules if engaged in by a lawyer if:

1. The lawyer orders the conduct; or

2. The lawyer has supervisory authority over the other lawyer or the non-lawyer, and knows or should have known of the conduct at a time when its consequences can be avoided or mitigated but fails to take reasonable remedial action.

DR 2-101. Publicity and Advertising

A. A lawyer on behalf of himself or herself or partners or associates, shall not use or disseminate or participate in the preparation or dissemination of any public communication containing statements or claims that are false, deceptive, misleading or cast reflection on the legal profession as a whole.

B. Advertising or other publicity by lawyers, including participation in public functions, shall not contain puffery, self-laudation, claims regarding the quality of the lawyers' legal services, or claims that cannot be measured or verified.

C. It is proper to include information, provided its dissemination does not violate the provisions of subdivisions (A) and (B) of this section, as to:

1. education, degrees and other scholastic distinctions, dates of admission to any bar; areas of the law in which the lawyer or law firm practices, as authorized by the Code of Professional Responsibility; public offices and teaching positions held; memberships in bar associations or other professional societies or organizations, including offices and committee assignments therein; foreign language fluency;

2. names of clients regularly represented, provided that the client has given prior written consent;

3. bank references; credit arrangements accepted; prepaid or group legal services programs in which the attorney or firm participates; and

4. legal fees for initial consultation; contingent fee rates in civil matters when accompanied by a statement disclosing whether percentages are computed before or after deduction of costs and disbursements; range of fees for services, provided that there be available to the public free of charge a written statement clearly describing the scope of each advertised service; hourly rates; and fixed fees for specified legal services.

D. Advertising and publicity shall be designed to educate the public to an awareness of legal needs and to provide information relevant to the selection of the most appropriate counsel. Information other than that specifically authorized in subdivision (C) of this section that is consistent with these purposes may be disseminated providing that it does not violate any other provisions of this Rule.

E. A lawyer or law firm advertising any fixed fee for specified legal services shall, at the time of fee publication, have available to the public a written statement clearly describing the scope of each advertised service, which statement shall be delivered to the client at the time of retainer for any such service.

1. So in original. No par. B has been enacted.

DR 2-101 N.Y. CODE OF PROFESSIONAL RESPONSIBILITY

Such legal services shall include all those services which are recognized as reasonable and necessary under local custom in the area of practice in the community where the services are performed.

F. If the advertisement is broadcast, it shall be prerecorded or taped and approved for broadcast by the lawyer, and a recording or videotape of the actual transmission shall be retained by the lawyer for a period of not less than one year following such transmission. All advertisements of legal services that are mailed, or are distributed other than by radio, television, directory, newspaper, magazine or other periodical, by a lawyer or law firm with an office for the practice of law in this state, shall also be subject to the following provisions:

1. A copy of each advertisement shall at the time of its initial mailing or distribution be filed with the Departmental Disciplinary Committee of the appropriate judicial department.

2. Such advertisement shall contain no reference to the fact of filing.

3. If such advertisement is directed to a predetermined addressee, a list, containing the names and addresses of all persons to whom the advertisement is being or will thereafter be mailed or distributed, shall be retained by the lawyer or law firm for a period of not less than one year following the last date of mailing or distribution.

4. The advertisements filed pursuant to this subdivision shall be open to public inspection.

5. The requirements of this subdivision shall not apply to such professional cards or other announcements the distribution of which is authorized by DR 2-102(A).

G. If a lawyer or law firm advertises a range of fees or an hourly rate for services, the lawyer or law firm may not charge more than the fee advertised for such services. If a lawyer or law firm advertises a fixed fee for specified legal services, or performs services described in a fee schedule, the lawyer or law firm may not charge more than the fixed fee for such stated legal service as set forth in the advertisement or fee schedule, unless the client agrees in writing that the services performed or to be performed were not legal services referred to or implied in the advertisement or in the fee schedule and, further, that a different fee arrangement shall apply to the transaction.

H. Unless otherwise specified in the advertisement, if a lawyer publishes any fee information authorized under this Disciplinary Rule in a publication which is published more frequently than once per month, the lawyer shall be bound by any representation made therein for a period of not less than 30 days after such publication. If a lawyer publishes any fee information authorized under this Rule in a publication which is published once per month or less frequently, the lawyer shall be bound by any representation made therein until the publication of the succeeding issue. If a lawyer publishes any fee information authorized under this Rule in a publication which has no fixed date for publication of a succeeding issue, the lawyer shall be bound by any representation made therein for a reasonable period of time after publication, but in no event less than 90 days.

I. Unless otherwise specified, if a lawyer broadcasts any fee information authorized under this Rule, the lawyer shall be bound by any representation made therein for a period of not less than 30 days after such broadcast.

J. A lawyer shall not compensate or give any thing of value to representatives of the press, radio, television or other communication medium in anticipation of or in return for professional publicity in a news item.

K. All advertisements of legal services shall include the name, office address and telephone number of the attorney or law firm whose services are being offered.

DR 2–102. Professional Notices, Letterheads, and Signs

A. A lawyer or law firm may use professional cards, professional announcement cards, office signs, letterheads or similar professional notices or devices, provided the same do not violate any statute or court rule, and are in accordance with DR 2–101, including the following:

1. A professional card of a lawyer identifying the lawyer by name and as a lawyer, and giving addresses, telephone numbers, the name of the law firm, and any information permitted under DR 2–105. A professional card of a law firm may also give the names of members and associates.

2. A professional announcement card stating new or changed associations or addresses, change of firm name, or similar matters pertaining to the professional offices of a lawyer or law firm. It may state biographical data, the names of members of the firm and associates and the names and dates of predecessor firms in a continuing line of succession. It shall not state the nature of the practice except as permitted under DR 2–105.

3. A sign in or near the office and in the building directory identifying the law office. The sign shall not state the nature of the practice, except as permitted under DR 2-105.

4. A letterhead identifying the lawyer by name and as a lawyer, and giving addresses, telephone numbers, the name of the law firm, associates and any information permitted under DR 2–105. A letterhead of a law firm may also give the names of members and associates, and names and dates relating to deceased and retired members. A lawyer may be designated "Of Counsel" on a letterhead if there is a continuing relationship with a lawyer or law firm, other than as a partner or associate. A lawyer or law firm may be designated as "General Counsel" or by similar professional reference on stationery of a client if the lawyer or the firm devotes a substantial amount of professional time in the representation of that client. The letterhead of a law firm may give the names and dates of predecessor firms in a continuing line of succession.

B. A lawyer in private practice shall not practice under a trade name, a name that is misleading as to the identity of the lawyer or lawyers practicing under such name, or a firm name containing names other than those of one or more of the lawyers in the firm, except that the name of a professional corporation may contain "P.C." or such symbols permitted by law, and, if otherwise lawful, a firm may use as, or continue to include in its name the name or names of one or more deceased or retired members of the firm or of a predecessor firm in a continuing line of succession. Such terms as "legal clinic", "legal aid", "legal service office", "legal assistance office", "defender office" and the like, may be used only by qualified legal assistance organizations described in DR 2–103(D), except that the term "legal clinic" may be used by any lawyer or law firm provided the name of a participating lawyer or firm is incorporated therein. A lawyer who assumes a judicial, legislative or public executive or administrative post or office shall not permit his or her name to remain in the name of a law firm or be used in professional notices of the firm during any significant period in which the lawyer is not actively and regularly practicing law as a member of the firm and, during such period, other members of the firm shall not use the lawyer's name in the firm name or in professional notices of the firm.

C. A lawyer shall not hold himself or herself out as having a partnership with one or more other lawyers unless they are in fact partners.

D. A partnership shall not be formed or continued between or among lawyers licensed in different jurisdictions unless all enumerations of the members and associates of the firm on its letterhead and in other permissible listings make clear the jurisdictional limitations on those members and associates of the firm not licensed to practice in all listed jurisdictions; however, the same firm name may be used in each jurisdiction.

DR 2–103. Solicitation and Recommendation of Professional Employment

A. A lawyer shall not, directly or indirectly, seek professional employment for the lawyer or a partner or associate of the lawyer from a person who has not sought advice regarding employment of the lawyer in violation of any statute or existing court rule in the judicial department in which the lawyer practices.

B. A lawyer shall not compensate or give anything of value to a person or organization to recommend or obtain employment by a client, or as a reward for having made a recommendation resulting in employment by a client, except by any of the organizations listed in DR 2–103(D).

C. A lawyer shall not request a person or organization to recommend or promote the use of the lawyer's services or those of the lawyer's partner or associate, or any other affiliated lawyer as a private practitioner, other than by advertising or publicity not proscribed by DR 2–101, except that:

1. The lawyer may request referrals from a lawyer referral service operated, sponsored or approved by a bar association and may pay its fees incident thereto.

2. The lawyer may cooperate with the legal service activities of any of the offices or organizations enumerated in DR 2–103(D)(1) through (4) and may perform legal services for those to whom the lawyer was recommended by such an office or organization to do such work if:

a. The person to whom the recommendation is made is a member or beneficiary of such office or organization; and

b. The lawyer remains free to exercise independent professional judgment on behalf of the client.

3. The lawyer may request such a recommendation from another lawyer or an organization performing legal services.

D. A lawyer or the lawyer's partner or associate or any other affiliated lawyer may be recommended, employed or paid by, or may cooperate with one of the following offices or organizations which promote the use of the lawyer's services or those of a partner or associate or any other affiliated lawyer if there is no interference with the exercise of independent professional judgment on behalf of the client:

1. A legal aid office or public defender office:

  a. Operated or sponsored by a duly accredited law school;

  b. Operated or sponsored by a bona fide, non-profit community organization;

  c. Operated or sponsored by a governmental agency; or

  d. Operated, sponsored, or approved by a bar association;

2. A military legal assistance office;

3. A lawyer referral service operated, sponsored or approved by a bar association;

4. Any bona fide organization which recommends, furnishes or pays for legal services to its members or beneficiaries provided the following conditions are satisfied:

  a. Neither the lawyer, nor the lawyer's partner, nor associate, nor any other affiliated lawyer nor any non-lawyer, shall have initiated or promoted such organization for the primary purpose of providing financial or other benefit to such lawyer, partner, associate or affiliated lawyer.

  b. Such organization is not operated for the purpose of procuring legal work or financial benefit for any lawyer as a private practitioner outside of the legal services program of the organization.

  c. The member or beneficiary to whom the legal services are furnished, and not such organization, is recognized as the client of the lawyer in the matter.

  d. Any member or beneficiary who is entitled to have legal services furnished or paid for by the organization may, if such member or beneficiary so desires, select counsel other than that furnished, selected or approved by the organization for the particular matter involved; and the legal service plan of such organization provides appropriate relief for any member or beneficiary who asserts a claim that representation by counsel furnished, selected or approved would be unethical, improper or inadequate under the circumstances of the matter involved; and the plan provides an appropriate procedure for seeking such relief.

  e. The lawyer does not know or have cause to know that such organization is in violation of applicable laws, rules of court or other legal requirements that govern its legal service operations.

  f. Such organization has filed with the appropriate disciplinary authority, to the extent required by such authority, at least annually a report with respect to its legal service plan, if any, showing its terms, its schedule of benefits, its subscription charges, agreements with counsel and financial results of its legal service activities or, if it has failed to do so, the lawyer does not know or have cause to know of such failure.

E. A lawyer shall not accept employment when the lawyer knows or it is obvious that the person who seeks services does so as a result of conduct prohibited under this Disciplinary Rule.

F. Advertising not proscribed under DR 2-101 shall not be deemed in violation of any provision of this Disciplinary Rule.

DR 2-104. Suggestion of Need of Legal Services

A. A lawyer who has given unsolicited advice to an individual to obtain counsel or take legal action shall not accept employment resulting from that advice, in violation of any statute or court rule.

B. A lawyer may accept employment by a close friend, relative, former client (if the advice is germane to the former employment) or one whom the lawyer reasonably believes to be a client.

C. A lawyer may accept employment which results from participation in activities designed to educate the public to recognize legal problems, to make intelligent selection of counsel or to utilize available legal services.

D. A lawyer who is recommended, furnished or paid by a qualified legal assistance organization enumerated in DR 2-103(D)(1) through (4) may represent a member or beneficiary thereof, to the extent and under the conditions prescribed therein.

E. Without affecting the right to accept employment, a lawyer may speak publicly or write for publication on legal topics so long as the lawyer does not undertake to give individual advice.

F. Subject to compliance with the provisions of DR 2-103(A), if success in asserting rights or defenses of a client in litigation in the nature of a class action is dependent upon the joinder of others, a lawyer may accept employment from those contacted for the purpose of obtaining their joinder.

DR 2-105. Identification of Practice and Specialty

A. A lawyer or law firm may publicly identify one or more areas of law in which the lawyer or the law firm practices, or may state that the practice of the lawyer or law firm is limited to one or more areas of law.

B. A lawyer who is certified as a specialist in a particular area of law or law practice by the authority having jurisdiction under the laws of this state over the subject of specialization by lawyers may hold himself or herself out as a specialist, but only in accordance with the rules prescribed by that authority.

DR 2-106. Fee for Legal Services

A. A lawyer shall not enter into an agreement for, charge or collect an illegal or excessive fee.

B. A fee is excessive when, after a review of the facts, a lawyer of ordinary prudence would be left with a definite and firm conviction that the fee is in excess of a reasonable fee. Factors to be considered as guides in determining the reasonableness of a fee include the following:

1. The time and labor required, the novelty and difficulty of the questions involved and the skill requisite to perform the legal service properly.

2. The likelihood, if apparent or made known to the client, that the acceptance of the particular employment will preclude other employment by the lawyer.

3. The fee customarily charged in the locality for similar legal services.

4. The amount involved and the results obtained.

5. The time limitations imposed by the client or by circumstances.

6. The nature and length of the professional relationship with the client.

7. The experience, reputation and ability of the lawyer or lawyers performing the services.

8. Whether the fee is fixed or contingent.

C. A lawyer shall not enter into an arrangement for, charge or collect:

1. A contingent fee for representing a defendant in a criminal case; or

2. Any fee in a domestic relations matter, the payment or amount of which is contingent upon the securing of a divorce or upon the amount of maintenance, support, equitable distribution, or property settlement; or

3. A fee proscribed by law or rule of court.

D. Promptly after a lawyer has been employed in a contingent fee matter, the lawyer shall provide the client with a writing stating the method by which the fee is to be determined, including the percentage or percentages that shall accrue to the lawyer in the event of settlement, trial or appeal, litigation and other expenses to be deducted from the recovery and whether such expenses are to be deducted before or after the contingent fee is calculated. Upon conclusion of a contingent fee matter, the lawyer shall provide the client with a written statement stating the outcome of the matter, and if there is a recovery, showing the remittance to the client and the method of its determination.

DR 2-107. Division of Fees Among Lawyers

A. A lawyer shall not divide a fee for legal services with another lawyer who is not a partner in or associate of the lawyer's law firm or law office, unless:

1. The client consents to employment of the other lawyer after a full disclosure that a division of fees will be made.

2. The division is in proportion to the services performed by each lawyer or, by a writing given to the client, each lawyer assumes joint responsibility for the representation.

3. The total fee of the lawyers does not exceed reasonable compensation for all legal services they rendered the client.

B. This Disciplinary Rule does not prohibit payment to a former partner or associate pursuant to a separation or retirement agreement.

DR 2-108. Agreement Restricting the Practice of a Lawyer

A. A lawyer shall not be a party to or participate in a partnership or employment agreement with another lawyer that restricts the right of a lawyer to practice law after the termination of a relationship created by the agreement, except as a condition to payment of retirement benefits.

B. In connection with the settlement of a controversy or suit, a lawyer shall not enter into an agreement that restricts the right of a lawyer to practice law.

DR 2-109. Acceptance of Employment

A.[1] A lawyer shall not accept employment on behalf of a person if the lawyer knows or it is obvious that such person wishes to:

[1] So in original. No par. B has been enacted.

DR 2-109 *N.Y. CODE OF PROFESSIONAL RESPONSIBILITY*

1. Bring a legal action, conduct a defense, or assert a position in litigation, or otherwise have steps taken for such person merely for the purpose of harassing or maliciously injuring any person.

2. Present a claim or defense in litigation that is not warranted under existing law, unless it can be supported by good faith argument for an extension, modification, or reversal of existing law.

DR 2-110. Withdrawal From Employment

A. In general. 1. If permission for withdrawal from employment is required by the rules of a tribunal, a lawyer shall not withdraw from employment in a proceeding before that tribunal without its permission.

2. Even when withdrawal is otherwise permitted or required under DR 2-110(A)(1), (B) or (C), a lawyer shall not withdraw from employment until the lawyer has taken steps to the extent reasonably practicable to avoid foreseeable prejudice to the rights of the client, including giving due notice to the client, allowing time for employment of other counsel, delivering to the client all papers and property to which the client is entitled and complying with applicable laws and rules.

3. A lawyer who withdraws from employment shall refund promptly any part of a fee paid in advance that has not been earned.

B. Mandatory withdrawal. A lawyer representing a client before a tribunal, with its permission if required by its rules, shall withdraw from employment, and a lawyer representing a client in other matters shall withdraw from employment, if:

1. The lawyer knows or it is obvious that the client is bringing the legal action, conducting the defense, or asserting a position in the litigation, or is otherwise having steps taken, merely for the purpose of harassing or maliciously injuring any person.

2. The lawyer knows or it is obvious that continued employment will result in violation of a Disciplinary Rule.

3. The lawyer's mental or physical condition renders it unreasonably difficult to carry out the employment effectively.

4. The lawyer is discharged by his or her client.

C. Permissive withdrawal. Except as stated in DR 2-110(A), a lawyer may withdraw from representing a client if withdrawal can be accomplished without material adverse effect on the interests of the client, or if:

1. The client:

a. Insists upon presenting a claim or defense that is not warranted under existing law and cannot be supported by good faith argument for an extension, modification, or reversal of existing law.

b. Persists in a course of action involving the lawyer's services that the lawyer reasonably believes is criminal or fraudulent.

c. Insists that the lawyer pursue a course of conduct which is illegal or prohibited under the Disciplinary Rules.

d. By other conduct renders it unreasonably difficult for the lawyer to carry out employment effectively.

e. Insists, in a matter not pending before a tribunal, that the lawyer engage in conduct which is contrary to the judgment and advice of the lawyer but not prohibited under the Disciplinary Rules.

f. Deliberately disregards an agreement or obligation to the lawyer as to expenses or fees.

g. Has used the lawyer's services to perpetrate a crime or fraud.

2. The lawyer's continued employment is likely to result in a violation of a Disciplinary Rule.

3. The lawyer's inability to work with co-counsel indicates that the best interests of the client likely will be served by withdrawal.

4. The lawyer's mental or physical condition renders it difficult for the lawyer to carry out the employment effectively.

5. The lawyer's client knowingly and freely assents to termination of the employment.

6. The lawyer believes in good faith, in a proceeding pending before a tribunal, that the tribunal will find the existence of other good cause for withdrawal.

DR 3–101. Aiding Unauthorized Practice of Law

A. A lawyer shall not aid a non-lawyer in the unauthorized practice of law.

B. A lawyer shall not practice law in a jurisdiction where to do so would be in violation of regulations of the profession in that jurisdiction.

DR 3–102. Dividing Legal Fees With a Non-lawyer

A.[1] A lawyer or law firm shall not share legal fees with a non-lawyer, except that:

1. An agreement by a lawyer with his or her firm, partner, or associate may provide for the payment of money, over a reasonable period of time after the lawyer's death, to the lawyer's estate or to one or more specified persons.

2. A lawyer who undertakes to complete unfinished legal business of a deceased lawyer may pay to the estate of the deceased lawyer that proportion of the total compensation which fairly represents the services rendered by the deceased lawyer.

3. A lawyer or law firm may include non-lawyer employees in a retirement plan, even though the plan is based in whole or in part on a profit-sharing arrangement.

DR 3–103. Forming a Partnership With a Non-lawyer

A.[1] A lawyer shall not form a partnership with a non-lawyer if any of the activities of the partnership consist of the practice of law.

DR 4–101. Preservation of Confidences and Secrets of a Client

A. "Confidence" refers to information protected by the attorney-client privilege under applicable law, and "secret" refers to other information gained in the professional relationship that the client has requested be held inviolate or the

---

1. So in original. No par. B has been enacted.

DR 4-101 N.Y. CODE OF PROFESSIONAL RESPONSIBILITY

disclosure of which would be embarrassing or would be likely to be detrimental to the client.

B. Except when permitted under DR 4-101(C), a lawyer shall not knowingly:

1. Reveal a confidence or secret of a client.

2. Use a confidence or secret of a client to the disadvantage of the client.

3. Use a confidence or secret of a client for the advantage of the lawyer or of a third person, unless the client consents after full disclosure.

C. A lawyer may reveal:

1. Confidences or secrets with the consent of the client or clients affected, but only after a full disclosure to them.

2. Confidences or secrets when permitted under Disciplinary Rules or required by law or court order.

3. The intention of a client to commit a crime and the information necessary to prevent the crime.

4. Confidences or secrets necessary to establish or collect the lawyer's fee or to defend the lawyer or his or her employees or associates against an accusation of wrongful conduct.

5. Confidences or secrets to the extent implicit in withdrawing a written or oral opinion or representation previously given by the lawyer and believed by the lawyer still to be relied upon by a third person where the lawyer has discovered that the opinion or representation was based on materially inaccurate information or is being used to further a crime or fraud.

D. A lawyer shall exercise reasonable care to prevent his or her employees, associates, and others whose services are utilized by the lawyer from disclosing or using confidences or secrets of a client, except that a lawyer may reveal the information allowed by DR 4-101(C) through an employee.

DR 5-101. Refusing Employment When the Interests of the Lawyer May Impair Independent Professional Judgment

A. Except with the consent of the client after full disclosure, a lawyer shall not accept employment if the exercise of professional judgment on behalf of the client will be or reasonably may be affected by the lawyer's own financial, business, property, or personal interests.

B. A lawyer shall not act, or accept employment that contemplates the lawyer's acting, as an advocate before any tribunal if the lawyer knows or it is obvious that the lawyer ought to be called as a witness on behalf of the client, except that the lawyer may act as an advocate and also testify:

1. If the testimony will relate solely to an uncontested issue.

2. If the testimony will relate solely to a matter of formality and there is no reason to believe that substantial evidence will be offered in opposition to the testimony.

3. If the testimony will relate solely to the nature and value of legal services rendered in the case by the lawyer or the lawyer's firm to the client.

4. As to any matter, if disqualification as an advocate would work a substantial hardship on the client because of the distinctive value of the lawyer as counsel in the particular case.

C. Neither a lawyer nor the lawyer's firm shall accept employment in contemplated or pending litigation if the lawyer knows or it is obvious that the lawyer or another lawyer in the lawyer's firm may be called as a witness other than on behalf of the client, and it is apparent that the testimony would or might be prejudicial to the client.

DR 5–102. Withdrawal as Counsel When the Lawyer Becomes a Witness

A. If, after undertaking employment in contemplated or pending litigation, a lawyer learns or it is obvious that the lawyer ought to be called as a witness on behalf of the client, the lawyer shall withdraw as an advocate before the tribunal, except that the lawyer may continue as an advocate and may testify in the circumstances enumerated in DR 5–101(B)(1) through (4).

B. If, after undertaking employment in contemplated or pending litigation, a lawyer learns or it is obvious that the lawyer or a lawyer in his or her firm may be called as a witness other than on behalf of the client, the lawyer may continue the representation until it is apparent that the testimony is or may be prejudicial to the client at which point the lawyer and the firm must withdraw from acting as an advocate before the tribunal.

DR 5–103. Avoiding Acquisition of Interest in Litigation

A. A lawyer shall not acquire a proprietary interest in the cause of action or subject matter of litigation he or she is conducting for a client, except that the lawyer may:

1. Acquire a lien granted by law to secure the lawyer's fee or expenses.

2. Except as provided in DR 2–106(C)(2) or (3), contract with a client for a reasonable contingent fee in a civil case.

B. While representing a client in connection with contemplated or pending litigation, a lawyer shall not advance or guarantee financial assistance to the client, except that:

1. A lawyer may advance or guarantee the expenses of litigation, including court costs, expenses of investigation, expenses of medical examination, and costs of obtaining and presenting evidence, provided the client remains ultimately liable for such expenses.

2. Unless prohibited by law or rule of court, a lawyer representing an indigent client on a pro bono basis may pay court costs and reasonable expenses of litigation on behalf of the client.

DR 5–104. Limiting Business Relations With a Client

A. A lawyer shall not enter into a business transaction with a client if they have differing interests therein and if the client expects the lawyer to exercise professional judgment therein for the protection of the client, unless the client has consented after full disclosure.

B. Prior to conclusion of all aspects of the matter giving rise to employment, a lawyer shall not enter into any arrangement or understanding with a client or a prospective client by which the lawyer acquires an interest in literary or media rights with respect to the subject matter of the employment or proposed employment.

DR 5-105. Refusing to Accept or Continue Employment if the Interests of Another Client May Impair the Independent Professional Judgment of the Lawyer

A. A lawyer shall decline proffered employment if the exercise of independent professional judgment in behalf of a client will be or is likely to be adversely affected by the acceptance of the proffered employment, or if it would be likely to involve the lawyer in representing differing interests, except to the extent permitted under DR 5-105(C).

B. A lawyer shall not continue multiple employment if the exercise of independent professional judgment in behalf of a client will be or is likely to be adversely affected by the lawyer's representation of another client, or if it would be likely to involve the lawyer in representing differing interests, except to the extent permitted under DR 5-105(C).

C. In the situations covered by DR 5-105(A) and (B), a lawyer may represent multiple clients if it is obvious that the lawyer can adequately represent the interest of each and if each consents to the representation after full disclosure of the possible effect of such representation on the exercise of the lawyer's independent professional judgment on behalf of each.

D. While lawyers are associated in a law firm, none of them shall knowingly accept or continue employment when any one of them practicing alone would be prohibited from doing so under DR 5-101(A), DR 5-105(A), (B) or (C), DR 5-108, or DR 9-101(B) except as otherwise provided therein.

DR 5-106. Settling Similar Claims of Clients

A.[1] A lawyer who represents two or more clients shall not make or participate in the making of an aggregate settlement of the claims of or against the clients, unless each client has consented to the settlement after being advised of the existence and nature of all the claims involved in the proposed settlement, of the total amount of the settlement, and of the participation of each person in the settlement.

DR 5-107. Avoiding Influence by Others Than the Client

A. Except with the consent of the client after full disclosure a lawyer shall not:

1. Accept compensation for legal services from one other than the client.

2. Accept from one other than the client any thing of value related to his or her representation of or employment by the client.

B. A lawyer shall not permit a person who recommends, employs, or pays the lawyer to render legal service for another to direct or regulate his or her professional judgment in rendering such legal services.

C. A lawyer shall not practice with or in the form of a professional corporation or association authorized to practice law for a profit, if:

1. A non-lawyer owns any interest therein, except that a fiduciary representative of the estate of a lawyer may hold the stock or interest of the lawyer for a reasonable time during administration;

---

1. So in original. No par. B has been enacted.

2. A non-lawyer is a corporate director or officer thereof; or

3. A non-lawyer has the right to direct or control the professional judgment of a lawyer.

DR 5–108. Conflict of Interest—Former Client

A.[1] Except with the consent of a former client after full disclosure a lawyer who has represented the former client in a matter shall not:

1. Thereafter represent another person in the same or a substantially related matter in which that person's interests are materially adverse to the interests of the former client.

2. Use any confidences or secrets of the former client except as permitted by DR 4–101(C) or when the confidence or secret has become generally known.

DR 5–109. Conflict of Interest—Organization as Client

A.[1] When a lawyer employed or retained by an organization is dealing with the organization's directors, officers, employees, members, shareholders or other constituents, and it appears that the organization's interests may differ from those of the constituents with whom the lawyer is dealing, the lawyer shall explain that the lawyer is the lawyer for the organization and not for any of the constituents.

DR 5–110. Membership in Legal Services Organization

A.[1] A lawyer may serve as a director, officer or member of a not-for-profit legal services organization, apart from the law firm in which the lawyer practices, notwithstanding that the organization serves persons having interests that differ from those of a client of the lawyer or the lawyer's firm, provided that the lawyer shall not knowingly participate in a decision or action of the organization

1. If participating in the decision or action would be incompatible with the lawyer's duty of loyalty to a client under Canon 5; or

2. Where the decision or action could have a material adverse effect on the representation of a client of the organization whose interests differ from those of a client of the lawyer or the lawyer's firm.

DR 6–101. Failing to Act Competently

A.[1] A lawyer shall not:

1. Handle a legal matter which the lawyer knows or should know that he or she is not competent to handle, without associating with a lawyer who is competent to handle it.

2. Handle a legal matter without preparation adequate in the circumstances.

3. Neglect a legal matter entrusted to the lawyer.

DR 6–102. Limiting Liability to Client

A.[1] A lawyer shall not seek, by contract or other means, to limit prospectively the lawyer's individual liability to a client for malpractice, or, without first advising that person that independent representation is appropriate in connection

---

1. So in original. No par. B has been enacted.

DR 6–102 *N.Y. CODE OF PROFESSIONAL RESPONSIBILITY*

therewith, to settle a claim for such liability with an unrepresented client or former client.

DR 7–101. Representing a Client Zealously

A. A lawyer shall not intentionally:

1. Fail to seek the lawful objectives of the client through reasonably available means permitted by law and the Disciplinary Rules, except as provided by DR 7–101(B). A lawyer does not violate this Disciplinary Rule, however, by acceding to reasonable requests of opposing counsel which do not prejudice the rights of the client, by being punctual in fulfilling all professional commitments, by avoiding offensive tactics, or by treating with courtesy and consideration all persons involved in the legal process.

2. Fail to carry out a contract of employment entered into with a client for professional services, but the lawyer may withdraw as permitted under DR 2–110, DR 5–102, and DR 5–105.

3. Prejudice or damage the client during the course of the professional relationship, except as required under DR 7–102(B).

B. In the representation of a client, a lawyer may:

1. Where permissible, exercise professional judgment to waive or fail to assert a right or position of the client.

2. Refuse to aid or participate in conduct that the lawyer believes to be unlawful, even though there is some support for an argument that the conduct is legal.

DR 7–102. Representing a Client Within the Bounds of the Law

A. In the representation of a client, a lawyer shall not:

1. File a suit, assert a position, conduct a defense, delay a trial, or take other action on behalf of the client when the lawyer knows or when it is obvious that such action would serve merely to harass or maliciously injure another.

2. Knowingly advance a claim or defense that is unwarranted under existing law, except that the lawyer may advance such claim or defense if it can be supported by good faith argument for an extension, modification, or reversal of existing law.

3. Conceal or knowingly fail to disclose that which the lawyer is required by law to reveal.

4. Knowingly use perjured testimony or false evidence.

5. Knowingly make a false statement of law or fact.

6. Participate in the creation or preservation of evidence when the lawyer knows or it is obvious that the evidence is false.

7. Counsel or assist the client in conduct that the lawyer knows to be illegal or fraudulent.

8. Knowingly engage in other illegal conduct or conduct contrary to a Disciplinary Rule.

B. A lawyer who receives information clearly establishing that:

1. The client has, in the course of the representation, perpetrated a fraud upon a person or tribunal shall promptly call upon the client to rectify the same,

N.Y. CODE OF PROFESSIONAL RESPONSIBILITY DR 7-106

and if the client refuses or is unable to do so, the lawyer shall reveal the fraud to the affected person or tribunal, except when the information is protected as a confidence or secret.

2. A person other than the client has perpetrated a fraud upon a tribunal shall promptly reveal the fraud to the tribunal.

DR 7-103. Performing the Duty of Public Prosecutor or Other Government Lawyer

A. A public prosecutor or other government lawyer shall not institute or cause to be instituted criminal charges when he or she knows or it is obvious that the charges are not supported by probable cause.

B. A public prosecutor or other government lawyer in criminal litigation shall make timely disclosure to counsel for the defendant, or to a defendant who has no counsel, of the existence of evidence, known to the prosecutor or other government lawyer, that tends to negate the guilt of the accused, mitigate the degree of the offense or reduce the punishment.

DR 7-104. Communicating With One of Adverse Interest

A.[1] During the course of the representation of a client a lawyer shall not:

1. Communicate or cause another to communicate on the subject of the representation with a party the lawyer knows to be represented by a lawyer in that matter unless the lawyer has the prior consent of the lawyer representing such other party or is authorized by law to do so.

2. Give advice to a person who is not represented by a lawyer, other than the advice to secure counsel, if the interests of such person are or have a reasonable possibility of being in conflict with the interests of the lawyer's client.

DR 7-105. Threatening Criminal Prosecution

A.[1] A lawyer shall not present, participate in presenting, or threaten to present criminal charges solely to obtain an advantage in a civil matter.

DR 7-106. Trial Conduct

A. A lawyer shall not disregard or advise the client to disregard a standing rule of a tribunal or a ruling of a tribunal made in the course of a proceeding, but the lawyer may take appropriate steps in good faith to test the validity of such rule or ruling.

B. In presenting a matter to a tribunal, a lawyer shall disclose:

1. Controlling legal authority known to the lawyer to be directly adverse to the position of the client and which is not disclosed by opposing counsel.

2. Unless privileged or irrelevant, the identities of the clients the lawyer represents and of the persons who employed the lawyer.

C. In appearing as a lawyer before a tribunal, a lawyer shall not:

1. State or allude to any matter that he or she has no reasonable basis to believe is relevant to the case or that will not be supported by admissible evidence.

---

1. So in original. No par. B has been enacted.

DR 7-106 *N.Y. CODE OF PROFESSIONAL RESPONSIBILITY*

2. Ask any question that he or she has no reasonable basis to believe is relevant to the case and that is intended to degrade a witness or other person.

3. Assert personal knowledge of the facts in issue, except when testifying as a witness.

4. Assert a personal opinion as to the justness of a cause, as to the credibility of a witness, as to the culpability of a civil litigant, or as to the guilt or innocence of an accused; but the lawyer may argue, upon analysis of the evidence, for any position or conclusion with respect to the matters stated herein.

5. Fail to comply with known local customs of courtesy or practice of the bar or a particular tribunal without giving to opposing counsel timely notice of the intent not to comply.

6. Engage in undignified or discourteous conduct which is degrading to a tribunal.

7. Intentionally or habitually violate any established rule of procedure or of evidence.

DR 7-107. Trial Publicity

A. A lawyer participating in or associated with a criminal or civil matter shall not make an extrajudicial statement that a reasonable person would expect to be disseminated by means of public communication if the lawyer knows or reasonably should know that it will have a substantial likelihood of materially prejudicing an adjudicative proceeding.

B. A statement ordinarily is likely to prejudice materially an adjudicative proceeding when it refers to a civil matter triable to a jury, a criminal matter, or any other proceeding that could result in incarceration, and the statement relates to:

1. The character, credibility, reputation or criminal record of a party, suspect in a criminal investigation or witness, or the identity of a witness, or the expected testimony of a party or witness.

2. In a criminal case or proceeding that could result in incarceration, the possibility of a plea of guilty to the offense or the existence or contents of any confession, admission, or statement given by a defendant or suspect or that person's refusal or failure to make a statement.

3. The performance or results of any examination or test or the refusal or failure of a person to submit to an examination or test, or the identity or nature of physical evidence expected to be presented.

4. Any opinion as to the guilt or innocence of a defendant or suspect in a criminal case or proceeding that could result in incarceration.

5. Information the lawyer knows or reasonably should know is likely to be inadmissible as evidence in a trial and would if disclosed create a substantial risk of prejudicing an impartial trial.

6. The fact that a defendant has been charged with a crime, unless there is included therein a statement explaining that the charge is merely an accusation and that the defendant is presumed innocent until and unless proven guilty.

N.Y. CODE OF PROFESSIONAL RESPONSIBILITY DR 7–108

C. Provided that the statement complies with DR 7–107(A), a lawyer involved with the investigation or litigation of a matter may state the following without elaboration:

1. The general nature of the claim or defense.

2. The information contained in a public record.

3. That an investigation of the matter is in progress.

4. The scheduling or result of any step in litigation.

5. A request for assistance in obtaining evidence and information necessary thereto.

6. A warning of danger concerning the behavior of a person involved, when there is reason to believe that there exists the likelihood of substantial harm to an individual or to the public interest.

7. In a criminal case:

a. The identity, age, residence, occupation and family status of the accused.

b. If the accused has not been apprehended, information necessary to aid in apprehension of that person.

c. The fact, time and place of arrest, resistance, pursuit, use of weapons, and a description of physical evidence seized, other than as contained only in a confession, admission, or statement.

d. The identity of investigating and arresting officers or agencies and the length of the investigation.

DR 7–108. Communication With or Investigation of Jurors

A. Before the trial of a case a lawyer connected therewith shall not communicate with or cause another to communicate with anyone the lawyer knows to be a member of the venire from which the jury will be selected for the trial of the case.

B. During the trial of a case:

1. A lawyer connected therewith shall not communicate with or cause another to communicate with any member of the jury.

2. A lawyer who is not connected therewith shall not communicate with or cause another to communicate with a juror concerning the case.

C. DR 7–108(A) and (B) do not prohibit a lawyer from communicating with members of the venire or jurors in the course of official proceedings.

D. After discharge of the jury from further consideration of a case with which the lawyer was connected, the lawyer shall not ask questions of or make comments to a member of that jury that are calculated merely to harass or embarrass the juror or to influence the juror's actions in future jury service.

E. A lawyer shall not conduct or cause, by financial support or otherwise, another to conduct a vexatious or harassing investigation of either a member of the venire or a juror.

F. All restrictions imposed by DR 7–108 upon a lawyer also apply to communications with or investigations of members of a family of a member of the venire or a juror.

G. A lawyer shall reveal promptly to the court improper conduct by a member of the venire or a juror, or by another toward a member of the venire or a juror or a member of his or her family of which the lawyer has knowledge.

DR 7–109. Contact With Witnesses

A. A lawyer shall not suppress any evidence that the lawyer or the client has a legal obligation to reveal or produce.

B. A lawyer shall not advise or cause a person to hide or to leave the jurisdiction of a tribunal for the purpose of making the person unavailable as a witness therein.

C. A lawyer shall not pay, offer to pay, or acquiesce in the payment of compensation to a witness contingent upon the content of his or her testimony or the outcome of the case. But a lawyer may advance, guarantee, or acquiesce in the payment of:

1. Expenses reasonably incurred by a witness in attending or testifying.

2. Reasonable compensation to a witness for the loss of time in attending or testifying.

3. A reasonable fee for the professional services of an expert witness.

DR 7–110. Contact With Officials

A. A lawyer shall not give or lend anything of value to a judge, official, or employee of a tribunal except as permitted by Section C(4) of Canon 5 of the Code of Judicial Conduct, but a lawyer may make a contribution to the campaign fund of a candidate for judicial office in conformity with Section B(2) under Canon 7 of the Code of Judicial Conduct.

B. In an adversary proceeding, a lawyer shall not communicate, or cause another to communicate, as to the merits of the cause with a judge or an official before whom the proceeding is pending, except:

1. In the course of official proceedings in the cause.

2. In writing if the lawyer promptly delivers a copy of the writing to opposing counsel or to an adverse party who is not represented by a lawyer.

3. Orally upon adequate notice to opposing counsel or to an adverse party who is not represented by a lawyer.

4. As otherwise authorized by law, or by Section A(4) under Canon 3 of the Code of Judicial Conduct.

DR 8–101. Action as a Public Official

A.[1] A lawyer who holds public office shall not:

1. Use the public position to obtain, or attempt to obtain, a special advantage in legislative matters for the lawyer or for a client under circumstances where the lawyer knows or it is obvious that such action is not in the public interest.

2. Use the public position to influence, or attempt to influence, a tribunal to act in favor of the lawyer or of a client.

---

1. So in original. No par. B has been enacted.

3. Accept any thing of value from any person when the lawyer knows or it is obvious that the offer is for the purpose of influencing the lawyer's action as a public official.

DR 8–102. Statements Concerning Judges and Other Adjudicatory Officers

A. A lawyer shall not knowingly make false statements of fact concerning the qualifications of a candidate for election or appointment to a judicial office.

B. A lawyer shall not knowingly make false accusations against a judge or other adjudicatory officer.

DR 8–103. Lawyers Candidate for Judicial Office

A.[1] A lawyer who is a candidate for judicial office shall comply with the applicable provisions of Canon 7 of the Code of Judicial Conduct.

DR 9–101. Avoiding Even the Appearance of Impropriety

A. A lawyer shall not accept private employment in a matter upon the merits of which the lawyer has acted in a judicial capacity.

B. Except as law may otherwise expressly permit:

1. A lawyer shall not represent a private client in connection with a matter in which the lawyer participated personally and substantially as a public officer or employee, and no lawyer in a firm with which that lawyer is associated may knowingly undertake or continue representation in such a matter unless:

   a. The disqualified lawyer is effectively screened from any participation, direct or indirect, including discussion, in the matter and is apportioned no part of the fee therefrom; and

   b. There are no other circumstances in the particular representation that create an appearance of impropriety.

2. A lawyer having information that the lawyer knows is confidential government information about a person, acquired when the lawyer was a public officer or employee, may not represent a private client whose interests are adverse to that person in a matter in which the information could be used to the material disadvantage of that person. A firm with which that lawyer is associated may knowingly undertake or continue representation in the matter only if the disqualified lawyer is effectively screened from any participation, direct or indirect, including discussion, in the matter and is apportioned no part of the fee therefrom.

3. A lawyer serving as a public officer or employee shall not:

   a. Participate in a matter in which the lawyer participated personally and substantially while in private practice or nongovernmental employment, unless under applicable law no one is, or by lawful delegation may be, authorized to act in the lawyer's stead in the matter; or

   b. Negotiate for private employment with any person who is involved as a party or as attorney for a party in a matter in which the lawyer is participating personally and substantially.

1. So in original. No par. B has been enacted.

DR 9–101 *N.Y. CODE OF PROFESSIONAL RESPONSIBILITY*

C. A lawyer shall not state or imply that the lawyer is able to influence improperly or upon irrelevant grounds any tribunal, legislative body, or public official.

D. A lawyer related to another lawyer as parent, child, sibling or spouse shall not represent in any matter a client whose interests differ from those of another party to the matter who the lawyer knows is represented by the other lawyer unless the client consents to the representation after full disclosure and the lawyer concludes that the lawyer can adequately represent the interests of the client.

DR 9–102. Preserving Identity of Funds and Property of Others; Fiduciary Responsibility; Maintenance of Bank Accounts; Recordkeeping; Examination of Records

A. Prohibition Against Commingling. A lawyer in possession of any funds or other property belonging to another person, where such possession is incident to his or her practice of law, is a fiduciary, and must not commingle such property with his or her own.

B. Separate Accounts. 1. A lawyer who is in possession of funds belonging to another person incident to the lawyer's practice of law, shall maintain in a bank or trust company within the State of New York in the lawyer's own name, or in the name of a firm of lawyers of which he or she is a member, or in the name of the lawyer or firm of lawyers by whom he or she is employed, a special account or accounts, separate from any business or personal accounts of the lawyer or lawyer's firm, and separate from any accounts which the lawyer may maintain as executor, guardian, trustee or receiver, or in any other fiduciary capacity, into which special account or accounts all funds held in escrow or otherwise entrusted to the lawyer or firm shall be deposited.

2. Other than accounts maintained by a lawyer as executor, guardian, trustee or receiver, or in any other such fiduciary capacity, all special accounts as well as all deposit slips relating to and checks drawn upon such special accounts, shall be designated in a manner sufficient to distinguish them from all other bank accounts maintained by the lawyer or the lawyer's firm.

3. Funds reasonably sufficient to maintain the account or to pay account charges may be deposited therein.

4. Funds belonging in part to a client or third person and in part presently or potentially to the lawyer or law firm shall be kept in such special account or accounts, but the portion belonging to the lawyer or law firm may be withdrawn when due unless the right of the lawyer or law firm to receive it is disputed by the client or third person, in which event the disputed portion shall not be withdrawn until the dispute is finally resolved.

C. Notification of Receipt of Property; Safekeeping; Rendering Accounts; Payment or Delivery of Property. A lawyer shall:

1. Promptly notify a client or third person of the receipt of funds, securities, or other properties in which the client or third person has an interest.

2. Identify and label securities and properties of a client or third person promptly upon receipt and place them in a safe deposit box or other place of safekeeping as soon as practicable.

3. Maintain complete records of all funds, securities, and other properties of a client or third person coming into the possession of the lawyer and render appropriate accounts to the client or third person regarding them.

4. Promptly pay or deliver to the client or third person as requested by the client or third person the funds, securities, or other properties in the possession of the lawyer which the client or third person is entitled to receive.

D. Required Bookkeeping Records. A lawyer shall maintain for seven years after the events which they record:

1. The records of all deposits in and withdrawals from the accounts specified in subdivision (B) of this Disciplinary Rule and of any other bank account which concerns or affects the lawyer's practice of law. These records shall specifically identify the date, source and description of each item deposited, as well as the date, payee and purpose of each withdrawal or disbursement.

2. A record for special accounts, showing the source of all funds deposited in such accounts, the names of all persons for whom the funds are or were held, the amount of such funds, the description and amounts, and the names of all persons to whom such funds were disbursed.

3. Copies of all retainer and compensation agreements with clients.

4. Copies of all statements to clients or other persons showing the disbursement of funds to them or on their behalf.

5. Copies of all bills rendered to clients.

6. Copies of all records showing payments to lawyers, investigators or other persons, not in the lawyer's regular employ, for services rendered or performed.

7. Copies of all retainer and closing statements filed with the Office of Court Administration.

8. All checkbooks and checkstubs, bank statements, prenumbered cancelled checks and duplicate deposit slips.

Lawyers shall make accurate entries of all financial transactions in their records of receipts and disbursements, in their special accounts, in their ledger books or similar records, and in any other books of account kept by them in the regular course of their practice, which entries shall be made at or near the time of the act, condition or event recorded.

E. Authorized Signatories. All special account withdrawals shall be made only to a named payee and not to cash. Such withdrawals shall be made by check or, with the prior written approval of the party entitled to the proceeds, by bank transfer. Only an attorney admitted to practice law in New York State shall be an authorized signatory of a special account.

F. Missing Clients. Whenever any sum of money is payable to a client and the lawyer is unable to locate the client, the lawyer shall apply to the court in which the action was brought, or, if no action was commenced, to the Supreme Court in the county in which the lawyer has his or her office, for an order directing payment to the lawyer of his or her fee and disbursements and to the clerk of the court of the balance due to the client.

G. Dissolution of a Firm. Upon the dissolution of any firm of lawyers, the former partners or members shall make appropriate arrangements for the maintenance by one of them or by a successor firm of the records specified in subdivision (D) of this Disciplinary Rule.

DR 9-102 *N.Y. CODE OF PROFESSIONAL RESPONSIBILITY*

H. Availability of Bookkeeping Records; Records Subject to Production in Disciplinary Investigations and Proceedings. The financial records required by this Disciplinary Rule shall be located, or made available, at the principal New York State office of the lawyers subject hereto and any such records shall be produced in response to a notice or subpoena duces tecum issued in connection with a complaint before or any investigation by the appropriate grievance or departmental disciplinary committee, or shall be produced at the direction of the appropriate Appellate Division before any person designated by it. All books and records produced pursuant to this subdivision shall be kept confidential, except for the purpose of the particular proceeding, and their contents shall not be disclosed by anyone in violation of the lawyer-client privilege.

I. Disciplinary Action. A lawyer who does not maintain and keep the accounts and records as specified and required by this Disciplinary Rule, or who does not produce any such records pursuant to this Rule, shall be deemed in violation of these Rules and shall be subject to disciplinary proceedings.

WASHINGTON, D.C. RULES OF PROFESSIONAL CONDUCT

Scope

[1] The Rules of Professional Conduct are rules of reason. They should be interpreted with reference to the purposes of legal representation and of the law itself. Some of the Rules are imperatives, cast in the terms "shall" or "shall not." These define proper conduct for purposes of professional discipline. Others, generally cast in the term "may," are permissive and define areas under the Rules in which the lawyer has professional discretion. No disciplinary action should be taken when the lawyer chooses not to act or acts within the bounds of such discretion. Other Rules define the nature of relationships between the lawyer and others. The Rules are thus partly obligatory and disciplinary and partly constitutive and descriptive in that they define a lawyer's professional role. Many of the Comments use the term "should." Comments do not add obligations to the Rules but provide guidance for interpreting the Rules and practicing in compliance with them.

[2] The Rules presuppose a larger legal context shaping the lawyer's role. That context includes court rules and statutes relating to matters of licensure, laws defining specific obligations of lawyers, and substantive and procedural law in general. Compliance with the Rules, as with all law in an open society, depends primarily upon understanding and voluntary compliance, secondarily upon reinforcement by peer and public opinion, and finally, when necessary, upon enforcement through disciplinary proceedings. The Rules do not, however, exhaust the moral and ethical considerations that should inform a lawyer, for no worthwhile human activity can be completely defined by legal rules. The Rules simply provide a framework for the ethical practice of law.

[3] Failure to comply with an obligation or prohibition imposed by a Rule is a basis for invoking the disciplinary process. The Rules presuppose that disciplinary assessment of a lawyer's conduct will be made on the basis of the facts and circumstances as they existed at the time of the conduct in question and in recognition of the fact that a lawyer often has to act upon uncertain or incomplete evidence of the situation. Moreover, the Rules presuppose that whether or not discipline should be imposed for a violation, and the severity of a sanction, depend on all the circumstances, such as the willfulness and seriousness of the violation, extenuating factors and whether there have been previous violations.

[4] Violation of a Rule does not necessarily give rise to a cause of action, nor does it create a presumption that a legal duty has been violated. Some violations may be subject to redress only through the disciplinary process, and other violations may be relevant to liability only to a client of the lawyer who commits the violation. In appropriate cases, violation of a Rule may be evidence admissible in connection with a claim that a substantive duty has been violated, but in other cases evidence of such violations may not be admissible on the issue of the liability of the lawyer to others. Such issues are to be resolved by the tribunal having jurisdiction with respect to the substantive claims. Furthermore, nothing in these Rules, the Comments associated with them, or this Scope section is intended to alter existing requirements that the testimony of expert witnesses or

other modes of proof must be employed in determining the scope of a lawyer's duty to others. Finally, nothing in the Rules or associated Comments or this Scope section is intended to confer rights on an adversary of a lawyer to enforce the Rules in a proceeding other than a disciplinary proceeding. A tribunal presented with claims that the conduct of a lawyer appearing before that tribunal requires, for example, disqualification of the lawyer and/or the lawyer's firm may take such action as seems appropriate in the circumstances, which may or may not involve disqualification.

[5] The Comment accompanying each Rule explains and illustrates the meaning and purpose of the Rule. This note on Scope provides general orientation. The Comments are intended as guides to interpretation, but the text of each Rule is controlling.

Terminology

[1] "Belief" or "believes" denotes that the person involved actually supposed the fact in question to be true. A person's belief may be inferred from circumstances.

[2] "Consent" denotes a client's uncoerced assent to a proposed course of action, following consultation with the lawyer regarding the matter in question.

[3] "Consult" or "consultation" denotes communication of information reasonably sufficient to permit the client to appreciate the significance of the matter in question.

[4] "Firm" or "law firm" denotes a lawyer or lawyers in a private firm, lawyers employed in the legal department of a corporation or other organization, and lawyers employed in a legal services organization. See Comment, Rule 1.10.

[5] "Fraud" or "fraudulent" denotes conduct having a purpose to deceive and not merely negligent misrepresentation or failure to apprise another of relevant information.

[6] "Knowingly," "known," or "knows" denotes actual knowledge of the fact in question. A person's knowledge may be inferred from circumstances.

[7] "Law clerk" denotes a person, typically a recent law school graduate, who acts, typically for a limited period, as confidential assistant to a judge or judges of a court; to an administrative law judge or a similar administrative hearing officer; or to the head of a governmental agency or to a member of a governmental commission, either of which has authority to adjudicate or to promulgate rules or regulations of general application.

[8] "Partner" denotes a member of a partnership and a shareholder in a law firm organized as a professional corporation.

[9] "Reasonable" or "reasonably" when used in relation to conduct by a lawyer denotes the conduct of a reasonably prudent and competent lawyer.

[10] "Reasonably should know" when used in reference to a lawyer denotes that a lawyer of reasonable prudence and competence would ascertain the matter in question.

[11] "Substantial" when used in reference to degree or extent denotes a material matter of clear and weighty importance.

[12] "Tribunal" denotes a court, regulatory agency, commission, and any other body or individual authorized by law to render decisions of a judicial or

quasi-judicial nature, based on information presented before it, regardless of the degree of formality or informality of the proceedings.

Note to the Reader

The *D.C. Rules of Professional Conduct* have a unique page numbering system as well as two lapses in sequential numbering within the *Rules* themselves.

These *Rules* are divided into nine sections. Each of the sections is numbered independently of the others with a roman numeral preceding an arabic numeral. The roman numeral refers to one of the nine sections: Client–Lawyer Relationship (I), Counselor (II), Advocate (III), Transactions with Persons Other than Clients (IV), Law Firms and Associations (V), Public Service (VI), Information About Legal Services (VII), Maintaining the Integrity of the Profession (VIII), and Nondiscrimination by Members of the Bar (IX); the arabic number is the actual page number within the section.

The *Rules* were drafted following the numbering system promulgated by the American Bar Association in its *Model Rules of Professional Conduct*. Following the recommendation of the D.C. Bar Board of Governors, the D.C. Court of Appeals in its Order of March 1, 1990, chose not to adopt several rules included in the ABA *Model* and also elected not to renumber the remaining rules sequentially. Therefore, the section entitled Information About Legal Services contains no Rules 7.2, 7.3, and 7.4, and the section entitled Maintaining the Integrity of the Profession contains no Rule 8.2. These omissions are deliberate and do not represent an error in this text.

The Editors

CLIENT–LAWYER RELATIONSHIP

RULE 1.1 Competence

(a) A lawyer shall provide competent representation to a client. Competent representation requires the legal knowledge, skill, thoroughness, and preparation reasonably necessary for the representation.

(b) A lawyer shall serve a client with skill and care commensurate with that generally afforded to clients by other lawyers in similar matters.

COMMENT:

Legal Knowledge and Skill

[1] In determining whether a lawyer employs the requisite knowledge and skill in a particular matter, relevant factors include the relative complexity and specialized nature of the matter, the lawyer's general experience, the lawyer's training and experience in the field in question, the preparation and study the lawyer is able to give the matter, and whether it is feasible to refer the matter to, or associate or consult with, a lawyer of established competence in the field in question. In many instances, the required proficiency is that of a general practitioner. Expertise in a particular field of law may be required in some circumstances. One such circumstance would be where the lawyer, by representations made to the client, has led the client reasonably to expect a special level of expertise in the matter undertaken by the lawyer.

[2] A lawyer need not necessarily have special training or prior experience to handle legal problems of a type with which the lawyer is unfamiliar. A newly admitted lawyer can be as competent as a practitioner with long experience. Some important legal skills, such as the analysis of precedent, the evaluation of evidence, and legal drafting, are required in all legal problems. Perhaps the most fundamental legal skill consists of determining what kind of legal problems a situation may involve, a skill that necessarily transcends any particular specialized knowledge. A lawyer can provide adequate representation in a wholly novel field through necessary study. Competent representation can also be provided through the association of a lawyer of established competence in the field in question.

[3] In an emergency a lawyer may give advice or assistance in a matter in which the lawyer does not have the skill ordinarily required where referral to or consultation or association with another lawyer would be impractical. Even in an emergency, however, assistance should be limited to that reasonably necessary in the circumstances, for ill-considered action under emergency conditions can jeopardize the client's interest.

[4] A lawyer may accept representation where the requisite level of competence can be achieved by reasonable preparation. This applies as well to a lawyer who is appointed as counsel for an unrepresented person. *See also* Rule 6.2.

Thoroughness and Preparation

[5] Competent handling of a particular matter includes inquiry into and analysis of the factual and legal elements of the problem, and use of methods and procedures meeting the standards of competent practitioners. It also includes adequate preparation, and continuing attention to the needs of the representation to assure that there is no neglect of such needs. The required attention and preparation are determined in part by what is at stake; major litigation and complex transactions ordinarily require more elaborate treatment than matters of lesser consequence.

Maintaining Competence

[6] To maintain the requisite knowledge and skill, a lawyer should engage in such continuing study and education as may be necessary to maintain competence, taking into account that the learning acquired through a lawyer's practical experience in actual representations may reduce or eliminate the need for special continuing study or education. If a system of peer review has been established, the lawyer should consider making use of it in appropriate circumstances.

RULE 1.2 Scope of Representation

(a) **A lawyer shall abide by a client's decisions concerning the objectives of representation, subject to paragraphs (c), (d), and (e), and shall consult with the client as to the means by which they are to be pursued. A lawyer shall abide by a client's decision whether to accept an offer of settlement of a matter. In a criminal case, the lawyer shall abide by the client's decision, after consultation with the lawyer, as to a plea to be entered, whether to waive jury trial, and whether the client will testify.**

(b) A lawyer's representation of a client, including representation by appointment, does not constitute an endorsement of the client's political, economic, social, or moral views or activities.

(c) A lawyer may limit the objectives of the representation if the client consents after consultation.

(d) A government lawyer's authority and control over decisions concerning the representation may, by statute or regulation, be expanded beyond the limits imposed by paragraphs (a) and (c).

(e) A lawyer shall not counsel a client to engage, or assist a client, in conduct that the lawyer knows is criminal or fraudulent, but a lawyer may discuss the legal consequences of any proposed course of conduct with a client and may counsel or assist a client to make a good-faith effort to determine the validity, scope, meaning, or application of the law.

(f) When a lawyer knows that a client expects assistance not permitted by the rules of professional conduct or other law, the lawyer shall consult with the client regarding the relevant limitations on the lawyer's conduct.

COMMENT:

Scope of Representation

[1] Both lawyer and client have authority and responsibility in the objectives and means of representation. The client has ultimate authority to determine the purposes to be served by legal representation, within the limits imposed by law and the lawyer's professional obligations. Within these limits, a client also has a right to consult with the lawyer about the means to be used in pursuing those objectives. At the same time, a lawyer is not required to pursue objectives or employ means simply because a client may wish that the lawyer do so. A clear distinction between objectives and means sometimes cannot be drawn, and in many cases the client-lawyer relationship partakes of a joint undertaking. In questions of means, the lawyer should assume responsibility for technical and legal tactical issues, but should defer to the client regarding such questions as the expense to be incurred and concern for third persons who might be adversely affected. Law defining the lawyer's scope of authority in litigation varies among jurisdictions.

[2] In a case in which the client appears to be suffering mental disability, the lawyer's duty to abide by the client's decisions is to be guided by reference to Rule 1.14.

Independence From Client's Views or Activities

[3] Legal representation should not be denied to people who are unable to afford legal services, or whose cause is controversial or the subject of popular disapproval. By the same token, representing a client does not constitute approval of the client's views or activities.

Services Limited in Objectives or Means

[4] The objectives or scope of services provided by the lawyer may be limited by agreement with the client or by terms under which the lawyer's services are made available to the client. For example, a retainer may be for a specifically defined purpose. Representation provided through a legal aid agency may be subject to limitations on the types of cases the agency handles. When a lawyer

has been retained by an insurer to represent an insured, the representation may be limited to matters related to the insurance coverage. The terms upon which representation is undertaken may exclude specific objectives or means. Such limitations may exclude objectives or means that the lawyer regards as repugnant or imprudent.

[5] An agreement concerning the scope of representation must accord with the Rules of Professional Conduct and other law. Thus, the client may not be asked to agree to representation so limited in scope as to violate Rule 1.1, or to surrender the right to terminate the lawyer's services or the right to settle litigation that the lawyer might wish to continue.

Criminal, Fraudulent, and Prohibited Transactions

[6] A lawyer is required to give an honest opinion about the actual consequences that appear likely to result from a client's conduct. The fact that a client uses advice in a course of action that is criminal or fraudulent does not, of itself, make a lawyer a party to the course of action. However, a lawyer may not knowingly assist a client in criminal or fraudulent conduct. There is a critical distinction between presenting an analysis of legal aspects of questionable conduct and recommending the means by which a crime or fraud might be committed with impunity.

[7] When the client's course of action has already begun and is continuing, the lawyer's responsibility is especially delicate. The lawyer is not permitted to reveal the client's wrongdoing, except where permitted by Rule 1.6. However, the lawyer is required to avoid furthering the purpose, for example, by suggesting how it might be concealed. A lawyer may not continue assisting a client in conduct that the lawyer originally supposes is legally proper but then discovers is criminal or fraudulent. Withdrawal from the representation, therefore, may be required.

[8] Where the client is a fiduciary, the lawyer may be charged with special obligations in dealings with a beneficiary.

[9] Paragraph (e) applies whether or not the defrauded party is a party to the transaction. Hence, a lawyer should not participate in a sham transaction; for example, a transaction to effectuate criminal or fraudulent escape of tax liability. Paragraph (e) does not preclude undertaking a criminal defense incident to a general retainer for legal services to a lawful enterprise. The last clause of paragraph (e) recognizes that determining the validity or interpretation of a statute or regulation may require a course of action involving disobedience of the statute or regulation or of the interpretation placed upon it by governmental authorities.

RULE 1.3 Diligence and Zeal

(a) A lawyer shall represent a client zealously and diligently within the bounds of the law.

(b) A lawyer shall not intentionally:

(1) Fail to seek the lawful objectives of a client through reasonably available means permitted by law and the disciplinary rules; or

(2) Prejudice or damage a client during the course of the professional relationship.

(c) A lawyer shall act with reasonable promptness in representing a client.

COMMENT:

[1] The duty of a lawyer, both to the client and to the legal system, is to represent the client zealously within the bounds of the law, including the Rules of Professional Conduct and other enforceable professional regulations, such as agency regulations applicable to lawyers practicing before the agency. This duty requires the lawyer to pursue a matter on behalf of a client despite opposition, obstruction, or personal inconvenience to the lawyer, and to take whatever lawful and ethical measures are required to vindicate a client's cause or endeavor. A lawyer should act with commitment and dedication to the interests of the client. However, a lawyer is not bound to press for every advantage that might be realized for a client. A lawyer has professional discretion in determining the means by which a matter should be pursued. *See* Rule 1.2. A lawyer's work load should be controlled so that each matter can be handled adequately.

[2] This duty derives from the lawyer's membership in a profession that has the duty of assisting members of the public to secure and protect available legal rights and benefits. In our government of laws and not of individuals, each member of our society is entitled to have such member's conduct judged and regulated in accordance with the law; to seek any lawful objective through legally permissible means; and to present for adjudication any lawful claim, issue, or defense.

[3] The bounds of the law in a given case are often difficult to ascertain. The language of legislative enactments and judicial opinions may be uncertain as applied to varying factual situations. The limits and specific meaning of apparently relevant law may be made doubtful by changing or developing constitutional interpretations, ambiguous statutes, or judicial opinions, and changing public and judicial attitudes.

[4] Where the bounds of law are uncertain, the action of a lawyer may depend on whether the lawyer is serving as advocate or adviser. A lawyer may serve simultaneously as both advocate and adviser, but the two roles are essentially different. In asserting a position on behalf of a client, an advocate for the most part deals with past conduct and must take the facts as the advocate finds them. By contrast, a lawyer serving as adviser primarily assists the client in determining the course of future conduct and relationships. While serving as advocate, a lawyer should resolve in favor of the client doubts as to the bounds of the law, but even when acting as an advocate, a lawyer may not institute or defend a proceeding unless the positions taken are not frivolous. *See* Rule 3.1. In serving a client as adviser, a lawyer, in appropriate circumstances, should give a lawyer's professional opinion as to what the ultimate decisions of the courts would likely be as to the applicable law.

[5] In the exercise of professional judgment, a lawyer should always act in a manner consistent with the best interests of the client. However, when an action in the best interests of the client seems to be unjust, a lawyer may ask the client for permission to forgo such action. If the lawyer knows that the client expects assistance that is not in accord with the Rules of Professional Conduct or other law, the lawyer must inform the client of the pertinent limitations on the lawyer's conduct. *See* Rule 1.2(e) and (f). Similarly, the lawyer's obligation not to prejudice the interests of the client is subject to the duty of candor toward the tribunal under Rule 3.3 and the duty to expedite litigation under Rule 3.2.

[6] The duty of a lawyer to represent the client with zeal does not militate against the concurrent obligation to treat with consideration all persons involved

in the legal process and to avoid the infliction of needless harm. Thus, the lawyer's duty to pursue a client's lawful objectives zealously does not prevent the lawyer from acceding to reasonable requests of opposing counsel that do not prejudice the client's rights, being punctual in fulfilling all professional commitments, avoiding offensive tactics, or treating all persons involved in the legal process with courtesy and consideration.

[7] Perhaps no professional shortcoming is more widely resented by clients than procrastination. A client's interests often can be adversely affected by the passage of time or the change of conditions; in extreme instances, as when a lawyer overlooks a statute of limitations, the client's legal position may be destroyed. Even when the client's interests are not affected in substance, however, unreasonable delay can cause a client needless anxiety and undermine confidence in the lawyer's trustworthiness. Neglect of client matters is a serious violation of the obligation of diligence.

[8] Unless the relationship is terminated as provided in Rule 1.16, a lawyer should carry through to conclusion all matters undertaken for a client. If a lawyer's employment is limited to a specific matter, the relationship terminates when the matter has been resolved. If a lawyer has served a client over a substantial period in a variety of matters, the client sometimes may assume that the lawyer will continue to serve on a continuing basis unless the lawyer gives notice of withdrawal. Doubt about whether a client-lawyer relationship still exists should be eliminated by the lawyer, preferably in writing, so that the client will not mistakenly suppose the lawyer is looking after the client's affairs when the lawyer has ceased to do so. For example, if a lawyer has handled a judicial or administrative proceeding that produced a result adverse to the client but has not been specifically instructed concerning pursuit of an appeal, the lawyer should advise the client of the possibility of appeal before relinquishing responsibility for the matter.

RULE 1.4 Communication

(a) A lawyer shall keep a client reasonably informed about the status of a matter and promptly comply with reasonable requests for information.

(b) A lawyer shall explain a matter to the extent reasonably necessary to permit the client to make informed decisions regarding the representation.

(c) A lawyer who receives an offer of settlement in a civil case or a proffered plea bargain in a criminal case shall inform the client promptly of the substance of the communication.

COMMENT:

[1] The client should have sufficient information to participate intelligently in decisions concerning the objectives of the representation and the means by which they are to be pursued, to the extent the client is willing and able to do so. For example, a lawyer negotiating on behalf of a client should provide the client with facts relevant to the matter, inform the client of communications from another party, and take other reasonable steps that permit the client to make a decision regarding a serious offer from another party. A lawyer who receives from opposing counsel an offer of settlement in a civil controversy or a proffered plea bargain in a criminal case is required to inform the client promptly of its substance. *See* Rule 1.2(a). Even when a client delegates authority to the lawyer, the client should be kept advised of the status of the matter.

[2] A client is entitled to whatever information the client wishes about all aspects of the subject matter of the representation unless the client expressly consents not to have certain information passed on. The lawyer must be particularly careful to ensure that decisions of the client are made only after the client has been informed of all relevant considerations. The lawyer must initiate and maintain the consultative and decision-making process if the client does not do so and must ensure that the ongoing process is thorough and complete.

[3] Adequacy of communication depends in part on the kind of advice or assistance involved. The guiding principle is that the lawyer should fulfill reasonable client expectations for information consistent with (1) the duty to act in the client's best interests, and (2) the client's overall requirements and objectives as to the character of representation.

[4] Ordinarily, the information to be provided is that appropriate for a client who is a comprehending and responsible adult. However, fully informing the client according to this standard may be impracticable, for example, where the client is a child or suffers from mental disability. See Rule 1.14. When the client is an organization or group, it is often impossible or inappropriate to inform every one of its members about its legal affairs; ordinarily, the lawyer should address communications to the appropriate officials of the organization. See Rule 1.13. Where many routine matters are involved, a system of limited or occasional reporting may be arranged with the client. Practical exigency may also require a lawyer to act for a client without prior consultation. When the lawyer is conducting a trial, it is often not possible for the lawyer to consult with the client and obtain the client's acquiescence in tactical matters arising during the course of trial. It is sufficient if the lawyer consults with the client in advance of trial on significant issues that can be anticipated as arising during the course of the trial, and consults during trial to the extent practical, given the nature of the trial process.

Withholding Information

[5] In rare circumstances, a lawyer may be justified in delaying transmission of information when the client would be likely to react imprudently to an immediate communication. Thus, a lawyer might withhold a psychiatric diagnosis of a client when the examining psychiatrist indicates that disclosure would harm the client. Similarly, a lawyer may be justified, for humanitarian reasons, in not conveying certain information, for example, where the information would merely be upsetting to a terminally ill client. A lawyer may not withhold information to serve the lawyer's own interest or convenience. Rules or court orders governing litigation (such as a protective order limiting access to certain types of discovery material to counsel only) may provide that information supplied to a lawyer may not be disclosed to the client. Rule 3.4(c) directs compliance with such rules or orders.

RULE 1.5 Fees

(a) A lawyer's fee shall be reasonable. The factors to be considered in determining the reasonableness of a fee include the following:

(1) The time and labor required, the novelty and difficulty of the questions involved, and the skill requisite to perform the legal service properly;

(2) The likelihood, if apparent to the client, that the acceptance of the particular employment will preclude other employment by the lawyer;

(3) The fee customarily charged in the locality for similar legal services;

(4) The amount involved and the results obtained;

(5) The time limitations imposed by the client or by the circumstances;

(6) The nature and length of the professional relationship with the client;

(7) The experience, reputation, and ability of the lawyer or lawyers performing the services; and

(8) Whether the fee is fixed or contingent.

(b) When the lawyer has not regularly represented the client, the basis or rate of the fee shall be communicated to the client, in writing, before or within a reasonable time after commencing the representation.

(c) A fee may be contingent on the outcome of the matter for which the service is rendered, except in a matter in which a contingent fee is prohibited by paragraph (d) or other law. A contingent fee agreement shall be in writing and shall state the method by which the fee is to be determined, including the percentage or percentages that shall accrue to the lawyer in the event of settlement, trial or appeal, litigation, and other expenses to be deducted from the recovery, and whether such expenses are to be deducted before or after the contingent fee is calculated. Upon conclusion of a contingent fee matter, the lawyer shall provide the client with a written statement stating the outcome of the matter and, if there is a recovery, showing the remittance to the client and the method of its determination.

(d) A lawyer shall not enter into an arrangement for, charge, or collect a contingent fee for representing a defendant in a criminal case.

(e) A division of a fee between lawyers who are not in the same firm may be made only if:

(1) The division is in proportion to the services performed by each lawyer or each lawyer assumes joint responsibility for the representation;

(2) The client is advised, in writing, of the identity of the lawyers who will participate in the representation, of the contemplated division of responsibility, and of the effect of the association of lawyers outside the firm on the fee to be charged;

(3) The client consents to the arrangement; and

(4) The total fee is reasonable.

COMMENT:

Basis or Rate of Fee

[1] When the lawyer has regularly represented a client, they ordinarily will have evolved an understanding concerning the basis or rate of the fee. In a new client-lawyer relationship, however, an understanding as to the fee should be promptly established. It is not necessary to recite all the factors that underlie the basis of the fee, but only those that are directly involved in its computation. It is sufficient, for example, to state that the basic rate is an hourly charge or a fixed amount or an estimated amount, or to identify the factors that may be

taken into account in finally fixing the fee. When developments occur during the representation that render an earlier estimate substantially inaccurate, a revised estimate should be provided to the client.

[2] A written statement concerning the fee, required to be furnished in advance in most cases by paragraph (b), reduces the possibility of misunderstanding. In circumstances in which paragraph (b) requires that the basis for the lawyer's fee be in writing, an individualized writing specific to the particular client and representation is generally not required. Unless there are unique aspects of the fee arrangement, the lawyer may utilize a standardized letter, memorandum, or pamphlet explaining the lawyer's fee practices, and indicating those practices applicable to the specific representation. Such publications would, for example, explain applicable hourly billing rates, if billing on an hourly rate basis is contemplated, and indicate what charges (such as filing fees, transcript costs, duplicating costs, long-distance telephone charges) are imposed in addition to hourly rate charges.

[3] Where the services to be rendered are covered by a fixed-fee schedule that adequately informs the client of the charges to be imposed, a copy of such schedule may be utilized to satisfy the requirement for a writing. Such services as routine real estate transactions, uncontested divorces, or preparation of simple wills, for example, may be suitable for description in such a fixed-fee schedule.

Terms of Payment

[4] A lawyer may require advance payment of a fee, but is obliged to return any unearned portion. See Rule 1.16(d). A lawyer may accept property in payment for services, such as an ownership interest in an enterprise. However, a fee paid in property instead of money may be subject to special scrutiny because it involves questions concerning both the value of the services and the lawyer's special knowledge of the value of the property.

[5] An agreement may not be made whose terms might induce the lawyer improperly to curtail services for the client or perform them in a way contrary to the client's interest. For example, a lawyer should not enter into an agreement whereby services are to be provided only up to a stated amount when it is foreseeable that more extensive services probably will be required, unless the situation is adequately explained to the client. Otherwise, the client might have to bargain for further assistance in the midst of a proceeding or transaction. However, it is proper to define the extent of services in light of the client's ability to pay. A lawyer should not exploit a fee arrangement based primarily on hourly charges by using wasteful procedures.

Contingent Fees

[6] Generally, contingent fees are permissible in all civil cases. However, paragraph (d) continues the prohibition, imposed under the previous Code of Professional Responsibility, against the use of a contingent fee arrangement by a lawyer representing a defendant in a criminal case. Applicable law may impose other limitations on contingent fees, such as a ceiling on the percentage. And in any case, if there is doubt whether a contingent fee is consistent with the client's best interests, the lawyer should explain any existing payment alternatives and their implications.

[7] Contingent fees in domestic relations cases, while rarely justified, are not prohibited by Rule 1.5. Contingent fees in such cases are permitted in order that

lawyers may provide representation to clients who might not otherwise be able to afford to contract for the payment of fees on a noncontingent basis.

[8] Paragraph (c) requires that the contingent fee arrangement be in writing. This writing must explain the method by which the fee is to be computed. The lawyer must also provide the client with a written statement at the conclusion of a contingent fee matter, stating the outcome of the matter and explaining the computation of any remittance made to the client.

Division of Fee

[9] A division of fee is a single billing to a client covering the fee of two or more lawyers who are not in the same firm. A division of fee facilitates association of more than one lawyer in a matter in which neither alone could serve the client as well, and most often is used when the fee is contingent and the division is between a referring lawyer and a trial specialist.

[10] Paragraph (e) permits the lawyers to divide a fee either on the basis of the proportion of services they render or by agreement between the participating lawyers if all assume responsibility for the representation as a whole. Joint responsibility for the representation entails the obligations stated in Rule 5.1 for purposes of the matter involved. Permitting a division on the basis of joint responsibility, rather than on the basis of services performed, represents a change from the basis for fee divisions allowed under the prior Code of Professional Responsibility. The change is intended to encourage lawyers to affiliate other counsel, who are better equipped by reason of experience or specialized background to serve the client's needs, rather than to retain sole responsibility for the representation in order to avoid losing the right to a fee.

[11] The concept of joint responsibility is not, however, merely a technicality or incantation. The lawyer who refers the client to another lawyer, or affiliates another lawyer in the representation, remains fully responsible to the client, and is accountable to the client for deficiencies in the discharge of the representation by the lawyer who has been brought into the representation. If a lawyer wishes to avoid such responsibility for the potential deficiencies of another lawyer, the matter must be referred to the other lawyer without retaining a right to participate in fees beyond those fees justified by services actually rendered.

[12] The concept of joint responsibility does not require the referring lawyer to perform any minimum portion of the total legal services rendered. The referring lawyer may agree that the lawyer to whom the referral is made will perform substantially all of the services to be rendered in connection with the representation, without review by the referring lawyer. Thus, the referring lawyer is not required to review pleadings or other documents, attend hearings or depositions, or otherwise participate in a significant and continuing manner. The referring lawyer does not, however, escape the implications of joint responsibility, see Comment [11], by avoiding direct participation.

[13] When fee divisions are based on assumed joint responsibility, the requirement of paragraph (a) that the fee be reasonable applies to the total fee charged for the representation by all participating lawyers.

[14] Paragraph (e) requires that the client be advised, in writing, of the fee division and states that the client must affirmatively consent to the proposed fee arrangement. The Rule does not require disclosure to the client of the share that each lawyer is to receive but does require that the client be informed of the

identity of the lawyers sharing the fee, their respective responsibilities in the representation, and the effect of the association of lawyers outside the firm on the fee charged.

Disputes Over Fees

[15] If a procedure has been established for resolution of fee disputes, such as an arbitration or mediation procedure established by the Bar, the lawyer should conscientiously consider submitting to it. Law may prescribe a procedure for determining a lawyer's fee, for example, in representation of an executor or administrator, a class, or a person entitled to a reasonable fee as part of the measure of damages. The lawyer entitled to such a fee and a lawyer representing another party concerned with the fee should comply with the prescribed procedure.

RULE 1.6 Confidentiality of Information

(a) Except when permitted under paragraph (c) or (d), a lawyer shall not knowingly:

(1) Reveal a confidence or secret of the lawyer's client;

(2) Use a confidence or secret of the lawyer's client to the disadvantage of the client;

(3) Use a confidence or secret of the lawyer's client for the advantage of the lawyer or of a third person.

(b) "Confidence" refers to information protected by the attorney-client privilege under applicable law, and "secret" refers to other information gained in the professional relationship that the client has requested be held inviolate, or the disclosure of which would be embarrassing, or would be likely to be detrimental, to the client.

(c) A lawyer may reveal client confidences and secrets, to the extent reasonably necessary:

(1) To prevent a criminal act that the lawyer reasonably believes is likely to result in death or substantial bodily harm absent disclosure of the client's secrets or confidences by the lawyer; or

(2) To prevent the bribery or intimidation of witnesses, jurors, court officials, or other persons who are involved in proceedings before a tribunal if the lawyer reasonably believes that such acts are likely to result absent disclosure of the client's confidences or secrets by the lawyer.

(d) A lawyer may use or reveal client confidences or secrets:

(1) With the consent of the client affected, but only after full disclosure to the client;

(2)(A) When permitted by these Rules or required by law or court order; and

(B) If a government lawyer, when permitted or authorized by law;

(3) To the extent reasonably necessary to establish a defense to a criminal charge, disciplinary charge, or civil claim, formally instituted against the lawyer, based upon conduct in which the client was involved, or to the extent reasonably necessary to respond to specific allegations by the client concerning the lawyer's representation of the client;

(4) When the lawyer has reasonable grounds for believing that a client has impliedly authorized disclosure of a confidence or secret in order to carry out the representation; or

(5) To the minimum extent necessary in an action instituted by the lawyer to establish or collect the lawyer's fee.

(e) A lawyer shall exercise reasonable care to prevent the lawyer's employees, associates, and others whose services are utilized by the lawyer from disclosing or using confidences or secrets of a client, except that a lawyer may reveal the information required to be disclosed by paragraph (c) and the information permitted to be disclosed by paragraph (d) through such persons.

(f) The lawyer's obligation to preserve the client's confidences and secrets continues after termination of the lawyer's employment.

(g) The obligation of a lawyer under paragraph (a) also applies to confidences and secrets learned prior to becoming a lawyer in the course of providing assistance to another lawyer.

(h) A lawyer who serves as a member of the D.C. Bar Lawyer Counseling Committee, or as a trained intervenor for that committee, shall be deemed to have a lawyer-client relationship with respect to any lawyer-counselee being counseled under programs conducted by or on behalf of the committee. Information obtained from another lawyer being counseled under the auspices of the committee, or in the course of and associated with such counseling, shall be treated as a confidence or secret within the terms of paragraph (b). Such information may be disclosed only to the extent permitted by this rule.

(i) The client of the government lawyer is the agency that employs the lawyer unless expressly provided to the contrary by appropriate law, regulation, or order.

COMMENT:

[1] The lawyer is part of a judicial system charged with upholding the law. One of the lawyer's functions is to advise clients so that they avoid any violation of the law in the proper exercise of their rights.

[2] The observance of the ethical obligation of a lawyer to hold inviolate confidential information of the client not only facilitates the full development of facts essential to proper representation of the client but also encourages people to seek early legal assistance.

[3] Almost without exception, clients come to lawyers in order to determine what their rights are and what is, in the maze of laws and regulations, deemed to be legal and correct. The common law recognizes that the client's confidences must be protected from disclosure. Based upon experience, lawyers know that almost all clients follow the advice given, and the law is upheld.

[4] A fundamental principle in the client-lawyer relationship is that the lawyer holds inviolate the client's secrets and confidences. The client is thereby encouraged to communicate fully and frankly with the lawyer even as to embarrassing or legally damaging subject matter.

Relationship Between Rule 1.6 and Attorney–Client Evidentiary Privilege and Work Product Doctrine

[5] The principle of confidentiality is given effect in two related bodies of law: the attorney-client privilege and the work product doctrine in the law of evidence and the rule of confidentiality established in professional ethics. The attorney-client privilege and the work product doctrine apply in judicial and other proceedings in which a lawyer may be called as a witness or otherwise required to produce evidence concerning a client. This Rule is not intended to govern or affect judicial application of the attorney-client privilege or work product doctrine. The privilege and doctrine were developed to promote compliance with law and fairness in litigation. In reliance on the attorney-client privilege, clients are entitled to expect that communications within the scope of the privilege will be protected against compelled disclosure. The attorney-client privilege is that of the client and not of the lawyer. The fact that in exceptional situations the lawyer under this Rule has limited discretion to disclose a client confidence does not vitiate the proposition that, as a general matter, the client has a reasonable expectation that information relating to the client will not be voluntarily disclosed and that disclosure of such information may be judicially compelled only in accordance with recognized exceptions to the attorney-client privilege and work product doctrine.

[6] The rule of client-lawyer confidentiality applies in situations other than those where evidence is sought from the lawyer through compulsion of law; furthermore, it applies not merely to matters communicated in confidence by the client (i.e., confidences) but also to all information gained in the course of the professional relationship that the client has requested be held inviolate, or the disclosure of which would be embarrassing or would be likely to be detrimental to the client (i.e., secrets). This ethical precept, unlike the evidentiary privilege, exists without regard to the nature or source of the information or the fact that others share the knowledge. It reflects not only the principles underlying the attorney-client privilege, but the lawyer's duty of loyalty to the client.

The Commencement of the Client–Lawyer Relationship

[7] Principles of substantive law external to these Rules determine whether a client-lawyer relationship exists. Although most of the duties flowing from the client-lawyer relationship attach only after the client has requested the lawyer to render legal services and the lawyer has agreed to do so, the duty of confidentiality imposed by this Rule attaches when the lawyer agrees to consider whether a client-lawyer relationship shall be established. Thus, a lawyer may be subject to a duty of confidentiality with respect to information disclosed by a client to enable the lawyer to determine whether representation of the potential client would involve a prohibited conflict of interest under Rule 1.7, 1.8, or 1.9.

Exploitation of Confidences and Secrets

[8] In addition to prohibiting the disclosure of a client's confidences and secrets, subparagraph (a)(2) provides that a lawyer may not use the client's confidences and secrets to the disadvantage of the client. For example, a lawyer who has learned that the client is investing in specific real estate may not seek to acquire nearby property where doing so would adversely affect the client's plan for investment. Similarly, information acquired by the lawyer in the course of representing a client may not be used to the disadvantage of that client even

after the termination of the lawyer's representation of the client. However, the fact that a lawyer has once served a client does not preclude the lawyer from using generally known information about the former client when later representing another client. Under subparagraphs (a)(3) and (d)(1) a lawyer may use a client's confidences and secrets for the lawyer's own benefit or that of a third party only after the lawyer has made full disclosure to the client regarding the proposed use of the information and obtained the client's affirmative consent to the use in question.

Authorized Disclosure

[9] A lawyer is impliedly authorized to make disclosures about a client when appropriate in carrying out the representation, except to the extent that the client's instructions or special circumstances limit that authority. In litigation, for example, a lawyer may disclose information by admitting a fact that cannot properly be disputed, or in negotiation by making a disclosure that facilitates a satisfactory conclusion.

[10] The obligation to protect confidences and secrets obviously does not preclude a lawyer from revealing information when the client consents after full disclosure, when necessary to perform the professional employment, when permitted by these Rules, or when required by law. Unless the client otherwise directs, a lawyer may disclose the affairs of the client to partners or associates of the lawyer's firm. It is a matter of common knowledge that the normal operation of a law office exposes confidential professional information to nonlawyer employees of the office, particularly secretaries and those having access to the files; and this obligates a lawyer to exercise care in selecting and training employees so that the sanctity of all confidences and secrets of clients may be preserved. If the obligation extends to two or more clients as to the same information, a lawyer should obtain the permission of all before revealing the information. A lawyer must always be sensitive to the rights and wishes of the client and act scrupulously in the making of decisions that may involve the disclosure of information obtained in the course of the professional relationship. Thus, in the absence of consent of the client after full disclosure, a lawyer should not associate another lawyer in the handling of a matter; nor should the lawyer, in the absence of consent, seek counsel from another lawyer if there is a reasonable possibility that the identity of the client or the client's confidences or secrets would be revealed to such lawyer. Proper concern for professional duty should cause a lawyer to shun indiscreet conversations concerning clients.

[11] Unless the client otherwise directs, it is not improper for a lawyer to give limited information from client files to an outside agency necessary for statistical, bookkeeping, accounting, data processing, banking, printing, or other legitimate purposes, provided the lawyer exercises due care in the selection of the agency and warns the agency that the information must be kept confidential.

Disclosure Adverse to Client

[12] The confidentiality rule is subject to limited exceptions. In becoming privy to information about a client, a lawyer may foresee that the client intends serious harm to another person. However, to the extent a lawyer is required or permitted to disclose a client's purposes, the client will be inhibited from revealing facts that would enable the lawyer to counsel against a wrongful course of action. The public is better protected if full and open communication

by the client is encouraged than if it is inhibited. Nevertheless, when the client's confidences or secrets are such that the lawyer knows or reasonably should know that the client or any other person is likely to kill or do substantial bodily injury to another unless the lawyer discloses client confidences or secrets, the lawyer may reveal the client's confidences and secrets if necessary to prevent harm to the third party.

[13] Several situations must be distinguished.

[14] First, the lawyer may not counsel or assist a client to engage in conduct that is criminal or fraudulent. *See* Rule 1.2(e). Similarly, a lawyer has a duty not to use false evidence of a nonclient and may permit introduction of the false evidence of a client only in extremely limited circumstances in criminal cases when the witness is the defendant client. *See* Rule 3.3(a)(4) and (b). This Rule is essentially a special instance of the duty prescribed in Rule 1.2(e) to avoid assisting a client in criminal or fraudulent conduct.

[15] Second, the lawyer may have been innocently involved in past conduct by the client that was criminal or fraudulent. In such a situation the lawyer has not violated Rule 1.2(e), because to "counsel or assist" criminal or fraudulent conduct requires knowing that the conduct is of that character.

[16] Third, the lawyer may learn that a client intends prospective conduct that is criminal and likely to result in death or substantial bodily harm unless disclosure of the client's intentions is made by the lawyer. As stated in paragraph (c), the lawyer has professional discretion to reveal information in order to prevent such consequences. The lawyer may make a disclosure in order to prevent homicide or serious bodily injury which the lawyer reasonably believes is intended by a client. The "reasonably believes" standard is applied because it is very difficult for a lawyer to "know" when such a heinous purpose will actually be carried out, for the client may have a change of mind.

[17] The lawyer's exercise of discretion in determining whether to make disclosures that are reasonably likely to prevent the death or substantial bodily injury of another requires consideration of such factors as the client's tendency to commit violent acts or, conversely, to make idle threats. In any case, a disclosure adverse to the client's interest should be no greater than the lawyer reasonably believes necessary to the purpose. A lawyer's decision not to take preventive action permitted by subparagraph (c)(1) does not violate this Rule.

Withdrawal

[18] If the lawyer's services will be used by the client in materially furthering a course of criminal or fraudulent conduct, the lawyer must withdraw, as stated in Rule 1.16(a)(1). If the client persists in a course of action involving the lawyer's services that the lawyer reasonably believes is criminal or fraudulent, or if the client has used the lawyer's services to perpetrate a crime or a fraud, the lawyer may (but is not required to) withdraw, as stated in Rule 1.16(b)(1) and (2).

[19] After withdrawal under either Rule 1.16(a)(1) or Rule 1.16(b)(1) or (2), the lawyer is required to refrain from making disclosure of the client's confidences, except as otherwise provided in Rule 1.6. Giving notice of withdrawal, without elaboration, is not a disclosure of a client's confidences and is not proscribed by this Rule or by Rule 1.16(d). Furthermore, a lawyer's statement to a court that withdrawal is based upon "irreconcilable differences between the lawyer and the client," as provided under paragraph [3] of the Comment to Rule

1.16, is not elaboration. Similarly, after withdrawal under either Rule 1.16(a)(1) or Rule 1.16(b)(1) or (2), the lawyer may retract or disaffirm any opinion, document, affirmation, or the like that contains a material misrepresentation by the lawyer that the lawyer reasonably believes will be relied upon by others to their detriment.

[20] Where the client is an organization, the lawyer may be in doubt whether contemplated conduct will actually be carried out by the organization. Where necessary to guide conduct in connection with this Rule, the lawyer may make inquiry within the organization. See Comment to Rule 1.13.

Dispute Concerning Lawyer's Conduct

[21] Where a legal claim or disciplinary charge alleges complicity of the lawyer in a client's conduct or other misconduct of the lawyer involving representation of the client, the lawyer may respond to the extent the lawyer reasonably believes necessary to establish a defense. The same is true with respect to a claim involving the conduct or representation of a former client. Charges, in defense of which a lawyer may disclose client confidences and secrets, can arise in a civil, criminal, or professional disciplinary proceeding, and can be based on a wrong allegedly committed by the lawyer against the client, or on a wrong alleged by a third person; for example, a person claiming to have been defrauded by the lawyer and client acting together.

[22] The lawyer may not disclose a client's confidences or secrets to defend against informal allegations made by third parties; the Rule allows disclosure only if a third party has formally instituted a civil, criminal, or disciplinary action against the lawyer. Even if the third party has formally instituted such a proceeding, the lawyer should advise the client of the third party's action and request that the client respond appropriately, if this is practicable and would not be prejudicial to the lawyer's ability to establish a defense.

[23] If a lawyer's client, or former client, has made specific allegations against the lawyer, the lawyer may disclose that client's confidences and secrets in establishing a defense, without waiting for formal proceedings to be commenced. The requirement of subparagraph (d)(3) that there be "specific" charges of misconduct by the client precludes the lawyer from disclosing confidences or secrets in response to general criticism by a client; an example of such a general criticism would be an assertion by the client that the lawyer "did a poor job" of representing the client. But in this situation, as well as in the defense of formally instituted third-party proceedings, disclosure should be no greater than the lawyer reasonably believes is necessary to vindicate innocence, the disclosure should be made in a manner that limits access to the information to the tribunal or other persons having a need to know it, and appropriate protective orders or other arrangements should be sought by the lawyer to the fullest extent practicable.

Fee Collection Actions

[24] Subparagraph (d)(5) permits a lawyer to reveal a client's confidences or secrets if this is necessary in an action to collect fees from the client. This aspect of the Rule expresses the principle that the beneficiary of a fiduciary relationship may not exploit it to the detriment of the fiduciary. Subparagraph (d)(5) should be construed narrowly; it does not authorize broad, indiscriminate disclosure of secrets or confidences. The lawyer should evaluate the necessity

for disclosure of information at each stage of the action. For example, in drafting the complaint in a fee collection suit, it would be necessary to reveal the "secrets" that the lawyer was retained by the client, that fees are due, and that the client has failed to pay those fees. Further disclosure of the client's secrets and confidences would be impermissible at the complaint stage. If possible, the lawyer should prevent even the disclosure of the client's identity through the use of John Doe pleadings.

[25] If the client's response to the lawyer's complaint raised issues implicating confidences or secrets, the lawyer would be permitted to disclose confidential or secret information pertinent to the client's claims or defenses. Even then, the Rule would require that the lawyer's response be narrowly tailored to meet the client's specific allegations, with the minimum degree of disclosure sufficient to respond effectively. In addition, the lawyer should continue, throughout the action, to make every effort to avoid unnecessary disclosure of the client's confidences and secrets and to limit the disclosure to those having the need to know it. To this end the lawyer should seek appropriate protective orders and make any other arrangements that would minimize the risk of disclosure of the confidential information in question, including the utilization of in camera proceedings.

Disclosures Otherwise Required or Authorized

[26] The attorney-client privilege is differently defined in various jurisdictions. If a lawyer is called as a witness to give testimony concerning a client, absent waiver by the client, subparagraph (d)(2) requires the lawyer to invoke the privilege when it is applicable. The lawyer may comply with the final orders of a court or other tribunal of competent jurisdiction requiring the lawyer to give information about the client. But a lawyer ordered by a court to disclose client confidences or secrets should not comply with the order until the lawyer has personally made every reasonable effort to appeal the order or has notified the client of the order and given the client the opportunity to challenge it.

[27] The Rules of Professional Conduct in various circumstances permit or require a lawyer to disclose information relating to the representation. *See* Rules 2.2, 2.3, 3.3, and 4.1. In addition to these provisions, a lawyer may be obligated or permitted by other provisions of law to give information about a client. Whether another provision of law supersedes Rule 1.6 is a matter of interpretation beyond the scope of these Rules, but a presumption exists against such a supersession.

Former Client

[28] The duty of confidentiality continues after the client-lawyer relationship has terminated.

Services Rendered in Assisting Another Lawyer Before Becoming a Member of the Bar

[29] There are circumstances in which a person who ultimately becomes a lawyer provides assistance to a lawyer while serving in a nonlawyer capacity. The typical situation is that of the law clerk or summer associate in a law firm or government agency. Paragraph (g) addresses the confidentiality obligations of such a person after becoming a member of the Bar; the same confidentiality obligations are imposed as would apply if the person had been a member of the

Bar at the time confidences or secrets were received. This resolution of the confidentiality obligation is consistent with the reasoning employed in D.C. Bar Legal Ethics Committee Opinion 84 (1980). For a related provision dealing with the imputation of disqualifications arising from prior participation as a law clerk, summer associate, or in a similar position, *see* Rule 1.10(b).

[30] Paragraph (h) adds a provision dealing specifically with the disclosure obligations of lawyers who are assisting in the counseling programs of the D.C. Bar's Lawyer Counseling Committee. Members of that committee, and lawyer-intervenors who assist the committee in counseling, may obtain information from lawyer-counselees who have sought assistance from the counseling programs offered by the committee. It is in the interests of the public to encourage lawyers who have alcohol or other substance abuse problems to seek counseling as a first step toward rehabilitation. Some lawyers who seek such assistance may have violated provisions of the Rules of Professional Conduct, or other provisions of law, including criminal statutes such as those dealing with embezzlement. In order for those who are providing counseling services to evaluate properly the lawyer-counselee's problems and enhance the prospects for rehabilitation, it is necessary for the counselors to receive completely candid information from the lawyer-counselee. Such candor is not likely if the counselor, for example, would be compelled by Rule 8.3 to report the lawyer-counselee's conduct to Bar Counsel, or if the lawyer-counselee feared that the counselor could be compelled by prosecutors or others to disclose information.

[31] These considerations make it appropriate to treat the lawyer-counselee relationship as a lawyer-client relationship, and to create an additional limited class of information treated as secrets or confidences subject to the protection of Rule 1.6. The scope of that information is set forth in paragraph (h).

[32] Rules established by the District of Columbia Court of Appeals with respect to the kinds of information protected from compelled disclosure may not be accepted by other forums or jurisdictions. Therefore, the protections afforded to lawyer-counselees by paragraph (h) may not be available to preclude disclosure in all circumstances. Furthermore, lawyers who are members of the bar of other jurisdictions may not be entitled under the ethics rules applicable to members of the bar in such other jurisdictions, to forgo reporting violations to disciplinary authorities pursuant to the other jurisdictions' counterparts to Rule 8.3.

Government Lawyers

[33] Subparagraph (d)(2) was revised, and paragraph (i) was added, to address the unique circumstances raised by attorney-client relationships within the government.

[34] Subparagraph (d)(2)(A) applies to both private and government attorney-client relationships. Subparagraph (d)(2)(B) applies to government lawyers only. It is designed to permit disclosures that are not required by law or court order under Rule 1.6(d)(2)(A), but which the government authorizes its attorneys to make in connection with their professional services to the government. Such disclosures may be authorized or required by statute, executive order, or regulation, depending on the constitutional or statutory powers of the authorizing entity. If so authorized or required, subparagraph (d)(2)(B) governs.

[35] The term "agency" in paragraph (i) includes, inter alia, executive and independent departments and agencies, special commissions, committees of the

legislature, agencies of the legislative branch such as the General Accounting Office, and the courts to the extent that they employ lawyers (e.g., staff counsel) to counsel them. The employing agency has been designated the client under this rule to provide a commonly understood and easily determinable point for identifying the government client.

[36] Government lawyers may also be assigned to provide an individual with counsel or representation in circumstances that make clear that an obligation of confidentiality runs directly to that individual and that subparagraph (d)(2)(A), not (d)(2)(B), applies. It is, of course, acceptable in this circumstance for a government lawyer to make disclosures about the individual representation to supervisors or others within the employing governmental agency so long as such disclosures are made in the context of, and consistent with, the agency's representation program. *See, e.g.*, 28 C.F.R. §§ 50.15 and 50.16. The relevant circumstances, including the agreement to represent the individual, may also indicate the extent to which the individual client to whom the government lawyer is assigned will be deemed to have granted or denied consent to disclosures to the lawyer's employing agency. Examples of such representation include representation by a public defender, a government lawyer representing a defendant sued for damages arising out of the performance of the defendant's government employment, and a military lawyer representing a court-martial defendant.

RULE 1.7 Conflict of Interest: General Rule

(a) A lawyer shall not represent a client with respect to a position to be taken in a matter if that position is adverse to a position taken or to be taken in the same matter by another client represented with respect to that position by the same lawyer.

(b) Except as permitted by paragraph (c) below, a lawyer shall not represent a client with respect to a matter if:

(1) A position to be taken by that client in that matter is adverse to a position taken or to be taken by another client in the same matter;

(2) Such representation will be or is likely to be adversely affected by representation of another client;

(3) Representation of another client will be or is likely to be adversely affected by such representation; or

(4) The lawyer's professional judgment on behalf of the client will be or reasonably may be adversely affected by the lawyer's responsibilities to or interests in a third party or the lawyer's own financial, business, property, or personal interests.

(c) A lawyer may represent a client with respect to a matter in the circumstances described in paragraph (b) above if:

(1) Each potentially affected client provides consent to such representation after full disclosure of the existence and nature of the possible conflict and the possible adverse consequences of such representation; and

(2) The lawyer is able to comply with all other applicable rules with respect to such representation.

Rule 1.7   WASH., D.C. RULES OF PROF. CONDUCT

COMMENT:

Representation Absolutely Prohibited

[1] Institutional interests in preserving confidence in the adversary process and in the administration of justice preclude permitting a lawyer to represent adverse positions in the same matter. For that reason, paragraph (a) prohibits such conflicting representations, with or without client consent.

[2] The prohibition applies whether the "matter" involved is litigation, an administrative proceeding, an application, the drafting of a contract, a negotiation, estates or family relations practice, or any other type of representation. The same lawyer should not espouse adverse positions with respect to the same matter during the course of any type of representation. However, if the adverse positions to be taken relate to different matters, the absolute prohibition of paragraph (a) is inapplicable, even though paragraphs (b) and (c) may apply.

[3] The concept of a "matter" is typically apparent in on-the-record adversary proceedings or other proceedings in which a written record of the position of parties exists. In other situations, it may not be clear to a lawyer whether the representation of one client is adverse to the interests of another client. For example, a lawyer may represent a client only with respect to one or a few of the client's areas of interest. Other lawyers, or nonlawyers (such as lobbyists), or employees of the client (such as government relations personnel) may be representing that client on many issues whose scope and content are unknown to the lawyer. A lawyer may not undertake a representation known to be adverse to the interests of another client, whether that representation is in a court proceeding, an on-the-record administrative hearing, a notice-and-comment rulemaking, or in an effort to influence policy or achieve a legislative result. However, clients often have many representatives acting for them, including multiple law firms, nonlawyer lobbyists, and client employees. A lawyer retained for a limited purpose may not be aware of the full range of a client's other interests or positions on issues. A lawyer is not required to inquire of a client concerning the full range of that client's interests in issues, unless it is clear to the lawyer or to any affiliated lawyer that there is a potential for concrete adversity between the interests of clients of the lawyer or firm. Unless a lawyer is aware that representing one client involves seeking a result to which another client is opposed, Rule 1.7 is not violated by a representation that eventuates in the lawyer's unwittingly taking a position for one client adverse to the interests of another client.

[4] The absolute prohibition of paragraph (a) applies only to situations in which a lawyer would be called upon to espouse adverse positions in the same matter. It is for this reason that paragraph (a) refers to adversity with respect to a "position taken or to be taken" in a matter rather than adversity with respect to the matter or the entire representation. This approach is intended to reduce the costs of litigation in other representations where parties have common, nonadverse interests on certain issues, but have adverse (or contingently or possibly adverse) positions with respect to other issues. If, for example, a lawyer would not be required to take adverse positions in providing joint representation of two clients in the liability phase of a case, it would be permissible to undertake such a limited representation. Then, after completion of the liability phase, and upon satisfying the requirements of paragraph (c) of this Rule, and of any other applicable Rules, the lawyer could represent either one of those parties as to the damages phase of the case, even though the other,

represented by separate counsel as to damages, might have an adverse position as to that phase of the case. Insofar as the absolute prohibition of paragraph (a) is concerned, a lawyer may represent two parties that may be adverse to each other as to some aspects of the case so long as the same lawyer does not represent both parties with respect to those positions. Such a representation comes within paragraph (b), rather than paragraph (a), and is therefore subject to the consent provisions of paragraph (c).

[5] The ability to represent two parties who have adverse interests as to portions of a case may be limited because the lawyer obtains confidences or secrets relating to a party while jointly representing both parties in one phase of the case. In some circumstances, such confidences or secrets might be useful, against the interests of the party to whom they relate, in a subsequent part of the case. Absent the consent of the party whose confidences or secrets are implicated, the subsequent adverse representation is governed by the "substantial relationship" test, which is set forth in Rule 1.9.

[6] The prohibition of paragraph (a) relates only to actual conflicts of positions, not to mere formalities. For example, a lawyer is not absolutely forbidden to provide joint or simultaneous representation if the clients' positions are only nominally but not actually adverse. Joint representation is commonly provided to incorporators of a business, to parties to a contract, in formulating estate plans for family members, and in other circumstances where the clients might be nominally adverse in some respect but have retained a lawyer to accomplish a common purpose. If no actual conflict of positions exists with respect to a matter, the absolute prohibition of paragraph (a) does not come into play. Thus, in the limited circumstances set forth in Opinion 143 of the D.C. Bar Legal Ethics Committee, this prohibition would not preclude the representation of both parties in an uncontested divorce proceeding, there being no actual conflict of positions based on the facts presented in Opinion 143.

Representation Conditionally Prohibited

[7] Paragraphs (b) and (c) are based upon two principles: (1) that a client is entitled to wholehearted and zealous representation of its interests, and (2) that the client as well as the lawyer must have the opportunity to judge and be satisfied that such representation can be provided. Consistent with these principles, paragraph (b) provides a general description of the types of circumstances in which representation is improper in the absence of informed consent. The underlying premise is that disclosure and consent are required before assuming a representation if there is any reason to doubt the lawyer's ability to provide wholehearted and zealous representation of a client or if a client might reasonably consider the representation of its interests to be adversely affected by the lawyer's assumption of the other representation in question. Although the lawyer must be satisfied that the representation can be wholeheartedly and zealously undertaken, if an objective observer would have any reasonable doubt on that issue, the client has a right to disclosure of all relevant considerations and the opportunity to be the judge of its own interests.

[8] A client may, on occasion, adopt unreasonable positions with respect to having the lawyer who is representing that client also represent other parties. Such an unreasonable position may be based on an aversion to the other parties being represented by a lawyer, or on some philosophical or ideological ground having no foundation in the rules regarding representation of conflicting inter-

ests. Whatever difficulties may be presented for the lawyer in such circumstances as a matter of client relations, the unreasonable positions taken by a client do not fall within the circumstances requiring notification and consent. Clients have broad discretion to terminate their representation by a lawyer and that discretion may generally be exercised on unreasonable as well as reasonable grounds.

[9] If the lawyer determines or can foresee that an issue with respect to the application of paragraph (b) exists, the only prudent course is for the lawyer to make disclosure, pursuant to paragraph (c), to each affected client and enable each to determine whether in its judgment the representation at issue is likely to affect its interests adversely.

[10] To give specific examples, paragraphs (b) and (c) require disclosure and consent in every case in which a client will take a position adverse to another client in a matter in which the one client is represented by the lawyer even though the lawyer does not represent the other client as to that position or even that matter. Paragraph (b) does not, however, purport to state a uniform rule applicable to cases in which two clients may be adverse to each other in a matter in which neither is represented by the lawyer or in a situation in which two or more clients may be direct business competitors. The matter in which two clients are adverse may be so unrelated or insignificant as to have no possible effect upon a lawyer's ability to represent both in other matters. The fact that two clients are business competitors, standing alone, is usually not a bar to simultaneous representation.

Situations That Frequently Arise

[11] A number of types of situations frequently arise in which disclosure and informed consent are usually required. These include joint representation of parties to criminal and civil litigation, joint representation of incorporators of a business, joint representation of a business or government agency and its employees, representation of family members seeking estate planning or the drafting of wills, joint representation of an insurer and an insured, representation in circumstances in which the personal or financial interests of the lawyer, or the lawyer's family, might be affected by the representation, and other similar situations in which experience indicates that conflicts are likely to exist or arise. For example, a lawyer might not be able to represent a client vigorously if the client's adversary is a person with whom the lawyer has longstanding personal or social ties. The client is entitled to be informed of such circumstances so that an informed decision can be made concerning the advisability of retaining the lawyer who has such ties to the adversary. The principles of disclosure and consent are equally applicable to all such circumstances, except that if the positions to be taken by two clients in a matter as to which the lawyer represents both are actually adverse, then, as provided in paragraph (a), the lawyer may not undertake or continue the representation with respect to those issues even if disclosure has been made and consent obtained.

Disclosure and Consent

[12] Disclosure and consent are not mere formalities. Adequate disclosure requires such disclosure of the parties and their interests and positions as to enable each potential client to make a fully informed decision as to whether to proceed with the contemplated representation. If a lawyer's obligation to one or

another client or to others or some other consideration precludes making such full disclosure to all affected parties, that fact alone precludes undertaking the representation at issue. Full disclosure also requires that clients be made aware of the possible extra expense, inconvenience, and other disadvantages that may arise if an actual conflict of position should later arise and the lawyer be required to terminate the representation.

[13] The Rule does not require that disclosure be in writing or in any other particular form in all cases. Nevertheless, it should be recognized that the form of disclosure sufficient for more sophisticated business clients may not be sufficient to permit less sophisticated clients to provide fully informed consent. For that reason, as well as for the lawyer's own protection, it would be prudent for the lawyer to provide potential joint clients with at least a written summary of the considerations disclosed.

[14] The term "consent" is defined in the Terminology section of these Rules. As indicated there, a client's consent must not be coerced either by the lawyer or by any other person. In particular, the lawyer should not use the client's investment in previous representation by the lawyer as leverage to obtain or maintain representation that may be contrary to the client's best interests. If a lawyer has reason to believe that undue influence has been used by anyone to obtain agreement to the representation, the lawyer should not undertake the representation.

Compliance With Other Applicable Rules

[15] Subparagraph (c)(2) is a reminder that disclosure and consent to representation do not diminish a lawyer's obligations to comply with the other Rules of Professional Conduct. For example, even if a client provides informed and uncoerced consent, a lawyer may not undertake or continue a representation if the lawyer is unable to comply with the obligations regarding diligence, communication of relevant information, and protection of client confidences provided in Rules 1.3, 1.4, and 1.6.

Withdrawal

[16] It is much to be preferred that a representation that is likely to lead to a conflict be avoided before the representation begins, and a lawyer should bear this fact in mind in considering whether disclosure should be made and consent obtained at the outset. If, however, a conflict only arises after a representation has been undertaken, and the conflict falls within paragraph (a), or informed and uncoerced consent is not or cannot be obtained pursuant to paragraph (c), then the lawyer should withdraw from the representation, complying with Rule 1.16. Where more than one client is involved and the lawyer withdraws because a conflict arises after representation has been undertaken, the question of whether the lawyer may continue to represent any of the clients is determined by Rule 1.9.

Imputed Disqualification

[17] All of the references in Rule 1.7 and its accompanying Comment to the limitation upon a "lawyer" must be read in light of the imputed disqualification provisions of Rule 1.10, which affect lawyers practicing in a firm.

[18] In the government lawyer context, Rule 1.7(b) is not intended to apply to conflicts between agencies or components of government (federal, state, or

local) where the resolution of such conflicts has been entrusted by law, order, or regulation to a specific individual or entity.

RULE 1.8 Conflict of Interest: Prohibited Transactions

(a) A lawyer shall not enter into a business transaction with a client or knowingly acquire an ownership, possessory, security, or other pecuniary interest adverse to a client unless:

(1) The transaction and terms on which the lawyer acquires the interest are fair and reasonable to the client and are fully disclosed and transmitted in writing to the client in a manner which can be reasonably understood by the client;

(2) The client is given a reasonable opportunity to seek the advice of independent counsel in the transaction; and

(3) The client consents in writing thereto.

(b) A lawyer shall not prepare an instrument giving the lawyer or a person related to the lawyer as parent, child, sibling, or spouse any substantial gift from a client, including a testamentary gift, except where the client is related to the donee.

(c) Prior to the conclusion of representation of a client, a lawyer shall not make or negotiate an agreement giving the lawyer literary or media rights to a portrayal or account based in substantial part on information relating to the representation.

(d) While representing a client in connection with contemplated or pending litigation or administrative proceedings, a lawyer shall not advance or guarantee financial assistance to the client, except that a lawyer may pay or otherwise provide:

(1) The expenses of litigation or administrative proceedings, including court costs, expenses of investigation, expenses of medical examination, costs of obtaining and presenting evidence; and

(2) Other financial assistance which is reasonably necessary to permit the client to institute or maintain the litigation or administrative proceeding.

(e) A lawyer shall not accept compensation for representing a client from one other than the client unless:

(1) The client consents after consultation;

(2) There is no interference with the lawyer's independence of professional judgment or with the client-lawyer relationship; and

(3) Information relating to representation of a client is protected as required by Rule 1.6.

(f) A lawyer who represents two or more clients shall not participate in making an aggregate settlement of the claims of or against the clients, or in a criminal case an aggregated agreement as to guilty or nolo contendere pleas, unless each client consents after consultation, including disclosure of the existence and nature of all the claims or pleas involved and of the participation of each person in the settlement.

(g) A lawyer shall not:

(1) Make an agreement prospectively limiting the lawyer's liability to a client for malpractice; or

(2) Settle a claim for such liability with an unrepresented client or former client without first advising that person in writing that independent representation is appropriate in connection therewith.

(h) A lawyer related to another lawyer as parent, child, sibling, or spouse shall not represent a client in a representation directly adverse to a person who the lawyer knows is represented by the other lawyer except upon consent by the client after consultation regarding the relationship.

(i) A lawyer shall not impose a lien upon any part of a client's files, except upon the lawyer's own work product, and then only to the extent that the work product has not been paid for. This work product exception shall not apply when the client has become unable to pay, or when withholding the lawyer's work product would present a significant risk to the client of irreparable harm.

COMMENT:

Transactions Between Client and Lawyer

[1] As a general principle, all transactions between client and lawyer should be fair and reasonable to the client. In such transactions a review by independent counsel on behalf of the client is often advisable. Paragraph (a) does not, however, apply to standard commercial transactions between the lawyer and the client for products or services that the client generally markets to others; for example, banking or brokerage services, medical services, products manufactured or distributed by the client, and utility services. In such transactions, the lawyer has no advantage in dealing with the client, and the restrictions in paragraph (a) are unnecessary and impracticable.

[2] A lawyer may accept a gift from a client, if the transaction meets general standards of fairness. For example, a simple gift such as a present given at a holiday or as a token of appreciation is permitted. If effectuation of a substantial gift requires preparing a legal instrument such as a will or conveyance, however, the client should be advised by the lawyer to obtain the detached advice that another lawyer can provide. Paragraph (b) recognizes an exception where the client is a relative of the donee or the gift is not substantial.

[3] This Rule does not prevent a lawyer from entering into a contingent fee arrangement with a client in a civil case, if the arrangement satisfies all the requirements of Rule 1.5(c).

Literary Rights

[4] An agreement by which a lawyer acquires literary or media rights concerning the conduct of the representation creates a conflict between the interests of the client and the personal interests of the lawyer. Measures that might otherwise be taken in the representation of the client may detract from the publication value of an account of the representation. Paragraph (c) does not prohibit a lawyer representing a client in a transaction concerning literary property from agreeing that the lawyer's fee shall consist of a share in ownership in the property, if the arrangement conforms to Rule 1.5.

Paying Certain Litigation Costs and Client Expenses

[5] Historically, under the Code of Professional Responsibility, lawyers could only advance the costs of litigation. The client remained ultimately responsible, and was required to pay such costs even if the client lost the case. That rule was modified by this court in 1980 in an amendment to DR 5–103(B) that eliminated the requirement that the client remain ultimately liable for costs of litigation, even if the litigation was unsuccessful. The provisions of Rule 1.8(d) embrace the result of the 1980 modification, but go further by providing that a lawyer may also pay certain expenses of a client that are not litigation expenses. Thus, under Rule 1.8(d), a lawyer may pay medical or living expenses of a client to the extent necessary to permit the client to continue the litigation. The payment of these additional expenses is limited to those strictly necessary to sustain the client during the litigation, such as medical expenses and minimum living expenses. The purpose of permitting such payments is to avoid situations in which a client is compelled by exigent financial circumstances to settle a claim on unfavorable terms in order to receive the immediate proceeds of settlement. This provision does not permit lawyers to "bid" for clients by offering financial payments beyond those minimum payments necessary to sustain the client until the litigation is completed. Regardless of the types of payments involved, assuming such payments are proper under Rule 1.8(d), client reimbursement of the lawyer is not required. However, no lawyer is required to pay litigation or other costs to a client. The Rule merely permits such payments to be made without requiring reimbursement by the client.

Person Paying for Lawyer's Services

[6] Paragraph (e) requires disclosure of the fact that the lawyer's services are being paid for by a third party. Such an arrangement must also conform to the requirements of Rule 1.6 concerning confidentiality and Rule 1.7 concerning conflict of interest. Where the client is a class, consent may be obtained on behalf of the class by court-supervised procedure.

Family Relationships Between Lawyers

[7] Paragraph (h) applies to related lawyers who are in different firms. Related lawyers in the same firm are governed by Rules 1.7, 1.9, and 1.10. Pursuant to the provisions of Rule 1.10, the disqualification stated in paragraph (h) is personal and is not imputed to members of firms with whom the lawyers are associated. Since each of the related lawyers is subject to paragraph (h), the effect is to require the consent of all materially affected clients.

Liens on Lawyer's Work Product

[8] Rule 1.16(d) requires a lawyer to surrender papers and property to which the client is entitled when representation of the client terminates. Paragraph (i) of this Rule states a narrow exception to Rule 1.16(d): a lawyer may retain the lawyer's own work product if the client has not paid for the work. However, if the client has paid for the work product, the client is entitled to receive it, even if the client has not previously seen or received a copy of the work product. Furthermore, the lawyer may not retain the work product for which the client has not paid, if the client has become unable to pay or if withholding the work product might irreparably harm the client's interest.

[9] Under Rule 1.16(d), for example, a lawyer would be required to return all papers received from a client, such as birth certificates, wills, tax returns, or "green cards." Rule 1.8(i) does not permit retention of such papers to secure payment of any fee due. Only the lawyer's own work product—results of factual investigations, legal research and analysis, and similar materials generated by the lawyer's own effort—could be retained. (The term "work product" as used in paragraph (i) is not limited to materials falling within the "work product doctrine," but includes any material generated by the lawyer whether or not in connection with pending or anticipated litigation.) And a lawyer could not withhold all of the work product merely because a portion of the lawyer's fees had not been paid.

[10] There are situations in which withholding the work product would not be permissible because of irreparable harm to the client. The possibility of involuntary incarceration or criminal conviction constitutes one category of irreparable harm. The realistic possibility that a client might irretrievably lose a significant right or become subject to a significant liability because of the withholding of the work product constitutes another category of irreparable harm. On the other hand, the mere fact that the client might have to pay another lawyer to replicate the work product does not, standing alone, constitute irreparable harm. These examples are merely indicative of the meaning of the term "irreparable harm," and are not exhaustive.

RULE 1.9 Conflict of Interest: Former Client

A lawyer who has formerly represented a client in a matter shall not thereafter represent another person in the same or a substantially related matter in which that person's interests are materially adverse to the interests of the former client unless the former client consents after consultation.

COMMENT:

[1] After termination of client-lawyer relationship, a lawyer may not represent another client except in conformity with the Rule. The principles in Rule 1.7 determine whether the interests of the present and former client are adverse. Thus, a lawyer could not properly seek to rescind on behalf of a new client a contract drafted on behalf of the former client. So also a lawyer who has prosecuted an accused person could not properly represent the accused in a subsequent civil action against the government concerning the same transaction.

[2] The scope of a "matter" for purposes of this Rule may depend on the facts of a particular situation or transaction. The lawyer's involvement in a matter can also be a question of degree. When a lawyer has been directly involved in a specific transaction, subsequent representation of other clients with materially adverse interests clearly is prohibited. On the other hand, a lawyer who recurrently handled a type of problem for a former client is not precluded from later representing another client in a wholly distinct problem of that type even though the subsequent representation involves a position adverse to the prior client. Similar considerations can apply to the reassignment of military lawyers between defense and prosecution functions within the same military jurisdiction. The underlying question is whether the lawyer was so involved in the matter that the subsequent representation can be justly regarded as a changing of sides in the matter in question. Rule 1.9 is intended to incorporate federal case law defining the "substantial relationship" test. *See, e.g., T.C.*

Theatre Corp. v. Warner Brothers Pictures, 113 F.Supp. 265 (S.D.N.Y.1953), and its progeny; *see also Conflicts of Interest in the Legal Profession,* 94 Harv. L.Rev. 1244, 1315–34 (1981).

[3] Disqualification from subsequent representation is for the protection of clients and can be waived by them. A waiver is effective only if there is disclosure of the circumstances, including the lawyer's intended role in behalf of the new client. The question of whether a lawyer is personally disqualified from representation in any matter on account of successive government and private employment is governed by Rule 1.11 rather than by Rule 1.9.

[4] With regard to an opposing party's raising a question of conflict of interest, see Comment to Rule 1.7. With regard to disqualification of a firm with which a lawyer is associated, see Rules 1.10 and 1.11

RULE 1.10 Imputed Disqualification: General Rule

(a) While lawyers are associated in a firm, none of them shall knowingly represent a client when any one of them practicing alone would be prohibited from doing so by Rules 1.7, 1.8(b), 1.9, or 2.2.

(b) When a lawyer becomes associated with a firm, the firm may not knowingly represent a person in a matter which is the same as, or substantially related to, a matter with respect to which the lawyer had previously represented a client whose interests are materially adverse to that person or about whom the lawyer has in fact acquired information protected by rule 1.6 that is material to the matter. The disqualification of the firm does not apply if the lawyer participated in a previous representation or acquired information under the circumstances covered by Rule 1.6(g).

(c) When a lawyer has terminated an association with a firm, the firm is not prohibited from thereafter representing a person with interests materially adverse to those of a client represented by the formerly associated lawyer during the association unless:

(1) The matter is the same or substantially related to that in which the formerly associated lawyer represented the client during such former association; or

(2) Any lawyer remaining in the firm has information protected by Rule 1.6 that is material to the matter.

(d) A disqualification prescribed by this rule may be waived by the affected client under the conditions stated in Rule 1.7.

COMMENT:

Definition of "Firm"

[1] For purposes of the Rules of Professional Conduct, the term "firm" includes lawyers in a private firm, and lawyers employed in the legal department of a corporation or other organization, or in a legal services organization, but does not include a government agency or other government entity. Whether two or more lawyers constitute a firm within this definition can depend on the specific facts. For example, two practitioners who share office space and occasionally consult or assist each other ordinarily would not be regarded as constituting a firm. However, if they present themselves to the public in a way suggesting that they are a firm or conduct themselves as a firm, they should be regarded as a firm for purposes of the Rules. The terms of any formal

agreement between associated lawyers are relevant in determining whether they are a firm, as is the fact that they have mutual access to confidential information concerning the clients they serve. Furthermore, it is relevant in doubtful cases to consider the underlying purpose of the Rule that is involved. A group of lawyers could be regarded as a firm for purposes of the Rule that the same lawyer should not represent opposing parties in litigation, while it might not be so regarded for purposes of the Rule that information acquired by one lawyer is attributed to another.

[2] With respect to the law department of an organization, there is ordinarily no question that the members of the department constitute a firm within the meaning of the Rules of Professional Conduct. However, there can be uncertainty as to the identity of the client. For example, it may not be clear whether the law department of a corporation represents a subsidiary or an affiliated corporation, as well as the corporation by which the members of the department are directly employed. A similar question can arise concerning an unincorporated association and its local affiliates.

[3] Similar questions can also arise with respect to lawyers in legal aid organizations. Lawyers employed in the same unit of a legal service organization constitute a firm, but not necessarily those employed in separate units. As in the case of independent practitioners, whether the lawyers should be treated as associated with each other can depend on the particular Rule that is involved, and on the specific facts of the situation.

[4] Where a lawyer has joined a private firm after having represented the government, the situation is governed by Rule 1.11. The individual lawyer involved is bound by the Rules generally, including Rules 1.6, 1.7, and 1.9.

[5] Different provisions are thus made for movement of a lawyer from one private firm to another and for movement of a lawyer from the government to a private firm. The government is entitled to protection of its client confidences, and therefore to the protections provided in Rules 1.6 and 1.11. However, if the more extensive disqualification in Rule 1.10 were applied to former government lawyers, the potential effect on the government would be unduly burdensome. The government deals with all private citizens and organizations, and thus has a much wider circle of adverse legal interests than does any private law firm. In these circumstances, the government's recruitment of lawyers would be seriously impaired if Rule 1.10 were applied to the government. On balance, therefore, the government is better served in the long run by the protections stated in Rule 1.11.

Principles of Imputed Disqualification

[6] The rule of imputed disqualification stated in paragraph (a) gives effect to the principle of loyalty to the client as it applies to lawyers who practice in a law firm. Such situations can be considered from the premise that a firm of lawyers is essentially one lawyer for purposes of the Rules governing loyalty to the client, or from the premise that each lawyer is vicariously bound by the obligation of loyalty owed by each lawyer with whom the lawyer is associated. Paragraph (a) operates only among the lawyers currently associated in a firm. When a lawyer moves from one firm to another, the situation is governed by paragraph (b) or (c).

Lawyers Moving Between Firms

[7] When lawyers have been associated in a firm but then end their association, however, the problem is more complicated. The fiction that the law firm is the same as a single lawyer is no longer wholly realistic. There are several competing considerations. First, the client previously represented must be reasonably assured that the principle of loyalty to the client is not compromised. Second, the rule of disqualification should not be so broadly cast as to preclude other persons from having reasonable choice of legal counsel. Third, the rule of disqualification should not unreasonably hamper lawyers from forming new associations and taking on new clients after having left a previous association. In this connection, it should be recognized that today many lawyers practice in firms, that many to some degree limit their practice to one field or another, and that many move from one association to another several times in their careers. If the concept of imputed disqualification were defined with unqualified rigor, the result would be radical curtailment of the opportunity of lawyers to move from one practice setting to another and of the opportunity of clients to change counsel.

[8] Reconciliation of these competing principles in the past has been attempted under two rubrics. One approach has been to seek *per se* rules of disqualification. For example, it has been held that a partner in a law firm is conclusively presumed to have access to all confidences concerning all clients of the firm. Under this analysis, if a lawyer has been a partner in one law firm and then becomes a partner in another law firm, there is a presumption that all confidences known by a partner in the first firm are known to all partners in the second firm. This presumption might properly be applied in some circumstances, especially where the client has been extensively represented, but may be unrealistic where the client was represented only for limited purposes. Furthermore, such a rigid rule exaggerates the difference between a partner and an associate in modern law firms.

[9] The other rubric formerly used for dealing with vicarious disqualification is the appearance of impropriety proscribed in Canon 9 of the Code of Professional Responsibility. Applying this rubric presents two problems. First, the appearance of impropriety can be taken to include any new client-lawyer relationship that might make a former client feel anxious. If that meaning were adopted, disqualification would become little more than a question of subjective judgment by the former client. Second, since "impropriety" is undefined, the term "appearance of impropriety" is question-begging. It therefore has to be recognized that the problem of imputed disqualification cannot be properly resolved either by simple analogy to a lawyer practicing alone or by the very general concept of appearance of impropriety.

[10] A rule based on a functional analysis is more appropriate for determining the question of vicarious disqualification. Two functions are involved: preserving confidentiality and avoiding positions adverse to a client.

Confidentiality

[11] Preserving confidentiality is a question of access to information. Access to information, in turn, is essentially a question of fact in particular circumstances, aided by inferences, deductions, or working presumptions that reasonably may be made about the way in which lawyers work together. A lawyer may have general access to files of all clients of a law firm and may

regularly participate in discussions of their affairs; it should be inferred that such a lawyer in fact is privy to all information about all the firm's clients. In contrast, another lawyer may have access to the files of only a limited number of clients and participate in discussion of the affairs of no other clients; in the absence of information to the contrary, it should be inferred that such a lawyer in fact is privy to information about the clients actually served but not those of other clients.

[12] Application of paragraphs (b) and (c) depends on a situation's particular facts. In any such inquiry, the burden of proof should rest upon the firm whose disqualification is sought.

[13] The provisions of paragraphs (b) and (c) which refer to possession of protected information operate to disqualify the firm only when the lawyer involved has actual knowledge of information protected by Rule 1.6. Thus, if a lawyer while with one firm acquired no knowledge of information relating to a particular client of the firm, and that lawyer later joined another firm, neither the lawyer individually nor the second firm is disqualified from representing another client in the same or a substantially related matter even though the interests of the two clients conflict.

[14] Independent of the question of disqualification of a firm, a lawyer changing professional association has a continuing duty to preserve confidentiality of information about a client formerly represented. *See* Rule 1.6.

Adverse Positions

[15] The second aspect of loyalty to a client is the lawyer's obligation to decline subsequent representations involving positions adverse to a former client arising in substantially related matters. This obligation requires abstention from adverse representations by the individual lawyer involved, and may also entail abstention of other lawyers through imputed disqualification. Hence, this aspect of the problem is governed by the principles of Rule 1.9. Thus, under paragraph (b), if a lawyer left one firm for another, the new affiliation would preclude the lawyer's new firm from continuing to represent clients with interests materially adverse to those of the lawyer's former clients in the same or substantially related matters. In this respect paragraph (b) is at odds with—and thus must be understood to reject—the dicta expressed in the "second" hypothetical in the second paragraph of footnote 5 of *Brown v. District of Columbia Board of Zoning Adjustment*, 486 A.2d 37, 42 n. 5 (D.C.App.1984) (en banc), premised on *LaSalle National Bank v. County of Lake*, 703 F.2d 252, 257–59 (7th Cir.1983).

[16] The concept of "former client" as used in paragraph (b) extends only to actual representation of the client by the newly affiliated lawyer while that lawyer was employed by the former firm. Thus, not all of the clients of the former firm during the newly affiliated lawyer's practice there are necessarily deemed former clients of the newly affiliated lawyer. Only those clients with whom the newly affiliated lawyer in fact personally had a lawyer-client relationship are former clients within the terms of paragraph (b).

[17] Conversely, when a lawyer terminates an association with a firm, paragraph (c) provides that the old firm may not thereafter represent clients whose interests are materially adverse to those of the formerly associated lawyer's client in respect to a matter that is the same or substantially related to a matter with respect to which the formerly associated lawyer represented the client during the former association. For example, if a lawyer who represented a

client in a litigation while with Firm A departs the firm, taking to the lawyer's new firm the litigation, Firm A may not, despite the departure of the lawyer, who takes the matter and the client to the new firm, undertake a representation adverse to the former client in that same litigation. See Rule 1.9 and the Comment thereto for the definition of "substantially related matter."

[18] The last sentence of paragraph (b) limits the imputation rule in certain limited circumstances. Those circumstances involve situations in which any secrets or confidences obtained were received before the lawyer had become a member of the Bar, but during a time when such person was providing assistance to another lawyer. The typical situation is that of the part-time or summer law clerk, or so-called summer associate. Other types of assistance to a lawyer, such as working as a paralegal or legal assistant, could also fall within the scope of this sentence. The limitation on the imputation rule is similar to the provision dealing with judicial law clerks under Rule 1.11(b). Not applying the imputation rule reflects a policy choice that imputation in such circumstances could unduly impair the mobility of persons employed in such nonlawyer positions once they become members of the Bar. The personal disqualification of the former nonlawyer is not affected, and the lawyer who previously held the nonlegal job may not be involved in any representation with respect to which the firm would have been disqualified but for the last sentence of paragraph (b). Rule 1.6(g) provides that the former nonlawyer is subject to the requirements of Rule 1.6 (regarding protection of client confidences and secrets) just as if the person had been a member of the Bar when employed in the prior position.

RULE 1.11 Successive Government and Private Employment

(a) A lawyer shall not accept other employment in connection with a matter which is the same as, or substantially related to, a matter in which the lawyer participated personally and substantially as a public officer or employee. Such participation includes acting on the merits of a matter in a judicial or other adjudicative capacity.

(b) If a lawyer is required to decline or to withdraw from employment under paragraph (a) on account of personal and substantial participation in a matter, no partner or associate of that lawyer, or lawyer with an of counsel relationship to that lawyer, may accept or continue such employment except as provided in paragraphs (c) and (d) below. The disqualification of such other lawyers does not apply if the sole form of participation was as a judicial law clerk.

(c) The prohibition stated in paragraph (b) shall not apply if the personally disqualified lawyer is screened from any form of participation in the matter or representation as the case may be, and from sharing in any fees resulting therefrom, and if the requirements of paragraphs (d) and (e) are satisfied.

(d) Except as provided in paragraph (e), when any of counsel, lawyer, partner, or associate of a lawyer personally disqualified under paragraph (a) accepts employment in connection with a matter giving rise to the personal disqualification, the following notifications shall be required:

(1) The personally disqualified lawyer shall submit to the public department or agency by which the lawyer was formerly employed and serve on each other party to any pertinent proceeding a signed document attesting that during the period of disqualification the personally disqualified lawyer will not participate in any manner in the matter or the representation,

will not discuss the matter or the representation with any partner, associate, or of counsel lawyer, and will not share in any fees for the matter or the representation.

(2) At least one affiliated lawyer shall submit to the same department or agency and serve on the same parties a signed document attesting that all affiliated lawyers are aware of the requirement that the personally disqualified lawyer be screened from participating in or discussing the matter or the representation and describing the procedures being taken to screen the personally disqualified lawyer.

(e) If a client requests in writing that the fact and subject matter of a representation subject to paragraph (d) not be disclosed by submitting the signed statements referred to in paragraph (d), such statements shall be prepared concurrently with undertaking the representation and filed with Bar Counsel under seal. If at any time thereafter the fact and subject matter of the representation are disclosed to the public or become a part of the public record, the signed statements previously prepared shall be promptly submitted as required by paragraph (d).

(f) Signed documents filed pursuant to paragraph (d) shall be available to the public, except to the extent that a lawyer submitting a signed document demonstrates to the satisfaction of the public department or agency upon which such documents are served that public disclosure is inconsistent with rule 1.6 or provisions of law.

(g) As used in this Rule, a "matter" is any judicial or other proceeding, application, request for a ruling or other determination, contract, claim, controversy, investigation, charge, accusation, arrest, or other particular matter involving a specific party or parties.

COMMENT:

[1] This Rule deals with lawyers who leave public office and enter other employment. It applies to judges and their law clerks as well as to lawyers who act in other public capacities. It is a counterpart of Rule 1.10(b), which applies to lawyers moving from one firm to another.

[2] A lawyer representing a government agency, whether employed or specially retained by the government, is subject to the Rules of Professional Conduct, including the prohibition against representing adverse interests stated in Rule 1.7 and the protections afforded former clients in Rule 1.9. In addition, such a lawyer is subject to this Rule 1.11 and to statutes and government regulations concerning conflict of interest. In the District of Columbia, where there are so many lawyers for the federal and D.C. governments and their agencies, a number of whom are constantly leaving government and accepting other employment, particular heed must be paid to the federal conflict-of-interest statutes. *See, e.g.,* 18 U.S.C. Chapter 11 and regulations and opinions thereunder.

[3] Rule 1.11, in paragraph (a), flatly forbids a lawyer to accept other employment in a matter in which the lawyer participated personally and substantially as a public officer or employee; participation specifically includes acting on a matter in a judicial capacity. There is no provision for waiver of the individual lawyer's disqualification. "Matter" is defined in paragraph (g) so as to encompass only matters that are particular to a specific party or parties. The making

of rules of general applicability and the establishment of general policy will ordinarily not be a "matter" within the meaning of Rule 1.11. When a lawyer is forbidden by paragraph (a) to accept private employment in a matter, the partners and associates of that lawyer are likewise forbidden, by paragraph (b), to accept the employment unless the screening and disclosure procedures described in paragraphs (c) through (f) are followed.

[4] The Rule forbids lawyers to accept other employment in connection with matters that are the same as or "substantially related" to matters in which they participated personally and substantially while serving as public officers or employees. The leading case defining "substantially related" matters in the context of former government employment is *Brown v. District of Columbia Board of Zoning Adjustment*, 486 A.2d 37 (D.C.App.1984) (en banc). There the D.C. Court of Appeals, en banc, held that in the "revolving door" context, a showing that a reasonable person could infer that, through participation in one matter as a public officer or employee, the former government lawyer "may have had access to information legally relevant to, or otherwise useful in" a subsequent representation, is prima facie evidence that the two matters are substantially related. If this prima facie showing is made, the former government lawyer must disprove any ethical impropriety by showing that the lawyer "could not have gained access to information during the first representation that might be useful in the later representation." *Id.* at 49–50. In *Brown*, the Court of Appeals announced the "substantially related" test after concluding that, under former DR 9-101(B), *see* "Revolving Door," 445 A.2d 615 (D.C.App.1982) (en banc) (per curiam), the term "matter" was intended to embrace all matters "substantially related" to one another—a test that originated in "side-switching" litigation between private parties. *See* Rule 1.9, Comment [2]; *Brown*, 486 A.2d at 39–40 n. 1, 41–42 & n. 4. Accordingly, the words "or substantially related to" in paragraph (a) are an express statement of the judicial gloss in *Brown* interpreting "matter."

[5] Paragraph (a)'s absolute disqualification of a lawyer from matters in which the lawyer participated personally and substantially carries forward a policy of avoiding both actual impropriety and the appearance of impropriety that is expressed in the federal conflict-of-interest statutes and was expressed in the former Code of Professional Responsibility. Paragraph (c) requires the screening of a disqualified lawyer from such a matter as a condition to allowing any lawyers in the disqualified lawyer's firm to participate in it. This procedure is permitted in order to avoid imposing a serious deterrent to lawyers' entering public service. Governments have found that they benefit from having in their service both younger and more experienced lawyers who do not intend to devote their entire careers to public service. Some lawyers might not enter into short-term public service if they thought that, as a result of their active governmental practice, a firm would hesitate to hire them because of a concern that the entire firm would be disqualified from matters as a result.

[6] There is no imputed disqualification and consequently no screening requirement in the case of a judicial law clerk. But such clerks are subject to a personal obligation not to participate in matters falling within paragraph (a), since participation by a law clerk is within the term "judicial or other adjudicative capacity."

[7] Paragraph (d) imposes a further requirement that must be met before lawyers affiliated with a disqualified lawyer may participate in the representa-

tion. Except to the extent that the exception in paragraph (e) is satisfied, both the personally disqualified lawyer and at least one affiliated lawyer must submit to the agency signed documents basically stating that the personally disqualified lawyer will be screened from participation in the matter. The personally disqualified lawyer must also state that the lawyer will not share in any fees paid for the representation in question. And the affiliated lawyer must describe the procedures to be followed to ensure that the personally disqualified lawyer is effectively screened.

[8] Paragraph (e) makes it clear that the lawyer's duty, under Rule 1.6, to maintain client confidences and secrets may preclude the submission of any notice required by paragraph (d). If the client requests in writing that the fact and subject matter of the representation not be disclosed, the lawyer must comply with that request. If the client makes such a request, the lawyer must abide by the client's wishes until such time as the fact and subject matter of the representation become public through some other means, such as a public filing. Filing a pleading or making an appearance in a proceeding before a tribunal constitutes a public filing. Once information concerning the representation is public, the notifications called for must be made promptly, and the lawyers involved may not honor a client request not to make the notifications. If a government agency has adopted rules governing practice before the agency by former government employees, members of the District of Columbia Bar are not exempted by Rule 1.11(e) from any additional or more restrictive notice requirements that the agency may impose. Thus the agency may require filing of notifications whether or not a client consents. While the lawyer cannot file a notification that the client has directed the lawyer not to file, the failure to file in accordance with agency rules may preclude the lawyer's representation of the client before the agency. Such issues are governed by the agency's rules, and Rule 1.11(e) is not intended to displace such agency requirements.

[9] Although paragraph (e) prohibits the lawyer from disclosing the fact and subject matter of the representation when the client has requested in writing that the information be kept confidential, it requires the lawyer to prepare the documents described in paragraph (d) as soon as the representation commences and to preserve the documents for possible submission to the agency and parties to any pertinent proceeding if and when the client does consent to their submission or the information becomes public.

[10] "Other employment" as used in paragraph (a), includes the representation of a governmental body other than an agency of the government by which the lawyer was employed as a public officer or employee.

[11] Paragraph (c) does not prohibit a lawyer from receiving a salary or partnership share established by prior independent agreement. It prohibits directly relating the attorney's compensation in any way to the fee in the matter in which the lawyer is disqualified.

RULE 1.12 Former Arbitrator

(a) Except as stated in paragraph (b), a lawyer shall not represent anyone in connection with a matter in which the lawyer participated personally and substantially as an arbitrator, unless all parties to the proceeding consent after disclosure.

(b) An arbitrator selected as a partisan of a party in a multimember arbitration panel is not prohibited from subsequently representing that party.

COMMENT:

[1] This Rule extends the basic requirements of Rule 1.11(a) to privately employed arbitrators. Paragraph (a) is substantially similar to Rule 1.11(a), except that it allows an arbitrator to represent someone in connection with a matter with which the lawyer was substantially involved while serving as an arbitrator if the parties to the arbitration consent. Paragraph (b) makes it clear that the prohibition set forth in paragraph (a) does not apply to partisan arbitrators serving on a multimember arbitration panel.

RULE 1.13 Organization as Client

(a) A lawyer employed or retained by an organization represents the organization acting through its duly authorized constituents.

(b) In dealing with an organization's directors, officers, employees, members, shareholders, or other constituents, a lawyer shall explain the identity of the client when it is apparent that the organization's interests may be adverse to those of the constituents with whom the lawyer is dealing.

(c) A lawyer representing an organization may also represent any of its directors, officers, employees, members, shareholders, or other constituents, subject to the provisions of Rule 1.7. If the organization's consent to the dual representation is required by Rule 1.7, the consent shall be given by an appropriate official of the organization other than the individual who is to be represented, or by the shareholders.

COMMENT:

The Entity as the Client

[1] An organizational client is a legal entity, but it cannot act except through its officers, directors, employees, shareholders, and other constituents.

[2] Officers, directors, employees, and shareholders are the constituents of the corporate organizational client. The duties defined in this Comment apply equally to unincorporated associations. "Other constituents" as used in this Comment means the positions equivalent to officers, directors, employees, and shareholders held by persons acting for organizational clients that are not corporations.

[3] When one of the constituents of an organizational client communicates with the organization's lawyer in that person's organizational capacity, the communication is protected by Rule 1.6. Thus, by way of example, if an organizational client requests its lawyer to investigate allegations of wrongdoing, interviews made in the course of that investigation between the lawyer and the client's employees or other constituents are covered by Rule 1.6. This does not mean, however, that constituents of an organizational client are the clients of the lawyer. The lawyer may not disclose to such constituents information relating to the representation except for disclosures explicitly or impliedly authorized by the organizational client in order to carry out the representation or as otherwise permitted by Rule 1.6.

[4] When constituents of the organization make decisions for it, the decisions ordinarily must be accepted by the lawyer even if their utility or prudence is doubtful. Decisions concerning policy and operations, including ones entailing serious risk, are not as such in the lawyer's province. However, different considerations arise when the lawyer knows that the organization may be

substantially injured by tortious or illegal conduct by a constituent member of an organization that reasonably might be imputed to the organization or that might result in substantial injury to the organization. In such a circumstance, it may be reasonably necessary for the lawyer to ask the constituent to reconsider the matter. If that fails, or if the matter is of sufficient seriousness and importance to the organization, it may be reasonably necessary for the lawyer to take steps to have the matter reviewed by a higher authority in the organization. Clear justification should exist for seeking review over the head of the constituent normally responsible for it. The stated policy of the organization may define circumstances and prescribe channels for such review, and a lawyer should encourage the formulation of such a policy. Even in the absence of organization policy, however, the lawyer may have an obligation to refer a matter to a higher authority, depending on the seriousness of the matter and whether the constituent in question has apparent motives to act at variance with the organization's interest. Review by the chief executive officer or by the board of directors may be required when the matter is of importance commensurate with their authority. At some point it may be useful or essential to obtain an independent legal opinion.

[5] In an extreme case, it may be reasonably necessary for the lawyer to refer the matter to the organization's highest authority. Ordinarily, that is the board of directors or similar governing body. However, applicable law may prescribe that under certain conditions highest authority reposes elsewhere; for example, in the independent directors of a corporation.

Relation to Other Rules

[6] This Rule does not limit or expand the lawyer's responsibility under Rules 1.6, 1.8, 1.16, 3.3, and 4.1. If the lawyer's services are being used by an organization to further a crime or fraud by the organization, Rule 1.2(e) can be applicable.

Government Agency

[7] Because the government agency that employs the government lawyer is the lawyer's client, the lawyer represents the agency acting through its duly authorized constituents. Any application of Rule 1.13 to government lawyers must, however, take into account the differences between government agencies and other organizations.

Clarifying the Lawyer's Role

[8] There are times when the organization's interest may be or become adverse to those of one or more of its constituents. In such circumstances the lawyer should advise any constituent, whose interest the lawyer finds adverse to that of the organization, of the conflict or potential conflict of interest, that the lawyer cannot represent such constituent, and that such person may wish to obtain independent representation. Care must be taken to assure that the individual understands that, when there is such adversity of interest, the lawyer for the organization cannot provide legal representation for that constituent individual, and that discussions between the lawyer for the organization and the individual may not be privileged.

[9] Whether such a warning should be given by the lawyer for the organization to any constituent individual may turn on the facts of each case.

Dual Representation

[10] Paragraph (c) recognizes that a lawyer for an organization may also represent a principal officer or major shareholder.

Derivative Actions

[11] Under generally prevailing law, the shareholders or members of a corporation may bring suit to compel the directors to perform their legal obligations in the supervision of the organization. Members of unincorporated associations have essentially the same right. Such an action may be brought nominally by the organization, but usually is, in fact, a legal controversy over management of the organization.

[12] The question can arise whether counsel for the organization may defend such an action. The proposition that the organization is the lawyer's client does not alone resolve the issue. Most derivative actions are a normal incident of an organization's affairs, to be defended by the organization's lawyer like any other suit. However, if the claim involves serious charges of wrongdoing by those in control of the organization, a conflict may arise between the lawyer's duty to the organization and the lawyer's relationship with the board. In those circumstances, Rule 1.7 governs whether lawyers who normally serve as counsel to the corporation can properly represent both the directors and the organization.

RULE 1.14 Client Under a Disability

(a) When a client's ability to make adequately considered decisions in connection with the representation is impaired, whether because of minority, mental disability, or for some other reason, the lawyer shall, as far as reasonably possible, maintain a normal client-lawyer relationship with the client.

(b) A lawyer may seek the appointment of a guardian or take other protective action with respect to a client, only when the lawyer reasonably believes that the client cannot adequately act in the client's own interest.

COMMENT:

[1] The normal client-lawyer relationship is based on the assumption that the client, when properly advised and assisted, is capable of making decisions about important matters. When the client is a minor or suffers from a mental disorder or disability, however, maintaining the ordinary client-lawyer relationship may not be possible in all respects. In particular, an incapacitated person may have no power to make legally binding decisions. Nevertheless, a client lacking legal competence often has the ability to understand, deliberate upon, and reach conclusions about matters affecting the client's own well-being. Furthermore, to an increasing extent the law recognizes intermediate degrees of competence. For example, children as young as five or six years of age, and certainly those of ten or twelve, are regarded as having opinions that are entitled to weight in legal proceedings concerning their custody. So also, it is recognized that some persons of advanced age can be quite capable of handling routine financial matters while needing special legal protection concerning major transactions.

[2] The fact that a client suffers a disability does not diminish the lawyer's obligation to treat the client with attention and respect. If the person has no guardian or legal representative, the lawyer often must act as de facto guardian. Even if the person does have a legal representative, the lawyer should as far as

possible accord the represented person the status of client, particularly in maintaining communication.

[3] If a legal representative has already been appointed for the client, the lawyer should ordinarily look to the representative for decisions on behalf of the client. If a legal representative has not been appointed, the lawyer should see to such an appointment where it would serve the client's best interests. Thus, if a disabled client has substantial property that should be sold for the client's benefit, effective completion of the transaction ordinarily requires appointment of a legal representative. In many circumstances, however, appointment of a legal representative may be expensive or traumatic for the client. Evaluation of these considerations is a matter of professional judgment on the lawyer's part.

Disclosure of the Client's Condition

[4] Rules of procedure in litigation generally provide that minors or persons suffering mental disability shall be represented by a guardian or next friend if they do not have a general guardian. However, disclosure of the client's disability can adversely affect the client's interests. For example, raising the question of disability could, in some circumstances, lead to proceedings for involuntary commitment. The lawyer's position in such cases is an unavoidably difficult one. The lawyer may seek guidance from an appropriate diagnostician.

RULE 1.15 Safekeeping Property

(a) A lawyer shall hold property of clients or third persons that is in the lawyer's possession in connection with a representation separate from the lawyer's own property. Funds shall be kept in a separate account maintained in a financial institution which is authorized by federal, District of Columbia, or state law to do business in the District of Columbia or the state in which the lawyer's or law firm's office is situated and which is a member of the federal deposit insurance corporation, or the federal savings and loan insurance corporation, or successor agencies, other property shall be identified as such and appropriately safeguarded. Complete records of such account funds and other property shall be kept by the lawyer and shall be preserved for a period of five years after termination of the representation.

(b) Upon receiving funds or other property in which a client or third person has an interest, a lawyer shall promptly notify the client or third person. Except as stated in this rule or otherwise permitted by law or by agreement with the client, a lawyer shall promptly deliver to the client or third person any funds or other property that the client or third person is entitled to receive and, upon request by the client or third person, shall promptly render a full accounting regarding such property, subject to rule 1.6.

(c) When in the course of representation a lawyer is in possession of property in which both the lawyer and another person claim interests, the property shall be kept separate by the lawyer until there is an accounting and severance of their interests. If a dispute arises concerning their respective interests, the portion in dispute shall be kept separate by the lawyer until the dispute is resolved, and any funds in dispute shall be deposited in a separate account meeting the requirements of paragraph (a).

(d) Advances of legal fees and costs become the property of the lawyer upon receipt. Any unearned amount of prepaid fees must be returned to the client at the termination of the lawyer's services in accordance with Rule 1.16(d).

(e) Nothing in this rule shall prohibit a lawyer or law firm from placing clients' funds which are nominal in amount or to be held for a short period of time in one or more interest-bearing accounts for the benefit of the charitable purposes of a court-approved "Interest on Lawyers Trust Account (IOLTA)" program.

COMMENT:

[1] A lawyer should hold property of others with the care required of a professional fiduciary. Securities should be kept in a safe deposit box, except when some other form of safekeeping is warranted by special circumstances. All property that is the property of clients or third persons should be kept separate from the lawyer's business and personal property and, if monies, in one or more trust accounts maintained with financial institutions meeting the requirements of paragraph (a). Separate trust accounts may be warranted when administering estate monies or acting in similar fiduciary capacities.

[2] The District of Columbia Court of Appeals has promulgated specific rules allowing lawyers to place clients' funds that are nominal in amount, or that are to be held for a short period of time, into interest-bearing accounts for the benefit of the charitable purposes of a court-approved "Interest on Lawyers Trust Account (IOLTA)" program. On February 22, 1985, the court added to DR 9–103 a new paragraph (C) that expressly permitted IOLTA accounts meeting the requirements of Appendix B to Rule X of the court's Rules Governing the Bar of the District of Columbia. Appendix B sets forth detailed rules to be followed in establishing and administering IOLTA accounts. Paragraph (e) of this Rule is substantially identical to DR 9–103(C). The rules contained in Appendix B to Rule X are hereby incorporated and must be followed in setting up IOLTA programs pursuant to paragraph (e).

[3] Lawyers often receive funds from third parties from which the lawyer's fee will be paid. If there is risk that the client may divert the funds without paying the fee, the lawyer is not required to remit the portion from which the fee is to be paid. However, a lawyer may not hold funds to coerce a client into accepting the lawyer's contention. The disputed portion of the funds should be kept in trust and the lawyer should suggest means for prompt resolution of the dispute, such as arbitration. The undisputed portion of the funds should be promptly distributed.

[4] Third parties, such as a client's creditors, may have just claims against funds or other property in a lawyer's custody. A lawyer may have a duty under applicable law to protect such third-party claims against wrongful interference by the client, and accordingly may refuse to surrender the property to the client. However, a lawyer should not unilaterally assume to arbitrate a dispute between the client and the third party.

[5] The obligations of a lawyer under this Rule are independent of those arising from activity other than rendering legal services. For example, a lawyer who serves as an escrow agent is governed by the applicable law relating to fiduciaries even though the lawyer does not render legal services in the transaction.

[6] A "clients' security fund" provides a means through the collective efforts of the Bar to reimburse persons who have lost money or property as a result of dishonest conduct of a lawyer. Where such a fund has been established, a lawyer should participate.

[7] With respect to property that constitutes evidence, such as the instruments or proceeds of crime, see Rule 3.4(a).

RULE 1.16 Declining or Terminating Representation

(a) Except as stated in paragraph (c), a lawyer shall not represent a client or, where representation has commenced, shall withdraw from the representation of a client if:

(1) The representation will result in violation of the rules of professional conduct or other law;

(2) The lawyer's physical or mental condition materially impairs the lawyer's ability to represent the client; or

(3) The lawyer is discharged.

(b) Except as stated in paragraph (c), a lawyer may withdraw from representing a client if withdrawal can be accomplished without material adverse effect on the interests of the client, or if:

(1) The client persists in a course of action involving the lawyer's services that the lawyer reasonably believes is criminal or fraudulent;

(2) The client has used the lawyer's services to perpetrate a crime or fraud;

(3) The client fails substantially to fulfill an obligation to the lawyer regarding the lawyer's services and has been given reasonable warning that the lawyer will withdraw unless the obligation is fulfilled;

(4) The representation will result in an unreasonable financial burden on the lawyer or obdurate or vexatious conduct on the part of the client has rendered the representation unreasonably difficult;

(5) The lawyer believes in good faith, in a proceeding before a tribunal, that the tribunal will find the existence of other good cause for withdrawal.

(c) When ordered to do so by a tribunal, a lawyer shall continue representation notwithstanding good cause for terminating the representation.

(d) In connection with any termination of representation, a lawyer shall take timely steps to the extent reasonably practicable to protect a client's interests, such as giving reasonable notice to the client, allowing time for employment of other counsel, surrendering papers and property to which the client is entitled, and refunding any advance payment of fee that has not been earned. The lawyer may retain papers relating to the client to the extent permitted by Rule 1.8(i).

COMMENT:

[1] A lawyer should not accept representation in a matter unless it can be performed competently, promptly, without improper conflict of interest, and to completion.

Mandatory Withdrawal

[2] A lawyer ordinarily must decline or withdraw from representation if the client demands that the lawyer engage in conduct that is illegal or violates the Rules of Professional Conduct or other law. The lawyer is not obliged to decline or withdraw simply because the client suggests such a course of conduct; a client may make such a suggestion in the hope that a lawyer will not be constrained by a professional obligation.

[3] When a lawyer has been appointed to represent a client, withdrawal ordinarily requires approval of the appointing authority. *See also* Rule 6.2. Difficulty may be encountered if withdrawal is based on the client's demand that the lawyer engage in unprofessional conduct. The court may wish an explanation for the withdrawal, while the lawyer may be bound to keep confidential the facts that would constitute such an explanation. The lawyer's statement that irreconcilable differences between the lawyer and client require termination of the representation ordinarily should be accepted as sufficient.

Discharge

[4] A client has a right to discharge a lawyer at any time, with or without cause, subject to liability for payment for the lawyer's services. Where future dispute about the withdrawal may be anticipated, it may be advisable to prepare a written statement reciting the circumstances.

[5] Whether a client can discharge appointed counsel may depend on applicable law. A client seeking to do so should be given a full explanation of the consequences. These consequences may include a decision by the appointing authority that appointment of successor counsel is unjustified, thus requiring the client to proceed pro se.

[6] If the client is mentally incompetent, the client may lack the legal capacity to discharge the lawyer, and in any event the discharge may be seriously adverse to the client's interests. The lawyer should make a special effort to help the client consider the consequences and, in an extreme case, may initiate proceedings for a conservatorship or similar protection of the client. *See* Rule 1.14.

Optional Withdrawal

[7] A lawyer may withdraw from representation in some circumstances. The lawyer has the option to withdraw if the withdrawal can be accomplished without material adverse effect on the client's interests. Withdrawal is also justified if the client persists in a course of action that the lawyer reasonably believes is criminal or fraudulent, for a lawyer is not required to be associated with such conduct even if the lawyer does not further it. Withdrawal is also permitted if the lawyer's services were misused in the past even if that would materially prejudice the client.

[8] A lawyer may withdraw if the client refuses to abide by the terms of an agreement relating to the representation, such as an agreement concerning the timely payment of the lawyer's fees, court costs or other out-of-pocket expenses of the representation, or an agreement limiting the objectives of the representation.

[9] If the matter is not pending in court, a lawyer will not have "other good cause for withdrawal" unless the lawyer is acting in good faith and the circum-

stances are exceptional enough to outweigh the material adverse effect on the interests of the client that withdrawal will cause.

Assisting the Client Upon Withdrawal

[10] Even if the lawyer has been unfairly discharged by the client, a lawyer must take all reasonable steps to mitigate the consequences to the client. The lawyer may retain papers as security for a fee only to the extent permitted by Rule 1.8(i).

Compliance With Requirements of a Tribunal

[11] Paragraph (c) reflects the possibility that a lawyer may, by appearing before a tribunal, become subject to the tribunal's power in some circumstances to prevent a withdrawal that would otherwise be proper. Paragraph (c) requires the lawyer who is ordered to continue a representation before a tribunal to do so. However, paragraph (c) is not intended to prevent the lawyer from challenging the tribunal's order as beyond its jurisdiction, arbitrary, or otherwise improper while, in the interim, continuing the representation.

COUNSELOR

RULE 2.1 Adviser

In representing a client, a lawyer shall exercise independent professional judgment and render candid advice. In rendering advice, a lawyer may refer not only to law but to other considerations such as moral, economic, social, and political factors, that may be relevant to the client's situation.

COMMENT:

Scope of Advice

[1] A client is entitled to straightforward advice expressing the lawyer's honest assessment. Legal advice often involves unpleasant facts and alternatives that a client may be disinclined to confront. In presenting advice, a lawyer endeavors to sustain the client's morale and may put advice in as acceptable a form as honesty permits. However, a lawyer should not be deterred from giving candid advice by the prospect that the advice will be unpalatable to the client.

[2] Advice couched in narrowly legal terms may be of little value to a client, especially where practical considerations, such as cost or effects on other people, are predominant. Purely technical legal advice, therefore, can sometimes be inadequate. It is proper for a lawyer to refer to relevant moral and ethical considerations in giving advice. Although a lawyer is not a moral adviser as such, moral and ethical considerations impinge upon most legal questions and may decisively influence how the law will be applied.

[3] A client may expressly or impliedly ask the lawyer for purely technical advice. When such a request is made by a client experienced in legal matters, the lawyer may accept it at face value. When such a request is made by a client inexperienced in legal matters, however, the lawyer's responsibility as adviser may include indicating that more may be involved than strictly legal considerations.

[4] Matters that go beyond strictly legal questions may also be in the domain of another profession. Family matters can involve problems within the

professional competence of psychiatry, clinical psychology, or social work; business matters can involve problems within the competence of the accounting profession or of financial specialists. Where consultation with a professional in another field is itself something a competent lawyer would recommend, the lawyer should make such a recommendation. At the same time, a lawyer's advice at its best often consists of recommending a course of action in the face of conflicting recommendations of experts.

Offering Advice

[5] In general, a lawyer is not expected to give advice until asked by the client. However, when a lawyer knows that a client proposes a course of action that is likely to result in substantial adverse legal consequences to the client, duty to the client under Rule 1.4 may require that the lawyer act if the client's course of action is related to the representation. A lawyer ordinarily has no duty to initiate investigation of a client's affairs or to give advice that the client has indicated is unwanted, but a lawyer may initiate advice to a client when doing so appears to be in the client's interest.

RULE 2.2 Intermediary

(a) A lawyer may act as intermediary between clients if:

(1) The lawyer consults with each client concerning the implications of the common representation, including the advantages and risks involved, and the effect on the attorney-client privileges, and obtains each client's consent to the common representation;

(2) The lawyer reasonably believes that the matter can be resolved on terms compatible with the clients' best interests, that each client will be able to make adequately informed decisions in the matter, and that there is little risk of material prejudice to the interests of any of the clients if the contemplated resolution is unsuccessful; and

(3) The lawyer reasonably believes that the common representation can be undertaken impartially and without improper effect on other responsibilities the lawyer has to any of the clients.

(b) A lawyer should, except in unusual circumstances that may make it infeasible, provide both clients with an explanation in writing of the risks involved in the common representation and of the circumstances that may cause separate representation later to be necessary or desirable. The consent of the clients shall also be in writing.

(c) While acting as intermediary, the lawyer shall consult with each client concerning the decisions to be made and the considerations relevant in making them, so that each client can make adequately informed decisions.

(d) A lawyer shall withdraw as intermediary if any of the clients so request, or if any of the conditions stated in paragraph (a) are no longer satisfied. Upon withdrawal, the lawyer shall not continue to represent any of the clients in the matter that was the subject of the intermediation.

COMMENT:

[1] A lawyer acts as intermediary under this Rule when the lawyer represents two or more parties with potentially conflicting interests. A key factor in defining the relationship is whether the parties share responsibility for the

lawyer's fee, but the common representation may be inferred from other circumstances. Because confusion can arise as to the lawyer's role where each party is not separately represented, it is important that the lawyer make clear the relationship.

[2] Because the potential for confusion is so great, paragraph (b) imposes the requirement that an explanation of the risks of the common representation be furnished in writing, except in unusual circumstances. The process of preparing the writing causes the lawyer involved to focus specifically on those risks, a process that may suggest to the lawyer that the particular situation is not suited to the use of the lawyer as an intermediary. In any event, the writing performs a valuable role in educating the client to such risks as may exist—risks that many clients may not otherwise comprehend. Mere agreement by a client to waive the requirement for a written analysis of the risks does not constitute the "unusual circumstances" that justify omitting the writing. The "unusual circumstances" requirement may be met in rare situations where an assessment of risks is not feasible at the beginning of the intermediary role. In such circumstances, the writing should be provided as soon as it becomes feasible to assess the risks with reasonable clarity. The consent required by paragraph (b) should refer to the disclosure upon which it is based.

[3] The Rule does not apply to a lawyer acting as arbitrator or mediator between or among parties who are not clients of the lawyer, even where the lawyer has been appointed with the concurrence of the parties. In performing such a role the lawyer may be subject to applicable codes of ethics, such as the Code of Ethics for Arbitration in Commercial Disputes prepared by a Joint Committee of the American Bar Association and the American Arbitration Association.

[4] A lawyer acts as intermediary in seeking to establish or adjust a relationship between clients on an amicable and mutually advantageous basis; for example, in helping to organize a business in which two or more clients are entrepreneurs, working out the financial reorganization of an enterprise in which two or more clients have an interest, arranging a property distribution in settlement of an estate, or mediating a dispute between clients. The lawyer seeks to resolve potentially conflicting interests by developing the parties' mutual interests. The alternative can be that each party may have to obtain separate representation, with the possibility in some situations of incurring additional cost, complication, or even litigation. Given these and other relevant factors, all the clients may prefer that the lawyer act as intermediary.

[5] In considering whether to act as intermediary between clients, a lawyer should be mindful that if the intermediation fails the result can be additional cost, embarrassment, and recrimination. In some situations the risk of failure is so great that intermediation is plainly impossible. For example, a lawyer cannot undertake common representation of clients between whom contentious litigation is imminent or who contemplate contentious negotiations. More generally, if the relationship between the parties has already assumed definite antagonism, the possibility that the clients' interests can be adjusted by intermediation ordinarily is not very good.

[6] The appropriateness of intermediation can depend on its form. Forms of intermediation range from informal arbitration where each client's case is presented by the respective client and the lawyer decides the outcome, to mediation, to common representation where the clients' interests are substantially though

Rule 2.2 *WASH., D.C. RULES OF PROF. CONDUCT*

not entirely compatible. One form may be appropriate in circumstances where another would not. Other relevant factors are whether the lawyer subsequently will represent both parties on a continuing basis and whether the situation involves creating a relationship between the parties or terminating one.

[7] Since the lawyer is required to be impartial between commonly represented clients, intermediation is improper when that impartiality cannot be maintained. For example, a lawyer who has represented one of the clients for a long period of time and in a variety of matters could have difficulty being impartial between that client and one to whom the lawyer has only recently been introduced.

Confidentiality and Privilege

[8] A particularly important factor in determining the appropriateness of intermediation is the effect on client-lawyer confidentiality and the attorney-client privilege. In a common representation, the lawyer is still required both to keep each client adequately informed and to maintain confidentiality of information relating to the representation. *See* Rules 1.4 and 1.6. Complying with both requirements while acting as intermediary requires a delicate balance. If the balance cannot be maintained, the common representation is improper. With regard to the attorney-client privilege, the prevailing rule is that as between commonly represented clients the privilege does not attach. Hence, it must be assumed that if litigation eventuates between the clients, the privilege will not protect any such communications, and the clients should be so advised.

Consultation

[9] In acting as intermediary between clients, the lawyer is required to consult with the clients on the implications of doing so, and proceed only upon consent based on such a consultation. The consultation should make clear that the lawyer's role is not that of partisanship normally expected in other circumstances.

[10] Paragraph (c) is an application of the principle expressed in Rule 1.4. Where the lawyer is intermediary, the clients ordinarily must assume greater responsibility for decisions than when each client is independently represented.

Withdrawal

[11] Common representation does not diminish the rights of each client in the client-lawyer relationship. Each has the right to loyal and diligent representation, the right to discharge the lawyer as stated in Rule 1.16, and the protection of Rule 1.9 concerning obligations to a former client.

RULE 2.3 Evaluation for Use by Third Persons

(a) A lawyer may undertake an evaluation of a matter affecting a client for the use of someone other than the client if:

(1) The lawyer reasonably believes that making the evaluation is compatible with other aspects of the lawyer's relationship with the client; and

(2) The client consents after consultation.

(b) Except as disclosure is required in connection with a report of an evaluation, information relating to the evaluation is otherwise protected by Rule 1.6.

COMMENT:

Definition

[1] An evaluation may be performed at the client's direction but for the primary purpose of establishing information for the benefit of third parties; for example, an opinion concerning the title of property rendered at the behest of a vendor for the information of a prospective purchaser, or at the behest of a borrower for the information of a prospective lender. In some situations, the evaluation may be required by a government agency; for example, an opinion concerning the legality of the securities registered for sale under the securities laws. In other instances, the evaluation may be required by a third person, such as a purchaser of a business.

[2] A legal evaluation should be distinguished from an investigation of a person with whom the lawyer does not have a client-lawyer relationship. For example, a lawyer retained by a purchaser to analyze a vendor's title to property does not have a client-lawyer relationship with the vendor. So also, an investigation into a person's affairs by a government lawyer, or by special counsel employed by the government, is not an evaluation as that term is used in this Rule. The question is whether the lawyer is retained by the person whose affairs are being examined. When the lawyer is retained by that person, the general Rules concerning loyalty to client and preservation of confidences apply, which is not the case if the lawyer is retained by someone else. For this reason, it is essential to identify the person by whom the lawyer is retained. This should be made clear not only to the person under examination, but also to others to whom the results are to be made available.

Duty to Third Person

[3] When the evaluation is intended for the information or use of a third person, a legal duty to that person may or may not arise. That legal question is beyond the scope of this Rule. However, since such an evaluation involves a departure from the normal client-lawyer relationship, careful analysis of the situation is required. The lawyer must be satisfied as a matter of professional judgment that making the evaluation is compatible with other functions undertaken in behalf of the client. For example, if the lawyer is acting as advocate in defending the client against charges of fraud, it would normally be incompatible with that responsibility for the lawyer to perform an evaluation for others concerning the same or a related transaction. Assuming no such impediment is apparent, however, the lawyer should advise the client of the implications of the evaluation, particularly the lawyer's responsibilities to third persons and the duty to disseminate the findings.

Access to and Disclosure of Information

[4] The quality of an evaluation depends on the freedom and extent of the investigation upon which it is based. Ordinarily a lawyer should have whatever latitude of investigation seems necessary as a matter of professional judgment. Under some circumstances, however, the terms of the evaluation may be limited. For example, certain issues or sources may be categorically excluded, or the scope of search may be limited by time constraints or the noncooperation of persons having relevant information. Any such limitations that are material to the evaluation should be described in the report. If after a lawyer has commenced an evaluation, the client refuses to comply with the terms upon which it

was understood the evaluation was to have been made, the lawyer's obligations are determined by law, having reference to the terms of the client's agreement and the surrounding circumstances.

Financial Auditors' Requests for Information

[5] When a question concerning the legal situation of a client arises at the insistence of the client's financial auditor and the question is referred to the lawyer, the lawyer's response may be made in accordance with procedures recognized in the legal profession. Such a procedure is set forth in the American Bar Association Statement of Policy Regarding Lawyers' Responses to Auditors' Requests for Information, adopted in 1975.

ADVOCATE

RULE 3.1 Meritorious Claims and Contentions

A lawyer shall not bring or defend a proceeding, or assert or controvert an issue therein, unless there is a basis for doing so that is not frivolous, which includes a good-faith argument for an extension, modification, or reversal of existing law. A lawyer for the defendant in a criminal proceeding, or for the respondent in a proceeding that could result in involuntary institutionalization, shall, if the client elects to go to trial or to a contested fact-finding hearing, nevertheless so defend the proceeding as to require that the government carry its burden of proof.

COMMENT:

[1] The advocate has a duty to use legal procedure for the fullest benefit of the client's cause, but also a duty not to abuse legal procedure. The law, both procedural and substantive, establishes the limits within which an advocate may proceed. However, the law is not always clear and never is static. Accordingly, in determining the proper scope of advocacy, account must be taken of the law's ambiguities and potential for change.

[2] The filing of an action or defense or similar action taken for a client is not frivolous merely because the facts have not first been fully substantiated or because the lawyer expects to develop vital evidence only by discovery. Such action is not frivolous even though the lawyer believes that the client's position ultimately will not prevail. The action is frivolous if the lawyer is unable either to make a good-faith argument on the merits of the action taken or to support the action taken by a good-faith argument for an extension, modification, or reversal of existing law.

[3] In criminal cases or proceedings in which the respondent can be involuntarily institutionalized, such as juvenile delinquency and civil commitment cases, the lawyer is not only permitted, but is indeed required, to put the government to its proof whenever the client elects to contest adjudication.

RULE 3.2 Expediting Litigation

(a) In representing a client, a lawyer shall not delay a proceeding when the lawyer knows or when it is obvious that such action would serve solely to harass or maliciously injure another.

(b) A lawyer shall make reasonable efforts to expedite litigation consistent with the interests of the client.

COMMENT:

[1] Dilatory practices bring the administration of justice into disrepute. Delay should not be indulged merely for the convenience of the advocates, or for the purpose of frustrating an opposing party's attempt to obtain rightful redress or repose. It is not a justification that similar conduct is often tolerated by the bench and bar. The question is whether a competent lawyer acting in good-faith would regard the course of action as having some substantial purpose other than delay. Realizing financial or other benefit from otherwise improper delay in litigation is not a legitimate interest of the client.

RULE 3.3 Candor Toward the Tribunal

(a) A lawyer shall not knowingly:

(1) Make a false statement of material fact or law to a tribunal;

(2) Counsel or assist a client to engage in conduct that the lawyer knows is criminal or fraudulent, but a lawyer may discuss the legal consequences of any proposed course of conduct with a client and may counsel or assist a client to make a good-faith effort to determine the validity, scope, meaning, or application of the law;

(3) Fail to disclose to the tribunal legal authority in the controlling jurisdiction not disclosed by opposing counsel and known to the lawyer to be dispositive of a question at issue and directly adverse to the position of the client; or

(4) Offer evidence that the lawyer knows to be false, except as provided in paragraph (b).

(b) When the witness who intends to give evidence that the lawyer knows to be false is the lawyer's client and is the accused in a criminal case, the lawyer shall first make a good-faith effort to dissuade the client from presenting the false evidence; if the lawyer is unable to dissuade the client, the lawyer shall seek leave of the tribunal to withdraw. If the lawyer is unable to dissuade the client or to withdraw without seriously harming the client, the lawyer may put the client on the stand to testify in a narrative fashion, but the lawyer shall not examine the client in such manner as to elicit testimony which the lawyer knows to be false, and shall not argue the probative value of the client's testimony in closing argument.

(c) The duties stated in paragraph (a) continue to the conclusion of the proceeding.

(d) A lawyer who receives information clearly establishing that a fraud has been perpetrated upon the tribunal shall promptly reveal the fraud to the tribunal unless compliance with this duty would require disclosure of information otherwise protected by Rule 1.6, in which case the lawyer shall promptly call upon the client to rectify the fraud.

COMMENT:

[1] This Rule defines the duty of candor to the tribunal. In dealing with a tribunal the lawyer is also required to comply with the general requirements of Rule 1.2(e) and (f). However, an advocate does not vouch for the evidence

submitted in a cause; the tribunal is responsible for assessing its probative value.

Representations by a Lawyer

[2] An assertion purported to be made by the lawyer, as in an affidavit by the lawyer or in a statement in open court, may properly be made only when the lawyer knows the assertion is true or believes it to be true on the basis of a reasonably diligent inquiry. There may be circumstances where failure to make a disclosure is the equivalent of an affirmative misrepresentation. The obligation prescribed in Rule 1.2(e) not to counsel a client to commit or assist the client in committing a fraud applies in litigation but is subject to Rule 3.3(b) and (d). Regarding compliance with Rule 1.2(e), see the Comment to that Rule. *See also* Comment to Rule 8.4(b).

Misleading Legal Argument

[3] Legal argument based on a knowingly false representation of law constitutes dishonesty toward the tribunal. A lawyer is not required to make a disinterested exposition of the law, but must recognize the existence of pertinent legal authorities. Furthermore, as stated in subparagraph (a)(3), an advocate has a duty to disclose directly adverse authority in the controlling jurisdiction that has not been disclosed by the opposing party and that is dispositive of a question at issue. The underlying concept is that legal argument is a discussion seeking to determine the legal premises properly applicable to the case.

False Evidence

[4] When evidence that a lawyer knows to be false is provided by a person who is not the client, the lawyer must refuse to offer it regardless of the client's wishes.

[5] When false evidence is offered by the client, however, a conflict may arise between the lawyer's duty to keep the client's revelations confidential and the duty of candor to the court. Upon ascertaining that material evidence is false, the lawyer should seek to persuade the client that the evidence should not be offered or, if it has been offered, that its false character should immediately be disclosed.

[6] Paragraph (d) provides that if a lawyer learns that a fraud has been perpetrated on the tribunal, the lawyer must reveal the fraud to the tribunal. However, if the notification of the tribunal would require disclosure of information protected by Rule 1.6, the lawyer may not inform the tribunal of the fraud; the lawyer's only duty in such an instance is to call upon the client to rectify the fraud. In other cases, the lawyer may learn of the client's intention to present false evidence before the client has had a chance to do so. In this situation, paragraphs (a)(4) and (b) forbid the lawyer to present the false evidence, except in rare instances where the witness is the accused in a criminal case, the lawyer is unsuccessful in dissuading the client from going forward, and the lawyer is unable to withdraw without causing serious harm to the client. The terms "criminal case" and "criminal defendant" as used in Rule 3.3 and its Comment include juvenile delinquency proceedings and the person who is the subject of such proceedings.

Perjury by a Criminal Defendant

[7] Paragraph (b) allows the lawyer to permit a client who is the accused in a criminal case to present false testimony in very narrowly circumscribed circumstances and in a very limited manner. Even in a criminal case the lawyer must seek to persuade the defendant-client to refrain from perjurious testimony. There has been dispute concerning the lawyer's duty when that persuasion fails. Paragraph (b) requires the lawyer to withdraw rather than offer the client's false testimony, if this can be done without seriously harming the client.

[8] Serious harm to the client sufficient to prevent the lawyer's withdrawal entails more than the usual inconveniences that necessarily result from withdrawal, such as delay in concluding the client's case or an increase in the costs of concluding the case. The term should be construed narrowly to preclude withdrawal only where the special circumstances of the case are such that the client would be significantly prejudiced, such as by express or implied divulgence of information otherwise protected by Rule 1.6. If the confrontation with the client occurs before trial, the lawyer ordinarily can withdraw. Withdrawal before trial may not be possible, however, either because trial is imminent, or because the confrontation with the client does not take place until the trial itself, or because no other counsel is available. In those rare circumstances in which withdrawal without such serious harm to the client is impossible, the lawyer may go forward with examination of the client and closing argument subject to the limitations of paragraph (b).

Refusing to Offer Proof of a Nonclient Known to Be False

[9] Generally speaking, a lawyer may not offer testimony or other proof, through a nonclient, that the lawyer knows to be false. Furthermore, a lawyer may not offer evidence of a client if the evidence is known by the lawyer to be false, except to the extent permitted by paragraph (b) where the client is a defendant in a criminal case.

RULE 3.4 Fairness to Opposing Party and Counsel

A lawyer shall not:

(a) Obstruct another party's access to evidence or alter, destroy, or conceal evidence, or counsel or assist another person to do so, if the lawyer reasonably should know that the evidence is or may be the subject of discovery or subpoena in any pending or imminent proceeding. Unless prohibited by law, a lawyer may receive physical evidence of any kind from the client or from another person. If the evidence received by the lawyer belongs to anyone other than the client, the lawyer shall make a good-faith effort to preserve it and to return it to the owner, subject to Rule 1.6;

(b) Falsify evidence, counsel or assist a witness to testify falsely, or offer an inducement to a witness that is prohibited by law;

(c) Knowingly disobey an obligation under the rules of a tribunal except for an open refusal based on an assertion that no valid obligation exists;

(d) In pretrial procedure, make a frivolous discovery request or fail to make reasonably diligent effort to comply with a legally proper discovery request by an opposing party;

(e) In trial, allude to any matter that the lawyer does not reasonably believe is relevant or that will not be supported by admissible evidence, assert personal knowledge of facts in issue except when testifying as a witness, or state a personal opinion as to the justness of a cause, the credibility of a witness, the culpability of a civil litigant, or the guilt or innocence of an accused; or

(f) Request a person other than a client to refrain from voluntarily giving relevant information to another party unless:

(1) The person is a relative or an employee or other agent of a client; and

(2) The lawyer reasonably believes that the person's interests will not be adversely affected by refraining from giving such information.

COMMENT:

[1] The procedure of the adversary system contemplates that the evidence in a case is to be marshaled competitively by the contending parties. Fair competition in the adversary system is secured by prohibitions against destruction or concealment of evidence, improperly influencing witnesses, obstructive tactics in discovery procedure, and the like.

[2] Documents and other items of evidence are often essential to establish a claim or defense. Subject to evidentiary privileges, the right of an opposing party, including the government, to obtain evidence through discovery or subpoena is an important procedural right. The exercise of that right can be frustrated if relevant material is altered, concealed, or destroyed. To the extent clients are involved in the effort to comply with discovery requests, the lawyer's obligations are to pursue reasonable efforts to assure that documents and other information subject to proper discovery requests are produced. Applicable law in many jurisdictions makes it an offense to destroy material for purpose of impairing its availability in a pending proceeding or a proceeding whose commencement can be foreseen. Falsifying evidence is also generally a criminal offense. Paragraph (a) applies to evidentiary material generally, including computerized information.

[3] Paragraph (a) permits, but does not require, the lawyer to accept physical evidence (including the instruments or proceeds of crime) from the client or any other person. Such receipt is, as stated in paragraph (a), subject to other provisions of law and the limitations imposed by paragraph (a) with respect to obstruction of access, alteration, destruction, or concealment, and subject also to the requirements of paragraph (a) with respect to return of property to its rightful owner, and to the obligation to comply with subpoenas and discovery requests. The term "evidence" includes any document or physical object that the lawyer reasonably should know may be the subject of discovery or subpoena in any pending or imminent litigation. *See* D.C. Bar Legal Ethics Committee Opinion No. 119 (Mar. 15, 1983) (test is whether destruction of document is directed at concrete litigation that is either pending or almost certain to be filed).

[4] A lawyer should ascertain that the lawyer's handling of documents or other physical objects does not violate any other law. Federal criminal law may forbid the destruction of documents or other physical objects in circumstances not covered by the ethical rule set forth in paragraph (a). *See, e.g.,* 18 U.S.C. § 1503 (obstruction of justice); 18 U.S.C. § 1505 (obstruction of proceedings before departments, agencies, and committees); 18 U.S.C. § 1510 (obstruction of criminal investigations). And it is a crime in the District of Columbia for one who knows or has reason to know that an official proceeding has begun or is

likely to be instituted to alter, destroy, or conceal a document with intent to impair its integrity or availability for use in the proceeding. D.C.Code § 22–723 (1981). Finally, some discovery rules having the force of law may prohibit the destruction of documents and other material even if litigation is not pending or imminent. This Rule does not set forth the scope of a lawyer's responsibilities under all applicable laws. It merely imposes on the lawyer an ethical duty to make reasonable efforts to comply fully with those laws. The provisions of paragraph (a) prohibit a lawyer from obstructing another party's access to evidence, and from altering, destroying, or concealing evidence. These prohibitions may overlap with criminal obstruction provisions and civil discovery rules, but they apply whether or not the prohibited conduct violates criminal provisions or court rules. Thus, the alteration of evidence by a lawyer, whether or not such conduct violates criminal law or court rules, constitutes a violation of paragraph (a).

[5] Because of the duty of confidentiality under Rule 1.6, the lawyer is generally forbidden to volunteer information about physical evidence received from a client without the client's consent after consultation. In some cases, the Office of Bar Counsel will accept physical evidence from a lawyer and then turn it over to the appropriate persons; in those cases this procedure is usually the best means of delivering evidence to the proper authorities without disclosing the client's confidences. However, Bar Counsel may refuse to accept evidence; thus lawyers should keep the following in mind before accepting evidence from a client, and should discuss with Bar Counsel's office the procedures that may be employed in particular circumstances.

[6] First, if the evidence received from the client is subpoenaed or otherwise requested through the discovery process while held by the lawyer, the lawyer will be obligated to deliver the evidence directly to the appropriate persons, unless there is a basis for objecting to the discovery request or moving to quash the subpoena. A lawyer should therefore advise the client of the risk that evidence may be subject to subpoena or discovery, and of the lawyer's duty to turn the evidence over in that event, before accepting it from the client.

[7] Second, if the lawyer has received physical evidence belonging to the client, for purposes of examination or testing, the lawyer may later return the property to the client pursuant to Rule 1.15, provided that the evidence has not been subpoenaed. The lawyer may not be justified in returning to a client physical evidence the possession of which by the client would be per se illegal, such as certain drugs and weapons. And if it is reasonably apparent that the evidence is not the client's property, the lawyer may not retain the evidence or return it to the client. Instead, the lawyer must under paragraph (a), make a good-faith effort to return the evidence to its owner.

[8] With regard to paragraph (b), it is not improper to pay a witness's expenses or to compensate a witness for loss of time in preparing to testify, in attending, or in testifying. A fee for the services of a witness who will be proffered as an expert may be made contingent on the outcome of the litigation, provided, however, that the fee, while conditioned on recovery, shall not be a percentage of the recovery.

[9] Paragraph (f) permits a lawyer to advise employees of a client to refrain from giving information to another party, for the employees may identify their interests with those of the client. *See also* Rule 4.2.

RULE 3.5 Impartiality and Decorum of the Tribunal

A lawyer shall not:

(a) Seek to influence a judge, juror, prospective juror, or other official by means prohibited by law;

(b) Communicate ex parte with such a person except as permitted by law; or

(c) Engage in conduct intended to disrupt a tribunal.

COMMENT:

[1] Many forms of improper influence upon a tribunal are proscribed by criminal law. Others are specified in the ABA Model Code of Judicial Conduct, with which an advocate should be familiar. A lawyer is required to avoid contributing to a violation of such provisions.

[2] The advocate's function is to present evidence and argument so that the cause may be decided according to law. Refraining from abusive or obstreperous conduct is a corollary of the advocate's right to speak on behalf of litigants. A lawyer may stand firm against abuse by a judge but should avoid reciprocation; the judge's default is no justification for similar dereliction by an advocate. An advocate can present the cause, protect the record for subsequent review, and preserve professional integrity by patient firmness no less effectively than by belligerence or theatrics.

RULE 3.6 Trial Publicity

A lawyer engaged in a case being tried to a judge or jury shall not make an extrajudicial statement that a reasonable person would expect to be disseminated by means of mass public communication if the lawyer knows or reasonably should know that the statement will create a serious and imminent threat to the impartiality of the judge or jury.

COMMENT:

[1] It is difficult to strike a proper balance between protecting the right to a fair trial and safeguarding the right of free expression, which are both guaranteed by the Constitution. On one hand, publicity should not be allowed to influence the fair administration of justice. On the other hand, litigants have a right to present their side of a dispute to the public, and the public has an interest in receiving information about matters that are in litigation. Often a lawyer involved in the litigation is in the best position to assist in furthering these legitimate objectives. No body of rules can simultaneously satisfy all interests of fair trial and all those of free expression.

[2] The special obligations of prosecutors to limit comment on criminal matters involve considerations in addition to those implicated in this Rule, and are dealt with in Rule 3.8. Furthermore, this Rule is not intended to abrogate special court rules of confidentiality in juvenile or other cases. Lawyers are bound by Rule 3.4(c) to adhere to any such rules that have not been found invalid.

[3] Because administrative agencies should have the prerogative to determine the ethical rules for prehearing publicity, this rule does not purport to apply to matters before administrative agencies.

RULE 3.7 Lawyer as Witness

(a) A lawyer shall not act as advocate at a trial in which the lawyer is likely to be a necessary witness except where:

(1) The testimony relates to an uncontested issue;

(2) The testimony relates to the nature and value of legal services rendered in the case; or

(3) Disqualification of the lawyer would work substantial hardship on the client.

(b) A lawyer may not act as advocate in a trial in which another lawyer in the lawyer's firm is likely to be called as a witness if the other lawyer would be precluded from acting as advocate in the trial by Rule 1.7 or Rule 1.9. The provisions of this paragraph (b) do not apply if the lawyer who is appearing as an advocate is employed by, and appears on behalf of, a government agency.

COMMENT:

[1] Combining the roles of advocate and witness can prejudice the opposing party and can involve a conflict of interest between the lawyer and client.

[2] The opposing party has proper objection where the combination of roles may prejudice that party's rights in the litigation. A witness is required to testify on the basis of personal knowledge, while an advocate is expected to explain and comment on evidence given by others. It may not be clear whether a statement by an advocate-witness should be taken as proof or as an analysis of the proof.

[3] Subparagraph (a)(1) recognizes that if the testimony will be uncontested, the ambiguities in the dual role are purely theoretical. Subparagraph (a)(2) recognizes that where the testimony concerns the extent and value of legal services rendered in the action in which the testimony is offered, permitting the lawyers to testify avoids the need for a second trial with new counsel to resolve that issue. Moreover, in such a situation the judge has firsthand knowledge of the matter in issue; hence, there is less dependence on the adversary process to test the credibility of the testimony.

[4] Apart from these two exceptions, subparagraph (a)(3) recognizes that a balancing is required between the interests of the client and those of the opposing party. Whether the opposing party is likely to suffer prejudice depends on the nature of the case, the importance and probable tenor of the lawyer's testimony, and the probability that the lawyer's testimony will conflict with that of other witnesses. Even if there is risk of such prejudice, in determining whether the lawyer should be disqualified due regard must be given to the effect of disqualification on the lawyer's client. It is relevant that one or both parties could reasonably foresee that the lawyer would probably be a witness.

[5] If the only reason for not permitting a lawyer to combine the roles of advocate and witness is possible prejudice to the opposing party, there is no reason to disqualify other lawyers in the testifying lawyer's firm from acting as advocates in that trial. In short, there is no general rule of imputed disqualification applicable to Rule 3.7. However, the combination of roles of advocate and witness may involve an improper conflict of interest between the lawyer and the client in addition to or apart from possible prejudice to the opposing party. Whether there is such a client conflict is determined by Rule 1.7 or 1.9. For

example, if there is likely to be a significant conflict between the testimony of the client and that of the lawyer, the representation is improper by the standard of Rule 1.7(b) without regard to Rule 3.7(a). The problem can arise whether the lawyer is called as a witness on behalf of the client or is called by the opposing party. Determining whether such a conflict exists is, in the first instance, the responsibility of the lawyer involved. See Comment to Rule 1.7. Rule 3.7(b) states that other lawyers in the testifying lawyer's firm are disqualified only when there is such a client conflict and the testifying lawyer therefore could not represent the client under Rule 1.7 or 1.9. The principles of client consent, embodied in Rules 1.7 and 1.9, also apply to paragraph (b). Thus, the reference to Rules 1.7 and 1.9 incorporates the client consent aspects of those Rules. Paragraph (b) is designed to provide protection for the client, not rights of disqualification to the adversary. Subject to the disclosure and consultation requirements of Rules 1.7 and 1.9, the client may consent to the firm's continuing representation, despite the potential problems created by the nature of the testimony to be provided by a lawyer in the firm.

[6] Even though a lawyer's testimony does not involve a conflict with the client's interests under Rule 1.7 or 1.9 and would not be precluded under Rule 3.7, the client's interests might nevertheless be harmed by the appearance as a witness of a lawyer in the firm that represents the client. For example, the lawyer's testimony would be vulnerable to impeachment on the grounds that the lawyer-witness is testifying to support the position of the lawyer's own firm. Similarly, a lawyer whose firm colleague is testifying in the case should recognize the possibility that the lawyer might not scrutinize the testimony of the colleague carefully enough and that this could prejudice the client's interests, whether the colleague is testifying for or against the client. In such instances, the lawyer should inform the client of any possible adverse effects on the client's interests that might result from the lawyer's relationship with the colleague-witness, so that the client may make a meaningful choice whether to retain the lawyer for the representation in question.

RULE 3.8 Special Responsibilities of a Prosecutor

The prosecutor in a criminal case shall not:

(a) In exercising discretion to investigate or to prosecute, improperly favor or invidiously discriminate against any person;

(b) File in court or maintain a charge that the prosecutor knows is not supported by probable cause;

(c) Prosecute to trial a charge that the prosecutor knows is not supported by evidence sufficient to establish a prima facie showing of guilt;

(d) Intentionally avoid pursuit of evidence or information because it may damage the prosecution's case or aid the defense;

(e) Intentionally fail to disclose to the defense, upon request and at a time when use by the defense is reasonably feasible, any evidence or information that the prosecutor knows or reasonably should know tends to negate the guilt of the accused or to mitigate the offense, or in connection with sentencing, intentionally fail to disclose to the defense upon request any unprivileged mitigating information known to the prosecutor and not reasonably available to the defense, except when the prosecutor is relieved of this responsibility by a protective order of the tribunal;

(f) Except for statements which are necessary to inform the public of the nature and extent of the prosecutor's action and which serve a legitimate law enforcement purpose, make extrajudicial comments which serve to heighten condemnation of the accused;

(g) In presenting a case to a grand jury, intentionally interfere with the independence of the grand jury, preempt a function of the grand jury, abuse the processes of the grand jury, or fail to bring to the attention of the grand jury material facts tending substantially to negate the existence of probable cause; or

(h) Peremptorily strike jurors on grounds of race, religion, national or ethnic background, or sex.

COMMENT:

[1] A prosecutor has the responsibility of a minister of justice and not simply that of an advocate. This responsibility carries with it specific obligations to see that the defendant is accorded procedural justice and that guilt is decided upon the basis of sufficient evidence. Precisely how far the prosecutor is required to go in this direction is a matter of debate and varies in different jurisdictions. Many jurisdictions have adopted the ABA Standards of Criminal Justice Relating to Prosecution Function, which in turn are the product of prolonged and careful deliberation by lawyers experienced in both criminal prosecution and defense. This Rule is intended to be a distillation of some, but not all, of the professional obligations imposed on prosecutors by applicable law. The Rule, however, is not intended either to restrict or to expand the obligations of prosecutors derived from the United States Constitution, federal or District of Columbia statutes, and court rules of procedure.

[2] Apart from the special responsibilities of a prosecutor under this Rule, prosecutors are subject to the same obligations imposed upon all lawyers by these Rules of Professional Conduct, including Rule 5.3, relating to responsibilities regarding nonlawyers who work for or in association with the lawyer's office. Indeed, because of the power and visibility of a prosecutor, the prosecutor's compliance with these Rules, and recognition of the need to refrain even from some actions technically allowed to other lawyers under the Rules, may, in certain instances, be of special importance. For example, Rule 3.6 prohibits extrajudicial statements that will have a substantial likelihood of destroying the impartiality of the judge or jury. In the context of a criminal prosecution, pretrial publicity can present the further problem of giving the public the incorrect impression that the accused is guilty before having been proven guilty through the due processes of the law. It is unavoidable, of course, that the publication of an indictment may itself have severe consequences for an accused. What is avoidable, however, is extrajudicial comment by a prosecutor that serves unnecessarily to heighten public condemnation of the accused without a legitimate law enforcement purpose before the criminal process has taken its course. When that occurs, even if the ultimate trial is not prejudiced, the accused may be subjected to unfair and unnecessary condemnation before the trial takes place. Accordingly, a prosecutor should use special care to avoid publicity, such as through televised press conferences, which would unnecessarily heighten condemnation of the accused.

[3] Nothing in this Comment, however, is intended to suggest that a prosecutor may not inform the public of such matters as whether an official investiga-

tion has ended or is continuing, or who participated in it, and the prosecutor may respond to press inquiries to clarify such things as technicalities of the indictment, the status of the matter, or the legal procedures that will follow. Also, a prosecutor should be free to respond, insofar as necessary, to any extrajudicial allegations by the defense of unprofessional or unlawful conduct on the part of the prosecutor's office.

RULE 3.9 Advocate in Nonadjudicative Proceedings

A lawyer representing a client before a legislative or administrative body in a nonadjudicative proceeding shall disclose that the appearance is in a representative capacity and shall conform to the provisions of Rules 3.3, 3.4(a) through (c), and 3.5.

COMMENT:

[1] In representation before bodies such as legislatures, municipal councils, and executive and administrative agencies acting in a rule-making or policy-making capacity, lawyers present facts, formulate issues, and advance argument in the matters under consideration. The decision-making body, like a court, should be able to rely on the integrity of the submissions made to it. A lawyer appearing before such a body should deal with it honestly and in conformity with applicable rules of procedure.

[2] Lawyers have no exclusive right to appear before nonadjudicative bodies, as they do before a court. The requirements of this Rule therefore may subject lawyers to regulations inapplicable to advocates, such as nonlawyer lobbyists, who are not lawyers. However, legislatures and administrative agencies have a right to expect lawyers to deal with them as they deal with courts.

[3] This Rule does not apply to representation of a client in a negotiation or other bilateral transaction with a government agency; representation in such a transaction is governed by Rules 4.1 through 4.4.

[4] This Rule is closely related to Rules 3.3 through 3.5, which deal with conduct regarding tribunals. The term "tribunal," as defined in the Terminology section of these Rules, refers to adjudicative or quasi-adjudicative bodies.

TRANSACTIONS WITH PERSONS OTHER THAN CLIENTS

RULE 4.1 Truthfulness in Statements to Others

In the course of representing a client, a lawyer shall not knowingly:

(a) Make a false statement of material fact or law to a third person; or

(b) Fail to disclose a material fact to a third person when disclosure is necessary to avoid assisting a criminal or fraudulent act by a client, unless disclosure is prohibited by Rule 1.6.

COMMENT:

Misrepresentation

[1] A lawyer is required to be truthful when dealing with others on a client's behalf, but generally has no affirmative duty to inform an opposing party of relevant facts. A misrepresentation can occur if the lawyer incorporates or affirms a statement of another person that the lawyer knows is false. Misrepre-

sentations can also occur by failure to act. The term "third person" as used in paragraphs (a) and (b) refers to any person or entity other than the lawyer's client.

Statements of Fact

[2] This Rule refers to material statements of fact. Whether a particular statement should be regarded as material, and as one of fact, can depend on the circumstances. Under generally accepted conventions in negotiation, certain types of statements ordinarily are not taken as statements of material fact. Estimates of price or value placed on the subject of a transaction and a party's intentions as to an acceptable settlement of a claim are in this category, and so is the existence of an undisclosed principal except where nondisclosure of the principal would constitute fraud. There may be other analogous situations.

Fraud by Client

[3] Paragraph (b) recognizes that substantive law may require a lawyer to disclose certain information to avoid being deemed to have assisted the client's crime or fraud. The requirement of disclosure created by this paragraph is, however, subject to the obligations created by Rule 1.6.

RULE 4.2 Communication Between Lawyer and Opposing Parties

(a) During the course of representing a client, a lawyer shall not communicate or cause another to communicate about the subject of the representation with a party known to be represented by another lawyer in the matter, unless the lawyer has the prior consent of the lawyer representing such other party or is authorized by law to do so.

(b) During the course of representing a client, a lawyer may communicate about the subject of the representation with a nonparty employee of the opposing party without obtaining the consent of that party's lawyer. However, prior to communicating with any such nonparty employee, a lawyer must disclose to such employee both the lawyer's identity and the fact that the lawyer represents a party with a claim against the employee's employer.

(c) For purposes of this Rule, the term "party" includes any person, including an employee of a party organization, who has the authority to bind a party organization as to the representation to which the communication relates.

(d) This Rule does not prohibit communication by a lawyer with government officials who have the authority to redress the grievances of the lawyer's client, whether or not those grievances or the lawyer's communications relate to matters that are the subject of the representation, provided that in the event of such communications the disclosures specified in (b) are made to the government official to whom the communication is made.

COMMENT:

[1] This Rule does not prohibit communication with a party, or an employee or agent of a party, concerning matters outside the representation. For example, the existence of a controversy between two organizations does not prohibit a lawyer for either from communicating with nonlawyer representatives of the other regarding a separate matter. Also, parties to a matter may communicate

Rule 4.2   WASH., D.C. RULES OF PROF. CONDUCT

directly with each other and a lawyer having independent justification for communicating with the other party is permitted to do so.

[2] In the case of an organization, this Rule prohibits communication by a lawyer for one party concerning the matter in representation with persons having the power to bind the organization as to the particular representation to which the communication relates. If an agent or employee of the organization with authority to make binding decisions regarding the representation is represented in the matter by separate counsel, the consent by that agent's or employee's counsel to a communication will be sufficient for purposes of this Rule.

[3] This Rule does not prohibit a lawyer from communicating with employees of an organization who have the authority to bind the organization with respect to the matters underlying the representation if they do not also have authority to make binding decisions regarding the representation itself. A lawyer may therefore communicate with such persons without first notifying the organization's lawyer. *See* D.C. Bar Legal Ethics Committee Opinion No. 129 (1983). But before communicating with such a "nonparty employee," the lawyer must disclose to the employee the lawyer's identity and the fact that the lawyer represents a party with a claim against the employer. It is preferable that this disclosure be made in writing. The notification requirements of Rule 4.2(b) apply to contacts with government employees who do not have the authority to make binding decisions regarding the representation.

[4] This Rule also covers any person, whether or not a party to a formal proceeding, who is represented by counsel concerning the matter in question.

[5] This Rule does not apply to the situation in which a lawyer contacts employees of an organization for the purpose of obtaining information generally available to the public, or obtainable under the Freedom of Information Act, even if the information in question is related to the representation. For example, a lawyer for a plaintiff who has filed suit against an organization represented by a lawyer may telephone the organization to request a copy of a press release regarding the representation, without disclosing the lawyer's identity, obtaining the consent of the organization's lawyer, or otherwise acting as paragraphs (a) and (b) of this Rule require.

[6] Paragraph (d) recognizes that special considerations come into play when a lawyer is seeking to redress grievances involving the government. It permits communications with those in government having the authority to redress such grievances (but not with any other government personnel) without the prior consent of the lawyer representing the government in such cases. However, a lawyer making such a communication without the prior consent of the lawyer representing the government must make the kinds of disclosures that are required by paragraph (b) in the case of communications with non-party employees.

[7] Paragraph (d) does not permit a lawyer to bypass counsel representing the government on every issue that may arise in the course of disputes with the government. It is intended to provide lawyers access to decision makers in government with respect to genuine grievances, such as to present the view that the government's basic policy position with respect to a dispute is faulty, or that government personnel are conducting themselves improperly with respect to aspects of the dispute. It is not intended to provide direct access on routine

disputes such as ordinary discovery disputes, extensions of time or other scheduling matters, or similar routine aspects of the resolution of disputes.

[8] This Rule is not intended to regulate the law enforcement activities of the United States or the District of Columbia. A body of law has been developed that recognizes both the authority of the government to seek to obtain statements from a suspect, and the Fifth and Sixth Amendment rights of the suspect. The Rules of Professional Conduct do not apply to government conduct that is valid under this body of law. Generally speaking, Rule 4.2 will apply once a defendant is formally charged, elects to be represented by counsel, and obtains or is appointed counsel. But there are situations in which a defendant who is represented by counsel will seek to communicate with the government without defense counsel's being aware of the communication. Some communications will serve to protect the defendant and to identify sham representations. Although communications between charged defendants and the government without notice to defense counsel must be viewed with suspicion, such communications cannot be prohibited in all instances.

RULE 4.3 Dealing With Unrepresented Person

In dealing on behalf of a client with a person who is not represented by counsel, a lawyer shall not:

(a) Give advice to the unrepresented person other than the advice to secure counsel, if the interests of such person are or have a reasonable possibility of being in conflict with the interests of the lawyer's client;

(b) State or imply to unrepresented persons whose interests are not in conflict with the interests of the lawyer's client that the lawyer is disinterested. When the lawyer knows or reasonably should know that the unrepresented person misunderstands the lawyer's role in the matter, the lawyer shall make reasonable efforts to correct the misunderstanding.

COMMENT:

[1] An unrepresented person, particularly one not experienced in dealing with legal matters, might assume that a lawyer will provide disinterested advice concerning the law even when the lawyer represents a client. In dealing personally with any unrepresented third party on behalf of the lawyer's client, a lawyer must take great care not to exploit these assumptions.

[2] This Rule distinguishes between situations involving unrepresented third parties whose interests may be adverse to those of the lawyer's client and those in which the third party's interests are not in conflict with the client's. In the former situation, the possibility of the lawyer's compromising the unrepresented person's interests is so great that the Rule prohibits the giving of any advice, apart from the advice that the unrepresented person obtain counsel. A lawyer is free to give advice to unrepresented persons whose interests are not in conflict with those of the lawyer's client, but only if it is made clear that the lawyer is acting in the interests of the client. Thus the lawyer should not represent to such persons, either expressly or implicitly, that the lawyer is disinterested. Furthermore, if it becomes apparent that the unrepresented person misunderstands the lawyer's role in the matter, the lawyer must take whatever reasonable, affirmative steps are necessary to correct the misunderstanding.

[3] This Rule is not intended to restrict in any way law enforcement efforts by government lawyers that are consistent with constitutional requirements and applicable federal law.

RULE 4.4 Respect for Rights of Third Persons

In representing a client, a lawyer shall not use means that have no substantial purpose other than to embarrass, delay, or burden a third person, or use methods of obtaining evidence that violate the legal rights of such a person.

COMMENT:

[1] Responsibility to a client requires a lawyer to subordinate the interests of others to those of the client, but that responsibility does not imply that a lawyer may disregard the rights of third persons. It is impractical to catalogue all such rights, but they include legal restrictions on methods of obtaining evidence from third persons.

LAW FIRMS AND ASSOCIATIONS

RULE 5.1 Responsibilities of a Partner or Supervisory Lawyer

(a) A partner in a law firm shall make reasonable efforts to ensure that the firm has in effect measures giving reasonable assurance that all lawyers in the firm conform to the rules of professional conduct.

(b) A lawyer having direct supervisory authority over another lawyer shall make reasonable efforts to ensure that the other lawyer conforms to the rules of professional conduct.

(c) A lawyer shall be responsible for another lawyer's violation of the rules of professional conduct if:

(1) The lawyer orders or, with knowledge of the specific conduct, ratifies the conduct involved; or

(2) The lawyer has direct supervisory authority over the other lawyer or is a partner in the law firm in which the other lawyer practices, and knows or reasonably should know of the conduct at a time when its consequences can be avoided or mitigated but fails to take reasonable remedial action.

COMMENT:

[1] Paragraphs (a) and (b) refer to lawyers who have supervisory authority over the professional work of a firm or legal department of a government agency. This includes members of a partnership and the shareholders in a law firm organized as a professional corporation; lawyers having supervisory authority in the law department of an enterprise or government agency; and lawyers who have intermediate managerial responsibilities in a firm.

[2] The measures required to fulfill the responsibility prescribed in paragraphs (a) and (b) can depend on the firm's structure and the nature of its practice. In a small firm, informal supervision and occasional admonition ordinarily might be sufficient. In a large firm, or in practice situations in which intensely difficult ethical problems frequently arise, more elaborate procedures may be necessary. Some firms, for example, have a procedure whereby junior

lawyers can make confidential referral of ethical problems directly to a designated senior partner or special committee. See Rule 5.2. Firms, whether large or small, may also rely on continuing legal education in professional ethics. In any event, the ethical atmosphere of a firm can influence the conduct of all its members and a lawyer having authority over the work of another may not assume that the subordinate lawyer will inevitably conform to the Rules.

[3] Paragraph (c) sets forth general principles of imputed responsibility for the misconduct of others. Subparagraph (c)(1) makes any lawyer who orders or, with knowledge, ratifies misconduct responsible for that misconduct. See also Rule 8.4(a). Subparagraph (c)(2) extends that responsibility to any lawyer who is a partner in the firm in which the misconduct takes place, or who has direct supervisory authority over the lawyer who engages in misconduct, when the lawyer knows or should reasonably know of the conduct and could intervene to ameliorate its consequences. Whether a lawyer has such supervisory authority in particular circumstances is a question of fact. A lawyer with direct supervisory authority is a lawyer who has an actual supervisory role with respect to directing the conduct of other lawyers in a particular representation. A lawyer who is technically a "supervisor" in organizational terms, but is not involved in directing the effort of other lawyers in a particular representation, is not a supervising lawyer with respect to that representation.

[4] The existence of actual knowledge is also a question of fact; whether a lawyer should reasonably have known of misconduct by another lawyer in the same firm is an objective standard based on evaluation of all the facts, including the size and organizational structure of the firm, the lawyer's position and responsibilities within the firm, the type and frequency of contacts between the various lawyers involved, the nature of the misconduct at issue, and the nature of the supervision or other direct responsibility (if any) actually exercised. The mere fact of partnership or a position as a principal in a firm is not sufficient, without more, to satisfy this standard. Similarly, the fact that a lawyer holds a position on the management committee of a firm, or heads a department of the firm, is not sufficient, standing alone, to satisfy this standard.

[5] Appropriate remedial action would depend on the immediacy of the involvement and the seriousness of the misconduct. The supervisor is required to intervene to prevent avoidable consequences of misconduct if the supervisor knows that the misconduct occurred. Thus, if a supervising lawyer knows that a subordinate misrepresented a matter to an opposing party in a negotiation, the supervisor as well as the subordinate has a duty to correct the resulting misapprehension.

[6] Professional misconduct by a lawyer under supervision could reveal a violation of paragraph (b) on the part of the supervisory lawyer even though it does not entail a violation of paragraph (c) because there was no direction, ratification, or knowledge of the violation.

[7] Apart from this Rule and Rule 8.4(a), a lawyer does not have disciplinary liability for the conduct of a partner, associate, or subordinate. Whether a lawyer may be liable civilly or criminally for another lawyer's conduct is a question of law beyond the scope of these Rules.

RULE 5.2 Responsibilities of a Subordinate Lawyer

(a) A lawyer is bound by the rules of professional conduct notwithstanding that the lawyer acted at the direction of another person.

(b) A subordinate lawyer does not violate the rules of professional conduct if that lawyer acts in accordance with a supervisory lawyer's reasonable resolution of an arguable question of professional duty.

COMMENT:

[1] Although a lawyer is not relieved of responsibility for a violation by the fact that the lawyer acted at the direction of a supervisor, that fact may be relevant in determining whether a lawyer had the knowledge required to render conduct a violation of the Rules. For example, if a subordinate filed a frivolous pleading at the direction of a supervisor, the subordinate would not be guilty of a professional violation unless the subordinate knew of the document's frivolous character.

[2] When lawyers in a supervisor-subordinate relationship encounter a matter involving professional judgment as to ethical duty, the supervisor may assume responsibility for making the judgment. Otherwise a consistent course of action or position could not be taken. If the question can reasonably be answered only one way, the duty of both lawyers is clear and they are equally responsible for fulfilling it. However, if the question is reasonably arguable, someone has to decide upon the course of action. That authority ordinarily reposes in the supervisor, and a subordinate may be guided accordingly. For example, if a question arises whether the interests of two clients conflict under Rule 1.7, the supervisor's reasonable resolution of the question should protect the subordinate professionally if the resolution is subsequently challenged.

RULE 5.3 Responsibilities Regarding Nonlawyer Assistants

With respect to a nonlawyer employed or retained by or associated with a lawyer:

(a) A partner in a law firm shall make reasonable efforts to ensure that the firm has in effect measures giving reasonable assurance that the person's conduct is compatible with the professional obligations of the lawyer;

(b) A lawyer having direct supervisory authority over the nonlawyer shall make reasonable efforts to ensure that the person's conduct is compatible with the professional obligations of the lawyer; and

(c) A lawyer shall be responsible for conduct of such a person that would be a violation of the rules of professional conduct if engaged in by a lawyer if:

(1) The lawyer requests or, with the knowledge of the specific conduct, ratifies the conduct involved; or

(2) The lawyer has direct supervisory authority over the person, or is a partner in the law firm in which the person is employed, and knows of the conduct at a time when its consequences can be avoided or mitigated but fails to take reasonable remedial action.

COMMENT:

[1] Lawyers generally employ assistants in their practice, including secretaries, investigators, law student interns, and paraprofessionals. Such assistants, whether employees or independent contractors, act for the lawyer in rendition of

the lawyer's professional services. A lawyer should give such assistants appropriate instruction and supervision concerning the ethical aspects of their employment, particularly regarding the obligation not to disclose information relating to representation of the client, and should be responsible for their work product. The measures employed in supervising nonlawyers should take account of the fact that they do not have legal training and are not subject to professional discipline.

[2] Just as lawyers in private practice may direct the conduct of investigators who may be independent contractors, prosecutors and other government lawyers may effectively direct the conduct of police or other governmental investigative personnel, even though they may not have, strictly speaking, formal authority to order actions by such personnel, who report to the chief of police or the head of another enforcement agency. Such prosecutors or other government lawyers have a responsibility with respect to police or investigative personnel, whose conduct they effectively direct, equivalent to that of private lawyers with respect to investigators whom they retain. See also Comments [3], [4], and [5] to Rule 5.1, in particular, the concept of what constitutes direct supervisory authority, and the significance of holding certain positions in a firm. Comments [3], [4], and [5] of Rule 5.1 apply as well to Rule 5.3.

RULE 5.4 Professional Independence of a Lawyer

(a) A lawyer or law firm shall not share legal fees with a nonlawyer, except that:

(1) An agreement by a lawyer with the lawyer's firm, partner, or associate may provide for the payment of money, over a reasonable period of time after the lawyer's death, to the lawyer's estate or to one or more specified persons;

(2) A lawyer who undertakes to complete unfinished legal business of a deceased lawyer may pay to the estate of the deceased lawyer that proportion of the total compensation which fairly represents the services rendered by the deceased lawyer;

(3) A lawyer or law firm may include nonlawyer employees in a compensation or retirement plan, even though the plan is based in whole or in part on a profit-sharing arrangement; and

(4) Sharing of fees is permitted in a partnership or other form of organization which meets the requirements of paragraph (b).

(b) A lawyer may practice law in a partnership or other form of organization in which a financial interest is held or managerial authority is exercised by an individual nonlawyer who performs professional services which assist the organization in providing legal services to clients, but only if:

(1) The partnership or organization has as its sole purpose providing legal services to clients;

(2) All persons having such managerial authority or holding a financial interest undertake to abide by these rules of professional conduct;

(3) The lawyers who have a financial interest or managerial authority in the partnership or organization undertake to be responsible for the nonlawyer participants to the same extent as if nonlawyer participants were lawyers under Rule 5.1;

(4) The foregoing conditions are set forth in writing.

(c) A lawyer shall not permit a person who recommends, employs, or pays the lawyer to render legal services for another to direct or regulate the lawyer's professional judgment in rendering such legal services.

COMMENT:

[1] The provisions of this Rule express traditional limitations on sharing fees with nonlawyers. (On sharing fees among lawyers not in the same firm, see Rule 1.5(e).) These limitations are to protect the lawyer's professional independence of judgment. Where someone other than the client pays the lawyer's fee or salary, or recommends employment of the lawyer, that arrangement does not modify the lawyer's obligation to the client. As stated in paragraph (c), such arrangements should not interfere with the lawyer's professional judgment.

[2] Traditionally, the canons of legal ethics and disciplinary rules prohibited lawyers from practicing law in a partnership that includes nonlawyers or in any other organization where a nonlawyer is a shareholder, director, or officer. Notwithstanding these strictures, the profession implicitly recognized exceptions for lawyers who work for corporate law departments, insurance companies, and legal service organizations.

[3] As the demand increased for a broad range of professional services from a single source, lawyers employed professionals from other disciplines to work for them. So long as the nonlawyers remained employees of the lawyers, these relationships did not violate the disciplinary rules. However, when lawyers and nonlawyers considered forming partnerships and professional corporations to provide a combination of legal and other services to the public, they faced serious obstacles under the former rules.

[4] This Rule rejects an absolute prohibition against lawyers and nonlawyers joining together to provide collaborative services, but continues to impose traditional ethical requirements with respect to the organization thus created. Thus, a lawyer may practice law in an organization where nonlawyers hold a financial interest or exercise managerial authority, but only if the conditions set forth in subparagraphs (b)(1), (b)(2), and (b)(3) are satisfied, and pursuant to subparagraph (b)(4), satisfaction of these conditions is set forth in a written instrument. The requirement of a writing helps ensure that these important conditions are not overlooked in establishing the organizational structure of entities in which nonlawyers enjoy an ownership or managerial role equivalent to that of a partner in a traditional law firm.

[5] Nonlawyer participants under Rule 5.4 ought not be confused with nonlawyer assistants under Rule 5.3. Nonlawyer participants are persons having managerial authority or financial interests in organizations that provide legal services. Within such organizations, lawyers with financial interests or managerial authority are held responsible for ethical misconduct by nonlawyer participants about which the lawyers know or reasonably should know. This is the same standard of liability contemplated by Rule 5.1, regarding the responsibilities of lawyers with direct supervisory authority over other lawyers.

[6] Nonlawyer assistants under Rule 5.3 do not have managerial authority or financial interests in the organization. Lawyers having direct supervisory authority over nonlawyer assistants are held responsible only for ethical misconduct by assistants about which the lawyers actually know.

[7] As the introductory portion of paragraph (b) makes clear, the purpose of liberalizing the rules regarding the possession of a financial interest or the exercise of management authority by a nonlawyer is to permit nonlawyer professionals to work with lawyers in the delivery of legal services without being relegated to the role of an employee. For example, the Rule permits economists to work in a firm with antitrust or public utility practitioners, psychologists or psychiatric social workers to work with family law practitioners to assist in counseling clients, nonlawyer lobbyists to work with lawyers who perform legislative services, certified public accountants to work in conjunction with tax lawyers or others who use accountants' services in performing legal services, and professional managers to serve as office managers, executive directors, or in similar positions. In all of these situations, the professionals may be given financial interests or managerial responsibility, so long as all of the requirements of paragraph (c) are met.

[8] Paragraph (b) does not permit an individual or entity to acquire all or any part of the ownership of a law partnership or other form of law practice organization for investment or other purposes. It thus does not permit a corporation, an investment banking firm, an investor, or any other person or entity to entitle itself to all or any portion of the income or profits of a law firm or other similar organization. Since such an investor would not be an individual performing professional services within the law firm or other organization, the requirements of paragraph (b) would not be met.

[9] The term "individual" in subparagraph (b) is not intended to preclude the participation in a law firm or other organization by an individual professional corporation in the same manner as lawyers who have incorporated as a professional corporation currently participate in partnerships that include professional corporations.

[10] Some sharing of fees is likely to occur in the kinds of organizations permitted by paragraph (b). Subparagraph (a)(4) makes it clear that such fee sharing is not prohibited.

RULE 5.5 Unauthorized Practice of Law

A lawyer shall not:

(a) Practice law in a jurisdiction where doing so violates the regulation of the legal profession in that jurisdiction; or

(b) Assist a person who is not a member of the bar in the performance of activity that constitutes the unauthorized practice of law.

COMMENT:

[1] The definition of the practice of law is established by law and varies from one jurisdiction to another. Whatever the definition, limiting the practice of law to members of the bar protects the public against rendition of legal services by unqualified persons. Paragraph (b) does not prohibit a lawyer from employing the services of paraprofessionals and delegating functions to them, so long as the lawyer supervises the delegated work and retains responsibility for their work. See Rule 5.3. Likewise, it does not prohibit lawyers from providing professional advice and instruction to nonlawyers whose employment requires knowledge of law; for example, claims adjusters, employees of financial or commercial institutions, social workers, accountants and persons employed in

government agencies. In addition, a lawyer may counsel nonlawyers who wish to proceed *pro se*.

RULE 5.6 Restrictions On Right to Practice

A lawyer shall not participate in offering or making:

(a) A partnership or employment agreement that restricts the rights of a lawyer to practice after termination of the relationship, except an agreement concerning benefits upon retirement; or

(b) An agreement in which a restriction on the lawyer's right to practice is part of the settlement of a controversy between parties.

COMMENT:

[1] An agreement restricting the right of partners or associates to practice after leaving a firm not only limits their professional autonomy but also limits the freedom of clients to choose a lawyer. Paragraph (a) prohibits such agreements except for restrictions incident to provisions concerning retirement benefits for service with the firm.

[2] Paragraph (b) prohibits a lawyer from agreeing not to represent other persons in connection with settling a claim on behalf of a client.

PUBLIC SERVICE

RULE 6.1 Pro Bono Publico Service

A lawyer should participate in serving those persons, or groups of persons, who are unable to pay all or a portion of reasonable attorneys' fees or who are otherwise unable to obtain counsel. A lawyer may discharge this responsibility by providing professional services at no fee, or at a substantially reduced fee, to persons and groups who are unable to afford or obtain counsel, or by active participation in the work of organizations that provide legal services to them. When personal representation is not feasible, a lawyer may discharge this responsibility by providing financial support for organizations that provide legal representation to those unable to obtain counsel.

COMMENT:

[1] This Rule reflects the long-standing ethical principle underlying Canon 2 of the previous Code of Professional Responsibility that "A lawyer should assist the legal profession in fulfilling its duty to make legal counsel available." The Rule incorporates the legal profession's historical commitment to the principle that all persons in our society should be able to obtain necessary legal services. The Rule also recognizes that the rights and responsibilities of individuals and groups in the United States are increasingly defined in legal terms and that, as a consequence, legal assistance in coping with the web of statutes, rules, and regulations is imperative for persons of modest and limited means, as well as for the relatively well-to-do. The Rule also recognizes that a lawyer's pro bono services are sometimes needed to assert or defend public rights belonging to the public generally where no individual or group can afford to pay for the services.

[2] This Rule carries forward the ethical precepts set forth in the Code. Specifically, the Rule recognizes that the basic responsibility for providing legal services for those unable to pay ultimately rests upon the individual lawyer, and

that every lawyer, regardless of professional prominence or professional work load, should find time to participate in or otherwise support the provision of legal services to the disadvantaged.

[3] The Rule also acknowledges that while the provision of free legal services to those unable to pay reasonable fees continues to be an obligation of each lawyer as well as the profession generally, the efforts of individual lawyers are often not enough to meet the need. Thus, it has been necessary for the profession and government to institute additional programs to provide legal services. Accordingly, legal aid offices, lawyer referral services, and other related programs have been developed, and others will be developed by the profession and government. Every lawyer should support all proper efforts to meet this need for legal services. A lawyer also should not refuse a request from a court or bar association to undertake representation of a person unable to obtain counsel except for compelling reasons such as those listed in Rule 6.2.

[4] This Rule expresses the profession's traditional commitment to make legal counsel available, but it is not intended that the Rule be enforced through disciplinary process. Neither is it intended to place any obligation on a government lawyer that is inconsistent with laws such as 18 U.S.C. §§ 203 and 205 limiting the scope of permissible employment or representational activities.

[5] In determining their responsibilities under this Rule, lawyers admitted to practice in the District of Columbia should be guided by the Resolutions on Pro Bono Services passed by the Judicial Conference of the District of Columbia and the D.C. Circuit in 1980 and 1981, respectively. Those resolutions call on members of the D.C. Bar, at a minimum, each year to (1) accept one court appointment, (2) provide 40 hours of pro bono legal service, or (3) when personal representation is not feasible, contribute the lesser of $200 or 1 percent of earned income to a legal assistance organization that services the community's economically disadvantaged, including pro bono referral and appointment offices sponsored by the Bar and the courts.

RULE 6.2 Accepting Appointments

A lawyer shall not seek to avoid appointment by a tribunal to represent a person except for good cause, such as:

(a) Representing the client is likely to result in violation of the rules of professional conduct or other law;

(b) Representing the client is likely to result in a substantial and unreasonable burden on the lawyer; or

(c) The client or the cause is so repugnant to the lawyer as to be likely to impair the client-lawyer relationship or the lawyer's ability to represent the client.

COMMENT:

[1] A lawyer ordinarily is not obliged to accept a client whose character or cause the lawyer regards as repugnant. The lawyer's freedom to select clients is, however, qualified. All lawyers have a responsibility to assist in providing pro bono publico service. See Rule 6.1. An individual lawyer fulfills this responsibility by accepting a fair share of unpopular matters or indigent or unpopular clients. A lawyer may also be subject to appointment by a court to serve unpopular clients or persons unable to afford legal services.

Appointed Counsel

[2] For good cause a lawyer may seek to decline an appointment to represent a person who cannot afford to retain counsel or whose cause is unpopular. Good cause exists if the lawyer could not handle the matter competently, see Rule 1.1, or if undertaking the representation would result in an improper conflict of interest; for example, when the client or the cause is so repugnant to the lawyer as to be likely to impair the client-lawyer relationship or the lawyer's ability to represent the client. A lawyer may also seek to decline an appointment if acceptance would be substantially and unreasonably burdensome, such as when it would impose a financial sacrifice so great as to be unjust.

[3] An appointed lawyer has the same obligations to the client as retained counsel, including the obligations of loyalty and confidentiality, and is subject to the same limitations on the client-lawyer relationship, such as the obligation to refrain from assisting the client in violation of the Rules.

RULE 6.3 Membership in Legal Services Organization

A lawyer may serve as a director, officer, or member of a legal services organization, apart from the law firm in which the lawyer practices, notwithstanding that the organization serves persons having interests adverse to a client of the lawyer. The lawyer shall not knowingly participate in a decision or action of the organization:

(a) If participating in the decision would be incompatible with the lawyer's obligations to a client under Rule 1.7; or

(b) Where the decision could have a material adverse effect on the representation of a client of the organization whose interests are adverse to a client of the lawyer.

COMMENT:

[1] Lawyers should be encouraged to support and participate in legal service organizations. A lawyer who is an officer or a member of such an organization does not thereby have a client-lawyer relationship with persons served by the organization. However, there is potential conflict between the interests of such persons and the interests of the lawyer's clients. If the possibility of such conflict disqualified a lawyer from serving on the board of a legal services organization, the profession's involvement in such organizations would be severely curtailed.

[2] It may be necessary in appropriate cases to reassure a client of the organization that the representation will not be affected by conflicting loyalties of a member of the board. Established, written policies in this respect can enhance the credibility of such assurances.

RULE 6.4 Law Reform Activities

(a) A lawyer should assist in improving the administration of justice. A lawyer may discharge this requirement by rendering services in activities for improving the law, the legal system, or the legal profession.

(b) A lawyer may serve as a director, officer, or member of an organization involved in reform of the law or its administration notwithstanding that the reform may affect the interests of a client of the lawyer. When the lawyer knows that the interests of a client may be materially benefited by a decision in which the lawyer participates, the lawyer shall disclose that fact but need not identify the client.

COMMENT:

[1] Changes in human affairs and imperfections in human institutions make necessary constant efforts to maintain and improve our legal system. This system should function in a manner that commands public respect and fosters the use of legal remedies to achieve redress of grievances. By reason of education and experience, lawyers are especially qualified to recognize deficiencies in the legal system and to initiate corrective measures therein. Thus, they should participate in proposing and supporting legislation and programs to improve the system, without regard to the general interests or desires of clients or former clients. Rules of law are deficient if they are not just, understandable, and responsive to the needs of society. If a lawyer believes that the existence or absence of a rule of law, substantive or procedural, causes or contributes to an unjust result, the lawyer should endeavor by lawful means to obtain appropriate changes in the law. This Rule expresses the policy underlying Canon 8 of the previous Code of Professional Responsibility that "A lawyer should assist in improving the legal system," but it is not intended that it be enforced through disciplinary process.

[2] Lawyers involved in organizations seeking law reform generally do not have a client-lawyer relationship with the organization. Otherwise, it might follow that a lawyer could not be involved in a bar association law reform program that might indirectly affect a client. *See also* Rule 1.2(b). For example, a lawyer specializing in antitrust litigation might be regarded as disqualified from participating in drafting revisions of rules governing that subject. In determining the nature and scope of participation in such activities, a lawyer should be mindful of obligations to clients under other Rules, particularly Rule 1.7. A lawyer is professionally obligated to protect the integrity of the program by making an appropriate disclosure within the organization when the lawyer knows a private client might be materially benefited.

INFORMATION ABOUT LEGAL SERVICES

RULE 7.1 Communications Concerning a Lawyer's Services

(a) A lawyer shall not make a false or misleading communication about the lawyer or the lawyer's services. A communication is false or misleading if it:

    (1) Contains a material misrepresentation of fact or law, or omits a fact necessary to make the statement considered as a whole not materially misleading; or

    (2) Contains an assertion about the lawyer or the lawyer's services that cannot be substantiated.

(b) A lawyer shall not seek by in-person contact, or through an intermediary, employment (or employment of a partner or associate) by a nonlawyer who has not sought the lawyer's advice regarding employment of a lawyer, if:

    (1) The solicitation involves use of a statement or claim that is false or misleading, within the meaning of paragraph (a);

    (2) The solicitation involves the use of undue influence;

(3) The potential client is apparently in a physical or mental condition which would make it unlikely that the potential client could exercise reasonable, considered judgment as to the selection of a lawyer;

(4) The solicitation involves use of an intermediary and the lawyer knows or could reasonably ascertain that such conduct violates the intermediary's contractual or other legal obligations; or

(5) The solicitation involves the use of an intermediary and the lawyer has not taken all reasonable steps to ensure that the potential client is informed of (a) the consideration, if any, paid or to be paid by the lawyer to the intermediary, and (b) the effect, if any, of the payment to the intermediary on the total fee to be charged.

(c) A lawyer shall not knowingly assist an organization that furnishes or pays for legal services to others to promote the use of the lawyer's services or those of the lawyer's partner or associate, or any other lawyer affiliated with the lawyer or the lawyer's firm, as a private practitioner, if the promotional activity involves the use of coercion, duress, compulsion, intimidation, threats, or vexatious or harassing conduct.

(d) No lawyer or any person acting on behalf of a lawyer shall solicit or invite or seek to solicit any person for purposes of representing that person for a fee paid by or on behalf of a client or under The Criminal Justice Act, D.C. Code Ann. § 11–2601 et seq., in any present or future case in the District of Columbia Courthouse, on the sidewalks on the north, south, and west sides of the courthouse, or within 50 feet of the building on the east side.

COMMENT:

[1] This Rule governs all communications about a lawyer's services, including advertising. It is especially important that statements about a lawyer or the lawyer's services be accurate, since many members of the public lack detailed knowledge of legal matters. Certain advertisements such as those that describe the amount of a damage award, the lawyer's record in obtaining favorable verdicts, or those containing client endorsements, unless suitably qualified, have a capacity to mislead by creating an unjustified expectation that similar results can be obtained for others. Advertisements comparing the lawyer's services with those of other lawyers are false or misleading if the claims made cannot be substantiated.

Advertising

[2] To assist the public in obtaining legal services, lawyers should be allowed to make known their services not only through reputation but also through organized information campaigns in the form of advertising. Advertising involves an active quest for clients, contrary to the tradition that a lawyer should not seek clientele. However, the public's need to know about legal services can be fulfilled in part through advertising. This need is particularly acute in the case of persons of moderate means who have not made extensive use of legal services. The interest in expanding public information about legal services ought to prevail over considerations of tradition.

[3] This Rule permits public dissemination of information concerning a lawyer's name or firm name, address, and telephone number; the kinds of services the lawyer will undertake; the basis on which the lawyer's fees are determined, including prices for specific services and payment and credit ar-

rangements; a lawyer's foreign language ability; names of references and, with their consent, names of clients regularly represented; and other information that might invite the attention of those seeking legal assistance.

[4] Questions of effectiveness and taste in advertising are matters of speculation and subjective judgment. Some jurisdictions have had extensive prohibitions against television advertising, against advertising going beyond specific facts about a lawyer, or against "undignified" advertising. Television is now one of the most powerful media for getting information to the public, particularly persons of low and moderate income; prohibiting television advertising, therefore, would impede the flow of information about legal services to many sectors of the public. Limiting the information that may be advertised has a similar effect and assumes that the Bar can accurately forecast the kind of information that the public would regard as relevant.

[5] There is no significant distinction between disseminating information and soliciting clients through mass media or through individual personal contact. In-person solicitation can, however, create additional problems because of the particular circumstances in which the solicitation takes place. This Rule prohibits in-person solicitation in circumstances or through means that are not conducive to intelligent, rational decisions.

Paying Others to Recommend a Lawyer

[6] A lawyer is allowed to pay for advertising permitted by this Rule. This Rule also permits a lawyer to pay another person for channeling professional work to the lawyer. Thus, an organization or person other than the lawyer may advertise or recommend the lawyer's services. Likewise, a lawyer may participate in lawyer referral programs and pay the usual fees charged by such programs. However, special concerns arise when a lawyer is making payments to intermediaries to recommend the lawyer's services to others. These concerns are particularly significant when the payments are not being made to a recognized or established agency or organization, such as an organized lawyer referral program. In employing intermediaries, the lawyer is bound by all of the provisions of this Rule. However, subparagraphs (b)(4) and (b)(5) contain provisions specifically relating to the use of intermediaries.

[7] Subparagraph (b)(4) forbids a lawyer to solicit clients through another person when the lawyer knows or could reasonably ascertain that such conduct violates a contractual or other legal obligation of that other person. For example, a lawyer may not solicit clients through hospital or court employees if solicitation by such employees is prohibited by their employment contracts or rules established by their employment. This prohibition applies whether or not the intermediary is being paid.

[8] Subparagraph (b)(5) imposes specific obligations on the lawyer who employs an intermediary to ensure that the potential client who is the target of the solicitation is informed of the consideration paid or to be paid by the lawyer to the intermediary, and any effect of the payment of such consideration on the total fee to be charged. The concept of payment, as incorporated in subparagraph (b)(5), includes giving anything of value to the recipient and is not limited to payments of money alone. For example, if an intermediary were provided the free use of an automobile in return for soliciting clients on behalf of the lawyer, the obligations imposed by subparagraph (b)(5) would apply and impose the specified disclosure requirements.

Solicitations in the Vicinity of the District of Columbia Courthouse

[9] Paragraph (d) is designed to prohibit unseemly solicitations of prospective clients in and around the District of Columbia Courthouse. The words "for a fee paid by or on behalf of a client or under the Criminal Justice Act" have been added to paragraph (d) as it was originally promulgated by the District of Columbia Court of Appeals in 1982. The purpose of the addition is to permit solicitation in the District of Columbia Courthouse for the purposes of pro bono representation. For the purposes of this Rule, pro bono representation, whether by individual lawyers or nonprofit organizations, is representation undertaken primarily for purposes other than a fee. That representation includes providing services free of charge for individuals who may be in need of legal assistance and may lack the financial means and sophistication necessary to have alternative sources of aid. Cases where fees are awarded under the Criminal Justice Act do not constitute pro bono representation for the purposes of this Rule. However, the possibility that fees may be awarded under the Equal Access to Justice Act and Civil Rights Attorneys' Fees Awards Act of 1976, as amended, or other statutory attorney fee statutes, does not prevent representation from constituting pro bono representation.

[Note: there is no Rule 7.2, 7.3, or 7.4.]

RULE 7.5 Firm Names and Letterheads

(a) A lawyer shall not use a firm name, letterhead, or other professional designation that violates Rule 7.1. A trade name may be used by a lawyer in private practice if it does not imply a connection with a government agency or with a public or charitable legal services organization and is not otherwise in violation of Rule 7.1.

(b) A law firm with offices in more than one jurisdiction may use the same name in each jurisdiction, but identification of the lawyers in an office of the firm shall indicate the jurisdictional limitations on those not licensed to practice in the jurisdiction where the office is located.

(c) The name of a lawyer holding a public office shall not be used in the name of a law firm, or in communications on its behalf, during any substantial period in which the lawyer is not actively and regularly practicing with the firm.

(d) Lawyers may state or imply that they practice in a partnership or other organization only when that is the fact.

COMMENT:

[1] A firm may be designated by the names of all or some of its members, by the names of deceased members where there has been a continuing succession in the firm's identity, or by a trade name such as the ABC Legal Clinic. Although the United States Supreme Court has held that legislation may prohibit the use of trade names in professional practice, use of such names in law practice is acceptable so long as it is not misleading. If a private firm uses a trade name that includes a geographical name such as Springfield Legal Clinic, an express disclaimer that it is a public legal aid agency may be required to avoid a misleading implication. It may be observed that any firm name including the name of a deceased partner is, strictly speaking, a trade name. The use of such names to designate law firms has proven a useful means of identification.

However, it is misleading to use the name of a lawyer not associated with the firm or a predecessor of the firm.

[2] With regard to paragraph (d), lawyers sharing office facilities, but who are not in fact partners, may not denominate themselves as, for example, Smith and Jones, for that title suggests partnership in the practice of law.

MAINTAINING THE INTEGRITY OF THE PROFESSION

RULE 8.1 Bar Admission and Disciplinary Matters

An applicant for admission to the bar, or a lawyer in connection with a bar admission application or in connection with a disciplinary matter, shall not:

(a) Knowingly make a false statement of material fact; or

(b) Fail to disclose a fact necessary to correct a misapprehension known by the lawyer or applicant to have arisen in the matter, or knowingly fail to respond reasonably to a lawful demand for information from an admissions or disciplinary authority, except that this rule does not require disclosure of information otherwise protected by Rule 1.6.

COMMENT:

[1] The duty imposed by this Rule extends to persons seeking admission to the Bar as well as to lawyers. Hence, if a person makes a material false statement in connection with an application for admission, it may be the basis for subsequent disciplinary action if the person is admitted, and in any event may be relevant in a subsequent admission application. The duty imposed by this Rule applies to a lawyer's own admission or discipline as well as that of others. Thus, it is a separate professional offense for a lawyer knowingly to make a misrepresentation or omission in connection with a disciplinary investigation of the lawyer's own conduct. This Rule also requires affirmative clarification of any misunderstanding on the part of the admissions or disciplinary authority of which the person involved becomes aware.

[2] This Rule is subject to the provisions of the Fifth Amendment of the United States Constitution and corresponding provisions of state constitutions. A person relying on such a provision in response to a question, however, should do so openly and not use the right of nondisclosure as a justification for failure to comply with this Rule.

[3] A lawyer representing an applicant for admission to the Bar, or representing a lawyer who is the subject of a disciplinary inquiry or proceeding, is governed by the Rules applicable to the client-lawyer relationship. For example, Rule 1.6 may prohibit disclosures, which would otherwise be required, by a lawyer serving in such representative capacity.

[Note: there is no Rule 8.2.]

RULE 8.3 Reporting Professional Misconduct

(a) A lawyer having knowledge that another lawyer has committed a violation of the rules of professional conduct that raises a substantial question as to that lawyer's honesty, trustworthiness, or fitness as a lawyer in other respects, shall inform the appropriate professional authority.

(b) A lawyer having knowledge that a judge has committed a violation of applicable rules of judicial conduct that raises a substantial question as to the judge's fitness for office shall inform the appropriate authority.

(c) This Rule does not require disclosure of information otherwise protected by Rule 1.6.

COMMENT:

[1] Self-regulation of the legal profession requires that members of the profession initiate disciplinary investigation when they know of a violation of the Rules of Professional Conduct. Lawyers have a similar obligation with respect to judicial misconduct. An apparently isolated violation may indicate a pattern of misconduct that only a disciplinary investigation can uncover. Reporting a violation is especially important where the victim is unlikely to discover the offense.

[2] A report about misconduct is not required where it would involve violation of Rule 1.6. However, a lawyer should encourage a client to consent to disclosure where prosecution would not substantially prejudice the client's interests.

[3] If a lawyer were obliged to report every violation of the Rules, the failure to report any violation would itself be a professional offense. Such a requirement existed in many jurisdictions but proved to be unenforceable. This Rule limits the reporting obligation to those offenses that a self-regulating profession must vigorously endeavor to prevent. A measure of judgment is, therefore, required in complying with the provisions of this Rule. The term "substantial" refers to the seriousness of the possible offense and not the quantum of evidence of which the lawyer is aware. A report should be made to the Office of Bar Counsel. A lawyer who believes that another lawyer has a significant problem of alcohol or other substance abuse which does not require reporting to Bar Counsel under this Rule, may nonetheless wish to report the perceived situation to the Lawyer Counseling Committee, operated by the D.C. Bar, which assists lawyers having such problems.

[4] The duty to report professional misconduct does not apply to a lawyer retained to represent a lawyer whose professional conduct is in question. Such a situation is governed by the Rules applicable to the client-lawyer relationship.

[5] Rule 1.6(h) brings within the protections of Rule 1.6 certain types of information gained by lawyers participating in lawyer counseling programs of the D.C. Bar Lawyer Counseling Committee. To the extent information concerning violations of the Rules of Professional Conduct fall within the scope of Rule 1.6(h), a lawyer-counselor would not be required or permitted to inform the "appropriate professional authority" referred to in Rule 8.3. Where disclosure is permissive under Rule 1.6 (see paragraph 1.6(c) for cases of permitted disclosures), discretion to disclose to the "appropriate professional authority" would also exist pursuant to paragraph 8.3(c). *See also* Comment to Rule 1.6, paragraphs [29], [30], and [31].

RULE 8.4 Misconduct

It is professional misconduct for a lawyer to:

(a) Violate or attempt to violate the rules of professional conduct, knowingly assist or induce another to do so, or do so through the acts of another;

(b) Commit a criminal act that reflects adversely on the lawyer's honesty, trustworthiness, or fitness as a lawyer in other respects;

(c) Engage in conduct involving dishonesty, fraud, deceit, or misrepresentation;

(d) Engage in conduct that seriously interferes with the administration of justice;

(e) State or imply an ability to influence improperly a government agency or official;

(f) Knowingly assist a judge or judicial officer in conduct that is a violation of applicable rules of judicial conduct or other law; or

(g) Seek or threaten to seek criminal charges or disciplinary charges solely to obtain an advantage in a civil matter.

COMMENT:

[1] Many kinds of illegal conduct reflect adversely on fitness to practice law, such as offenses involving fraud and the offense of willful failure to file an income tax return. However, some kinds of offenses carry no such implication. Traditionally, the distinction was drawn in terms of offenses involving "moral turpitude." That concept can be construed to include offenses concerning some matters of personal morality, such as adultery and comparable offenses, that have no specific connection to fitness for the practice of law. Although a lawyer is personally answerable to the entire criminal law, a lawyer should be professionally answerable only for offenses that indicate lack of those characteristics relevant to law practice. Offenses involving violence, dishonesty, breach of trust, or serious interference with the administration of justice are in that category. A pattern of repeated offenses, even ones of minor significance when considered separately, can indicate indifference to legal obligation.

[2] Paragraph (d)'s prohibition of conduct that "seriously interferes with the administration of justice" includes conduct proscribed by the previous Code of Professional Responsibility under DR 1-102(A)(5) as "prejudicial to the administration of justice." The extensive case law on that standard, as set forth below, is hereby incorporated into this Rule.

[3] The majority of these cases involve a lawyer's failure to cooperate with Bar Counsel. A lawyer's failure to respond to Bar Counsel's inquiries or subpoenas may constitute misconduct, see *In re Cope*, 455 A.2d 1357 (D.C.1983); *In re Haupt*, 444 A.2d 317 (D.C.1982); *In re Lieber*, 442 A.2d 153 (D.C.1982); *In re Whitlock*, 441 A.2d 989 (D.C.1982); *In re Spencer*, No. M-112-82 (D.C. June 4, 1982); *In re L. Smith*, No. M-91-82 (D.C.App. Mar. 9, 1982); *In re Walsh*, No. M-70(81) (D.C. Sept. 25, 1981) en banc; *In re Schattman*, No. M-63-81 (D.C. June 2, 1981); *In re Russell*, 424 A.2d 1087 (D.C.1980); *In re Willcher*, 404 A.2d 185 (D.C.1979); *In re Carter*, No. D-31-79 (D.C. Oct. 28, 1979); *In re Bush* (Bush II), No. S-58-79 (D.C. Oct. 1, 1979); *In re Tucker*, No. M-13-75/S-56-78 (D.C. Nov. 15, 1978), as may the failure to abide by agreements made with Bar Counsel. *In re Harmon*, M-79-81 (D.C. Dec. 14, 1981) (breaking promise to Bar Counsel to offer complainant refund of fee or vigorous representation constitutes conduct prejudicial to the administration of justice).

[4] A lawyer's failure to appear in court for a scheduled hearing is another common form of conduct deemed prejudicial to the administration of justice. *See In re Evans*, No. M-126-82 (D.C. Dec. 18, 1982); *In re Doud*, Bar Docket No.

442–80 (Sept. 23, 1982); *In re Bush* (Bush III), No. S–58–79/D/39/80 (D.C. Apr. 30, 1980); *In re Molovinsky*, No. M–31–79 (D.C. Aug. 23, 1979). Similarly, failure to obey court orders may constitute misconduct under paragraph (d). *Whitlock*, 441 A.2d at 989–91; *In re Brown*, Bar Docket No. 222-78 (Aug. 4, 1978); *In re Bush* (Bush I), No. DP–22–75 (D.C. July 26, 1977).

[5] While the above categories—failure to cooperate with Bar Counsel and failure to obey court orders—encompass the major forms of misconduct proscribed by paragraph (d), that provision is to be interpreted flexibly and includes any improper behavior of an analogous nature. For example, the failure to turn over the assets of a conservatorship to the court or to the successor conservator has been held to be conduct "prejudicial to the administration of justice." *In re Burka*, 423 A.2d 181 (D.C.App.1980). In *Russell, supra,* the court found that failure to keep the Bar advised of respondent's changes of address, after being warned to do so, was also misconduct under that standard. And in *Schattman, supra,* it was held that a lawyer's giving a worthless check in settlement of a claim against the lawyer by a client was improper.

RULE 8.5 Jurisdiction

A lawyer admitted to practice in this jurisdiction is subject to the disciplinary authority of this jurisdiction although engaged in practice elsewhere.

COMMENT:

[1] In modern practice lawyers frequently act outside the territorial limits of the jurisdiction in which they are licensed to practice, either in another state or outside the United States. In doing so, they remain subject to the governing authority of the jurisdiction in which they are licensed to practice. Similarly, if their activity in the non-licensing jurisdiction is substantial and continuous, it may constitute practice of law in that jurisdiction. See Rule 5.5.

[2] If the Rules of Professional Conduct in the two jurisdictions differ, principles of conflict of laws may apply. Similar problems can arise when a lawyer is licensed to practice in more than one jurisdiction.

[3] Where the lawyer is licensed to practice law in two jurisdictions that impose conflicting obligations, applicable rules of choice of law may govern the situation. A related problem arises with respect to practice before a federal tribunal, where the general authority of the states to regulate the practice of law must be reconciled with such authority, as federal tribunals may have to regulate practice before them.

NONDISCRIMINATION BY MEMBERS OF THE BAR

RULE 9.1 DISCRIMINATION IN EMPLOYMENT

A lawyer shall not discriminate against any individual in conditions of employment because of the individual's race, color, religion, national origin, sex, age, marital status, sexual orientation, family responsibility, or physical handicap.

COMMENT:

[1] This provision is modeled after the D.C. Human Rights Act, D.C.Code § 1–2512 (1981), though in some respects more limited in scope. There are also

provisions of federal law that contain certain prohibitions on discrimination in employment. The rule is not intended to create ethical obligations that exceed those imposed on a lawyer by applicable law.

[2] A similar rule has been adopted by the highest court in Vermont. A similar rule is also under consideration for adoption by the courts in New York based on the recommendations of the New York State Bar Association.

[3] The investigation and adjudication of discrimination claims may involve particular expertise of the kind found within the D.C. Office of Human Rights and the federal Equal Employment Opportunity Commission. Such experience may involve, among other things, methods of analysis of statistical data regarding discrimination claims. These agencies also have, in appropriate circumstances, the power to award remedies to the victims of discrimination, such as reinstatement or back pay, which extend beyond the remedies that are available through the disciplinary process. Remedies available through the disciplinary process include such sanctions as disbarment, suspension, censure, and admonition, but do not extend to monetary awards or other remedies that could alter the employment status to take into account the impact of prior acts of discrimination.

[4] If proceedings are pending before other organizations, such as the D.C. Office of Human Rights or the Equal Employment Opportunity Commission, the processing of complaints by Bar Counsel may be deferred or abated where there is substantial similarity between the complaint filed with Bar Counsel and material allegations involved in such other proceedings. *See* § 19(d) of Rule XI of the Rules Governing the Bar of the District of Columbia.

A.B.A. ASPIRATIONAL GOALS ON LAWYER ADVERTISING

Copyright © American Bar Association 1988. All rights reserved. Reprinted with permission.

Editors Note: Because some lawyers believe that legal advertising should be more dignified than other types of advertising, the American Bar Association's Commission on Advertising has drafted nonregulatory "Aspirational Goals on Lawyer Advertising." These goals are not intended to be binding, because the Commission concluded that binding regulations would raise serious antitrust and First Amendment issues:

Preamble

During the past decade, the courts have sought to define the nature and extent of permissible advertising by lawyers. In a series of decisions, the U.S. Supreme Court has held that lawyer advertising which is not false or misleading is commercial speech entitled to protection under the First Amendment of the U.S. Constitution.

Pending further clarification by the courts, some advertising practices exist which may be detrimental. Some forms of advertising may adversly affect public perceptions about the justice system itself. For example, empirical evidence suggests that undignified advertising can detract from the public's confidence in the legal profession and respect for the justice system.

Under present case law, the matter of dignity is widely believed to be so subjective as to be beyond the scope of constitutionally permitted regulation. Nevertheless, it seems entirely proper for the organized bar to suggest non-binding aspirational goals urging lawyers who wish to advertise to do so in a dignified manner. Although only aspirational, such goals must be scrupulously sensitive to fundamental constitutional rights of lawyers and the needs of the public.

It is the role and responsibility of lawyers to provide legal services to the public. It has been demonstrated by responsible studies that people sometimes do not receive needed legal services, either because they are unaware of available services, don't understand how they can benefit from those services or don't understand how to obtain them. Therefore, it is also the legal profession's responsibility to inform the public about the availability of legal services and how to obtain and use them.

Advertising is one of many methods by which lawyers can inform the public about legal services. Although most people find a lawyer through word-of-mouth networks of family, friends and work associates, when properly done, advertising can help people to better understand the legal services available to them and how to obtain those services.

A.B.A. ASPIRATIONAL GOALS IN ADVERTISING

When properly done, advertising can also be a productive way for lawyers to build and maintain their client bases. Advertising and other forms of marketing can enable lawyers to attain efficiencies of scale which may help make legal services more affordable. As the Supreme Court pointed out in *Bates v. State Bar of Arizona*, 433 U.S. 350, 377 (1977), it is "entirely possible that advertising will serve to reduce, not advance, the cost of legal services to the consumer."

Lawyers are at all times officers of the court, and as such, they have a special obligation to assure that their conduct conforms to the highest ideals of the legal profession. Thus, lawyers who advertise should be mindful not only of the effect their advertising may have on their own professional image but also of the effect it may have on the public's overall perception of the judicial system.

If lawyer advertising avoids false, misleading or deceptive representations, or coercive or misleading solicitation, it advances the goal of bringing needed legal services to more people than are now being served.

However, when advertising though not false, misleading or deceptive degenerates into undignified and unprofessional presentations, the public is not served, the lawyer who advertised does not benefit and the image of the judicial system may be harmed.

Accordingly, lawyer advertising should exemplify the inherent dignity and professionalism of the legal community. Dignified lawyer advertising tends to inspire public confidence in the professional competence and ability of lawyers and portrays the commitment of lawyers to serve clients' legal needs in accordance with the ethics and public service tradition of a learned profession.

Lawyer advertising is a key facet of the marketing and delivery of legal services to the public. The professional conduct rules for lawyers adopted by the states regulate some aspects of lawyer advertising, but they also leave lawyers much latitude to decide how to advertise. The following Aspirational Goals are presented in an effort to suggest how lawyers can achieve the beneficial goals of advertising while minimizing or eliminating altogether its negative implications.

These aspirational goals are not intended to establish mandatory requirements which might form the basis for disciplinary enforcement. Rules of Professional Conduct and Disciplinary Rules of Codes of Professional Responsibility in effect in all jurisdictions establish the standards which all lawyers who advertise must meet. Rather, these aspirational goals are intended to provide suggested objectives which all lawyers who engage in advertising their services should be encouraged to achieve in order that lawyer advertising may be more effective and reflect the professionalism of the legal community.

A.B.A. ASPIRATIONAL GOALS IN ADVERTISING

Aspirational Goals

1. Lawyer advertising should encourage and support the public's confidence in the individual lawyer's competence and integrity as well as the commitment of the legal profession to serve the public's legal needs in the tradition of the law as a learned profession.

2. Since advertising may be the only contact many people have with lawyers, advertising by lawyers should help the public understand its legal rights and the judicial process and should uphold the dignity of the legal profession.

3. While "dignity" and "good taste" are terms open to subjective interpretation, lawyers should consider that advertising which reflects the ideals stated in these Aspirational Goals is likely to be dignified and suitable to the profession.

4. Since advertising must be truthful and accurate, and not false or misleading, lawyers should realize that ambiguous or confusing advertising can be misleading.

5. Particular care should be taken in describing fees and costs in advertisements. If an advertisement states a specific fee for a particular service, it should make clear whether or not all problems of that type can be handled for that specific fee. Similar care should be taken in describing the lawyer's areas of practice.

6. Lawyers should consider that the use of inappropriately dramatic music, unseemly slogans, hawkish spokespersons, premium offers, slapstick routines or outlandish settings in advertising does not instill confidence in the lawyer or the legal profession and undermines the serious purpose of legal services and the judicial system.

7. Advertising developed with a clear identification of its potential audience is more likely to be understandable, respectful and appropriate to that audience, and, therefore, more effective. Lawyers should consider using advertising and marketing professionals to assist in identifying and reaching an appropriate audience.

8. How advertising conveys its message is as important as the message itself. Again, lawyers should consider using professional consultants to help them develop and present a clear message to the audience in an effective and appropriate way.

9. Lawyers should design their advertising to attract legal matters which they are competent to handle.

10. Lawyers should be concerned with making legal services more affordable to the public. Lawyer advertising may be designed to build up client bases so that efficiencies of scale may be achieved that will translate into more affordable legal services.

AMERICAN BAR ASSOCIATION STANDARDS RELATING TO THE ADMINISTRATION OF CRIMINAL JUSTICE †

SECOND EDITION *

Approved February 1979

CHAPTER 3. THE PROSECUTION FUNCTION

		Page
Part I.	General Standards	405
3–1.1	The Function of the Prosecutor	405
3–1.2	Conflicts of Interest	405
3–1.3	Public Statements	405
3–1.4	Duty to Improve the Law	406

† Permission to reprint has been granted by Section on Criminal Justice of the American Bar Association. This material is reprinted from "Prosecution and Defense Function," Chapters 3 and 4, of *Standards Relating to the Administration of Criminal Justice*, 2d Edition, Tentative Draft Approved February 12, 1979 (with the exception of 4–7.7).

* The first edition of the American Bar Association Standards Relating to the Administration of Criminal Justice was printed in eighteen separate volumes as the sets of standards were completed and approved by the ABA House of Delegates between 1968 and 1973. The second edition, however, is printed in a comprehensive two-volume publication, thus affording the user immediate access to all of the Association's standards in the area of criminal justice. Existing volumes of the original standards will become chapters in the second edition, arranged generally in the order of a case's progression through the criminal justice system. The A.B.A. is now working on a third edition. Those chapters of the second edition are as follows:

Chapter 1: Urban Police Function

Chapter 2: Electronic Surveillance

Chapter 3: Prosecution Function

Chapter 4: Defense Function

Chapter 5: Providing Defense Services

Chapter 6: Special Functions of the Trial Judge

Chapter 7: *reserved for expansion*

Chapter 8: Fair Trial and Free Press

Chapter 9: Grand Jury

Chapter 10: Pretrial Release

Chapter 11: Discovery and Procedure Before Trial

Chapter 12: Speedy Trial

Chapter 13: Joinder and Severance

Chapter 14: Pleas of Guilty

Chapter 15: Trial by Jury

Chapter 16: *reserved for expansion*

Chapter 17: *reserved for expansion*

Chapter 18: Sentencing Alternatives and Procedures

Chapter 19: Probation

Chapter 20: Appellate Review of Sentences

Chapter 21: Criminal Appeals

Chapter 22: Postconviction Remedies

Chapter 23: *reserved for expansion*

Chapter 24: *reserved for expansion*

ABA STANDARDS

		Page
Part II.	**Organization of the Prosecution Function**	406
3-2.1	Prosecution Authority to Be Vested in a Public Official	406
3-2.2	Interrelationship of Prosecution Offices Within a State	406
3-2.3	Assuring High Standards of Professional Skill	406
3-2.4	Special Assistants, Investigative Resources, Experts	407
3-2.5	Prosecutor's Handbook; Policy Guidelines and Procedures	407
3-2.6	Training Programs	407
3-2.7	Relations With Police	407
3-2.8	Relations With the Courts and Bar	408
3-2.9	Prompt Disposition of Criminal Charges	408
3-2.10	Supersession and Substitution of Prosecutor	408
Part III.	**Investigation for Prosecution Decision**	409
3-3.1	Investigative Function of Prosecutor	409
3-3.2	Relations With Prospective Witnesses	409
3-3.3	Relations With Expert Witnesses	409
3-3.4	Decision to Charge	410
3-3.5	Relations With Grand Jury	410
3-3.6	Quality and Scope of Evidence Before Grand Jury	410
3-3.7	Quality and Scope of Evidence for Information	411
3-3.8	Discretion as to Noncriminal Disposition	411
3-3.9	Discretion in the Charging Decision	411
3-3.10	Role in First Appearance and Preliminary Hearing	412
3-3.11	Disclosure of Evidence by the Prosecutor	412
Part IV.	**Plea Discussions**	413
3-4.1	Availability for Plea Discussions	413
3-4.2	Fulfillment of Plea Discussions	413
3-4.3	Record of Reasons for Nolle Prosequi Disposition	413
Part V.	**The Trial**	413
3-5.1	Calendar Control	413
3-5.2	Courtroom Decorum	414
3-5.3	Selection of Jurors	414
3-5.4	Relations With Jury	414
3-5.5	Opening Statement	415
3-5.6	Presentation of Evidence	415
3-5.7	Examination of Witnesses	415
3-5.8	Argument to the Jury	416
3-5.9	Facts Outside the Record	416
3-5.10	Comments by Prosecutor After Verdict	416
Part VI.	**Sentencing**	416
3-6.1	Role in Sentencing	416
3-6.2	Information Relevant to Sentencing	417

PART I. GENERAL STANDARDS

Standard 3–1.1 The Function of the Prosecutor

(a) The office of prosecutor is charged with responsibility for prosecutions in its jurisdiction.

(b) The prosecutor is both an administrator of justice and an advocate. The prosecutor must exercise sound discretion in the performance of his or her functions.

(c) The duty of the prosecutor is to seek justice, not merely to convict.

(d) It is the duty of the prosecutor to know and be guided by the standards of professional conduct as defined in the codes and canons of the legal profession, and in this chapter. The prosecutor should make use of the guidance afforded by an advisory council of the kind described in standard 4–1.4.

(e) As used in this chapter, the term "unprofessional conduct" denotes conduct which, in either identical or similar language, is or should be made subject to disciplinary sanctions pursuant to codes of professional responsibility in force in each jurisdiction. Where other terms are used, the standard is intended as a guide to honorable professional conduct and performance. These standards are not intended as criteria for the judicial evaluation of alleged misconduct of the prosecutor to determine the validity of a conviction. They may or may not be relevant in such judicial evaluation, depending upon all the circumstances.

Standard 3–1.2 Conflicts of Interest

A prosecutor should avoid the appearance or reality of a conflict of interest with respect to official duties. In some instances, as defined in codes of professional responsibility, failure to do so will constitute unprofessional conduct.

Standard 3–1.3 Public Statements

(a) The prosecutor should not exploit the office by means of personal publicity connected with a case before trial, during trial, or thereafter.

(b) The prosecutor should comply with the chapter on Fair Trial and Free Press in these standards. In some instances, as defined in codes of professional responsibility, failure to do so will constitute unprofessional conduct.

(c) In order to assure a fair trial for the accused, the prosecutor and police should cooperate in achieving compliance with the chapter on Fair Trial and Free Press of these standards and codes of professional responsibility.

Standard 3–1.4 Duty to Improve the Law

It is an important function of the prosecutor to seek to reform and improve the administration of criminal justice. When inadequacies or injustices in the substantive or procedural law come to the prosecutor's attention, he or she should stimulate efforts for remedial action.

PART II. ORGANIZATION OF THE PROSECUTION FUNCTION

Standard 3–2.1 Prosecution Authority to Be Vested in a Public Official

The prosecution function should be performed by a public prosecutor who is a lawyer subject to the standards of professional conduct and discipline.

Standard 3–2.2 Interrelationship of Prosecution Offices Within a State

(a) Local authority and responsibility for prosecution is properly vested in a district, county, or city attorney. Wherever possible, a unit of prosecution should be designed on the basis of population, caseload, and other relevant factors sufficient to warrant at least one full-time prosecutor and the supporting staff necessary to effective prosecution.

(b) In some states, conditions such as geographical area and population may make it appropriate to create a statewide system of prosecution in which the state attorney general is the chief prosecutor and the local prosecutors are deputies.

(c) In all states, there should be coordination of the prosecution policies of local prosecution offices to improve the administration of justice and assure the maximum practicable uniformity in the enforcement of the criminal law throughout the state. A state council of prosecutors should be established in each state.

(d) In cases where questions of law of statewide interest or concern arise which may create important precedents, the prosecutor should consult and advise with the attorney general of the state.

(e) A central pool of supporting resources and manpower, including laboratories, investigators, accountants, special counsel, and other experts to the extent needed, should be maintained by the state government and should be available to all local prosecutors.

Standard 3–2.3 Assuring High Standards of Professional Skill

(a) The function of public prosecution requires highly developed professional skills. This objective can best be achieved by promoting continuity of service and broad experience in all phases of the prosecution function.

(b) Wherever feasible, the offices of chief prosecutor and staff should be full-time occupations.

(c) Professional competence should be the only basis for selection for prosecutorial office. Prosecutors should select their staffs on the basis of professional competence without regard to partisan political influence.

(d) In order to achieve the objective of professionalism and to encourage competent lawyers to accept such offices, compensation for prosecutors and their staffs should be commensurate with the high responsibilities of the office and comparable to the compensation of their peers in the private sector.

Standard 3-2.4 Special Assistants, Investigative Resources, Experts

(a) Funds should be provided to enable a prosecutor to appoint special assistants from among the trial bar experienced in criminal cases, as needed for the prosecution of a particular case or to assist generally.

(b) Funds should be provided to the prosecutor for the employment of a regular staff of professional investigative personnel and other necessary supporting personnel, under the prosecutor's direct control, to the extent warranted by the responsibilities and scope of the office. The prosecutor should also be provided with funds for the employment of qualified experts as needed for particular cases.

Standard 3-2.5 Prosecutor's Handbook; Policy Guidelines and Procedures

(a) Each prosecutor's office should develop a statement of:
  (i) general policies to guide the exercise of prosecutorial discretion, and
  (ii) procedures of the office.

The objectives of these policies as to discretion and procedures should be to achieve a fair, efficient, and effective enforcement of the criminal law.

(b) In the interest of continuity and clarity, such statement of policies and procedures should be maintained in an office handbook. This handbook should be available to the public, except for subject matters declared "confidential," when it is reasonably believed that public access to their contents would adversely affect the prosecution function.

Standard 3-2.6 Training Programs

Training programs should be established within the prosecutor's office for new personnel and for continuing education of the staff. Continuing education programs for prosecutors should be substantially expanded and public funds should be provided to enable prosecutors to attend such programs.

Standard 3-2.7 Relations With Police

(a) The prosecutor should provide legal advice to the police concerning police functions and duties in criminal matters.

(b) The prosecutor should cooperate with police in providing the services of the prosecutor's staff to aid in training police in the performance of their function in accordance with law.

Standard 3-2.8 Relations With the Courts and Bar

(a) It is unprofessional conduct for a prosecutor intentionally to misrepresent matters of fact or law to the court.

(b) A prosecutor's duties necessarily involve frequent and regular official contacts with the judge or judges of the prosecutor's jurisdiction. In such contacts the prosecutor should carefully strive to preserve the appearance as well as the reality of the correct relationship which professional traditions and canons require between advocates and judges.

(c) It is unprofessional conduct for a prosecutor to engage in unauthorized ex parte discussions with or submission of material to a judge relating to a particular case which is or may come before the judge.

(d) In the prosecutor's necessarily frequent contacts with other members of the bar, the prosecutor should strive to avoid the appearance as well as the reality of any relationship which would tend to cast doubt on the independence and integrity of the office.

Standard 3-2.9 Prompt Disposition of Criminal Charges

(a) A prosecutor should not intentionally use procedural devices for delay for which there is no legitimate basis.

(b) The prosecution function should be so organized and supported with staff and facilities as to enable it to dispose of all criminal charges promptly. The prosecutor should be punctual in attendance in court and in the submission of all motions, briefs, and other papers. The prosecutor should emphasize to all witnesses the importance of punctuality in attendance in court.

(c) It is unprofessional conduct intentionally to misrepresent facts or otherwise mislead the court in order to obtain a continuance.

Standard 3-2.10 Supersession and Substitution of Prosecutor

(a) Procedures should be established by appropriate legislation to the end that the governor or other elected state official is empowered by law to suspend and supersede a local prosecutor upon making a public finding, after reasonable notice and hearing, that the prosecutor is incapable of fulfilling the duties of office.

(b) The governor or other elected official should be empowered by law to substitute special counsel in the place of the local prosecutor in a particular case, or category of cases, upon making a public finding that this is required for the protection of the public interest.

PART III. INVESTIGATION FOR PROSECUTION DECISION

Standard 3-3.1 Investigative Function of Prosecutor

(a) A prosecutor ordinarily relies on police and other investigative agencies for investigation of alleged criminal acts, but the prosecutor has an affirmative responsibility to investigate suspected illegal activity when it is not adequately dealt with by other agencies.

(b) It is unprofessional conduct for a prosecutor knowingly to use illegal means to obtain evidence or to employ or instruct or encourage others to use such means.

(c) A prosecutor should not discourage or obstruct communication between prospective witnesses and defense counsel. It is unprofessional conduct for the prosecutor to advise any person or cause any person to be advised to decline to give to the defense information which such person has the right to give.

(d) It is unprofessional conduct for a prosecutor to secure the attendance of persons for interviews by use of any communication which has the appearance or color of a subpoena or similar judicial process unless the prosecutor is authorized by law to do so.

(e) It is unprofessional conduct for a prosecutor to promise not to prosecute for prospective criminal activity, except where such activity is part of an officially supervised investigative and enforcement program.

(f) Unless a prosecutor is prepared to forgo impeachment of a witness by the prosecutor's own testimony as to what the witness stated in an interview or to seek leave to withdraw from the case in order to present the impeaching testimony, a prosecutor should avoid interviewing a prospective witness except in the presence of a third person.

Standard 3-3.2 Relations With Prospective Witnesses

(a) It is unprofessional conduct to compensate a witness, other than an expert, for giving testimony, but it is not improper to reimburse an ordinary witness for the reasonable expenses of attendance upon court, attendance for depositions pursuant to statute or court rule, or attendance for pretrial interviews. Payments to a witness may be for transportation and loss of income, provided there is no attempt to conceal the fact of reimbursement.

(b) Whenever a prosecutor knows or has reason to believe that the conduct of a witness to be interviewed may be the subject of a criminal prosecution, the prosecutor or the prosecutor's investigator should advise the witness concerning possible self-incrimination and the possible need for counsel.

Standard 3-3.3 Relations With Expert Witnesses

(a) A prosecutor who engages an expert for an opinion should respect the independence of the expert and should not seek to dictate the formation of the expert's opinion on the subject. To the extent necessary, the prosecutor should explain to the expert his or her role in the trial as an impartial expert called to aid the fact finders and the manner in which the examination of witnesses is conducted.

(b) It is unprofessional conduct for a prosecutor to pay an excessive fee for the purpose of influencing the expert's testimony or to fix the amount of the fee contingent upon the testimony the expert will give or the result in the case.

Standard 3-3.4 Decision to Charge

(a) The decision to institute criminal proceedings should be initially and primarily the responsibility of the prosecutor.

(b) Absent exceptional circumstances, no arrest warrant or search warrant should issue without the approval of the prosecutor.

(c) The prosecutor should establish standards and procedures for evaluating complaints to determine whether criminal proceedings should be instituted.

(d) Where the law permits a citizen to complain directly to a judicial officer or the grand jury, the citizen complainant should be required to present the complaint for prior approval to the prosecutor, and the prosecutor's action or recommendation thereon should be communicated to the judicial officer or grand jury.

Standard 3-3.5 Relations With Grand Jury

(a) Where the prosecutor is authorized to act as legal adviser to the grand jury, the prosecutor may appropriately explain the law and express an opinion on the legal significance of the evidence but should give due deference to its status as an independent legal body.

(b) The prosecutor should not make statements or arguments in an effort to influence grand jury action in a manner which would be impermissible at trial before a petit jury.

(c) The prosecutor's communications and presentations to the grand jury should be on the record.

Standard 3-3.6 Quality and Scope of Evidence Before Grand Jury

(a) A prosecutor should present to the grand jury only evidence which the prosecutor believes would be admissible at trial. However, in appropriate cases, the prosecutor may present witnesses to summarize admissible evidence available to the prosecutor which the prosecutor believes he or she will be able to present at trial.

(b) No prosecutor should knowingly fail to disclose to the grand jury evidence which will tend substantially to negate guilt.

(c) A prosecutor should recommend that the grand jury not indict if it is believed the evidence presented does not warrant an indictment under governing law.

THE PROSECUTION FUNCTION   Standard 3-3.9

(d) If the prosecutor believes that a witness is a potential defendant, the prosecutor should not seek to compel the witness's testimony before the grand jury without informing the witness that he or she may be charged and that the witness should seek independent legal advice concerning his or her rights.

(e) The prosecutor should not compel the appearance of a witness before the grand jury whose activities are the subject of the inquiry if the witness states in advance that if called he or she will exercise the constitutional privilege not to testify, unless the prosecutor intends to seek a grant of immunity according to the law.

Standard 3-3.7   Quality and Scope of Evidence for Information

Where the prosecutor is empowered to charge by information, the prosecutor's decisions should be governed by the principles embodied in standards 3-3.6 and 3-3.9.

Standard 3-3.8   Discretion as to Noncriminal Disposition

(a) The prosecutor should explore the availability of noncriminal disposition, including programs of rehabilitation, formal or informal, in deciding whether to press criminal charges. Especially in the case of a first offender, the nature of the offense may warrant noncriminal disposition.

(b) Prosecutors should be familiar with the resources of social agencies which can assist in the evaluation of cases for diversion from the criminal process.

Standard 3-3.9   Discretion in the Charging Decision

(a) It is unprofessional conduct for a prosecutor to institute, or cause to be instituted, or to permit the continued pendency of criminal charges when it is known that the charges are not supported by probable cause. A prosecutor should not institute, cause to be instituted, or permit the continued pendency of criminal charges in the absence of sufficient admissible evidence to support a conviction.

(b) The prosecutor is not obliged to present all charges which the evidence might support. The prosecutor may in some circumstances and for good cause consistent with the public interest decline to prosecute, notwithstanding that sufficient evidence may exist which would support a conviction. Illustrative of the factors which the prosecutor may properly consider in exercising his or her discretion are:

   (i) the prosecutor's reasonable doubt that the accused is in fact guilty;

   (ii) the extent of the harm caused by the offense;

   (iii) the disproportion of the authorized punishment in relation to the particular offense or the offender;

   (iv) possible improper motives of a complainant;

(v) reluctance of the victim to testify;

(vi) cooperation of the accused in the apprehension or conviction of others; and

(vii) availability and likelihood of prosecution by another jurisdiction.

(c) In making the decision to prosecute, the prosecutor should give no weight to the personal or political advantages or disadvantages which might be involved or to a desire to enhance his or her record of convictions.

(d) In cases which involve a serious threat to the community, the prosecutor should not be deterred from prosecution by the fact that in the jurisdiction juries have tended to acquit persons accused of the particular kind of criminal act in question.

(e) The prosecutor should not bring or seek charges greater in number or degree than can reasonably be supported with evidence at trial.

Standard 3-3.10 Role in First Appearance and Preliminary Hearing

(a) A prosecutor who is present at the first appearance (however denominated) of the accused before a judicial officer should not communicate with the accused unless a waiver of counsel has been entered, except for the purpose of aiding in obtaining counsel or in arranging for the pretrial release of the accused.

(b) The prosecutor should cooperate in good faith in arrangements for release under the prevailing system for pretrial release.

(c) The prosecutor should not encourage an uncounseled accused to waive preliminary hearing.

(d) The prosecutor should not seek a continuance solely for the purpose of mooting the preliminary hearing by securing an indictment.

(e) Except for good cause, the prosecutor should not seek delay in the preliminary hearing after an arrest has been made if the accused is in custody.

(f) The prosecutor should ordinarily be present at a preliminary hearing where such hearing is required by law.

Standard 3-3.11 Disclosure of Evidence by the Prosecutor

(a) It is unprofessional conduct for a prosecutor intentionally to fail to make disclosure to the defense, at the earliest feasible opportunity, of the existence of evidence which tends to negate the guilt of the accused as to the offense charged or which would tend to reduce the punishment of the accused.

(b) The prosecutor should comply in good faith with discovery procedures under the applicable law.

(c) It is unprofessional conduct for a prosecutor intentionally to avoid pursuit of evidence because he or she believes it will damage the prosecution's case or aid the accused.

PART IV. PLEA DISCUSSIONS

Standard 3-4.1 Availability for Plea Discussions

(a) The prosecutor should make known a general policy or willingness to consult with defense counsel concerning disposition of charges by plea.

(b) It is unprofessional conduct for a prosecutor to engage in plea discussions directly with an accused who is represented by counsel, except with counsel's approval. Where the defendant has properly waived counsel, the prosecuting attorney may engage in plea discussions with the defendant, although ordinarily a verbatim record of such discussions should be made and preserved.

(c) It is unprofessional conduct for a prosecutor knowingly to make false statements or representations in the course of plea discussions with defense counsel or the accused.

Standard 3-4.2 Fulfillment of Plea Discussions

(a) It is unprofessional conduct for a prosecutor to make any promise or commitment concerning the sentence which will be imposed or concerning a suspension of sentence. A prosecutor may properly advise the defense what position will be taken concerning disposition.

(b) It is unprofessional conduct for a prosecutor to imply a greater power to influence the disposition of a case than is actually possessed.

(c) It is unprofessional conduct for a prosecutor to fail to comply with a plea agreement, unless a defendant fails to comply with a plea agreement or other extenuating circumstances are present.

Standard 3-4.3 Record of Reasons for Nolle Prosequi Disposition

Whenever felony criminal charges are dismissed by way of nolle prosequi (or its equivalent), the prosecutor should make a record of the reasons for the action.

PART V. THE TRIAL

Standard 3-5.1 Calendar Control

Control over the trial calendar should be vested in the court. The prosecuting attorney should be required to file with the court as a public record periodic reports setting forth the reasons for delay as to each case for which the prosecuting attorney has not requested trial within a prescribed time following charging. The prosecuting attorney should also advise the court of facts relevant in determining the order of cases on the calendar.

Standard 3-5.2 Courtroom Decorum

(a) The prosecutor should support the authority of the court and the dignity of the trial courtroom by strict adherence to the rules of decorum and by manifesting an attitude of professional respect toward the judge, opposing counsel, witnesses, defendants, jurors, and others in the courtroom.

(b) When court is in session the prosecutor should address the court, not opposing counsel, on all matters relating to the case.

(c) It is unprofessional conduct for a prosecutor to engage in behavior or tactics purposefully calculated to irritate or annoy the court or opposing counsel.

(d) A prosecutor should comply promptly with all orders and directives of the court, but the prosecutor has a duty to have the record reflect adverse rulings or judicial conduct which the prosecutor considers prejudicial. The prosecutor has a right to make respectful requests for reconsideration of adverse rulings.

(e) A prosecutor should be punctual in all court appearances and in the submission of all motions, briefs, and other papers.

(f) Prosecutors should cooperate with courts and the organized bar in developing codes of decorum and professional etiquette for each jurisdiction.

Standard 3-5.3 Selection of Jurors

(a) The prosecutor should prepare himself or herself prior to trial to discharge effectively the prosecution function in the selection of the jury and the exercise of challenges for cause and peremptory challenges.

(b) In those cases where it appears necessary to conduct a pretrial investigation of the background of jurors, investigatory methods of the prosecutor should neither harass nor unduly embarrass potential jurors or invade their privacy and, whenever possible, should be restricted to an investigation of records and sources of information already in existence.

(c) The opportunity to question jurors personally should be used solely to obtain information for the intelligent exercise of challenges. A prosecutor should not intentionally use the voir dire to present factual matter which the prosecutor knows will not be admissible at trial or to argue the prosecution's case to the jury.

Standard 3-5.4 Relations With Jury

(a) It is unprofessional conduct for a prosecutor to communicate privately with persons summoned for jury duty or impaneled as jurors concerning a case prior to or during trial. The prosecutor should avoid the reality or appearance of any such improper communications.

(b) The prosecutor should treat jurors with deference and respect, avoiding the reality or appearance of currying favor by a show of undue solicitude for their comfort or convenience.

(c) After discharge of the jury from further consideration of a case, it is unprofessional conduct for the prosecutor to intentionally make comments to or ask questions of a juror for the purpose of harassing or embarrassing the juror in any way which will tend to influence judgment in future jury service.

Standard 3-5.5 Opening Statement

The prosecutor's opening statement should be confined to a brief statement of the issues in the case and to remarks on evidence the prosecutor intends to offer which the prosecutor believes in good faith will be available and admissible. It is unprofessional conduct to allude to any evidence unless there is a good faith and reasonable basis for believing that such evidence will be tendered and admitted in evidence.

Standard 3-5.6 Presentation of Evidence

(a) It is unprofessional conduct for a prosecutor knowingly to offer false evidence, whether by documents, tangible evidence, or the testimony of witnesses, or fail to seek withdrawal thereof upon discovery of its falsity.

(b) It is unprofessional conduct for a prosecutor knowingly and for the purpose of bringing inadmissible matter to the attention of the judge or jury to offer inadmissible evidence, ask legally objectionable questions, or make other impermissible comments or arguments in the presence of the judge or jury.

(c) It is unprofessional conduct for a prosecutor to permit any tangible evidence to be displayed in the view of the judge or jury which would tend to prejudice fair consideration by the judge or jury until such time as a good faith tender of such evidence is made.

(d) It is unprofessional conduct to tender tangible evidence in the view of the judge or jury if it would tend to prejudice fair consideration by the judge or jury unless there is a reasonable basis for its admission in evidence. When there is any substantial doubt about the admissibility of such evidence, it should be tendered by an offer of proof and a ruling obtained.

Standard 3-5.7 Examination of Witnesses

(a) The interrogation of all witnesses should be conducted fairly, objectively, and with due regard for the dignity and legitimate privacy of the witness, and without seeking to intimidate or humiliate the witness unnecessarily. Proper cross-examination can be conducted without violating rules of decorum.

(b) The prosecutor's brief that the witness is telling the truth does not preclude cross-examination, but may affect the method and scope of cross-examination. A prosecutor should not use the power of cross-examination to discredit or undermine a witness if the prosecutor knows the witness is testifying truthfully.

(c) A prosecutor should not call a witness who the prosecutor knows will claim a valid privilege not to testify for the purpose of impressing upon the jury the fact of the claim of privilege. In some instances, as defined in codes of professional responsibility, doing so will constitute unprofessional conduct.

(d) It is unprofessional conduct for a prosecutor to ask a question which implies the existence of a factual predicate for which a good faith belief is lacking.

Standard 3-5.8 Argument to the Jury

(a) The prosecutor may argue all reasonable inferences from evidence in the record. It is unprofessional conduct for the prosecutor intentionally to misstate the evidence or mislead the jury as to the inferences it may draw.

(b) It is unprofessional conduct for the prosecutor to express his or her personal belief or opinion as to the truth or falsity of any testimony or evidence or the guilt of the defendant.

(c) The prosecutor should not use arguments calculated to inflame the passions or prejudices of the jury.

(d) The prosecutor should refrain from argument which would divert the jury from its duty to decide the case on the evidence, by injecting issues broader than the guilt or innocence of the accused under the controlling law, or by making predictions of the consequences of the jury's verdict.

(e) It is the responsibility of the court to insure that final argument to the jury is kept within proper, accepted bounds.

Standard 3-5.9 Facts Outside the Record

It is unprofessional conduct for the prosecutor intentionally to refer to or argue on the basis of facts outside the record whether at trial or on appeal, unless such facts are matters of common public knowledge based on ordinary human experience or matters of which the court may take judicial notice.

Standard 3-5.10 Comments by Prosecutor After Verdict

The prosecutor should not make public comments critical of a verdict, whether rendered by judge or jury.

PART VI. SENTENCING

Standard 3-6.1 Role in Sentencing

(a) The prosecutor should not make the severity of sentences the index of his or her effectiveness. To the extent that the prosecutor becomes involved in the sentencing process, he or she should seek to assure that a fair and informed judgment is made on the sentence and to avoid unfair sentence disparities.

THE DEFENSE FUNCTION

(b) Where sentence is fixed by the court without jury participation, the prosecutor should be afforded the opportunity to address the court at sentencing and to offer a sentencing recommendation. When requested by the court to furnish a sentencing recommendation, the prosecutor should have the obligation to do so.

(c) Where sentence is fixed by the jury, the prosecutor should present evidence on the issue within the limits permitted in the jurisdiction, but the prosecutor should avoid introducing evidence bearing on sentence which will prejudice the jury's determination of the issue of guilt.

Standard 3–6.2 Information Relevant to Sentencing

(a) The prosecutor should assist the court in basing its sentence on complete and accurate information for use in the presentence report. The prosecutor should disclose to the court any information in the prosecutor's files relevant to the sentence. If incompleteness or inaccurateness in the presentence report comes to the prosecutor's attention, the prosecutor should take steps to present the complete and correct information to the court and to defense counsel.

(b) The prosecutor should disclose to the defense and to the court at or prior to the sentencing proceeding all information in the prosecutor's files which is relevant to the sentencing issue.

CHAPTER 4. THE DEFENSE FUNCTION *

		Page
Part I.	**General Standards**	418
4–1.1	Role of Defense Counsel	418
4–1.2	Delays; Punctuality	419
4–1.3	Public Statements	419
4–1.4	Advisory Councils on Professional Conduct	420
4–1.5	Trial Lawyer's Duty to Administration of Justice	420
4–1.6	Client Interests Paramount	420
Part II.	**Access to Counsel**	420
4–2.1	Communication	420
4–2.2	Referral Service for Criminal Cases	421
4–2.3	Prohibited Referrals	421
Part III.	**Lawyer-Client Relationship**	421
4–3.1	Establishment of Relationship	421
4–3.2	Interviewing the Client	422
4–3.3	Fees	422
4–3.4	Obtaining Publication Rights From the Accused	422
4–3.5	Conflict of Interest	422
4–3.6	Prompt Action to Protect the Accused	423

* The A.B.A. is now in the process of preparing the third edition of its Standards for Criminal Justice. As part of this effort, it approved new Standards of the Defense Function on February 11, 1991. However, the Commentary to this Standard is not yet available. When the Commentary is completed, a subsequent edition of this Supplement will reprint the revised Standards.

Standard 4–1.1   *ABA STANDARDS*

		Page
4–3.7	Advice and Service on Anticipated Unlawful Conduct	424
4–3.8	Duty to Keep Client Informed	424
4–3.9	Obligations to Client and Duty to Court	424

Part IV. Investigation and Preparation — 424

4–4.1	Duty to Investigate	424
4–4.2	Illegal Investigation	424
4–4.3	Relations With Prospective Witnesses	425
4–4.4	Relations With Expert Witnesses	425
4–4.5	Compliance With Discovery Procedure	425

Part V. Control and Direction of Litigation — 425

4–5.1	Advising the Defendant	425
4–5.2	Control and Direction of the Case	426

Part VI. Disposition Without Trial — 426

4–6.1	Duty to Explore Disposition Without Trial	426
4–6.2	Conduct of Discussions	426

Part VII. Trial — 427

4–7.1	Courtroom Decorum	427
4–7.2	Selection of Jurors	427
4–7.3	Relations With Jury	428
4–7.4	Opening Statement	428
4–7.5	Presentation of Evidence	428
4–7.6	Examination of Witnesses	429
4–7.7	Testimony by the Defendant	430
4–7.8	Argument to the Jury	432
4–7.9	Facts Outside the Record	432
4–7.10	Posttrial Motions	432

Part VIII. After Conviction — 432

4–8.1	Sentencing	432
4–8.2	Appeal	433
4–8.3	Counsel on Appeal	433
4–8.4	Conduct of Appeal	433
4–8.5	Post-Conviction Remedies	433
4–8.6	Challenges to the Effectiveness of Counsel	433

PART I. GENERAL STANDARDS

Standard 4–1.1 Role of Defense Counsel

(a) Counsel for the accused is an essential component of the administration of criminal justice. A court properly constituted to hear a criminal case must be viewed as a tripartite entity consisting of the judge (and jury, where appropriate), counsel for the prosecution, and counsel for the accused.

(b) The basic duty the lawyer for the accused owes to the administration of justice is to serve as the accused's counselor and advocate with courage, devotion, and to the utmost of his or her learning and ability and according to law.

THE DEFENSE FUNCTION **Standard 4–1.3**

(c) The defense lawyer, in common with all members of the bar, is subject to standards of conduct stated in statutes, rules, decisions of courts, and codes, canons, or other standards of professional conduct. The defense lawyer has no duty to execute any directive of the accused which does not comport with law or such standards. The defense lawyer is the professional representative of the accused, not the accused's alter ego.

(d) It is unprofessional conduct for a lawyer intentionally to misrepresent matters of fact or law to the court.

(e) It is the duty of every lawyer to know the standards of professional conduct as defined in codes and canons of the legal profession and in this chapter. The functions and duties of defense counsel are governed by such standards whether defense counsel is assigned or privately retained.

(f) As used in this chapter, the term "unprofessional conduct" denotes conduct which, in either identical or similar language, is or should be made subject to disciplinary sanctions pursuant to codes of professional responsibility. Where other terms are used, the standard is intended as a guide to honorable professional conduct and performance. These standards are not intended as criteria for the judicial evaluation of alleged misconduct of counsel to determine the validity of a conviction. They may or may not be relevant in such judicial evaluation, depending upon all the circumstances.

Standard 4–1.2 Delays; Punctuality

(a) Defense counsel should avoid unnecessary delay in the disposition of cases. Defense counsel should be punctual in attendance upon court and in the submission of all motions, briefs, and other papers. Defense counsel should emphasize to the client and all witnesses the importance of punctuality in attendance in court.

(b) It is unprofessional conduct for defense counsel intentionally to misrepresent facts or otherwise mislead the court in order to obtain a continuance.

(c) Defense counsel should not intentionally use procedural devices for delay for which there is no legitimate basis.

(d) A lawyer should not accept more employment than the lawyer can discharge within the spirit of the constitutional mandate for speedy trial and the limits of the lawyer's capacity to give each client effective representation. It is unprofessional conduct to accept employment for the purpose of delaying trial.

Standard 4–1.3 Public Statements

(a) The lawyer representing an accused should avoid personal publicity connected with the case before trial, during trial, and thereafter.

(b) The lawyer should comply with the standards on Fair Trial and Free Press herein. In some instances, as defined in codes of professional responsibility, his failure to do so will constitute unprofessional conduct.

Standard 4-1.4 Advisory Councils on Professional Conduct

(a) In every jurisdiction an advisory body of lawyers selected for their experience, integrity, and standing at the trial bar should be established as an advisory council on problems of professional conduct in criminal cases. This council should provide prompt and confidential guidance and advice to lawyers seeking assistance in the application of standards of professional conduct in criminal cases.

(b) Communications between a lawyer and such an advisory council should have the same privilege for protection of the client's confidences as exist between lawyer and client. The council should be bound by statute or rule of court in the same manner as a lawyer is bound not to reveal any disclosure of the client except

(i) if the client challenges the effectiveness of the lawyer's conduct of the case and the lawyer relies on the guidance received from the council, and

(ii) if the lawyer's conduct is called into question in an authoritative disciplinary inquiry or proceeding.

Standard 4-1.5 Trial Lawyer's Duty to Administration of Justice

(a) The bar should encourage through every available means the widest possible participation in the defense of criminal cases by experienced trial lawyers. Lawyers active in general trial practice should be encouraged to qualify themselves for participation in criminal cases both by formal training and through experience as associate counsel.

(b) All qualified trial lawyers should stand ready to undertake the defense of an accused regardless of public hostility toward the accused or personal distaste for the offense charged or the person of the defendant.

(c) Qualified trial lawyers should not assert or announce a general unwillingness to appear in criminal cases. Law firms should encourage partners and associates to appear in criminal cases.

Standard 4-1.6 Client Interests Paramount

The duties of a lawyer to a client are to represent the client's legitimate interests, and considerations of personal and professional advantage should not influence the lawyer's advice or performance.

PART II. ACCESS TO COUNSEL

Standard 4-2.1 Communication

Every jurisdiction should guarantee by statute or rule of court the right of an accused person to prompt and effective communication with a lawyer and should require that reasonable access to a telephone or other facilities be provided for that purpose.

Standard 4-2.2 Referral Service for Criminal Cases

(a) To assist persons who wish to retain counsel privately and who do not know a lawyer or how to engage one, every jurisdiction should have a referral service for criminal cases. The referral service should maintain a list of lawyers willing and qualified to undertake the defense of a criminal case; it should be so organized that it can provide prompt service at all times.

(b) The availability of the referral service should be publicized. In addition, notices containing the essential information about the referral service and how to contact it should be posted conspicuously in police stations, jails, and wherever else it is likely to give effective notice.

Standard 4-2.3 Prohibited Referrals

(a) It is unprofessional conduct for a lawyer to accept referrals by agreement or as a regular practice from law enforcement personnel, bondsmen, or court personnel.

(b) Regulations and licensing requirements governing the conduct of law enforcement personnel, bondsmen, court personnel, and others in similar positions should prohibit their referring an accused to any particular lawyer and should require them, when asked to suggest the name of an attorney, to direct the accused to the referral service or to the local bar association if no referral service exists.

PART III. LAWYER–CLIENT RELATIONSHIP

Standard 4-3.1 Establishment of Relationship

(a) Defense counsel should seek to establish a relationship of trust and confidence with the accused. The lawyer should explain the necessity of full disclosure of all facts known to the client for an effective defense, and the lawyer should explain the obligation of confidentiality which makes privileged the accused's disclosures relating to the case.

(b) The conduct of the defense of a criminal case requires trained professional skill and judgment. Therefore, the technical and professional decisions must rest with the lawyer without impinging on the right of the accused to make the ultimate decisions on certain specified matters, as delineated in chapter 5, part II.

(c) To ensure the privacy essential for confidential communication between lawyer and client, adequate facilities should be available for private discussions between counsel and accused in jails, prisons, courthouses, and other places where accused persons must confer with counsel.

(d) Personnel of jails, prisons, and custodial institutions should be prohibited by law or administrative regulations from examining or otherwise interfering with any communication or correspondence between

Standard 4-3.1

client and lawyer relating to legal action arising out of charges or incarceration.

Standard 4-3.2 Interviewing the Client

(a) As soon as practicable the lawyer should seek to determine all relevant facts known to the accused. In so doing, the lawyer should probe for all legally relevant information without seeking to influence the direction of the client's responses.

(b) It is unprofessional conduct for the lawyer to instruct the client or to intimate to the client in any way that the client should not be candid in revealing facts so as to afford the lawyer free rein to take action which would be precluded by the lawyer's knowing of such facts.

Standard 4-3.3 Fees

(a) In determining the amount of the fee in a criminal case, it is proper to consider the time and effort required, the responsibility assumed by counsel, the novelty and difficulty of the questions involved, the skill requisite to proper representation, the likelihood that other employment will be precluded, the fee customarily charged in the locality for similar services, the gravity of the charge, the experience, reputation, and ability of the lawyer, and the capacity of the client to pay the fee.

(b) It is unprofessional conduct for a lawyer to imply that compensation of the lawyer is for anything other than professional services rendered by the lawyer or by others for the lawyer.

(c) It is unprofessional conduct for a lawyer to enter into an agreement for, charge, or collect an illegal or clearly excessive fee.

(d) It is unprofessional conduct for a lawyer to divide a fee with a nonlawyer, except as permitted by the Code of Professional Responsibility. A lawyer may share a fee with another lawyer only on the basis of their respective services and responsibility in a case, in accordance with the Code of Professional Responsibility.

(e) It is unprofessional conduct for a lawyer to enter into an arrangement for, charge, or collect a contingent fee for representing a defendant in a criminal case.

Standard 4-3.4 Obtaining Publication Rights From the Accused

It is unprofessional conduct for a lawyer, prior to conclusion of all aspects of the matter giving rise to his or her employment, to enter into any agreement or understanding with a client or a prospective client by which the lawyer acquires an interest in publication rights with respect to the subject matter of the employment or proposed employment.

Standard 4-3.5 Conflict of Interest

(a) At the earliest feasible opportunity defense counsel should disclose to the defendant any interest in or connection with the case or any other matter that might be relevant to the defendant's selection of a lawyer to represent him or her.

(b) Except for preliminary matters such as initial hearings or applications for bail, a lawyer or lawyers who are associated in practice should not undertake to defend more than one defendant in the same criminal case if the duty to one of the defendants may conflict with the duty to another. The potential for conflict of interest in representing multiple defendants is so grave that ordinarily a lawyer should decline to act for more than one of several codefendants except in unusual situations when, after careful investigation, it is clear that:

(i) no conflict is likely to develop;

(ii) the several defendants give an informed consent to such multiple representation; and

(iii) the consent of the defendants is made a matter of judicial record. In determining the presence of consent by the defendants, the trial judge should make appropriate inquiries respecting actual or potential conflicts of interest of counsel and whether the defendants fully comprehend the difficulties that an attorney sometimes encounters in defending multiple clients.

In some instances, accepting or continuing employment by more than one defendant in the same criminal case is unprofessional conduct.

(c) In accepting payment of fees by one person for the defense of another, a lawyer should be careful to determine that he or she will not be confronted with a conflict of loyalty since the lawyer's entire loyalty is due the accused. It is unprofessional conduct for the lawyer to accept such compensation except with the consent of the accused after full disclosure. It is unprofessional conduct for a lawyer to permit a person who recommends, employs, or pays the lawyer to render legal services for another to direct or regulate the lawyer's professional judgment in rendering such legal services.

(d) It is unprofessional conduct for a lawyer to defend a criminal case in which the lawyer's partner or other professional associate is or has been the prosecutor.

Standard 4-3.6 Prompt Action to Protect the Accused

(a) Many important rights of the accused can be protected and preserved only by prompt legal action. The lawyer should inform the accused of his or her rights forthwith and take all necessary action to vindicate such rights. The lawyer should consider all procedural steps which in good faith may be taken, including, for example, motions seeking pretrial release of the accused, obtaining psychiatric examination of the accused when a need appears, moving for change of venue or continuance, moving to suppress illegally obtained evidence, moving for severance from jointly charged defendants, and seeking dismissal of the charges.

(b) A lawyer should not act as surety on a bail bond either for the accused or for others.

Standard 4-3.7 Advice and Service on Anticipated Unlawful Conduct

(a) It is a lawyer's duty to advise a client to comply with the law, but the lawyer may advise concerning the meaning, scope, and validity of a law.

(b) It is unprofessional conduct for a lawyer to counsel a client in or knowingly assist a client to engage in conduct which the lawyer knows to be illegal or fraudulent.

(c) It is unprofessional conduct for a lawyer to agree in advance of the commission of a crime that the lawyer will serve as counsel for the defendant, except as part of a bona fide effort to determine the validity, scope, meaning, or application of the law, or where the defense is incident to a general retainer for legal services to a person or enterprise engaged in legitimate activity.

(d) A lawyer may reveal the expressed intention of a client to commit a crime and the information necessary to prevent the crime, and the lawyer must do so if the contemplated crime is one which would seriously endanger the life or safety of any person or corrupt the processes of the courts and the lawyer believes such action on his or her part is necessary to prevent it.

Standard 4-3.8 Duty to Keep Client Informed

The lawyer has a duty to keep the client informed of the developments in the case and the progress of preparing the defense.

Standard 4-3.9 Obligations to Client and Duty to Court

Once a lawyer has undertaken the representation of an accused, the duties and obligations are the same whether the lawyer is privately retained, appointed, or serving in a legal aid or defender program.

PART IV. INVESTIGATION AND PREPARATION

Standard 4-4.1 Duty to Investigate

It is the duty of the lawyer to conduct a prompt investigation of the circumstances of the case and to explore all avenues leading to facts relevant to the merits of the case and the penalty in the event of conviction. The investigation should always include efforts to secure information in the possession of the prosecution and law enforcement authorities. The duty to investigate exists regardless of the accused's admissions or statements to the lawyer of facts constituting guilt or the accused's stated desire to plead guilty.

Standard 4-4.2 Illegal Investigation

It is unprofessional conduct for a lawyer knowingly to use illegal means to obtain evidence or information or to employ, instruct, or encourage others to do so.

Standard 4-4.3 Relations With Prospective Witnesses

(a) It is unprofessional conduct to compensate a witness, other than an expert, for giving testimony, but it is not improper to reimburse a witness for the reasonable expenses of attendance upon court, including transportation and loss of income, attendance for depositions pursuant to statute or court rule, or attendance for pretrial interviews, provided there is no attempt to conceal the fact of reimbursement.

(b) It is not necessary for the lawyer or the lawyer's investigator, in interviewing a prospective witness, to caution the witness concerning possible self-incrimination and the need for counsel.

(c) A lawyer should not discourage or obstruct communication between prospective witnesses and the prosecutor. It is unprofessional conduct to advise any person, other than a client, or cause such person to be advised to decline to give to the prosecutor or counsel for codefendants information which such person has a right to give.

(d) Unless the lawyer for the accused is prepared to forgo impeachment of a witness by the lawyer's own testimony as to what the witness stated in an interview or to seek leave to withdraw from the case in order to present such impeaching testimony, the lawyer should avoid interviewing a prospective witness except in the presence of a third person.

Standard 4-4.4 Relations With Expert Witnesses

(a) A lawyer who engages an expert for an opinion should respect the independence of the expert and should not seek to dictate the formation of the expert's opinion on the subject. To the extent necessary, the lawyer should explain to the expert his or her role in the trial as an impartial witness called to aid the fact finders and the manner in which the examination of witnesses is conducted.

(b) It is unprofessional conduct for a lawyer to pay an excessive fee for the purpose of influencing the expert's testimony or to fix the amount of the fee contingent upon the testimony the expert will give or the result in the case.

Standard 4-4.5 Compliance With Discovery Procedure

The lawyer should comply in good faith with discovery procedures under the applicable law.

PART V. CONTROL AND DIRECTION OF LITIGATION

Standard 4-5.1 Advising the Defendant

(a) After informing himself or herself fully on the facts and the law, the lawyer should advise the accused with complete candor concerning all aspects of the case, including a candid estimate of the probable outcome.

Standard 4–5.1   *ABA STANDARDS*

(b) It is unprofessional conduct for the lawyer intentionally to understate or overstate the risks, hazards, or prospects of the case to exert undue influence on the accused's decision as to his or her plea.

(c) The lawyer should caution the client to avoid communication about the case with witnesses, except with the approval of the lawyer, to avoid any contact with jurors or prospective jurors, and to avoid either the reality or the appearance of any other improper activity.

Standard 4–5.2 Control and Direction of the Case

(a) Certain decisions relating to the conduct of the case are ultimately for the accused and others are ultimately for defense counsel. The decisions which are to be made by the accused after full consultation with counsel are:

   (i) what pleas to enter;

   (ii) whether to waive jury trial; and

   (iii) whether to testify in his or her own behalf.

(b) The decisions on what witnesses to call, whether and how to conduct cross-examination, what jurors to accept or strike, what trial motions should be made, and all other strategic and tactical decisions are the exclusive province of the lawyer after consultation with the client.

(c) If a disagreement on significant matters of tactics or strategy arises between the lawyer and the client, the lawyer should make a record of the circumstances, the lawyer's advice and reasons, and the conclusion reached. The record should be made in a manner which protects the confidentiality of the lawyer-client relationship.

PART VI. DISPOSITION WITHOUT TRIAL

Standard 4–6.1 Duty to Explore Disposition Without Trial

(a) Whenever the nature and circumstances of the case permit, the lawyer for the accused should explore the possibility of an early diversion of the case from the criminal process through the use of other community agencies.

(b) A lawyer may engage in plea discussions with the prosecutor, although ordinarily the client's consent to engage in such discussions should be obtained in advance. Under no circumstances should a lawyer recommend to a defendant acceptance of a plea unless a full investigation and study of the case has been completed, including an analysis of controlling law and the evidence likely to be introduced at trial.

Standard 4–6.2 Conduct of Discussions

(a) In conducting discussions with the prosecutor the lawyer should keep the accused advised of developments at all times and all proposals made by the prosecutor should be communicated promptly to the accused.

THE DEFENSE FUNCTION   **Standard 4–7.2**

(b) It is unprofessional conduct for a lawyer knowingly to make false statements concerning the evidence in the course of plea discussions with the prosecutor.

(c) It is unprofessional conduct for a lawyer to seek or accept concessions favorable to one client by any agreement which is detrimental to the legitimate interests of any other client.

PART VII. TRIAL

Standard 4–7.1 Courtroom Decorum

(a) As an officer of the court the lawyer should support the authority of the court and the dignity of the trial courtroom by strict adherence to the rules of decorum and by manifesting an attitude of professional respect toward the judge, opposing counsel, witnesses, jurors, and others in the courtroom.

(b) When court is in session defense counsel should address the court and should not address the prosecutor directly on any matter relating to the case.

(c) It is unprofessional conduct for a lawyer to engage in behavior or tactics purposefully calculated to irritate or annoy the court or the prosecutor.

(d) The lawyer should comply promptly with all orders and directives of the court, but the lawyer has a duty to have the record reflect adverse rulings or judicial conduct which the lawyer considers prejudicial to his or her client's legitimate interests. The lawyer has a right to make respectful requests for reconsiderations of adverse rulings.

(e) Lawyers should cooperate with courts and the organized bar in developing codes of decorum and professional etiquette for each jurisdiction.

Standard 4–7.2 Selection of Jurors

(a) The lawyer should prepare himself or herself prior to trial to discharge effectively his or her function in the selection of the jury, including the raising of any appropriate issues concerning the method by which the jury panel was selected and the exercise of both challenges for cause and peremptory challenges.

(b) In those cases where it appears necessary to conduct a pretrial investigation of the background of jurors, investigatory methods of the lawyer should neither harass nor unduly embarrass potential jurors or invade their privacy and, whenever possible, should be restricted to an investigation of records and sources of information already in existence.

(c) The opportunity to question jurors personally should be used solely to obtain information for the intelligent exercise of challenges. A lawyer should not intentionally use the voir dire to present factual matter which the lawyer knows will not be admissible at trial or to argue the lawyer's case to the jury.

Standard 4-7.3 Relations With Jury

(a) It is unprofessional conduct for the lawyer to communicate privately with persons summoned for jury duty or impaneled as jurors concerning the case prior to or during the trial. The lawyer should avoid the reality or appearance of any such improper communications.

(b) The lawyer should treat jurors with deference and respect, avoiding the reality or appearance of currying favor by a show of undue solicitude for their comfort or convenience.

(c) After discharge of the jury from further consideration of a case, it is unprofessional conduct for a lawyer to intentionally make comments to or ask questions of a juror for the purpose of harassing or embarrassing the juror in any way which will tend to influence judgment in future jury service. If the lawyer believes that the verdict may be subject to legal challenge, the lawyer may properly, if no statute or rule prohibits such course, communicate with jurors to determine whether such challenge may be available.

Standard 4-7.4 Opening Statement

The lawyer's opening statement should be confined to a brief statement of the issues in the case and evidence the lawyer intends to offer which the lawyer believes in good faith will be available and admissible. It is unprofessional conduct to allude to any evidence unless there is a good faith and reasonable basis for believing such evidence will be tendered and admitted in evidence.

Standard 4-7.5 Presentation of Evidence

(a) It is unprofessional conduct for a lawyer knowingly to offer false evidence, whether by documents, tangible evidence, or the testimony of witnesses, or fail to seek withdrawal thereof upon discovery of its falsity.

(b) It is unprofessional conduct for a lawyer knowingly and for the purpose of bringing inadmissible matter to the attention of the judge or jury to offer inadmissible evidence, ask legally objectionable questions, or make other impermissible comments or arguments in the presence of the judge or jury.

(c) It is unprofessional conduct to permit any tangible evidence to be displayed in the view of the judge or jury which would tend to prejudice fair consideration of the case by the judge or jury until such time as a good faith tender of such evidence is made.

(d) It is unprofessional conduct to tender tangible evidence in the presence of the judge or jury if it would tend to prejudice fair consideration of the case unless there is a reasonable basis for its admission in

Standard 4-7.6 Examination of Witnesses

evidence. When there is any substantial doubt about the admissibility of such evidence it should be tendered by an offer of proof and a ruling obtained.

Standard 4-7.6 Examination of Witnesses

(a) The interrogation of all witnesses should be conducted fairly, objectively, and with due regard for the dignity and legitimate privacy of the witness, and without seeking to intimidate or humiliate the witness unnecessarily. Proper cross-examination can be conducted without violating rules of decorum.

(b) A lawyer's belief or knowledge that the witness is telling the truth does not preclude cross-examination, but should, if possible, be taken into consideration by counsel in conducting the cross-examination.*

---

* Commentary [by the ABA]

Undermining a Truthful Witness

The mere fact that defense counsel can, by use of impeachment, impair or destroy the credibility of an adverse witness does not impose on counsel a duty to do so. Cross-examination and impeachment are legal tools that are a monopoly of licensed lawyers, given primarily for the purpose of exposing falsehood. A prosecution witness, for example, may testify in a manner that confirms precisely what the defense lawyer has learned from the defendant and has substantiated by investigation. But defense counsel may believe that the temperament, personality, or inexperience of the witness provide an opportunity, by adroit cross-examination, to confuse the witness and undermine the witness's testimony in the eyes of the jury. If defense counsel can provide an effective defense for the accused and also avoid confusion or embarrassment of the witness, counsel should seek to do so.

Another example of a situation where restraint may be called for is where a witness whose testimony the lawyer believes to be truthful is subject to impeachment by revealing to the jury that the witness was convicted of a crime many years earlier. The use of this conventional method of impeachment against a witness who has testified truthfully should be avoided if it is possible for defense counsel to do so without jeopardizing the defense of the accused. In deciding whether to use such impeachment, counsel undoubtedly will want to consider the tactical implications, since the jury may recognize the undue humiliation to the witness and thus react adversely to the lawyer.

There also is a public policy factor underlying restraint in use of impeachment powers vested in a lawyer. The policy of the law is to encourage witnesses to come forward and give evidence in litigation. If witnesses are subjected to needless humiliation when they testify, the existing human tendency to avoid "becoming involved" will be increased.

Notwithstanding the foregoing comments, there unquestionably are many cases where defense counsel cannot provide the accused with a defense at all if counsel is precluded from engaging in vigorous cross-examination of witnesses either believed or known to have testified truthfully. For example, where the defendant has admitted guilt to the lawyer and does not plan to testify, and the lawyer simply intends to put the state to its proof and raise a reasonable doubt, skillful cross-examination of the prosecution's witnesses is essential. Indeed, were counsel in this circumstance to forgo vigorous cross-examination of the prosecution's witnesses, counsel would violate the clear duty of zealous representation that is owed to the client. Justice White, in a 1967 Supreme Court opinion, addressed the sometimes professional obligation of defense counsel to impeach truthful witnesses:

> "[A]bsent a voluntary plea of guilty, we * * * insist that [defense counsel] defend his client whether he is innocent or guilty. The State has the obligation to present the evidence. Defense counsel need present nothing, even if he knows what the truth is. He need not furnish any witnesses to the police, or reveal any confidences of his client, or furnish any other information to help the prosecution's case. If he can confuse a witness, even a truthful one, or make him appear at a disadvantage, unsure or indecisive, that will be his normal course. Our interest in not convicting the innocent permits

Standard 4-7.6   *ABA STANDARDS*

(c) A lawyer should not call a witness who the lawyer knows will claim a valid privilege not to testify, for the purpose of impressing upon the jury the fact of the claim of privilege. In some instances, doing so will constitute unprofessional conduct.

(d) It is unprofessional conduct for a lawyer to ask a question which implies the existence of a factual predicate for which a good faith belief is lacking.

Standard 4-7.7 Testimony by the Defendant

(a) If the defendant has admitted to defense counsel facts which establish guilt and counsel's independent investigation established that the admissions are true but the defendant insists on the right to trial, counsel must strongly discourage the defendant against taking the witness stand to testify perjuriously.

(b) If, in advance of trial, the defendant insists that he or she will take the stand to testify perjuriously, the lawyer may withdraw from the case, if that is feasible, seeking leave of the court if necessary, but the court should not be advised of the lawyer's reason for seeking to do so.

(c) If withdrawal from the case is not feasible or is not permitted by the court, or if the situation arises immediately preceding trial or during the trial and the defendant insists upon testifying perjuriously in his or her own behalf, it is unprofessional conduct for the lawyer to lend aid to the perjury or use the perjured testimony. Before the defendant takes the stand in these circumstances, the lawyer should make a record of the fact that the defendant is taking the stand against the advice of counsel in some appropriate manner without

counsel to put the State to its proof, to put the State's case in the worst possible light, *regardless* of what he thinks or knows to be *the truth.* Undoubtedly there are some limits which defense counsel must observe but more often than not, defense counsel will cross-examine a prosecution witness, and impeach him if he can, even if he thinks the witness is telling the truth, just as he will attempt to destroy a witness who he thinks is lying. In this respect, as part of our modified adversary system and as part of the duty imposed on the most honorable defense counsel, we countenance or require conduct which in many instances has little, if any, relation to the search for truth."

Forcing Claim of Privilege Before the Jury

Although the situation arises more frequently for the prosecutor than it does for defense counsel, it is equally unprofessional for either to call a witness he or she knows will assert a claim of privilege in order to encourage the jury to draw inferences from the fact that the witness claims a privilege. If there is genuine doubt whether the witness will claim the privilege or whether the validity of the privilege will be recognized, the matter should be resolved out of the presence of the jury.

Unfounded Question

It is an improper tactic for either the prosecutor or defense counsel to attempt to communicate impressions by innuendo through questions that would be to the defendant's advantage to answer in the negative, for example, "Have you ever been convicted of the crime of robbery?" or "Weren't you a member of the Communist Party?" or "Did you tell Mr. X that . . .?" when the questioner has no evidence to support the innuendo. Generally, a question may be asked on cross-examination if, as recommended in paragraph (d), a "good faith belief" in the factual predicate implied in the question is present.

revealing the fact to the court. The lawyer may identify the witness as the defendant and may ask appropriate questions of the defendant when it is believed that the defendant's answers will not be perjurious. As to matters for which it is believed the defendant will offer perjurious testimony, the lawyer should seek to avoid direct examination of the defendant in the conventional manner; instead, the lawyer should ask the defendant if he or she wishes to make any additional statement concerning the case to the trier or triers of the facts. A lawyer may not later argue the defendant's known false version of facts to the jury as worthy of belief, and may not recite or rely upon the false testimony in his or her closing argument.*

* Ed. Note: Standard 4-7.7 was not enacted by the ABA House of Delegates during the February, 1979 meeting. This Standard 4-7.7 is printed for informational purposes only. It has not been approved by the ABA House of Delegates, and conflicts with Model Rule 3.3, Comment 11.

In ABA Formal Opinion 87-353 (Apr. 20, 1987), the ABA Standing Committee on Ethics and Professional Responsibility ruled that under Model Rule 3.3(a)(2), the lawyer "can no longer rely on the narrative approach [proposed by Defense Function Standard 7.7] to insulate him from a charge of assisting a client's perjury." The Formal Opinion also stated:

"Rule 3.3(a)(2) and (4) complement each other. While (a)(4), itself, does not expressly require disclosure by the lawyer to the tribunal of the client's false testimony after the lawyer has offered it and learns of its falsity, such disclosure will be the only 'reasonable remedial [measure]' the lawyer will be able to take if the client is unwilling to rectify the perjury. Paragraph (a)(2) requires disclosure only when it is necessary to 'avoid assisting' client perjury. When a lawyer knows a client has committed perjury, disclosure is necessary to avoid such assistance."

The Opinion added that the lawyer must "know" of the client's perjury. "The lawyer's suspicions are not enough." The obligation of Rule 3.3(b) continues only to the conclusion of the proceeding.

In 1986 the ABA Standing Committee on Association Standards for Criminal Justice explained:

"The commentary to rule 3.3, which was also approved by the House of Delegates, makes it quite clear that 'the general rule—that an advocate must disclose the existence of perjury with respect to a material fact, even that of a client—applies to defense counsel in criminal cases, as well as in other instances.' The commentary also states that 'the definition of the lawyer's ethical duty in such a situation may be qualified by constitutional provisions of due process and the right to counsel in criminal cases. In some jurisdictions these provisions have been construed to require that counsel present an accused as a witness if the accused wishes to testify, even if counsel knows the testimony will be false. The obligation of the advocate under these Rules is subordinate to such a constitutional requirement.'"

Model Rule 3.3 and its supporting commentary therefore adopts a stance incompatible with bracketed standard 4-7.7. That standard suggested that if a lawyer were unsuccessful in dissuading a defendant from offering perjurious testimony, the lawyer could nonetheless allow the defendant to testify in a narrative fashion after separately recording that defendant was taking the stand against the advice of counsel. Model Rule 3.3 eschews this approach and requires that counsel disclose proposed perjury, absent constitutional rulings to the contrary. Currently, no approved ABA Standard for Criminal Justice addresses the perjurious defendant issue and users of these standards are directed to Rule 3.3 of the Model Rules of Professional Conduct, which is the sole ABA authority on the subject.

Although proposed bracketed standard 4-7.7 ceased to be official policy of the ABA in 1979, some courts have nevertheless endorsed the standard's recommended procedures. *See, e.g., Coleman v. State,* 621 P.2d 869 (Alaska 1980); *State v. Fosnight,* 235 Kan. 52, 679 P.2d 174 (1984); *In the Matter of Goodwin,* 279 S.C. 274, 305 S.E.2d 578 (1983). . . .

Standard 4-7.8 Argument to the Jury

(a) In closing argument to the jury the lawyer may argue all reasonable inferences from the evidence in the record. It is unprofessional conduct for a lawyer intentionally to misstate the evidence or mislead the jury as to the inferences it may draw.

(b) It is unprofessional conduct for a lawyer to express a personal belief or opinion in his or her client's innocence or personal belief or opinion in the truth or falsity of any testimony or evidence, or to attribute the crime to another person unless such an inference is warranted by the evidence.

(c) A lawyer should not make arguments calculated to inflame the passions or prejudices of the jury.

(d) A lawyer should refrain from argument which would divert the jury from its duty to decide the case on the evidence by injecting issues broader than the guilt or innocence of the accused under the controlling law or by making predictions of the consequences of the jury's verdict.

Standard 4-7.9 Facts Outside the Record

It is unprofessional conduct for a lawyer intentionally to refer to or argue on the basis of facts outside the record, unless such facts are matters of common public knowledge based on ordinary human experience or matters of which the court can take judicial notice.

Standard 4-7.10 Posttrial Motions

The trial lawyer's responsibility includes presenting appropriate motions, after verdict and before sentence, to protect the defendant's rights.

PART VIII. AFTER CONVICTION

Standard 4-8.1 Sentencing

(a) The lawyer for the accused should be familiar with the sentencing alternatives available to the court and should endeavor to learn its practices in exercising sentencing discretion. The consequences of the various dispositions available should be explained fully by the lawyer to the accused.

(b) Defense counsel should present to the court any ground which will assist in reaching a proper disposition favorable to the accused. If a presentence report or summary is made available to the defense lawyer, he or she should seek to verify the information contained in it and should be prepared to supplement or challenge it if necessary. If there is no presentence report or if it is not disclosed, the lawyer should submit to the court and the prosecutor all favorable information relevant to sentencing and in an appropriate case be prepared to suggest a program of rehabilitation based on the lawyer's exploration of employment, educational, and other opportunities made available by community services.

(c) Counsel should alert the accused to the right of allocution, if any, and to the possible dangers of making a judicial confession in the course of allocution which might tend to prejudice an appeal.

Standard 4-8.2 Appeal

(a) After conviction, the lawyer should explain to the defendant the meaning and consequences of the court's judgment and defendant's right of appeal. The lawyer should give the defendant his or her professional judgment as to whether there are meritorious grounds for appeal and as to the probable results of an appeal. The lawyer should also explain to the defendant the advantages and disadvantages of an appeal. The decision whether to appeal must be the defendant's own choice.

(b) The lawyer should take whatever steps are necessary to protect the defendant's right of appeal.

Standard 4-8.3 Counsel on Appeal

Appellate counsel should not seek to withdraw from a case solely on the basis of his or her own determination that the appeal lacks merit.

Standard 4-8.4 Conduct of Appeal

(a) Appellate counsel should be diligent in perfecting an appeal and expediting its prompt submission to the appellate court.

(b) Appellate counsel should be scrupulously accurate in referring to the record and the authorities upon which counsel relies in the presentation to the court of briefs and oral argument.

(c) It is unprofessional conduct for a lawyer intentionally to refer to or argue on the basis of facts outside the record on appeal, unless such facts are matters of common public knowledge based on ordinary human experience or matters of which the court may take judicial notice.

Standard 4-8.5 Post-Conviction Remedies

After a conviction is affirmed on appeal, appellate counsel should determine whether there is any ground for relief under other post-conviction remedies. If there is a reasonable prospect of a favorable result counsel should explain to the defendant the advantages and disadvantages of taking such action. Appellate counsel is not obligated to represent the defendant in a post-conviction proceeding unless counsel has agreed to do so. In other respects the responsibility of a lawyer in a post-conviction proceeding should be guided generally by the standards governing the conduct of lawyers in criminal cases.

Standard 4-8.6 Challenges to the Effectiveness of Counsel

(a) If a lawyer, after investigation, is satisfied that another lawyer who served in an earlier phase of the case did not provide effective assistance, he or she should not hesitate to seek relief for the defendant on that ground.

Standard 4-8.6 *ABA STANDARDS*

(b) If a lawyer, after investigation, is satisfied that another lawyer who served in an earlier phase of the case provided effective assistance, he or she should so advise the client and may decline to proceed further.

(c) A lawyer whose conduct of a criminal case is drawn into question is entitled to testify concerning the matters charged and is not precluded from disclosing the truth concerning the accusation, even though this involves revealing matters which were given in confidence.

SELECTED FEDERAL STATUTES AND RULES

1. BRIBERY, GRAFT, AND CONFLICTS OF INTEREST, 18 U.S.C.A. §§ 201–18—Excerpts

§ 202. Definitions

(a) For the purpose of sections 203, 205, 207, 208, and 209 of this title the term "special Government employee" shall mean an officer or employee of the executive or legislative branch of the United States Government, of any independent agency of the United States or of the District of Columbia, who is retained, designated, appointed, or employed to perform, with or without compensation, for not to exceed one hundred and thirty days during any period of three hundred and sixty-five consecutive days, temporary duties either on a full-time or intermittent basis, a part-time United States commissioner, or a part-time United States magistrate, or, regardless of the number of days of appointment, an independent counsel appointed under chapter 40 of title 28 and any person appointed by that independent counsel under section 594(c) of title 28. Notwithstanding the next preceding sentence, every person serving as a part-time local representative of a Member of Congress in the Member's home district or State shall be classified as a special Government employee. Notwithstanding section 29(c) and (d) of the Act of August 10, 1956 (70A Stat. 632; 5 U.S.C. 30r(c) and (d)), a Reserve officer of the Armed Forces, or an officer of the National Guard of the United States, unless otherwise an officer or employee of the United States, shall be classified as a special Government employee while on active duty solely for training. A Reserve officer of the Armed Forces or an officer of the National Guard of the United States who is voluntarily serving a period of extended active duty in excess of one hundred and thirty days shall be classified as an officer of the United States within the meaning of section 203 and sections 205 through 209 and 218. A Reserve officer of the Armed Forces or an officer of the National Guard of the United States who is serving involuntarily shall be classified as a special Government employee. The terms "officer or employee" and "special Government employee" as used in sections 203, 205, 207 through 209, and 218, shall not include enlisted members of the Armed Forces.

(b) For the purposes of sections 205 and 207 of this title, the term "official responsibility" means the direct administrative or operating authority, whether intermediate or final, and either exercisable alone or with others, and either personally or through subordinates, to approve, disapprove, or otherwise direct Government action.

§ 203. Compensation to Members of Congress, officers, and others in matters affecting the Government

(a) Whoever, otherwise than as provided by law for the proper discharge of official duties, directly or indirectly—

(1) demands, seeks, receives, accepts, or agrees to receive or accept any compensation for any representational services, as agent or attorney or otherwise, rendered or to be rendered either personally or by another—

(A) at a time when such person is a Member of Congress, Member of Congress Elect, Delegate, Delegate Elect, Resident Commissioner, or Resident Commissioner Elect; or

(B) at a time when such person is an officer or employee of the United States in the executive, legislative, or judicial branch of the Government, or in any agency of the United States,

in relation to any proceeding, application, request for a ruling or other determination, contract, claim, controversy, charge, accusation, arrest or other particular matter in which the United States is a party or has a direct and substantial interest, before any department, agency, court, court-martial, officer, or any civil, military, or naval commission; or

(2) knowingly gives, promises, or offers any compensation for any such representational services rendered or to be rendered at a time when the person to whom the compensation is given, promised, or offered, is or was such a Member, Member Elect, Delegate, Delegate Elect, Commissioner, officer, or employee;

shall be subject to the penalties set forth in section 216 of this title.

(b) Whoever, otherwise than as provided by law for the proper discharge of official duties, directly or indirectly—

(1) demands, seeks, receives, accepts, or agrees to receive or accept any compensation for any representational services, as agent or attorney or otherwise, rendered or to be rendered either personally or by another, at a time when such person is an officer or employee of the District of Columbia, in relation to any proceeding, application, request for a ruling or other determination, contract, claim, controversy, charge, accusation, arrest, or other particular matter in which the District of Columbia is a party or has a direct and substantial interest, before any department, agency, court, officer, or commission; or

(2) knowingly gives, promises, or offers any compensation for any such services rendered or to be rendered at a time when the person to whom the compensation is given, promised, or offered, is or was an officer or employee of the District of Columbia;

shall be subject to the penalties set forth in section 216 of this title.

(c) A special Government employee shall be subject to subsections (a) and (b) only in relation to a particular matter involving a specific party or parties—

(1) in which such employee has at any time participated personally and substantially as a Government employee or as a special Government employee through decision, approval, disapproval, recommendation, the rendering of advice, investigation or otherwise; or

(2) which is pending in the department or agency of the Government in which such employee is serving except that paragraph (2) of this subsection shall not apply in the case of a special Government employee who has served in such department or agency no more than sixty days during the immediately preceding period of three hundred and sixty-five consecutive days.

(d) Nothing in this section prevents an officer or employee, including a special Government employee, from acting, with or without compensation, as agent or attorney for or otherwise representing his parents, spouse, child, or any person for whom, or for any estate for which, he is serving as guardian, executor, administrator, trustee, or other personal fiduciary except—

(1) in those matters in which he has participated personally and substantially as a Government employee, through decision, approval, disapproval, recommendation, the rendering of advice, investigation, or otherwise; or

(2) in those matters that are the subject of his official responsibility,

subject to approval by the Government official responsible for appointment to his position.

(e) Nothing in this section prevents a special Government employee from acting as agent or attorney for another person in the performance of work under a grant by, or a contract with or for the benefit of, the United States if the head of the department or agency concerned with the grant or contract certifies in writing that the national interest so requires and publishes such certification in the Federal Register.

(f) Nothing in this section prevents an individual from giving testimony under oath or from making statements required to be made under penalty of perjury.

§ 204. Practice in United States Claims Court or the United States Court of Appeals for the Federal Circuit by Members of Congress

Whoever, being a Member of Congress or Member of Congress Elect, practices in the United States Claims Court or the United States Court of Appeals for the Federal Circuit shall be subject to the penalties set forth in section 216 of this title.

§ 205. Activities of officers and employees in claims against and other matters affecting the Government

(a) Whoever, being an officer or employee of the United States in the executive, legislative, or judicial branch of the Government or in any agency of the United States, other than in the proper discharge of his official duties—

(1) acts as agent or attorney for prosecuting any claim against the United States, or receives any gratuity, or any share of or interest in any such claim, in consideration of assistance in the prosecution of such claim; or

(2) acts as agent or attorney for anyone before any department, agency, court, court-martial, officer, or any civil, military, or naval commission in connection with any covered matter in which the United States is a party or has a direct and substantial interest;

shall be subject to the penalties set forth in section 216 of this title.

(b) Whoever, being an officer or employee of the District of Columbia or an officer or employee of the Office of the United States Attorney for the District of Columbia, otherwise than in the proper discharge of official duties—

(1) acts as agent or attorney for prosecuting any claim against the District of Columbia, or receives any gratuity, or any share of or interest in any such claim in consideration of assistance in the prosecution of such claim; or

(2) acts as agent or attorney for anyone before any department, agency, court, officer, or any commission in connection with any covered matter in which the District of Columbia is a party or has a direct and substantial interest;

shall be subject to the penalties set forth in section 216 of this title.

(c) A special Government employee shall be subject to subsections (a) and (b) only in relation to a covered matter involving a specific party or parties—

(1) in which he has at any time participated personally and substantially as a Government employee or special Government employee through decision, approval, disapproval, recommendation, the rendering of advice, investigation, or otherwise; or

(2) which is pending in the department or agency of the Government in which he is serving.

Paragraph (2) shall not apply in the case of a special Government employee who has served in such department or agency no more than sixty days during the immediately preceding period of three hundred and sixty-five consecutive days.

(d) Nothing in subsection (a) or (b) prevents an officer or employee, if not inconsistent with the faithful performance of his duties, from acting without compensation as agent or attorney for, or otherwise representing, any person who is the subject of disciplinary, loyalty, or other personnel administration proceedings in connection with those proceedings.

(e) Nothing in subsection (a) or (b) prevents an officer or employee, including a special Government employee, from acting, with or without compensation, as agent or attorney for, or otherwise representing, his parents, spouse, child, or any person for whom, or for any estate for which, he is serving as guardian, executor, administrator, trustee, or other personal fiduciary except—

(1) in those matters in which he has participated personally and substantially as a Government employee or special Government employee through decision, approval, disapproval, recommendation, the rendering of advice, investigation, or otherwise, or

(2) in those matters which are the subject of his official responsibility,

subject to approval by the Government official responsible for appointment to his position.

(f) Nothing in subsection (a) or (b) prevents a special Government employee from acting as agent or attorney for another person in the performance of work under a grant by, or a contract with or for the benefit of, the United States if the head of the department or agency concerned with the grant or contract certifies in writing that the national interest so requires and publishes such certification in the Federal Register.

(g) Nothing in this section prevents an officer or employee from giving testimony under oath or from making statements required to be made under penalty for perjury or contempt.

(h) For the purpose of this section, the term "covered matter" means any judicial or other proceeding, application, request for a ruling or other determination, contract, claim, controversy, investigation, charge, accusation, arrest, or other particular matter.

§ 207. Restrictions on former officers, employees, and elected officials of the executive and legislative branches

(a) Restrictions on all officers and employees of the executive branch and certain other agencies.—

(1) **Permanent restrictions on representation on particular matters.**—Any person who is an officer or employee (including any special Government employee) of the executive branch of the United States (including any independent agency of the United States), or of the District of Columbia, and who, after the termination of his or her service or employment with the United States or the District of Columbia, knowingly makes, with the intent to influence, any communication to or appearance before any officer or employee of any department, agency, court, or court-martial of the United States or

the District of Columbia, on behalf of any other person (except the United States or the District of Columbia) in connection with a particular matter—

> (A) in which the United States or the District of Columbia is a party or has a direct and substantial interest,
>
> (B) in which the person participated personally and substantially as such officer or employee, and
>
> (C) which involved a specific party or specific parties at the time of such participation,

shall be punished as provided in section 216 of this title.

(2) **Two-year restrictions concerning particular matters under official responsibility.**—Any person subject to the restrictions contained in paragraph (1) who, within 2 years after the termination of his or her service or employment with the United States or the District of Columbia, knowingly makes, with the intent to influence, any communication to or appearance before any officer or employee of any department, agency, court, or court-martial of the United States or the District of Columbia, on behalf of any other person (except the United States or the District of Columbia), in connection with a particular matter—

> (A) in which the United States or the District of Columbia is a party or has a direct and substantial interest,
>
> (B) which such person knows or reasonably should know was actually pending under his or her official responsibility as such officer or employee within a period of 1 year before the termination of his or her service or employment with the United States or the District of Columbia, and
>
> (C) which involved a specific party or specific parties at the time it was so pending,

shall be punished as provided in section 216 of this title.

(3) **Clarification of restrictions.**—The restrictions contained in paragraphs (1) and (2) shall apply—

> (A) in the case of an officer or employee of the executive branch of the United States (including any independent agency), only with respect to communications to or appearances before any officer or employee of any department, agency, court, or court-martial of the United States on behalf of any other person (except the United States), and only with respect to a matter in which the United States is a party or has a direct and substantial interest; and
>
> (B) in the case of an officer or employee of the District of Columbia, only with respect to communications to or appearances before any officer or employee of any department, agency, or court of the District of Columbia on behalf of any other person

(except the District of Columbia), and only with respect to a matter in which the District of Columbia is a party or has a direct and substantial interest.

(b) One-year restrictions on aiding or advising.—

(1) In general.—Any person who is a former officer or employee of the executive branch of the United States (including any independent agency) and is subject to the restrictions contained in subsection (a)(1), or any person who is a former officer or employee of the legislative branch or a former Member of Congress, who personally and substantially participated in any ongoing trade or treaty negotiation on behalf of the United States within the 1-year period preceding the date on which his or her service or employment with the United States terminated, and who had access to information concerning such trade or treaty negotiation which is exempt from disclosure under section 552 of title 5, which is so designated by the appropriate department or agency, and which the person knew or should have known was so designated, shall not, on the basis of that information, knowingly represent, aid, or advise any other person (except the United States) concerning such ongoing trade or treaty negotiation for a period of 1 year after his or her service or employment with the United States terminates. Any person who violates this subsection shall be punished as provided in section 216 of this title.

(2) Definition.—For purposes of this paragraph—

(A) the term "trade negotiation" means negotiations which the President determines to undertake to enter into a trade agreement pursuant to section 1102 of the Omnibus Trade and Competitiveness Act of 1988, and does not include any action taken before that determination is made; and

(B) the term "treaty" means an international agreement made by the President that requires the advice and consent of the Senate.

(c) One-year restrictions on certain senior personnel of the executive branch and independent agencies.—

(1) Restrictions.—In addition to the restrictions set forth in subsections (a) and (b), any person who is an officer or employee (including any special Government employee) of the executive branch of the United States (including an independent agency), who is referred to in paragraph (2), and who, within 1 year after the termination of his or her service or employment as such officer or employee, knowingly makes, with the intent to influence, any communication to or appearance before any officer or employee of the department or agency in which such person served within 1 year before such termination, on behalf of any other person (except the United States), in connection with any matter on which such person seeks official action by any officer or employee of such department or agency, shall be punished as provided in section 216 of this title.

(2) **Persons to whom restrictions apply.**—(A) Paragraph (1) shall apply to a person (other than a person subject to the restrictions of subsection (d))—

(i) employed at a rate of pay specified in or fixed according to subchapter II of chapter 53 of title 5,

(ii) employed in a position which is not referred to in clause (i) and for which the basic rate of pay, exclusive of any locality-based pay adjustment under section 5302 of title 5 (or any comparable adjustment pursuant to interim authority of the President), is equal to or greater than the rate of basic pay payable for level V of the Executive Schedule;

(iii) appointed by the President to a position under section 105(a)(2)(B) of title 3 or by the Vice President to a position under section 106(a)(1)(B) of title 3, or

(iv) employed in a position which is held by an active duty commissioned officer of the uniformed services who is serving in a grade or rank for which the pay grade (as specified in section 201 of title 37) is pay grade O-7 or above.

(B) Paragraph (1) shall not apply to a special Government employee who serves less than 60 days in the 1-year period before his or her service or employment as such employee terminates.

(C) At the request of a department or agency, the Director of the Office of Government Ethics may waive the restrictions contained in paragraph (1) with respect to any position, or category of positions, referred to in clause (ii) or (iv) of subparagraph (A), in such department or agency if the Director determines that—

(i) the imposition of the restrictions with respect to such position or positions would create an undue hardship on the department or agency in obtaining qualified personnel to fill such position or positions, and

(ii) granting the waiver would not create the potential for use of undue influence or unfair advantage.

(d) **Restrictions on very senior personnel of the executive branch and independent agencies.**—

(1) **Restrictions.**—In addition to the restrictions set forth in subsections (a) and (b), any person who—

(A) serves in the position of Vice President of the United States,

(B) is employed in a position in the executive branch of the United States (including any independent agency) at a rate of pay payable for level I of the Executive Schedule or employed in a position in the Executive Office of the President at a rate of pay payable for level II of the Executive Schedule, or

(C) is appointed by the President to a position under section 105(a)(2)(A) of title 3 or by the Vice President to a position under section 106(a)(1)(A) of title 3,

and who, within 1 year after the termination of that person's service in that position, knowingly makes, with the intent to influence, any communication to or appearance before any person described in paragraph (2), on behalf of any other person (except the United States), in connection with any matter on which such person seeks official action by any officer or employee of the executive branch of the United States, shall be punished as provided in section 216 of this title.

(2) **Persons who may not be contacted.**—The persons referred to in paragraph (1) with respect to appearances or communications by a person in a position described in subparagraph (A), (B), or (C) of paragraph (1) are—

(A) any officer or employee of any department or agency in which such person served in such position within a period of 1 year before such person's service or employment with the United States Government terminated, and

(B) any person appointed to a position in the executive branch which is listed in sections 5312, 5313, 5314, 5315, or 5316 of title 5.

(e) **Restrictions on members of Congress and officers and employees of the legislative branch.**—

(1) **Members of congress and elected officers.**—(A) Any person who is a Member of Congress or an elected officer of either House of Congress and who, within 1 year after that person leaves office, knowingly makes, with the intent to influence, any communication to or appearance before any of the persons described in subparagraph (B) or (C), on behalf of any other person (except the United States) in connection with any matter on which such former Member of Congress or elected officer seeks action by a Member, officer, or employee of either House of Congress, in his or her official capacity, shall be punished as provided in section 216 of this title.

(B) The persons referred to in subparagraph (A) with respect to appearances or communications by a former Member of Congress are any Member, officer, or employee of either House of Congress, and any employee of any other legislative office of the Congress.

(C) The persons referred to in subparagraph (A) with respect to appearances or communications by a former elected officer are any Member, officer, or employee of the House of Congress in which the elected officer served.

(2) **Personal staff.**—(A) Any person who is an employee of a Senator or an employee of a Member of the House of Representatives and who, within 1 year after the termination of that employment, knowingly makes, with the intent to influence, any communication to or appearance before any of the persons described in subparagraph (B), on behalf of any other person (except the United States) in connection with any matter on which such former employee seeks action by a Member, officer, or employee of either House of Congress, in his or her official capacity, shall be punished as provided in section 216 of this title.

(B) The persons referred to in subparagraph (A) with respect to appearances or communications by a person who is a former employee are the following:

(i) the Senator or Member of the House of Representatives for whom that person was an employee; and

(ii) any employee of that Senator or Member of the House of Representatives.

(3) **Committee staff.**—Any person who is an employee of a committee of Congress and who, within 1 year after the termination of that person's employment on such committee, knowingly makes, with the intent to influence, any communication to or appearance before any person who is a Member or an employee of that committee or who was a Member of the committee in the year immediately prior to the termination of such person's employment by the committee, on behalf of any other person (except the United States) in connection with any matter on which such former employee seeks action by a Member, officer, or employee of either House of Congress, in his or her official capacity, shall be punished as provided in section 216 of this title.

(4) **Leadership staff.**—(A) Any person who is an employee on the leadership staff of the House of Representatives or an employee on the leadership staff of the Senate and who, within 1 year after the termination of that person's employment on such staff, knowingly makes, with the intent to influence, any communication to or appearance before any of the persons described in subparagraph (B), on behalf of any other person (except the United States) in connection with any matter on which such former employee seeks action by a Member, officer, or employee of either House of Congress, in his or her official capacity, shall be punished as provided in section 216 of this title.

(B) The persons referred to in subparagraph (A) with respect to appearances or communications by a former employee are the following:

(i) in the case of a former employee on the leadership staff of the House of Representatives, those persons are any Member of the leadership of the House of Representatives and any employee on the leadership staff of the House of Representatives; and

(ii) in the case of a former employee on the leadership staff of the Senate, those persons are any Member of the leadership of the Senate and any employee on the leadership staff of the Senate.

(5) **Other legislative offices.**—(A) Any person who is an employee of any other legislative office of the Congress and who, within 1 year after the termination of that person's employment in such office, knowingly makes, with the intent to influence, any communication to or appearance before any of the persons described in subparagraph (B), on behalf of any other person (except the United States) in connection with any matter on which such former employee seeks action by any officer or employee of such office, in his or her official capacity, shall be punished as provided in section 216 of this title.

(B) The persons referred to in subparagraph (A) with respect to appearances or communications by a former employee are the employees and officers of the former legislative office of the Congress of the former employee.

(6) **Limitation on restrictions.**—(A) The restrictions contained in paragraphs (2), (3), and (4) apply only to acts by a former employee who, for at least 60 days, in the aggregate, during the 1-year period before that former employee's service as such employee terminated, was paid a rate of basic pay equal to or greater than an amount which is 75 percent of the basic rate of pay payable for a Member of the House of Congress in which such employee was employed.

(B) The restrictions contained in paragraph (5) apply only to acts by a former employee who, for at least 60 days, in the aggregate, during the 1-year period before that former employee's service as such employee terminated, was employed in a position for which the rate of basic pay, exclusive of any locality-based pay adjustment under section 5302 of title 5 (or any comparable adjustment pursuant to interim authority of the President), is equal to or greater than the basic rate of pay payable for level V of the Executive Schedule.

(7) **Definitions.**—As used in this subsection—

(A) the term "committee of Congress" includes standing committees, joint committees, and select committees;

(B) a person is an employee of a House of Congress if that person is an employee of the Senate or an employee of the House of Representatives;

(C) the term "employee of the House of Representatives" means an employee of a Member of the House of Representatives, an employee of a committee of the House of Representatives, an employee of a joint committee of the Congress whose pay is disbursed by the Clerk of the House of Representatives, and an employee on the leadership staff of the House of Representatives;

(D) the term "employee of the Senate" means an employee of a Senator, an employee of a committee of the Senate, an employee of a joint committee of the Congress whose pay is disbursed by the Secretary of the Senate, and an employee on the leadership staff of the Senate;

(E) a person is an employee of a Member of the House of Representatives if that person is an employee of a Member of the House of Representatives under the clerk hire allowance;

(F) a person is an employee of a Senator if that person is an employee in a position in the office of a Senator;

(G) the term "employee of any other legislative office of the Congress" means an officer or employee of the Architect of the Capitol, the United States Botanic Garden, the General Accounting Office, the Government Printing Office, the Library of Congress, the Office of Technology Assessment, the Congressional Budget Office, the Copyright Royalty Tribunal, the United States Capitol Police, and any other agency, entity, or office in the legislative branch not covered by paragraph (1), (2), (3), or (4) of this subsection;

(H) the term "employee on the leadership staff of the House of Representatives" means an employee of the office of a Member of the leadership of the House of Representatives described in subparagraph (L), and any elected minority employee of the House of Representatives;

(I) the term "employee on the leadership staff of the Senate" means an employee of the office of a Member of the leadership of the Senate described in subparagraph (M);

(J) the term "Member of Congress" means a Senator or a Member of the House of Representatives;

(K) the term "Member of the House of Representatives" means a Representative in, or a Delegate or Resident Commissioner to, the Congress;

(L) the term "Member of the leadership of the House of Representatives" means the Speaker, majority leader, minority leader, majority whip, minority whip, chief deputy majority whip, chief deputy minority whip, chairman of the Democratic Steering Committee, chairman and vice chairman of the Democratic Caucus, chairman, vice chairman, and secretary of the Republican Conference, chairman of the Republican Research Committee, and chairman of the Republican Policy Committee, of the House of Representatives (or any similar position created on or after the effective date set forth in section 102(a) of the Ethics Reform Act of 1989);

(M) the term "Member of the leadership of the Senate" means the Vice President, and the President pro tempore, Deputy President pro tempore, majority leader, minority leader, majority whip, minority whip, chairman and secretary of the Conference of the Majority, chairman and secretary of the Conference of the Minority, chairman and co-chairman of the Majority Policy Committee, and chairman of the Minority Policy Committee, of the Senate (or any similar position created on or after the effective date set forth in section 102(a) of the Ethics Reform Act of 1989).

(f) Restrictions relating to foreign entities.—

(1) Restrictions.—Any person who is subject to the restrictions contained in subsection (c), (d), or (e) and who knowingly, within 1 year after leaving the position, office, or employment referred to in such subsection—

(A) represents a foreign entity before any officer or employee of any department or agency of the United States with the intent to influence a decision of such officer or employee in carrying out his or her official duties, or

(B) aids or advises a foreign entity with the intent to influence a decision of any officer or employee of any department or agency of the United States, in carrying out his or her official duties,

shall be punished as provided in section 216 of this title.

(2) Definition.—For purposes of this subsection, the term "foreign entity" means the government of a foreign country as defined in section 1(e) of the Foreign Agents Registration Act of 1938, as amended, or a foreign political party as defined in section 1(f) of that Act.

(g) Special rules for detailees.—For purposes of this section, a person who is detailed from one department, agency, or other entity to another department, agency, or other entity shall, during the period such person is detailed, be deemed to be an officer or employee of both departments, agencies, or such entities.

(h) Designations of separate statutory agencies and bureaus.—

(1) Designations.—For purposes of subsection (c) and except as provided in paragraph (2), whenever the Director of the Office of Government Ethics determines that an agency or bureau within a department or agency in the executive branch exercises functions which are distinct and separate from the remaining functions of the department or agency and that there exists no potential for use of undue influence or unfair advantage based on past Government service, the Director shall by rule designate such agency or bureau as a separate department or agency. On an annual basis the Director of the Office of Government Ethics shall review the designations and determinations made under this subparagraph and, in consultation with the department or agency concerned, make such additions and deletions as are necessary. Departments and agencies shall cooperate to the fullest extent with the Director of the Office of Government Ethics in the exercise of his or her responsibilities under this paragraph.

(2) **Inapplicability of designations.**—No agency or bureau within the Executive Office of the President may be designated under paragraph (1) as a separate department or agency. No designation under paragraph (1) shall apply to persons referred to in subsection (c)(2)(A)(i) or (iii).

(i) **Definitions.**—For purposes of this section—

(1) the term "officer or employee", when used to describe the person to whom a communication is made or before whom an appearance is made, with the intent to influence, shall include—

(A) in subsections (a), (c), and (d), the President and the Vice President; and

(B) in subsection (f), the President, the Vice President, and Members of Congress;

(2) the term "participated" means an action taken as an officer or employee through decision, approval, disapproval, recommendation, the rendering of advice, investigation, or other such action; and

(3) the term "particular matter" includes any investigation, application, request for a ruling or determination, rulemaking, contract, controversy, claim, charge, accusation, arrest, or judicial or other proceeding.

(j) **Exceptions.**—

(1) **Official government duties.**—The restrictions contained in this section shall not apply to acts done in carrying out official duties on behalf of the United States or the District of Columbia or as an elected official of a State or local government.

(2) **State and local governments and institutions, hospitals, and organizations.**—The restrictions contained in subsections (c), (d), and (e) shall not apply to acts done in carrying out official duties as an employee of—

(A) an agency or instrumentality of a State or local government if the appearance, communication, or representation is on behalf of such government, or

(B) an accredited, degree-granting institution of higher education, as defined in section 1201(a) of the Higher Education Act of 1965, or a hospital or medical research organization, exempted and defined under section 501(c)(3) of the Internal Revenue Code of 1986, if the appearance, communication, or representation is on behalf of such institution, hospital, or orgnization.

(3) **International organizations.**—The restrictions contained in this section shall not apply to an appearance or communication on behalf of, or advice or aid to, an international organization in which

the United States participates, if the Secretary of State certifies in advance that such activity is in the interests of the United States.

(4) **Special knowledge.**—The restrictions contained in subsections (c), (d), and (e) shall not prevent an individual from making or providing a statement, which is based on the individual's own special knowledge in the particular area that is the subject of the statement, if no compensation is thereby received.

(5) **Exception for scientific or technological information.**—The restrictions contained in subsections (a), (c), and (d) shall not apply with respect to the making of communications solely for the purpose of furnishing scientific or technological information, if such communications are made under procedures acceptable to the department or agency concerned or if the head of the department or agency concerned with the particular matter, in consultation with the Director of the Office of Government Ethics, makes a certification, published in the Federal Register, that the former officer or employee has outstanding qualifications in a scientific, technological, or other technical discipline, and is acting with respect to a particular matter which requires such qualifications, and that the national interest would be served by the participation of the former officer or employee. For purposes of this paragraph, the term "officer or employee" includes the Vice President.

(6) **Exception for testimony.**—Nothing in this section shall prevent an individual from giving testimony under oath, or from making statements required to be made under penalty of perjury. Notwithstanding the preceding sentence—

(A) a former officer or employee of the executive branch of the United States (including any independent agency) who is subject to the restrictions contained in subsection (a)(1) with respect to a particular matter may not, except pursuant to court order, serve as an expert witness for any other person (except the United States) in that matter; and

(B) a former officer or employee of the District of Columbia who is subject to the restrictions contained in subsection (a)(1) with respect to a particular matter may not, except pursuant to court order, serve as an expert witness for any other person (except the District of Columbia) in that matter.

§ 208. Acts affecting a personal financial interest

(a) Except as permitted by subsection (b) hereof, whoever, being an officer or employee of the executive branch of the United States Government, or of any independent agency of the United States, a Federal Reserve bank director, officer, or employee, or an officer or employee of the District of Columbia, including a special Government employee, participates personally and substantially as a Government officer or employee, through decision, approval, disapproval, recommendation, the rendering of advice, investigation, or otherwise, in a judicial or other proceeding, application, request for a ruling or other determination, contract, claim, controversy, charge, accusation, arrest, or other particular matter in which, to his knowledge, he, his spouse, minor child, general partner, organization in which he is serving as officer, director, trustee, general partner or employee, or any person or organization with whom he is negotiating or has any arrangement concerning prospective employment, has a financial interest—

Shall be subject to the penalties set forth in section 216 of this title.

(b) Subsection (a) shall not apply—

(1) if the officer or employee first advises the Government official responsible for appointment to his or her position of the nature and circumstances of the judicial or other proceeding, application, request for a ruling or other determination, contract, claim, controversy, charge, accusation, arrest, or other particular matter and makes full disclosure of the financial interest and receives in advance a written determination made by such official that the interest is not so substantial as to be deemed likely to affect the integrity of the services which the Government may expect from such officer or employee;

(2) if, by regulation issued by the Director of the Office of Government Ethics, applicable to all or a portion of all officers and employees covered by this section, and published in the Federal Register, the financial interest has been exempted from the requirements of subsection (a) as being too remote or too inconsequential to affect the integrity of the services of the Government officers or employees to which such regulation applies:

(3) in the case of a special Government employee serving on an advisory committee within the meaning of the Federal Advisory Committee Act (including an individual being considered for an appointment to such a position), the official responsible for the employee's appointment, after review of the financial disclosure report filed by the individual pursuant to section 107 of the Ethics in Government Act of 1978, certifies in writing that the need for the individual's services outweighs the potential for a conflict of interest created by the financial interest involved; or

(4) the financial interest that would be affected by the particular matter involved is that resulting solely from the interest of the officer or employee, or his or her spouse or minor child, in birthrights—

(A) in an Indian tribe, band, nation, or other organized group or community, including any Alaska Native village corporation as defined in or established pursuant to the Alaska Native Claims Settlement Act, which is recognized as eligible for the special programs and services provided by the United States to Indians because of their status as Indians,

(B) in an Indian allotment the title to which is held in trust by the United States or which is inalienable by the allottee without the consent of the United States, or

(C) in an Indian claims fund held in trust or administered by the United States,

if the particular matter does not involve the Indian allotment or claims fund or the Indian tribe, band, nation, organized group or community, or Alaska Native village corporation as a specific party or parties.

(c)(1) For the purpose of paragraph (1) of subsection (b), in the case of class A and B directors of Federal Reserve Banks, the Board of Governors of the Federal Reserve System shall be deemed to be the Government official responsible for appointment.

(2) The potential availability of an exemption under any particular paragraph of subsection (b) does not preclude an exemption being granted pursuant to another paragraph of subsection (b).

(d)(1) Upon request, a copy of any determination granting an exemption under subsection (b)(1) or (b)(3) shall be made available to the public by the agency granting the exemption pursuant to the procedures set forth in section 105 of the Ethics in Government Act of 1978. In making such determination available, the agency may withhold from disclosure any information contained in the determination that would be exempt from disclosure under section 552 of title 5. For purposes of determinations under subsection (b)(3), the information describing each financial interest shall be no more extensive than that required of the individual in his or her financial disclosure report under the Ethics in Government Act of 1978.

(2) The Office of Government Ethics, after consultation with the Attorney General, shall issue uniform regulations for the issuance of waivers and exemptions under subsection (b) which shall—

(A) list and describe exemptions; and

(B) provide guidance with respect to the types of interests that are not so substantial as to be deemed likely to affect the integrity of the services the Government may expect from the employee.

§ 209. Salary of Government officials and employees payable only by United States

(a) Whoever receives any salary, or any contribution to or supplementation of salary, as compensation for his services as an officer or employee of the executive branch of the United States Government, of any independent agency of the United States, or of the District of Columbia, from any source other than the Government of the United

§ 209

States, except as may be contributed out of the treasury of any State, county, or municipality; or

Whoever, whether an individual, partnership, association, corporation, or other organization pays, or makes any contribution to, or in any way supplements the salary of, any such officer or employee under circumstances which would make its receipt a violation of this subsection—

Shall be subject to the penalties set forth in Section 216 of this title.

(b) Nothing herein prevents an officer or employee of the executive branch of the United States Government, or of any independent agency of the United States, or of the District of Columbia, from continuing to participate in a bona fide pension, retirement, group life, health or accident insurance, profit-sharing, stock bonus, or other employee welfare or benefit plan maintained by a former employer.

(c) This section does not apply to a special Government employee or to an officer or employee of the Government serving without compensation, whether or not he is a special Government employee, or to any person paying, contributing to, or supplementing his salary as such.

(d) This section does not prohibit payment or acceptance of contributions, awards, or other expenses under the terms of Chapter 41 of title 5.

(e) This section does not prohibit the payment of actual relocation expenses incident to participation, or the acceptance of same by a participant in an executive exchange or fellowship program in an executive agency: *Provided,* That such program has been established by statute or Executive order of the President, offers appointments not to exceed three hundred and sixty-five days, and permits no extensions in excess of ninety additional days or, in the case of participants in overseas assignments, in excess of three hundred and sixty-five days.

(f) This section does not prohibit acceptance or receipt, by any officer or employee injured during the commission of an offense described in section 351 or 1751 of this title, of contributions or payments from an organization which is described in section 501(c)(3) of the Internal Revenue Code of 1954 and which is exempt from taxation under section 501(a) of such Code.

2. 18 U.S.C.A. § 1905

§ 1905. Disclosure of Confidential Information Generally

Whoever, being an officer or employee of the United States or of any department or agency thereof, or agent of the Department of Justice as defined in the Antitrust Civil Process Act (15 U.S.C. 1311–1314), publishes, divulges, discloses, or makes known in any manner or to any extent not authorized by law any information coming to him in the course of his employment or official duties or by reason of any examination or investigation made by, or return, report or record made to or filled with, such department or agency or officer or employee thereof, which information concerns or relates to the trade secrets, processes, operations, style of work, or apparatus, or to the identity, confidential statistical data, amount or source of any income, profits, losses, or expenditures of any person, firm, partnership, corporation, or association; or permits any income return or copy thereof or any book containing any abstract or particulars thereof to be seen or examined by any person except as provided by law; shall be fined not more than $1,000, or imprisoned not more than one year, or both; and shall be removed from office or employment.

3. 28 U.S.C.A. §§ 47, 144, 372, 454–55

§ 47. Disqualification of Trial Judge to Hear Appeal

No judge shall hear or determine an appeal from the decision of a case or issue tried by him.

§ 144. Bias or Prejudice of Judge

Whenever a party to any proceeding in a district court makes and files a timely and sufficient affidavit that the judge before whom the matter is pending has a personal bias or prejudice either against him or in favor of any adverse party, such judge shall proceed no further therein, but another judge shall be assigned to hear such proceeding.

The affidavit shall state the facts and the reasons for the belief that bias or prejudice exists, and shall be filed not less than ten days before the beginning of the term at which the proceeding is to be heard, or good cause shall be shown for failure to file it within such time. A party may file only one such affidavit in any case. It shall be accompanied by a certificate of counsel of record stating that it is made in good faith.

§ 372. Retirement for Disability; Substitute Judge on Failure to Retire; Judicial Discipline

(a) * * *

(b) * * *

(c)(1) Any person alleging that a circuit, district, or bankruptcy judge, or a magistrate, has engaged in conduct prejudicial to the effective and expeditious administration of the business of the courts, or alleging that such a judge or magistrate is unable to discharge all the duties of office by reason of mental or physical disability, may file with the clerk of the court of appeals for the circuit a written complaint containing a brief statement of the facts constituting such conduct. * * *

(2) Upon receipt of a complaint filed under paragraph (1) of this subsection, the clerk shall promptly transmit such complaint to the chief judge of the circuit, or, if the conduct complained of is that of the chief judge, to that circuit judge in regular active service next senior in date of commission (hereafter, for purposes of this subsection only, included in the term "chief judge"). The clerk shall

simultaneously transmit a copy of the complaint to the judge or magistrate whose conduct is the subject of the complaint.

(3) After expeditiously reviewing a complaint, the chief judge, by written order stating his reasons, may—

> (A) dismiss the complaint, if he finds it to be (i) not in conformity with paragraph (1) of this subsection, (ii) directly related to the merits of a decision or procedural ruling, or (iii) frivolous; or
>
> (B) conclude the proceeding if he finds that appropriate corrective action has been taken.

The chief judge shall transmit copies of his written order to the complainant and to the judge or magistrate whose conduct is the subject of the complaint.

(4) If the chief judge does not enter an order under paragraph (3) of this subsection, such judge shall promptly—

> (A) appoint himself and equal numbers of circuit and district judges of the circuit to a special committee to investigate the facts and allegations contained in the complaint;
>
> (B) certify the complaint and any other documents pertaining thereto to each member of such committee; and
>
> (C) provide written notice to the complainant and the judge or magistrate whose conduct is the subject of the complaint of the action taken under this paragraph.

* * *

(5) Each committee appointed under paragraph (4) of this subsection shall conduct an investigation as extensive as it considers necessary, and shall expeditiously file a comprehensive written report thereon with the judicial council of the circuit. Such report shall present both the findings of the investigation and the committee's recommendations for necessary and appropriate action by the judicial council of the circuit.

(6) Upon receipt of a report filed under paragraph (5) of this subsection, the judicial council—

> (A) may conduct any additional investigation which it considers to be necessary;
>
> (B) shall take such action as is appropriate to assure the effective and expeditious administration of the business of the courts within the circuit, including, but not limited to, any of the following actions:
>
>> (i) directing the chief judge of the district of the magistrate whose conduct is the subject of the complaint to take such action as the judicial council considers appropriate;
>>
>> (ii) certifying disability of a judge appointed to hold office during good behavior whose conduct is the subject of the

complaint, pursuant to the procedures and standards provided under subsection (b) of this section;

(iii) requesting that any such judge appointed to hold office during good behavior voluntarily retire, with the provision that the length of service requirements under section 371 * of this title shall not apply;

(iv) ordering that, on a temporary basis for a time certain, no further cases be assigned to any judge or magistrate whose conduct is the subject of a complaint;

(v) censuring or reprimanding such judge or magistrate by means of private communication;

(vi) censuring or reprimanding such judge or magistrate by means of public announcement; or

(vii) ordering such other action as it considers appropriate under the circumstances, except that (I) in no circumstances may the council order removal from office of any judge appointed to hold office during good behavior, and (II) any removal of a magistrate shall be in accordance with section 631 of this title and any removal of a bankruptcy judge shall be in accordance with section 152 of this title; and

(C) may dismiss the complaint; and

(D) shall immediately provide written notice to the complainant and to such judge or magistrate of the action taken under this paragraph.

(7)(A) In addition to the authority granted under paragraph (6) of this subsection, the judicial council may, in its discretion, refer any complaint under this subsection, together with the record of any associated proceedings and its recommendations for appropriate action, to the Judicial Conference of the United States.

(B) In any case in which the judicial council determines, on the basis of a complaint and an investigation under this subsection, or on the basis of information otherwise available to the council, that a judge appointed to hold office during good behavior has engaged in conduct—

(i) which might constitute one or more grounds for impeachment under article II of the Constitution; or

(ii) which, in the interest of justice, is not amenable to resolution by the judicial council,

the judicial council shall promptly certify such determination, together with any complaint and a record of any associated proceedings, to the Judicial Conference of the United States.

* Ed. Note: Section 371 refers to age and service requirements for purposes of a retirement annuity.

§ 372   TITLE 28 U.S.C.A.

(C) A judicial council acting under authority of this paragraph shall, unless contrary to the interests of justice, immediately submit written notice to the complainant and to the judge or magistrate whose conduct is the subject of the action taken under this paragraph.

(8)(A) Upon referral or certification of any matter under paragraph (7) of this subsection, the Judicial Conference, after consideration of the prior proceedings and such additional investigation as it considers appropriate, shall by majority vote take such action, as described in paragraph (6)(B) of this subsection, as it considers appropriate. If the Judicial Conference concurs in the determination of the council, or makes its own determination, that consideration of impeachment may be warranted, it shall so certify and transmit the determination and the record of proceedings to the House of Representatives for whatever action the House of Representatives considers to be necessary. * * *

(9)(A) In conducting any investigation under this subsection, the judicial council, or a special committee appointed under paragraph (4) of this subsection, shall have full subpoena powers as provided in section 332(d) of this title.

(B) In conducting any investigation under this subsection, the Judicial Conference, or a standing committee appointed by the Chief Justice under section 331 of this title, shall have full subpoena powers as provided in that section.

(10) A complainant, judge, or magistrate aggrieved by a final order of the chief judge under paragraph (3) of this subsection may petition the judicial council for review thereof. A complainant, judge, or magistrate aggrieved by an action of the judicial council under paragraph (6) of this subsection may petition the Judicial Conference of the United States for review thereof. The Judicial Conference, or the standing committee established under section 331 of this title, may grant a petition filed by a complainant, judge, or magistrate under this paragraph. Except as expressly provided in this paragraph, all orders and determinations, including denials of petitions for review, shall be final and conclusive and shall not be judicially reviewable on appeal or otherwise.

(11) Each judicial council and the Judicial Conference may prescribe such rules for the conduct of proceedings under this subsection, including the processing of petitions for review, as each considers to be appropriate. Such rules shall contain provisions requiring that—

    (A) adequate prior notice of any investigation be given in writing to the judge or magistrate whose conduct is the subject of the complaint;

(B) the judge or magistrate whose conduct is the subject of the complaint be afforded an opportunity to appear (in person or by counsel) at proceedings conducted by the investigating panel, to present oral and documentary evidence, to compel the attendance of witnesses or the production of documents, to cross-examine witnesses, and to present argument orally or in writing; and

(C) the complainant be afforded an opportunity to appear at proceedings conducted by the investigating panel, if the panel concludes that the complainant could offer substantial information.

Any such rule shall be made or amended only after giving appropriate public notice and an opportunity for comment. Any rule promulgated under this subsection shall be a matter of public record, and any such rule promulgated by a judicial council may be modified by the Judicial Conference. * * *

(12) No judge or magistrate whose conduct is the subject of an investigation under this subsection shall serve upon a special committee appointed under paragraph (4) of this subsection, upon a judicial council, upon the Judicial Conference, or upon the standing committee established under section 331 of this title, until all related proceedings under this subsection have been finally terminated.

(13) No person shall be granted the right to intervene or to appear as amicus curiae in any proceeding before a judicial council or the Judicial Conference under this subsection.

(14) Except as provided in paragraph (8), all papers, documents, and records of proceedings related to investigations conducted under this subsection shall be confidential and shall not be disclosed by any person in any proceeding except to the extent that—

* * *

(B) the judicial council of the circuit, the Judicial Conference of the United States, or the Senate or the House of Representatives by resolution, releases any such material which is believed necessary to an impeachment investigation or trial of a judge under article I of the Constitution; or

(C) authorized in writing by the judge or magistrate who is the subject of the complaint and by the chief judge of the circuit, the Chief Justice, or the chairman of the standing committee established under section 331 of this title.

(15) Each written order to implement any action under paragraph (6)(B) of this subsection, which is issued by a judicial council, the Judicial Conference, or the standing committee established under section 331 of this title, shall be made available to the public through the appropriate clerk's office of the court of appeals for the circuit. Unless contrary in the interests of justice, each such order issued

§ 372   TITLE 28 U.S.C.A.

under this paragraph shall be accompanied by written reasons therefor.

* * *

(17) Except as expressly provided in this subsection, nothing in this subsection shall be construed to affect any other provision of this title, the Federal Rules of Civil Procedure, the Federal Rules of Criminal Procedure, the Federal Rules of Appellate Procedure, or the Federal Rules of Evidence.

(18) The United States Claims Court, the Court of International Trade, and the Court of Appeals for the Federal Circuit shall each prescribe rules, consistent with the foregoing provisions of this subsection, establishing procedures for the filing of complaints with respect to the conduct of any judge of such court and for the investigation and resolution of such complaints. In investigating and taking action with respect to any such complaint, each such court shall have the powers granted to a judicial council under this subsection.

§ 454. Practice of Law by Justices and Judges

Any justice or judge appointed under the authority of the United States who engages in the practice of law is guilty of a high misdemeanor.

§ 455. Disqualification of Justice, Judge, or Magistrate

(a) Any justice, judge, or magistrate of the United States shall disqualify himself in any proceeding in which his impartiality might reasonably be questioned.

(b) He shall also disqualify himself in the following circumstances:

(1) Where he has a personal bias or prejudice concerning a party, or personal knowledge of disputed evidentiary facts concerning the proceeding;

(2) Where in private practice he served as lawyer in the matter in controversy, or a lawyer with whom he previously practiced law served during such association as a lawyer concerning the matter, or the judge or such lawyer has been a material witness concerning it;

(3) Where he has served in governmental employment and in such capacity participated as counsel, adviser or material witness concerning the proceeding or expressed an opinion concerning the merits of the particular case in controversy;

(4) He knows that he, individually or as a fiduciary, or his spouse or minor child residing in his household, has a financial interest in the subject matter in controversy or in a party to the proceeding, or any other interest that could be substantially affected by the outcome of the proceeding;

(5) He or his spouse, or a person within the third degree of relationship to either of them, or the spouse of such a person:

(i) Is a party to the proceeding, or an officer, director, or trustee of a party;

(ii) Is acting as a lawyer in the proceeding;

(iii) Is known by the judge to have an interest that could be substantially affected by the outcome of the proceeding;

(iv) Is to the judge's knowledge likely to be a material witness in the proceeding.

(c) A judge should inform himself about his personal and fiduciary financial interests, and make a reasonable effort to inform himself about the personal financial interests of his spouse and minor children residing in his household.

(d) For the purposes of this section the following words or phrases shall have the meaning indicated:

(1) "proceeding" includes pretrial, trial, appellate review, or other stages of litigation;

(2) the degree of relationship is calculated according to the civil law system;

(3) "fiduciary" includes such relationships as executor, administrator, trustee, and guardian;

(4) "financial interest" means ownership of a legal or equitable interest, however small, or a relationship as director, adviser, or other active participant in the affairs of a party, except that:

(i) Ownership in a mutual or common investment fund that holds securities is not a "financial interest" in such securities unless the judge participates in the management of the fund;

(ii) An office in an educational, religious, charitable, fraternal, or civic organization is not a "financial interest" in securities held by the organization;

(iii) The proprietary interest of a policyholder in a mutual insurance company, of a depositor in a mutual savings association, or a similar proprietary interest, is a "financial interest" in the organization only if the outcome of the proceeding could substantially affect the value of the interest;

(iv) Ownership of government securities is a "financial interest" in the issuer only if the outcome of the proceeding could substantially affect the value of the securities.

(e) No justice, judge, or magistrate shall accept from the parties to the proceeding a waiver of any ground for disqualification enumerated in subsection (b). Where the ground for disqualification arises only under subsection (a), waiver may be accepted provided it is preceded by a full disclosure on the record of the basis for disqualification.

(f) Notwithstanding the preceding provisions of this section, if any justice, judge, magistrate, or bankruptcy judge to whom a matter has been assigned would be disqualified, after substantial judicial time has been devoted to the matter, because of the appearance or discovery after the matter was assigned to him or her, that he or she individually or as a fiduciary, or his or her spouse or minor child residing in his or her household, has a financial interest in a party (other than an interest that could be substantially affected by the outcome), disqualification is not required if the justice, judge, magistrate, bankruptcy judge, spouse or minor child, as the case may be, divests himself or herself of the interest that provides the grounds for the disqualification.

4. 5 U.S.C.A. Appendix 6, §§ 101–112

FINANCIAL DISCLOSURE REQUIREMENTS OF FEDERAL PERSONNEL

§ 101. Persons required to file

(a) Within thirty days of assuming the position of an officer or employee described in subsection (f), an individual shall file a report containing the information described in section 102(b) unless the individual has left another position described in subsection (f) within thirty days prior to assuming such new position or has already filed a report under this title with respect to nomination for the new position or as a candidate for the position.

(b)(1) Within five days of the transmittal by the President to the Senate of the nomination of an individual (other than an individual nominated for appointment to a position as a Foreign Service Officer or a grade or rank in the uniformed services for which the pay grade prescribed by section 201 of title 37, United States Code, is 0–6 or below) to a position, appointment to which requires the advice and consent of the Senate, such individual shall file a report containing the information described in section 102(b). Such individual shall, not later than the date of the first hearing to consider the nomination of such individual, make current the report filed pursuant to this paragraph by filing the information required by section 102(a)(1)(A) with respect to income and honoraria received as of the date which occurs five days before the date of such hearing. Nothing in this Act shall prevent any Congressional committee from requesting, as a condition of confirmation, any additional financial information from any Presidential nominee whose nomination has been referred to that committee.

(2) An individual whom the President or the President-elect has publicly announced he intends to nominate to a position may file the report required by paragraph (1) at any time after that public announcement, but not later than is required under the first sentence of such paragraph.

(c) Within thirty days of becoming a candidate as defined in section 301 of the Federal Campaign Act of 1971, in a calendar year for nomination or election to the office of President, Vice President, or Member of Congress, or on or before May 15 of that calendar year, whichever is later, but in no event later than 30 days before the election, and on or before May 15 of each successive year an individual continues to be a candidate, an individual other than an incumbent President, Vice President, or Member of Congress shall file a report containing the information described in section 102(b). Notwithstanding the preceding sentence, in any calendar year in which an individual continues to be a candidate for any office but all elections for such office relating to such candidacy were held in prior calendar years, such individual need not file a report unless he becomes a candidate for another vacancy in that office or another office during that year.

(d) Any individual who is an officer or employee described in subsection (f) during any calendar year and performs the duties of his position or office for a period in excess of sixty days in that calendar year shall file on or before May 15 of the succeeding year a report containing the information described in section 102(a).

(e) Any individual who occupies a position described in subsection (f) shall, on or before the thirtieth day after termination of employment in such position, file a report containing the information described in section 102(a) covering the preceding calendar year if the report required by subsection (d) has not been filed and covering the portion of the calendar year in which such termination occurs up to the date the individual left such office or position, unless such individual has accepted employment in another position described in subsection (f).

(f) The officers and employees referred to in subsections (a), (d), and (e) are—

(1) the President;

(2) the Vice President;

(3) each officer or employee in the executive branch, including a special Government employee as defined in section 202 of title 18, United States Code, whose position is classified at GS–16 or above of the General Schedule prescribed by section 5332 of title 5, United States Code, or the rate of basic pay for which is fixed (other than under the General Schedule) at a rate equal to or greater than the minimum rate of basic pay fixed for GS–16; each member of a uniformed service whose pay grade is at or in excess of 0–7 under section 201 of title 37, United States Code; and each officer or employee in any other position determined by the Director of the Office of Government Ethics to be of equal classification;

(4) each employee appointed pursuant to section 3105 of title 5, United States Code;

(5) any employee not described in paragraph (3) who is in a position in the executive branch which is excepted from the competitive service by reason of being of a confidential or policymaking character, except that the Director of the Office of Government Ethics may, by regulation, exclude from the application of this paragraph any individual, or group of individuals, who are in such positions, but only in cases in which the Director determines such exclusion would not affect adversely the integrity of the Government or the public's confidence in the integrity of the Government;

(6) the Postmaster General, the Deputy Postmaster General, each Governor of the Board of Governors of the United States Postal Service and each officer or employee of the United States Postal Service or Postal Rate Commission whose basic rate of pay is equal to or greater than the minimum rate of basic pay fixed for GS–16;

(7) the Director of the Office of Government Ethics and each designated agency ethics official;

(8) any civilian employee not described in paragraph (3), employed in the Executive Office of the President (other than a special government employee) who holds a commission of appointment from the President;

(9) a Member of Congress as defined under section 109(12);

(10) an officer or employee of the Congress as defined under section 109(13);

(11) a judicial officer as defined under section 109(10); and

(12) a judicial employee as defined under section 109(8).

(g) Reasonable extensions of time for filing any report may be granted under procedures prescribed by the supervising ethics office for each branch, but the total of such extensions shall not exceed ninety days.

(h) The provisions of subsections (a), (b), and (e) shall not apply to an individual who, as determined by the designated agency ethics official or Secretary concerned (or in the case of a Presidential appointee under subsection (b), the Director of the Office of Government Ethics), the congressional ethics committees, or the Judicial Conference is not reasonably expected to perform the duties of his office or position for more than sixty days in a calendar year, except that if such individual performs the duties of his office or position for more than sixty days in a calendar year—

(1) the report required by subsections (a) and (b) shall be filed within fifteen days of the sixtieth day, and

(2) the report required by subsection (e) shall be filed as provided in such subsection.

(i) The supervising ethics office for each branch may grant a publicly available request for a waiver of any reporting requirement under this section for an individual who is expected to perform or has performed the duties of his office or position less than one hundred and thirty days in a calendar year, but only if the supervising ethics office determines that—

(1) such individual is not a full-time employee of the Government,

(2) such individual is able to provide services specially needed by the Government,

(3) it is unlikely that the individual's outside employment or financial interests will create a conflict of interest, and

(4) public financial disclosure by such individual is not necessary in the circumstances.

§ 102. Contents of reports

(a) Each report filed pursuant to section 101(d) and (e) shall include a full and complete statement with respect to the following:

(1)(A) The source, type, and amount or value of income (other than income referred to in subparagraph (B)) from any source (other than from current employment by the United States Government), and the source, date, and amount of honoraria from any source, received during the preceding calendar year, aggregating $200 or more in value and, effective January 1, 1991, the source, date, and amount of payments made to charitable organizations in lieu of honoraria, and the reporting individual shall simultaneously file with the applicable supervising ethics office, on a confidential basis, a corresponding list of recipients of all such payments, together with the dates and amounts of such payments.

(B) The source and type of income which consists of dividends, rents, interest, and capital gains, received during the preceding calendar year which exceeds $200 in amount or value, and an indication of which of the following categories the amount or value of such item of income is within:

(i) not more than $1,000,

(ii) greater than $1,000 but not more than $2,500,

(iii) greater than $2,500 but not more than $5,000,

(iv) greater than $5,000 but not more than $15,000,

(v) greater than $15,000 but not more than $50,000,

(vi) greater than $50,000 but not more than $100,000,

(vii) greater than $100,000 but not more than $1,000,000, or

(viii) greater than $1,000,000.

(2)(A) The identity of the source and a brief description (including a travel itinerary, dates, and nature of expenses provided) of any gifts of transportation, lodging, food, or entertainment aggregating $250 or more in value received from any source other than a relative of the reporting individual during the preceding calendar year, except that any food, lodging, or entertainment received as personal hospitality of any individual need not be reported, and any gift with a fair market value of $75 or less need not be aggregated for purposes of this subparagraph.

(B) The identity of the source, a brief description, and the value of all gifts other than transportation, lodging, food, or entertainment aggregating $100 or more in value received from any source other than a relative of the reporting individual during the preceding calendar year, except that any gift with a fair market value of $75 or less need not be aggregated for purposes of this subparagraph.

(C) The identity of the source and a brief description (including a travel itinerary, dates, and nature of expenses provided) of reimbursements received from any source aggregating $250 or more in value and received during the preceding calendar year.

(D) In an unusual case, a gift need not be aggregated under subparagraph (A) or (B) if a publicly available request for a waiver is granted.

(3) The identity and category of value of any interest in property held during the preceding calendar year in a trade or business, or for investment or the production of income, which has a fair market value which exceeds $1,000 as of the close of the preceding calendar year, excluding any personal liability owned to the reporting individual by a spouse, or by a parent, brother, sister, or child of the reporting individual or of the reporting individual's spouse, or any deposits aggregating $5,000 or less in a personal savings account. For purposes of this paragraph, a personal savings account shall include any certificate of deposit or any other form of deposit in a bank, savings and loan association, credit union, or similar financial institution.

(4) The identity and category of value of the total liabilities owed to any creditor other than a spouse, or a parent, brother, sister, or child of the reporting individual or of the reporting individual's spouse which exceed $10,000 at any time during the preceding calendar year, excluding—

(A) any mortgage secured by real property which is a personal residence of the reporting individual or his spouse; and

(B) any loan secured by a personal motor vehicle, household furniture, or appliances, which loan does not exceed the purchase price of the item which secures it.

With respect to revolving charge accounts, only those with an outstanding liability which exceeds $10,000 as of the close of the preceding calendar year need be reported under this paragraph.

(5) Except as provided in this paragraph, a brief description, the date, and category of value of any purchase, sale or exchange during the preceding calendar year which exceeds $1,000—

(A) in real property, other than property used solely as a personal residence of the reporting individual or his spouse; or

(B) in stocks, bonds, commodities futures, and other forms of securities.

Reporting is not required under this paragraph of any transaction solely by and between the reporting individual, his spouse, or dependent children.

(6)(A) The identity of all positions held on or before the date of filing during the current calendar year (and, for the first report filed by an individual, during the two-year period preceding such calendar year) as an officer, director, trustee, partner, proprietor, representative, employee, or consultant of any corporation, company, firm, partnership, or other business enterprise, any non-profit organization, any labor organization, or any educational or other institution other than the United States. This subparagraph shall not require the reporting of positions held in any religious, social, fraternal, or political entity and positions solely of an honorary nature.

(B) If any person, other than the United States Government, paid a nonelected reporting individual compensation in excess of $5,000 in any of the two calendar years prior to the calendar year during which the individual files his first report under this title, the individual shall include in the report—

(i) the identity of each source of such compensation; and

(ii) a brief description of the nature of the duties performed or services rendered by the reporting individual for each such source.

The preceding sentence shall not require any individual to include in such report any information which is considered confidential as a result of a privileged relationship, established by law, between such individual and any person nor shall it require an individual to report any information with respect to any person for whom services were provided by any firm or association of which such individual was a member, partner, or employee unless such individual was directly involved in the provision of such services.

(7) A description of the date, parties to, and terms of any agreement or arrangement with respect to (A) future employment; (B) a leave of absence during the period of the reporting individual's Government service; (C) continuation of payments by a former employer other than the United States Government; and (D) continuing participation in an employee welfare or benefit plan maintained by a former employer.

(b)(1) Each report filed pursuant to subsections (a), (b), and (c) of section 101 shall include a full and complete statement with respect to the information required by—

　(A) paragraph (1) of subsection (a) for the year of filing and the preceding calendar year,

　(B) paragraphs (3) and (4) of subsection (a) as of the date specified in the report but which is less than thirty-one days before the filing date, and

　(C) paragraphs (6) and (7) of subsection (a) as of the filing date but for periods described in such paragraphs.

(2)(A) In lieu of filling out one or more schedules of a financial disclosure form, an individual may supply the required information in an alternative format, pursuant to either rules adopted by the supervising ethics office for the branch in which such individual serves or pursuant to a specific written determination by such office for a reporting individual.

(B) In lieu of indicating the category of amount or value of any item contained in any report filed under this title, a reporting individual may indicate the exact dollar amount of such item.

(c) In the case of any individual described in section 101(e), any reference to the preceding calendar year shall be considered also to include that part of the calendar year of filing up to the date of the termination of employment.

(d)(1) The categories for reporting the amount or value of the items covered in paragraphs (3), (4), and (5) of subsection (a) are as follows:

　(A) not more than $15,000;

　(B) greater than $15,000 but not more than $50,000;

　(C) greater than $50,000 but not more than $100,000;

　(D) greater than $100,000 but not more than $250,000;

　(E) greater than $250,000 but not more than $500,000;

　(F) greater than $500,000 but not more than $1,000,000; and

　(G) greater than $1,000,000.

(2) For the purposes of paragraph (3) of subsection (a) if the current value of an interest in real property (or an interest in a real estate partnership) is not ascertainable without an appraisal, an individual may list (A) the date of purchase and the purchase price of the interest in the real property, or (B) the assessed value of the real property for tax purposes, adjusted to reflect the market value of the property used for the assessment if the assessed value is computed at less than 100 percent of such market value, but such individual shall include in his report a full and complete description of the method used to determine such assessed value, instead of specifying a category of value pursuant to paragraph (1) of this subsection. If the current value of any other item required to be reported under paragraph (3) of subsection (a) is not ascertainable without an appraisal, such individual may list the book value of a corporation whose stock is not publicly traded, the net worth of a business partnership, the equity value of an individually owned business, or with respect to other holdings, any recognized indication of value, but such individual shall include in his report a full and complete description of the method used in determining such value. In lieu of any value referred to in the preceding sentence, an individual may list the assessed value of the item for tax purposes, adjusted to reflect the market value of the item used for the assessment if the assessed value is computed at less than 100 percent of such market value, but a full and complete description of the method used in determining such assessed value shall be included in the report.

(e)(1) Except as provided in the last sentence of this paragraph, each report required by section 101 shall also contain information listed in paragraphs (1) through (5) of subsection (a) of this section respecting the spouse or dependent child of the reporting individual as follows:

(A) The source of items of earned income earned by a spouse from any person which exceed $1,000 and the source and amount of any honoraria received by a spouse, except that, with respect to earned income (other than honoraria), if the spouse is self-employed in business or a profession, only the nature of such business or profession need be reported.

(B) All information required to be reported in subsection (a)(1)(B) with respect to income derived by a spouse or dependent child from any asset held by the spouse or dependent child and reported pursuant to subsection (a)(3).

(C) In the case of any gifts received by a spouse or dependent child which are not received totally independent of the relationship of the spouse or dependent child to the reporting individual, the identity of the source and a brief description of gifts of transportation, lodging, food, or entertainment and a brief description and the value of other gifts.

(D) In the case of any reimbursements received by a spouse or dependent child which are not received totally independent of the relationship of the spouse or dependent child to the reporting individual, the identity of the source and a brief description of each such reimbursement.

(E) In the case of items described in paragraphs (3) through (5) of subsection (a), all information required to be reported under these paragraphs other than items (i) which the reporting individual certifies represent the spouse's or dependent child's sole financial interest or responsibility and which the reporting individual has no knowledge of, (ii) which are not in any way, past or present, derived from the income, assets, or activities of the reporting individual, and (iii) from which the reporting individual neither derives, nor expects to derive, any financial or economic benefit.

Reports required by subsections (a), (b), and (c) of section 101 shall, with respect to the spouse and dependent child of the reporting individual, only contain information listed in paragraphs (1), (3), and (4) of subsection (a), as specified in this paragraph.

(2) No report shall be required with respect to a spouse living separate and apart from the reporting individual with the intention of terminating the marriage or providing for permanent separation; or with respect to any income or obligations of an individual arising from the dissolution of his marriage or the permanent separation from his spouse.

(f)(1) Except as provided in paragraph (2), each reporting individual shall report the information required to be reported pursuant to subsections (a), (b), and (c) of this section with respect to the holdings of and the income from a trust or other financial arrangement from which income is received by, or with respect to which a beneficial interest in principal or income is held by, such individual, his spouse, or any dependent child.

(2) A reporting individual need not report the holdings of or the source of income from any of the holdings of—

(A) any qualified blind trust (as defined in paragraph (3));

(B) a trust—

(i) which was not created directly by such individual, his spouse, or any dependent child, and

(ii) the holdings or sources of income of which such individual, his spouse, and any dependent child have no knowledge of; or

(C) an entity described under the provisions of paragraph (8),

but such individual shall report the category of the amount of income received by him, his spouse, or any dependent child from the trust or other entity under subsection (a)(1)(B) of this section.

(3) For purposes of this subsection, the term "qualified blind trust" includes any trust in which a reporting individual, his spouse, or any minor or dependent child has a beneficial interest in the principal or income, and which meets the following requirements:

(A)(i) The trustee of the trust and any other entity designated in the trust instrument to perform fiduciary duties is a financial institution, an attorney, a certified public accountant, a broker, or an investment advisor who—

(I) is independent of and not associated with any interested party so that the trustee or other person cannot be controlled or influenced in the administration of the trust by any interested party; and

(II) is not and has not been an employee of or affiliated with any interested party and is not a partner of, or involved in any joint venture or other investment with, any interested party; and

(III) is not a relative of any interested party.

(ii) Any officer or employee of a trustee or other entity who is involved in the management or control of the trust—

(I) is independent of and not associated with any interested party so that such officer or employee cannot be controlled or influenced in the administration of the trust by any interested party;

(II) is not a partner of, or involved in any joint venture or other investment with, any interested party; and

(III) is not a relative of any interested party.

(B) Any asset transferred to the trust by an interested party is free of any restriction with respect to its transfer or sale unless such restriction is expressly approved by the supervising ethics office of the reporting individual.

(C) The trust instrument which establishes the trust provides that—

(i) except to the extent provided in subparagraph (B) of this paragraph, the trustee in the exercise of his authority and discretion to manage and control the assets of the trust shall not consult or notify any interested party;

(ii) the trust shall not contain any asset the holding of which by an interested party is prohibited by any law or regulation;

(iii) the trustee shall promptly notify the reporting individual and his supervising ethics office when the holdings of any particular asset transferred to the trust by any interested party are disposed of or when the value of such holding is less than $1,000;

(iv) the trust tax return shall be prepared by the trustee or his designee, and such return and any information relating thereto (other than the trust income summarized in appropriate categories necessary to complete an interested party's tax return), shall not be disclosed to any interested party;

(v) an interested party shall not receive any report on the holdings and sources of income of the trust, except a report at the end of each calendar quarter with respect to the total cash value of the interest of the interested party in the trust or the net income or loss of the trust or any reports necessary to enable the interested party to complete an individual tax return required by law or to provide the information required by subsection (a)(1) of this section, but such report shall not identify any asset or holding;

(vi) except for communications which solely consist of requests for distributions of cash or other unspecified assets of the trust, there shall be no direct or indirect communication between the trustee and an interested party with respect to the trust unless such communication is in writing and unless it relates only (I) to the general financial interest and needs of the interested party (including, but not limited to, an interest in maximizing income or long-term capital gain), (II) to the notification of the trustee of a law or regulation subsequently applicable to the reporting individual which prohibits the interested party from holding an asset, which notification directs that the asset not be held by the trust, or (III) to directions to the trustee to sell all of an asset initially placed in the trust by an interested party which in the determination of the reporting individual creates a conflict of interest or the appearance thereof due to the subsequent assumption of duties by the reporting individual (but nothing herein shall require any such direction); and

(vii) the interested parties shall make no effort to obtain information with respect to the holdings of the trust, including obtaining a copy of any trust tax return filed or any information relating thereto except as otherwise provided in this subsection.

(D) The proposed trust instrument and the proposed trustee is approved by the reporting individual's supervising ethics office.

(E) For purposes of this subsection, 'interested party' means a reporting individual, his spouse, and any minor or dependent child; 'broker' has the meaning set forth in section 3(a)(4) of the Securities and Exchange Act of 1934 (15 U.S.C. 78c(a)(4)); and 'investment adviser' includes any investment adviser who, as determined under regulations prescribed by the supervising ethics office, is generally involved in his role as such an adviser in the management or control of trusts.

(F) Any trust qualified by a supervising ethics office before the effective date of title II of the Ethics Reform Act of 1989 shall continue to be governed by the law and regulations in effect immediately before such effective date.

(4)(A) An asset placed in a trust by an interested party shall be considered a financial interest of the reporting individual, for the purposes of any applicable conflict of interest statutes, regulations, or rules of the Federal Government (including section 208 of title 18, United States Code), until such time as the reporting individual is notified by the trustee that such asset has been disposed of, or has a value of less than $1,000.

(B)(i) The provisions of subparagraph (A) shall not apply with respect to a trust created for the benefit of a reporting individual, or the spouse, dependent child, or minor child of such a person, if the supervising ethics office for such reporting individual finds that—

(I) the assets placed in the trust consist of a well-diversified portfolio of readily marketable securities;

(II) none of the assets consist of securities of entities having substantial activities in the area of the reporting individual's primary area of responsibility;

(III) the trust instrument prohibits the trustee, notwithstanding the provisions of paragraphs (3)(C)(iii) and (iv) of this subsection, from making public or informing any interested party of the sale of any securities;

(IV) the trustee is given power of attorney, notwithstanding the provisions of paragraph (3)(C)(v) of this subsection, to prepare on behalf of any interested party the personal income tax returns and similar returns which may contain information relating to the trust; and

(V) except as otherwise provided in this paragraph, the trust instrument provides (or in the case of a trust established prior to the effective date of this Act which by its terms does not permit amendment, the trustee, the reporting individual, and any any other interested party agree in writing) that the trust shall be administered in accordance with the requirements of this subsection and the trustee of such trust meets the requirements of paragraph (3)(A).

(ii) In any instance covered by subparagraph (B) in which the reporting individual is an individual whose nomination is being considered by a congressional committee, the reporting individual shall inform the congressional committee considering his nomination before or during the period of such individual's confirmation hearing of his intention to comply with this paragraph.

(5)(A) The reporting individual shall, within thirty days after a qualified blind trust is approved by his supervising ethics office, file with such office a copy of—

(i) the executed trust instrument of such trust (other than those provisions which relate to the testamentary disposition of the trust assets), and

(ii) a list of the assets which were transferred to such trust, including the category of value of each asset as determined under subsection (d) of this section.

This subparagraph shall not apply with respect to a trust meeting the requirements for being considered a qualified blind trust under paragraph (7) of this subsection.

(B) The reporting individual shall, within thirty days of transferring an asset (other than cash) to a previously established qualified blind trust, notify his supervising ethics office of the identity of each such asset and the category of value of each asset as determined under subsection (d) of this section.

(C) Within thirty days of the dissolution of a qualified blind trust, a reporting individual shall—

(i) notify his supervising ethics office of such dissolution, and

(ii) file with such office a copy of a list of the assets of the trust at the time of such dissolution and the category of value under subsection (d) of this section of each such asset.

(D) Documents filed under subparagraphs (A), (B), and (C) of this paragraph and the lists provided by the trustee of assets placed in the trust by an interested party which have been sold shall be made available to the public in the same manner as a report is made available under section 105 and the provisions of that section shall apply with respect to such documents and lists.

(E) A copy of each written communication with respect to the trust under paragraph (3)(C)(vi) shall be filed by the person initiating the communication with the reporting individual's supervising ethics office within five days of the date of the communication.

(6)(A) A trustee of a qualified blind trust shall not knowingly and willfully, or negligently, (i) disclose any information to an interested party with respect to such trust that may not be disclosed under paragraph (3) of this subsection; (ii) acquire any holding the ownership of which is prohibited by the trust instrument; (iii) solicit advice from any interested party with respect to such trust, which solicitation is prohibited by paragraph (3) of this subsection or the trust agreement; or (iv) fail to file any document required by this subsection.

(B) A reporting individual shall not knowingly and willfully, or negligently, (i) solicit or receive any information with respect to a qualified blind trust of which he is an interested party that may not be disclosed under paragraph (3)(C) of this subsection or (ii) fail to file any document required by this subsection.

(C)(i) The Attorney General may bring a civil action in any appropriate United States district court against any individual who knowingly and willfully violates the provisions of subparagraph (A) or (B) of this paragraph. The court in which such action is brought may assess against such individual a civil penalty in any amount not to exceed $10,000.

(ii) The Attorney General may bring a civil action in any appropriate United States district court against any individual who negligently violates the provisions of subparagraph (A) or (B) of this paragraph. The court in which such action is brought may assess against such individual a civil penalty in any amount not to exceed $5,000.

(7) Any trust may be considered to be a qualified blind trust if—

(A) the trust instrument is amended to comply with the requirements of paragraph (3) or, in the case of a trust instrument which does not by its terms permit amendment, the trustee, the reporting individual, and any other interested party agree in writing that the trust shall be administered in accordance with the requirements of this subsection and the trustee of such trust meets the requirements of paragraph (3)(A); except that in the case of any interested party who is a dependent child, a parent or guardian of such child may execute the agreement referred to in this subparagraph;

(B) a copy of the trust instrument (except testamentary provisions) and a copy of the agreement referred to in subparagraph (A), and a list of the assets held by the trust at the time of approval by the supervising ethics office, including the category of value of each asset as determined under subsection (d) of this section, are filed with such office and made available to the public as provided under paragraph (5)(D) of this subsection; and

(C) the supervising ethics office determines that approval of the trust arrangement as a qualified blind trust is in the particular case appropriate to assure compliance with applicable laws and regulations.

(8) A reporting individual shall not be required to report the financial interests held by a widely held investment fund (whether such fund is a mutual fund, regulated investment company, pension or deferred compensation plan, or other investment fund), if—

(A)(i) the fund is publicly traded; or

(ii) the assets of the fund are widely diversified; and

(B) the reporting individual neither exercises control over nor has the ability to exercise control over the financial interests held by the fund.

(g) Political campaign funds, including campaign receipts and expenditures, need not be included in any report filed pursuant to this title.

(h) A report filed pursuant to subsection (a), (d), or (e) of section 101 need not contain the information described in subparagraphs (A), (B), and (C) of subsection (a)(2) with respect to gifts and reimbursements received in a period when the reporting individual was not an officer or employee of the Federal Government.

(i) A reporting individual shall not be required under this title to report—

(1) financial interests in or income derived from—

(A) any retirement system under title 5, United States Code (including the Thrift Savings Plan under subchapter III of chapter 84 of such title); or

(B) any other retirement system maintained by the United States for officers or employees of the United States, including the President, or for members of the uniformed services; or

(2) benefits received under the Social Security Act.

§ 103. Filing of reports

(a) Except as otherwise provided in this section, the reports required under this title shall be filed by the reporting individual with the designated agency ethics official at the agency by which he is employed (or in the case of an individual described in section 101(e), was employed) or in which he will serve. The date any report is received (and the date of receipt of any supplemental report) shall be noted on such report by such official.

(b) The President, the Vice President, and independent counsel and persons appointed by independent counsel under chapter 40 of title 28, United States Code, shall file reports required under this title with the Director of the Office of Government Ethics.

(c) Copies of the reports required to be filed under this title by the Postmaster General, the Deputy Postmaster General, the Governors of the Board of Governors of the United States Postal Service, designated agency ethics officials, employees described in section 105(a)(2)(A) or (B), 106(a)(1)(A) or (B), or 107(a)(1)(A) or (b)(1)(A)(i), of title 3, United States Code, candidates for the office of President or Vice President and officers and employees in (and nominees to) offices or positions which require confirmation by the Senate or by both Houses of Congress other than individuals nominated to be judicial officers and those referred to in subsection (f) shall be transmitted to the Director of the Office of Government Ethics. The Director shall forward a copy of the report of each nominee to the congressional committee considering the nomination.

(d) Reports required to be filed under this title by the Director of the Office of Government Ethics shall be filed in the Office of Government Ethics and, immediately after being filed, shall be made available to the public in accordance with this title.

(e) Each individual identified in section 101(c) who is a candidate for nomination or election to the Office of President or Vice President shall file the reports required by this title with the Federal Election Commission.

(f) Reports required of members of the uniformed services shall be filed with the Secretary concerned.

(g) Each supervising ethics office shall develop and make available forms for reporting the information required by this title.

(h)(1) The reports required under this title shall be filed by a reporting individual with—

(A)(i)(I) the Clerk of the House of Representatives, in the case of a Representative in Congress, a Delegate to Congress, the Resident

Commissioner from Puerto Rico, an officer or employee of the Congress whose compensation is disbursed by the Clerk of the House of Representatives, an officer or employee of the Architect of the Capitol, the United States Botanic Garden, the Congressional Budget Office, the Government Printing Office, the Library of Congress, or the Copyright Royalty Tribunal (including any individual terminating service, under section 101(e), in any office or position referred to in this subclause), or an individual described in section 101(c) who is a candidate for nomination or election as a Representative in Congress, a Delegate to Congress, or the Resident Commissioner from Puerto Rico; and

(II) the Secretary of the Senate, in the case of a Senator, an officer or employee of the Congress whose compensation is disbursed by the Secretary of the Senate, an officer or employee of the General Accounting Office, the Office of Technology Assessment, or the Office of the Attending Physician (including any individual terminating service, under section 101(e), in any office or position referred to in this subclause), or an individual described in section 101(c) who is a candidate for nomination or election as a Senator; and

(ii) in the case of an officer or employee of the Congress as described under section 101(f)(10) who is employed by an agency or commission established in the legislative branch after the date of the enactment of the Ethics Reform Act of 1989—

(I) the Secretary of the Senate or the Clerk of the House of Representatives, as the case may be, as designated in the statute establishing such agency or commission; or

(II) if such statute does not designate such committee, the Secretary of the Senate for agencies and commissions established in even numbered calendar years, and the Clerk of the House of Representatives for agencies and commissions established in odd numbered calendar years; and

(B) the Judicial Conference with regard to a judicial officer or employee described under paragraphs (11) and (12) of section 101(f) (including individuals terminating service in such office or position under section 101(e) or immediately preceding service in such office or position).

(2) The date any report is received (and the date of receipt of any supplemental report) shall be noted on such report by such committee.

(i) A copy of each report filed under this title by a Member or an individual who is a candidate for the office of Member shall be sent by the Clerk of the House of Representatives or Secretary of the Senate, as the case may be, to the appropriate State officer designated under section 316(a) of the Federal Election Campaign Act of 1971 of the State represented by the Member or in which the individual is a candidate, as

§ 103   TITLE 5 U.S.C.A.

the case may be, within the 7–day period beginning on the day the report is filed with the Clerk or Secretary.

(j)(1) A copy of each report filed under this title with the Clerk of the House of Representatives shall be sent by the Clerk to the Committee on Standards of Official Conduct of the House of Representatives within the 7–day period beginning on the day the report is filed.

(2) A copy of each report filed under this title with the Secretary of the Senate shall be sent by the Secretary to the Select Committee on Ethics of the Senate within the 7–day period beginning on the day the report is filed.

(k) In carrying out their responsibilities under this title with respect to candidates for office, the Clerk of the House of Representatives and the Secretary of the Senate shall avail themselves of the assistance of the Federal Election Commission. The Commission shall make available to the Clerk and the Secretary on a regular basis a complete list of names and addresses of all candidates registered with the Commission, and shall cooperate and coordinate its candidate information and notification program with the Clerk and the Secretary to the greatest extent possible.

§ 104. Failure to file or filing false reports

(a) The Attorney General may bring a civil action in any appropriate United States district court against any individual who knowingly and willfully falsifies or who knowingly and willfully fails to file or report any information that such individual is required to report pursuant to section 102. The court in which such action is brought may assess against such individual a civil penalty in any amount, not to exceed $10,000.

(b) The head of each agency, each Secretary concerned, the Director of the Office of Government Ethics, each congressional ethics committee, or the Judicial Conference, as the case may be, shall refer to the Attorney General the name of any individual which such official or committee has reasonable cause to believe has willfully failed to file a report or has willfully falsified or willfully failed to file information required to be reported.

(c) The President, the Vice President, the Secretary concerned, the head of each agency, the Office of Personnel Management, a congressional ethics committee, and the Judicial Conference may take any appropriate personnel or other action in accordance with applicable law or regulation against any individual failing to file a report or falsifying or failing to report information required to be reported.

(d)(1) Any individual who files a report required to be filed under this title more than 30 days after the later of—

(A) the date such report is required to be filed pursuant to the provisions of this title and the rules and regulations promulgated thereunder; or

(B) if a filing extension is granted to such individual under section 101(g), the last day of the filing extension period,

shall * * * pay a filing fee of $200 to the miscellaneous receipts of the General Treasury.

(2) The supervising ethics office may waive the filing fee under this subsection in extraordinary circumstances.

§ 105. Custody of and public access to reports

(a) Each agency, each supervising ethics office in the executive or judicial branch, the Clerk of the House of Representatives, and the Secretary of the Senate shall make available to the public, in accordance with subsection (b), each report filed under this title with such agency or office or with the Clerk or the Secretary of the Senate, except that—

(1) this section does not require public availability of a report filed by any individual in the Central Intelligence Agency, the Defense Intelligence Agency, or the National Security Agency, or any individual engaged in intelligence activities in any agency of the United States, if the President finds or has found that, due to the nature of the office or position occupied by such individual, public disclosure of such report would, be revealing the identity of the individual or other sensitive information, compromise the national interest of the United States; and such individuals may be authorized, notwithstanding section 104(a), to file such additional reports as are necessary to protect their identity from public disclosure if the President first finds or has found that such filing is necessary in the national interest; and

(2) any report filed by an independent counsel whose identity has not been disclosed by the division of the court under chapter 40 of title 28, United States Code, and any report filed by any person appointed by that independent counsel under such chapter, shall not be made available to the public under this title.

(b)(1) Each agency, each supervising ethics office in the executive or judicial branch, the Clerk of the House of Representatives, and the Secretary of the Senate shall, within thirty days after any report is received under this title by such agency or office or by the Clerk or the Secretary of the Senate, as the case may be, permit inspection of such report by or furnish a copy of such report to any person requesting such inspection or copy. The agency, office, Clerk, or Secretary of the Senate, as the case may be, may require a reasonable fee to be paid in any amount which is found necessary to recover the cost of reproduction or mailing of such report excluding any salary of any employee involved in such reproduction or mailing. A copy of such report may be furnished without charge or at a reduced charge if it is determined that waiver or reduction of the fee is in the public interest.

(2) Notwithstanding paragraph (1), a report may not be made available under this section to any person nor may any copy thereof be provided under this section to any person except upon a written application by such person stating—

(A) that person's name, occupation and address;

(B) the name and address of any other person or organization on whose behalf the inspection or copy is requested; and

(C) that such person is aware of the prohibitions on the obtaining or use of the report.

Any such application shall be made available to the public throughout the period during which the report is made available to the public.

(c)(1) It shall be unlawful for any person to obtain or use a report—

(A) for any unlawful purpose;

(B) for any commercial purpose, other than by news and communications media for dissemination to the general public;

(C) for determining or establishing the credit rating of any individual; or

(D) for use, directly or indirectly, in the solicitation of money for any political, charitable, or other purpose.

(2) The Attorney General may bring a civil action against any person who obtains or uses a report for any purpose prohibited in paragraph (1) of this subsection. The court in which such action is brought may assess against such person a penalty in any amount not to exceed $10,000. Such remedy shall be in addition to any other remedy available under statutory or common law.

(d) Any report filed with or transmitted to an agency or supervising ethics office or to the Clerk of the House of Representatives or the Secretary of the Senate pursuant to this title shall be retained by such agency or office or by the Clerk or the Secretary of the Senate, as the case may be. Such report shall be made available to the public for a period of six years after receipt of the report. After such six-year period the report shall be destroyed unless needed in an ongoing investigation, except that in the case of an individual who filed the report pursuant to section 101(b) and was not subsequently confirmed by the Senate, or who filed the report pursuant to section 101(c) and was not subsequently elected, such report shall be destroyed one year after the individual either is no longer under consideration by the Senate or is no longer a candidate for nomination or election to the Office of President, Vice President, or as a Member of Congress, unless needed in an ongoing investigation.

§ 106. Review of reports

(a)(1) Each designated agency ethics official or Secretary concerned shall make provisions to ensure that each report filed with him under this title is reviewed within sixty days after the date of such filing, except that the Director of the Office of Government Ethics shall review only those reports required to be transmitted to him under this title within sixty days after the date of transmittal.

(2) Each congressional ethics committee and the Judicial Conference shall make provisions to ensure that each report filed under this title is reviewed within sixty days after the date of such filing.

(b)(1) If after reviewing any report under subsection (a), the Director of the Office of Government Ethics, the Secretary concerned, the designated agency ethics official, a person designated by the congressional ethics committee, or a person designated by the Judicial Conference, as the case may be, is of the opinion that on the basis of information contained in such report the individual submitting such report is in compliance with applicable laws and regulations, he shall state such opinion on the report, and shall sign such report.

(2) If the Director of the Office of Government Ethics, the Secretary concerned, the designated agency ethics official, a person designated by the congressional ethics committee, or a person designated by the Judicial Conference, after reviewing any report under subsection (a)—

(A) believes additional information is required to be submitted, he shall notify the individual submitting such report what additional information is required and the time by which it must be submitted, or

(B) is of the opinion, on the basis of information submitted, that the individual is not in compliance with applicable laws and regulations, he shall notify the individual, afford a reasonable opportunity for a written or oral response, and after consideration of such response, reach an opinion as to whether or not, on the basis of information submitted, the individual is in compliance with such laws and regulations.

(3) If the Director of the Office of Government Ethics, the Secretary concerned, the designated agency ethics official, a person designated by a congressional ethics committee, or a person designated by the Judicial Conference, reaches an opinion under paragraph (2)(B) that an individual is not in compliance with applicable laws and regulations, the official or committee shall notify the individual of that opinion and, after an opportunity for personal consultation (if practicable), determine and notify the individual of which steps, if any, would in the opinion of such official or committee be appropriate for assuring compliance with such

laws and regulations and the date by which such steps should be taken. Such steps may include, as appropriate—

(A) divestiture,

(B) restitution,

(C) the establishment of a blind trust,

(D) request for an exemption under section 208(b) of title 18, United States Code, or

(E) voluntary request for transfer, reassignment, limitation of duties, or resignation.

The use of any such steps shall be in accordance with such rules or regulations as the supervising ethics office may prescribe.

(4) If steps for assuring compliance with applicable laws and regulations are not taken by the date set under paragraph (3) by an individual in a position in the executive branch (other than in the Foreign Service or the uniformed services), appointment to which requires the advice and consent of the Senate, the matter shall be referred to the President for appropriate action.

(5) If steps for assuring compliance with applicable laws and regulations are not taken by the date set under paragraph (3) by a member of the Foreign Service or the uniformed services, the Secretary concerned shall take appropriate action.

(6) If steps for assuring compliance with applicable laws and regulations are not taken by the date set under paragraph (3) by any other officer or employee, the matter shall be referred to the head of the appropriate agency, the congressional ethics committee, or the Judicial Conference, for appropriate action; except that in the case of the Postmaster General or Deputy Postmaster General, the Director of the Office of Government Ethics shall recommend to the Governors of the Board of Governors of the United States Postal Service the action to be taken.

(7) Each supervising ethics office may render advisory opinions interpreting this title within its respective jurisdiction. Notwithstanding any other provision of law, the individual to whom a public advisory opinion is rendered in accordance with this paragraph, and any other individual covered by this title who is involved in a fact situation which is indistinguishable in all material aspects, and who acts in good faith in accordance with the provisions and findings of such advisory opinion shall not, as a result of such act, be subject to any penalty or sanction provided by this title.

§ 107. Confidential reports and other additional requirements

(a)(1) Each supervising ethics office may require officers and employees under its jurisdiction (including special Government employees as defined in section 202 of title 18, United States Code) to file confidential financial disclosure reports, in such form as the supervising ethics office may prescribe. The information required to be reported under this subsection by the officers and employees of any department or agency shall be set forth in rules or regulations prescribed by the supervising ethics office, any may be less extensive than otherwise required by this title, or more extensive when determined by the supervising ethics office to be necessary and appropriate in light of sections 202 through 209 of title 18, United States Code, regulations promulgated thereunder, or the authorized activities of such officers or employees. Any individual required to file a report pursuant to section 101 shall not be required to file a confidential report pursuant to this subsection, except with respect to information which is more extensive than information otherwise required by this title. Subsections (a), (b), and (d) of section 105 shall not apply with respect to any such report.

(2) Any information required to be provided by an individual under this subsection shall be confidential and shall not be disclosed to the public.

(3) Nothing in this subsection exempts any individual otherwise covered by the requirement to file a public financial disclosure report under this title from such requirement.

(b) The provisions of this title requiring the reporting of information shall supersede any general requirement under any other provision of law or regulation with respect to the reporting of information required for purposes of preventing conflicts of interest or apparent conflicts of interest. Such provisions of this title shall not supersede the requirements of section 7342 of title 5, United States Code.

(c) Nothing in this Act requiring reporting of information shall be deemed to authorize the receipt of income, gifts, or reimbursements; the holding of assets, liabilities, or positions; or the participation in transactions that are prohibited by law, Executive order, rule, or regulation.

§ 108. Authority of Comptroller General

(a) The Comptroller General shall have access to financial disclosure reports filed under this title for the purposes of carrying out his statutory responsibilities.

(b) No later than December 31, 1992, and regularly thereafter, the Comptroller General shall conduct a study to determine whether the provisions of this title are being carried out effectively.

§ 109. Definitions

For the purposes of this title, the term—

(1) "congressional ethics committees" means the Select Committee on Ethics of the Senate and the Committee on Standards of Official Conduct of the House of Representatives;

(2) "dependent child" means, when used with respect to any reporting individual, any individual who is a son, daughter, stepson, or stepdaughter and who—

(A) is unmarried and under age 21 and is living in the household of such reporting individual; or

(B) is a dependent of such reporting individual within the meaning of section 152 of the Internal Revenue Code of 1986;

(3) "designated agency ethics official" means an officer or employee who is designated to administer the provisions of this title within an agency;

(4) "executive branch" includes each Executive agency (as defined in section 105 of title 5, United States Code), other than the General Accounting Office, and any other entity or administrative unit in the executive branch;

(5) "gift" means a payment, advance, forbearance, rendering, or deposit of money, or any thing of value, unless consideration of equal or greater value is received by the donor, but does not include—

(A) bequest and other forms of inheritance;

(B) suitable mementos of a function honoring the reporting individual;

(C) food, lodging, transportation, and entertainment provided by a foreign government within a foreign country or by the United States Government, the District of Columbia, or a State or local government or political subdivision thereof;

(D) food and beverages which are not consumed in connection with a gift of overnight lodging;

(E) communications to the offices of a reporting individual, including subscriptions to newspapers and periodicals; or

(F) consumable products provided by home-State businesses to the offices of a reporting individual who is an elected official, if those products are intended for consumption by persons other than such reporting individual;

(6) "honoraria" has the meaning given such term in section 505 of this Act;

(7) "income" means all income from whatever source derived, including but not limited to the following items: compensation for services, including fees, commissions, and similar items; gross income derived from business (and net income if the individual elects to include it); gains derived from dealings in property; interest; rents; royalties; dividends; annuities; income from life insurance and endowment contracts; pensions; income from discharge of indebtedness; distributive share of partnership income; and income from an interest in an estate or trust;

(8) "judicial employee" means any employee of the judicial branch of the Government, of the United States Sentencing Commission, of the Tax Court, of the Claims Court, of the Court of Veterans Appeals, or of the United States Court of Military Appeals, who is not a judicial officer and who is authorized to perform adjudicatory functions with respect to proceedings in the judicial branch, or who is paid at a rate of basic pay equal to or greater than the minimum rate of basic pay in effect for grade GS–16 of the General Schedule;

(9) "Judicial Conference" means the Judicial Conference of the United States;

(10) "judicial officer" means the Chief Justice of the United States, the Associate Justices of the Supreme Court, and the judges of the United States courts of appeals, United States district courts, including the district courts in Guam, the Northern Mariana Islands, and the Virgin Islands, Court of Appeals for the Federal Circuit, Court of International Trade, Tax Court, Claims Court, Court of Veterans Appeals, United States Court of Military Appeals, and any court created by Act of Congress, the judges of which are entitled to hold office during good behavior;

(11) "legislative branch" includes—

(A) the Architect of the Capitol;

(B) the Botanic Gardens;

(C) the Congressional Budget Office;

(D) the General Accounting Office;

(E) the Government Printing Office;

(F) the Library of Congress;

(G) the United States Capitol Police;

(H) the Office of Technology Assessment; and

(I) any other agency, entity, office, or commission established in the legislative branch;

(12) "Member of Congress" means a United States Senator, a Representative in Congress, a Delegate to Congress, or the Resident Commissioner from Puerto Rico;

(13) "officer or employee of the Congress" means—

(A) any individual described under subparagraph (B), other than a Member of Congress or the Vice President, whose compensation is disbursed by the Secretary of the Senate or the Clerk of the House of Representatives;

(B)(i) each officer or employee of the legislative branch who is compensated for at least 60 days at a rate of basic pay equal to or greater than the annual rate of basic pay in effect for grade GS–16 of the General Schedule; and

(ii) at least one principal assistant designated for purposes of this paragraph by each Member who does not have an employee compensated at a rate equal to or in excess of the annual rate of basic pay in effect for grade GS–16 of the General Schedule;

(14) "personal hospitality of any individual" means hospitality extended for a nonbusiness purpose by an individual, not a corporation or organization, at the personal residence of that individual or his family or on property or facilities owned by that individual or his family;

(15) "reimbursement" means any payment or other thing of value received by the reporting individual, other than gifts, to cover travel-related expenses of such individual other than those which are—

(A) provided by the United States Government, the District of Columbia, or a State or local government or political subdivision thereof;

(B) required to be reported by the reporting individual under section 7342 of title 5, United States Code; or

(C) required to be reported under section 304 of the Federal Election Campaign Act of 1971 (2 U.S.C. 434);

(16) "relative" means an individual who is related to the reporting individual, as father, mother, son, daughter, brother, sister, uncle, aunt, great aunt, great uncle, first cousin, nephew, niece, husband, wife, grandfather, grandmother, grandson, granddaughter, father-in-law, mother-in-law, son-in-law, daughter-in-law, brother-in-law, sister-in-law, stepfather, stepmother, stepson, stepdaughter, stepbrother, stepsister, half brother, half sister, or who is the grandfather or grandmother of the spouse of the reporting individual, and shall be deemed to include the fiance or fiancee of the reporting individual;

(17) "Secretary concerned" has the meaning set forth in section 101(8) of title 10, United States Code, and, in addition, means—

(A) the Secretary of Commerce, with respect to matters concerning the National Oceanic and Atmospheric Administration;

(B) the Secretary of Health and Human Services, with respect to matters concerning the Public Health Service; and

(C) the Secretary of State, with respect to matters concerning the Foreign Service;

(18) "supervising ethics office" means—

(A) the Select Committee on Ethics of the Senate, for Senators, officers and employees of the Senate, and other officers or employees of the legislative branch required to file financial disclosure reports with the Secretary of the Senate pursuant to section 103(h) of this title;

(B) the Committee on Standards of Official Conduct of the House of Representatives, for Members, officers and employees of the House of Representatives and other officers or employees of the legislative branch required to file financial disclosure reports with the Clerk of the House of Representatives pursuant to section 103(h) of this title;

(C) the Judicial Conference for judicial officers and judicial employees; and

(D) the Office of Government Ethics for all executive branch officers and employees; and

(19) "value" means a good faith estimate of the dollar value if the exact value is neither known nor easily obtainable by the reporting individual.

§ 110. Notice of actions taken to comply with ethics agreements

(a) In any case in which an individual agrees with that individual's designated agency ethics official, the Office of Government Ethics, a Senate confirmation committee, a congressional ethics committee, or the Judicial Conference of the United States, to take any action to comply with this Act or any other law or regulation governing conflicts of interest of, or establishing standards of conduct applicable with respect to, officers or employees of the Government, that individual shall notify in writing the designated agency ethics official, the Office of Government Ethics, the appropriate committee of the Senate, the congressional ethics committee, or the Judicial Conference of the United States, as the case may be, of any action taken by the individual pursuant to that agreement. Such notification shall be made not later than the date specified in the agreement by which action by the individual must be taken, or not later than three months after the date of the agreement, if no date for action is so specified.

(b) If an agreement described in subsection (a) requires that the individual recuse himself or herself from particular categories of agency or other official action, the individual shall reduce to writing those subjects regarding which the recusal agreement will apply and the process by which it will be determined whether the individual must recuse himself or herself in a specific instance. An individual shall be considered to have complied with the requirements of subsection (a) with respect to such recusal agreement if such individual files a copy of the document setting forth the information described in the preceding sentence with such individual's designated agency ethics official or the appropriate supervising ethics office within the time prescribed in the last sentence of subsection (a).

§ 111. Administration of provisions

The provisions of this title shall be administered by—

(1) the Director of the Office of Government Ethics, the designated agency ethics official, or the Secretary concerned, as appropriate, with regard to officers and employees described in paragraphs (1) through (8) of section 101(f);

(2) the Senate Select Committee on Ethics and the Committee on Standards of Official Conduct of the House of Representatives, as appropriate, with regard to officers and employees described in paragraphs (9) and (10) of section 101(f); and

(3) the Judicial Conference of the United States and clerk of the applicable court, as appropriate, in the case of an officer or employee described in paragraphs (11) and (12) of section 101(f).

* * *

5. SAMPLE FEDERAL DISTRICT COURT RULES

UNITED STATES DISTRICT COURTS FOR THE SOUTHERN AND EASTERN DISTRICTS OF NEW YORK

Effective October 15, 1988

RULE 2. Admission to the Bar

(a) A member in good standing of the bar of the state of New York, or a member in good standing of the bar of the United States District Court in New Jersey, Connecticut or Vermont and of the bar of the State in which such district court is located, provided such district court by its rule extends a corresponding privilege to members of the bar of this court, may be admitted to practice in this court on compliance with the following provisions:

Each applicant for admission shall file with the clerk, at least ten (10) days prior to hearing (unless, for good cause shown, the judge shall shorten the time), a verified written petition for admission stating: (1) applicant's residence and office address; (2) the time when, and court where, admitted; (3) applicant's legal training and experience; (4) whether applicant has ever been held in contempt of court, and if so, the nature of the contempt and the final disposition thereof; (5) whether applicant has ever been censured, suspended or disbarred by any court, and if so, the facts and circumstances connected therewith; and (6) that applicant has read and is familiar with (a) the provisions of the Judicial Code (Title 28, U.S.C.) which pertain to the jurisdiction of, and practice in, the United States District Courts; (b) the Federal Rules of Civil Procedure for the district courts; (c) the Federal Rules of Criminal Procedure for the district courts; (d) the Federal Rules of Evidence for the United States Courts and Magistrates; (e) the Rules of the United States District Court for the Southern and Eastern Districts of New York; and (f) that applicant has read the Code of Professional Responsibility of the American Bar Association, and will faithfully adhere thereto.

The petition shall be accompanied by a certificate of the clerk of the court for each of the states in which the applicant is a member of the bar, which has been issued within thirty (30) days and states that the applicant is a member in good standing of the bar of that state court. The petition shall also be accompanied by an affidavit of an attorney of this court who has known the applicant for at least one year, stating when the affiant was admitted to practice in this court, how long and under what circumstances the attorney has known the applicant, and what the attorney knows of the applicant's character and experience at the bar. Such petition shall be placed at the head of the calendar and, on the call thereof, the attorney whose affidavit accompanied the petition shall personally move the admission of the applicant. If the petition is granted, the applicant shall take the oath of office and sign the roll of attorneys.

(b) [Southern District only] A member in good standing of the bar of either the Southern or Eastern District of New York may be admitted to the bar of the other district without formal application (1) upon filing in that district a certificate of the clerk of the United States District Court for the district in which the applicant is a member of the bar, issued within thirty (30) days and states that the applicant is a member in good standing of the bar of that court and (2) upon taking the oath of office, signing the roll of attorneys of that district, and paying the fee required in that district.

(b) [Eastern District only] A member in good standing of the bar of any district court in the Second Circuit may be admitted to the bar of the Eastern District of New York without formal application:

(1) upon filing in the Eastern District a certificate of the Clerk of the United States District Court for the district in which the attorney is a member of the bar, issued within thirty days, that the applicant is a member in good standing of the bar of that court and that the attorney was required to present a certificate of good standing in a state bar within the Second Circuit in order to be admitted to membership in the federal bar in question; and

(2) upon taking the oath of office, signing the roll of attorneys of this district, and paying the fee required in this district.

(c) A member in good standing of the bar of any state or of any United States District Court may be permitted to argue or try a particular case in whole or in part as counsel or advocate, upon motion and upon filing with the Clerk of the District Court a certificate of the court for each of the states in which the applicant is a member of the bar, which has been issued within thirty (30) days and states that the applicant is a member in good standing of the bar of that state court. Only an

Rule 2   *DISTRICT RULES*

attorney of this court may enter appearances for parties, sign stipulations or receive payments upon judgments, decrees or orders.

(d) If an attorney changes his or her residence or office address, the attorney shall immediately notify the clerk of the district in which the attorney is admitted.

6. FEDERAL RULES OF APPELLATE PROCEDURE

RULE 45. Duties of Clerks

(a) **General Provisions.** * * * Neither the clerk nor any deputy clerk shall practice as an attorney or counselor in any court while continuing in office. * * *

RULE 46. Attorneys

(a) **Admission to the Bar of a Court of Appeals; Eligibility; Procedure for Admission.** An attorney who has been admitted to practice before the Supreme Court of the United States, or the highest court of a state, or another United States court of appeals, or a United States district court (including the district courts for the Canal Zone, Guam and the Virgin Islands), and who is of good moral and professional character, is eligible for admission to the bar of a court of appeals.

An applicant shall file with the clerk of the court of appeals, on a form approved by the court and furnished by the clerk, an application for admission containing the applicant's personal statement showing his eligibility for membership. At the foot of the application the applicant shall take and subscribe to the following oath or affirmation: I, _____, do solemnly swear (or affirm) that I will demean myself as an attorney and counselor of this court, uprightly and according to law; and that I will support the Constitution of the United States.

Thereafter, upon written or oral motion of a member of the bar of the court, the court will act upon the application. An applicant may be admitted by oral motion in open court, but it is not necessary that the applicant appear before the court for the purpose of being admitted, unless the court shall otherwise order. An applicant shall upon admission pay to the clerk the fee prescribed by rule or order of the court.

(b) **Suspension or Disbarment.** When it is shown to the court that any member of its bar has been suspended or disbarred from practice in any other court of record, or has been guilty of conduct unbecoming a member of the bar of the court, the member will be subject to suspension or disbarment by the court. The member shall be afforded an opportunity to show good cause, within such time as the court shall prescribe, why the member should not be suspended or disbarred. Upon the member's response to the rule to show cause, and after hearing, if requested, or upon expiration of the time prescribed for a response if no response is made, the court shall enter an appropriate order.

(c) Disciplinary Power of the Court Over Attorneys. A court of appeals may, after reasonable notice and an opportunity to show cause to the contrary, and after hearing, if requested, take any appropriate disciplinary action against any attorney who practices before it for conduct unbecoming a member of the bar or for failure to comply with these rules or any rule of the court.

7. U.S. SUPREME COURT RULES

RULE 7. Prohibition Against Practice

.1. The Clerk shall not practice as an attorney or counselor while holding office.

.2. No law clerk, secretary to a Justice, or other employee of this Court shall practice as an attorney or counselor in any court or before any agency of government while employed at the Court; nor shall any person after leaving employment in this Court participate by way of any form of professional consultation or assistance, in any case pending before this Court or in any case being considered for filing in this Court, until two years have elapsed after separation; nor shall a former employee ever participate, by way of any form of professional consultation or assistance, in any case that was pending in this Court during the employee's tenure.

RULE 8. Disbarment and Disciplinary Action

.1. Whenever it is shown to the Court that a member of the Bar of this Court has been disbarred or suspended from practice in any court of record, or has engaged in conduct unbecoming a member of the Bar of this Court, that member will be suspended from practice before this Court forthwith and will be afforded the opportunity to show cause, within 40 days, why a disbarment order should not be entered. Upon response, or upon the expiration of the 40 days if no response is made, the Court will enter an appropriate order.

.2. The Court may, after reasonable notice and an opportunity to show cause why disciplinary action should not be taken, and after a hearing if material facts are in dispute, take any appropriate disciplinary action against any attorney who practices before it for conduct unbecoming a member of the Bar or for failure to comply with these Rules or any Rule of the Court.

ABA MODEL CODE OF JUDICIAL CONDUCT (1990)

[The Model Code of Judicial Conduct was adopted by the House of Delegates of the American Bar Association in August 1990. It is designed to replace the previous code, which had been adopted in 1972 and last amended in 1984. The Model Code of Judicial Conduct is copyrighted by the American Bar Association, and reprinted here with permission. Portions of the previous (1972) Judicial Code are quoted in the margin.]

PREAMBLE

[1] Our legal system is based on the principle that an independent, fair and competent judiciary will interpret and apply the laws that govern us. The role of the judiciary is central to American concepts of justice and the rule of law. Intrinsic to all sections of this Code are the precepts that judges, individually and collectively, must respect and honor the judicial office as a public trust and strive to enhance and maintain confidence in our legal system. The judge is an arbiter of facts and law for the resolution of disputes and a highly visible symbol of government under the rule of law.

[2] The Code of Judicial Conduct is intended to establish standards for ethical conduct of judges. It consists of broad statements called Canons, specific rules set forth in Sections under each Canon, a Terminology Section, an Application Section and Commentary. The text of the Canons and the Sections, including the Terminology and Application Sections, is authoritative. The Commentary, by explanation and example, provides guidance with respect to the purpose and meaning of the Canons and Sections. The Commentary is not intended as a statement of additional rules. When the text uses "shall" or "shall not," it is intended to impose binding obligations the violation of which can result in disciplinary action. When "should" or "should not" is used, the text is intended as hortatory and as a statement of what is or is not appropriate conduct but not as a binding rule under which a judge may be disciplined. When "may" is used, it denotes permissible discretion or, depending on the context, it refers to action that is not covered by specific proscriptions.

[3] The Canons and Sections are rules of reason. They should be applied consistent with constitutional requirements, statutes, other court rules and decisional law and in the context of all relevant circumstances. The Code is to be construed so as not to impinge on the essential independence of judges in making judicial decisions.

[4] The Code is designed to provide guidance to judges and candidates for judicial office and to provide a structure for regulating conduct through disciplinary agencies. It is not designed or intended as a basis for civil liability or criminal prosecution. Furthermore, the purpose of the Code would be subverted if the Code were invoked by lawyers for mere tactical advantage in a proceeding.

[5] The text of the Canons and Sections is intended to govern conduct of judges and to be binding upon them. It is not intended, however, that every transgression will result in disciplinary action. Whether disciplinary action is appropriate, and the degree of discipline to be imposed, should be determined through a reasonable and reasoned application of the text and should depend on

MODEL CODE OF JUDICIAL CONDUCT

such factors as the seriousness of the transgression, whether there is a pattern of improper activity and the effect of the improper activity on others or on the judicial system. See ABA Standards Relating to Judicial Discipline and Disability Retirement.[1]

[6] The Code of Judicial Conduct is not intended as an exhaustive guide for the conduct of judges. They should also be governed in their judicial and personal conduct by general ethical standards. The Code is intended, however, to state basic standards which should govern the conduct of all judges and to provide guidance to assist judges in establishing and maintaining high standards of judicial and personal conduct.

TERMINOLOGY

Terms explained below are noted with an asterisk (*) in the Sections where they appear. In addition, the Sections where terms appear are referred to after the explanation of each term below.

[1] "**Appropriate authority**" denotes the authority with responsibility for initiation of disciplinary process with respect to the violation to be reported. See Sections 3D(1) and 3D(2).

[2] "**Candidate**." A candidate is a person seeking selection for or retention in judicial office by election or appointment. A person becomes a candidate for judicial office as soon as he or she makes a public announcement of candidacy, declares or files as a candidate with the election or appointment authority, or authorizes solicitation or acceptance of contributions or support. The term "candidate" has the same meaning when applied to a judge seeking election or appointment to nonjudicial office. See Preamble and Sections 5A, 5B, 5C and 5E.

[3] "**Continuing part-time judge**." A continuing part-time judge is a judge who serves repeatedly on a part-time basis by election or under a continuing appointment, including a retired judge subject to recall who is permitted to practice law. See Application Section C.

[4] "**Court personnel**" does not include the lawyers in a proceeding before a judge. See Sections 3B(7)(c) and 3B(9).

[5] "**De minimis**" † denotes an insignificant interest that could not raise reasonable question as to a judge's impartiality. See Sections 3E(1)(c) and 3E(1)(d).

---

1. Judicial disciplinary procedures adopted in the jurisdictions should comport with the requirements of due process. The ABA Standards Relating to Judicial Discipline and Disability Retirement are cited as an example of how these due process requirements may be satisfied.

† **Editors' note:** In contrast, Canon 3C(3)(c) of the ABA Model Code of Judicial Conduct (1972, as amended) defined "financial interest" very differently; there was no such thing as a "de minimis" legal or equitable interest. It provided:

(c) "financial interest" means ownership of a legal or equitable interest, however small, or a relationship as director, advisor, or other active participant in the affairs of a party, except that:

(i) ownership in a mutual or common investment fund that holds securities is not a "financial interest" in such securities unless the judge participates in the management of the fund;

(ii) an office in an educational, religious, charitable, fraternal, or civic organization is not a "financial interest" in securities held by the organization;

(iii) the proprietary interest of a policy holder in a mutual insurance company, of a depositor in a mutual savings association, or a similar proprietary interest, is a "financial interest" in the

[6] **"Economic interest"** † denotes ownership of a more than de minimis legal or equitable interest, or a relationship as officer, director, advisor or other active participant in the affairs of a party, except that:

(i) ownership of an interest in a mutual or common investment fund that holds securities is not an economic interest in such securities unless the judge participates in the management of the fund or a proceeding pending or impending before the judge could substantially affect the value of the interest;

(ii) service by a judge as an officer, director, advisor or other active participant in an educational, religious, charitable, fraternal or civic organization, or service by a judge's spouse, parent or child as an officer, director, advisor or other active participant in any organization does not create an economic interest in securities held by that organization;

(iii) a deposit in a financial institution, the proprietary interest of a policy holder in a mutual insurance company, of a depositor in a mutual savings association or of a member in a credit union, or a similar proprietary interest, is not an economic interest in the organization unless a proceeding pending or impending before the judge could substantially affect the value of the interest;

(iv) ownership of government securities is not an economic interest in the issuer unless a proceeding pending or impending before the judge could substantially affect the value of the securities. See Sections 3E(1)(c) and 3E(2).

[7] **"Fiduciary"** includes such relationships as executor, administrator, trustee, and guardian. See Sections 3E(2) and 4E.

[8] **"Knowingly,"** "knowledge," "known" or "knows" denotes actual knowledge of the fact in question. A person's knowledge may be inferred from circumstances. See Sections 3D, 3E(1), and 5A(3).

[9] **"Law"** denotes court rules as well as statutes, constitutional provisions and decisional law. See Sections 2A, 3A, 3B(2), 3B(6), 4B, 4C, 4D(5), 4F, 4I, 5A(2), 5A(3), 5B(2), 5C(1), 5C(3) and 5D.

[10] **"Member of the candidate's family"** denotes a spouse, child, grandchild, parent, grandparent or other relative or person with whom the candidate maintains a close familial relationship. See Section 5A(3)(a).

[11] **"Member of the judge's family"** denotes a spouse, child, grandchild, parent, grandparent, or other relative or person with whom the judge maintains a close familial relationship. See Sections 4D(3), 4E and 4G.

[12] **"Member of the judge's family residing in the judge's household"** denotes any relative of a judge by blood or marriage, or a person treated by a judge as a member of the judge's family, who resides in the judge's household. See Sections 3E(1) and 4D(5).

[13] **"Nonpublic information"** denotes information that, by law, is not available to the public. Nonpublic information may include but is not limited to:

organization only if the outcome of the proceeding could substantially affect the value of the interest;

(iv) ownership of government securities is a "financial interest" in the issuer only if the outcome of the proceeding could substantially affect the value of the securities.

[14] **"Periodic part-time judge."** A periodic part-time judge is a judge who serves or expects to serve repeatedly on a part-time basis but under a separate appointment for each limited period of service or for each matter. See Application Section D.

[15] **"Political organization"** denotes a political party or other group, the principal purpose of which is to further the election or appointment of candidates to political office. See Sections 5A(1), 5B(2) and 5C(1).

[16] **"Pro tempore part-time judge."** A pro tempore part-time judge is a judge who serves or expects to serve once or only sporadically on a part-time basis under a separate appointment for each period of service or for each case heard. See Application Section E.

[17] **"Public election."** This term includes primary and general elections; it includes partisan elections, nonpartisan elections and retention elections. See Section 5C.

[18] **"Require."** The rules prescribing that a judge "require" certain conduct of others are, like all of the rules in this Code, rules of reason. The use of the term "require" in that context means a judge is to exercise reasonable direction and control over the conduct of those persons subject to the judge's direction and control. See Sections 3B(3), 3B(4), 3B(5), 3B(6), 3B(9) and 3C(2).

[19] **"Third degree of relationship."** The following persons are relatives within the third degree of relationship: great-grandparent, grandparent, parent, uncle, aunt, brother, sister, child, grandchild, great-grandchild, nephew or niece. See Section 3E(1)(d).

CANON 1

A Judge Shall Uphold the Integrity and Independence of the Judiciary

A. An independent and honorable judiciary is indispensable to justice in our society. A judge should participate in establishing, maintaining and enforcing high standards of conduct, and shall personally observe those standards so that the integrity and independence of the judiciary will be preserved. The provisions of this Code are to be construed and applied to further that objective.

Commentary:

[1] Deference to the judgments and rulings of courts depends upon public confidence in the integrity and independence of judges. The integrity and independence of judges depends in turn upon their acting without fear or favor. Although judges should be independent, they must comply with the law, including the provisions of this Code. Public confidence in the impartiality of the judiciary is maintained by the adherence of each judge to this responsibility. Conversely, violation of this Code diminishes public confidence in the judiciary and thereby does injury to the system of government under law.

CANON 2

A Judge Shall Avoid Impropriety and the Appearance of Impropriety in All of the Judge's Activities

A. A judge shall respect and comply with the law* and shall act at all times in a manner that promotes public confidence in the integrity and impartiality of the judiciary.

Commentary:

[1] Public confidence in the judiciary is eroded by irresponsible or improper conduct by judges. A judge must avoid all impropriety and appearance of impropriety. A judge must expect to be the subject of constant public scrutiny. A judge must therefore accept restrictions on the judge's conduct that might be viewed as burdensome by the ordinary citizen and should do so freely and willingly.

[2] The prohibition against behaving with impropriety or the appearance of impropriety applies to both the professional and personal conduct of a judge. Because it is not practicable to list all prohibited acts, the proscription is necessarily cast in general terms that extend to conduct by judges that is harmful although not specifically mentioned in the Code. Actual improprieties under this standard include violations of law, court rules or other specific provisions of this Code. The test for appearance of impropriety is whether the conduct would create in reasonable minds a perception that the judge's ability to carry out judicial responsibilities with integrity, impartiality and competence is impaired.

[3] See also Commentary under Section 2C.

B. A judge shall not allow family, social, political or other relationships to influence the judge's judicial conduct or judgment. A judge shall not lend the prestige of judicial office to advance the private interests of the judge or others; nor shall a judge convey or permit others to convey the impression that they are in a special position to influence the judge. A judge shall not testify voluntarily as a character witness.

Commentary:

[1] Maintaining the prestige of judicial office is essential to a system of government in which the judiciary functions independently of the executive and legislative branches. Respect for the judicial office facilitates the orderly conduct of legitimate judicial functions. Judges should distinguish between proper and improper use of the prestige of office in all of their activities. For example, it would be improper for a judge to allude to his or her judgeship to gain a personal advantage such as deferential treatment when stopped by a police officer for a traffic offense. Similarly, judicial letterhead must not be used for conducting a judge's personal business.

[2] A judge must avoid lending the prestige of judicial office for the advancement of the private interests of others. For example, a judge must not use the judge's judicial position to gain advantage in a civil suit involving a member of the judge's family. In contracts for publication of a judge's writings,

---

* See, Terminology.

a judge should retain control over the advertising to avoid exploitation of the judge's office. As to the acceptance of awards, see Section 4D(5)(a) and Commentary.

[3] Although a judge should be sensitive to possible abuse of the prestige of office, a judge may, based on the judge's personal knowledge, serve as a reference or provide a letter of recommendation. However, a judge must not initiate the communication of information to a sentencing judge or a probation or corrections officer but may provide to such persons information for the record in response to a formal request.

[4] Judges may participate in the process of judicial selection by cooperating with appointing authorities and screening committees seeking names for consideration, and by responding to official inquiries concerning a person being considered for a judgeship. See also Canon 5 regarding use of a judge's name in political activities.

[5] A judge must not testify voluntarily as a character witness because to do so may lend the prestige of the judicial office in support of the party for whom the judge testifies. Moreover, when a judge testifies as a witness, a lawyer who regularly appears before the judge may be placed in the awkward position of cross-examining the judge. A judge may, however, testify when properly summoned. Except in unusual circumstances where the demands of justice require, a judge should discourage a party from requiring the judge to testify as a character witness.

C. A judge shall not hold membership in any organization that practices invidious discrimination on the basis of race, sex, religion or national origin.

Commentary:

[1] Membership of a judge in an organization that practices invidious discrimination gives rise to perceptions that the judge's impartiality is impaired. Section 2C refers to the current practices of the organization. Whether an organization practices invidious discrimination is often a complex question to which judges should be sensitive. The answer cannot be determined from a mere examination of an organization's current membership rolls but rather depends on how the organization selects members and other relevant factors, such as that the organization is dedicated to the preservation of religious, ethnic or cultural values of legitimate common interest to its members, or that it is in fact and effect an intimate, purely private organization whose membership limitations could not be constitutionally prohibited. Absent such factors, an organization is generally said to discriminate invidiously if it arbitrarily excludes from membership on the basis of race, religion, sex or national origin persons who would otherwise be admitted to membership. See *New York State Club Ass'n. Inc. v. City of New York*, 108 S.Ct. 2225, 101 L.Ed.2d 1 (1988); *Board of Directors of Rotary International v. Rotary Club of Duarte*, 481 U.S. 537, 107 S.Ct. 1940 (1987), 95 L.Ed.2d 474; *Roberts v. United States Jaycees*, 468 U.S. 609, 104 S.Ct. 3244, 82 L.Ed.2d 462 (1984).

[2] Although Section 2C relates only to membership in organizations that invidiously discriminate on the basis of race, sex, religion or national origin, a judge's membership in an organization that engages in any discriminatory membership practices prohibited by the law of the jurisdiction also violates Canon 2 and Section 2A and gives the appearance of impropriety. In addition, it would be a violation of Canon 2 and Section 2A for a judge to arrange a meeting

at a club that the judge knows practices invidious discrimination on the basis of race, sex, religion or national origin in its membership or other policies, or for the judge to regularly use such a club. Moreover, public manifestation by a judge of the judge's knowing approval of invidious discrimination on any basis gives the appearance of impropriety under Canon 2 and diminishes public confidence in the integrity and impartiality of the judiciary, in violation of Section 2A.

[3] When a person who is a judge on the date this Code becomes effective [in the jurisdiction in which the person is a judge][1] learns that an organization to which the judge belongs engages in invidious discrimination that would preclude membership under Section 2C or under Canon 2 and Section 2A, the judge is permitted, in lieu of resigning, to make immediate efforts to have the organization discontinue its invidiously discriminatory practices, but is required to suspend participation in any other activities of the organization. If the organization fails to discontinue its invidiously discriminatory practices as promptly as possible (and in all events within a year of the judge's first learning of the practices), the judge is required to resign immediately from the organization.

CANON 3

A Judge Shall Perform the Duties of Judicial Office Impartially and Diligently

A. JUDICIAL DUTIES IN GENERAL. The judicial duties of a judge take precedence over all the judge's other activities. The judge's judicial duties include all the duties of the judge's office prescribed by law *. In the performance of these duties, the following standards apply.

B. ADJUDICATIVE RESPONSIBILITIES.

(1) A judge shall hear and decide matters assigned to the judge except those in which disqualification is required.

(2) A judge shall be faithful to the law * and maintain professional competence in it. A judge shall not be swayed by partisan interests, public clamor or fear of criticism.

(3) A judge shall require * order and decorum in proceedings before the judge.

(4) A judge shall be patient, dignified and courteous to litigants, jurors, witnesses, lawyers and others with whom the judge deals in an official capacity, and shall require * similar conduct of lawyers, and of staff, court officials and others subject to the judge's direction and control.

Commentary:

[1] The duty to hear all proceedings fairly and with patience is not inconsistent with the duty to dispose promptly of the business of the court. Judges can be efficient and businesslike while being patient and deliberate.

[2] A judge must refrain from speech, gestures or other conduct that could reasonably be perceived as sexual harassment and must require the same standard of conduct of others subject to the judge's direction and control.

---

1. The language within the brackets should be deleted when the jurisdiction adopts this provision.

* See, Terminology.

(5) A judge shall perform judicial duties without bias or prejudice. A judge shall not, in the performance of judicial duties, by words or conduct manifest bias or prejudice, including but not limited to bias or prejudice based upon race, sex, religion, national origin, disability, age, sexual orientation or socioeconomic status, and shall not permit staff, court officials and others subject to the judge's direction and control to do so.

Commentary:

[1] A judge must perform judicial duties impartially and fairly. A judge who manifests bias on any basis in a proceeding impairs the fairness of the proceeding and brings the judiciary into disrepute. Facial expression and body language, in addition to oral communication, can give to parties or lawyers in the proceeding, jurors, the media and others an appearance of judicial bias. A judge must be alert to avoid behavior that may be perceived as prejudicial.

(6) A judge shall require * lawyers in proceedings before the judge to refrain from manifesting, by words or conduct, bias or prejudice based upon race, sex, religion, national origin, disability, age, sexual orientation or socioeconomic status, against parties, witnesses, counsel or others. This Section 3B(6) does not preclude legitimate advocacy when race, sex, religion, national origin, disability, age, sexual orientation or socioeconomic status, or other similar factors, are issues in the proceeding.

(7) A judge shall accord to every person who has a legal interest in a proceeding, or that person's lawyer, the right to be heard according to law *. A judge shall not initiate, permit, or consider ex parte communications, or consider other communications made to the judge outside the presence of the parties concerning a pending or impending proceeding except that:

(a) Where circumstances require, ex parte communications for scheduling, administrative purposes or emergencies that do not deal with substantive matters or issues on the merits are authorized; provided:

(i) the judge reasonably believes that no party will gain a procedural or tactical advantage as a result of the ex parte communication, and

(ii) the judge makes provision promptly to notify all other parties of the substance of the ex parte communication and allows an opportunity to respond.

(b) A judge may obtain the advice of a disinterested expert on the law * applicable to a proceeding before the judge if the judge gives notice to the parties of the person consulted and the substance of the advice, and affords the parties reasonable opportunity to respond.

(c) A judge may consult with court personnel * whose function is to aid the judge in carrying out the judge's adjudicative responsibilities or with other judges.

(d) A judge may, with the consent of the parties, confer separately with the parties and their lawyers in an effort to mediate or settle matters pending before the judge.

* See, Terminology.

Canon 3 *ABA*

 (e) **A judge may initiate or consider any ex parte communications when expressly authorized by law * to do so.**

Commentary:

 [1] The proscription against communications concerning a proceeding includes communications from lawyers, law teachers, and other persons who are not participants in the proceeding, except to the limited extent permitted.

 [2] To the extent reasonably possible, all parties or their lawyers shall be included in communications with a judge.

 [3] Whenever presence of a party or notice to a party is required by Section 3B(7), it is the party's lawyer, or if the party is unrepresented the party, who is to be present or to whom notice is to be given.

 [4] An appropriate and often desirable procedure for a court to obtain the advice of a disinterested expert on legal issues is to invite the expert to file a brief *amicus curiae.*

 [5] Certain ex parte communication is approved by Section 3B(7) to facilitate scheduling and other administrative purposes and to accommodate emergencies. In general, however, a judge must discourage ex parte communication and allow it only if all the criteria stated in Section 3B(7) are clearly met. A judge must disclose to all parties all ex parte communications described in Sections 3B(7)(a) and 3B(7)(b) regarding a proceeding pending or impending before the judge.

 [6] A judge must not independently investigate facts in a case and must consider only the evidence presented.

 [7] A judge may request a party to submit proposed findings of fact and conclusions of law, so long as the other parties are apprised of the request and are given an opportunity to respond to the proposed findings and conclusions.

 [8] A judge must make reasonable efforts, including the provision of appropriate supervision, to ensure that Section 3B(7) is not violated through law clerks or other personnel on the judge's staff.

 [9] If communication between the trial judge and the appellate court with respect to a proceeding is permitted, a copy of any written communication or the substance of any oral communication should be provided to all parties.

 (8) **A judge shall dispose of all judicial matters promptly, efficiently and fairly.**

Commentary:

 [1] In disposing of matters promptly, efficiently and fairly, a judge must demonstrate due regard for the rights of the parties to be heard and to have issues resolved without unnecessary cost or delay. Containing costs while preserving fundamental rights of parties also protects the interests of witnesses and the general public. A judge should monitor and supervise cases so as to reduce or eliminate dilatory practices, avoidable delays and unnecessary costs. A judge should encourage and seek to facilitate settlement, but parties should not feel coerced into surrendering the right to have their controversy resolved by the courts.

 [2] Prompt disposition of the court's business requires a judge to devote adequate time to judicial duties, to be punctual in attending court and expeditious

* See, Terminology.

in determining matters under submission, and to insist that court officials, litigants and their lawyers cooperate with the judge to that end.

(9) A judge shall not, while a proceeding is pending or impending in any court, make any public comment that might reasonably be expected to affect its outcome or impair its fairness or make any nonpublic comment that might substantially interfere with a fair trial or hearing. The judge shall require * similar abstention on the part of court personnel * subject to the judge's direction and control. This Section does not prohibit judges from making public statements in the course of their official duties or from explaining for public information the procedures of the court. This Section does not apply to proceedings in which the judge is a litigant in a personal capacity.

Commentary:

[1] The requirement that judges abstain from public comment regarding a pending or impending proceeding continues during any appellate process and until final disposition. This Section does not prohibit a judge from commenting on proceedings in which the judge is a litigant in a personal capacity, but in cases such as a writ of mandamus where the judge is a litigant in an official capacity, the judge must not comment publicly. The conduct of lawyers relating to trial publicity is governed by [Rule 3.6 of the ABA Model Rules of Professional Conduct]. (Each jurisdiction should substitute an appropriate reference to its rule.)

(10) A judge shall not commend or criticize jurors for their verdict other than in a court order or opinion in a proceeding, but may express appreciation to jurors for their service to the judicial system and the community.

Commentary:

[1] Commending or criticizing jurors for their verdict may imply a judicial expectation in future cases and may impair a juror's ability to be fair and impartial in a subsequent case.

(11) A judge shall not disclose or use, for any purpose unrelated to judicial duties, nonpublic information * acquired in a judicial capacity.

C. ADMINISTRATIVE RESPONSIBILITIES.

(1) A judge shall diligently discharge the judge's administrative responsibilities without bias or prejudice and maintain professional competence in judicial administration, and should cooperate with other judges and court officials in the administration of court business.

(2) A judge shall require * staff, court officials and others subject to the judge's direction and control to observe the standards of fidelity and diligence that apply to the judge and to refrain from manifesting bias or prejudice in the performance of their official duties.

(3) A judge with supervisory authority for the judicial performance of other judges shall take reasonable measures to assure the prompt disposition of matters before them and the proper performance of their other judicial responsibilities.

* See, Terminology.

Canon 3 ABA

(4) A judge shall not make unnecessary appointments. A judge shall exercise the power of appointment impartially and on the basis of merit. A judge shall avoid nepotism and favoritism. A judge shall not approve compensation of appointees beyond the fair value of services rendered.

Commentary:

[1] Appointees of a judge include assigned counsel, officials such as referees, commissioners, special masters, receivers and guardians and personnel such as clerks, secretaries and bailiffs. Consent by the parties to an appointment or an award of compensation does not relieve the judge of the obligation prescribed by Section 3C(4).

D. **DISCIPLINARY RESPONSIBILITIES.**

(1) A judge who receives information indicating a substantial likelihood that another judge has committed a violation of this Code should take appropriate action. A judge having knowledge * that another judge has committed a violation of this Code that raises a substantial question as to the other judge's fitness for office shall inform the appropriate authority *.

(2) A judge who receives information indicating a substantial likelihood that a lawyer has committed a violation of the Rules of Professional Conduct [substitute correct title if the applicable rules of lawyer conduct have a different title] should take appropriate action. A judge having knowledge * that a lawyer has committed a violation of the Rules of Professional Conduct [substitute correct title if the applicable rules of lawyer conduct have a different title] that raises a substantial question as to the lawyer's honesty, trustworthiness or fitness as a lawyer in other respects shall inform the appropriate authority *.

(3) Acts of a judge, in the discharge of disciplinary responsibilities, required or permitted by Sections 3D(1) and 3D(2) are part of a judge's judicial duties and shall be absolutely privileged, and no civil action predicated thereon may be instituted against the judge.

Commentary:

[1] Appropriate action may include direct communication with the judge or lawyer who has committed the violation, other direct action if available, and reporting the violation to the appropriate authority or other agency or body.

E. **DISQUALIFICATION.**

(1) A judge shall disqualify himself or herself in a proceeding in which the judge's impartiality might reasonably be questioned, including but not limited to instances where:

Commentary:

[1] Under this rule, a judge is disqualified whenever the judge's impartiality might reasonably be questioned, regardless whether any of the specific rules in Section 3E(1) apply. For example, if a judge were in the process of negotiating for employment with a law firm, the judge would be disqualified from any matters in which that law firm appeared, unless the disqualification was waived by the parties after disclosure by the judge.

* See, Terminology.

[2] A judge should disclose on the record information that the judge believes the parties or their lawyers might consider relevant to the question of disqualification, even if the judge believes there is no real basis for disqualification.

[3] By decisional law, the rule of necessity may override the rule of disqualification. For example, a judge might be required to participate in judicial review of a judicial salary statute, or might be the only judge available in a matter requiring immediate judicial action, such as a hearing on probable cause or a temporary restraining order. In the latter case, the judge must disclose on the record the basis for possible disqualification and use reasonable efforts to transfer the matter to another judge as soon as practicable.

(a) the judge has a personal bias or prejudice concerning a party or a party's lawyer, or personal knowledge * of disputed evidentiary facts concerning the proceeding;

(b) the judge served as a lawyer in the matter in controversy, or a lawyer with whom the judge previously practiced law served during such association as a lawyer concerning the matter, or the judge has been a material witness concerning it;

Commentary:

[1] A lawyer in a government agency does not ordinarily have an association with other lawyers employed by that agency within the meaning of Section 3E(1)(b); a judge formerly employed by a government agency, however, should disqualify himself or herself in a proceeding if the judge's impartiality might reasonably be questioned because of such association.

(c) the judge knows * that he or she, individually or as a fiduciary, or the judge's spouse, parent or child wherever residing, or any other member of the judge's family residing in the judge's household *, has an economic interest * in the subject matter in controversy or in a party to the proceeding or has any other more than de minimis * interest that could be substantially affected by the proceeding;

(d) the judge or the judge's spouse, or a person within the third degree of relationship * to either of them, or the spouse of such a person:

(i) is a party to the proceeding, or an officer, director or trustee of a party;

(ii) is acting as a lawyer in the proceeding;

(iii) is known * by the judge to have a more than de minimis * interest that could be substantially affected by the proceeding;

(iv) is to the judge's knowledge * likely to be a material witness in the proceeding.

Commentary:

The fact that a lawyer in a proceeding is affiliated with a law firm with which a relative of the judge is affiliated does not of itself disqualify the judge. Under appropriate circumstances, the fact that "the judge's impartiality might reasonably be questioned" under Section 3E(1), or that the relative is known by the judge to have an interest in the law firm that could be "substantially affected by the

* See, Terminology.

outcome of the proceeding" under Section 3E(1)(d)(iii) may require the judge's disqualification.

(2) A judge shall keep informed about the judge's personal and fiduciary* economic interests*, and make a reasonable effort to keep informed about the personal economic interests of the judge's spouse and minor children residing in the judge's household.

F. REMITTAL OF DISQUALIFICATION. A judge disqualified by the terms of Section 3E may disclose on the record the basis of the judge's disqualification and may ask the parties and their lawyers to consider, out of the presence of the judge, whether to waive disqualification. If following disclosure of any basis for disqualification other than personal bias or prejudice concerning a party, the parties and lawyers, without participation by the judge, all agree that the judge should not be disqualified, and the judge is then willing to participate, the judge may participate in the proceeding. The agreement shall be incorporated in the record of the proceeding.

Commentary:

A remittal procedure provides the parties an opportunity to proceed without delay if they wish to waive the disqualification. To assure that consideration of the question of remittal is made independently of the judge, a judge must not solicit, seek or hear comment on possible remittal or waiver of the disqualification unless the lawyers jointly propose remittal after consultation as provided in the rule. A party may act through counsel if counsel represents on the record that the party has been consulted and consents. As a practical matter, a judge may wish to have all parties and their lawyers sign the remittal agreement.

CANON 4

A Judge Shall So Conduct the Judge's Extra-Judicial Activities as to Minimize the Risk of Conflict With Judicial Obligations

A. EXTRA-JUDICIAL ACTIVITIES IN GENERAL. A judge shall conduct all of the judge's extra-judicial activities so that they do not:

(1) cast reasonable doubt on the judge's capacity to act impartially as a judge;

(2) demean the judicial office; or

(3) interfere with the proper performance of judicial duties.

Commentary:

[1] Complete separation of a judge from extra-judicial activities is neither possible nor wise; a judge should not become isolated from the community in which the judge lives.

[2] Expressions of bias or prejudice by a judge, even outside the judge's judicial activities, may cast reasonable doubt on the judge's capacity to act impartially as a judge. Expressions which may do so include jokes or other remarks demeaning individuals on the basis of their race, sex, religion, national

* See, Terminology.

origin, disability, age, sexual orientation or socioeconomic status. See Section 2C and accompanying Commentary.

B. AVOCATIONAL ACTIVITIES. A judge may speak, write, lecture, teach and participate in other extra-judicial activities concerning the law*, the legal system, the administration of justice and non-legal subjects, subject to the requirements of this Code.

Commentary:

[1] As a judicial officer and person specially learned in the law, a judge is in a unique position to contribute to the improvement of the law, the legal system, and the administration of justice, including revision of substantive and procedural law and improvement of criminal and juvenile justice. To the extent that time permits, a judge is encouraged to do so, either independently or through a bar association, judicial conference or other organization dedicated to the improvement of the law. Judges may participate in efforts to promote the fair administration of justice, the independence of the judiciary and the integrity of the legal profession and may express opposition to the persecution of lawyers and judges in other countries because of their professional activities.

[2] In this and other Sections of Canon 4, the phrase "subject to the requirements of this Code" is used, notably in connection with a judge's governmental, civic or charitable activities. This phrase is included to remind judges that the use of permissive language in various Sections of the Code does not relieve a judge from the other requirements of the Code that apply to the specific conduct.

C. GOVERNMENTAL, CIVIC OR CHARITABLE ACTIVITIES.

(1) A judge shall not appear at a public hearing before, or otherwise consult with, an executive or legislative body or official except on matters concerning the law *, the legal system or the administration of justice or except when acting pro se in a matter involving the judge or the judge's interests.

Commentary:

See Section 2B regarding the obligation to avoid improper influence.

(2) A judge shall not accept appointment to a governmental committee or commission or other governmental position that is concerned with issues of fact or policy on matters other than the improvement of the law *, the legal system or the administration of justice. A judge may, however, represent a country, state or locality on ceremonial occasions or in connection with historical, educational or cultural activities.

Commentary:

[1] Section 4C(2) prohibits a judge from accepting any governmental position except one relating to the law, legal system or administration of justice as authorized by Section 4C(3). The appropriateness of accepting extra-judicial assignments must be assessed in light of the demands on judicial resources created by crowded dockets and the need to protect the courts from involvement in extra-judicial matters that may prove to be controversial. Judges should not

* See, Terminology.

Canon 4   *ABA*

accept governmental appointments that are likely to interfere with the effectiveness and independence of the judiciary.

[2] Section 4C(2) does not govern a judge's service in a nongovernmental position. See Section 4C(3) permitting service by a judge with organizations devoted to the improvement of the law, the legal system or the administration of justice and with educational, religious, charitable, fraternal or civic organizations not conducted for profit. For example, service on the board of a public educational institution, unless it were a law school, would be prohibited under Section 4C(2), but service on the board of a public law school or any private educational institution would generally be permitted under Section 4C(3).

(3) A judge may serve as an officer, director, trustee or non-legal advisor of an organization or governmental agency devoted to the improvement of the law *, the legal system or the administration of justice or of an educational, religious, charitable, fraternal or civic organization not conducted for profit, subject to the following limitations and the other requirements of this Code.

Commentary:

[1] Section 4C(3) does not apply to a judge's service in a governmental position unconnected with the improvement of the law, the legal system or the administration of justice; see Section 4C(2).

[2] See Commentary to Section 4B regarding use of the phrase "subject to the following limitations and the other requirements of this Code." As an example of the meaning of the phrase, a judge permitted by Section 4C(3) to serve on the board of a fraternal institution may be prohibited from such service by Sections 2C or 4A if the institution practices invidious discrimination or if service on the board otherwise casts reasonable doubt on the judge's capacity to act impartially as a judge.

[3] Service by a judge on behalf of a civic or charitable organization may be governed by other provisions of Canon 4 in addition to Section 4C. For example, a judge is prohibited by Section 4G from serving as a legal advisor to a civic or charitable organization.

(a) A judge shall not serve as an officer, director, trustee or non-legal advisor if it is likely that the organization

(i) will be engaged in proceedings that would ordinarily come before the judge, or

(ii) will be engaged frequently in adversary proceedings in the court of which the judge is a member or in any court subject to the appellate jurisdiction of the court of which the judge is a member.

Commentary:

[1] The changing nature of some organizations and of their relationship to the law makes it necessary for a judge regularly to reexamine the activities of each organization with which the judge is affiliated to determine if it is proper for the judge to continue the affiliation. For example, in many jurisdictions charitable hospitals are now more frequently in court than in the past. Similarly, the boards of some legal aid organizations now make policy decisions that may

* See, Terminology.

have political significance or imply commitment to causes that may come before the courts for adjudication.

(b) A judge as an officer, director, trustee or non-legal advisor, or as a member or otherwise:

(i) may assist such an organization in planning fund-raising and may participate in the management and investment of the organization's funds, but shall not personally participate in the solicitation of funds or other fund-raising activities, except that a judge may solicit funds from other judges over whom the judge does not exercise supervisory or appellate authority;

(ii) may make recommendations to public and private fund-granting organizations on projects and programs concerning the law*, the legal system or the administration of justice;

(iii) shall not personally participate in membership solicitation if the solicitation might reasonably be perceived as coercive or, except as permitted in Section 4C(3)(b)(i), if the membership solicitation is essentially a fund-raising mechanism;

(iv) shall not use or permit the use of the prestige of judicial office for fund-raising or membership solicitation.

Commentary:

[1] A judge may solicit membership or endorse or encourage membership efforts for an organization devoted to the improvement of the law, the legal system or the administration of justice or a nonprofit educational, religious, charitable, fraternal or civic organization as long as the solicitation cannot reasonably be perceived as coercive and is not essentially a fund-raising mechanism. Solicitation of funds for an organization and solicitation of memberships similarly involve the danger that the person solicited will feel obligated to respond favorably to the solicitor if the solicitor is in a position of influence or control. A judge must not engage in direct, individual solicitation of funds or memberships in person, in writing or by telephone except in the following cases: 1) a judge may solicit for funds or memberships other judges over whom the judge does not exercise supervisory or appellate authority, 2) a judge may solicit other persons for membership in the organizations described above if neither those persons nor persons with whom they are affiliated are likely ever to appear before the court on which the judge serves and 3) a judge who is an officer of such an organization may send a general membership solicitation mailing over the judge's signature.

[2] Use of an organization letterhead for fund-raising or membership solicitation does not violate Section 4C(3)(b) provided the letterhead lists only the judge's name and office or other position in the organization, and, if comparable designations are listed for other persons, the judge's judicial designation. In addition, a judge must also make reasonable efforts to ensure that the judge's staff, court officials and others subject to the judge's direction and control do not solicit funds on the judge's behalf for any purpose, charitable or otherwise.

[3] A judge must not be a speaker or guest of honor at an organization's fund-raising event, but mere attendance at such an event is permissible if otherwise consistent with this Code.

* See, Terminology.

Canon 4 ABA

D. **FINANCIAL ACTIVITIES.**

(1) A judge shall not engage in financial and business dealings that:

(a) may reasonably be perceived to exploit the judge's judicial position, or

(b) involve the judge in frequent transactions or continuing business relationships with those lawyers or other persons likely to come before the court on which the judge serves.

Commentary:

[1] The Time for Compliance provision of this Code (Application, Section F) postpones the time for compliance with certain provisions of this Section in some cases.

[2] When a judge acquires in a judicial capacity information, such as material contained in filings with the court, that is not yet generally known, the judge must not use the information for private gain. See Section 2B; see also Section 3B(11).

[3] A judge must avoid financial and business dealings that involve the judge in frequent transactions or continuing business relationships with persons likely to come either before the judge personally or before other judges on the judge's court. In addition, a judge should discourage members of the judge's family from engaging in dealings that would reasonably appear to exploit the judge's judicial position. This rule is necessary to avoid creating an appearance of exploitation of office or favoritism and to minimize the potential for disqualification. With respect to affiliation of relatives of judge with law firms appearing before the judge, see Commentary to Section 3E(1) relating to disqualification.

[4] Participation by a judge in financial and business dealings is subject to the general prohibitions in Section 4A against activities that tend to reflect adversely on impartiality, demean the judicial office, or interfere with the proper performance of judicial duties. Such participation is also subject to the general prohibition in Canon 2 against activities involving impropriety or the appearance of impropriety and the prohibition in Section 2B against the misuse of the prestige of judicial office. In addition, a judge must maintain high standards of conduct in all of the judge's activities, as set forth in Canon 1. See Commentary for Section 4B regarding use of the phrase "subject to the requirements of this Code."

(2) A judge may, subject to the requirements of this Code, hold and manage investments of the judge and members of the judge's family *, including real estate, and engage in other remunerative activity.

Commentary:

[1] This Section provides that, subject to the requirements of this Code, a judge may hold and manage investments owned solely by the judge, investments owned solely by a member or members of the judge's family, and investments owned jointly by the judge and members of the judge's family.

(3) A judge shall not serve as an officer, director, manager, general partner, advisor or employee of any business entity except that a judge may, subject to the requirements of this Code, manage and participate in:

* See, Terminology.

(a) a business closely held by the judge or members of the judge's family*, or

(b) a business entity primarily engaged in investment of the financial resources of the judge or members of the judge's family.

Commentary:

[1] Subject to the requirements of this Code, a judge may participate in a business that is closely held either by the judge alone, by members of the judge's family, or by the judge and members of the judge's family.

[2] Although participation by a judge in a closely-held family business might otherwise be permitted by Section 4D(3), a judge may be prohibited from participation by other provisions of this Code when, for example, the business entity frequently appears before the judge's court or the participation requires significant time away from judicial duties. Similarly, a judge must avoid participating in a closely-held family business if the judge's participation would involve misuse of the prestige of judicial office.

(4) A judge shall manage the judge's investments and other financial interests to minimize the number of cases in which the judge is disqualified. As soon as the judge can do so without serious financial detriment, the judge shall divest himself or herself of investments and other financial interests that might require frequent disqualification.

(5) A judge shall not accept, and shall urge members of the judge's family residing in the judge's household* not to accept, a gift, bequest, favor or loan from anyone except for:

Commentary:

[1] Section 4D(5) does not apply to contributions to a judge's campaign for judicial office, a matter governed by Canon 5.

[2] Because a gift, bequest, favor or loan to a member of the judge's family residing in the judge's household might be viewed as intended to influence the judge, a judge must inform those family members of the relevant ethical constraints upon the judge in this regard and discourage those family members from violating them. A judge cannot, however, reasonably be expected to know or control all of the financial or business activities of all family members residing in the judge's household.

(a) a gift incident to a public testimonial, books, tapes and other resource materials supplied by publishers on a complimentary basis for official use, or an invitation to the judge and the judge's spouse or guest to attend a bar-related function or an activity devoted to the improvement of the law*, the legal system or the administration of justice;

Commentary:

[1] Acceptance of an invitation to a law-related function is governed by Section 4D(5)(a); acceptance of an invitation paid for by an individual lawyer or group of lawyers is governed by Section 4D(5)(h).

[2] A judge may accept a public testimonial or a gift incident thereto only if the donor organization is not an organization whose members comprise or

* See, Terminology.

Canon 4   *ABA*

frequently represent the same side in litigation, and the testimonial and gift are otherwise in compliance with other provisions of this Code. See Sections 4A(1) and 2B.

(b) a gift, award or benefit incident to the business, profession or other separate activity of a spouse or other family member of a judge residing in the judge's household, including gifts, awards and benefits for the use of both the spouse or other family member and the judge (as spouse or family member), provided the gift, award or benefit could not reasonably be perceived as intended to influence the judge in the performance of judicial duties;

(c) ordinary social hospitality;

(d) a gift from a relative or friend, for a special occasion, such as a wedding, anniversary or birthday, if the gift is fairly commensurate with the occasion and the relationship;

Commentary:

[1] A gift to a judge, or to a member of the judge's family living in the judge's household, that is excessive in value raises questions about the judge's impartiality and the integrity of the judicial office and might require disqualification of the judge where disqualification would not otherwise be required. See, however, Section 4D(5)(e).

(e) a gift, bequest, favor or loan from a relative or close personal friend whose appearance or interest in a case would in any event require disqualification under Section 3E;

(f) a loan from a lending institution in its regular course of business on the same terms generally available to persons who are not judges;

(g) a scholarship or fellowship awarded on the same terms and based on the same criteria applied to other applicants; or

(h) any other gift, bequest, favor or loan, only if: the donor is not a party or other person who has come or is likely to come or whose interests have come or are likely to come before the judge; and, if its value exceeds $150.00, the judge reports it in the same manner as the judge reports compensation in Section 4H.

Commentary:

[1] Section 4D(5)(h) prohibits judges from accepting gifts, favors, bequests or loans from lawyers or their firms if they have come or are likely to come before the judge; it also prohibits gifts, favors, bequests or loans from clients of lawyers or their firms when the clients' interests have come or are likely to come before the judge.

E. **FIDUCIARY ACTIVITIES.**

(1) **A judge shall not serve as executor, administrator or other personal representative, trustee, guardian, attorney in fact or other fiduciary *, except for the estate, trust or person of a member of the judge's family *,**

* See, Terminology.

and then only if such service will not interfere with the proper performance of judicial duties.

(2) A judge shall not serve as a fiduciary * if it is likely that the judge as a fiduciary will be engaged in proceedings that would ordinarily come before the judge, or if the estate, trust or ward becomes involved in adversary proceedings in the court on which the judge serves or one under its appellate jurisdiction.

(3) The same restrictions on financial activities that apply to a judge personally also apply to the judge while acting in a fiduciary * capacity.

Commentary:

[1] The Time for Compliance provision of this Code (Application, Section F) postpones the time for compliance with certain provisions of this Section in some cases.

[2] The restrictions imposed by this Canon may conflict with the judge's obligation as a fiduciary. For example, a judge should resign as trustee if detriment to the trust would result from divestiture of holdings the retention of which would place the judge in violation of Section 4D(4).

F. SERVICE AS ARBITRATOR OR MEDIATOR. A judge shall not act as an arbitrator or mediator or otherwise perform judicial functions in a private capacity unless expressly authorized by law *.

Commentary:

Section 4F does not prohibit a judge from participating in arbitration, mediation or settlement conferences performed as part of judicial duties.

G. PRACTICE OF LAW. A judge shall not practice law. Notwithstanding this prohibition, a judge may act pro se and may, without compensation, give legal advice to and draft or review documents for a member of the judge's family *.

Commentary:

[1] This prohibition refers to the practice of law in a representative capacity and not in a pro se capacity. A judge may act for himself or herself in all legal matters, including matters involving litigation and matters involving appearances before or other dealings with legislative and other governmental bodies. However, in so doing, a judge must not abuse the prestige of office to advance the interests of the judge or the judge's family. See Section 2(B).

[2] The Code allows a judge to give legal advice to and draft legal documents for members of the judge's family, so long as the judge receives no compensation. A judge must not, however, act as an advocate or negotiator for a member of the judge's family in a legal matter.

* * *

[3] Canon 6, new in the 1972 Code, reflected concerns about conflicts of interest and appearances of impropriety arising from compensation for off-the-bench activities. Since 1972, however, reporting requirements that are much more comprehensive with respect to what must be reported and with whom reports must be filed have been adopted by many jurisdictions. The Committee

* See, Terminology.

Canon 4   *ABA*

believes that although reports of compensation for extra-judicial activities should be required, reporting requirements preferably should be developed to suit the respective jurisdictions, not simply adopted as set forth in a national model code of judicial conduct. Because of the Committee's concern that deletion of this Canon might lead to the misconception that reporting compensation for extra-judicial activities is no longer important, the substance of Canon 6 is carried forward as Section 4H in this Code for adoption in those jurisdictions that do not have other reporting requirements. In jurisdictions that have separately established reporting requirements, Section 4H(2) (Public Reporting) may be deleted and the caption for Section 4H modified appropriately.

* * *

H. COMPENSATION, REIMBURSEMENT AND REPORTING.

(1) COMPENSATION AND REIMBURSEMENT. A judge may receive compensation and reimbursement of expenses for the extra-judicial activities permitted by this Code, if the source of such payments does not give the appearance of influencing the judge's performance of judicial duties or otherwise give the appearance of impropriety.

(a) Compensation shall not exceed a reasonable amount nor shall it exceed what a person who is not a judge would receive for the same activity.

(b) Expense reimbursement shall be limited to the actual cost of travel, food and lodging reasonably incurred by the judge and, where appropriate to the occasion, by the judge's spouse or guest. Any payment in excess of such an amount is compensation.

(2) PUBLIC REPORTS. A judge shall report the date, place and nature of any activity for which the judge received compensation, and the name of the payor and the amount of compensation so received. Compensation or income of a spouse attributed to the judge by operation of a community property law is not extra-judicial compensation to the judge. The judge's report shall be made at least annually and shall be filed as a public document in the office of the clerk of the court on which the judge serves or other office designated by law *.

Commentary:

[1] See Section 4D(5) regarding reporting of gifts, bequests and loans.

[2] The Code does not prohibit a judge from accepting honoraria or speaking fees provided that the compensation is reasonable and commensurate with the task performed. A judge should ensure, however, that no conflicts are created by the arrangement. A judge must not appear to trade on the judicial position for personal advantage. Nor should a judge spend significant time away from court duties to meet speaking or writing commitments for compensation. In addition, the source of the payment must not raise any question of undue influence or the judge's ability or willingness to be impartial.

I. Disclosure of a judge's income, debts, investments or other assets is required only to the extent provided in this Canon and in Sections 3E and 3F, or as otherwise required by law *.

* See, Terminology.

Commentary:

[1] Section 3E requires a judge to disqualify himself or herself in any proceeding in which the judge has an economic interest. See "economic interest" as explained in the Terminology Section. Section 4D requires a judge to refrain from engaging in business and from financial activities that might interfere with the impartial performance of judicial duties; Section 4H requires a judge to report all compensation the judge received for activities outside judicial office. A judge has the rights of any other citizen, including the right to privacy of the judge's financial affairs, except to the extent that limitations established by law are required to safeguard the proper performance of the judge's duties.

CANON 5 [2]

A Judge or Judicial Candidate Shall Refrain From Inappropriate Political Activity

A. ALL JUDGES AND CANDIDATES.

(1) Except as authorized in Sections 5B(2), 5C(1) and 5C(3), a judge or a candidate * for election or appointment to judicial office shall not:

(a) act as a leader or hold an office in a political organization *;

(b) publicly endorse or publicly oppose another candidate for public office;

(c) make speeches on behalf of a political organization;

(d) attend political gatherings; or

(e) solicit funds for, pay an assessment to or make a contribution to a political organization or candidate, or purchase tickets for political party dinners or other functions.

Commentary:

[1] A judge or candidate for judicial office retains the right to participate in the political process as a voter.

---

* See, Terminology.

2. **Introductory Note to Canon 5:** There is wide variation in the methods of judicial selection used, both among jurisdictions and within the jurisdictions themselves. In a given state, judges may be selected by one method initially, retained by a different method, and selected by still another method to fill interim vacancies.

According to figures compiled in 1987 by the National Center for State Courts, 32 states and the District of Columbia use a merit selection method (in which an executive such as a governor appoints a judge from a group of nominees selected by a judicial nominating commission) to select judges in the state either initially or to fill an interim vacancy. Of those 33 jurisdictions, a merit selection method is used in 18 jurisdictions to choose judges of courts of last resort, in 13 jurisdictions to choose judges of intermediate appellate courts, in 12 jurisdictions to choose judges of general jurisdiction courts and in 5 jurisdictions to choose judges of limited jurisdiction courts.

Methods of judicial selection other than merit selection include nonpartisan election (10 states use it for initial selection at all court levels, another 10 states use it for initial selection for at least one court level) and partisan election (8 states use it for initial selection at all court levels, another 7 states use it for initial selection for at least one level). In a small minority of the states, judicial selection methods include executive or legislative appointment (without nomination of a group of potential appointees by a judicial nominating commission) and court selection. In addition, the federal judicial system utilizes an executive appointment method. See State Court Organization 1987 (National Center for State Courts, 1988).

Canon 5   *ABA*

[2] Where false information concerning a judicial candidate is made public, a judge or another judicial candidate having knowledge of the facts is not prohibited by Section 5A(1) from making the facts public.

[3] Section 5A(1)(a) does not prohibit a candidate for elective judicial office from retaining during candidacy a public office such as county prosecutor, which is not "an office in a political organization."

[4] Section 5A(1)(b) does not prohibit a judge or judicial candidate from privately expressing his or her views on judicial candidates or other candidates for public office.

[5] A candidate does not publicly endorse another candidate for public office by having that candidate's name on the same ticket.

(2) A judge shall resign from judicial office upon becoming a candidate* for a non-judicial office either in a primary or in a general election, except that the judge may continue to hold judicial office while being a candidate for election to or serving as a delegate in a state constitutional convention if the judge is otherwise permitted by law* to do so.

(3) A candidate* for a judicial office:

(a) shall maintain the dignity appropriate to judicial office and act in a manner consistent with the integrity and independence of the judiciary, and shall encourage members of the candidate's family* to adhere to the same standards of political conduct in support of the candidate as apply to the candidate;

Commentary:

[1] Although a judicial candidate must encourage members of his or her family to adhere to the same standards of political conduct in support of the candidate that apply to the candidate, family members are free to participate in other political activity.

(b) shall prohibit employees and officials who serve at the pleasure of the candidate*, and shall discourage other employees and officials subject to the candidate's direction and control from doing on the candidate's behalf what the candidate is prohibited from doing under the Sections of this Canon;

(c) except to the extent permitted by Section 5C(2), shall not authorize or knowingly* permit any other person to do for the candidate* what the candidate is prohibited from doing under the Sections of this Canon;

(d) shall not:

(i) make pledges or promises of conduct in office other than the faithful and impartial performance of the duties of the office;

(ii) make statements that commit or appear to commit the candidate with respect to cases, controversies or issues that are likely to come before the court; or

(iii) knowingly* misrepresent the identity, qualifications, present position or other fact concerning the candidate or an opponent;

Commentary:

[1] Section 5A(3)(d) prohibits a candidate for judicial office from making statements that appear to commit the candidate regarding cases, controversies or

* See, Terminology.

issues likely to come before the court. As a corollary, a candidate should emphasize in any public statement the candidate's duty to uphold the law regardless of his or her personal views. See also Section 3B(9), the general rule on public comment by judges. Section 5A(3)(d) does not prohibit a candidate from making pledges or promises respecting improvements in court administration. Nor does this Section prohibit an incumbent judge from making private statements to other judges or court personnel in the performance of judicial duties. This Section applies to any statement made in the process of securing judicial office, such as statements to commissions charged with judicial selection and tenure and legislative bodies confirming appointment. See also Rule 8.2 of the ABA Model Rules of Professional Conduct.

(e) may respond to personal attacks or attacks on the candidate's record as long as the response does not violate Section 5A(3)(d).

B. CANDIDATES SEEKING APPOINTMENT TO JUDICIAL OR OTHER GOVERNMENTAL OFFICE.

(1) A candidate * for appointment to judicial office or a judge seeking other governmental office shall not solicit or accept funds, personally or through a committee or otherwise, to support his or her candidacy.

(2) A candidate * for appointment to judicial office or a judge seeking other governmental office shall not engage in any political activity to secure the appointment except that:

(a) such persons may:

(i) communicate with the appointing authority, including any selection or nominating commission or other agency designated to screen candidates;

(ii) seek support or endorsement for the appointment from organizations that regularly make recommendations for reappointment or appointment to the office, and from individuals to the extent requested or required by those specified in Section 5B(2)(a); and

(iii) provide to those specified in Sections 5B(2)(a)(i) and 5B(2)(a)(ii) information as to his or her qualifications for the office;

(b) a non-judge candidate * for appointment to judicial office may, in addition, unless otherwise prohibited by law *:

(i) retain an office in a political organization *,

(ii) attend political gatherings, and

(iii) continue to pay ordinary assessments and ordinary contributions to a political organization or candidate and purchase tickets for political party dinners or other functions.

Commentary:

[1] Section 5B(2) provides a limited exception to the restrictions imposed by Sections 5A(1) and 5D. Under Section 5B(2), candidates seeking reappointment to the same judicial office or appointment to another judicial office or other governmental office may apply for the appointment and seek appropriate support.

[2] Although under Section 5B(2) nonjudge candidates seeking appointment to judicial office are permitted during candidacy to retain office in a political organization, attend political gatherings and pay ordinary dues and assessments,

* See, Terminology.

they remain subject to other provisions of this Code during candidacy. See Sections 5B(1), 5B(2)(a), 5E and Application Section.

C. JUDGES AND CANDIDATES SUBJECT TO PUBLIC ELECTION.

(1) A judge or a candidate * subject to public election * may, except as prohibited by law *:

(a) at any time

(i) purchase tickets for and attend political gatherings;

(ii) identify himself or herself as a member of a political party; and

(iii) contribute to a political organization *;

(b) when a candidate for election

(i) speak to gatherings on his or her own behalf;

(ii) appear in newspaper, television and other media advertisements supporting his or her candidacy;

(iii) distribute pamphlets and other promotional campaign literature supporting his or her candidacy; and

(iv) publicly endorse or publicly oppose other candidates for the same judicial office in a public election in which the judge or judicial candidate is running.

Commentary:

[1] Section 5C(1) permits judges subject to election at any time to be involved in limited political activity. Section 5D, applicable solely to incumbent judges, would otherwise bar this activity.

(2) A candidate * shall not personally solicit or accept campaign contributions or personally solicit publicly stated support. A candidate may, however, establish committees of responsible persons to conduct campaigns for the candidate through media advertisements, brochures, mailings, candidate forums and other means not prohibited by law. Such committees may solicit and accept reasonable campaign contributions, manage the expenditure of funds for the candidate's campaign and obtain public statements of support for his or her candidacy. Such committees are not prohibited from soliciting and accepting reasonable campaign contributions and public support from lawyers. A candidate's committees may solicit contributions and public support for the candidate's campaign no earlier than [one year] before an election and no later than [90] days after the last election in which the candidate participates during the election year. A candidate shall not use or permit the use of campaign contributions for the private benefit of the candidate or others.

Commentary:

[1] Section 5C(2) permits a candidate, other than a candidate for appointment, to establish campaign committees to solicit and accept public support and reasonable financial contributions. At the start of the campaign, the candidate must instruct his or her campaign committees to solicit or accept only contributions that are reasonable under the circumstances. Though not prohibited,

* See, Terminology.

campaign contributions of which a judge has knowledge, made by lawyers or others who appear before the judge, may be relevant to disqualification under Section 3E.

[2] Campaign committees established under Section 5C(2) should manage campaign finances responsibly, avoiding deficits that might necessitate post-election fund-raising, to the extent possible.

[3] Section 5C(2) does not prohibit a candidate from initiating an evaluation by a judicial selection commission or bar association, or, subject to the requirements of this Code, from responding to a request for information from any organization.

(3) Except as prohibited by law *, a candidate * for judicial office in a public election * may permit the candidate's name: (a) to be listed on election materials along with the names of other candidates for elective public office, and (b) to appear in promotions of the ticket.

Commentary:

[1] Section 5C(3) provides a limited exception to the restrictions imposed by Section 5A(1).

D. INCUMBENT JUDGES. A judge shall not engage in any political activity except (i) as authorized under any other Section of this Code, (ii) on behalf of measures to improve the law *, the legal system or the administration of justice, or (iii) as expressly authorized by law.

Commentary:

[1] Neither Section 5D nor any other section of the Code prohibits a judge in the exercise of administrative functions from engaging in planning and other official activities with members of the executive and legislative branches of government. With respect to a judge's activity on behalf of measures to improve the law, the legal system and the administration of justice, see Commentary to Section 4B and Section 4C(1) and its Commentary.

E. APPLICABILITY. Canon 5 generally applies to all incumbent judges and judicial candidates *. A successful candidate, whether or not an incumbent, is subject to judicial discipline for his or her campaign conduct; an unsuccessful candidate who is a lawyer is subject to lawyer discipline for his or her campaign conduct. A lawyer who is a candidate for judicial office is subject to [Rule 8.2(b) of the ABA Model Rules of Professional Conduct]. (An adopting jurisdiction should substitute a reference to its applicable rule.)

APPLICATION OF THE CODE OF JUDICIAL CONDUCT

A. Anyone, whether or not a lawyer, who is an officer of a judicial system [3] and who performs judicial functions, including an officer such as a

* See, Terminology.

3. Applicability of this Code to administrative law judges should be determined by each adopting jurisdiction. Administrative law judges generally are affiliated with the executive branch of government rather than the judicial branch and each adopting jurisdiction should consider the unique characteristics of particular administrative law judge positions in adopting and adapting the Code for administrative law judges. See, e.g., Model Code of Judicial Conduct for Federal Administrative Law Judges, endorsed by the National Conference of Administrative Law Judges in February 1989.

magistrate, court commissioner, special master or referee, is a judge within the meaning of this Code. All judges shall comply with this Code except as provided below.

Commentary:

[1] The four categories of judicial service in other than a full-time capacity are necessarily defined in general terms because of the widely varying forms of judicial service. For the purposes of this Section, as long as a retired judge is subject to recall the judge is considered to "perform judicial functions." The determination of which category and, accordingly, which specific Code provisions apply to an individual judicial officer, depend upon the facts of the particular judicial service.

B. **RETIRED JUDGE SUBJECT TO RECALL.** A retired judge subject to recall who by law is not permitted to practice law is not required to comply:

(1) except while serving as a judge, with Section 4F; and

(2) at any time with Section 4E.

C. **CONTINUING PART–TIME JUDGE.** A continuing part-time judge *:

(1) is not required to comply

(a) except while serving as a judge, with Section 3B(9); and

(b) at any time with Sections 4C(2), 4D(3), 4E(1), 4F, 4G, 4H, 5A(1), 5B(2) and 5D.

(2) shall not practice law in the court on which the judge serves or in any court subject to the appellate jurisdiction of the court on which the judge serves, and shall not act as a lawyer in a proceeding in which the judge has served as a judge or in any other proceeding related thereto.

Commentary:

[1] When a person who has been a continuing part-time judge is no longer a continuing part-time judge, including a retired judge no longer subject to recall, that person may act as a lawyer in a proceeding in which he or she has served as a judge or in any other proceeding related thereto only with the express consent of all parties pursuant to [Rule 1.12(a) of the ABA Model Rules of Professional Conduct]. (An adopting jurisdiction should substitute a reference to its applicable rule).

D. **PERIODIC PART–TIME JUDGE.** A periodic part-time judge *:

(1) is not required to comply

(a) except while serving as a judge, with Section 3B(9);

(b) at any time, with Sections 4C(2), 4C(3)(a), 4D(1)(b), 4D(3), 4D(4), 4D(5), 4E, 4F, 4G, 4H, 5A(1), 5B(2) and 5D.

(2) shall not practice law in the court on which the judge serves or in any court subject to the appellate jurisdiction of the court on which the judge serves, and shall not act as a lawyer in a proceeding in which the judge has served as a judge or in any other proceeding related thereto.

* See, Terminology.

Commentary:

[1] When a person who has been a periodic part-time judge is no longer a periodic part-time judge (no longer accepts appointments), that person may act as a lawyer in a proceeding in which he or she has served as a judge or in any other proceeding related thereto only with the express consent of all parties pursuant to [Rule 1.12(a) of the ABA Model Rules of Professional Conduct]. (An adopting jurisdiction should substitute a reference to its applicable rule).

E. PRO TEMPORE PART-TIME JUDGE. A pro tempore part-time judge *:

(1) is not required to comply

(a) except while serving as a judge, with Sections 2A, 2B, 3B(9) and 4C(1);

(b) at any time with Sections 2C, 4C(2), 4C(3)(a), 4C(3)(b), 4D(1)(b), 4D(3), 4D(4), 4D(5), 4E, 4F, 4G, 4H, 5A(1), 5A(2), 5B(2) and 5D.

(2) A person who has been a pro tempore part-time judge * shall not act as a lawyer in a proceeding in which the judge has served as a judge or in any other proceeding related thereto except as otherwise permitted by [Rule 1.12(a) of the ABA Model Rules of Professional Conduct]. (An adopting jurisdiction should substitute a reference to its applicable rule.)

F. TIME FOR COMPLIANCE. A person to whom this Code becomes applicable shall comply immediately with all provisions of this Code except Sections 4D(2), 4D(3) and 4E and shall comply with these Sections as soon as reasonably possible and shall do so in any event within the period of one year.

Commentary:

[1] If serving as a fiduciary when selected as judge, a new judge may, notwithstanding the prohibitions in Section 4E, continue to serve as fiduciary but only for that period of time necessary to avoid serious adverse consequences to the beneficiary of the fiduciary relationship and in no event longer than one year. Similarly, if engaged at the time of judicial selection in a business activity, a new judge may, notwithstanding the prohibitions in Section 4D(3), continue in that activity for a reasonable period but in no event longer than one year.

---

* See, Terminology.

CALIFORNIA CODE OF JUDICIAL CONDUCT

PREFACE

Formal standards of judicial conduct have existed for more than fifty years. The original Canons of Judicial Ethics were modified and adopted in 1949 for application in California by the Conference of California Judges (California Judges Association).

In 1969 the American Bar Association determined the current needs and problems warranted revision of the Canons. In the revision process, a special American Bar Association committee, headed by former California Chief Justice Roger Traynor, sought and considered the views of the bench and bar and other interested persons. The American Bar Association Code of Judicial Conduct was adopted by the House of Delegates of the American Bar Association August 16, 1972.

The California Code of Judicial Conduct is adapted from the American Bar Association Code of Judicial Conduct of 1972 and supersedes all prior Canons. The Code was adopted on September 10, 1974 and became effective January 1, 1975.

Revisions of the Code are made by vote of the membership of the California Judges Association by plebiscite or at its Annual Business Meeting.

This edition includes all revisions made through the Association's 1989 Annual Meeting. In 1986, the Code was re-cast in gender-neutral form.

Note: Sections designated as "Commentary" were adopted from the original ABA Code. Sections designated as "California Commentary" were adopted by the California Judges Association.

PREAMBLE

The California Judges Association, mindful that the character and conduct of a judge should never be objects of indifference, and that declared ethical standards should become habits of life, adopts these principles which should govern the personal practice of members of the judiciary. The administration of justice requires adherence by the judiciary to the highest ideals of personal and official conduct. The office of judge casts upon the incumbents duties in respect to their conduct which concern their relation to the state, its inhabitants, and all who come in contact with them. The Association adopts this Code of Judicial Conduct as a proper guide and reminder for justices and judges of courts in California and for aspirants to judicial office, and as indicating what the people have a right to expect from them.

CANON 1

Judges Should Uphold the Integrity and Independence of the Judiciary

An independent and honorable judiciary is indispensable to justice in our society. Judges should participate in establishing, maintaining, and enforcing, and should themselves observe, high standards of conduct so that the integrity and independence of the judiciary may be preserved. The provisions of this Code should be construed and applied to further that objective.

CANON 2

Judges Should Avoid Impropriety and the Appearance of Impropriety in All Their Activities

A. Judges should respect and comply with the law and should conduct themselves at all times in a manner that promotes public confidence in the integrity and impartiality of the judiciary.

B. Judges should not allow their families, social, or other relationships to influence their judicial conduct or judgment. Judges should not lend the prestige of their office to advance the private interests of others; nor should judges convey or permit others to convey the impression that they are in a special position to influence them. Judges should not testify voluntarily as character witnesses.

C. It is inappropriate for a judge to hold membership in any organization, excluding religious organizations, that practices invidious discrimination on the basis of race, sex, religion or national origin.

Commentary

Public confidence in the judiciary is eroded by irresponsible or improper conduct by judges. Judges must avoid all impropriety and appearance of impropriety. Judges must expect to be the subject of constant public scrutiny. Judges must therefore accept restrictions on their conduct that might be viewed as burdensome by the ordinary citizen and should do so freely and willingly.

The testimony of judges as character witnesses injects the prestige of their office into the proceeding in which they testify and may be misunderstood to be an official testimonial. This Canon, however, does not afford judges a privilege against testifying in response to an official summons.

California Commentary

Membership in an organization that practices invidious discrimination may give rise to perceptions by minorities, women and others, that the judge's impartiality is impaired. Whether an organization practices invidious discrimination is often a complex question to which judges should be sensitive. The answer cannot be determined from a mere examination of an organization's current membership rolls, but rather depends on the history of the organization's selection of members and other relevant factors.

CANON 3

Judges Should Perform the Duties of Their Office Impartially and Diligently

The judicial duties of a judge take precedence over all other activities. The judge's judicial duties include all the duties of office prescribed by law. In the performance of these duties, the following standards apply:

A. Adjudicative Responsibilities

(1) Judges should be faithful to the law and maintain professional competence in it. Judges should be unswayed by partisan interest, public clamor, or fear of criticism.

Canon 3   *CALIFORNIA CODE*

(2) Judges should maintain order and decorum in proceedings before them.

(3) Judges should be patient, dignified, and courteous to litigants, jurors, witnesses, lawyers, and others with whom judges deal in their official capacity, and should require similar conduct of lawyers, and the staff, court officials, and others subject to their direction and control.

Commentary

The duty to hear all proceedings fairly and with patience is not inconsistent with the duty to dispose promptly of the business of the court. Courts can be efficient and businesslike while being patient and deliberate.

(4) Judges should accord to every person who is legally interested in a proceeding, or that person's lawyer, full right to be heard according to law, and except as authorized by law, neither initiate nor consider ex parte or other communications concerning a pending or impending proceeding. Judges, however, may obtain the advice of a disinterested expert on the law applicable to a proceeding before them if they give notice to the parties of the person consulted and the substance of the advice, and afford the parties reasonable opportunity to respond.

Commentary

The proscription against communications concerning a proceeding includes communications from lawyers, law teachers, and other persons who are not participants in the proceeding except to the limited extent permitted. It does not preclude judges from consulting with other judges, or with court personnel whose function is to aid judges in carrying out their adjudicative responsibilities.

An appropriate and often desirable procedure for a court to obtain the advice of a disinterested expert on legal issues is to invite the expert to file a brief amicus curiae.

(5) Judges should dispose promptly of the business of the court.

Commentary

Prompt disposition of the court's business requires judges to devote adequate time to their duties, to be punctual in attending court and expeditious in determining matters under submission, and to insist that court officials, litigants and their lawyers cooperate with the judges to that end.

(6) Judges should abstain from public comment about a pending or impending proceeding in any court, and should require similar abstention on the part of court personnel subject to their direction and control. This subsection does not prohibit judges from making public statements in the course of their official duties or from explaining for public information the procedures of the court.

Commentary

"Court personnel" does not include the lawyers in a proceeding before a judge. The conduct of lawyers is governed by DR 7-107 of the Code of Professional Responsibility.

(7) Unless otherwise provided by law or by the California Rules of Court or Standards, judges should prohibit broadcasting, televising,

JUDICIAL CONDUCT   Canon 3

recording, or taking photographs in the courtroom during sessions of court or recesses between sessions, and also prohibit such activities in areas immediately adjacent thereto if such activities disturb or are likely to disturb the court proceedings, except that judges may authorize:

(a) the use of electronic or photographic means for the presentation of evidence, for the perpetuation of a record, or for other purposes of judicial administration;

(b) the broadcasting, televising, recording or photographing of investitive, ceremonial, or naturalization proceedings;

(c) the photographic or electronic recording and reproduction of appropriate court proceedings under the following conditions:

   (i) the means of recording will not distract participants or impair the dignity of the proceeding;

   (ii) the parties have consented, and the consent to being depicted or recorded has been obtained from each witness appearing in the recording and reproduction;

   (iii) the reproduction will not be exhibited until after the proceeding has been concluded and all direct appeals have been exhausted; and

   (iv) the reproduction will be exhibited only for instructional purposes in educational institutions.

(d) Judges should comply with any additional and more restrictive requirements of applicable statutes and California Rules of Court.

Commentary

Temperate conduct of judicial proceedings is essential to the fair administration of justice. The recording and reproduction of a proceeding should not distort or dramatize the proceeding.

B. Administrative Responsibilities.

(1) Judges should diligently discharge their administrative responsibilities, maintain professional competence in judicial administration, and facilitate the performance of the administrative responsibilities of other judges and court officials.

(2) Judges should require their staff and court officials subject to their direction and control to observe the standards of fidelity and diligence that apply to them.

(3) Judges should take or initiate appropriate disciplinary measure against a judge or lawyer for unprofessional conduct of which they may become aware.

Commentary

Disciplinary measures may include reporting a lawyer's misconduct to an appropriate disciplinary body.

(4) Judges should not make unnecessary appointments. They should exercise their power of appointment only on the basis of merit, avoiding nepotism and favoritism. They should not approve compensation of appointees beyond the fair value of services rendered.

Commentary

Appointees of judges include officials such as attorneys, referees, commissioners, special masters, receivers, guardians and personnel such as clerks, secretaries, and bailiffs. Consent by the parties to an appointment or an award of compensation does not relieve judges of the obligation prescribed by this subsection.

C. Disqualification.*

(1) Judges should disqualify themselves in a proceeding in which their disqualification is required by law, or their impartiality might reasonably be questioned, including but not limited to instances where:

(a) the judge has a personal bias or prejudice concerning a party;

California Commentary

CCP § 170.1 contains the comparable California statutory disqualification. Section 170.1 provides in subdivision (a)(6) in part that:

> For any reason (A) the judge believes his or her recusal would further the interests of justice, (B) the judge believes there is a substantial doubt as to his or her capacity to be impartial, or (C) a person aware of the facts might reasonably entertain a doubt that the judge would be able to be impartial. . . .

(b) the judge served as lawyer in the matter in controversy, or the judge has been a material witness concerning it;

California Commentary

Subdivision (a)(2) of Section 170.1 of the California Code of Civil Procedure contains disqualifications in addition to those enumerated in Canon 3C(1)(b). A California judge should carefully consider CCP § 170.1, subdivisions (a)(2), (a)(2)(A), and (a)(2)(B) in connection with Canon 3C(1)(b).

CCP § 170.1, subdivision (a)(2) provides for disqualification when:

The judge served as a lawyer in the proceeding or in any other proceeding involving the same issues, he or she served as a lawyer for any party in the present proceeding or gave advice to any party in the present proceeding upon any matter involved in the action or proceeding.

A judge shall be deemed to have served as a lawyer in the proceeding if within the last two years:

(A) A party to the proceeding or an officer, director, or trustee of a party was a client of the judge when the judge was in the private practice of law or a client of a lawyer with whom the judge was associated in the private practice of law, or

(B) A lawyer in the proceeding was associated in the private practice of law with the judge.

A judge who served as a lawyer for or officer of a public agency which is a party to the proceeding shall be deemed to have served as a lawyer in the proceeding if or she personally advised or in any way represented the public agency concerning the factual or legal issues in the proceeding.

---

* Each California Commentary to Canon 3C on Disqualification has been revised to reflect differences between the Canon and the Code of Civil Procedure 170 et seq. (September 15, 1986).

JUDICIAL CONDUCT Canon 3

(c) the judge knows that, individually or as a fiduciary, the judge or the judge's spouse or minor child residing in the judge's household, has a financial interest in the subject matter in controversy or in a party to the proceeding, or any other interest that could be substantially affected by the outcome of the proceeding;

California Commentary

Canon 3C(1)(c) contains slightly different grounds for disqualification than does California Code of Civil Procedure Section 170.1(a)(3) which provides that a judge shall be disqualified if:

The judge has a financial interest in the subject matter in a proceeding or in a party to the proceeding.

A judge shall be deemed to have a financial interest within the meaning of this paragraph if:

(A) A spouse or minor child living in the household has a financial interest; or

(B) The judge or the spouse of the judge is a fiduciary who has a financial interest.

A judge has a duty to make reasonable efforts to inform himself or herself about his or her personal and fiduciary interests and those of his or her spouse and the personal financial interest of children living in the household.

CCP § 170.5(b) provides that:

"Financial interest" means ownership of more than a one percent legal or equitable interest in a party, or a legal or equitable interest in a party of a fair market value in excess of one thousand five hundred dollars ($1500) or a relationship as director, advisor or other active participant in the affairs of a party, except as follows:

(1) Ownership in a mutual or common investment fund that holds securities is not a "financial interest" in those securities unless the judge participates in the management of the fund.

(2) An office in an educational, religious, charitable, fraternal or civic organization is not a "financial interest" in securities held by the organization.

(3) The proprietary interest of a policyholder in a mutual insurance company, or a depositor in a mutual savings association, or a similar proprietary interest, is a "financial interest" in the organization only if the outcome of the proceeding could substantially affect the value of the interest.

(d) the judge or the judge's spouse, or a person within the third degree of relationship to either of them, or the spouse of such a person:

(i) is a party to the proceeding, or an officer, director, or a trustee of a party;

(ii) is acting as a lawyer in the proceeding;

Commentary

The fact that a lawyer in a proceeding is affiliated with a law firm with which a lawyer-relative of the judge is affiliated does not of itself disqualify the judge. Under appropriate circumstances, the fact that "their impartiality might reasonably be questioned" under Canon 3C(1), or that the lawyer-relative is known by the judge to have an interest in the law firm that could be "substantially affected by the outcome of the proceeding" under Canon 3C(1)(d)(iii) may require the judge's disqualification.

(iii) is known by the judge to have an interest that could be substantially affected by the outcome of the proceeding;

(iv) is to the judge's knowledge likely to be a material witness in the proceeding;

(e) the judge has personal knowledge of disputed evidentiary facts concerning the proceedings;

(2) Judges should inform themselves about their personal and fiduciary financial interests, and make a reasonable effort to inform themselves about the personal financial interests of their spouses and minor children residing in their households.

(3) For the purposes of this section:

(a) the degree of relationship is calculated according to the civil law system;

Commentary

According to the civil law system, the third degree of relationship test would, for example, disqualify the judge if the judge's or the judge's spouse's parent, grandparent, aunt, uncle, sibling or niece's husband or nephew's wife were a party or lawyer in the proceeding, but would not disqualify the judge if a cousin were a party or lawyer in the proceeding.

California Commentary

Canon 3C(1)(d) contains the same grounds for disqualification as does the California Code of Civil Procedure Section 170.1(a)(4) and (5).

(b) "fiduciary" includes such relationships as executor, administrator, trustee, and guardian;

(c) "financial interest" means ownership of a legal or equitable interest, however small, or a relationship as director, advisor, or other active participant in the affairs of a party, except that:

(i) ownership in a mutual or common investment fund that holds securities is not a "financial interest" in such securities unless the judge participates in the management of the fund;

(ii) an office in an educational, religious, charitable, fraternal, or civic organization is not a "financial interest" in securities held by the organization;

(iii) the proprietary interest of a policy holder in a mutual insurance company, of a depositor in a mutual savings association, or a similar proprietary interest, is a "financial interest" in the organization only if the outcome of the proceeding could substantially affect the value of the interest;

California Commentary

Canons 3C(3)(b) and (c) contain substantially the same disqualifications previously quoted in Section 170.5(b)(1), (2) and (3).

(iv) ownership of government securities is a "financial interest" in the issuer only if the outcome of the proceeding could substantially affect the value of the securities.

D. Remittal of Disqualification

A judge disqualified for any reason other than those expressed in Canon 3C(1)(a) or Canon 3C(1)(b) may, instead of withdrawing from the proceeding, disclose on the record the basis of the disqualification, and may ask the parties and their lawyers whether they wish to waive the disqualification. If the parties and lawyers, independently of the judge's participation, all agree in writing to waive the disqualification, the judge may participate in the proceeding. The waiver agreement, signed by all parties and lawyers, shall recite the basis for the disqualification and shall be incorporated in the record of the proceeding.

The judge shall not seek to induce a waiver and shall avoid any effort to discover which lawyers or parties favored or opposed a waiver of disqualification.

Commentary

This procedure is designed to minimize the chance that a party or lawyer will feel coerced into an agreement. When a party is not immediately available, the judge, without violating this section, may proceed on the written assurance of the lawyer that the party's consent will be subsequently filed.

California Commentary

The Canon precludes waivers of disqualification in situations involving personal bias or personal participation in the matter. Code of Civil Procedure Section 170.3 does not contain those limitations on the waiver procedure. Code of Civil Procedure Section 170.3 does not contain those limitations on the waiver procedure.

1. The Canon permits waivers of disqualifications only in situations involving financial interest or relationship. CCP § 170.3 does not contain those limitations.

2. CCP § 170.3(b)(1) requires the waiver of disqualification to recite the basis for the disqualification and is effective only when signed by all parties and their attorneys and filed in the record.

3. The Canon provides that the waiver agreement shall be entered into "independent of participation by the judge," whereas CCP § 170.3(b)(1) permits the judge to disclose the basis for disqualification on the record and permits the judge to ask the parties and their attorneys whether they wish to waive the disqualification. Section 170.3(b)(2), however, states the judge shall not seek to induce a waiver and shall avoid any effort to discover which lawyers or parties favored or opposed a waiver of disqualification.

CANON 4

Judges May Engage in Activities to Improve the Law, the Legal System, and the Administration of Justice

Judges, subject to the proper performance of their judicial duties, may engage in the following quasi-judicial activities, if in doing so they

Canon 4 CALIFORNIA CODE

do not cast doubt on their capacity to decide impartially any issue that may come before them:

A. They may speak, write, lecture, teach, and participate in other activities concerning the law, the legal system, and the administration of justice.

B. They may appear at a public hearing before an executive or legislative body or official on matters concerning the law, the legal system, and the administration of justice, and they may otherwise consult with an executive or legislative body or official, but only on matters concerning the administration of justice.

California Commentary

This Canon is not intended to prevent judges from making an appearance in the management of their personal affairs, provided they do not exploit their judicial position; for example, judges may properly appear before zoning boards acting with respect to property in which they own an interest.

C. Judges may serve as members, officers, or directors of an organization or governmental agency devoted to the improvement of the law, the legal system, or the administration of justice. They may assist such an organization in raising funds and may participate in their management and investment, but should not personally participate in public fund raising activities. They may make recommendations to public and private fund granting agencies on projects and programs concerning the law, the legal system, and the administration of justice.

Commentary

As judicial officers and persons specially learned in the law, judges are in a unique position to contribute to the improvement of the law, the legal system, and the administration of justice, including revision of substantive and procedural law and improvement of criminal and juvenile justice. To the extent that their time permits, they are encouraged to do so, either independently or through a bar association, judicial conference, or other organization dedicated to the improvement of the law.

Extra-judicial activities are governed by Canon 5.

CANON 5

Judges Should Regulate Their Extra-Judicial Activities to Minimize the Risk of Conflict With Their Judicial Duties

A. **Avocational Activities.** Judges may write, lecture, teach, and speak on non-legal subjects, and engage in the arts, sports, and other social and recreational activities, if such avocational activities do not detract from the dignity of their office or interfere with the performance of their judicial duties.

Commentary

Complete separation of judges from extra-judicial activities is neither possible nor wise. They should not become isolated from the society in which they live.

B. Civic and Charitable Activities. Judges may participate in civic and charitable activities that do not reflect adversely upon their impartiality or interfere with the performance of their judicial duties. Judges may serve as officers, directors, trustees, or non-legal advisors of educational, religious, charitable, fraternal, or civic organizations not conducted for the economic or political advantage of their members, subject to the following limitations:

(1) Judges should not serve if it is likely that the organization will be engaged in proceedings that would ordinarily come before them or will be regularly engaged in adversary proceedings in any court.

Commentary

The changing nature of some organizations and of their relationship to the law makes it necessary for judges regularly to reexamine the activities of each organization with which they are affiliated to determine if it is proper for them to continue their relationship with the organization. For example, in many jurisdictions charitable hospitals are now more frequently in court than in the past. Similarly, the boards of some legal aid organizations now make policy decisions that may have political significance or imply commitment to causes that may come before the courts for adjudication.

(2) Judges should not solicit funds for any educational, religious, charitable, fraternal, or civic organization, or use or permit the use of the prestige of their office for that purpose, but they may be listed as officers, directors, or trustees of such organization. They should not be the principal speaker or the guest of honor at an organization's fund-raising events, but they may attend such events.

(3) Judges should not give investment advice to such an organization, but they may serve on its board of directors or trustees even though it has the responsibility for approving investment decisions.

Commentary

Judges' participation in organizations devoted to quasi-judicial activities is governed by Canon 4.

C. Financial Activities

(1) Judges should refrain from financial and business dealings that tend to reflect adversely on their impartiality, interfere with the proper performance of their judicial duties, exploit their judicial position, or involve them in frequent transactions with lawyers or persons likely to come before the courts on which they serve.

(2) Subject to the requirements of subsection (1), judges may hold and manage investments, including real estate, and engage in other remunerative activities, but should not participate in, nor permit their names to be used in connection with, any business venture or commercial advertising program, with or without compensation, in such a way as would justify a reasonable inference that the power or prestige of their office is being utilized to promote a business or commercial product. Judges should not serve as officers, directors, managers or employees of a

business affected with a public interest including, without limitation, a financial institution, insurance company, or public utility.

(3) Judges should manage their investments and other financial interests to minimize the number of cases in which they are disqualified. As soon as they can do so without serious financial detriment, they should divest themselves of investments and other financial interest that might require frequent disqualification.

(4) Neither judges nor members of their families residing in their households should accept a gift, bequest, favor, or loan from anyone except as follows:

(a) judges may accept a gift incident to a public testimonial to them; books supplied by publishers on a complimentary basis for official use; or an invitation to judges and their spouses to attend a bar-related function or activity devoted to the improvement of the law, the legal system, or the administration of justice;

(b) judges or members of their families residing in their households may accept ordinary social hospitality; a gift, bequest, favor, or loan from a relative; a wedding or engagement gift; a loan from a lending institution in its regular course of business on the same terms generally available to persons who are not judges; or a scholarship or fellowship awarded on the same terms applied to other applicants;

(c) judges or members of their families residing in their households may accept any other gift, bequest, favor, or loan only if the donor is not a party or other person whose interests have come or are likely to come before the judge.

Commentary

This subsection does not apply to contributions to any judge's campaign for judicial office, a matter governed by Canon 7.

(5) For the purposes of this section "members of their families residing in their households" means any relative of a judge by blood or marriage, or a person treated by a judge as a member of the judge's family, who resides in the judge's household.

(6) Judges are not required by this Code to disclose their income, debts, or investments.

Commentary

Canon 3 requires judges to disqualify themselves in any proceeding in which they have a financial interest, however small. Canon 5 requires judges to refrain from engaging in business and from financial activities that might interfere with the impartial performance of their judicial duties. Judges have the rights of ordinary citizens, including the right to privacy of their financial affairs. Owning and receiving income from investments do not as such affect the performance of a judge's duties.

(7) Neither confidential information acquired by judges in their official capacity nor intentions with respect to rulings to be made by them

should be used or disclosed by judges in financial dealings or for any other purpose until such information is a matter of public record.

D. Fiduciary Activities. Except as provided in Canon 5B, judges should not serve as executors, administrators, trustees, guardians, or other fiduciaries, except for the estate, trust, or person of members of their families, and then only if such service will not interfere with the proper performance of their judicial duties. "Members of their families" include a spouse, child, grandchild, parent, grandparent, or other relative or person with whom the judge maintains a close family-like relationship. As family fiduciaries, judges are subject to the following restrictions:

(1) Judges should not serve if it is likely that as a fiduciary they will be engaged in proceedings that would ordinarily come before them.

Commentary

The Effective Date of Compliance provision of this Code qualifies this subsection with regard to a judge who is an executor, administrator, trustee, or other fiduciary at the time this Code becomes effective.

(2) While acting as a fiduciary, judges are subject to the same restrictions on financial activities that apply to them in their personal capacities.

Commentary

Judges' obligations under this Canon and their obligations as a fiduciary may come into conflict. For example, judges should resign as trustees if such service would result in detriment to the trust because the judge had to divest it of holdings whose retention would place the judge in violation of Canon 5C(3).

E. Arbitration. Judges should not act as arbitrators or mediators, other than in their official capacity as judges.

F. Practice of Law. Judges should not practice law.

G. Extra-judicial Appointments. Judges should not accept appointment to a governmental committee, commission, or other position that is concerned with issues of fact or policy on matters other than the improvement of the law, the legal system, or the administration of justice. Judges, however, may represent their county, state, or locality on ceremonial occasions or in connection with historical, educational, and cultural activities.

Commentary

Valuable services have been rendered in the past to the states and the nation by judges appointed by the executive to undertake important extra-judicial assignments. The appropriateness of conferring these assignments on judges must be reassessed, however, in light of demands on the judiciary created by today's crowded dockets and the need to protect the courts from involvement in extra-judicial matters that may prove to be controversial. Judges should not be expected or permitted to accept governmental appointments that could interfere with the effectiveness and independence of the judiciary.

CANON 6

Compensation and Expense Reimbursement for Quasi-Judicial and Extra-Judicial Activities

Judges may receive compensation and reimbursement of expenses for the quasi-judicial and extra-judicial activities permitted by this Code, if the source of such payments does not give the appearance of influencing the judges in their judicial duties or otherwise give the appearance of impropriety, subject to the following restrictions:

A. Compensation. Compensation should not exceed a reasonable amount nor should it exceed what a person who is not a judge would receive for the same activity.

B. Expense Reimbursement. Expense reimbursement should be limited to the actual cost of travel, food, and lodging reasonably incurred by the judge and, where appropriate to the occasion, by the judge's spouse. Any payment in excess of such an amount is compensation.

Commentary

Subject to Canon 5C(1), the foregoing restrictions shall not apply to the sale or distribution of publications authored by a judge which are available to the general public.

CANON 7

Judges Should Refrain From Political Activity Inappropriate to Their Judicial Office

Judges are entitled to entertain their personal views on political questions. They are not required to surrender their rights or opinions as citizens. They should avoid political activity which may give rise to a suspicion of political bias or impropriety.

A. Political Conduct in General

(1) Judges and candidates for election to judicial office should not:

(a) act as leaders or hold any office in a political organization;

(b) make speeches for a political organization or candidate for non-judicial office or publicly endorse a candidate for non-judicial office;

(c) personally solicit funds for or pay an assessment to a political organization or non-judicial candidate; make contributions to a political party or organization or to a non-judicial candidate in excess of five hundred dollars per year per political party or organization or candidate, or in excess of an aggregate of one thousand dollars per year for all political parties or organizations or candidates.

California Commentary

Although attendance at political gatherings is not prohibited, any such attendance should be restricted in such a manner as not to constitute a public endorsement of a cause or candidate otherwise prohibited by these Canons.

Subject to the monetary limitation herein to political contributions, a judge may purchase tickets for political dinners or other similar dinner functions. Any admission price to such a political dinner or function, in excess of the actual cost of the meal shall be considered a political contribution. The prohibition in 7A(1)(c) does not preclude judges from contributing to a campaign fund for distribution among judges who are candidates for reelection or retention.

(2) Judges who are candidates for election or reelection or non-judges who are candidates for judicial office, may speak to political gatherings only on their own behalf.

(3) Except as otherwise permitted in this Code, judges should not engage in any political activity, other than on behalf of measures to improve the law, the legal system or the administration of justice.

California Commentary

The term "political activity" should not be construed so narrowly as to prevent private comment.

This provision does not prohibit a judge from signing a petition to qualify a measure for the ballot without the use of the judge's official title.

Compliance With the Code of Judicial Conduct

Anyone, whether or not a lawyer, who is an officer of a judicial system performing judicial functions, including an officer such as a referee in bankruptcy, special master, court commissioner, or magistrate, is a judge for the purpose of this Code. All judges should comply with this Code except as provided below.

A. Part-time Judge. A part-time judge is a judge who serves on a continuing or periodic basis, but is permitted by law to devote time to some other profession or occupation and whose compensation for that reason is less than that of a full-time judge. Part-time judges:

(1) are not required to comply with Canon 5C(2), 5D, 5E, 5F, and 5G.

(2) should not practice law in the court on which they serve or in any court subject to the appellate jurisdiction of the court on which they serve, or act as a lawyer in a proceeding in which they have served as a judge or in any other proceeding related thereto.

B. Judge Pro Tempore. A judge pro tempore is a person appointed to act temporarily as a judge, except that officers of the judicial system performing judicial functions, as defined above, shall not be deemed judges pro tempore qualifying for the exceptions contained herein.

(1) While acting as such, judges pro tempore are not required to comply with Canons 5C(2), (3), 5D, 5E, 5F, 5G, and 7, except that they may not engage in political activity while performing judicial functions.

Canon 7   *CALIFORNIA CODE*

(2) Persons who have been judges pro tempore should not act as lawyers in a proceeding in which they have served as judges or in any other proceeding related thereto.

C. Retired Judge. Retired judges, upon recall to judicial service, during such service or prior to such service if they consider themselves available for such service, shall comply with all the provisions of this Code. However, they shall not be required to comply with Canon 5C(2), 5D, 5E, and 5G.

Effective Date of Compliance

Persons to whom this Code becomes applicable should arrange their affairs as soon as reasonably possible to comply with it. If, however, the demands on their time and the possibility of conflicts of interest are not substantial, a person who holds judicial office on the date this Code becomes effective may continue to act as an executor, administrator, trustee, of other fiduciary for the estate or person of one who is not a member of their family.

CALIFORNIA RULES ON CONFIDENTIALITY OF PROCEEDINGS BEFORE THE COMMISSION ON JUDICIAL PERFORMANCE

Rule 902. Confidentiality of Proceedings

(a) Except as provided in this rule, all papers filed with and proceedings before the Commission, or before the masters appointed by the Supreme Court pursuant to rule 907, shall be confidential until a record is filed by the Commission in the Supreme Court. Upon a recommendation of censure, all papers filed with and proceedings before the Commission or masters shall remain confidential until the judge who is the subject of the proceedings files a petition in the Supreme Court to modify or reject the Commission's recommendation or until the time for filing a petition expires.

Information released by the Commission under this subdivison in proceedings resulting in a recommendation of censure shall make appropriate reference to a petition for review in the Supreme Court filed by the judge, if any is filed, to the end that the public will perceive that the Commission's recommendation and findings are wholly or partly contested by the judge.

(b) The Commission may release information regarding its proceedings under the following circumstances:

(1) If a judge is publicly charged with involvement in proceedings before the Commission resulting in substantial unfairness to him, the Commission may, at the request of the judge involved, issue a short statement of clarification and correction.

(2) If a judge is publicly associated with having engaged in serious reprehensible conduct or having committed a major offense, and after a preliminary investigation or a formal hearing it is determined there is no basis for further proceedings or recommendation of discipline, the Commission may issue a short explanatory statement.

(3) When a formal hearing has been ordered in a proceeding in which the subject matter is generally known to the public and in which there is broad public interest, and in which confidence in the administration of justice is threatened due to lack of information concerning the status of the proceeding and the requirements of due process, the Commission may issue one or more short announcements confirming the hearing, clarifying the procedural aspects, and defending the right of a judge to a fair hearing.

(4) If a judge retires or resigns from judicial office following institution of formal proceedings the Commission may, in the interest of justice or to maintain confidence in the administration of justice,

Rule 902

release information concerning the investigation and proceedings to a public entity.

(5) Upon completion of an investigation or proceeding, the Commission shall disclose to the person complaining against the judge that after an investigation of the charges the Commission (i) has found no basis for action against the judge, (ii) has taken an appropriate corrective action, the nature of which shall not be disclosed, or (iii) has filed a recommendation for the censure, removal, or retirement of the judge. The name of the judge shall not be used in any written communication to the complainant unless the record has been filed in the Supreme Court.

Adopted, eff. Nov. 11, 1966. As amended, eff. July 1, 1971; July 1, 1977; Jan. 1, 1978; July 1, 1978; July 1, 1985.

AMERICAN BAR ASSOCIATION CANONS OF PROFESSIONAL ETHICS *

Preamble.

In America, where the stability of Courts and of all departments of government rests upon the approval of the people, it is peculiarly essential that the system for establishing and dispensing Justice be developed to a high point of efficiency and so maintained that the public shall have absolute confidence in the integrity and impartiality of its administration. The future of the Republic, to a great extent, depends upon our maintenance of Justice pure and unsullied. It cannot be so maintained unless the conduct and the motives of the members of our profession are such as to merit the approval of all just men.

No code or set of rules can be framed, which will particularize all the duties of the lawyer in the varying phases of litigation or in all the relations of professional life. The following canons of ethics are adopted by the American Bar Association as a general guide, yet the enumeration of particular duties should not be construed as a denial of the existence of others equally imperative, though not specifically mentioned.

1. The Duty of the Lawyer to the Courts

It is the duty of the lawyer to maintain towards the Courts a respectful attitude, not for the sake of the temporary incumbent of the judicial office, but for the maintenance of its supreme importance. Judges, not being wholly free to defend themselves, are peculiarly entitled to receive the support of the Bar against unjust criticism and clamor. Whenever there is proper ground for serious complaint of a judicial officer, it is the right and duty of the lawyer to submit his grievances to the proper authorities. In such cases, but not otherwise, such charges should be encouraged and the person making them should be protected.

2. The Selection of Judges

It is the duty of the Bar to endeavor to prevent political considerations from outweighing judicial fitness in the selections of Judges. It should protest earnestly and actively against the appointment or election of those who are unsuitable for the Bench; and it should strive to have elevated thereto only those willing to forego other employments, wheth-

---

* These Canons, to and including Canon 32 and the recommended oath, were adopted by the American Bar Association at Its Thirty-First Annual Meeting at Seattle, Washington, on August 27, 1908. * * *

[The Canons were applied, as amended, until the adoption of the Code in 1970]. Reprinted with permission. Copyright © American Bar Association.

er of a business, political or other character, which may embarrass their free and fair consideration of questions before them for decision. The aspiration of lawyers for judicial position should be governed by an impartial estimate of their ability to add honor to the office and not by a desire for the distinction the position may bring to themselves.

3. Attempts to Exert Personal Influence on the Court

Marked attention and unusual hospitality on the part of a lawyer to a Judge, uncalled for by the personal relations of the parties, subject both the Judge and the lawyer to misconstructions of motive and should be avoided. A lawyer should not communicate or argue privately with the Judge as to the merits of a pending cause, and he deserves rebuke and denunciation for any device or attempt to gain from a Judge special personal consideration or favor. A self-respecting independence in the discharge of professional duty, without denial or diminution of the courtesy and respect due the Judge's station, is the only proper foundation for cordial personal and official relations between Bench and Bar.

4. When Counsel for an Indigent Prisoner

A lawyer assigned as counsel for an indigent prisoner ought not to ask to be excused for any trivial reason, and should always exert his best efforts in his behalf.

5. The Defense or Prosecution of Those Accused of Crime

It is the right of the lawyer to undertake the defense of a person accused of crime, regardless of his personal opinion as to the guilt of the accused; otherwise innocent persons, victims only of suspicious circumstances, might be denied proper defense. Having undertaken such defense, the lawyer is bound, by all fair and honorable means, to present every defense that the law of the land permits, to the end that no person may be deprived of life or liberty, but by due process of law.

The primary duty of a lawyer engaged in public prosecution is not to convict, but to see that justice is done. The suppression of facts or the secreting of witnesses capable of establishing the innocence of the accused is highly reprehensible.

6. Adverse Influences and Conflicting Interests

It is the duty of a lawyer at the time of retainer to disclose to the client all the circumstances of his relations to the parties, and any interest in or connection with the controversy, which might influence the client in the selection of counsel.

It is unprofessional to represent conflicting interests, except by express consent of all concerned given after a full disclosure of the facts. Within the meaning of this canon, a lawyer represents conflicting interests when, in behalf of one client, it is his duty to contend for that which duty to another client requires him to oppose.

CANONS OF PROFESSIONAL ETHICS

The obligation to represent the client with undivided fidelity and not to divulge his secrets or confidences forbids also the subsequent acceptance of retainers or employment from others in matters adversely affecting any interest of the client with respect to which confidence has been reposed.

7. Professional Colleagues and Conflicts of Opinion

A client's proffer of assistance of additional counsel should not be regarded as evidence of want of confidence, but the matter should be left to the determination of the client. A lawyer should decline association as colleague if it is objectionable to the original counsel, but if the lawyer first retained is relieved, another may come into the case.

When lawyers jointly associated in a cause cannot agree as to any matter vital to the interest of the client, the conflict of opinion should be frankly stated to him for his final determination. His decision should be accepted unless the nature of the difference makes it impracticable for the lawyer whose judgment has been overruled to co-operate effectively. In this event it is his duty to ask the client to relieve him.

Efforts, direct or indirect, in any way to encroach upon the professional employment of another lawyer, are unworthy of those who should be brethren at the Bar; but, nevertheless, it is the right of any lawyer, without fear or favor, to give proper advice to those seeking relief against unfaithful or neglectful counsel, generally after communication with the lawyer of whom the complaint is made.

8. Advising Upon the Merits of a Client's Cause

A lawyer should endeavor to obtain full knowledge of his client's cause before advising thereon, and he is bound to give a candid opinion of the merits and probable result of pending or contemplated litigation. The miscarriages to which justice is subject, by reason of surprises and disappointments in evidence and witnesses, and through mistakes of juries and errors of Courts, even though only occasional, admonish lawyers to beware of bold and confident assurances to clients, especially where the employment may depend upon such assurance. Whenever the controversy will admit of fair adjustment, the client should be advised to avoid or to end the litigation.

9. Negotiations With Opposite Party

A lawyer should not in any way communicate upon the subject of controversy with a party represented by counsel; much less should he undertake to negotiate or compromise the matter with him, but should deal only with his counsel. It is incumbent upon the lawyer most particularly to avoid everything that may tend to mislead a party not represented by counsel, and he should not undertake to advise him as to the law.

10. Acquiring Interest in Litigation

The lawyer should not purchase any interest in the subject matter of the litigation which he is conducting.

11. Dealing With Trust Property

The lawyer should refrain from any action whereby for his personal benefit or gain he abuses or takes advantage of the confidence reposed in him by his client.

Money of the client or collected for the client or other trust property coming into the possession of the lawyer should be reported and accounted for promptly, and should not under any circumstances be commingled with his own or be used by him.

12. Fixing the Amount of the Fee

In fixing fees, lawyers should avoid charges which overestimate their advice and services, as well as those which undervalue them. A client's ability to pay cannot justify a charge in excess of the value of the service, though his poverty may require a less charge, or even none at all. The reasonable requests of brother lawyers, and of their widows and orphans without ample means, should receive special and kindly consideration.

In determining the amount of the fee, it is proper to consider: (1) the time and labor required, the novelty and difficulty of the questions involved and the skill requisite properly to conduct the cause; (2) whether the acceptance of employment in the particular case will preclude the lawyer's appearance for others in cases likely to arise out of the transaction, and in which there is a reasonable expectation that otherwise he would be employed, or will involve the loss of other employment while employed in the particular case or antagonisms with other clients; (3) the customary charges of the Bar for similar services; (4) the amount involved in the controversy and the benefits resulting to the client from the services; (5) the contingency or the certainty of the compensation; and (6) the character of the employment, whether casual or for an established and constant client. No one of these considerations in itself is controlling. They are mere guides in ascertaining the real value of the service.

In determining the customary charges of the Bar for similar services, it is proper for a lawyer to consider a schedule of minimum fees adopted by a Bar Association, but no lawyer should permit himself to be controlled thereby or to follow it as his sole guide in determining the amount of his fee.

In fixing fees it should never be forgotten that the profession is a branch of the administration of justice and not a mere money-getting trade.

CANONS OF PROFESSIONAL ETHICS

13. Contingent Fees

A contract for a contingent fee, where sanctioned by law, should be reasonable under all the circumstances of the case, including the risk and uncertainty of the compensation, but should always be subject to the supervision of a court, as to its reasonableness.

14. Suing a Client for a Fee

Controversies with clients concerning compensation are to be avoided by the lawyer so far as shall be compatible with his self-respect and with his right to receive reasonable recompense for his services; and lawsuits with clients should be resorted to only to prevent injustice, imposition or fraud.

15. How Far a Lawyer May Go in Supporting a Client's Cause

Nothing operates more certainly to create or to foster popular prejudice against lawyers as a class, and to deprive the profession of that full measure of public esteem and confidence which belongs to the proper discharge of its duties than does the false claim, often set up by the unscrupulous in defense of questionable transactions, that it is the duty of the lawyer to do whatever may enable him to succeed in winning his client's cause.

It is improper for a lawyer to assert in argument his personal belief in his client's innocence or in the justice of his cause.

The lawyer owes "entire devotion to the interest of the client, warm zeal in the maintenance and defense of his rights and the exertion of his utmost learning and ability," to the end that nothing be taken or be withheld from him, save by the rules of law, legally applied. No fear of judicial disfavor or public unpopularity should restrain him from the full discharge of his duty. In the judicial forum the client is entitled to the benefit of any and every remedy and defense that is authorized by the law of the land, and he may expect his lawyer to assert every such remedy or defense. But it is steadfastly to be borne in mind that the great trust of the lawyer is to be performed within and not without the bounds of the law. The office of attorney does not permit, much less does it demand of him for any client, violation of law or any manner of fraud or chicane. He must obey his own conscience and not that of his client.

16. Restraining Clients from Improprieties

A lawyer should use his best efforts to restrain and to prevent his clients from doing those things which the lawyer himself ought not to do, particularly with reference to their conduct towards Courts, judicial officers, jurors, witnesses and suitors. If a client persists in such wrongdoing the lawyer should terminate their relation.

17. Ill-Feeling and Personalities Between Advocates

Clients, not lawyers, are the litigants. Whatever may be the ill-feeling existing between clients, it should not be allowed to influence counsel in their conduct and demeanor toward each other or toward suitors in the case. All personalities between counsel should be scrupulously avoided. In the trial of a cause it is indecent to allude to the personal history or the personal peculiarities and idiosyncrasies of counsel on the other side. Personal colloquies between counsel which cause delay and promote unseemly wrangling should also be carefully avoided.

18. Treatment of Witnesses and Litigants

A lawyer should always treat adverse witnesses and suitors with fairness and due consideration, and he should never minister to the malevolence or prejudices of a client in the trial or conduct of a cause. The client cannot be made the keeper of the lawyer's conscience in professional matters. He has no right to demand that his counsel shall abuse the opposite party or indulge in offensive personalities. Improper speech is not excusable on the ground that it is what the client would say if speaking in his own behalf.

19. Appearance of Lawyer as Witness for His Client

When a lawyer is a witness for his client, except as to merely formal matters, such as the attestation or custody of an instrument and the like, he should leave the trial of the case to other counsel. Except when essential to the ends of justice, a lawyer should avoid testifying in court in behalf of his client.

20. Newspaper Discussion of Pending Litigation

Newspaper publications by a lawyer as to pending or anticipated litigation may interefere with a fair trial in the Courts and otherwise prejudice the due administration of justice. Generally they are to be condemned. If the extreme circumstances of a particular case justify a statement to the public, it is unprofessional to make it anonymously. An *ex parte* reference to the facts should not go beyond quotation from the records and papers on file in the court; but even in extreme cases it is better to avoid any *ex parte* statement.

21. Punctuality and Expedition

It is the duty of the lawyer not only to his client, but also to the Courts and to the public to be punctual in attendance, and to be concise and direct in the trial and disposition of causes.

22. Candor and Fairness

The conduct of the lawyer before the Court and with other lawyers should be characterized by candor and fairness.

It is not candid or fair for the lawyer knowingly to misquote the contents of a paper, the testimony of a witness, the language or the argument of opposing counsel, or the language of a decision or a textbook; or with knowledge of its invalidity, to cite as authority a decision that has been overruled, or a statute that has been repealed; or in argument to assert as a fact that which has not been proved, or in those jurisdictions where a side has the opening and closing arguments to mislead his opponent by concealing or withholding positions in his opening argument upon which his side then intends to rely.

It is unprofessional and dishonorable to deal other than candidly with the facts in taking the statements of witnesses, in drawing affidavits and other documents, and in the presentation of causes.

A lawyer should not offer evidence which he knows the Court should reject, in order to get the same before the jury by argument for its admissibility, nor should he address to the Judge arguments upon any point not properly calling for determination by him. Neither should he introduce into an argument, addressed to the court, remarks or statements intended to influence the jury or bystanders.

These and all kindred practices are unprofessional and unworthy of an officer of the law charged, as is the lawyer, with the duty of aiding in the administration of justice.

23. Attitude Toward Jury

All attempts to curry favor with juries by fawning, flattery or pretended solicitude for their personal comfort are unprofessional. Suggestions of counsel, looking to the comfort or convenience of jurors, and propositions to dispense with argument, should be made to the Court out of the jury's hearing. A lawyer must never converse privately with jurors about the case; and both before and during the trial he should avoid communicating with them, even as to matters foreign to the cause.

24. Right of Lawyer to Control the Incidents of the Trial

As to incidental matters pending the trial, not affecting the merits of the cause, or working substantial prejudice to the rights of the client, such as forcing the opposite lawyer to trial when he is under affliction or bereavement; forcing the trial on a particular day to the injury of the opposite lawyer when no harm will result from a trial at a different time; agreeing to an extension of time for signing a bill of exceptions, cross interrogatories and the like, the lawyer must be allowed to judge. In such matters no client has a right to demand that his counsel shall be illiberal, or that he do anything therein repugnant to his own sense of honor and propriety.

25. Taking Technical Advantage of Opposite Counsel; Agreements With Him

A lawyer should not ignore known customs or practice of the Bar or of a particular Court, even when the law permits, without giving timely notice to the opposing counsel. As far as possible, important agreements, affecting the rights of clients, should be reduced to writing; but it is dishonorable to avoid performance of an agreement fairly made because it is not reduced to writing, as required by rules of Court.

26. Professional Advocacy Other Than Before Courts

A lawyer openly, and in his true character may render professional services before legislative or other bodies, regarding proposed legislation and in advocacy of claims before departments of government, upon the same principles of ethics which justify his appearance before the Courts; but it is unprofessional for a lawyer so engaged to conceal his attorneyship, or to employ secret personal solicitations, or to use means other than those addressed to the reason and understanding, to influence action.

27. Advertising, Direct or Indirect

It is unprofessional to solicit professional employment by circulars, advertisements, through touters or by personal communications or interviews not warranted by personal relations. Indirect advertisements for professional employment such as furnishing or inspiring newspaper comments, or procuring his photograph to be published in connection with causes in which the lawyer has been or is engaged or concerning the manner of their conduct, the magnitude of the interest involved, the importance of the lawyer's position, and all other like self-laudation, offend the traditions and lower the tone of our profession and are reprehensible; but the customary use of simple professional cards is not improper.

Publication in reputable law lists in a manner consistent with the standards of conduct imposed by these canons of brief biographical and informative data is permissible. Such data must not be misleading and may include only a statement of the lawyer's name and the names of his professional associates; addresses, telephone numbers, cable addresses; branches of the profession practiced; date and place of birth and admission to the bar; schools attended; with dates of graduation, degrees and other educational distinctions; public or quasi-public offices; posts of honor; legal authorships; legal teaching positions; memberships and offices in bar associations and committees thereof, in legal and scientific societies and legal fraternities; foreign language ability; the fact of listings in other reputable law lists; the names and addresses of references; and, with their written consent, the names of clients regularly represented. A certificate of compliance with the Rules and Standards issued by the Standing Committee on Law Lists may be treated as evidence that such list is reputable.

It is not improper for a lawyer who is admitted to practice as a proctor in admiralty to use that designation on his letterhead or shingle or for a lawyer who has complied with the statutory requirements of admission to practice before the patent office, to so use the designation "patent attorney" or "patent lawyer" or "trademark attorney" or "trademark lawyer" or any combination of those terms.

28. Stirring Up Litigation, Directly or Through Agents

It is unprofessional for a lawyer to volunteer advice to bring a lawsuit, except in rare cases where ties of blood, relationship or trust make it his duty to do so. Stirring up strife and litigation is not only unprofessional, but it is indictable at common law. It is disreputable to hunt up defects in titles or other causes of action and inform thereof in order to be employed to bring suit or collect judgment, or to breed litigation by seeking out those with claims for personal injuries or those having any other grounds of action in order to secure them as clients, or to employ agents or runners for like purposes, or to pay or reward, directly or indirectly, those who bring or influence the bringing of such cases to his office, or to remunerate policemen, court or prison officials, physicians, hospital *attachés* or others who may succeed, under the guise of giving disinterested friendly advice, in influencing the criminal, the sick and the injured, the ignorant or others, to seek his professional services. A duty to the public and to the profession devolves upon every member of the Bar having knowledge of such practices upon the part of any practitioner immediately to inform thereof, to the end that the offender may be disbarred.

29. Upholding the Honor of the Profession

Lawyers should expose without fear or favor before the proper tribunals corrupt or dishonest conduct in the profession, and should accept without hesitation employment against a member of the Bar who has wronged his client. The counsel upon the trial of a cause in which perjury has been committed owe it to the profession and to the public to bring the matter to the knowledge of the prosecuting authorities. The lawyer should aid in guarding the Bar against the admission to the profession of candidates unfit or unqualified because deficient in either moral character or education. He should strive at all times to uphold the honor and to maintain the dignity of the profession and to improve not only the law but the administration of justice.

30. Justifiable and Unjustifiable Litigations

The lawyer must decline to conduct a civil cause or to make a defense when convinced that it is intended merely to harass or to injure the opposite party or to work oppression or wrong. But otherwise it is his right, and, having accepted retainer, it becomes his duty to insist upon the judgment of the Court as to the legal merits of his client's claim. His appearance in Court should be deemed equivalent to an assertion on his honor that in his opinion his client's case is one proper for judicial determination.

31. Responsibility for Litigation

No lawyer is obliged to act either as adviser or advocate for every person who may wish to become his client. He has the right to decline employment. Every lawyer upon his own responsibility must decide what employment he will accept as counsel, what causes he will bring into Court for plaintiffs, what cases he will contest in Court for defendants. The responsibility for advising as to questionable transactions, for bringing questionable suits, for urging questionable defenses, is the lawyer's responsibility. He cannot escape it by urging as an excuse that he is only following his client's instructions.

32. The Lawyer's Duty in Its Last Analysis

No client, corporate or individual, however powerful, nor any cause, civil or political, however important, is entitled to receive nor should any lawyer render any service or advice involving disloyalty to the law whose ministers we are, or disrespect of the judicial office, which we are bound to uphold, or corruption of any person or persons exercising a public office or private trust, or deception or betrayal of the public. When rendering any such improper service or advice, the lawyer invites and merits stern and just condemnation. Correspondingly, he advances the honor of his profession and the best interests of his client when he renders service or gives advice tending to impress upon the client and his undertaking exact compliance with the strictest principles of moral law. He must also observe and advise his client to observe the statute law, though until a statute shall have been construed and interpreted by competent adjudication, he is free and is entitled to advise as to its validity and as to what he conscientiously believes to be its just meaning and extent. But above all a lawyer will find his highest honor in a deserved reputation for fidelity to private trust and to public duty, as an honest man and as a patriotic and loyal citizen.

33. Partnerships—Names

Partnerships among lawyers for the practice of their profession are very common and are not to be condemned. In the formation of partnerships and the use of partnership names care should be taken not to violate any law, custom, or rule of court locally applicable. Where partnerships are formed between lawyers who are not all admitted to practice in the courts of the state, care should be taken to avoid any misleading name or representation which would create a false impression as to the professional position or privileges of the member not locally admitted. In the formation of partnerships for the practice of law, no

CANONS OF PROFESSIONAL ETHICS

person should be admitted or held out as a practitioner or member who is not a member of the legal profession duly authorized to practice, and amenable to professional discipline. In the selection and use of a firm name, no false, misleading, assumed or trade name should be used. The continued use of the name of a deceased or former partner, when permissible by local custom, is not unethical, but care should be taken that no imposition or deception is practiced through this use. When a member of the firm, on becoming a judge, is precluded from practicing law, his name should not be continued in the firm name.

Partnerships between lawyers and members of other professions or non-professional persons should not be formed or permitted where any part of the partnership's employment consists of the practice of law.

34. Division of Fees

No division of fees for legal services is proper, except with another lawyer, based upon a division of service or responsibility.

35. Intermediaries

The professional services of a lawyer should not be controlled or exploited by any lay agency, personal or corporate, which intervenes between client and lawyer. A lawyer's responsibilities and qualifications are individual. He should avoid all relations which direct the performance of his duties by or in the interest of such intermediary. A lawyer's relation to his client should be personal, and the responsibility should be direct to the client. Charitable societies rendering aid to the indigents are not deemed such intermediaries.

A lawyer may accept employment from any organization, such as an association, club or trade organization, to render legal services in any matter in which the organization, as an entity, is interested, but this employment should not include the rendering of legal services to the members of such an organization in respect to their individual affairs.

36. Retirement From Judicial Position or Public Employment

A lawyer should not accept employment as an advocate in any matter upon the merits of which he has previously acted in a judicial capacity.

A lawyer, having once held public office or having been in the public employ, should not after his retirement accept employment in connection with any matter which he has investigated or passed upon while in such office or employ.

37. Confidences of a Client

It is the duty of a lawyer to preserve his client's confidences. This duty outlasts the lawyer's employment, and extends as well to his employees; and neither of them should accept employment which involves or may involve the disclosure or use of these confidences, either for the private advantage of the lawyer or his employees or to the disadvantage of the client, without his knowledge and consent, and even though there are other available sources of such information. A lawyer should not continue employment when he discovers that this obligation prevents the performance of his full duty to his former or to his new client.

If a lawyer is accused by his client, he is not precluded from disclosing the truth in respect to the accusation. The announced intention of a client to commit a crime is not included within the confidences which he is bound to respect. He may properly make such disclosures as may be necessary to prevent the act or protect those against whom it is threatened.

38. Compensation, Commissions and Rebates

A lawyer should accept no compensation, commissions, rebates or other advantages from others without the knowledge and consent of his client after full disclosure.

39. Witnesses

A lawyer may properly interview any witness or prospective witness for the opposing side in any civil or criminal action without the consent of opposing counsel or party. In doing so, however, he should scrupulously avoid any suggestion calculated to induce the witness to suppress or deviate from the truth, or in any degree to affect his free and untrammeled conduct when appearing at the trial or on the witness stand.

40. Newspapers

A lawyer may with propriety write articles for publications in which he gives information upon the law; but he should not accept employment from such publications to advise inquirers in respect to their individual rights.

41. Discovery of Imposition and Deception

When a lawyer discovers that some fraud or deception has been practiced, which has unjustly imposed upon the court or a party, he should endeavor to rectify it; at first by advising his client, and if his client refuses to forego the advantage thus unjustly gained, he should promptly inform the injured person or his counsel, so that they may take appropriate steps.

42. Expenses of Litigation

A lawyer may not properly agree with a client that the lawyer shall pay or bear the expenses of litigation; he may in good faith advance expenses as a matter of convenience, but subject to reimbursement.

43. Approved Law Lists

It shall be improper for a lawyer to permit his name to be published in a law list the conduct, management or contents of which are calculated or likely to deceive or injure the public or the profession, or to lower the dignity or standing of the profession.

44. Withdrawal From Employment as Attorney or Counsel

The right of an attorney or counsel to withdraw from employment, once assumed, arises only from good cause. Even the desire or consent of the client is not always sufficient. The lawyer should not throw up the unfinished task to the detriment of his client except for reasons of honor or self-respect. If the client insists upon an unjust or immoral course in the conduct of his case, or if he persists over the attorney's remonstrance in presenting frivolous defenses, or if he deliberately disregards an agreement or obligation as to fees or expenses, the lawyer may be warranted in withdrawing on due notice to the client, allowing him time to employ another lawyer. So also when a lawyer discovers that his client has no case and the client is determined to continue it; or even if the lawyer finds himself incapable of conducting the case effectively. Sundry other instances may arise in which withdrawal is to be justified. Upon withdrawing from a case after a retainer has been paid, the attorney should refund such part of the retainer as has not been clearly earned.

45. Specialists

The canons of the American Bar Association apply to all branches of the legal profession; specialists in particular branches are not to be considered as exempt from the application of these principles.

46. Notice to Local Lawyers

A lawyer available to act as an associate of other lawyers in a particular branch of the law or legal service may send to local lawyers only and publish in his local legal journal, a brief and dignified announcement of his availability to serve other lawyers in connection therewith. The announcement should be in a form which does not constitute a statement or representation of special experience or expertness.

47. Aiding the Unauthorized Practice of Law

No lawyer shall permit his professional services, or his name, to be used in aid of, or to make possible, the unauthorized practice of law by any lay agency, personal or corporate.

PARALLEL TABLES BETWEEN THE ABA CANONS OF PROFESSIONAL ETHICS AND THE ABA MODEL CODE OF PROFESSIONAL RESPONSIBILITY *

CANONS OF PROFESSIONAL ETHICS TO CODE OF PROFESSIONAL RESPONSIBILITY

Preamble
Preamble
DR 1-102(A)(5)
EC 7-20
EC 7-39
EC 8-1
EC 9-1
EC 9-2

Canon 1
DR 1-103(B)
EC 7-36
EC 8-6
DR 7-106(C)(6)
DR 8-102(B)

Canon 2
EC 8-6
DR 8-102(A)

Canon 3
EC 7-34
EC 7-35
EC 7-36
DR 7-110

Canon 4
EC 2-29
EC 7-1
EC 7-19
DR 2-110(C)
DR 7-101(A)(1)

Canon 5
EC 1-5
DR 1-102(A)(4)

EC 2-29
EC 7-1
EC 7-4
EC 7-13
EC 7-19
EC 7-27
DR 7-101(A)(1)
DR 7-102(A)(3)-(7)
DR 7-103
DR 7-109(A)-(B)
EC 8-5

Canon 6
EC 4-1
EC 4-5
DR 4-101(B)
EC 5-1
EC 5-3
EC 5-14
EC 5-15
EC 5-16
EC 5-17
EC 5-19
DR 5-101(A)
DR 5-105
DR 5-106
EC 8-8

Canon 7
EC 2-28
EC 2-29
EC 2-30
EC 2-32
DR 2-108
DR 2-110(C)(3)
EC 4-2

EC 5-11
EC 5-12
DR 7-101(A)(2)

Canon 8
EC 2-9
EC 7-5
EC 7-8

Canon 9
EC 7-18
DR 7-104

Canon 10
EC 5-7
DR 5-103(A)

Canon 11
EC 4-5
DR 4-101(B)(3)
EC 9-5
DR 9-102

Canon 12
EC 2-16
EC 2-17
EC 2-18
EC 2-25
DR 2-106

Canon 13
EC 2-20
DR 2-106
EC 5-7
DR 5-103(A)(2)

* Compiled by Olavi Maru, Reference Librarian, William Nelson Cromwell Library, American Bar Foundation

PARALLEL TABLES

Canon 14
EC 2–23
EC 5–7
DR 5–103(A)(1)

Canon 15
EC 1–5
DR 1–102(A)(4)
EC 7–1
EC 7–2
EC 7–3
EC 7–4
EC 7–5
EC 7–6
EC 7–19
EC 7–24
EC 7–26
DR 7–101(A)(1)
DR 7–101(B)(2)
DR 7–102(A)(2)
DR 7–102(A)(3)–(7)
DR 7–106(C)(4)
EC 9–2

Canon 16
EC 2–32
DR 2–110(C)(1)(b)
EC 7–28
DR 7–101(A)(2)
EC 8–5

Canon 17
EC 1–5
EC 7–10
EC 7–37
EC 7–38
DR 7–101(A)(1)

Canon 18
EC 1–5
EC 7–10
EC 7–25
EC 7–36
DR 7–101(A)(1)
DR 7–106(C)(2)

Canon 19
EC 5–9
EC 5–10
DR 5–101(B)
DR 5–102

Canon 20
EC 7–33
DR 7–107

Canon 21
EC 6–4
DR 6–101(A)(3)
EC 7–20
EC 7–38
DR 7–101(A)(1)

Canon 22
EC 1–5
DR 1–102(A)(4)
EC 7–6
EC 7–25
EC 7–26
EC 7–27
DR 7–102(A)(3)–(7)
DR 7–106(C)(1)
EC 8–5

Canon 23
EC 7–29
EC 7–31
EC 7–36
DR 7–108

Canon 24
EC 7–7
EC 7–9
EC 7–10
EC 7–38
DR 7–101(A)(1)
DR 7–101(B)(1)

Canon 25
EC 7–38
DR 7–101(A)(1)
DR 7–106(C)(5)

Canon 26
EC 7–15
EC 7–16
EC 7–36
DR 7–106(B)(2)
DR 7–107(F)
DR 7–107(H)
DR 7–107(I)
DR 7–110(B)
EC 8–4

Canon 27
EC 2–2
EC 2–3
EC 2–4
EC 2–8
EC 2–9
EC 2–10
EC 2–14
DR 2–101
DR 2–102(A)
DR 2–102(E)
DR 2–103(A)
DR 2–105(A)

Canon 28
EC 1–4
EC 1–5
EC 2–1
EC 2–2
EC 2–3
EC 2–4
EC 2–8
DR 1–103(A)–(B)
DR 2–103(A)
DR 2–104(A)

Canon 29
EC 1–2
EC 1–3
EC 1–4
DR 1–101(B)
DR 1–103(A)
DR 1–103(B)
EC 2–28
DR 7–102(A)(3)–(7)

CANONS OF PROFESSIONAL ETHICS

Canon 29—Cont'd
DR 7–102(B)(2)
EC 8–1
EC 8–2
EC 8–5
EC 8–7
EC 8–9
EC 9–2
EC 9–6

Canon 30
EC 1–5
DR 1–102(A)(4)
EC 2–3
EC 2–30
DR 2–109(A)(1)
EC 7–1
EC 7–4
EC 7–19
DR 7–101(A)(1)
DR 7–102(A)(1)

Canon 31
EC 2–26
EC 2–27
EC 2–28
EC 2–29
DR 2–109(A)(2)
EC 7–1
EC 7–4
EC 7–5
EC 7–14
EC 7–19
DR 7–101(B)(2)
DR 7–102(A)(2)

Canon 32
EC 1–5
DR 1–102(A)(5)
EC 7–1
EC 7–5
EC 7–19
DR 7–102(A)(3)–(7)
EC 8–5

Canon 33
EC 2–11
EC 2–12
EC 2–13
DR 2–102(B)
DR 2–102(C)
DR 2–102(D)
EC 3–8
DR 3–103
DR 5–107(C)

Canon 34
EC 2–22
DR 2–103(B)
DR 2–107(A)
EC 3–8
DR 3–102

Canon 35
DR 2–103(D)
DR 2–104(A)(2)
DR 2–104(A)(3)
EC 5–1
EC 5–13
EC 5–21
EC 5–22
EC 5–23
EC 5–24
DR 5–107(B)
DR 5–107(C)(3)

Canon 36
EC 9–3
DR 9–101

Canon 37
Canon 4 generally
EC 2–32
DR 2–110
DR 4–101(B)
DR 4–101(B)(2)–(3)
DR 4–101(C)
DR 4–101(D)
DR 7–101(A)(2)

Canon 38
EC 2–21
EC 5–21
DR 5–107(A)(2)

Canon 39
EC 1–5
DR 1–102(A)(4)
EC 7–28
DR 7–102(A)(3)–(7)
DR 7–109(C)

Canon 40
EC 2–2
EC 2–5
DR 2–104(A)(4)

Canon 41
DR 7–102(B)(1)
EC 8–5

Canon 42
EC 5–8
DR 5–103(B)

Canon 43
DR 2–102(A)(6)

Canon 44
EC 1–5
DR 1–102(A)(5)
EC 2–31
EC 2–32
DR 2–110
EC 5–15
EC 5–19
EC 5–21
DR 5–102
DR 5–105(B)
DR 5–105(D)
EC 7–8
DR 7–101(A)(2)

Canon 45
Preliminary statement

PARALLEL TABLES

Canon 46	Canon 47	Canon 47
EC 2–14	EC 1–5	EC 3–1 through EC 3–9
DR 2–105(A)(3)	DR 1–102(A)(5)	DR 3–101

PARALLEL TABLES BETWEEN THE ABA MODEL CODE OF PROFESSIONAL RESPONSIBILITY AND THE ABA CANONS OF PROFESSIONAL ETHICS

Code	Canons	Code	Canons	Code	Canons
Preamble	Preamble	Canon 2			31
Preliminary		EC 2–1	28	EC 2–30	7
Statement	45	EC 2–2	27		30
Canon 1			28	EC 2–31	44
EC 1–2	29		40	EC 2–32	7
EC 1–3	29	EC 2–3	27		16
EC 1–4	28		28		37
	29		30		44
EC 1–5	5	EC 2–4	27	DR 2–101	27
	15		28	DR 2–102	
	17	EC 2–5	40	(A)	27
	18	EC 2–8	27	(A)(6)	43
	22		28	(B)	33
	28	EC 2–9	8	(C)	33
	30		27	(D)	33
	32	EC 2–10	27	(E)	27
	39	EC 2–11	33	DR 2–103	
	44	EC 2–12	33	(A)	27
	47	EC 2–13	33		28
DR 1–101		EC 2–14	27	(B)	34
(B)	29		46	(D)	35
DR 1–102		EC 2–16	12	DR 2–104	
(A)(4)	5	EC 2–17	12	(A)	28
	15	EC 2–18	12	(A)(2)	35
	22	EC 2–20	13	(A)(3)	35
	30	EC 2–21	38	(A)(4)	40
	39	EC 2–22	34	DR 2–105	
(A)(5)	Preamble	EC 2–23	14	(A)	27
	32	EC 2–25	12	(A)(3)	46
	44	EC 2–26	31	DR 2–106	12
	47	EC 2–27	31		13
DR 1–103		EC 2–28	7	DR 2–107	
(A)	28		29	(A)	34
	29		31	DR 2–108	7
(B)	1	EC 2–29	4	DR 2–109	
	28		5	(A)(1)	30
	29		7	(A)(2)	31

551

CANONS OF PROFESSIONAL ETHICS

Code	Canons	Code	Canons	Code	Canons
Canon 2—Cont'd		EC 5–17	6		31
DR 2–110	37	EC 5–19	6	EC 7–5	8
	44		44		15
DR 2–110(C)	4	EC 5–21	35		31
(C)(1)(b)	16		38		32
(C)(3)	7		44	EC 7–6	15
Canon 3		EC 5–22	35		22
EC 3–1		EC 5–23	35	EC 7–7	24
through		EC 5–24	35	EC 7–8	8
EC 3–9	47	DR 5–101			44
EC 3–8	33	(A)	6	EC 7–9	24
	34	(B)	19	EC 7–10	17
DR 3–101	47	DR 5–102	19		18
DR 3–102	34		44		24
DR 3–103	33	DR 5–103		EC 7–13	*5
Canon 4	37	(A)	10	EC 7–14	31
EC 4–1	6	(A)(1)	14	EC 7–15	26
EC 4–2	7	(A)(2)	13	EC 7–16	26
EC 4–5	6	(B)	42	EC 7–18	9
	11	DR 5–105	6	EC 7–19	4
DR 4–101		(B)	44		5
(B)	6	(D)	44		15
	37	DR 5–106	6		30
(B)(2)	37	DR 5–107			31
(B)(3)	11	(A)(2)	38		32
	37	(B)	35	EC 7–20	Preamble
(C)	37	(C)	33		21
(D)	37	(C)(3)	35	EC 7–24	15
Canon 5		Canon 6		EC 7–25	18
EC 5–1	6	EC 6–4	21		22
	35	DR 6–101		EC 7–26	15
EC 5–3	6	(A)(3)	21		22
EC 5–7	10	Canon 7		EC 7–27	2
	13	EC 7–1	4		22
	14		5	EC 7–28	16
EC 5–8	42		15		39
EC 5–9	19		30	EC 7–29	23
EC 5–11	7		31	EC 7–31	23
EC 5–12	7		32	EC 7–33	20
EC 5–13	35	EC 7–2	15	EC 7–34	3
EC 5–14	6	EC 7–3	15	EC 7–35	3
EC 5–15	6	EC 7–4	5	EC 7–36	1
	44		15		3
EC 5–16	6		30		18

PARALLEL TABLES

Code	Canons	Code	Canons	Code	Canons
Canon 7—Cont'd		(A)(3)–(7)	5		29
EC 7–36	23		15	EC 8–2	29
	26		22	EC 8–4	26
EC 7–37	17		29	EC 8–5	5
EC 7–38	17		32		16
	21		39		22
	24	(B)(1)	41		29
	25	(B)(2)	29		32
EC 7–39	Preamble	DR 7–103	5		41
DR 7–101		DR 7–104	9	EC 8–6	1
(A)(1)	4	DR 7–106			2
	5	(B)(2)	26	EC 8–7	29
	15	(C)(1)	22	EC 8–8	6
	17	(C)(2)	18	EC 8–9	29
	18	(C)(4)	15	DR 8–102	
	21	(C)(5)	25	(A)	2
	24	(C)(6)	1	(B)	1
	25	DR 7–107	20	Canon 9	
	30	(F)	26	EC 9–1	Preamble
(A)(2)	7	(H)	26	EC 9–2	Preamble
	16	(I)	26		15
	37	DR 7–108	23		29
	44	DR 7–109		EC 9–3	36
(B)(1)	24	(A)–(B)	5	EC 9–5	11
(B)(2)	15	(C)	39	EC 9–6	29
	31	DR 7–110	3	DR 9–101	36
DR 7–102		(B)	26	DR 9–102	11
(A)(1)	30	Canon 8			
(A)(2)	15	EC 8–1	Preamble		
	31				

553

AMERICAN BAR ASSOCIATION STANDING COMMITTEE ON ETHICS AND PROFESSIONAL RESPONSIBILITY

COMPOSITION AND JURISDICTION *

The Standing Committee on Ethics and Professional Responsibility, which consists of eight members, shall:

(1) by the concurrence of a majority of its members, express its opinion on proper professional or judicial conduct, either on its own initiative or when requested to do so by a member of the bar or by an officer or a committee of a state or local bar association, except that an opinion may not be issued on a question that is pending before a court;

(2) periodically publish its issued opinions to the legal profession in summary or complete form and, on request, provide copies of opinions to members of the bar;

(3) on request, advise or otherwise help (a) state or local bar associations, (b) courts, or (c) committees or commissions charged with responsibility for issuance of ethics opinions, the discipline of lawyers or the discipline or removal of judges, in their activities relating to the interpretation of the Model Rules of Professional Conduct, the former Model Code of Professional Responsibility and the Code of Judicial Conduct.

(4) recommend appropriate amendments to or clarifications of the Model Rules of Professional Responsibility or the Code of Judicial Conduct, if it considers them advisable; and

(5) adopt such rules as it considers appropriate relating to the procedures to be used in expressing opinions, effective when approved by the Board of Governors.

RULES OF PROCEDURE

1. The Committee may express its opinion on proper professional and judicial conduct. The Model Rules of Professional Conduct, and the Code of Judicial Conduct, as those Codes may be amended or superseded, contain the standards to be applied. For as long as a significant number of jurisdictions continue to base their professional standards on the predecessor Model Code of Professional Responsibility, the Committee will continue to refer to the Model Code in its opinions.

2. The Committee shall issue an opinion upon a request from a member of the bar, an officer or committee of a state or local bar association, the president of the American Bar Association, or a court or a judge of a court. The Committee may issue opinions on its own initiative.

---

* As defined by the By-Laws of the American Bar Association, Article 30.7, revised effective July 21, 1971. Formerly called the Standing Committee on Professional Ethics.

ETHICS AND PROFESSIONAL RESPONSIBILITY

3. The Committee may issue opinions of two kinds: Formal Opinions and Informal Opinions. Formal Opinions are those upon subjects determined by the Committee to be of widespread interest or unusual importance. Other opinions are Informal Opinions. The Committee shall assign to each opinion a non-duplicative identifying number, with distinction between Formal Opinions and Informal Opinions.

4. The Committee is not obliged to issue an opinion as to completed conduct unless the request is from an ethics committee, grievance committee, or similar committee of, or from the chief officer of, a bar association having disciplinary jurisdiction over the person whose conduct is the subject of the request, or is from a court, committee, or commission having disciplinary jurisdiction over a judge whose conduct is the subject of the request. The Committee is not obliged to issue an opinion as to the proposed conduct of someone other than the person requesting the opinion. The Committee will not issue an opinion on a question that is pending before a court. The Committee will not issue an opinion on a question of law.

5. As a condition of issuing an opinion, the Committee may require that the request be submitted in writing, with information sufficiently specific to enable adequate consideration by the Committee and to show eligibility under these rules.

6. The Committee shall not issue an opinion with respect to judicial conduct until the proposed opinion has been submitted to the Judges' Advisory Committee and the Committee has considered any objection or comment from the Judges' Advisory Committee and any member of it. The Committee may assume that the Judges' Advisory Committee has no objection or comment if none is received by the Committee within 30 days after the submission.

7. If the Committee determines that the issuance of a requested opinion is not appropriate under these rules, or that the information submitted is not sufficient, the Committee shall promptly notify the person requesting the opinion.

8. The Committee shall issue an opinion only with concurrence of five members at a meeting or with the concurrence of six members other than at a meeting. If a member specifically so requests, the Committee shall not issue an opinion unless approved at a meeting. A member may express a dissent or a special concurrence, which shall be appended to an opinion if the member specifically so directs.

9. The chairperson may assign to one or more members the responsibility of preparing a proposed opinion for consideration and action by the Committee. The Committee shall issue a requested opinion without undue delay after sufficient information is received.

10. A Formal Opinion overrules an earlier Formal Opinion or Informal Opinion to the extent of conflict. An Informal Opinion overrules an

earlier Informal Opinion to the extent of conflict but does not overrule an earlier Formal Opinion.

11. Opinions of the Committee issued before the effective dates of the Model Rules of Professional Conduct, the predecessor Model Code of Professional Responsibility and of the Code of Judicial Conduct continue in effect to the extent not inconsistent with those Codes and not overruled by a later opinion.

12. The Committee shall make opinions available for publication in the *American Bar Association Journal*, with Formal Opinions for publication in full and with Informal Opinions for publication in summary. The Committee shall cause Formal Opinions and Informal Opinions to be published in loose-leaf form. Before publication of opinions, the Committee shall remove information identifying the person who requested or was the subject of the opinion.

13. The Committee shall treat as confidential its files relating to requests for opinions.

ETHICS AND PROFESSIONAL RESPONSIBILITY

The ABA House of Delegates, at its August 1988 meeting, adopted as ABA policy a recommendation that state and local bar associations "encourage their members to accept as a guide for their individual conduct, and to comply with, a lawyers' creed of professionalism." The ABA Torts and Insurance Practice Section, which had sought and won the ABA's approval of such a policy, also set forth an example of such a "Lawyer's Creed of Professionalism." This document is published below in full text. The House of Delegates made clear that "nothing in such a creed shall be deemed to supersede or in any way amend the Model Rules of Professional Conduct or other disciplinary codes, alter existing standards of conduct against which lawyer negligence might be judged or become a basis for the imposition of civil liability of any kind."

Lawyer's Creed Of Professionalism *

Preamble

As a lawyer I must strive to make our system of justice work fairly and efficiently. In order to carry out that responsibility, not only will I comply with the letter and spirit of the disciplinary standards applicable to all lawyers, but I will also conduct myself in accordance with the following Creed of Professionalism when dealing with my client, opposing parties, their counsel, the courts and the general public.

A. With respect to my client:

1. I will be loyal and committed to my client's cause, but I will not permit that loyalty and commitment to interfere with my ability to provide my client with objective and independent advice;

2. I will endeavor to achieve my client's lawful objectives in business transactions and in litigation as expeditiously and economically as possible;

3. In appropriate cases, I will counsel my client with respect to mediation, arbitration and other alternative methods of resolving disputes;

4. I will advise my client against pursuing litigation (or any other course of action) that is without merit and against insisting on tactics which are intended to delay resolution of the matter or to harass or drain the financial resources of the opposing party;

5. I will advise my client that civility and courtesy are not to be equated with weakness;

6. While I must abide by my client's decision concerning the objectives of the representation, I nevertheless will counsel my client that a

---

* Not adopted by the ABA House of Delegates. Not American Bar Association Policy. Reprinted with permission.

willingness to initiate or engage in settlement discussions is consistent with zealous and effective representation.

B. With respect to opposing parties and their counsel:

1. I will endeavor to be courteous and civil, both in oral and in written communications;

2. I will not knowingly make statements of fact or of law that are untrue;

3. In litigation proceedings I will agree to reasonable requests for extensions of time or for waiver of procedural formalities when the legitimate interests of my client will not be adversely affected;

4. I will endeavor to consult with opposing counsel before scheduling depositions and meetings and before re-scheduling hearings, and I will cooperate with opposing counsel when scheduling changes are requested;

5. I will refrain from utilizing litigation or any other course of conduct to harass the opposing party;

6. I will refrain from engaging in excessive and abusive discovery, and I will comply with all reasonable discovery requests;

7. I will refrain from utilizing delaying tactics;

8. In depositions and other proceedings, and in negotiations, I will conduct myself with dignity, avoid making groundless objections and refrain from engaging in acts of rudeness or disrespect;

9. I will not serve motions and pleadings on the other party, or his counsel, at such a time or in such a manner as will unfairly limit the other party's opportunity to respond;

10. In business transactions I will not quarrel over matters of form or style, but will concentrate on matters of substance and content;

11. I will clearly identify, for other counsel or parties, all changes that I have made in documents submitted to me for review.

C. With respect to the courts and other tribunals:

1. I will be a vigorous and zealous advocate on behalf of my client, while recognizing, as an officer of the court, that excessive zeal may be detrimental to my client's interests as well as to the proper functioning of our system of justice;

2. Where consistent with my client's interests, I will communicate with opposing counsel in an effort to avoid litigation and to resolve litigation that has actually commenced;

3. I will voluntarily withdraw claims or defenses when it becomes apparent that they do not have merit or are superfluous;

4. I will refrain from filing frivolous motions;

ETHICS AND PROFESSIONAL RESPONSIBILITY

5. I will make every effort to agree with other counsel, as early as possible, on a voluntary exchange of information and on a plan for discovery;

6. I will attempt to resolve, by agreement, my objections to matters contained in my opponent's pleadings and discovery requests;

7. When scheduling hearings or depositions have to be canceled, I will notify opposing counsel, and, if appropriate, the court (or other tribunal) as early as possible;

8. Before dates for hearings or trials are set—or if that is not feasible, immediately after such dates have been set—I will attempt to verify the availability of key participants and witnesses so that I can promptly notify the court (or other tribunal) and opposing counsel of any likely problem in that regard;

9. In civil matters, I will stipulate to facts as to which there is no genuine dispute;

10. I will endeavor to be punctual in attending court hearings, conferences and depositions;

11. I will at all times be candid with the court.

D. With respect to the public and to our system of justice:

1. I will remember that, in addition to commitment to my client's cause, my responsibilities as a lawyer include a devotion to the public good;

2. I will endeavor to keep myself current in the areas in which I practice and, when necessary, will associate with, or refer my client to, counsel knowledgeable in another field of practice;

3. I will be mindful of the fact that, as a member of a self-regulating profession, it is encumbent on me to report violations by fellow lawyers of any disciplinary rule;

4. I will be mindful of the need to protect the image of the legal profession in the eyes of the public and will be so guided when considering methods and content of advertising;

5. I will be mindful that the law is a learned profession and that among its desirable goals are devotion to public service, improvement of administration of justice, and the contribution of uncompensated time and civic influence on behalf of those persons who cannot afford adequate legal assistance.

Lawyers' Pledge Of Professionalism

1. I will remember that the practice of law is first and foremost a profession, and I will subordinate business concerns to professionalism concerns.

...ll encourage respect for ... and our legal system ...ugh my words and actions.

3. I will remember my responsibilities to serve as an officer of the court and protector of individual rights.

4. I will contribute time and resources to public service, public education, charitable, and *pro bono* activities in my community.

5. I will work with the other participants in the legal system, including judges, opposing counsel and those whose practices are different from mine, to make our legal system more accessible and responsive.

6. I will resolve matters expeditiously and without unnecessary expense.

7. I will resolve disputes through negotiation whenever possible.

8. I will keep my clients well-informed and involved in making the decisions that affect them.

9. I will continue to expand my knowledge of the law.

10. I will achieve and maintain proficiency in my practice.

11. I will be courteous to those with whom I come into contact during the course of my work.

12. I will honor the spirit and intent, as well as the requirements, of the applicable rules or code of professional conduct for my jurisdiction, and I will encourage others to do the same.

†